Advanced Topics in Dataflow Computing and Multithreading

Guang R. Gao
McGill University, Montreal

Lubomir Bic
University of California, Irvine

Jean-Luc Gaudiot
University of Southern California

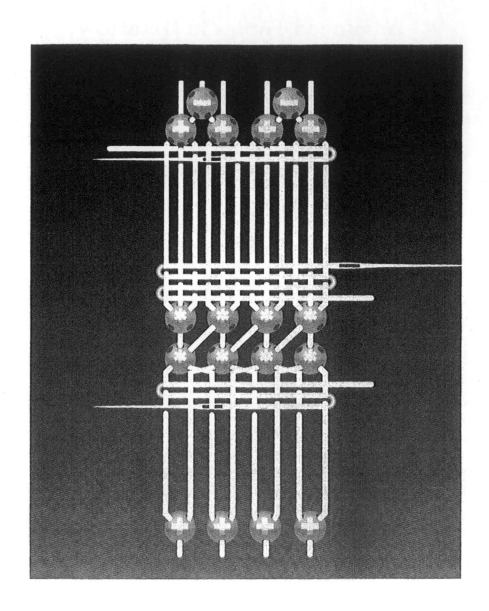

Advanced Topics in Dataflow Computing and Multithreading

Guang R. Gao
McGill University, Montreal

Lubomir Bic
University of California, Irvine

Jean-Luc Gaudiot
University of Southern California

IEEE
COMPUTER
SOCIETY
http://computer.org

WILEY-
INTERSCIENCE
A JOHN WILEY & SONS, INC., PUBLICATION

Library of Congress Cataloging-in-Publication Data

Advanced topics in dataflow computing and multithreading / [edited by]
Guang R. Gao, Lubomir Bic, and Jean-Luc Gaudiot.
     p. cm.
Includes bibliographic references.
ISBN 978-0-8186-6542-4
    1. Computer architecture.   2. Parallel processing (Electronic
computers)   3. Data structures (Computer science)   I. Gao, Guang R.,
II. Bic, Lubomir, 1951– .   III. Gaudiot, Jean-Luc.
QA76.9.A73A356   1995
004 ' .35—dc20

                      94-25601
                        CIP

IEEE Computer Society Press
10662 Los Vaqueros Circle
P.O. Box 3014
Los Alamitos, CA 90720-1314

Technical Editor: Jon T. Butler
Production Editors: Bob Werner and Edna Straub
Cover: Alex Torres

 The Institute of Electrical and Electronics Engineers, Inc

Contents

Foreword

Dataflow ideas have become intertwined with the main stream of computer system thought in areas as diverse as compiler construction and database access. This book provides, in a single volume, reports from many of the world's projects engaged in the current evolution and application of dataflow concepts. Their subject matter emphasizes the broad reach of dataflow principles in program representation from language design to processor architecture and compiler optimization techniques.

A basic question in computer architecture has been how to build effective large-scale parallel computers, with performance and programmability being central issues. The field continues in a state of flux. The data parallel model, although specialized, is applied with success to significant scientific computations.

At the same time, many computer scientists proclaim the advantages of the shared memory model even though its support for concurrent processing fails to satisfy basic principles of modular program construction. A general semantic model of program execution is needed that can serve as a guide and specification for future large-scale computer systems, and serve as a standard target for the compilation of high-level languages. Dataflow concepts have shown how functional programming ideas may be directed to exploit the power of parallel computers, and have the potential to lead to an important universal semantic model of computation. The reports published here are stepping stones along the way.

Jack B. Dennis
Belmont, Massachusetts
April 1995

Introduction

This book is the second in a series. It contains invited refereed papers representing recent advances in dataflow and multithreaded computing. Earlier versions of these papers were presented at the *Second International Workshop on Dataflow Computers*, organized in conjunction with the *19th Annual International Symposium on Computer Architecture*, at Hamilton Island, Australia, May 25–26, 1992. The previous dataflow workshop was held in Eilat, Israel, May 1989.[1]

Since the first workshop, there have been significant developments in both fundamental research and practical realizations of dataflow models of computation. In particular, there has been active research and development in multithreaded architectures that evolved from the dataflow model. These developments have also had considerable impact on the conception of high-performance architectures in the "post-RISC" era, where dataflow models and multithreading seem to provide a promising solution for the so-called von Neumann bottleneck. These activities have attracted growing interest from university researchers, government laboratory scientists, and computer manufacturers.

It is easy to imagine that a powerful multithreaded architecture based on the dataflow model with supercomputer performance will be integrated on a single chip by the end of this decade. As research activities are pursued and evolve, novel ideas will continue to emerge, while new challenges also continue to arise. The objective of this workshop was to provide a forum for the exchange of information on the modeling, design, and implementation of dataflow and multithreaded computers.

This book is divided into five sections, corresponding to the major efforts in the field. Papers within each section are presented in alphabetical order by the authors' names.

The first section contains four papers in the area of processor design. The paper by M. Amamiya presents a design principle of massively parallel distributed memory multiprocessor architecture—the Datarol-II project. Then, a report is presented on Arvind's multithreaded architecture design, the Start project. The next paper, by S. Sakai, examines the two basic functions in a massively parallel computer based on multithreading—the synchronization and pipelined design. Finally, Terada et al. describe their Qx-series superpipelined data-driven VLSI processors.

The second section contains five papers covering the area of language and programming issues. The paper by J.B. Dennis discusses the representation of signal processing operations in streams in the functional programming style and the related compilation issues. The paper by M. Iwata and H. Terada shows how the principles of data-driven computation are suited to the development of well-structured software. Next, R. Jagannathan presents a virtual architecture for executing a GLU (Granular Lucid) program in parallel and studies its performance. The paper by Sato et al. describes a distributed data structure, called Q-structure, and its implementation in the EM-4 dataflow machine. Finally, A. Sohn and J.-L. Gaudiot demonstrate how data-driven principles can be applied to nonnumeric computations.

Section 3 consists of four papers dealing with the issues of compiling for dataflow and other parallel machines. The first paper by Bic et al. presents an approach to automatically parallelize dataflow programs for execution on conventional multiprocessors. The paper by Culler et al. studies the behavior of a large dataflow program, compiled into threads, on the CM-5 massively parallel computer. Mitrovic

---

[1] *Advances in Dataflow Computing*, J.-L. Gaudiot and L. Bic, eds., Prentice Hall, 1991.

describes issues and solutions arising in compiling SISAL programs for a simulated coarse-grain dataflow machine called ADAM. In a similar manner, the last paper by Wail and Abramson presents problems and solutions in compiling Pascal programs for a dataflow machine and demonstrates that an imperative language may be quite suitable to the programming of such machines.

Section 4 contains six papers related to issues of scheduling and resource management. The first paper by Buck and Lee presents an analytical model for the behavior of dataflow graphs. It allows both long-term and short-term averages of tokens produced and consumed by actors to be determined, thus providing a basis for scheduling of dataflow graphs in bounded memory. Haines and Böhm compare a centralized work distribution scheme (single master) with a distributed one (tree-structure) and show the trade-offs between the two. The paper by Maquelin is devoted to load management in the ADAM machine—a coarse-grain dataflow computer. The proposed hardware-supported throttling mechanism is suitable to control the amount of parallelism not only for iterative loops but also for recursion and higher-order functions. The next paper, by Snelling and Gurd, presents a comprehensive approach to understanding the various schemes for workload management. It analyzes and compares these in the context of both dataflow and thread-based systems. Sterling et al. describe their Anida abstract architecture and show its performance by a combination of analytical models and simulation results. Trade-offs between granularity and loss of parallelism are investigated. Finally, the paper by Theobald, Gao, and Hendren presents a study of limits of instruction level parallelism in benchmark programs and its smoothability under a variety of abstract architecture models.

In section 5, issues of performance and program behavior are discussed. In the first paper by Böhm and Hiromoto, two FFT algorithms (recursive and iterative) are programmed in Id and executed on a Motorola Monsoon dataflow machine. The paper by Gottlieb and Biran investigates the issues of locality in a multithreaded machine and proposes a model for exposing locality for a given program execution. In the third paper of this section, Najjar, Miller, and Böhm examine the locality in dataflow graphs. They analyze the effect of increasing process granularity on communication latency in a data-driven environment. Finally, the last paper by Zeng and Egan compares the performance of an explicitly parallelized code with one written in SISAL and demonstrates that, with comparatively little effort, much better speedup is achievable using the latter.

As the editors of the monograph, we are very pleased with the depth and breadth of the work reported by all authors. It reflects the state of the art as well as future trends in the field of dataflow and multithreaded computing. Perhaps it provides an answer to the question raised by J. Gurd in his foreword to a similar book based on the first dataflow workshop three years ago—has dataflow computing research reached its adulthood? It seems it has!

We would like to thank Kevin Theobald at McGill University for his help in organizing the Second International Workshop on Dataflow Computers, held on Hamilton Island, Australia in 1992 and which served as the basis for this volume, and for his subsequent assistance with compiling, reviewing, and editing this compendium of research contributions.

Design Principle of Massively Parallel Distributed-Memory Multiprocessor Architecture

Makoto Amamiya and Tetsuo Kawano
Department of Information Systems
Kyushu University
Kasuga Fukuoka 816 Japan

In this paper, we discuss the design principles of massively parallel distributed-memory multiprocessor architecture and propose the Datarol-II architecture. We present the architecture of the massively parallel Datarol-II machine and show a Datarol-II processor design, including communication protocol and handling mechanisms of remote memory access and remote process/procedure invocation. Last, we show several evaluations of the Datarol-II processor from the viewpoint of effect on thread execution, effect of implicit register loading, and swapping cost by software simulation.

1. Introduction

Distributed-memory multiprocessor architecture is essential in developing massively parallel machines. One of the most important design issues in such a distributed-memory multiprocessor architecture is a latency problem, which is caused by remote procedure invocation and remote memory access. These conditions occur often in massively parallel execution, thus causing processes to suspend their executions until the response to the remote memory accesses or remote process/procedure invocations is received. Therefore, a new processor architecture should be developed to perform efficient context switching among fine-grain concurrent processes in order to solve this latency problem.

We propose a massively parallel distributed-memory multiprocessor architecture, called *Datarol-II*, which is tolerable to the latency caused by remote memory access and remote process invocation. Datarol-II is an advanced version of the *Datarol* architecture [3], which was designed to implement the distributed-memory massively parallel multiprocessor system. The original Datarol machine architecture *Datarol-I* [2, 3], was designed to support ultra-multiprocessing, in which a number of fine-grain processes can be executed in a highly concurrent fashion. The primary idea behind the Datarol-I architecture is to implement an efficient multithread execution control by introducing a continuation-based computation mechanism, by-reference execution control mechanism, and multiple register-sets, all of which enable us to eliminate redundant execution control in conventional dataflow architecture.

The two major architectural differences between Datarol-II and Datarol-I are: (a) the Datarol-II processor is designed to support efficient execution for both fine-grain and coarse-grain parallelisms; and (b) the Datarol-II processor integrates hardware modules for communication control and memory access control, which handle remote memory access and remote process communication in parallel. In order to control concurrent executions among various grain sizes of processes, the execution control mechanism of the Datarol-II processor is designed in such a manner that if the thread is a little bit long and has locality, it can execute a thread exclusively, while, if the

1

thread has no locality, it can switch the thread or process with very small overhead. Due to this mechanism, Datarol-II has features which are tolerable to remote memory access and remote process/procedure invocation latencies.

Although the Datarol-II processor is designed to execute each thread exclusively, the design is also based on the conjecture that the thread length is not so long in massively parallel computations. The thread length may be less than twenty or thirty instructions. It may be assumed that, in a distributed-memory multiprocessor environment, it will be very hard for programmers to construct such massively parallel programs with long threads. Therefore, implementing high-efficient thread switching is more important than implementing high-speed sequential execution in each thread.

The massively parallel Datarol-II machine is constructed with several thousand Datarol-II processors, in which each has local memory and is connected in a two- or three-dimensional mesh. It is constructed with three modules: Communication Control Module (CM), Memory Module (MM), and Processor Module (PM).

The Datarol-II processor executes a multithread control-flow program called Datarol. The execution of Datarol consists of program-count-based sequential execution and continuation-based thread initiation, i.e., thread synchronization and split-phase operations.

The execution of fine-grain sequential threads by a program-counter-based mechanism is referred to as *short-cycle* execution. In order to reduce the overhead of context switching, an implicit register-loading mechanism is embedded in the execution pipeline. In this mechanism, data is automatically loaded into registers from the local memory in the background of the instruction execution. A two-level hierarchical memory system is implemented in order to reduce memory access latency. A load control mechanism is introduced to improve the memory access locality. This mechanism makes the hierarchical memory system work effectively and prevents the hardware resources from suffering overload.

The Datarol-II processor also performs the continuation-based execution in a circular pipeline known as *long-cycle* execution. Since a token in the circular pipeline triggers a "thread" execution, which contains several instructions, the number of tokens in a circular pipeline of Datarol-II is much smaller than the number of tokens found in a dataflow machine. This decreases the overhead of a synchronization unit.

The Datarol-II processor achieves high-speed context switching and effective multiprocess execution by implementing these hierarchical memory systems and thread-level circular pipeline execution schemes.

. Motivation and Overview of Datarol Architecture

One of the important issues in designing a parallel computer is to make it scalable, that is, to achieve higher performance when more processors are added to the computer. In order to achieve this goal, a processing element should be designed to exploit program parallelism as much as possible. For this application there are several fundamental problems that must be solved: multiprocessing [4], long memory access latency, remote process/procedure call latency, and waiting time for events synchronization. These problems are strongly related to each other and conventional control-flow multiprocessor architectures attempt to compromise between them. Processor idling time, which is caused during the long-latency remote memory access and remote process call, could be avoided by a split transaction or multiphase operation. However, these operations require a highly efficient synchronization mechanism for switching the processor execution.

Dataflow multiprocessors avoid this contradiction by performing the context switching at instruction level via hardware. They are more tolerable to memory-access, process-call latencies, and synchronization overhead. Furthermore, the parallelism inherent in programs is maximally exploited without the need to be explicitly specified in programs. Dynamic dataflow architecture supports parallel execution in both function instance level and instruction level.

However, the following drawbacks of dataflow architecture have to be eliminated in order to develop massively parallel computers:

- The dataflow model requires a great deal of low-level communications because each instruction has to transfer its context by means of a token. This large communication overhead should be reduced by eliminating redundant dataflow synchronizations.

- The pure fine-grain dataflow execution scheme employs a by-value data access mechanism and this causes explicit data copying. This explicit data copying is redundant and should be eliminated by introducing by-reference data access in which data are accessed only when they are needed [1].

- Matching the memory mechanism requires complex and expensive hardware. This also makes it difficult to use caches.

Furthermore, since dataflow machines are implemented as a circular pipeline, they have the following problems:

- Dataflow machines are ineffective when they execute sequential programs because the circular pipeline is fully loaded only when a program provides sufficient parallelism. When a program is inherently sequential, a lot of bubbles occur in the instruction-execution stream.

- Latency in a thread execution is relatively long. This latency is caused by multi-staging the circular pipeline and queuing process.

- The synchronization unit, or matching-store mechanism, causes pipeline bottleneck. Since each instruction requires synchronization, i.e., one or two packets trigger one instruction, the number of input packets in the synchronization unit is more than that of executing instructions. Moreover, it is difficult to speed up the synchronization unit because it uses memory.

2.1 Concept of Datarol

The Datarol architecture model [3] was proposed to solve the problems stated previously. The idea of Datarol is to remove redundant dataflow by introducing hardware registers and a by-reference data access mechanism. The Datarol program is a multi-thread control-flow program which reflects the dataflow inherent in its source program. Datarol instructions are similar to conventional three-address instructions. Their execution is performed in four phases: instruction fetch, operand fetch, execute, and result write. The difference in this model is that each instruction explicitly specifies its succeeding instructions by a set of continuation points. The set of continuation points exploits parallelism inherent in programs.

The general Datarol instruction is expressed as

l:[*] *op rs1 rs2 rd*-> *D* [1]

---

[1] [] means this is optional.

where l is a label of this instruction and D is a set of labels of instruction which should be executed after this instruction. D is called a set of continuation points, and an instruction $e \in D$ is called a dependent of l. This expression means that the instruction *op* operates on two operands *rs1*, *rs2*, and stores its result to *rd*. *rs1*, *rs2*, and *rd* denote the respective register names.

Other instructions are switch and link instructions. Switch instructions, $l : sw\ b \rightarrow D_t, D_f$, transfer control to continuations D_t or D_f depending on the Boolean value b. Link and rlink instructions, which are used for function application, are represented as $l : [*]\ link\ r_{s1}\ r_{s2}\ n$ and $l : [*]\ rlink\ r_{s1}\ r_d\ n$. The meaning of these instructions are discussed later.

The tag "*" indicates that the operand of an instruction triggered by an op-token is not assured to exist in the specified register. The tag "*" is optional. When the tag is shown, the arrival of the partner operand is verified. If the partner operand has not been written in the register, the execution of this instruction will suspend until the partner operand arrives.

It should be noted that Datarol instructions are position independent, i.e., any instruction can be placed in any position in an instruction memory because its succeeding instructions are explicitly specified as continuation points.

This Datarol model offers the following features:

- Even if the result value produced by an instruction is referred to by several instructions, it is not necessary to make copies of the result value since the by-reference mechanism permits those instructions to share the result value. The result value is accessed only when it is needed.

- The address of a register, which is shared between consecutive instructions, can be determined and allocated at compile time, and no run time memory allocation is necessary. This significantly reduces the hardware cost needed for matching memory operations.

- The by-reference mechanism ensures that the operand data is written into a register only when the data is produced by an instruction, and is made available for the succeeding instructions. Therefore, if an operand is a dependent of its partner operand, the availability of the operand need not be checked. This reduces the overhead of matching memory operation.

The important advantage of the Datarol model is that the execution of the program is performed in a circular pipeline and execution of a thread is not exclusive, but can be interleaved with executions of other threads. Thus, multiple threads, whether they are in the same process instance or not, can be interleaved, and, therefore, they can be executed without context switching overhead. Circular pipeline stages will be set in full if sufficient parallelism resides in the execution of concurrent processes. This is quite different from other multithreading architectures such as Monsoon [13] and EM-4 [14].

2.2 Optimization of Datarol Architecture

The motivation for designing an optimized Datarol processor, which we call Datarol-II, is to improve the efficiency in the execution of sequential program code while preserving high efficiency in the execution of parallel threads and/or processes.

A previous version of Datarol, called Datarol-I, has the same circular pipeline problems as mentioned in Section 2.1. In order to solve these problems, the instructions of a sequential thread are arranged into consecutive memory addresses. Datarol-II executes these instructions in serial order until it encounters the termination point of the thread. This serial order execution reduces latency in sequential execution of a thread, and construction of instructions into one thread enables the use of high-speed registers within an execution unit. In addition to this thread construction, the compiler interleaves several threads of the same process into one combined thread without changing the order of instructions in each interleaved thread. Instructions of several threads can be interleaved in such a way that independent instructions are interleaved in order to avoid bubbles in the execution pipeline, i.e., instruction fetch, operand fetch, execution pipe, and result write. This is an easy task for compilers since every instruction is position independent and can be moved anywhere.

Moreover, thread-level continuation-based execution reduces the number of input packets to a synchronization unit, since a packet triggers a "thread"-level execution. This prevents the synchronization unit from being bottlenecked in a circular pipeline.

A Datarol-II machine instruction, which is a slight modification of Datarol-I instruction, is described as:

$$[l:] \ [!] \ op \ rs1 \ rs2 \ rd \ [-> \ (dest, \ mc, \ join) \ ]$$

Here, $(dest, mc, join)$ means the continuation. Notice that the format of continuation is different from that of Datarol-I. The continuation consists of a destination address $(dest)$, a matching counter address (mc), and the number of join $(join)$. In Datarol-II machine instructions, label and continuation are also optional. Tag "!" indicates that the thread execution terminates at this instruction.

The execution of Datarol-II code is triggered by a packet which contains a thread-ID. The thread-ID consists of a process instance name and an entry address of Instruction Memory. The execution proceeds in serial order of the instruction address until it reaches a termination point. This serial execution cycle is called a short-cycle execution. When an instruction specifies a continuation explicitly during the short-cycle execution, the continuation is set aside from the short-cycle execution. Instructions which cause remote memory access or a remote process call will specify a continuation. These instructions do not necessarily terminate the thread execution, but the thread execution continues from the instruction of the next address. When a remote access is completed, the number of join $join$ is compared with the matching counter mc. If the synchronization operation succeeds, a thread-ID of the continuation thread, which is specified by $dest$ is put into a queue. When an execution reaches a termination point, the processor takes another thread-ID from the queue and switches to this thread.

A load control mechanism is introduced in order to prevent hardware resources from being overloaded. When a Datarol-II processor receives a call packet, it allocates a new instance and sends a reply packet to the caller. After sending the reply packet, the processor checks its load level. If the load level is lower than the threshold, the initial thread of the new instance is invoked. Otherwise, invocation of the initial thread is delayed until the load level reaches lower than the threshold. Thus, Datarol-II processor controls its load and limits the number of active threads.

The memory unit of the Datarol-II processor has a two-level hierarchical memory system, operand memory, and register buffer in order to provide high-speed memory access from the execution unit. The thread-based execution and load control mechanism improve the memory access locality, allowing the hierarchical memory system to perform more effectively.

In the Datarol architecture, each instance has its own logical registers. Since the data values of the logical registers are stored in the memory unit, the register

Instruction	Semantics
op *rs1 rs2 rd*	arithmetic and logical instructions
op *rs1 # rd*	arithmetic and logical instructions with immediate data
start (*dest, mc, join*)	start new thread
brz *rs1 dest*	branch if *rs1* is zero
brnz *rs1 dest*	branch if *rs1* is not zero
call *rs1 rd*-> (*dest,mc,join*)	activate new instance
link *rs1 rs2 slot*	link *rs2* value to *rs1*
rlink *rs1 rd slot*-> (*dest,mc,join*)	link *rd* address to *rs1*
receive *rs1* -> (*dest,mc,join*)	receive parameter, *rs1*
return *rs1 rs2*	return *rs2* value to *rs1*
rins	release current instance
alloc *rs1 rd*-> (*dest,mc,join*)	allocate structure memory
free *rs1*	free structure memory
read *rs1 rd*-> (*dest,mc,join*)	read structure memory
iread *rs1 rd*-> (*dest,mc,join*)	
ifread *rs1 rd*-> (*dest,mc,join*)	
write *rs1 rs2*	write structure memory
iwrite *rs1 rs2*	
ifwrite *rs1 rs2*	

Table 1: Datarol-II machine instructions.

values have to be loaded from the memory unit to the registers, which are accessed by the execution unit. These register-loading processes are overhead to the context switching. In order to overcome this overhead, an implicit register-loading mechanism is embedded in the execution pipeline. Due to this mechanism, register values are loaded from the memory unit, resulting in small overhead when the registers are accessed. Thus, the Datarol-II processor performs very fast context switching. This implicit register-loading mechanism is described in Section 4.

. Datarol-II Program

3.1 Instruction Set

Table 1 shows the Datarol-II machine instruction set.

Remote memory access and remote call instructions specify a continuation, (*dest, mc, join*), and they are operated as split-phase transactions. The continuation consists of a thread-entry address (*dest*), matching counter address (*mc*), and the number of join (*join*). Each instance has its own matching counters, and they are used to control the thread activation. When a reply packet comes back, the number of join, *join* is compared with the corresponding matching counter (*mc*). If join synchronization succeeds, the continuation thread which starts from *dest* is invoked.

A start instruction initiates the new-thread execution whose entry is specified by continuation. Branch instructions, brz and brnz, also initiate a new thread. Termination flags of every branch of instructions are on. When the branch condition is true, the thread execution starting from *dest* is initiated. Otherwise the thread execution continues to the next address of the branch instruction.

The call instruction activates an instance of the function specified by *rs1* and sets the instance name to *rd*. The call operation is a split-phase operation, and a continuation thread is invoked when the *rd* is available. The link instruction sends the value of *rs2* to the *slot*-th parameter of another instance that is specified by *rs1*. The rlink instruction sends its instance name and *rd* address. The return instruction returns *rs2* value to the register of its caller instance. The register name is specified by *rs1*, whose value is passed by rlink. The receive instruction receives a thread parameter, which is passed through register *rs1*. The rins instruction releases the instance.

Arithmetic and logical instructions are the same as the conventional three-address type instructions.

3.2 Sample Program

An example of a program for function fib(n) which calculates Fibonacci numbers. This function is defined as follows:

fib(n) = if n < 2 then n else fib(n-1)+fib(n-2);

Figure 1 shows a Datarol-II program of fib(n).

```
; *** Initial thread ***
Fib:    receive r1 -> (Th1, 0, 0) ; receive n
      ! receive r2 -> (Th7, 1, 2) ; receive return register name
; *** thread 1 ***
Th1:    lti r1 2 t1
      ! brnz t1 Th6
; *** thread 2 ***
Th2:    set Fib t1
        call t1 r3 -> (Th3, 0, 0)    ; get new ins for fib(n-1)
      ! call t1 r4 -> (Th4, 0, 0)    ; get new ins for fib(n-2)
; *** thread 3 ***
Th3:    addi r1 -1 t1                ; link for fib(n-1)
        link r3 t1 1
      ! rlink r3 r5 2 -> (Th5, 2, 2)
; *** thread 4 ***
Th4:    addi r1 -2 t1                ; link for fib(n-2)
        link r4 t1 1
      ! rlink r4 r6 2 -> (Th5, 2, 2)
; *** thread 5 ***
Th5:    add r5 r6 r7                 ; add fib(n-1) and fib(n-2)
      ! start (Th7, 1, 2)
; *** thread 6 ***
Th6:    mov r1 r7                    ; case of (n < 2)
      ! start (Th7, 1, 2)
; *** thread 7 ***
Th7:    return r2 r7                 ; return result
      ! rins                        ; release this instance
```

Figure 1: Sample program fib(n).

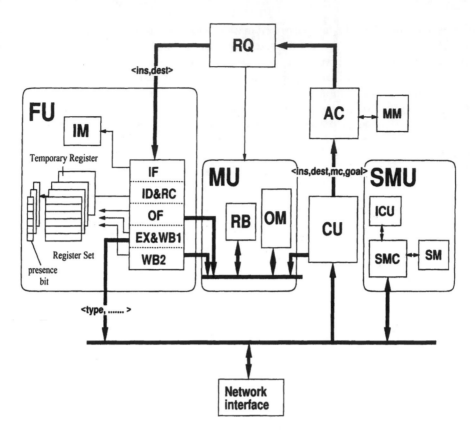

Figure 2: Datarol-II processor element.

4. Architecture of Datarol-II Processor

4.1 Overview of Datarol-II Processor

The Datarol-II machine is a massively parallel distributed-memory multiprocessor system in which thousands of processing elements (PE) are connected through a mesh-connection network. The structure of Datarol-II PE is shown in Figure 2. Datarol-II PE consists of: Function Unit (FU), Communication Unit (CU), Activation Controller (AC), Ready Queue (RQ), Memory Unit (MU), and Structure Memory Unit (SMU).

CU handles input packets sent to the PE. When CU gets a packet, it checks the type of the packet and writes the packet data into MU. Then CU issues the thread-invocation request to AC. The thread-invocation request consists of: thread entry address (*dest*), matching counter address (*mc*), and the number of join (*join*).

AC controls thread activation and has Matching Memory (MM). MM holds the value of the matching counter, which is used for join. AC, when it gets a thread-invocation request, accesses the MM and checks whether the requested thread is ready to run. If the thread is ready to run, AC puts the thread-ID into RQ. The thread-ID consists of instance number and thread entry address (*dest*).

FU has several register sets, dequeues a thread-ID from RQ, and sets an entry address of the thread to the Instruction Pointer (IP). At the same time, FU allocates a free register set and triggers execution of the thread. The thread execution starts from the entry address pointed to by IP, and proceeds in sequential order until it encounters an instruction whose termination bit is "on." This short-cycle execution mechanism is similar to conventional sequential execution. When the short-cycle execution encounters an instruction whose termination bit is on, FU dequeues the next available thread from RQ and switches the execution context to the new thread.

When a remote memory access instruction or a procedure call instruction is issued during the short-cycle execution, its request packet is delivered to another PE, and the continuation point is set into the destination register. An execution starts from the continuation point when a return packet has arrived. The return packet has an instance number and a register name in which the return value is stored. When a return packet has arrived, CU gets this continuation by reading the destination register, and sends the continuation to AC in order to invoke the continuation thread. Then, CU writes the return value to the destination register.

4.2 Memory Unit

In Datarol architecture, each instance has its own logical register. MU holds the name of this register in Operand Memory (OM). In fine-grain program execution, memory accesses are so frequently issued that the memory access latency has to be kept as short as possible. A high-speed memory called "Register Buffer" (RB) is introduced in order to achieve faster memory access from the FU. RB is accessed by a page number and an offset address which corresponds to the logical register name. Each page holds the register values of each instance. Before FU starts a new thread execution, register values for the new instance have been loaded into RB by the RB preloading mechanism, which is triggered by RQ. This RB preloading mechanism enables FU to read register values very fast during the thread execution.

4.3 Function Unit

FU has several register sets,[2] and each register has a presence bit which indicates whether the register value is valid or not (see Figure 2). FU also has temporary registers which are used to pass the value from an instruction to other instructions in the same thread. When FU starts execution of a new thread, one of the free register sets is chosen and allocated to the new thread. If a register set has already been allocated to that instance, FU reuses it. Otherwise, one of the register sets is selected and all of its presence bits are cleared. Each instance has its own logical registers. In this case, register values are stored in MU and the register values in MU are loaded into FU-registers before registers are accessed. This register loading is performed automatically by hardware when a register is accessed, and the register-loading operation is performed in the FU register in cooperation with the MU.

FU is constructed as a five-stage pipeline consisting of: Instruction Fetch (IF), Instruction Decode and Register Check (ID&RC), Operand Fetch (OF), Execution and Write Back 1 (EX&WB1), and Write Back 2 (WB2). IF stage fetches the IM cell whose address is specified by IP, and passes the fetched instruction to ID&RC stage. If the termination bit of the fetched instruction is on, FU dequeues a new thread-ID from RQ and sets the thread-ID in IP. Otherwise, IP is incremented. ID&RC stage decodes the instruction, then determines the source and destination register addresses and checks the presence bit of the source registers. In the OF stage, source register values are read from the register set or MU according to the result of the RC stage. One MU access is performed within one clock. If two source registers are needed to be read from MU, pipeline interlock occurs. The EX&WB1 stage executes the instruction. When the OF stage reads the source register value from MU, the read

---

[2]Four register sets is considered in current implementation.

data is stored in the corresponding register. The result data is stored in both the register set and MU, in WB2 stage. Since only one MU access is permitted in single cycle, if MU access occurs at the OF stage and WB2 stage at the same time, pipeline interlock occurs, and access in the OF stage is delayed.

In this pipeline, no explicit load/store instructions are necessary since MU access is performed implicitly in a background operation. Data accesses to MU is performed in parallel with the foreground execution so that the load/store overhead is hidden.

Branch instruction causes the creation of a new thread. Branch address is determined at the EX stage, and the new thread invocation packet is sent to CU. Since the termination bit of the branch instruction is set "on," the thread execution terminates at the branch instruction.

4.4 Structure Memory Unit

The Structure Memory Unit (SMU) supports synchronized memory access by using the I-structure mechanism. SMU also controls the PE load and book keeping of an instance.

Each memory cell has a two-bit tag: presence bit (pr) and pending bit (pe). This tag represents:

00: *Empty*

Neither read nor write access has arrived yet.

01: *Suspended*

Read access has already arrived but write access has not arrived yet.

10: *Full*

Write access has already arrived.

When a synchronized read access is issued to an *Empty* cell, its tag is changed to *Suspended* and a read access packet is stored into the cell. The read access packet contains a register name to which the result of the memory access is written. Table 2 shows memory access protocols. A load control mechanism is introduced in SMU. When SMU gets a call packet, it allocates a new instance and sends a reply packet which contains a new instance number. Then, SMU invokes an initial thread of the new instance. If the PE load is too heavy, SMU delays the invocation of the initial thread and stores the delayed threads in SM. When PE load gets light, SMU invokes the delayed initial threads.

4.5 Function Call Mechanism

The function call in the Datarol-II machine is performed as follows:

1. In a caller instance, say ins_p, a call instruction is executed in FU and FU issues a call packet to network.

2. Since network has a load distribution mechanism, the call packet is delivered to the lightest loaded processor, say PE_c.

3. In the callee processor, PE_c, the call packet is received at SMU. In the SMU, a new instance is allocated, and its name, say ins_c, is returned to the caller instance.

4. The callee processor initiates an initial thread of ins_c. In the initial thread, receive instructions are executed. A receive instruction sets a thread entry address (*dest*) and its synchronization condition (*mc, join*).

Protocol	Before		After		Action
	pr	*pe*	*pr*	*pe*	
write	—	—	1	0	Write data
iwrite	0	0	1	0	Write data
	0	1	1	0	Resume read access and write data
	1	0	—	—	Error
ifwrite	0	0	1	0	Write data
	0	1	0	0	Resume read access
	1	0	—	—	Error
read	0	—	0	—	Return empty value
	1	0	1	0	Read data
iread	0	0	0	1	Pending read access
	0	1	—	—	Error
	1	0	1	0	Read data
ifread	0	0	0	1	Pending read access
	0	1	—	—	Error
	1	0	0	0	Read data

Table 2: Structure memory access protocols.

5. When the caller processor gets a reply packet, the processor initiates a continuation thread, which contains link and rlink operations. The link instruction sends a $rs2$ to ins_c ($rs1$) as a *slot*-th parameter. The rlink instruction stores in a register a continuation thread which will be initiated when return data arrives, and then sends the register name to which the return data is written.

6. When the callee processor receives a link packet, the *slot*-th register value of ins_c is read, and its values are sent to AC to request a thread initiation. Then, CU writes the link data to MU.

7. When AC gets a thread initiation request, (ins, $dest$, mc, $join$), if $join$ is not zero, AC performs a join operation. AC increments the matching counter which is specified by ins and mc. If the value of the counter reaches $join$, the join is established and a thread-ID, which consists of ins and $dest$ is put into RQ. If $join$ is zero, AC puts the thread-ID into RQ without a synchronizing operation.

8. The callee thread is then initiated by link packets. When the callee thread meets a return instruction, a return packet is sent to ins_p. When the execution of ins_c reaches a rins instruction, that instance is released.

9. The caller instance gets a return packet and initiates a continuation thread which corresponds to the result data.

5. Evaluation

In this section, several evaluations of Datarol-II architecture are shown by software simulation. A software simulator of Datarol-II machine has been developed for this purpose. The simulation of the Datarol-II machine system occurs at the register transfer level. Two benchmark programs are used: fib(n) and queen(n). The program

Type	(A) No. of Instructions	(B) No. of AC Input Packets	(C)(B)/(A)	(D) No. of Matching
Dataflow	17752	24656	1.39	6904
Datarol-I	17752	22706	1.28	5917
Datarol-II	17752	9863	0.56	2959

Table 3: Load balance of FU and AC.

fib(n) calculates Fibonacci numbers as described in Section 3.2. Since this program consists of short threads, it requires fast context switching for efficient execution. The program queen(n) finds all solutions for the N-queen problem. This program creates a large number of threads, and a multitude of instances running concurrently because many instances are executed in random, and their memory accesses are less local.

5.1 Threading Effect
Dataflow-based processors, which are implemented as a circular pipeline, experience bottleneck in this pipeline due to the synchronization mechanism by AC in a Datarol-II processor as well as matching-store mechanism in dataflow. Suppose N instructions execute a thread, and the ratio k of the instructions require the operand check, then the synchronization mechanism has to handle $(1+k)N$ packets. Since the synchronization mechanism is, in general, implemented by using random access memory, speed-up of the synchronization is difficult. Thus, the packet handling speed is slower than that of the instruction execution.

Table 3 shows a balance between FU operations and AC matching operations for the program fib(15). In this table, column (A) shows the total number of executed instructions, and column (B) shows the total number of input packets to the matching-store in conventional dataflow machines and AC in the Datarol-I machine. The ratio (B)/(A) is important since it means load balance between the execution unit and synchronization unit. As the ratio (B)/(A) is more than one in these machines, the speed of matching-store limits the pipeline and consequently the speed of these machines. On the other hand, as the ratio (B)/(A) is 0.56 and less than one in Datarol-II, Datarol-II can use the execution unit at higher speeds and achieves higher performance.

5.2 Effect of Implicit Register Loading
In the Datarol-II processor, register values are loaded from MU during the thread execution automatically. The register loading is implicitiy performed without explicit load instruction. The register-loading mechanism is embedded in the execution pipeline in order to hide register loading overhead.

Figure 3 shows the effect of implicit register loading in comparison to explicit loading by load instructions embedded in Datarol codes. In the explicit loading case, load instructions are inserted in the Datarol code. In this program code, every thread execution loads register values from MU explicitly when the thread execution initiates. On the other hand, in the implicit loading case, since the register-loading operations are performed in background of the thread execution, the total thread execution is achieved in a significantly shorter amount of time.

Figure 4 shows the FU and RB utilization ratio for the execution of queen(6). In this case, FU and RB keep a high utilization ratio during the entire period of execution. This data shows the Datarol-II machine makes good use of the RB bandwidth.

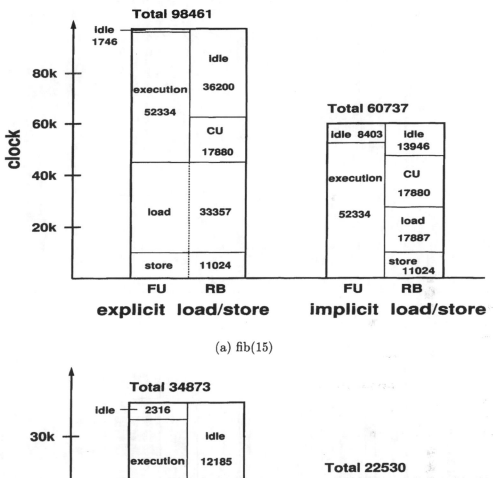

(a) fib(15)

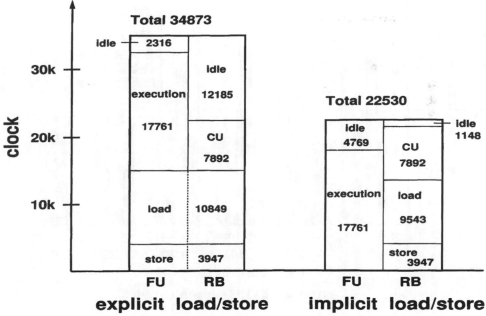

(b) queen(6)

Figure 3: Explicit load vs. implicit load.

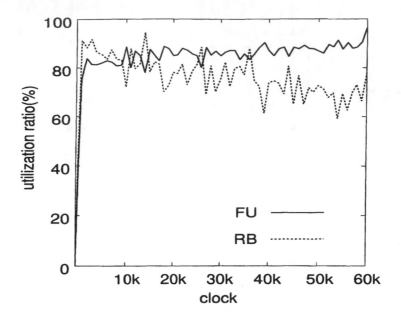

Figure 4: Utilization ratio of FU and RB.

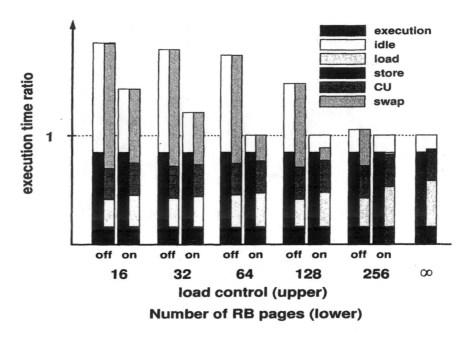

Figure 5: Effect of the number of RB pages.

5.3 Swapping Cost

In the evaluation of Sections 5.1 and 5.2, sufficient RB pages are assumed to exist and no data transfer between the RB and OM. In this section, we evaluate the data transfer cost between RB and OM, in the case of a limited number of RB pages. This cost is referred to as "swapping cost."

Little locality of data access will be expected in dataflow-based execution. When a dataflow machine uses a hierarchical memory system, like a cache, it causes a great increase in execution time because of thrashing.

A two-level hierarchical memory system, which consists of RB and OM, is introduced in Datarol-II. A load control mechanism is also introduced in order to avoid the thrashing between RB and OM. Figure 5 shows the execution times of queen(6) in the case of a various number of RB pages and whether the load control is on or off. When the load control is off, the execution time increases when there is a decrease in RB pages. When the number of RB pages is less than 128, the swapping occurs frequently and execution time increases greatly. When the load control is on, swapping is suppressed. In this case, if the number of RB is more than 64, the swapping time is hidden in the execution time. Even if the RB would require high-speed random access memory, 64 pages will be an acceptable size.

6. Related Work

Datarol-I was designed to achieve efficient context switching and high throughput for highly parallel programs. Datarol-II performs efficient execution both in intra-thread serial execution and in inter-thread concurrent execution. The intra-thread serial execution has a high-speed performance due to a RISC-type execution mechanism in the short-cycle. The inter-thread concurrent execution also achieves high throughput due to the ultra-multiprocessing mechanism inherited from the Datarol-I architecture.

Similar architectures are Monsoon [13], *T [12], EM-4 [14], J-Machine [6], and Epsilon-2 [8].

Monsoon is also designed to support multithread execution by introducing a synchronizing join operator. Monsoon uses ordinary random access memory for join counter management and performs its join operation as one of its general instructions. The join operation in Datarol-II machines is done in the Activation Controller (AC), which uses a special synchronization bit table called Matching Memory (MM), and AC performs the synchronization control in parallel with FU operations in a circular pipeline.

*T has a data processor (dP) and synchronization co-processor (sP), which are connected with a thread queue. *T is very similar to Datarol-II in this way. However, *T has the same join mechanism as Monsoon. Although *T performs join operations in sP, it still uses ordinary random access memory for the join counter, and this slows down the join operation since one join operation takes a few instruction steps, i.e., load, increment, test and store. Even though the join operation is done in sP, in parallel with dP, it should be done in one cycle in order to create a balance with high-speed thread switching in dP. Furthermore, *T requires longer threads for efficient execution than that of Datarol-II, since *T uses a conventional processor for dP.

Activation Controller in Datarol-II, on the other hand, is performed in one cycle since the test-and-set operation is done only for a one bit field in MM, and this mechanism is easily implemented by hardware logic.

EM-4 implements similar synchronization operations by a direct matching mechanism, which uses a direct address assignment of matching-store to the operand address of instruction which requires synchronization between operands. This causes the problem of inefficient memory usage, since memory cells cannot be assigned a continuous address and also one memory cell is used exclusively by only one instruction. AC-memory bit address assignment in Datarol, on the other hand, is independent of the instruction address and operand address, and, therefore, bit address assignment is continuous and the same bit is shared by several instructions.

EM-4 uses high-speed registers only within the strongly connected block which corresponds to the thread in Datarol-II. Since the execution unit is directly connected to the synchronization unit, it causes a pipeline bubble when it fails in operand matching. Moreover, EM-4 has no hierarchical memory system and it requires a large amount of high-speed memory. Datarol-II is more tolerable to the pipeline bubble, since Datarol-II uses registers for both intra-thread and inter-thread within an instance, and RQ works as a buffer between the execution unit and the synchronization unit. Furthermore, Datarol-II offers more flexible memory usage since the hierarchical memory system and the on-demand implicit data swapping control are incorporated into Datarol-II.

J-Machine has a feature for handling messages and low overhead remote procedure calls. However, J-Machine has no special features for efficient synchronization operation like *T, EM-4, and Datarol.

7. Conclusions

A design principle of massively parallel distributed-memory architecture was discussed, and the Datarol-II architecture, which meets this criteria, was proposed and implemented. Datarol-II inherits the highly concurrent execution mechanism from the Datarol-I architecture, which offers high throughput execution of multiple threads due to its continuation-based ultra-multiprocessing mechanism. In addition to this efficient multithread execution, Datarol-II also performs high-speed single-thread execution by introducing the short-cycle RISC-type execution mechanism.

The Datarol-II processor is an optimized version of Datarol-I. The key issues of optimization are: (1) employment of an efficient thread execution mechanism which does not specify the continuation point explicitly, and (2) load control mechanism which improves locality of memory access and enables the configuration of hierarchical memory.

The Datarol-II processor consists of: Function Unit, Memory Unit, Activation Controller, Communication Unit, Ready Queue, and Structure Memory Unit. The Function Unit performs program-counter-based short-cycle execution within a thread as well as continuation-based long-cycle execution among threads. The Memory Unit has a two-level hierarchical memory system, RB and OM, and it provides high-speed memory access. The Structure Memory Unit provides synchronized memory access by an I-structure-based mechanism. This construction of the processor is highly suitable for massively parallel execution since this processor provides high throughput execution of multiple threads due to its continuation-based execution mechanism.

We have evaluated the Datarol-II processor by software simulation for simple program samples. The simulation results showed that (1) thread level continuation-based execution, which reduces the number of input packets to a synchronization unit, prevents the pipeline in the synchronization unit from bottlenecking; (2) the implicit register-loading mechanism hides the memory access overhead, which is caused by context switching; and (3) the load control mechanism, which reduces the traffic between RB and OM, makes the hierarchical memory system work more effectively.

Currently, we are pursuing further simulation experiments using various applications in order to evaluate the performance of the Datarol-II processor in greater detail.

References

[1] M. Amamiya, "Dataflow Computing and Parallel Reduction Machine," *Future Generation Computer Systems*, Vol. 4, No. 1, 1988, pp. 53–67.

[2] M. Amamiya and R. Taniguchi, "Datarol: A Massively Parallel Architecture for Functional Language," *Proc. IEEE 2nd Symp. Parallel and Distributed Processing*, IEEE CS Press, Los Alamitos, Calif., 1990, pp. 726–735.

[3] M. Amamiya, "An Ultra-Multiprocessing Architecture for Functional Languages," in *Advanced Topics in Data-Flow Computing*, J.-L. Gaudiot and L. Bic, Eds. Prentice-Hall, Englewood Cliffs, N.J., 1991.

[4] Arvind and R. Iannucci, "Two Fundamental Issues in Multiprocessing," *Proc. DFVLR Conf. on Parallel Processing in Science and Engineering*, Bon-Bad Godesberg, Germany, 1987.

[5] D.E. Culler et al., "Fine-grain Parallelism with Minimal Hardware Support: A Compiler-Control Threaded Abstract Machine," *Proc. 4th ASPLOS*, ACM Press, New York, N.Y., 1991, pp. 164–175.

[6] W.J. Dally et al., "The J-Machine: A Fine-grain Concurrent Computer," *Proc. 11th IFIP*, 1989, pp. 1147–1153.

[7] T. von Eicken et al., "Active Messages: a Mechanism for Integrated Communication and Computation," *Proc. 19th Ann. Int'l Symp. Computer Architecture*, ACM Press, New York, N.Y., 1992, pp. 256–266.

[8] V.G. Grafe and J.E. Hoch, "The Epsilon-2 Multi-Processor System," *J. Parallel and Distributed Computing*, Vol. 10, 1990, pp. 309–318.

[9] S.W. Keckler and W.J. Dally, "Processor Coupling: Integrating Compile Time and Runtime Scheduling for Parallelism," *Proc. 19th Ann. Int'l Symp. Computer Architecture*, ACM Press, New York, N.Y., 1992, pp. 202–213.

[10] S. Kusakabe et al., "Parallelism Control and Storage Management in Datarol PE," *Proc. IFIP World Congress*, Vol. 1, 1992, pp. 535–541.

[11] R.S. Nikhil and Arvind, "Can dataflow subsume von Neumann computing?," *Proc. 16th Ann. Int'l Symp. Computer Architecture*, IEEE CS Press, Los Alamitos, Calif., 1989, pp. 262–272.

[12] R.S. Nikhil, G.M. Papadopoulos, and Arvind, "*T: A Multithread Massively Parallel Architecture," *Proc. 19th Ann. Int'l Symp. Computer Architecture*, ACM Press, New York, N.Y., 1992, pp. 156–167.

[13] G.M. Papadopoulos and D.E. Culler, "Monsoon: an Explicit Token-Store Architecture," *Proc. 17th Ann. Int'l Symp. Computer Architecture*, IEEE CS Press, Los Alamitos, Calif., 1990, pp. 82–91.

[14] S. Sakai et al., "An Architecture of a Dataflow Single Chip Processor," *Proc. 16th Ann. Int'l Symp. Computer Architecture*, IEEE CS Press, Los Alamitos, Calif., 1989, pp. 46–53.

[15] T. Tachibana, R. Taniguchi, and M. Amamiya, "Compiling Method of Functional Programming Language *Valid* by Dataflow Analysis—Extraction of Datarol Program," *J. Information Processing* (in Japanese), Vol. 30, No. 12, 1989, pp. 1628–1638.

[16] R. Taniguchi, T. Kawano, and M. Amamiya, "A Distributed-Memory Multi-Thread Multiprocessor Architecture for Computer Vision and Image Processing: Optimized Version of AMP," *Proc. 26th ICSS*, Vol. 1, 1993, pp. 151–160.

StarT the Next Generation: Integrating Global Caches and Dataflow Architecture

Boon Seong Ang, Arvind, and Derek Chiou
Laboratory for Computer Science
Massachusetts Institute of Technology

The implicitly parallel programming model provides an attractive approach to deal with the complexity of parallel programming. Implementing this model efficiently, especially on stock processors, remains a big challenge, partly because of the fine granularity of the parallelism exploited. The Monsoon [27] project was designed to address and investigate support for fine-grain parallelism, and has yielded very encouraging results [13].

*Our experience with Monsoon and *T [24], [28], a follow-up project after Monsoon, suggests that provision for global shared memory is an area where both the Monsoon and *T architectures can be improved. Starting with the split-phase approach used in Monsoon and *T, we propose to augment global memory access by including coherent global caches.*

The rapid improvements in stock microprocessors, and the high cost and effort required to develop a competitive microprocessor, presents practical constraints on what can be built in any experimental architecture project. We propose a machine that attempts to include as many of the desired features as possible within the constraint of using a stock microprocessor. This machine will allow us to continue research into the dataflow approach to parallel computing as well as provide a prototype of a commercial product.

1. Introduction

The dataflow approach to parallel computing has been very successful in at least two important aspects: (1) exposing parallelism and (2) using fine-grain parallelism to tolerate long latency operations and synchronization waits. These features have been demonstrated in several studies on real machines [13], [9]. There are, however, still several obstacles in making the dataflow approach a truly viable solution to parallel computing.

The biggest challenge is to find a way of executing dataflow style code efficiently on a wide variety of platforms. One approach is to improve the compilation of dataflow style languages to reduce synchronization requirements, instruction counts, non-local communication, and so on. Research efforts are underway to try to achieve this goal without affecting the ability to expose parallelism and tolerate latency. Another approach is to identify the basic architectural mechanisms that will efficiently support the dataflow style of fine-grain parallel execution. For pragmatic reasons, the resulting architecture should be as close to conventional architectures as possible to take advantage of the decades of experience in building and programming conventional processors, as well as to make maximum use of existing hardware and software subsystems.

This paper will concentrate on architectural features that are needed to support fine-grain parallel execution. We discuss the lessons we have learned from the Monsoon project [27], [13] and the early phases of implementing the *T Multithreaded architecture [24]. Drawing on these experiences, and the basic requirements of any parallel computation, we suggest a desirable set of features to be incorporated in our current machine called *T-NG (StarT, the Next Generation). Essentially *T-NG has better provision for global shared memory than either Monsoon or 88110MP [28], a Motorola 88110 based implementation of the abstract *T model presented in [24]. Our proposal adds caching of global memory in a way that allows it to coexist with the split-phase transactions and the multithreaded approach used in Monsoon and the 88110MP.

The rapid improvements in stock microprocessors and the high cost and complexity of developing a modern microprocessor impose practical constraints on what can be built in any experimental project that wishes to have competitive performance. *T-NG has to work within these constraints, and thus represents many compromises. Nevertheless, it incorporates many of the desired features. We hope that the importance of the missing features can be investigated through the effects of their absence. The machine will also provide the platform to continue research into compilation technology.

The rest of the paper is organized as follows: Section 2 describes some of the models for parallel programming. Section 3 describes the architectural concerns of running fine-grain parallel programs, especially on stock hardware. It also describes architectural modifications that would allow dataflow programs to run much more efficiently and how those modifications may help other programming paradigms as well. Section 4 examines Monsoon, an implementation of a processor designed to exploit fine-grain parallelism, and how it performed. That section ends with a discussion of the deficiencies of Monsoon, and how they may be fixed. Section 5 describes *T, an architecture that addresses some of Monsoon's weaknesses while moving towards a conventional microprocessor based machine. The initial plan was to build *T around Motorola's MC88110 microprocessor. However, for reasons beyond the control of the project, these plans had to be abandoned in late 1993. While drawing up new implementation plans centered around the Power PC architecture family, we took the opportunity to explore incorporating global caches into our new machine. Section 6 gives a high-level view of this machine. *T-NG is an ongoing project; thus, the discussed implementation should not be assumed to be final. Finally, we conclude this paper with a brief look at related work.

2. Parallel Programming

Writing parallel programs is currently much more difficult than writing sequential programs. The difficulty arises from three problems: (1) managing the control flow along multiple threads of execution, (2) managing the placement and access of global data, (3) timing events in such a way that parallel speedup is achieved. While it is possible for a programmer to explicitly choreograph a parallel program by indicating which tasks execute when, how tasks communicate and synchronize, and where data should be placed and how it can be accessed, such an undertaking is extremely complex. Several parallel programming models have thus emerged in an attempt to cope with these difficulties. We discuss some of these below.

2.1 Data Parallel Model

The data parallel programming model, exemplified by languages such as CM Fortran, Fortran 90, Fortran D, and High Performance Fortran (HPF), is a very popular model of parallel programming. The data parallel programming model maintains the single thread of execution abstraction of sequential programming. That single thread of execution, however, can perform the same operation in parallel on a selected subset of array elements (hence the name, *data parallel*). Conceptually each data element resides on a specific virtual processor. Periodically, data elements have to be moved to a virtual processor that needs them for computation. Since the cost of data movement is high, the initial data placement and the data movement operations must be planned very carefully to achieve high performance. Currently, the programmer has to help with the placement of global data by providing directives (automating the data placement process is currently an active area of research). Once the placement is specified, the compiler takes care of the tedious task of generating the actual memory access code.

SIMD machines, like the CM-2, provide a direct hardware implementation of this programming model. Processors in the machine operate in lock-step, with a single instruction stream controlling the operation of all the processors. General communication, i.e., an arbitrary permutation of array elements, is very expensive. For example, general communication on the CM-2 takes about 80 times as long as a primitive arithmetic operation; nearest neighbor communication is an order of magnitude faster, but still takes about four times that of a primitive arithmetic operation. A program must keep general communication of data to a minimum in order to achieve reasonable performance. Unfortunately, some programs are not amenable to this type of tuning.

The data parallel programming model has been implemented on various types of MIMD machines such as distributed memory, message passing machines (e.g., CM-5, Paragon), cache-coherent shared memory machines, and dataflow machines (e.g., EM-4 [34]). Although each processor has its own thread of control during execution, the program still follows a single thread of control logically. In order to preserve the lock-step execution semantics of data parallel programs, implementations on MIMD machines have to perform explicit barrier synchronization periodically. Barriers can be implemented in software on top of the communication facilities of the machine [34]. Many global communication primitives have the implicit effect of barrier synchronization, making the removal of redundant explicit barriers a compiler optimization. For machines that do not have very high performance networks, specialized global synchronization hardware as found on the CM-5 is sometimes provided. On the other hand, the ability of each processor to have its own thread of control makes MIMD machines much more efficient at executing conditionals than SIMD machines.

Some distributed memory machines favor large messages over small ones due to poor network interfaces. On such machines, the compiler or the programmer has the added burden of grouping small messages together (i.e., *message vectorization*). Managing the global movement of data remains the biggest issue in the implementation of data parallel model. Split-C is a language that provides a convenient way of expressing global data movement in the data parallel model [8].

Placement of data is significantly easier on shared memory machines than on distributed memory machines. Shared memory machines are somewhat more tolerant of dynamic data communication requirements, but still require good temporal and spatial locality to perform well. Careful orchestration of data access pattern is still important on these machines.

The data parallel programming model, because of its closeness to sequential languages, and because of its good performance for a certain class of programs (mostly dense matrix computations) on a fairly wide range of hardware platforms, has gained wide acceptance. The data parallel model is, however, restricted in the forms of parallelism that it can exploit due to its single thread of control. It is also restricted in the class of programs that it can efficiently execute due to data placement requirements. Any sort of irregularity rapidly decreases the efficiency of data parallel programs, even though there may be considerable parallelism in the underlying algorithms. As far as we know, no one has even attempted to express a symbolic code, such as a compiler, in the data parallel model. These types of programs need both a more general model of parallel computing as well as a machine that can support general communication efficiently.

2.2 Control Parallel Model

Programming models that try to exploit task level parallelism represent a large departure from the data parallel programming model. These models do not restrict parallelism to concurrent operation on arrays. Instead, they attempt to make full use of multiple threads of control. "Data parallelism" can still be exploited since it can be expressed as multiple threads of execution on different array elements. These models, however, are more complicated than the data parallel model, since they must manage multiple threads of control. In the next few paragraphs, we discuss several programming models that fall into this general category, but differ from one another in some significant aspects.

Communicating Sequential Processes (CSP)-based programming languages, such as Ada and Occam, offer one approach to control parallel programming. The multiple threads of control are exposed at the source language level. These threads are called *tasks* in Ada and *processes* in Occam. Communication between processes is through fixed channels, and synchronization is achieved through the use of blocking sends and receives. Globally shared memory is usually not supported in this model. Any shared data have to be communicated through messages managed by the programmer. The network of processes and channels corresponding to a program are statically mapped onto physical processors and channels. A very simple scheduler on each processor schedules processes and manages communication. While this programming model puts the power of writing parallel programs in the programmer's hands, it does not provide very much support in managing the complexity of parallel programming.

PVM [12] represents another approach to parallel programming which is closely related to the CSP model. This model is implemented via libraries on top of conventional sequential languages like C or Fortran. PVM consists mostly of send and receive functions. Messages have to be explicitly received. Receives can be blocking or non-blocking and can specify a message sender processor and/or a message type to receive, but are not required to do so. Shared memory is not directly supported by PVM. There are other parallel programming "languages"/packages that are similarly implemented via libraries on top of C that do support the abstraction of shared memory. An example is the Argonne National Laboratory's (ANL) parallel processing macro package, Parmacs, used in the SPLASH benchmarks [36]. The management of multiple threads of control is still the programmer's responsibility in all these packages.

In an effort to exploit finer-grain parallelism, several programming models take a much more dynamic view of thread creation and synchronization. Each processor keeps a pool of threads and does "multithreaded execution." This allows the idle cycles in one thread, due to such things as waiting for synchronization or remote memory operations, to be used by other threads to perform useful work. A very dynamic form of scheduling is required by this model. In general, management of threads can be done in user code, in the operating system, or by a system supplied run-time system (RTS). Having the user manage threads is impractical, tedious, and error prone. Having the operating system manage the threads imposes extremely high overheads. Both methods are prone to deadlocks and race conditions. A better solution is to hide this complexity from the user and have the system software, either compiler, run time system, or both handle this task. When the compiler generates threads, it is able to adhere to certain restrictions that allow the RTS to ensure that deadlocks and races do not occur. The TAM model, which we will discuss later, embodies many of these features [9].

2.3 Implicitly Parallel Model

Id, a parallel language based on functional languages, represents an effort at exploiting fine-grain parallelism while keeping the task of parallel programming manageable [21]. The implicitly parallel programming model offered by Id insulates the programmer from the concerns of managing parallel threads of control and global data. Instead of a data parallel, or task-level model, the programmer is provided with a data-driven model. In writing code with the functional subset of Id, the programmer only has to think about expressing data dependencies, a task that is inherent in any form of programming. The functional nature of the language allows the compiler to extract fine-grain parallelism and generate code that takes advantage of multiple threads of execution via multithreading. In Id, synchronization is managed automatically by the compiler, allowing fine-grain producer-consumer synchronization. The programming model provides global shared memory by default, and thus, the programmer does not have to manage data movement explicitly.

The functional nature of Id is the key that provides automatic extraction of parallelism. Other functional languages, notably SISAL [7], are similarly able to exploit implicit parallelism. Id goes one step further by providing non-strict procedure calls, which allow a call to begin execution before all the arguments have arrived, thus pushing the idea of an eager, data-driven execution to its limits.

The implicitly parallel approach provides a model that takes full advantage of all forms of available parallelism, while hiding the complexity of multiple threads of control. It is more general than the data parallel model in the forms of parallelism it can exploit, while avoiding the coding complexity of the control parallel models. Having such positive traits, the implicitly parallel approach will be a clear winner if the model could be implemented efficiently. Here, however, lies the difficulty encountered in this approach. The fine granularity of the parallelism makes efficient implementation on commercial parallel machines difficult. Since synchronization is pervasive, threads are switched frequently. Compile time information for managing locality is simply not available under such dynamic conditions, and this makes it difficult to generate efficient code.

The implicitly parallel model also requires a global shared address space and word-level memory accesses. Commercially available parallel machines either do not support these abstractions or do so poorly, thus increasing the difficulty in efficient implementation. Despite these problems, considerable progress has been made. The Monsoon dataflow machine, which we will discuss in greater detail in Section 4, is a demonstration that hardware can be built to support such a programming model. Much work still has to be done to deliver the promises of implicit parallel programming. The potential payback of taking advantage of all forms of useful parallelism implicitly, without the complexity for the programmer, is a great incentive to continue research in this area. This paper will deal with some of these difficulties and propose means of overcoming them.

3. Fine-Grain Parallel Programs on Stock Hardware

A natural question to ask dataflow architecture researchers is "why not use stock hardware?" Given the availability of very high performance microprocessors, it is a very relevant question. The problem is that the demands of fine-grain parallel execution are different than the demands made by sequential code. Current microprocessors are optimized for the latter. It is a challenge to determine whether processor features for fine-grain codes can coexist with existing features for sequential codes.

3.1 What Is Fine-Grain Parallel Execution?

Dataflow graphs offer perhaps the most mature model for fine-grain parallelism. These graphs are usually generated by a compiler from a functional language (see [4] for an example). We briefly explain the execution of a dataflow graph.

The nodes of a dataflow graph specify the operations to be performed on the values that flow on *tokens* along arcs between the nodes. Each token also carries a *continuation* consisting of a node number, an instruction pointer, and a frame pointer. A continuation specifies the computation to be done with the value on the token. Execution starts with a pool of initial tokens. When a token is processed, a waiting/matching store is checked to see if the token's partner, if any, is already present. If not, the token is inserted into the waiting/matching store, and the next token is processed. If the synchronization is successful (the correct partner token is found), the node is fired (*executed*) and the resulting values are put back into the pool. The order in which tokens are processed does not affect the result of the computation, but may greatly affect the running time and the resources required. To avoid deadlocks, it is essential that a value that fails to synchronize (i.e., one or more of its partners has not yet been processed) should not block the processing of other tokens.

Our dataflow graphs allow global memory in the form of I-structures which are write-once, read-many-times data structures. Accessing an I-structure location is done by splitting the read operation into two separate phases (see [4] for details). In the first phase, the read (fetch) is initiated and the processor is then relinquished to another thread. The read request consists of a continuation and the address to be read. In the second phase, the read is performed and the result is returned (actually forwarded) to the waiting node, specified in the continuation supplied on the request tokens.

In such a *split-phase* operation, the actual reading of the value may occur on some processor other than the one where the read is initiated. Depending on the dynamic execution order, a value to be read may not have been written yet. If it is unknown whether a value being read has already been written, the reads and write require some synchronization. Synchronizing reads (e.g., I-structures) may take an arbitrary amount of time to complete, since an arbitrary amount of time may elapse before the value is actually written. In the case where a read arrives before the write of a location, the second phase of the read request is deferred (i.e., queued up) until the write occurs. It is important to note that deadlocks are not possible (as long as the program does not include any cyclic data dependence) because the node waiting for a reply does not block any processor or memory operations. Once the write is completed, the request is satisfied in the usual manner.

If every node of the dataflow graph is a simple operation like add or memory fetch, an inordinate number of synchronizations need to be performed, because almost every instruction requires synchronization. It is easy to see, however, that a node could consist of more than one operation. Operations within a node could themselves be organized as a dataflow graph or as a simple linear sequence of instructions. We call the latter case, where the nodes in the dataflow graph are sequences of instructions, *multithreading*, and each of the linear instruction sequences, *threads*. This model of multithreading is essentially identical to the Threaded Abstract Machine (TAM) proposed by Culler et al. [9]. TAM distinguishes between inlet threads and computation threads—the former are threads executed in response to incoming messages. A thread scheduling model is also part of TAM. There are several other variants of multithreaded models—depending on whether threads are allowed to be suspended and resumed, and the types of instructions that can be included in a thread (see, for example, Traub [38] or Iannucci[14]). Nikhil [22] is a good introduction to compiling an implicitly parallel language into multithreaded code.

3.2 What Architectural Support Does Multithreading Require?

Multithreading requires some hardware support to run efficiently. In the following, we discuss the categories of hardware support that would be useful, and how current stock processors fail to provide that support.

3.2.1 Message Passing

Messages are used to start threads, to make a request or reply, or to pass information. Since every instance of a dataflow graph node could potentially be executed on a different processor, a huge number of interprocessor messages could be generated by a multithreaded program. A good network interface is probably the single largest improvement that can be made to a processor to support multithreading [28]. A fast processor/network interface that requires the fewest number of processor cycles to send and receive messages would be vital. The efficiency of the interface can be measured in terms of the number of processor cycles needed to send a certain unit of data, say a 64-bit word. The raw network latency is somewhat less critical, since multithreading can be used to tolerate it.

The fastest possible network interface can format and send a message in a single cycle. Given a standard RISC processor, formatting and sending a message in a single cycle would require using registers to provide the necessary pieces of the message, forcing large hardware modifications to insert the network interface into the processor itself. It is possible, however, to get a reasonable network interface through a normal memory bus. The cost of sending a message could still be low as the processor does not have to wait for the message to actually get out of the chip. The latency of receiving a message, however, cannot be hidden, and may be significant. Pipelined memory systems in a modern aggressive microprocessor add many stages between the processor and the memory bus, and may also introduce the possibility of out-of-order stores. These make sense for executing long sequential threads, but hurt the performance of a bus-based messaging interface.

Most commercial parallel machines take a substantial amount of time to get to the network, say 50 cycles or more if external hardware support is available (see CM-5 for example), or thousands of cycles if software gets involved (see Paragon, for example). This level of processor latency encountered in accessing the network makes communication very expensive and, thus, limits compilation options.

3.2.2 Thread Creation

In order to execute threads, they need to be created. When a multithreaded program first starts execution, an initial pool of threads is produced by the startup system code. The running program is then responsible for generating its own threads to get its job done. A mechanism for creating threads is a *fork*, which allows the running thread to split itself and execute down two paths. A minimal encoding of fork will require an instruction pointer which indicates one branch of the fork—the other branch being implicitly the next instruction. Thus, forking can be performed by a single instruction which takes an instruction pointer as an argument. Clearly, the cost of thread creation determines the rate at which parallelism can be expanded. It also determines whether it is worth spawning parallel threads at all.

Stock processors do not have any special support for thread creation. Creating a thread requires software conventions and some sort of thread queue which, on stock hardware, also needs to be managed by software.

3.2.3 Synchronization   When more than one value used for the same computation arrive on separate, arbitrarily ordered messages, the values must be *synchronized*. Synchronization ensures that the necessary values are available before continuing past the synchronization point. In a dataflow graph, each node must synchronize all of the incoming values before it can be fired. Though the frequency of synchronization events vary greatly from program to program, our preliminary compiler work indicates that synchronization events occur around once per 10 abstract dataflow instructions, which would expand to no more than 40 RISC instructions. This makes synchronization a very frequent event.

Synchronization required for multithreading can be emulated with software counters in normal memory locations. We call these locations *synchronization counters*. The essence of synchronization is an atomic read-modify-write to a the memory location, followed by a branch on the result. Synchronization is best viewed as a memory-to-memory operation because it is rare that the same synchronization counter is accessed more than once in a thread. Thus, a typical sequence of instruction to implement a synchronization will include a load, a decrement, a jump conditional, and a store, with the additional requirement that atomic access to the counter is maintained between the load and the store. Such a sequence of instruction is not very cheap, particularly when this is expected to happen every 50 or so instructions. Thus, specialized hardware support in this area is highly desirable.

Most stock processors have some hardware support for synchronization, in the form of test-and-set, exchange-reg-with-mem, load-locked/store-conditional, memory-barrier, etc. These instructions essentially enforce some atomicity constraints which would be hard to emulate otherwise. They do not, however, provide the type of synchronization we require. Also, these multicycle instructions usually disrupt the processor pipeline. It is probable that emulating synchronization using the scheme discussed in the previous paragraph will be easier and more efficient than using these specialized synchronization instructions.

3.2.4 Context Switching   Whenever a synchronization event fails or a thread terminates, a *context switch* must occur. A context switch conceptually requires the previous state to be saved and the new state to be installed into the processor. Of course, only the state that has been modified and needs to be preserved for later use needs to be saved. The cost of each context switch depends on the size of context to save and restore. This is related to the size of the thread, with shorter threads having smaller states. However, shorter threads also entail more frequent context switching. In general, the lower frequency of context switching for longer threads tend to outweigh the increased cost per switch, making it cheaper to run longer threads. Multithreading with short threads is therefore at a disadvantage.

This disadvantage is aggravated on commercial microprocessors by the principles behind their design, namely, to run long threads and expect infrequent context switches. Accordingly, the processor is optimized to take advantage of that locality with a sophisticated memory hierarchy that makes frequent access to the lower hierarchy a costly event. In some sense, stock processors are designed to make context switching *expensive* in order to process long threads more efficiently.

Faster context switching can take on many different flavors. The simplest technique is to eliminate the memory hierarchy and allow the processor to address a monolithic memory directly. Thus, context switching amounts to loading a program counter and a frame base register. The obvious problem with this is the less competitive speed and bandwidth of the large memory as compared to registers and cache. While very long pipelines and multiple banks of memory could conceivably alleviate this problem, elimination of the local state will probably slow down sequential threads.

Another solution is to have multiple register files, each dedicated to a thread, and to switch between them. One might interleave threads in the pipeline and force a context switch every cycle [37], [3], or one might switch to another thread on encountering a long latency operation [2]. On the University of Tokyo's UNIRED-II processor [35] the frequency of thread switching depends on the number of active threads. One might also allow one register file to be swapped while another is in use. Another possible related solution is the Named State Register File [25] which uses a cache instead of a register file and has multiple register contexts to allow very rapid switching between threads. Yet another solution is to permit multiple instruction streams to execute on the same set of execution units. If sufficient load-store unit bandwidth is available, this could allow the overlap of useful computation with context switching overhead, thus effectively masking the cost of context switching.

3.2.5 Thread and Message Scheduling

The pool of ready threads in our model needs to be scheduled for execution in some way. The ordering method could be as simple as LIFO or FIFO or could be very complicated, such as taking the content of the threads into account. As mentioned earlier, a bad schedule could explode the amount of resources required to run the program. Since messages/tokens often contain very small amounts of work, it is generally too expensive to allow software to do much scheduling.

Automatic hardware scheduling of the "next" thread upon thread completion or suspension takes far fewer cycles than any software scheduler. Hardware queues are, however, less flexible in terms of the ways in which the thread queues can be managed. No commercial processor has direct hardware support for thread queues.

3.2.6 Global Memory

Access to global shared memory is a fundamental issue of parallel processing. It is very important for the parallel execution of most high level languages. Thus, we discuss the issues in greater detail in the next section.

3.3 Accessing Global Memory

Researchers generally agree that it is important to support the abstraction of a global shared memory for the programmer even though reality dictates that the memory has to be physically distributed on any scalable machine. There are several ways of supporting the global shared memory abstraction on machines with physically distributed memory. The two basic methods for accessing global memory are (1) protocols built on top of message passing and (2) global caching. The method provided has become the most popular way of differentiating parallel computers. In this section, we will discuss the strengths and weaknesses of these two methods.

3.3.1 Global Shared Memory Through Message Passing

Message passing alone allows us to implement certain forms of global shared memory. A processor *a* which desires the value from a location in the memory of processor *b* can send a message to *b* requesting that value. After *b* receives the request, it replies to *a* with the desired value.

What does *a* do while it is waiting for *b* to respond? It could just wait for the result, not doing anything in the meantime. Just waiting, however, is prone to deadlock, since *b* could be waiting for *a* to return a result before it responds to *a*'s request. Either an alternative path for other processors to access *b*'s memory is required, or all processors must periodically satisfy other processors' requests. The former solution is used by *T (discussed in Section 5) and is showing up in commercial machines such as the Cray T3D [16]. This solution works as long as the value to be read is available. The latter solution, periodic polling, makes code generation more difficult and degrades sequential thread performance. Even if the polled message is just put aside, it can still negatively affect the caching behavior of thread in the processor pipeline.

In general, if the value to be read is not yet available, it is necessary to suspend the current thread and schedule another. This requirement stems from the fact that processor *a* may be required to execute a thread that creates, directly or indirectly, the value being read. If the processor is not relinquished, deadlock is possible. The request and reply messages must contain some information, a continuation, to indicate what should be done with the data when it returns to the requesting processor. Separating the request for a global memory location from its actual use is essentially the dataflow split-phase operation.

Switching threads has another good property; it overlaps computation and communication, potentially increasing processor efficiency. Reading a value from another processor can take more than a hundred cycles in most parallel machines of reasonable size. It involves two message launches, two network trips, execution of two message handlers, a load, and perhaps a context switch at the destination. Waiting for every global read will clearly destroy any chances of performance for the vast majority of programs. Switching threads, however, requires a context switch, scheduling a new thread, and other such overhead. If the aggregate overhead of switching a thread is longer than the total latency of remotely accessing the global location, it is not worth switching threads.

It is clear that the performance of global memory through message passing depends heavily on the performance of context switching and the processor/network interface (of course, the basic bandwidth of the network is also important, but is generally not the limiting factor). The faster the context switch, the greater the overlap of communication and computation. If switching cannot be done quickly, communication cannot be overlapped with computation since the latency of remote fetches is effectively added to the total computation time, often negating any advantage of using a parallel machine. Machines that do not have some special hardware for handling memory requests from other processors must context switch twice when doing a split-phase operation, first when the remote processor switches contexts to handle the request and second when the requesting processor switches contexts to accept the response. For these reasons, emulating word-level access to global memory on message-passing machines using stock processors is generally inefficient. These characteristics bias the compilers to generate long threads and large messages, hallmarks of coarse-grain parallelism, to achieve acceptable performance.

3.3.2 Global Shared Memory Through Caching The other basic approach to providing global shared memory is through the use of global caching, i.e., caching global data in computation processors' local caches. The requesting processor a performs a load on a global location exactly as it would a local location, i.e., it checks the cache first. If the value is found in the cache, the computation continues as it would in a sequential machine; the value is put into a register directly. If the value is not in the cache, however, the value is fetched from its remote location through the standard memory bus interface of a. There must be some device sitting on the memory bus which recognizes global addresses, satisfying the requests by communicating with the memory of processor b that actually owns the desired value.

In the simplest case, when a misses on a global location in the cache, a waits until the value is returned to it. If a never hits in the cache, the situation becomes exactly the same as for message passing when context switching takes longer than the round-trip message time. Clearly, the more a hits in the cache, the fewer remote fetches of cache data need to be done. Any miss of global values in the cache, assuming that a waits for the value, add the fetch latency to the critical path. The execution time includes all the latency from accesses to global memory.

Since current processors have scoreboarding, they can execute past a load until the loading data is actually needed. Future microprocessors will allow multiple outstanding memory operations. All of these features allow some overlap of communication and computation. How much is actually achievable depends on the program behavior. The potential for overlap, however, is still far less than in the split-phase model.

There are several reasons for stalling the processor on a miss rather than switching threads. The most important reason is that if the processor suspends the waiting thread and switches to another thread, there is no guarantee that the cache line fetched from the remote location will still be in the cache by the time the suspended thread is resumed. Additional mechanisms such as locking a cache line (analogous to locking a page of physical memory during a page fault), or placing the fetched line in some buffer that will not be flushed would be needed. Such schemes need to be careful not to introduce deadlocks. [17] describes how this problem is dealt with in Alewife. A second reason is that unless multiple hardware contexts are provided, thread switching can be expensive, especially since code compiled for such machines usually keeps as much valid state in registers as possible. A third reason is that most code compiled for such machines is not multithreaded at the processor level; there is usually only one single thread running on each physical processor.

The big problem with global caching is keeping the caches coherent. If two processors each have a copy of a cache line, and one modifies that line, the other processor must somehow be automatically notified of the change. If the notification is not automatic, there is no point to general purpose global caching since processors must then always check to see if the cached object is up-to-date. Some scheme for dealing with the coherency of data is needed (see DASH [20], [19], KSR [6], SCI [33], and Alewife [1] for examples of specific coherency protocols). Cache coherency protocols for managing cache coherency in a distributed memory machine are very complicated. Also, support for global coherent cached memory traditionally requires a fairly sizable investment in hardware.

When there is sufficient locality in the code, global caching works well (see DASH results for examples). Prefetches can also be used to bring data into the cache before they are actually needed. However, the performance is sensitive to the nature of the code, and how code and data is distributed. The same study described examples like the MP3D code in the SPLASH [36] benchmarks where poor locality killed performance.

3.3.3 Split-Phase versus Global Caching It is clear that both split-phase operations and global caching have their respective advantages and disadvantages. Split-phase operations can hide communication latency but demand fast context switching and network interfaces. Using proper message handlers, messages of any size and I-structure synchronized accesses can be supported. Global caching may reduce the average latency but does not hide it when a cache miss occurs. It is limited to cache-line sized accesses and requires more hardware support than message passing.

Is there a clear winner between the two methods? The short answer is no. We will discuss that question in greater depth in Section 5.4.

3.4 Does Hardware Support for Fine-Grain Parallelism Help Other Programming Models?

It is not difficult to see that all the hardware modifications proposed above would help execution of programs written under other paradigms. The question is by how much. The relative importance of these features crucially depends upon the programs to be run. In parallel computing, much more so than in sequential computing, programmers take into account the characteristics of the machine on which the program is to be run. Thus, it is difficult to determine the importance of each feature simply by studying the behavior of existing parallel applications. In some sense, many programming paradigms evolved to run on the available parallel hardware, and, thus, do not context switch, synchronize, or access the network very much. Thus, the impact of the described modifications would be modest for most paradigms other than fine-grain parallel execution.

Context switching and synchronization support only helps if you plan on switching contexts and synchronizing very often. Unless the threads are generated automatically, it is unlikely that a programmer will write a program with a large number of threads or complex synchronization. It is simply not feasible for a user to manage fine-grain parallel execution. Context switching and synchronization support, therefore, are much less important in data parallel and control parallel models.

A fast network interface, on the other hand, could potentially help other paradigms a great deal. Every parallel program has to access the network sometime, and if that access time was reduced, less care would be required to minimize communication. Performance would increase on codes that use the network extensively.

Support for shared memory will also help the compiler writers of almost all the high-level languages, including HPF. The global shared memory abstraction greatly simplifies access to distributed memory.

Even if all the features discussed in the previous sections could be included in a modern RISC processor without negatively affecting its performance, it would still be difficult to convince the manufacturer to include these features in his next generation processor. There is never sufficient silicon to include all one wants. However, if a feature, such as a better network interface, is useful for most programming models, its inclusion is more likely to be acceptable.

4. Monsoon: A Proof-of-Concept Dataflow Machine

Monsoon [10], [27], [39] is an existence proof that dataflow hardware is buildable. It incorporates both fast messaging and fast context switching as well as supports fast synchronization, all deemed desirable for fine-grain parallel codes. Monsoon was designed at MIT and built by Motorola. It was designed to run pure dynamic dataflow code, such as Id [21] programs compiled in that style. It is based on an eight-stage pipelined processing node running at 10 MHz (see Figure 1). Monsoon's pipeline

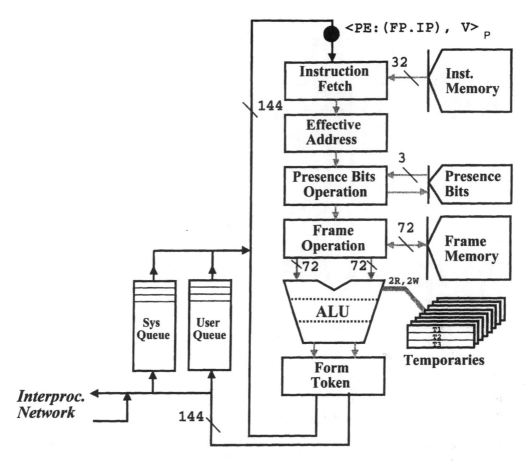

Figure 1: A Monsoon node (taken from [10]).

stages are interleaved like the Denelcor HEP [37]—a single thread can only execute during one out of every eight cycles. The global memory in Monsoon is supported in the form of I-structure boards, each of which contains four million 64-bit words. In addition, presence bits are associated with each word of I-structure memory. The I-structure boards perform the necessary manipulation of presence bits, including the "deferred list" management [10]. Monsoon processors and I-structure boards are connected by a 100 MBytes/second/port network built out of PaRC switches. The largest configuration built contains eight Monsoon processing elements and eight I-structure boards each. One such system is located at MIT and the other at Los Alamos National Laboratory.

Monsoon demonstrates the feasibility of dataflow architectures as discussed in the previous section. Our performance studies to date show good speedups and cycle counts. For up to the largest machine configuration of eight processors, Monsoon is able to achieve linear speedup for most programs (see Figure 2). We are able to explain the causes for less than perfect speedup [13]. Also, cycle counts of programs executed on Monsoon are only three times that of corresponding fully optimized C/Fortran programs executed on a typical RISC processor (see Figure 3). This demonstrates that with the proper architecture, it is possible to take advantage of fine-grain parallelism without paying an unduly high price.

Program	Configuration							
	1 PE		2 PE		4 PE		8 PE	
	$\frac{1PE}{1PE}$	$\times 10^6$ Critical Path	$\frac{1PE}{2PE}$	$\times 10^6$ Critical Path	$\frac{1PE}{4PE}$	$\times 10^6$ Critical Path	$\frac{1PE}{8PE}$	$\times 10^6$ critical Path
4 × 4 Blocked-MM 500 × 500	1	1057	1.99	531	3.90	271	7.74	137
Gamteb-2c 40000 particles	1	590	1.95	303	3.81	155	7.35	80.3
Simple 100 iters, 100 × 100	1	4681	1.86	2518	3.45	1355	6.27	747
Paraffins $n = 22$	1	322	1.99	162	3.92	82.2	7.25	44.4

Figure 2: Speedup Results: Id on Monsoon (taken from [13]).

Program	MIPS R3000 (25 MHz)		1 PE Monsoon (10 MHz)	
	$(\times 10^6$ Cycles)	Seconds	$(\times 10^6$ Cycles)	Seconds
Matrix-Multiply, 500 × 500				
double precision	1198	202.3	1768	176.8
single precision	915	153.1	—	—
4 × 4 Blocked-MM, 500 × 500				
double precision	954	61.4	1058	105.8
single precision	741	44.9	—	—
Gamteb-2c 40000 particles	265	11.1	590	59.0
Simple, 100 iters, 100 × 100				
double precision	1787	86.5	4682	468.2
single precision	1745	84.1	—	—
Paraffins $n = 22$	102	12.0	322	32.2

Figure 3: Performance of Fortran/C on the MIPS R3000 vs. Id on 1 processor Monsoon (taken from [13]).

4.1 Where Monsoon Succeeded

Since Monsoon was designed to execute dataflow code, its performance doing that is excellent. Monsoon's strengths can be categorized as follows:

4.1.1 Excellent Processor/Network Interface Integration

Monsoon is capable of sending a message to the network in a single instruction. There are many variations of the send instruction. The basic send instruction takes a *token* which is a tuple containing a continuation (instruction pointer and global frame pointer) and a value. The message is sent to the specified processor and, when scheduled, results in the execution of the continuation specified in the message. Variants of the send instruction allow us to encode operations, such as remote fetch, into a single instruction. For more complicated continuation manipulation, a specific functional unit (called the pointer increment unit) is available. Monsoon's functional unit and token formation unit were optimized for the message operations that would be most common in compiled Id code.

4.1.2 Implicit Forks   In order to expose parallelism to keep its pipelines busy and to tolerate latency, Monsoon must be able to fork off work. It does so by allowing instructions to produce up to two tokens in the last stage of the pipeline. This feature allows parallelism to expand quickly, with little added overhead. Since only one token can reenter the pipeline, one token is designated to be inserted into a token queue. The designation is encoded into the instruction being executed.

4.1.3 Fast Hardware Synchronization   Frequent use of cheap messaging and forking requires cheap synchronization. Monsoon has specialized hardware support for synchronization which consists of two components: a few bits of state (called presence bits) associated with each word of memory and a stage of the processor pipeline dedicated to synchronization. Instruction execution can be made conditional upon the presence bits of a memory location referenced by the instruction. Instructions can also alter the presence bits based on the previous values of these bits. For example, if synchronization fails, the presence bits are set and a *bubble* (i.e., a nop) is sent down the rest of the pipeline. If synchronization succeeds, the presence bits are cleared and the operation is continued down the pipeline. Bubbles affect performance, but are much more efficient means of synchronization than if the operation was simulated with a sequence of RISC style instructions.

How instructions react to specific presence bit states and how they mutate that state can be changed by a system programmer. Monsoon's instruction set is modifiable because it uses loadable microcode. The microcode is the instruction decode tables for the processor pipeline. See [26] for more details.

4.1.4 Fast Context Switch   Monsoon is able to support very short threads because it is able to switch contexts very quickly. Monsoon performs context switching at two levels. First, its interleaved pipeline switches context every cycle, interleaving eight threads at a time, making these context switches free. Tokens that produce result tokens are generally allowed to put one result token back into the pipeline as soon as it is produced, allowing threading. If the current thread does not produce any other tokens, effectively terminating the thread, a token is taken automatically from the token queue for execution. Incoming network tokens are allowed to enter the pipeline at regular intervals, taking advantage of the fact that there is no cost to do so.

Associated with each of the eight threads is an extremely lightweight context, consisting of a single accumulator value (the value carried on the token being processed) and three registers. The second level of context switching occurs when a thread ends. If there are useful values in the registers, they have to be explicitly stored away by the thread. This context switch is not free, unlike the cycle-by-cycle interleaving, but the small context makes the switch very cheap nevertheless. Pure dataflow code does not make use of the temporary registers at all; it uses only single-instruction threads. While this means that context switching is free, this style of execution fails to exploit the advantages of state that may be passed through the registers.

4.1.5 Hardware Managed Token Queues   Monsoon has hardware managed token queues to store additional tokens that cannot be executed immediately in the pipeline. Additional tokens are produced since an instruction can produce up to two tokens and only one can reenter the pipeline. Also, if the pipeline is completely full, the network is allowed to occasionally interrupt the processor, forcing the executing token to be pushed onto the token queue. There are two queues available which can be accessed in either FIFO or LIFO mode.

4.1.6 Support for Global Shared Memory   Global shared memory is supported by split-phase operations which are implemented by fast messaging, fast context switching, and fast synchronization. Split-phase operations are implemented as specialized send instructions, which automatically set the instruction pointer to point to the correct handler. The fast synchronization mechanism of Monsoon quickly integrates the returned value into the computation. Since the messaging and synchronization mechanisms were designed with split-phase operations in mind, they implement the necessary functionality very efficiently and are extremely tolerant of memory latency.

4.2 Where Monsoon Failed

Though Monsoon showed that architectures that run dataflow code well can be built, it has several weaknesses that prevent it from being a truly practical architecture. Many of these defects were intended to simplify implementation and are not fundamental in nature. The weaknesses are described below.

4.2.1 Poor Single Threaded Performance   Monsoon's single thread performance was poor. There are two basic reasons for the poor performance: an interleaved pipeline and a weak instruction set. Each is described more fully below.

- *Interleaved Pipeline:* The latency incurred by any specific thread is eight times the number of instructions to execute. Execution of two contiguous instructions in a thread are separated by seven cycles where instructions from other threads can be executed. If there is sufficient parallelism in the machine during this time, the overall performance of the machine is not degraded. In most programs, however, there are critical sections where shared resources are accessed. This happens within the run-time system, for instance, and can occur in user code as well. The extra thread latency can constrict the expansion of parallelism since the available parallelism is sequentialized through an expanded critical section. This problem can increase the total run time of a program. It can also increase the processor resources and parallelism required by a program, since eight threads need to be active to keep the machine busy.

  The interleaving used by Monsoon was expedient, as it simplified the pipeline. There is no reason why an aggressive implementation could not have a normal, non-interleaved pipeline and yet have the context switching capabilities of Monsoon.

- *Weak Instruction Set:* There are several problems with Monsoon's instruction set, which can be divided between those that are specific implementation problems and those that arise out of more fundamental architectural decisions.

  Among the implementation problems are Monsoon's instruction encoding, particularly its memory addressing modes. These are weak and inflexible, requiring address computation to be done separately from reads and requiring indirect reads to take two cycles. RISC-like three-address instruction sets are more powerful, as they can specify more general arguments and more general destinations. In fact, the EM-4 [30] has exactly that sort of instruction set. Monsoon is also capable of such instructions, but its instruction set is inherently limited in power because the number of registers is very small (three per thread), and the local memory is not addressable via these registers.

A more fundamental problem with the instruction set is the coupling of both synchronization and data delivery in the form of a token. This issue is related to the assumption about the frequency of synchronization which will be discussed in the next section. The immediate effect of this duality of token is that it makes it difficult for the compiler to perform certain types of optimizations. For example, if the compiler is able to determine that some synchronization is redundant, it is sometimes not able to optimize these synchronizations out because the data still need to be delivered.

4.2.2 Optimized for Synchronization

Monsoon's architecture was optimized for synchronization. Most instructions were expected to synchronize, and, thus, context switches were expected to be very frequent. This assumption justifies the automatic context switching found in Monsoon, which in turn increases the amount of necessary synchronization.

Due to both the necessity of forking to exploit instruction-level parallelism and the interleaved nature of the pipeline, synchronization is required much more often than would be necessary in a sequential processor that assumes a sequential instruction stream. The pure dataflow model also increases the number of forks, and subsequent synchronizations. Conventional RISC processors, on the other hand, exploit instruction level parallelism within a sequential instruction stream using pipelining and superscalar organization, and do not require explicit synchronization. The required coordination is managed in hardware resulting in a more efficient strategy for exploiting instruction level parallelism.

Since the synchronization section of the pipeline is tightly coupled to the execution units of the pipelines, a miss in the matching section causes a bubble in the execution units. This bubble degrades performance; approximately 10% to 30% of all cycles executed bubble the execution units. The obvious solution of decoupling the matching section from the execution unit is difficult, however, and can still result in bubbles, either in the execution units or matching sections.

Moving more towards a model that has better threading support (by increasing available state) and less support for synchronization would probably have overall benefits. If everything is balanced, that is context switching and synchronization become less frequent as context switching and synchronization costs go up, there would be no difference in performance. The compiler, however, is generally able to reduce synchronization events when it is allowed to thread an instruction stream. This threading will benefit machines optimized for long threads.

4.2.3 Unrealistic Memory Hierarchy

Another artifact of Monsoon's full custom nature is its memory hierarchy, which was implemented using fast static RAMs to save on design time and complexity. Some argue that the hierarchy is unrealistic. One could argue, however, that Monsoon's frame memory, 256 Kwords = 2 MBytes, is *smaller* than caches in modern processors. Monsoon's frame memory can be considered a cache. Since I-structure memory was not cached and resided some 30 cycles away from the processors, it is clear from our performance studies that multithreading allows us to tolerate latency reasonably well.

The presence bit pipeline stage, which read-modifies-writes memory on every cycle is unconventional and may be difficult to build. Some modern RISC processors, however, support read-modify-write for byte writes, proving it may be possible to implement the presence bit stage in a fast pipeline. Until an actual high-speed machine is built with the support we want, it is difficult to say for sure whether it is an obstacle to high-speed implementation.

4.2.4 Little Control Over Thread Scheduling

In Monsoon, token scheduling cannot really be controlled by the programmer. The token queues are completely hardware managed; software is not permitted to read or write the token queue. In general, it is a bad idea if any significant storage in the machine is not easily accessible by software. The compiler can decide which token in a two-token-producing instruction gets pushed onto the queue, but there is no way to select the "best" token to execute next. However, executing a "bad" sequence of tokens could dramatically increase run-time or resource usage of the entire program. It would be desirable to have more flexibility in managing the execution order, such as the ability to examine and reorder the token queues.

4.3 Pragmatic Issues

Since Monsoon is a fully custom processor, it cannot leverage commercial processor hardware and software efforts, dooming it to technology generations behind the current state of the art. While this is not a technical point, it is nevertheless an overriding practical consideration. Most parallel computer builders acknowledge the need to use a commercial processor, or a commercial processor with very simple changes, in order to be competitive in performance. Custom processors lag behind commercial processors in raw speed (cycle time).

It is difficult to justify the efforts involved in building experimental machines and software systems if commercially available sequential machines perform better. The time spent doing even simple support software can be substantial; Monsoon's basic software, such as the microcode generator, client/server software, and I/O took huge amounts of effort, probably well over 10 man years. Hence, even though there is a greater possibility of speedup for custom processors, their cost in terms of hardware and software development as well as their lower clock speed make them uncompetitive. Thus, it was imperative that our next machine be very close to a conventional processor, allowing us to use the basic support software and requiring only a custom compiler and run-time system.

*T: Modified Stock Processors

*T is an attempt to build a truly general building block for a parallel computer, one that will run any type of parallel code reasonably well [24]. It also tries to correct some of the shortcomings of pure-dataflow, while at the same time bringing dataflow architecture closer to RISC architecture. The architecture can be viewed as a RISC processor augmented with coprocessors for handling various types of messages. *T supports the multithreaded model which was introduced in the dataflow community towards the end of the 80s [15], [23], [31] and gained wide acceptance over the past few years [9], [32], [38], [29].

From a parallel system building viewpoint, using a commercial microprocessor with very limited changes allows the use of software and hardware built for the commercial microprocessor. Changes will have to be made for the parallel machine, but substantial reuse of many components is likely. The effort of the project can thus be focused on relevant research issues rather then spent on bringing up the system from ground zero.

Another motivation for using stock processors is to build a general purpose machine that can easily support other parallel execution paradigms. As most other styles of parallel execution are characterized by fairly coarse-grain parallelism with long sequential threads between synchronization points, a RISC style microprocessor will execute them efficiently. Finally, as stated in the previous section, the rapid rate at which stock microprocessors are improving makes it difficult for projects that build custom hardware to demonstrate a clear advantage, as they will be obsolete by the time they are built.

The original *T design logically partitions a node into three parts: the data processor (*dP*), the synchronization processor (*sP*), and the remote memory processor (*RMem*) (see Figure 4). Each processor is responsible for a different aspect of the computation. The synchronization processor's job is to receive messages from the network, write incoming values into frame memory for the data processor, synchronize the values with other input values for waiting threads, and notify the data processor when a thread is ready to execute by posting a continuation. The remote memory processor's job is to handle remote memory requests from other nodes. The data processor's job is to actually execute the user's program.

5.1 *T: An Architecture for Multithreading

The *sP* must be able to implement the functionality of four new instructions: `start`, `post`, `next`, and `join`. The `start` instruction starts a new thread in a different context by sending arguments to that new thread. If the context in question is on a different processor, a message is automatically formatted to start the thread on that processor. The `post` instruction takes a continuation (instruction pointer-frame pointer pair) as its argument and puts it into the *dP*'s continuation queue, essentially passing work to the *dP*. The `next` instruction terminates the current thread, finds the next thread in the continuation queue and starts that next thread running. The `join` instruction increments a memory value and conditionally on the resulting value jumps to a given instruction pointer. The *sP* may be viewed as a stripped down dataflow processor or a processor designed to execute short threads to completion.

The *RMem* needs to be able to send a message to resume a thread on the requester. *RMem* essentially behaves like the I-structure controller in Monsoon. The *dP* implements the functionality of the `start` and `next` operations as well. It must also be able to initiate remote loads `rload` and stores `rstore`. The `rload` operation takes a global address and a continuation. Its effect is to pass the contents of the address to the continuation. The `rstore` operation is basically the same as the `rload`—an acknowledgment after the store has been completed is sent to the continuation.

This design is motivated from the need to cater to both long and short threads. Fine-grain parallel execution introduces many frequent interrupts in the form of incoming messages from other processors. Stock microprocessors are however optimized to run long threads. To resolve this problem, any functionality that would require the *dP* to switch contexts often has been moved to the *sP* or *RMem*. This allows the functionality requirements of the *dP* to match that of stock microprocessors more closely.

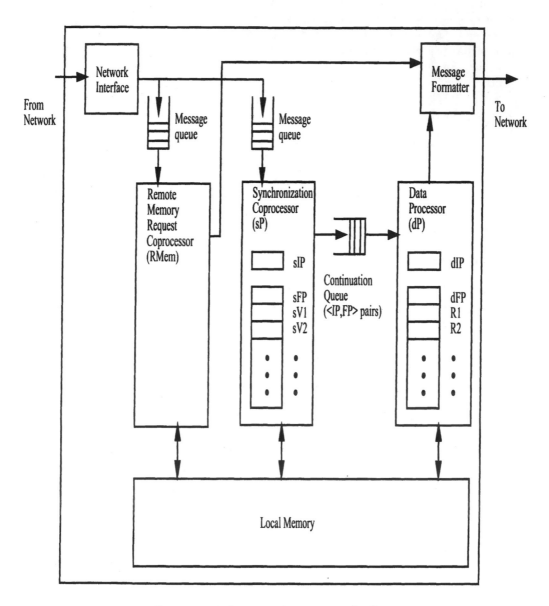

Figure 4: A *T node (taken from [24]).

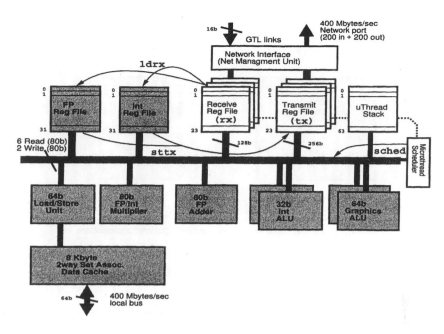

Figure 5: The 88110MP (taken from [28]).

5.2 88110MP: A Realization of *T

The 88110MP *T was based on a modified Motorola MC88110 (88110MP) and the Arctic [5] network routing chip. The 88110MP contains a MC88110 core along with an internal network interface operating as a functional unit and hardware support for thread scheduling. A diagram of an 88110MP processor is shown in Figure 5. The network interface is accessed via register operations, and is thus very fast. It utilizes the MC88110's dual instruction issue capability and wide internal datapath allowing up to 256 bits to be moved into the network buffer each cycle. A simple message could be formatted and launched in 6 cycles. Reading an incoming message is also done with simple register operations, albeit at a slightly lower bandwidth of 128 bits/cycle.

The 88110MP parallel machine consists of *nodes* connected by the Arctic network. The Arctic network is related to the Monsoon network but provides twice as much bandwidth per link (200 MBytes/sec/link). Each node consists of two 88110MP processors sitting on a shared memory bus (see Figure 6)—one node acts as a *RMem* while the other acts both as a *dP* and an *sP*. The remote memory processor would handle remote memory requests from other processors. We used a full 88110MP as an *RMem* for simplicity's sake. Since a memory controller, arithmetic operations and network capabilities are required of an *RMem*, it was easier and cheaper, at our quantities, to use a full 88110MP rather than build a separate part. The data processor would read messages from the network, run the message handlers associated with them, and also enqueue and run the ready threads. Of course, this division of labor is arbitrary and can easily be changed.

The 88110MP *T could execute the TAM execution model, based on *active messages* [40], in a fashion similar to the implementation running on the CM-5 [9]. *T's superior network interface would give it a significant advantage over the CM-5. Other parallel programming models were also considered and partially implemented for the

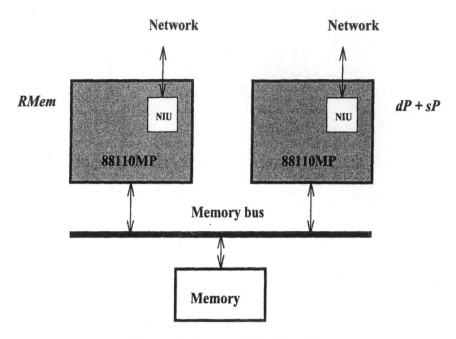

Figure 6: An 88110MP *T node.

88110MP *T. Unfortunately, the 88110MP project was canceled by Motorola because Motorola has shifted their emphasis from the 88110 architecture family to the PowerPC architecture family.

5.3 Evaluation of the 88110MP *T Architecture

In this section we will evaluate the 88110MP *T architecture on the criteria enumerated in Section 3. We will also compare the 88110MP *T to Monsoon. *T and Monsoon are very different machines, and not surprisingly, each is superior in some area. Monsoon is clearly better at switching contexts, synchronization, and accessing the network. *T is much better at single threaded performance. Though *T has fewer of the desirable traits to run multithreaded codes than Monsoon, it allows us to see how well multithreaded code will run on an almost stock processor, and how they should be augmented further.

5.3.1 Network Interface The network interface on the 88110MP *T is much more aggressive then those available on other RISC style machines. Its short message launch time of approximately 6 cycles is an order of magnitude better than the CM-5's 40 cycles [9]. Additional hardware support is provided to aid message construction. Its performance, however, is still worse than Monsoon's or EM-4's, where short messages are sent in a single cycle.

5.3.2 Thread Creation The 88110MP *T supports the instruction `fork` which pushes a continuation specified in registers onto a continuation stack (described later in this section). It also contains some special features in the network interface that facilitate header construction. Even though Monsoon can fork a thread in fewer cycles than *T, the superior single thread performance of *T reduces the need for forks, as explained below.

In traditional dataflow code, instruction-level parallelism is expressed in the dataflow graph, requiring forking and synchronization. Sequential processors exploit instruction-level parallelism in hardware using a variety of non-trivial mechanisms. Thus, the code can be sequentialized into a thread, eliminating synchronization requirements within a thread. The processor is able to dynamically extract this parallelism. Forking is still required, but not to exploit instruction level parallelism.

5.3.3 Synchronization

The 88110MP *T does not have full hardware support for synchronization. It has a conditional post instruction, cpost, that conditionally performs a post based on the value of a register. No support, however, is provided for atomic update to a synchronization counter. Just as in thread creation, however, the need for synchronization in the 88110MP is less because of superior single-thread performance. Within a thread, synchronization between each instruction is implicit. Though Monsoon has better synchronization capabilities, it does not necessarily translate into superior overall performance.

*T also does not have hardware supported presence bits for I-structures. It is easy to simulate presence bits by allocating them out of ordinary memory. I-structure-like synchronization can be performed by a *RMem*. This may not be too inefficient because we expect network access overhead and network latency will dominate the extra instructions executed by the *RMem*.

5.3.4 Context Switching

No special hardware support is provided in the 88110MP *T for context switching. It adopts a software solution, relying on the compiler to generate code for saving registers value at the end of a thread, and loading registers at the beginning of a thread. The effect of this choice is not clear. On the one hand, it seems that if threads are short, the number of values to be saved or restored for each thread is not very large. Since the save/restore code is compiler generated, only the relevant register values are saved/restored, not the entire register file. On the other hand, fine-grain threads are not expected to be very long, making such switches frequent. Further study, with actual experimental data, is needed to see if this is an adequate solution.

Thread switching also requires a switch (jump) in the instruction stream. If threads are short, such switches become frequent. The 88110MP *T has no modifications to its instruction fetch unit. It would have been desirable for the hardware to prefetch instructions for the next thread to be executed, thus eliminating the possible bubbles due to a jump.

The non-interleaved pipeline on the 88110MP is of obvious benefit to code segments that need to be sequential, such as critical sections (especially prevalent in run-time system code). Though 88110MP does not have multiple register contexts, the total number of registers are no less than Monsoon or any other microprocessor. There is always tension, when there are a fixed number of registers, between giving all the registers to one thread or dividing the registers among multiple threads. We do not understand this trade-off very well, but sequential codes or parallel codes derived from them obviously benefit from having the entire register state.

5.3.5 Thread/Message Queue Management

The 88110MP *T has hardware support for managing continuations. A fork pushes a continuation onto a stack, while a `sched` instruction selects either an incoming message or the top of the continuation stack. It is also possible to explicitly read the continuation stack, opening the possibility to explicitly control thread scheduling. Scheduling during run-time, however, unless very simple, can become very inefficient very quickly. There is much opportunity for research in this area.

Monsoon's token queues do not require explicit instructions to manipulate, and thus have higher performance. *T's offers greater flexibility, however, which could turn into a great advantage.

5.3.6 Global Shared Memory   The 88110MP *T only supported split-phase access to global memory. `start` instructions were to be used to initiate all phases of a split-phase transaction. *T includes an $RMem$ processor that allows access to the remote memory even if the data processor is busy; thus, the dP is not required to poll the network periodically.

Monsoon's support for split-phase operations, however, is superior to the 88110MP *T's support. Monsoon's split-phase operations are primitive instructions; all the information needed for an access are encoded within a single instruction. On *T, the request is a generic message which takes about six cycles to construct.

It is, however, not hard to design a RISC style instruction which encodes all the necessary information so that initiating a request takes only 1 instruction. Consider, for example, `rload rGAdd rIP rFP`, which loads from the address specified in `rGAdd`, and invoke a continuation with ip = `rIP` and fp = `rFP` when the value is returned.

Monsoon also has the advantage that for a read, the value that is returned comes in the form of a token and, thus, incurs no additional processing cost. *T relegates the task of dealing with the returned value to the sP which will store it into some frame slot. To the extent that the sP is considered "extra hardware" whose cycles are "free," this task incurs no extra cost. However, the value has to be loaded into a register from frame memory before it can be used by the dP. Depending on how code is generated, testing of synchronization counters by the dP may be needed.

The design of *T specifically states that global caching is an orthogonal issue that would not be explored due to time constraints. When the 88110MP was designed, global caching was again ignored for expediency. We feel that global caching has great potential to reduce communication requirements which could reduce critical paths. The next section analyzes global caching and compares it to split-phase operations when solving the DAXPY inner loop.

5.4 Comparing Split-Phase and Global Caching on DAXPY

The DAXPY loop may be written as follows in a high-level language.

```
for i = 0 to N-1 do
Y[i] = a * X[i] + Y[i]
```

The assembly code for both a uniprocessor version of DAXPY and a multithreaded version of DAXPY are taken from [24] and given in the appendix. The assembly code for a global cache coherent machine would look very similar to the uniprocessor version.

If we assume the loop is unrolled k times, then in each iteration there will be `cmp` + (`fmul` + `fadd` + `add` + `add`)*k arithmetic operations, $2k$ `rload`'s and k `rstore`'s, and 1 conditional jump instruction. The multithreaded version, in addition, will have 4 local loads for the loop constants, $2k$ local loads for the actual values of $X[i]$ and $Y[i]$, and 2 local stores to store back pointers to $X[i + k]$ and $Y[i + k]$. It will also have a `next` instruction, which we count as a branch instruction.

| | Arith | Br | Local | | Remote | |
			Load	Store	Load	Store
Global cache processor	$1 + 4k$	1	0	0	$2kl$	k
*T	$1 + 4k$	2	$4 + 2k$	2	$2kn$	kn

Figure 7: Instruction cycles in the inner loop of DAXPY unrolled k times, where l is the average latency and n is the cost of sending a message.

The behavior of remote memory references is very different between global caching and split-phase operations. In global caching, a remote memory reference is actually made only when a reference misses in the cache. Let us assume that l is the average latency of accessing global memory through the cache, taking miss ratios into account. Therefore, the total number of cycles for a single iteration of the inner loop on a global cached machine would be

$$(1 + 4k) + (2kl + k) + 1$$

$$= 2kl + 5k + 2$$

We assume that all arithmetic instructions take one cycle. In the split-phase case, every remote memory reference goes to the network. Assuming there is enough parallelism, the processor only sees the number of cycles it must spend formatting and sending the messages. Again, assuming that arithmetic and local memory operations take one cycle, and it takes n cycles to format and send a message, the total number of cycles for a single iteration of the inner loop on a message passing machine would be

$$(1 + 4k) + (2kn + kn) + 1 + (4 + 2k + 2) + 1$$

$$= 3kn + 6k + 9$$

This information is summarized in Figure 7.

To see where *T beats a global cached machine, we simply add up the two rows and see when *T's row is less. For *T to win, the following equation must be true.

$$3kn + 6k + 9 < 2kl + 5k + 2$$

$$3kn + k + 7 < 2kl$$

Clearly, the performance of the global cached machine is tied directly to its miss ratio and the amount of time it takes to get a global value. If the miss ratio is low and the time to get a global value is reasonable, there is no way for *T to win in terms of the number of cycles. *T can win if l is large or if n is especially small.

Let us assume that $k = 4$. Now the equation can be rewritten to

$$12n + 11 < 8l$$

For *T to beat the global cached machine, $(n < 2/3l - 1)$. If the miss ratio is an optimistic 1% and the global fetch latency is 100 cycles, there is no way for *T to win. For reasonable values of n, such as 6, l must be more than 10, which would imply miss rates close to 10% on global cached machines with global round-trip latencies of 100 cycles. There is no temporal locality, i.e., if Y is not reused soon, it is very possible for the cache to never hit, favoring *T. If Y is reused, however, *T will most likely lose. If you had a processor where memory accesses can be overlapped, which is very likely in the next generation of processors, then it will be even harder for split-phase transactions to beat global caching in accessing global memory. For stock processors, global caching is likely to win, because n is generally closer to 60 than to 6.

This analysis shows that dynamic program behavior has to be taken into account. This example is too simple to show the full potential of efficient message passing and split-phase transactions. Split-phase operations hide communication latency, but do not reduce communication. Global caching reduces communication, but does not hide communication latency. The former requires some hardware support to run well while the later requires some hardware support to run at all. Clearly the two methods are complementary, solving different problems. A machine with the ability to perform both kinds of remote accesses would be much more flexible, performing better on a larger set of problems, than a machine with just one sort of access. Others have come to exactly the same conclusion [2], [18] as well. Therefore, our next machine, described in the following section, will support both split-phase transactions and global caching.

6. StarT, the Next Generation

We plan to build another parallel machine called *T-NG (StarT, the Next Generation) in collaboration with Motorola. The machine design is heavily influenced by the *T work described in the previous section. The main difference between the original *T and *T-NG, motivated by the analysis presented in the previous section, is the addition of coherent caches for global shared memory. Full support for message passing is to be retained in this new model.

Adding global caches does not create a fundamental shift in our software model for *T. Cache coherency has always been considered an orthogonal issue. Compiler implementations, however, will have to take temporal locality of memory references into account to exploit this new feature. Global locations that are known to be already written and likely to be reused should be accessed through the cache coherency interface, while locations that may not have been "filled" should probably be accessed via split-phase operations.

We plan to implement *T-NG within the next two years, using some 64-bit processor from the IBM and Motorola PowerPC family. This choice is natural given our collaboration with Motorola, and the expected cost/performance of these processors. We are constrained to make no modification to either the processor or the operating system. Thus, all the hardware support for the desired features must be built around the processor. The PowerPC architecture has no on-chip network interface. Thus an external network interface unit (NIU) that communicates via existing memory datapaths must be provided.

In order to support global caching, we must provide an external piece of hardware to detect requests for a global location and to satisfy those requests. We call this piece of hardware the Shared Memory Unit (SMU). The logical place for the SMU is off the main memory bus of the processor. For reasons that will become clear shortly, the SMU will also have an NIU for accessing the network.

The basic building block, called a *site*, will consist of several PowerPC processors connected by a snoopy bus to memory and an SMU (see Figure 8). Some of the

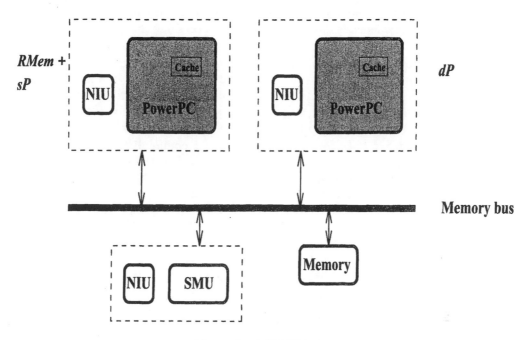

Figure 8: A *T-NG site.

processors will have NIU's, which may be connected through the second-level cache interface. There are many possible configurations for a site. For discussion purposes, we will assume that a site contains two processors and both processors have an NIU. Furthermore, we will designate one of the two processors as the compute processor (*dP*) and the other as remote memory processor (*RMem*) which will also provide the functionality of the synchronization processor (*sP*). An entire processor is not required for an *RMem*. Using a full processor, however, is the simplest and cheapest solution in terms of the engineering effort required, since it already contains the memory bus interface required to access local memory, and has the computation power to run cache coherency protocols and operate on presence bits in software.

Sites will be connected through a network built from the same Arctic [5] chips that we had planned to use in the 88110MP-based *T machine. As stated earlier it will have at least double the bandwidth (200 MBytes/sec/link) as the Monsoon network. The network will probably be configured as a FAT tree.

Before we describe how message passing and global caching will be supported on this machine, we want to emphasize that our approach is minimalist. For example, we will not consider any external custom device whose complexity may approach that of the processor. However, we still have several options for site configurations which we will discuss at the end of this section.

6.1 Message Passing and Split-Phase Transactions on *T-NG

Our basic message passing primitive is the `start` operation. The `start` operation takes a continuation and some arguments and sends those arguments to the processor specified by the continuation and executes that continuation with the arguments. Since we are not permitted to change the processor architecture, `start` must be emulated in software. We can, of course, optimize each instance of the `start` instruction to execute as efficiently as possible in its context. However, the efficiency of the **start** instruction crucially depends upon the overhead of accessing the network through the NIU.

The NIU must be memory mapped since that is the only way to get large amounts of information in and out of the processor. The NIU may have its own memory to provide some message buffering. It will have an input queue and an output queue that allows the processor to send and receive messages respectively. The NIU has to be able to function at the processor's clock rate as well as the network's clock rate.

To execute a **start** operation, the processor must communicate data to the NIU by writing it to the memory mapped locations assigned to the output buffer on the NIU. Once the message is completely written, the processor then writes to some special location to indicate that the message is ready to be sent. Since many modern microprocessors do not preserve ordering on memory operations, care has to be exercised to ensure that the **send** command is not seen by the NIU before the message is fully written to the NIU buffers. Ensuring correct order may require execution of processor synchronization instructions.

On receiving the **send** command, the NIU formats the message for the network and negotiates with its Arctic to send that message. The NIU may support the retransmission of messages to provide fault-tolerance for the network. It may also be able to enforce end-to-end FIFO transmission of user messages.

Receiving a message is trickier than sending one. Either the NIU must interrupt the processor or the processor must poll the NIU sufficiently frequently to avoid buffer overflows. Interrupts in fast processors are generally extremely expensive; thus, we will probably rely on polling to service the network. A software convention, that polls sufficiently frequently, will have to be obeyed by dP threads. Since we expect the data processors to execute long threads, even polling can be both expensive and disruptive. In cases when a message is detected, even minimal handling may be disruptive, due to cache thrashing, context switching, etc.

A simple solution to the polling problem is to not accept incoming messages on the dP. All messages intended for a dP must be sent to the $RMem$ associated with that dP. If $RMem$'s are programmed to execute only short threads, and they poll the network at the termination of each thread, polling will not be disruptive to the $RMem$. However, the $RMem$ has to pass on at least some of the messages to its dP. Message passing between processors on the same site can be done via the normal (snoopy) bus-based shared memory. The latency to receive a message would be much higher, but the processor receiving a message would not be forced to poll periodically. Many of the returning messages may not require immediate action, such as those messages that unsuccessfully synchronize. If an $RMem$ is delegated to performing those tasks, the overhead on the processor receiving the message is reduced. Each task passed from the $RMem$ to the dP thus has more "weight" and will probably be, on average, a longer thread. The problem with this scheme is that thread operands must be copied at least once, from the $RMem$'s cache to the dP's cache, thus increasing overall overhead.

Split-phase operations are special cases of the **start** instruction. Essentially, a split-phase operation is a **start** operation from the request processor to the home processor, and another **start** operation from the home processor back to the request processor. Split-phase handlers must be written to provide the desired functionality. Active Messages [40] provide a good abstraction for handling all incoming messages, including split-phase operations. An Active Message contains an instruction pointer for a handler which will process the message.

6.2 Global Caching on *T-NG

To implement shared memory, we will assume two things: the address space, both virtual and physical, is partitioned into local and global memory, and every global address has an owner site, which we will call the home site of the address. For simplicity, we will only consider the case where the home node of a global memory location does not change during the execution of a program. However, it should be possible to build software/OS that supports migration of global memory addresses at the page level.

The SMUs together with the *RMem*s implement global caching. The SMU detects a memory operation to global shared memory, and carries out the necessary action to complete the operation. It must be able to capture a global address, and format and send the message to fetch/store the requested/supplied data. Most of the processing needed to run cache coherency protocols is done in software on the *RMem* at the home site. To the first order, the complexity of the SMU is not related to the complexity of the cache coherence protocols.

The *RMem* maintains the coherence directory for all the addresses it owns, runs most of the coherence protocol, and supplies the requested data or performs the requested write. Memory for keeping the coherence directory will be part of the user's virtual memory. Implementing the coherence protocols in software will allow us to fix bugs and to experiment with different coherence protocols.

If a global address makes it to the memory bus, the corresponding memory operation could not have been satisfied in the on-chip cache or the second-level cache. Completing the operation requires sending a request to the *RMem* that owns the cache line. If a reply to the operation is expected, the SMU receives the reply and puts it onto the processor bus.

The SMU behaves like a cache on the processor bus. In addition to the tasks mentioned earlier, it keeps track of operations in progress, and associates some state with each active operation to keep the cache coherent protocols manageable. The SMU will also handle cache coherence requests arriving from the network from the various *RMem*s, such as requests to flush/invalidate cache copies of global data. Because of the need to send and receive remote requests, the SMU will need network access and will be provided with its own NIU.

6.2.1 Implementing Suspendable Global Loads

We hope to extend the functionality of our global coherent caching to allow a thread switch in case of a cache miss. A cache miss would effectively be turned into a split-phase transaction; the current thread would be suspended until the value is returned and another thread is scheduled in its place. We call this hybrid approach to caching the *suspending* approach, and name the corresponding load instruction sgload. Converting a cache miss to a split-phase transaction will allow us to cache locations of I-structure memory as well, and will provide a better means of masking latency. Without such a feature, in general, it is not possible to cache I-structure memory. Of course, it would be desirable to have the option of using normal blocking cache coherency as well as normal split-phase transactions. Alewife [1] already has a feature that allows thread switching on a global cache miss, but since the switching is done in hardware, only a small constant number of switches can occur. Our scheme will allow the user to retain control over thread switching.

The SMU will support the sgload instruction in the simplest fashion possible. If the SMU can notify the user code when a miss has occurred, the software on the requesting processor can take all the other required actions. Since the processor cannot tell if its `sgload` request was satisfied from the cache or through the SMU, a predefined pattern will be used by the SMU to indicate a missing value. The software tests the returned value against the predefined pattern, and switches the thread in case a missing value is detected. If the processor initiates a split-phase transaction for the missing value, the scheme can be made to work even if the predefined pattern is the actual content of the requested location, since the handler for the return of the value will not check the value against any pattern. The main cost is an unnecessary global cache line fetch. With the proper selection of the predefined pattern, we hope to avoid this problem all together.

Another possible implementation of the `sgload` instruction could have the SMU interrupt the processor when a miss occurs. We expect, however, that interrupts will be quite expensive. This solution also requires that the SMU has the ability to interrupt the processor. If the miss ratio is very low, however, this scheme will probably perform better than the first one.

More sophisticated implementations of `sgload` seem to require much more hardware support on the processor side. In one extreme the processor can provide the illusion of multiple, unlimited number of register contexts, and switch among them transparently. However, since we cannot modify the processor, we will not explore these variations here.

Our `sgload` implementation is very much a hack made necessary by our need to use a stock microprocessor. Performance will be far from optimal, since each `sgload` must be checked at some point to make sure the obtained value is valid. It is also possible for the test to fail, if the value is actually the test pattern. The implementation, however, will allow our ideas for caching I-structures to be tried without changes to the microprocessor core and the on-chip cache.

6.3 Alternative Site Configurations

Up to this point, we have assumed that there are exactly two processors per site and that both processors have NIUs. It is possible that there may be more processors per site, and that not all processors will have NIUs. If there are more than two processors per site, but all processors still have NIUs, *T-NG can run pretty much the same as described in the previous sections. The correct mix of *dP*s and *RMem*s will have to be determined, but the ratio is changeable in software.

If there are processors that do not have an NIU, certain problems arise. Such a configuration is shown in Figure 9.

There must be at least one processor per site that has an NIU to communicate with other processors. *RMem*s must each have a NIU in order to perform their duties; thus, at least one of the processors with an NIU will be assigned to being the *RMem*. The SMU's NIU will probably be usable as well in this case. A processor without an NIU cannot send or receive messages directly, and must rely on an *RMem* or the SMU for messaging capabilities. All message traffic must go through the snoopy bus, however, further degrading performance. A processor that wants to send out a message in this case would write out a message using normal snoopy bus memory writes, then writing a "send" signal, again on the bus, to indicate that the message is fully formatted and ready to send. Again, writing out messages from a processor to the snoopy bus is not straightforward, due to the fact that the issue order of the writes may not be the order in which the stores are seen on the bus.

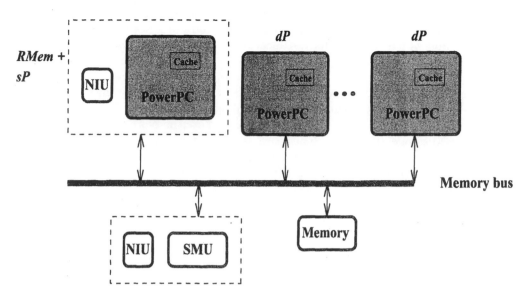

Figure 9: An alternative *T-NG site.

7. Conclusion

In this paper we examined the problems of supporting fine-grain parallelism on a machine built out of stock processors. We discussed the lessons we learned from the Monsoon project. Monsoon was a fully custom, pure dataflow machine. Though it was very successful running fine-grain parallel code, for pragmatic reasons we were forced to move to machines built from stock processors. We also briefly presented the *T model which was motivated by the desire to create a better building block for parallel machines. We then discussed our first implementation of a *T node which was based on a Motorola 88110 RISC processor. This project was abandoned in favor of a move towards the PowerPC architecture family. We took the opportunity to incorporate global caching into the *T model. The resulting model is called *T-NG for *T, the Next Generation.

There are many machines that have much in common with *T-NG. Japan's Electrotechnical Laboratory's (ETL) EM-4 [30] and its descendant architectures are custom machines designed to execute multithreaded code. In fact, those architectures are far more aggressive since their network interfaces are embedded into the processing pipeline itself. A message can be sent in a single instruction. Synchronization is built into the processor as well. *T-NG's hardware support for messaging is far less aggressive, since we use stock processors, but it will use state-of-the-art processing elements and will support global caching.

The machines that are most similar to *T-NG are MIT's Alewife [1] and Stanford's FLASH [18]. Both machines support global cached memory as well as message passing, and both are based on stock processors. Alewife's processor is modified to some degree for better support of cache coherency. It has greater support for user-level interrupts, including a division of the Sparc register set into four parts instead of using Sparc register windows, and has a few extra signaling pins. FLASH uses one stock processor and one very heavily modified processor (called MAGIC) to build a processing node. It is important to note that our implementation is far less aggressive than FLASH and, in many ways, Alewife. We plan to use completely stock processors running on a stock memory bus which will hopefully reduce development time relative to Alewife and FLASH. It will be interesting to see how close to FLASH and Alewife in performance *T-NG can get.

It is exciting to see that parallel architectures are converging. The machines mentioned in the previous paragraph differ only in detail from *T-NG. They all attempt to integrate shared memory with message passing, and are therefore significantly different from pure message passing machines, such as the J-machine [11], dataflow machines like Monsoon, and pure shared memory machines such as DASH. Eventual success of these attempts will depend very much on the quality of the hardware implementations, and the system software that is provided for using these machines.

Appendix: DAXPY Assembly Code

The loop compiled to uniprocessor code looks like this. (This code segment is lifted nearly verbatim from [24].)

```
        load rXP, dFP[XP]  -- load ptr to X
        load rYP, dFP[YP]  -- load ptr to Y
        load rA, dFP[A]  -- load loop const: a
        load rYlim, dFP[YLim]  -- load loop const: Y ptr limit
        cmp rB,rYP,rYLim  -- compare ptr to Y with limit
        jgt rB, OUT  -- zero-trip loop if greater

    LOOP:
        load rXI, rXP  -- X[i] into rXI (L1)
        load rYI, rYP  -- Y[i] into rYI (L2)
        add rXP,rXP,8  -- incr ptr to X
        fmul rTmp,rA,rXI  -- a*X[i]
        fadd rTmp,rTmp,rYI  -- a*X[i] + Y[i]
        store rYP, rTmp  -- store into Y[i] (S1)
        add rYP,rYP,8  -- incr ptr to Y

        cmp rB,rYP,rYLim  -- compare ptr to Y with limit
        jle rB, LOOP  -- fall out of loop if greater

    OUT:
        ... loop sequel ...
```

The loop compiled to *T code looks like this. (This code segment is again lifted nearly verbatim from [24].

```
;;
;; Synchronization Processor Message Handlers
;; L1_S:
 store sFP[XI], rV1 -- store away incoming X[I]
 join c1, 2, CONTINUE_D -- attempt continuation of loop
 next -- next message

L2_S:
 store sFP[YI], rV1 -- store away incoming Y[I]
 join c1, 2, CONTINUE_D -- attempt continuation of loop
 next -- next message

S1_S:
 load rN, sFP[N] -- total number of stores
 join c2, rN, OUT$_D$ -- sequel when all stores complete
;;
;; Data Processor Threads
;;
 load rXP, dFP[XP] -- load ptr to X
 load rYP, dFP[YP] -- load ptr to Y
 load rYlim, dFP[YLim] -- load loop const: Y ptr limit
 cmp rB,rYP,rYLim -- compare ptr to Y with limit
 jgt rB, OUT_D -- zero-trip loop if greater

LOOP_D:
 rload rXP, L1_S -- initiate load X[i] (L1)
 rload rYP, L2_S -- initiate load Y[i] (L2)
 next

CONTINUE_D:
 load rA, dFP[A] -- load loop const: a
 load rXP, dFP[XP] -- load ptr to X
 load rYP, dFP[YP] -- load ptr to Y
 load rYLim, dFP[YLim] -- load loop const: Y ptr limit

 load rXI, dFP[XI] -- load copy of X[I]
 load rYI, dFP[YI] -- load copy of Y[I]

 fmul rTmp,rA,rXI -- a*X[i]
 fadd rTmp,rTmp,rYI -- a*X[i] + Y[i]
 rstore rYP, rTmp,S1_S -- store into Y[i] (S1)
 add rXP,rXP,8 -- increment ptr to X
 add rYP,rYP,8 -- increment ptr to Y
 store dFP[XP], rXP -- store ptr to X
 store dFP[YP], rYP -- store ptr to Y

 cmp rB,rYP,rYLim -- compare ptr to Y with limit
 jle rB, LOOP_D -- fall out of loop if greater
 next

OUT_D:
 {\it ... loop sequel ...}
```

Acknowledgments

We would like to thank R.S. Nikhil and Greg Papadopoulos for permitting us to use diagrams and codes from their papers in this document. We would also like to thank Jamey Hicks, R.S. Nikhil, Shail Aditya, R. Paul Johnson, and Yuli Zhou, for reading various drafts of this paper and offering helpful comments.

The discussion on *T-NG has involved many people, both within our group and at Motorola. We have had very extensive discussions with Mike Beckerle, Bob Greiner and Jamey Hicks at Motorola and with Greg Papadopoulos, James Hoe, Chris Joerg, and Andy Boughton at MIT.

This paper describes research done at the Laboratory for Computer Science of the Massachusetts Institute of Technology. Funding for the Laboratory is provided in part by the Advanced Research Projects Agency of the Department of Defense under the Office of Naval Research contract N00014-92-J-1310.

References

[1] A. Agarwal et al., "The MIT Alewife Machine: A Large-Scale Distributed-Memory Multiprocessor," *Proc. Workshop on Scalable Shared Memory Multiprocessors*. Kluwer Academic Publishers, Norwel, Mass., 1991.

[2] A. Agarwal et al., "Sparcle: An Evolutionary Processor Design for Large-Scale Multiprocessors," *IEEE Micro*, June 1993, pp. 48–61.

[3] R. Alverson et al., "The Tera Computer System," *Proc. Int'l Conf. Supercomputing '90*, IEEE CS Press, Los Alamitos, Calif., 1990, pp. 1–6.

[4] Arvind and R.S. Nikhil, "Executing a Program on the MIT Tagged-Token Dataflow Architecture," *IEEE Trans. Computers*, Vol. 39, No. 3, Mar. 1990, pp. 300–318.

[5] A. Boughton et al., "Arctic User's Manual," CSG Memo 353, Laboratory for Computer Science, MIT, Feb. 1994.

[6] H. Burkhardt III et al., "Overview of the KSR1 Computer System," *Technical Report KSR-TR-9202001*, Kendall Square Research, Boston, Mass., Feb. 1992.

[7] D. Cann, "Retire Fortran? A Debate Rekindled," *Comm. ACM*, Vol. 35, No. 8, Aug. 1992, pp. 81–89.

[8] D.E. Culler et al., "Parallel Programming in Split-C," *Proc. Supercomputing '93*, IEEE CS Press, Los Alamitos, Calif., 1993, pp. 262–273.

[9] D.E. Culler et al., "TAM—A Compiler Controlled Threaded Abstract Machine," *J. Parallel and Distributed Computing*, Vol. 18, No. 3, 1993, pp. 347–370.

[10] D.E. Culler and G.M. Papadopoulos, "The Explicit Token Store," *J. Parallel and Distributed Computing*, Vol. 10, No. 4, 1990, pp. 289–308.

[11] W.J. Dally et al., "Architecture of a Message-Driven Processor," *IEEE Micro*, Vol. 12, No. 2, 1992, pp. 23–39.

[12] A. Geist et al., "PVM 3 User's Guide and Reference Manual," Technical Report 12187, ORNL, May 1993.

[13] J. Hicks et al., "Performance Studies of the Monsoon Dataflow Processor," *J. Parallel and Distributed Computing*, Vol. 18, No. 3, 1993, pp. 273–300.

[14] R.A. Iannucci, "Toward a Dataflow/von Neumann Hybrid Architecture," *Proc. 15th Ann. Int'l Symp. Computer Architecture*, 1988, IEEE CS Press, Los Alamitos, Calif., pp. 131–140.

[15] R.A. Iannucci, *Parallel Machine, Parallel Machine Languages: The Emergence of Hybrid Dataflow Computer Architectures*, Kluwer Academic Publishers, Norwell, Mass., 1990.

[16] R.E. Kessler and J.L. Schwarzmeier, "Cray T3D: A New Dimension for Cray Research," *Proc. CompCon93*, IEEE CS Press, Los Alamitos, Calif., 1993, pp. 176–182.

[17] J. Kubiatowicz, D. Chaiken, and A. Agrawal, "Closing the Window of Vulnerability in Multiphase Memory Transactions," *Proc. 5th Int'l Conf. Architectural Support for Programming Languages and Operating Systems*, ACM Press, New York, N.Y., 1992.

[18] J. Kuskin et al., "The Stanford FLASH Multiprocessor," *21st Ann. Int'l Symp. Computer Architecture*, IEEE CS Press, Los Alamitos, Calif., 1994, pp. 302–313.

[19] D. Lenoski et al., "The Directory-Based Cache Coherence Protocol for the DASH Multiprocessor," *Proc. 17th Ann. Int'l Symp. Computer Architecture*, IEEE CS Press, Los Alamitos, Calif., 1990, pp. 148–159.

[20] D. Lenoski et al., "The DASH Prototype: Implementation and Performance," *Proc. 18th Ann. Int'l Symp. Computer Architecture*, IEEE CS Press, Los Alamitos, Calif., 1991, pp. 92–103.

[21] R.S. Nikhil, *Id Reference Manual, Version 90.1*, CSG Memo 284-2, Laboratory for Computer Science, MIT, Cambridge Mass., Sept. 1990.

[22] R.S. Nikhil, "The Parallel Programming Language Id and its Compilation for Parallel Machines," *Int'l J. of High Speed Computing*, Vol. 5, No. 2, 1993, pp. 171–223.

[23] R.S. Nikhil and Arvind, "Can Dataflow Subsume von Neumann Computing?" *Proc. 16th Ann. Int'l Symp. Computer Architecture*, IEEE CS Press, Los Alamitos, Calif., 1989, pp. 262–272.

[24] R.S. Nikhil, G.M. Papdopoulos, and Arvind, "*T: A Multithreaded Massively Parallel Architecture," *Proc. 19th Ann. Int'l Symp. Computer Architecture*, ACM Press, New York, N.Y., 1992, pp. 156–167.

[25] P.R. Nuth, *The Named-State Register File*, Ph.D. thesis, Department of EECS, MIT, Cambridge, Mass., Aug. 1993.

[26] G.M. Papadopoulos, "Program Development and Performance Monitoring on the Monsoon Dataflow Multiprocessor," in *Instrumentation for Future Parallel Computing Systems*, M. Simmons, R. Koskela, and I. Bucher, Eds., Addison-Wesley Publishing Company, Reading, Mass., 1989.

[27] G.M. Papadopoulos, *Implementation of a General-Purpose Dataflow Multiprocessor*, MIT Press, Cambridge, Mass., 1992.

[28] G.M. Papadopoulos et al., "*T: Integrated Building Blocks for Parallel Computing," *Proc. Supercomputing '93*, IEEE CS Press, Los Alamitos, Calif., 1993, pp. 624–635.

[29] G.M. Papadopoulos and K.R. Traub, "Multithreading: A Revisionist View of Dataflow Architectures," *Proc. 18th Ann. Int'l Symp. Computer Architecture*, ACM Press, New York, N.Y., 1991, pp. 342–351.

[30] S. Sakai et al., "An Architecture of a Dataflow Single Chip Processor," *Proc. 16th Ann. Int'l Symp. Computer Architecture*, IEEE CS Press, Los Alamitos, Calif., 1989, pp. 46–53.

[31] M. Sato et al., "Thread-based Programming for the EM-4 Hybrid Dataflow Machine," *Proc. 19th Ann. Int'l Symp. Computer Architecture*, ACM Press, New York, N.Y., 1992, pp. 146–155.

[32] K.E. Schauser, D.E. Culler, and T. von Eicken, "Compiler-Controlled Multithreading for Lenient Parallel Languages," *Proc. Symp. Functional Programming Languages and Computer Architecture*, Cambridge, Mass., 1991, pp. 50–72.

[33] *IEEE Standard for Scalable Coherent Interface (SCI)*. IEEE, New York, N.Y., 1993. (IEEE Std 1596-1992).

[34] A. Shaw et al., "Performance of Data-Parallel Primitives on the EM-4 Dataflow Parallel Supercomputer," *Proceedings of Frontiers '92: The 4th Symp. Frontiers of Massively Parallel Computation*, IEEE CS Press, Los Alamitos, Calif., 1992, pp. 302–309.

[35] K. Shimada, H. Koike, and H. Tanaka, "UNIREDII: The High Performance Inference Processor for the Parallel Inference Machine PIE64," *Proc. Int'l Conf. Fifth Generation Computer Systems*, 1992, pp. 715–722.

[36] J.P. Singh, W.D. Weber, and A. Guta, "SPLASH: Stanford Parallel Applications for Shared Memory," Technical Report CSL-TR-91-469, Stanford University, 1991.

[37] B.J. Smith, "Architecture and Applications of the HEP Multiprocessor System," in *Real-time Signal Processing IV*, Aug. 1981, Vol. 298, pp. 241–248.

[38] K.R. Traub, "Multi-thread Code Generation for Dataflow Architectures from Non-Strict Programs," *Proc. Symp. Functional Programming Languages and Computer Architecture*, 1991, pp. 73–101.

[39] K.R. Traub et al., "Overview of the Monsoon Project," *Proc. 1991 IEEE Int'l Conf. Computer Design*, IEEE CS Press, Los Alamitos, Calif., 1991, pp. 150–155.

[40] T. von Eicken et al., "Active Messages: A Mechanism for Integrated Communication and Computation," *Proc. 19th Ann. Int'l Symp. Computer Architecture*, ACM Press, New York, N.Y., 1992, pp. 256–266.

Synchronization and Pipeline Design for a Multithreaded Massively Parallel Computer*

Shuichi Sakai[†]
Computation Structure Group
Laboratory for Computer Science
Massachusetts Institute of Technology

This paper examines two basic functions in a massively parallel computer—synchronizations and pipelining—and proposes efficient implementations. The data-driven synchronization mechanisms which currently exist are carefully analyzed from the viewpoint of efficiency and hardware complexity, and the optimized synchronization mechanism is proposed. The pipeline structure for a massively parallel computer containing the proposed synchronization is presented. Performance improvement methods for this pipeline are proposed, cost-effectiveness of the proposed method is considered, and related issues are listed. Lastly, future problems including software issues are presented.

1. Introduction

The main stream of research and development of dataflow architectures is being shifted from pure dataflow computers toward multithreaded computers. This tide includes: (1) the activities at MIT, from TTDA [2] to the Hybrid Architecture [5] and Monsoon [8], [13], and from Monsoon to *T [15], [16]; (2) the activities in ETL, from the SIGMA-1 [4] to the EM-4 [7], and from the EM-4 to the EM-5 [12]; and the activities in Sandia National Laboratory, from the Epsilon-1 to the Epsilon-2 [9]. Clearly these multithreaded architectures still maximally exploit the advantages of dataflow architectures; they tolerate long latencies by cheap local synchronization, and they are suited to the programming model which naturally extracts maximum parallelism. In addition, they are also advantageous for local sequential computation, since they include a von Neumann architecture (typically, a RISC architecture) which efficiently executes sequential threads with a set of registers and an advanced-control pipeline.

The concept of multithreading is not exclusive to the extension of dataflow architectures. For instance, the Denelcor HEP [1] and the Tera Computing System [6] are multithreaded computers in the sense that they execute and control multiple threads in a single pipeline. Dally's J-machine [17] does not interleave multiple threads, but it can switch between threads very quickly; thus, we can say that it actually supports the multithreaded computation. In addition, Dally's new machine, called the M-machine, has a mechanism of thread-interleaving [18] where many threads can exist inside a processor chip at the same time.

---

*This paper describes research done at the Laboratory for Computer Science of the Massachusetts Institute of Technology. Funding for the Laboratory is provided in part by the Advanced Research Projects Agency of the Department of Defense under Office of Naval Research contract N00014-89-J-1988.

[†]Now in Massively Parallel Architecture Laboratory, Real World Computing, Tsukuba Mitsui Building 16F, 1-6-1, Takezono, Tsukuba, Ibaraki 305, Japan.

In all of these machines, the common and central design decisions are how to design an efficient synchronization mechanism and how to pipeline the machine? These two functions seriously influence the performance of the multithreaded system.

This paper examines the functions of synchronization and pipelining, and proposes ultimately efficient mechanisms for them. Firstly, the data-driven synchronization mechanisms which were already proposed are carefully reconsidered from the viewpoint of efficiency and hardware complexity, and the new synchronization mechanism is proposed in Section 2. Secondly, the pipeline structure for a processing element of a massively parallel computer including the proposed synchronization is presented in Section 3. Thirdly, methods to improve performance proposed this pipeline are proposed in Section 4. Cost-effectiveness of synchronization and pipelining are also considered, and related issues are listed. Lastly, future problems including software issues are presented.

The mechanisms proposed here can be implemented using the current VLSI technology. We can provide an ultra-high-performance massively parallel system such that the communication/synchronization performance is strictly comparable to the computation performance, and the latency of each processor (time from packet input to result packet output) is fairly short, e.g., less than or equal to 5 RISC clocks.

2. Optimizing Data-Driven Synchronization

2.1 Data-Driven Synchronizations
This subsection summarizes the data-driven synchronizations which have already been proposed and reexamines their merits and defects.[1]

Earlier version of dynamic dataflow machines used associative mechanisms, such as hashing mechanisms, to implement data-driven synchronization (token matching). For instance, Manchester Dataflow Machine [3] uses a parallel hash table to provide a pseudo-associative access for token matching. Another example is the SIGMA-1 [4] system whose processor contains a chained hash mechanism. Matching by hashing has the following advantages.

- Efficient use of memory.

- Flexibility to implement different matching schemes; sticky token matching for example.

On the other hand, there are several drawbacks.

- Complexity.

- In case of a hash miss, pipeline bubbles are generated or an exception occurs.

- Difficulty to understand what is happening.

In the next generation dataflow machines, these defects were eliminated by introducing a frame-based matching. The explicit token store (ETS) in Monsoon [8], the direct matching in the EM-4 [7] and the direct match in the Epsilon [9] are such mechanisms.

Here the former two are briefly described and criticized in preparation for proposing a new scheme of a data-driven synchronization.

---

[1] Here, the author concentrates on the data-driven synchronizations on a dynamic dataflow model. We have another model, *a static model.* Although a modern "static architecture" [10] is also a challenging architecture, this paper does not include the architectural optimization of it.

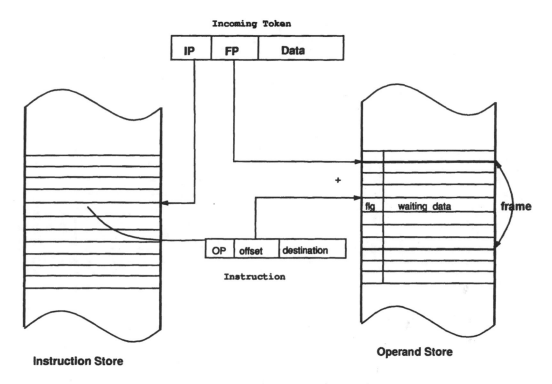

Figure 1: Explicit token store.

(1) *Explicit Token Store in Monsoon*

Figure 1 illustrates how matching is operated in Monsoon. The method by which tokens find their partners is called the Explicit Token Store (ETS) [8].

In Monsoon, an area for matching is exclusively reserved for a single function instance. This area is called a frame and a frame is allocated at the function invocation time. Matching occurs at a certain word in the frame.

In ETS, every token has a field of IP and FP. The IP is an instruction pointer which points the address of the instruction invoked by this packet, and the FP is a frame pointer which points the top of the frame. As each instruction has a field which indicates the offset of matching, the matching address can be calculated by adding FP and the offset (see Figure 1). Each data word in the frame is associated with a flag memory word where the synchronization flag is stored. In the case of a dyadic matching, Monsoon test-and-sets this flag in a single cycle. If the partner has already arrived, it clears the flag, reads the partner data and executes an instruction. If the partner has not yet arrived, then the token data will be stored in the memory word of matching address and the flag is set.

At the end of the function execution, the frame is released for a future reuse. The advantages of ETS are as follows.

- It does not need any associative mechanisms.

- It does not generate a pipeline bubble caused by a hash miss.

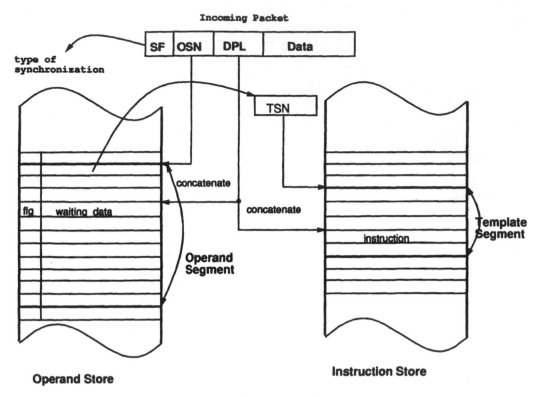

Figure 2: Direct matching.

- The location of the matching is written in the instruction, so debugging and tracing are quite easy.

- A frame word can be reused even by another instruction in the same function instance, if there is an ordering between two nodes.

However, ETS has a few defects as described below.

- An instruction fetch is always necessary, even if the matching fails.

- An instruction fetch and matching must be serialized, and the former always occurs before the latter occurs. This makes pipeline length longer and thus causes a long turnaround.

These two defects are the result of storing the frame offset with the instruction; it is necessary to fetch the instruction offset pair to find the match location.

(2) *Direct Matching in EM-4*

The direct matching in EM-4 [7] is also a data-driven synchronization without using associative mechanisms.

Figure 2 shows the direct matching scheme.

Similar to ETS, a matching area is exclusively reserved for a single function instance. This area is called an *operand segment* while the code block corresponding to it is called a *template segment*. Matching occurs at a certain word in the frame. At the function invocation time, one operand segment is reserved for the new function instance and the top address of the template segment is written to the top address word of the operand segment. The top address of the template segment is called TSN, *template segment number.*

In direct matching, every token contains two fields, OSN and DPL. OSN is an operand segment number (same as a frame pointer in ETS) which points to the top of the operand segment. The DPL serves both a displacement of the instruction and that of the matching. This displacement is common for both matching and an instruction fetch, i.e., the matching offset in the operand segment is the same as the instruction offset in the template segment.

Each packet also has a field of SF, a *synchronization flag.* This field indicates the type of the synchronization. In the EM-4, the SF contains two bits representing four synchronization types: monadic, dyadic left, dyadic right, and immediate.

The matching address is produced simply by concatenating the OSN and the DPL. Instruction address is derived by concatenating the TSN, which is fetched from the top word of the operand segment, and the DPL (see Figure 2).

Each data word in an operand segment also includes a synchronization flag. A dyadic matching in the EM-4 is performed by a test-and-set of the flag. If the flag has already been set, the partner data will be read, the flag will be cleared, and the instruction will be executed. Otherwise the arriving data will be stored there and the flag will be set.

At the end of function execution, the operand segment is released for a future reuse.

The advantages of the direct matching are as follows.

- It does not need any associative mechanisms.

- It does not generate a pipeline bubble caused by a hash miss.

- An instruction fetch is not necessary, if the matching fails. This solves the first defect of ETS.

- After a TSN fetch, matching and an instruction fetch can be performed in parallel. This partly solves the second defect of ETS.[2]

- The location of the matching is completely written in the packet, so debugging and tracing are quite easy.

However, the direct matching has a few drawbacks as described below.

- A TSN fetch is necessary before an instruction fetch. Although these can easily be pipelined, this makes the turnaround one cycle longer.

- The reuse of a frame word within the same function instance is impossible, since it is bound to a single instruction which has the same offset as the matching word.

- At the time of a function invocation, a TSN must be written to the first word of the operand segment. This overhead is usually negligible, since it happens once per one function. If the function body is quite small, this may be a problem.

---

[2]In the EM-4, matching and an instruction fetch are not operated in parallel, because of its narrow memory bandwidth. However, it has to be emphasized that, in principle, the direct matching can provide parallel operations of matching and an instruction fetch, if the memory bandwidth is sufficiently high or if the Harvard architecture is adopted.

- Each instruction must have exactly one frame slot. This reduces the memory efficiency.

Both in Monsoon and in the EM-4, a dyadic matching is performed only in a single clock cycle. Memory read-modify-write is thus carried out in a single clock cycle and the pipeline pitch of these two machines cannot be shorter than it.

After the development of these machines, more innovative computers were proposed and are now being built by the same groups. One is *T [15], [16] and the other is the EM-5 [12]. In these two machines, the data-driven synchronizations are improved so as to eliminate the defects listed above.

(3) *T Message Synchronization*

The data-driven synchronization in *T is based on ETS, but is more flexible. For thread-based computation, cases where more than two messages must be synchronized are the common case. To perform synchronization of n-messages efficiently and flexibly, *T will provide a general join by a sequence of instructions at the starting/resuming time of each thread. Each message in *T includes the FP and IP, just like ETS in Monsoon. The join reads a flag (or a counter), updates it, and performs a conditional branch if the synchronization is completed. This method makes the turnaround longer, but gains flexibility.

(4) *Advanced Direct Matching in the EM-5*

The EM-5 adopts an improved synchronization method, called an *advanced direct matching*. Unlike the previous mechanisms, the matching and the instruction fetch are completely independent within the advanced direct matching.

This method is based on the direct matching. Each token packet contains the OSN and the displacement in the operand segment (ODPL). Furthermore, it contains the TSN and the displacement of the template segment (TDPL). There are thus two offset fields, so the address of the instruction is completely independent of the matching.

The advanced direct matching uses the SF field in each packet, which indicates the type of the synchronization.

Figure 3 illustrates the advanced direct matching in the EM-5. At a function's invocation time, a frame is allocated for it. When each token arrives at a processor, an instruction fetch occurs using TSN and TDPL. At the same time, matching occurs using OSN and ODPL.

As the packet in the advanced direct matching holds all information necessary for an instruction fetch and matching, it is a superset of both ETS and the direct matching, i.e., it receives all the advantages which are listed in (1) and in (2). In addition, the advanced direct matching has the following advantages.

- An instruction fetch is not necessary for matching. A token whose partner has not arrived yet does not fetch an instruction.

- A matching and a speculative instruction fetch can be performed completely in parallel, which shortens the turnaround.

- It is not necessary to write TSN at a function invocation.

- There are no TSN fetches.

These advantages are derived at the cost of the additional address field in a packet, i.e., an additional offset and a TSN field. In each instruction which outputs a packet,

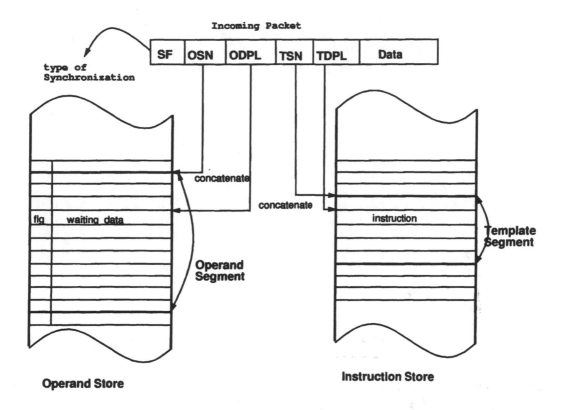

Figure 3: Advanced direct matching.

there is also an additional field containing the TDPL. Whether this cost is reasonable or not will be discussed in Section 4.

2.2 Optimized Synchronization

Before proposing a new method, we have to understand the differences between the synchronization requirements in an original dataflow architecture, and those in a multithreaded architecture. The additional requirements (or conditions) for "multithreaded" synchronization are as follows.

1. In a multithreaded architecture, multiway join occurs more frequently. This is because a long thread may need a lot of data for all of its operations. In addition, the size of messages may not be fixed, i.e., the amount of data included in a message will vary from one to many, depending on the system's data distribution method and its operand passing method.

2. Multithreaded architectures may not need as many data-driven synchronizations as the conventional dataflow architectures. This is because a node inside a thread does not need data matching.

3. To exploit locality, a cache and a register set are introduced for a fast single-thread execution. Synchronization should be comparable in the speed to these local storages.

The first condition may force us to use a counter-type join logic in addition to (or instead of) the traditional dyadic matching logic. In addition, we have to prepare multiple data words for waiting data storage at one synchronization. The second condition will make us reconsider the cost-effectiveness of synchronization. If a synchronization occurs usually once per ten thousand cycles, we may not need a special mechanism for it. The third condition will force us to make a short-pitch pipelined implementation of synchronization. It will also force us to perform the synchronization in parallel with an instruction fetch and a decode.

In this subsection, an ultimately efficient synchronization is proposed. Discussions on cost-effectiveness will be made in Section 4.

Figure 4 shows the optimized data-driven synchronization for massively parallel multithreaded computers.

Each message (or each packet) contains the (TSN, TDPL) pair (i.e., instruction address), and the (OSN, ODPL) pair,[3] just like the advanced direct matching shown in 2.1. In addition, the packet has a synchronization flag field (SF) which indicates the type of the synchronization. This flag field is larger than that in the advanced direct matching (more than 3 bits), representing (1) a monadic synchronization, (2) dyadic left data, (3) dyadic right data, (4) a synchronization for more than two messages, (5) a signal synchronization, (6) dyadic data with an immediate left, or (7) dyadic data with an immediate right. We may consider a larger field for this flag for representing a sticky token, representing a triadic synchronization, etc.

We use an instruction cache and a data cache, respectively, to shorten local memory latency. These will be separate on-chip caches just as in a typical RISC chip. In addition, it is advantageous to have another independent cache, a *flag cache*, to speedup synchronization.

Suppose a single clock cycle means time enough for a cache read (or write). When a message comes into the synchronization part in a processor, an instruction can immediately be fetched. The operational sequence of an instruction fetch and a decode are completely independent of that of the synchronization until the execution occurs. We can thus concentrate on the data-driven synchronization.

Actually, there are five types of data-driven synchronizations according to the SF. We describe the mechanism for each case.

1. *Monadic Synchronization*

   In case of monadic operations or in case that a single message contains all data which are necessary for certain thread execution. Synchronizations are not necessary. Besides fetching an instruction and decoding it, nothing happens before the execution. Note that all the synchronization stages of a pipeline should be bypassed to reduce latency.

2. *Dyadic Synchronization*

   A dyadic synchronization is the same as the dyadic matching in conventional dataflow machines. Although this can be implemented by a multiway join described below, this should be distinctively implemented, since dyadic synchronizations occur so frequently that its efficiency influences the overall performance of the machine considerably.

---

[3]All the addresses are virtualized, so there is an address translation mechanism for each cache.

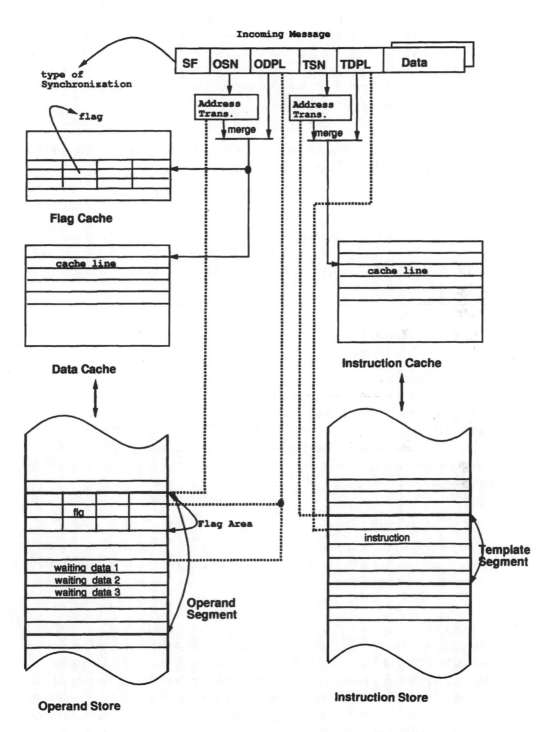

Figure 4: Optimized data-driven synchronization.

The operations of a dyadic synchronization are (1) read a flag from a flag cache (if it fails, a cache line is read from the main memory), (2) check whether the flag shows the existence of the partner or not, (3) clear the flag if the partner exists or to set the flag if it does not exist, (4) read data from the data cache (if it fails, a cache line is read from the main memory) whose address is (OSN, ODPL), and (5)write message data to the data cache whose address is (OSN, ODPL) if the partner does not exist.

These operations can be parallelized, i.e., (1) and (4) are parallelized, and (3) and (5) are parallelized. So the synchronization sequence is:

> *clock 1:* (1) and (4)
>
> *clock 2:* (3) and (5) following (2)

As (2) is simple and the address has been held since (1), (2) and (3) can be performed in a single cycle.

To make a complete pipeline, it is necessary to have a dual port flag cache and a dual port data cache.

3. *Multiway Join (≥3)*

There are two ways to synchronize more than two messages. One is to make a tree of dyadic synchronizations. Each node of the tree performs a dyadic synchronization and a store of message data to certain words of the frame. This method requires no additional hardware. However, it needs many instruction execution cycles and additional packet flow, since there may be many intermediate nodes dedicated to the synchronization. More precisely, an $n - ary$ join needs $n - 1$ instructions and $n - 2$ additional packet flows.

To perform the multiway join more efficiently and more flexibly, it is necessary to use a join-counter logic. In this case, each flag is used for a counter indicating the number of messages which have already arrived or the number of messages which will have to arrive before execution.

The operations of a multiway join with this counter are (1) read a flag from a flag cache (if it fails, a cache line is read from the main memory), (2) increment the counter and compare the result with some constant (or to decrement the counter and compare the result with zero), (3) clear the flag if the partner exists or to set the flag to the new value derived from (2) if it does not exist, (4) read waiting data from the data cache (if it fails, a cache line is read from the main memory), (5) write message data to the data cache (if it fails, a cache line is read from the main memory).

Here, (4) can be performed by the executor, not by the synchronization logic. However, the speculative data fetch will be effective, since (4) can be performed in parallel with the flag memory write.

The operations here can also be parallelized. The synchronization sequence is:

clock 1: (1) and (5)

clock 2: (2) and (4)

clock 3: (3) and (4)

clock 4 and after: (4), if necessary

In case of the multiway join, the counter update and branch are more time-consuming than the flag-check and branch in the dyadic synchronization. This is the reason why (2) takes one independent clock cycle.

If the size of the message data is more than one, (5) will take more than one cycle. In this case, data write occurs in clock 2 or after clock 2. This will delay the sequence of (4).

4. *Signal Synchronization*

The operations of a signal synchronization with a lot of tokens are similar to those of the multiway join. However, it does not need to access a data memory at all.

What happens in this case is a sequential operation of (1)(2)(3) of the multiway join.

5. *Counter Overflow*

In a multiway join (also in a signal synchronization), the counter overflow may occur when the number of messages which should be synchronized at the same point exceeds the number which can be represented by the flag.

In this case a join-tree is constructed, each node of which performs a smaller join.

One question is the size of the flag. If the flag is too small, we have to make a high tree which causes overhead. If the flag is too large, memory efficiency is degraded. For instance, if the flag is 4-bit wide, then it can perform 16 way join with a single node, 256 way join with a two-layer tree, etc. Although 4 bits seem sufficiently for a multiway join, a good size must be experimentally determined.

Note that the synchronization does not use instructions at all. Instructions such as Post, Start, Join and Next [15] do not exist here. This reduces the execution cycles of a processor. The synchronization for a certain thread can totally be pipelined with the other threads. This highly increases the system throughput. It also can be parallelized with the instruction fetch and the decode for the same message. This highly decreases the processing latency. The advantages of this optimized synchronization are as follows.

1. *Efficiency*
   The proposed method is ultimately efficient, because of the following: (1) it provides highly parallel and pipelinable operation mechanisms: parallel execution of instruction fetch/decode and synchronization, parallel execution of flag memory accesses and data memory accesses, and pipelined execution between multiple threads; (2) it provides five kinds of synchronization mechanisms which can optimally be adopted for the synchronization type; and (3) it does not need any instructions which will increase the latency and a whole cycle time.

2. *Flexibility*
   The proposed method provides five kinds of synchronization. The counter type synchronization especially makes it fairly flexible for complex synchronizations.

3. *Simplicity*
   As each message has both the address of instruction and the synchronization, this mechanism simplifies the synchronization itself and eases the understanding of what is happening in the synchronization stages. To design and to debug are both much easier than the other data-driven methods.

3. Pipeline Design

3.1 Basic Methodologies

Conventional dataflow machines and the HEP [1] have a pipeline where multiple threads share its slots at the same time. The pipeline of this type is called a *circular pipeline* [3]. The circular pipeline has several advantages as follows.

- It exploits the parallel activities maximally in a single pipeline. There is no overhead of a context switching.

- It achieves the natural and efficient combination of computation and communication by providing continuous operations from the network to the instruction executor and from the instruction executor to the network. There are no interruptions between a network and a processor.

- It can provide an excellent throughput without preparing complex interlocking mechanisms and branch prediction mechanisms.

Because of these advantages, the circular pipeline has been regarded as an excellent structure for parallel computation. Two of the representative dataflow machines, the SIGMA-1 [4] and Monsoon [8] have this type of pipeline.

Figure 5 shows the pipeline structure of Monsoon. It has eight stages, each of which can be occupied by an independent thread in a completely non-blocking way.

However, there are several drawbacks in a "pure" circular pipeline [11].

- The circular pipeline does not perform an advanced control. Advanced control here means a look-ahead control containing an instruction prefetch.

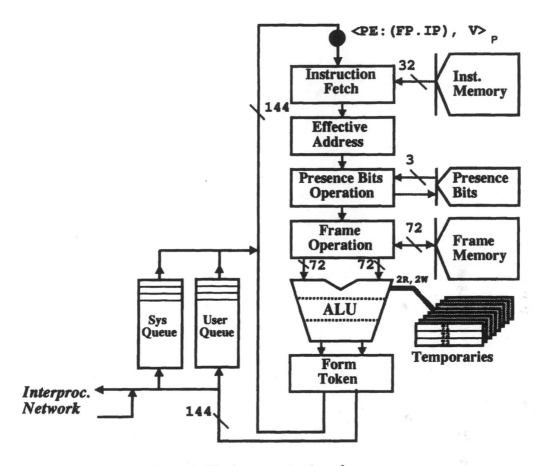

Figure 5: Pipeline organization of monsoon.

- There may be a lot of empty slots in the circular pipeline if there is not enough parallelism.

- Throughput of the circular pipeline is limited by the speed of global data handling, such as a packet flow and main memory access.

- Resource management is inefficient with the circular pipeline, since it has to lock the pipeline resources for a series of indivisible operations which cannot be interleaved.

Briefly, the circular pipeline is not suited to a local sequential execution nor is it suited to a less parallel execution.

To overcome these defects is one of the most essential reasons of proposing multi-threaded computers. Multithreaded computers typically have a RISC-type von Neumann pipeline in addition to the packet-based circular pipeline.

For instance, Figure 6 illustrates the pipeline structure of the EM-4 [7]. The processor of the EM-4 has two-layered nested pipeline, i.e., the packet-based circular

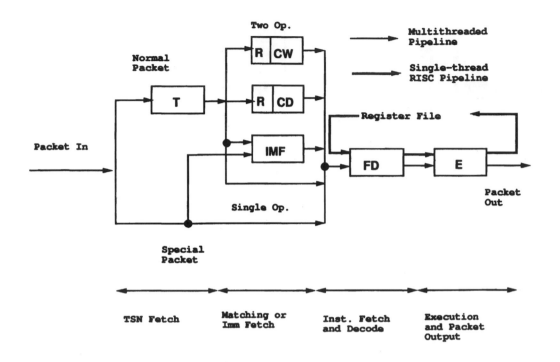

Figure 6: Pipeline organization of the EM-4.

pipeline includes the RISC-pipeline. The former performs a multithreaded pipelining as fast as or faster than a conventional dataflow pipeline, while the latter performs a register-based advanced-control pipelining as fast as a conventional RISC pipeline. In addition, the multithreaded pipeline of the EM-4 has several bypassing routes, which shortens a latency of a packet with a simple request.

The EM-5 [12] will have a faster and more complex pipeline based on the EM-4 layered-pipeline, i.e., the matching stage will be faster because of the introduction of the advanced direct matching, and the execution part will perform integer operations, floating operations, and load/store in parallel.[4]

The *T [15], [16] will also have a RISC pipeline inside its processor. Actually, the *T processor is an extension of a MC88110, a commercial RISC processor which will provide the peak performance of 100 MFLOPS for double precision floating point calculations. In the *T, there are no additional pipeline stages for message handling and synchronization. They are implemented by special instructions which are executed in a superscalar style with special register sets. The turnaround and the number of instructions executed for such operations are both larger than the EM-5 pipeline. However,

---

[4]The basic concept of the EM-5 pipeline design is the same as the EM-4, so this paper will not describe its structure more closely.

it could exploit the parallelism between thread execution and message handling by its superscalar mechanism.

3.2 Optimized Pipeline

The previous architectures have shown that the pipeline for a multithreaded processor should be a combination of two types of pipelines. One is a multithreaded circular pipeline and the other is a RISC type single-threaded pipeline with an advanced control. The former should be fairly fast with the optimized data-driven synchronization stages proposed in Section 2.2.

Before proposing an ultimately efficient pipeline for a multithreaded computer, we have to show the requirements for a pipeline of multithreaded computers.

1. *High throughput for both multithreaded execution and single-threaded execution.*
   In the normal case, the throughput should be one result per one RISC clock, which indicates the pitch for both pipelines.

2. *Short turnaround from message input to result write to message output, and from instruction fetch to result write.*
   For single-thread execution, the turnaround of operations inside a processor must be equal to or less than a normal RISC processor. For multithread execution, result message should be output as soon as possible after the input message enters.

To meet the first requirement, a pipeline pitch must be as short as possible.

Cache read and write should be pipelined. There are three independent caches to implement the optimized synchronization described in Section 2.2. Among those, the flag cache is accessed by the read-flag stage and write-flag stage. The data cache is accessed by the read-data stages, write-data stages, and, possibly, load/store stages.[5] To achieve the short pitch pipeline, the former cache must be dual-port and the latter will preferably be dual- or tri-ported, in order to avoid memory-request contentions at the same time.

The executor should also be highly pipelined as is shown in the current RISC processors, e.g., floating point pipelines and load/store pipelines.

To meet the latter requirement, intra-processor parallelism should be pursued as much as possible.

As was already shown in the optimization of synchronizations, the synchronization and the instruction fetch/decode should be operated in parallel. In the executor, many operations should be executed in parallel, e.g., superscaler execution of integer instructions and parallel execution of floating point instructions and integer instructions. In addition, for a multithreaded computer, generating packets should be carried out in parallel with the instruction execution.

To meet the latter requirement, bypassing mechanisms are sometimes necessary. For instance, remote fetch of the data should not be performed by a long pipeline.

Figure 7 illustrates the optimized pipeline for an element of a massively parallel multithreaded computer.

When a message enters, the processor performs the multithreaded pipeline as follows. The first stages of the pipeline carry out a synchronization and an instruction fetch and an instruction decode as was stated in Section 2.2. There were several kinds of parallelism in it, i.e., parallelism among the flag handling, the data read/write, and

---

[5] Note that the frame is used as a working area for the executor as well as a synchronization area.

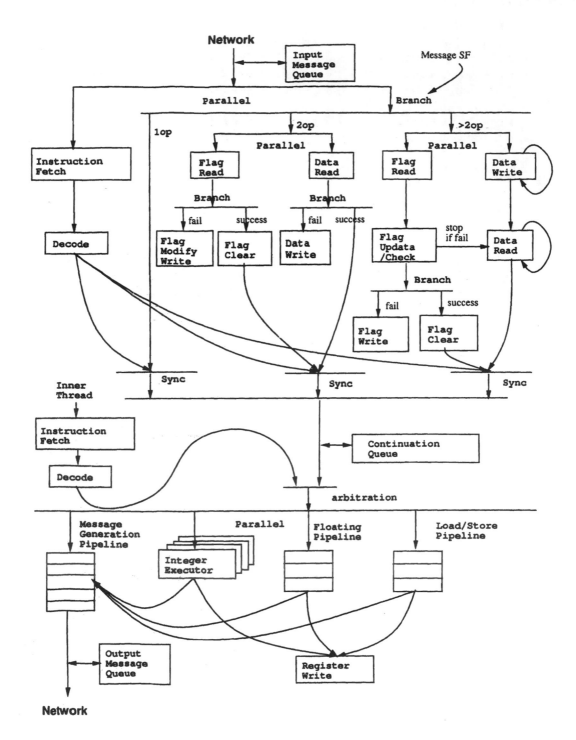

Figure 7: Optimized pipeline.

the instruction fetch/decode. In addition there are some bypassing routes. Continuously the latter stages execute the instruction invoked by the message. If the thread contains more than one instruction, an instruction fetch for the second instruction occurs while the decode of the first instruction is carried out. Third instruction fetch occurs while the first one is executed and the second one is in the decode stage.

The instructions can be issued in parallel in the executor as long as the operand data exist and the functional unit is available. Intra-processor parallelism can be extracted in this way, just as in the current RISC processor. In order to fetch instructions for incoming messages in parallel with the previous thread execution, the instruction cache should also be dual-ported.

Thread execution proceeds in this way. The packet turnaround time (the time from packet input to the first packet output, if the first instruction is a packet output instruction) is (1) 4 clocks for a monadic node, (2) 4 clocks for a dyadic node, and (3) $4 + (s - 2)$ clocks for a s-adic node if the processor and the network have no other activities. The typical throughput is n instructions per clock where n is an average execution parallelism utilized in a processor.

There are three queues illustrated in Figure 7: the Input Message Queue, the Continuation Queue, and the Output Message Queue. These queues absorb the speed gap between the network and the synchronization part, between the synchronization part and the execution part, and between the execution part and the network. To omit one or two queues is possible, depending on the typical throughput of each part.

4. Discussions

4.1 Architectural Tuning

(1) *Priority Control*

Although the proposed pipeline is fairly efficient, there are cases where a certain thread should be executed before the current thread execution is finished. For example, suppose that a certain remote fetch is critical for the whole computation time. If the remote fetch message is blocked at the entrance of the executor by a long thread, the overall performance will be degraded.

To solve this situation, two ways can be considered: independent execution or preemption. In the former, the processor may have an extra pipeline (including extra registers and data paths for executing) which is dedicated to the priority operations. The I-structure handling of *T uses this [15]. In the latter, the processor should have a fairly fast context switching mechanism. To exploit the ultimate pipeline shown in Section 3, the overhead of switching context must be zero or one clock cycle. The instruction insertion mechanism with multiple register sets [19] will be adopted for this.

In either case, efficient priority queues are necessary in a message waiting section and sometimes in an interconnection network.

(2) *Load/Store Overhead Between Synchronization and Execution*

In the pipeline described in Section 3.3, all message data must be stored before execution. However, if the synchronization succeeds, they can be sent directly to the registers of the execution unit, instead of store and load after the synchronization.

(3) *More Flexible Thread-Interleaving*

In the previous discussions, the author did not mention more complex situations where we can adopt a much finer control of threads. This can improve performance with a fairly small amount of control logic.

Here is a simple example. A floating point pipeline can be shared by more than two threads at the same time.

Another example is to execute parallel activities between threads in the multiple execution units (e.g., integer units, a floating point unit, a load/store unit).

4.2 Cost-Effectiveness

If threads are usually long, then the instruction executions can be pipelined in a single thread in most of the computation time. In this case, people may say that the synchronization mechanism and the pipeline proposed here may be an "overdesign."

However, as for the number of transistors, these mechanisms cost fairly small. The direct matching in the EM-4 only costed 3,610 CMOS gates [7], which are relatively small in comparison with the other units, e.g., integer units. The proposed mechanisms will need slightly larger amounts of hardware, since the pipeline pitch is about half that of the EM-4, and, thus, additional pipeline registers will be necessary; however, it is clearly not a great deal of a VLSI area. The logic is quite simple, since there are no interlocks necessary for coordinating more than one thread. In addition, no interrupt mechanisms exist instead of the error handlings and exceptions.

The extra hardware will also be required for implementing a multiport cache: multiple buses, multiset decoders and arbitration logic. However, these are simple circuits and all the buses are inside the chip. This part thus does not affect the pin limitation of VLSI design.

The last question is the bandwidth of an interconnection network and a memory. The message needs extra fields for the proposed synchronization method: in comparison with ETS, this needs the frame offset and the SF. However, in a multithreaded computer, this field can be fairly small, since synchronizations in a frame are much less frequent than in a conventional dataflow computers, and, thus, the address space necessary for a synchronization is small.

An extra field for a TDPL in an instruction memory is also a small problem for the same reason.

In addition, because of highly extracting intra-processor parallelism, the thread execution time becomes short in this architecture. Therefore, to shorten a pipeline is significant for performance, and we must have synchronization mechanisms with fairly short turnaround.

Therefore, we got the conclusion that the proposed synchronization and the proposed pipeline are both implementable at a reasonable cost; they are cost-effective in VLSI design of a multithreaded computer.

4.3 Related Issues

Here, we concentrate on a local data-driven synchronization. However, we have to optimize the I-structure/M-structure type synchronization for a large data structure handling. In addition, a multithreaded computer should have a fast global synchronization mechanism in case of a barrier in a program. These issues are orthogonal to the issues described in this paper. They can be independently pursued and added to the pipeline described in Section 3.3.

Optimization of the cache structure is another significant issue, since the pipeline cannot work well if cache misses are frequent. Scheduling techniques to increase the cache hit ratio without degrading the parallelism must be considered closely.

In an actual machine, naming mechanisms including virtualization should be implemented.[6] To optimize, the physical distribution of data influences the performance of the pipeline.

---

[6] Here, how to implement the virtual memory is not examined. It must be closely considered, combined with the implementation of caches.

5. Conclusion

This paper made a proposal about two fundamental mechanisms for a multithreaded massively parallel computer: synchronizations and pipelining. The synchronization proposed here is based on frame and is highly parallel and pipelinable. It provides one synchronization per each RISC clock cycle and its latency is typically 4 cycles if the target words are in caches.

With this synchronization mechanism, pipelines can be ultimately optimized. This paper showed such an optimized pipeline in a processor of a multithreaded massively parallel computer. The operations are highly parallelized (matching and an instruction fetch/decode are operated in parallel, instruction execution and packet generation are in parallel, etc.) and the pipeline pitch is ultimately shortened to a cache cycle. The latency of each processor is also ultimately shortened, i.e., less than or equal to 5 RISC clocks.

Future problems are: (1) quantitative evaluations of the proposed mechanisms, by analyses based on a queueing model and by simulations; (2) close consideration of the related issues, including virtual memory/cache design, priority handling mechanisms, task partitioning and optimization of granularity, work load balancing, data distribution, I/O and other scheduling problems; and (3) feasibility study by constructing a prototype system and examinations of its efficiency and cost-effectiveness, with state-of-the-art VLSI implementation and practical application programs.

Acknowledgment

The author wishes to thank Professor Arvind, Professor Gregory M. Papadopoulos, and Dr. George A. Boughton in MIT, and Dr. Toshitsugu Yuba, Dr. Toshio Shimada, and Dr. Yoshinori Yamaguchi in ETL for supporting this research. He would like to thank the members of Computation Structure Group in MIT-LCS and the members of the Computer Architecture Section in ETL for the fruitful discussions. He also would like to express his sincere appreciations to Professor Jack B. Dennis in MIT, and Dr. Rishiyur S. Nikhil of DEC for his helpful comments.

References

[1] B.J. Smith, "A Pipelined, Shared Resource MIMD Computer," *Proc. Int'l Conf. Parallel Processing*, IEEE CS Press, Los Alamitos, Calif., 1978, pp. 6–8.

[2] Arvind, V. Kathail, and K. Pingali, "A Data-flow Architecture with Tagged Tokens," Tech. Rep. TR-174, Lab. Computer Science, MIT, Cambridge, Mass., 1980.

[3] J. Gurd, C.C. Kirkham, and I. Watson, "The Manchester Prototype Dataflow Computer," *Comm. ACM*, Vol. 21, No. 1, 1985, pp. 34–53.

[4] K. Hiraki et al.,"The SIGMA-1 Dataflow Supercomputer: A Challenge for New Generation Supercomputing Systems," *J. Information Processing*, Vol. 10, No. 4, 1987, pp. 219–226.

[5] R.A. Iannucci, "Toward a Dataflow/von Neumann Hybrid Architecture," *Proc. 15th Ann. Int'l Symp. Computer Architecture*, IEEE CS Press, Los Alamitos, Calif., 1988, pp. 131–140.

[6] M.R. Thistle and B.J. Smith, "A Processor Architecture for Horizon," *Proc. IEEE Supercomputing Conference*, IEEE CS Press, Los Alamitos, Calif., 1988, pp. 35–41.

[7] S. Sakai et al., "An Architecture of a Single Chip Dataflow Processor," *Proc. 16th Ann. Int'l Symp. Computer Architecture*, IEEE CS Press, Los Alamitos, Calif., 1989, pp. 46–53.

[8] G.M. Papadopoulos and D.E. Culler, "Monsoon: An Explicit Token Store Architecture," *Proc. 17th Ann. Int'l Symp. Computer Architecture*, IEEE CS Press, Los Alamitos, Calif., 1990, pp. 82–91.

[9] V.G. Grafe et al., "The Epsilon Project," in *Advanced Topics in Data-Flow Computing*, Chap. 6, Prentice Hall, Englewood Cliffs, N.J., 1991.

[10] J.B. Dennis, "The Evolution of 'Static' Data-Flow Architecture," in *Advanced Topics in Data-Flow Computing*, Chap. 2, Prentice Hall, Englewood Cliffs, N.J., 1991.

[11] S. Sakai et al., "Pipeline Optimization of a Data-Flow Machine," in *Advanced Topics in Data-Flow Computing*, Chap. 8, Prentice Hall, Englewood Cliffs, N.J., 1991, pp. 225–246.

[12] S. Sakai, Y. Kodama, and Y. Yamaguchi, "Architectural Design of a Parallel Supercomputer EM-5," *Proc. JSPP91*, 1991, pp. 149–156.

[13] G.M. Papadopoulos and K.R. Traub, "Multithreading: A Revisionist View of Dataflow Architecture," *Proc. 18th Ann. Int'l Symp. Computer Architecture*, ACM Press, New York, N.Y., 1991, pp. 342–351.

[14] M. Sato et al., "Thread-based Programming for the EM-4 Hybrid Dataflow Machine," *Proc. 19th Ann. Int'l Symp. Computer Architecture*, ACM Press, New York, N.Y., 1992, pp. 146–155.

[15] R.S. Nikhil, G.M. Papadopoulos, and Arvind, "*T: A Multithreaded Massively Parallel Architecture," *Proc. 19th Ann. Int'l Symp. Computer Architecture*, ACM Press, New York, N.Y., 1992, pp. 156–167.

[16] G.M. Papadopoulos et al., "*T: Integrated Building Blocks for Parallel Computing," *Proc. Supercomputing '93*, ACM Press, New York, N.Y., 1993, pp. 624–635.

[17] W. Dally et al., "The J-Machine: A Fine-Grain Concurrent Computer," *Proc. IFIP 89*, 1989, pp. 1147–1153.

[18] S.W. Keckler and W.J. Dally, "Processor Coupling: Integrating Compile Time and Runtime Parallelism," *Proc. 19th Ann. Int'l Symp. Computer Architecture*, ACM Press, New York, N.Y., 1992, pp. 202–213.

[19] K. Toda et al., "Parallel Multi-Context Architecture with High-Speed Synchronization Mechanism," *Proc. 5th Int'l Parallel Processing Symp.*, IEEE CS Press, Los Alamitos, Calif., 1991, pp. 336–343.

Superpipelined Dynamic Data-Driven VLSI Processors

Hiroaki Terada and Makoto Iwata
Department of Information Systems Engineering
Faculty of Engineering, Osaka University
2-1 Yamadaoka, Suita, 565 Japan

Souichi Miyata
IC Group, SHARP Corp.
2613-1 Ichinomoto-cho, Tenri, 632 Japan

Shinji Komori
LSI Laboratory, Mitsubishi Electric Corp.
4-1 Mizuhara, Itami, 664 Japan

This paper first describes structural features of the Qx-series data-driven processors in which an autonomous and distributed control scheme is deployed extensively by introducing a self-timed elastic pipeline scheme. Several VLSI versions of the processor implementation will then be described to show the objectives of the Qx development project.

1. Introduction

Achieving ultimate processor performance under certain technological constraints has been a challenge for processor architecture designers. However, as far as conventional sequential processors are concerned, it seems that little has been done in assessing adequacy of their basic structures to VLSI technology. For example, if we examine the basic differences between RISC and CISC processors from the standpoint of hardware structures, it is apparent that they share the same structural principles such as:

1. a system clock synchronizing entire subsystems,

2. passive busses spanning all the functional modules, and

3. centralized control steering all the sequencing within the processor.

The only perceptible difference between these two camps is merely a relative compromise made between attainable net performance and permissible logical complexity in implementing the same structure onto a limited chip area.

If we ask ourselves the same question in implementing data-driven processors on silicon wafers, many instructive lessons can be learned. First of all, there is no need to synchronize all the functional modules comprising the data-driven primitive processing under severe clock skew constraints since the data-driven execution itself is basically a non-deterministic process. That is, data-driven primitive operations are initiated only when they are ready to be executed and can be executed independently of each other. Secondly, because of inherited latency tolerant nature of the data-driven primitive processing, very long pipelines could be accommodated instead of providing immediate communication paths between functional modules over heavily capacitive loaded bus systems. And finally, the pipelines can be controlled distributively and autonomously

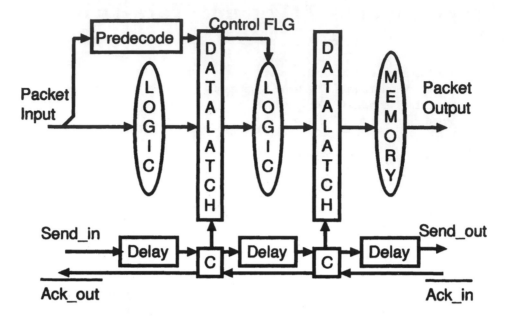

Figure 1: Basic pipeline structure with self-timed clocking.

since packets flowing through the pipes are always accompanied by necessary information on the data-driven primitive operations to be applied consecutively along the pipes.

With these contrasting features pertinent to data-driven primitive processing in mind, in the earliest stage of the Qx development project, it was decided not to follow any traditional hardware structures but to employ a superpipelined structure based on a self-timed data-transfer scheme in order to minimize unwanted extrinsic degradation on device switching speed by keeping all the wiring lengths as short as possible. In the section that follows, a self-timed elastic pipeline control scheme will be described first to demonstrate its capability in realizing distributed and autonomous control for various functions necessary to implement a data-driven processor. Then, examples of the VLSI-oriented data-driven processors already built as well as those currently being developed will be introduced briefly.

2. Self-Timed Elastic Pipeline and Its Variations

2.1 Elastic Pipeline Structure

The clock skew problem is one of the hardest obstacles for a fast clocked VLSI processor to overcome. The self-timed clocking scheme appears to be the best remedy for this problem since it makes use of skewed clocks itself in an advantageous way [1]–[5]. As seen in Figure 1, each latch in the pipeline is equipped with a localized latch trigger generator depicted by box C. It is controlled by an availability signal (Send-in) from preceding stage(s) and an acknowledge signal (Ack-in) from succeeding stage(s) and generates latch trigger as well as Send-out and Ack-out signals. An example of basic logic diagram for the box C is shown in Figure 2 in an actual form as it is used in Qv-1 described later. There are many variations of the basic box in order to realize diverse controlling functions necessary for controlling the pipelines [6].

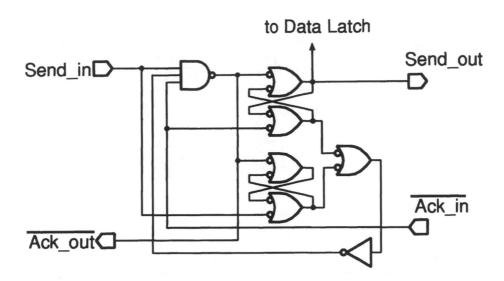

Figure 2: An example of basic C-element.

It can be seen that the pipeline is elastic since an input data packet being fed to the pipeline will be processed in consecutive stages and proceeds through the pipeline in a handshake fashion until an occupied stage, from which no Ack-in signal is being sent back, is reached. Thus, along with the data-driven primitive processing capability, the pipeline exhibits a sort of elasticity so that it behaves like a variable-length cascaded data latches or a queue (FIFO). This behavior also works favorably as a dynamic buffering function distributed throughout the processor and serves to smooth out fluctuating packet flow in a data-driven processor. Since this self-timed data transfer scheme is used throughout the data-driven VLSI processors developed so far in the project, they are collectively named as Q (queue) series processors.

2.2 Variations of the Elastic Pipeline Structure

By taking advantage of entirely localized data transfer control capability of the elastic pipeline, it is possible to construct several interesting structures for implementing pipelined data-driven processors. Examples of a straightforward modification are shown in Figures 3 and 4 which diversify and join/replicate packets, respectively. Although not shown here, it is also possible to derive more sophisticated mutually interacting pipelined structures such as a folded-pipeline structure [5] and a catalytic ring composition [4]. The folded-pipeline structure is actually deployed in some of the Q series processors to implement a queue-buffer (QB) function which is equivalent to a physically variable length FIFO buffer storage with a very short fall-through time.

In addition to versatile logical functioning, the self-timed pipeline has other physical advantages such as minimized wiring lengths and power consumption proportional to the packet flow rate. Minimum wiring length assures that any improvement in intrinsic device switching speed achieved by finer design rules could directly result in a faster processing rate through the pipeline since extrinsic degradation due to capac-

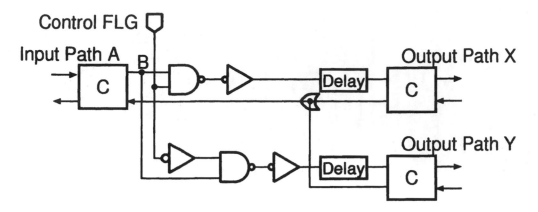

Figure 3: Branch component.

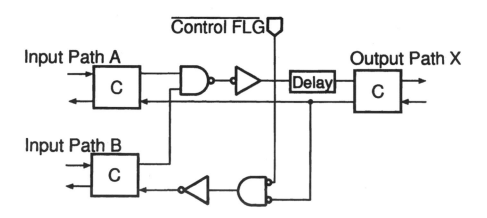

Figure 4: MERGE component.

itive loading of the gates is kept close to the theoretical minimum. It is also easily understood that, if CMOS technology is employed, the pipeline will theoretically consume no power when it is idling. In order to facilitate this feature, the latches in some of the Q series processor are designed so that their operational modes can be switched between static (during low flow rate) and dynamic (during high flow rate) flip-flops according to instantaneous packet flow rate through the pipeline. This also serves to cutting power consumption in the latches even when they are working at a faster packet transfer rate.

3. Qx Developments

The Qx development project was inaugurated in April 1983 as a collaborative research project under MITI (Ministry of International Trade and Industry) subsidy and was organized jointly by Sharp Corporation, Matsushita Electric Industrial Co., Sanyo Electric Co., and Mitsubishi Electric Co. Several researchers from Osaka University

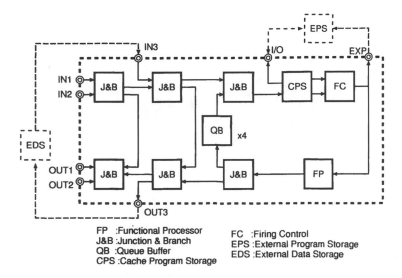

Figure 5: Block diagram of the Qv-1.

participated in the project as an advisory staff group. In April 1986, the project was completed when a prototype data-driven processor Qp (Queue-prototype) was built in the form of a bread-board set-up composed almost of discrete ICs. Four of the prototype processors were connected by a shuffle network and a demonstrative computer graphics program was run on the multiprocessor system that produced several illuminated spheres generated by a ray-tracing algorithm. Although the system was allowed to accommodate a bare minimum of four processors, linear scaling effect against the number of processors was demonstrated in a visual form by the rate of scanning lines displayed on the screen.

Stimulated by this rather unexpected success, Sharp Corp. and Mitsubishi Electric decided to fabricate jointly a VLSI version of the bread-board since it was originally designed to be a VLSI-oriented processor that the possible feasibility of the design could only be verified by doing real integration. In the following sections, some of the VLSI processors built according to the Qx design philosophy will be presented briefly in a chronological order.

3.1 VLSI Emulator: Qv-1

The first version of the Q-series VLSI-oriented processor Qv-1 (Figure 5) was developed jointly in early 1988 by Sharp and Mitsubishi as a 5-chip-set emulator [7], [8]. Since the Qv-1 was originally intended to serve not only as a VLSI prototype but also as an emulator by which performance measurements can be carried out by observing several internal test points, that would not be accessible if the system would be totally integrated as single chip. Therefore, the emulator is still in use as a convenient vehicle for evaluating and understanding performance of the basic ring-shaped superpipeline structure. Due to heavy off-chip communication penalty among separate chips comprising the main data-driven processing loop, the system itself can run at a maximum packet flow rate of around 20 mega packets per second. However, the internal packet flow rate in each of the constituent chips was designed to be able to operate at a rate of around 50 mega packets and thus paved the way to develop faster single chip versions [9], [10].

Peak performance	20 MFLOPS
Program memory	
on-chip	1K steps
external	512K steps
Data memory	
external	4G bytes
External memory	
Transfer rate	10 M bytes/sec
Board size	48 cm × 38.5 cm

Table 1: Specifications of the Qv-1.

It will be noted that the processor is organized as a unit-processing element in a multiprocessor system since it is equipped with a combination of 2×2 switches which comprises an integral portion of the processor. Presently, the packet header contains a field that can identify up to 1,024 destinations or processing elements. Specifications for the Qv-1 are summarized in Table 1.

3.2 First Commercial DDP Chips: Sharp LH993XX Chip-Set

In 1991, the 5-chip-set Qv-1 was reorganized by Sharp Corp. into 4-chip-set version in order to house the processor chips comprising a data-driven processor on a standard printed circuit board compatible with VME standard. In this version (Figure 6), the QB (queue buffer) or a simple physically variable length FIFO buffer described in the previous section, and the J&B (junction and branch) or a combined merging and diverting functions as depicted in Figures 3 and 4, respectively, are integrated onto one chip while other functional chips, namely, CPS (cache program storage), FC (firing control), and FP (functional processor), remain the same as their counterparts in the original Qv-1. The processor board is paired with an EDS (external data storage) board mounted in a piggyback fashion. The main purpose of the 4-chip-set version was to meet urgent application demands with a back-end accelerator attached to existing workstations and personal computers.

3.3 32-Bit Single Chip Dynamic Data-Driven Processor: RAPID

In parallel with the Qv-1 development, Mitsubishi attempted to integrate substantial parts of the Qv-1 onto single chip and gave birth to a RAPID (Ring Architecture Pipeline Intensive Data-driven) processor [11]–[14]. In this version (Figure 7), FALU and PM pipelines are arranged in parallel since these functions are mutually independent and can be executed simultaneously without causing any interference between the processes. Another improvement to the original Qv-1 is also found in FC, as shown in Figure 8, in which an associative memory with a limited capacity is attached to the original hashed address-based matching memory [12]. This avoids recirculation of packets around the loop, which occurred in the original Qv-1 when a hashed address collision took place. In this revised organization, the collision packets are dealt with by the associative memory function. It has been shown by executing several benchmark problems that the associative memory with a relatively small capacity results in significant overall improvement in performance [15].

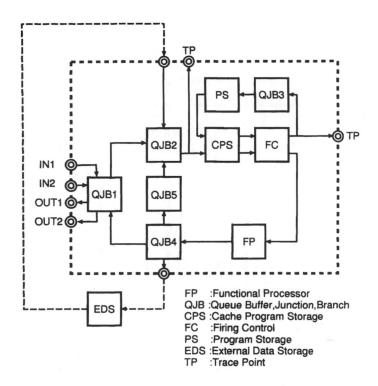

FP   :Functional Processor
QJB :Queue Buffer,Junction,Branch
CPS :Cache Program Storage
FC   :Firing Control
PS   :Program Storage
EDS :External Data Storage
TP   :Trace Point

Figure 6: Block diagram of an SBC.

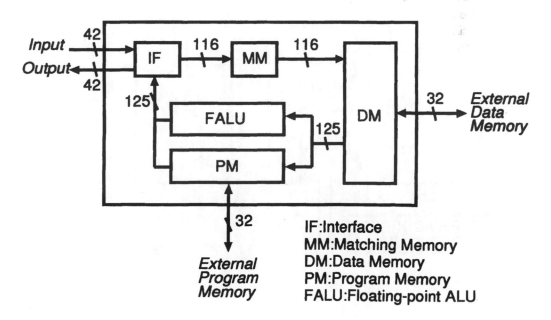

IF:Interface
MM:Matching Memory
DM:Data Memory
PM:Program Memory
FALU:Floating-point ALU

Figure 7: Block diagram of the single chip dynamic data-driven processor RAPID.

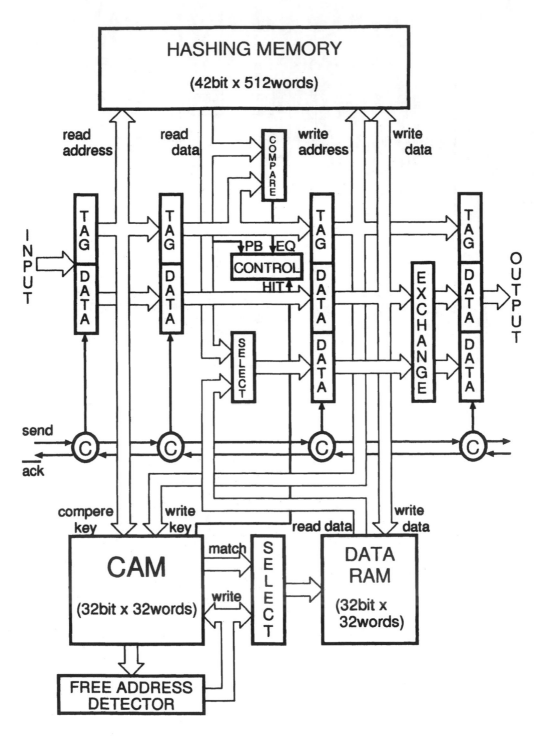

Figure 8: Block diagram of a matching memory in the RAPID.

Process	0.8μ double polysilicon double metal CMOS
Performance	50 MFLOPS
DM (on chip)	128 w × 8 bank × 32 b
PM (on chip)	512 w × 32 b
MM (RAM)	512 w × 56 b
MM (CAM)	32 w × 32 b
Transistor count	700,000
Chip size	14.65 mm × 14.65 mm

Table 2: Specifications of the RAPID.

Unit	No. of Stages
IF (interface)	8
MM (matching memory)	6
DM (data memory)	8
PM (program memory)	(8)
FALU (floating-point ALU)	12
Total	34

Table 3: Pipeline configuration in the RAPID.

Table 2 summarizes specifications of the RAPID. The pipeline configuration in the RAPID is shown in Table 3.

In this version, the switching network portion of the original Qv-1 was deliberately omitted from the RAPID chip and a separate router chip [13] was developed which allowed more flexible and efficient multiprocessor configurations than those realizable by combining simple 2 × 2 switches. This also helped to decrease pin count of the RAPID chip and to increase economy when the chips are organized in a simple manner such as a cascaded in-line connection.

3.4 12-Bit Single Chip Processor: QV3-S

In the original Qv-1, a fully fledged 32-bit floating point processor is incorporated in order to boast general purpose processing capabilities of the data-driven processors. However, for many dedicated applications, more simple arithmetical and/or logical operations will suffice as in the case of built-in signal processing functions and some logical inference systems. Sharp pursued this direction and a 12-bit single chip data-driven processor QV3-S is being developed. As the block diagram of the processor (Figure 9) shows, some of the functional modules, like PS and FC or FP and a part of B (branch) functions, are merged into composite blocks by virtue of a narrower data bandwidth and thus allow simpler layout on a chip. Since the chip has relatively simple structure in comparison with other Qx processors, it is expected that an enhanced operational packet rates beyond 100 mega transfers per second could be achieved by fabricating the chip with the latest semiconductor processing facility.

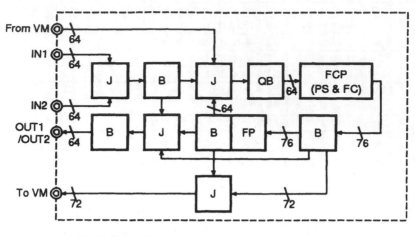

FP : Functional Processor
QB : Queue Buffer
FCP : Firing Control Combined with Program Storage
FC : Firing Control
PS : Program Storage
VM : Video Memory

Figure 9: Block diagram of a 12-bit single chip dynamic data-driven processor.

Specifications for the QV3-S are summarized in Table 4. Table 5 shows the pipeline configuration in the QV3-S.

Process	0.8μ double polysilicon double metal CMOS
Performance	40 MOPS
PS (on chip)	1 Kw × 42 b
FC (on chip)	1 Kw × 40 b
VM (external)	16 Mw × 12 b
Transistor count	700,000

Table 4: Specifications of the QV3-S.

Unit	No. of Stages
J+B (joint & branch)	2
QB (queue buffer)	16
FCP (PS + FC) (program storage + firing control)	14
FP (functional processor)	16
Total	48

Table 5: Pipeline configuration of the QV3-S.

4. Conclusion

In this paper, we have attempted to show how the data-driven processing is a natural fit for VLSI implementations by introducing autonomously and distributively controlled self-timed superpipeline structures. We firmly believe that the scheme will be proven to be more and more effective with continuous advancements in fabrication technology. It is also noted, along with performance improvements in a data-driven processor per se, that any data-driven program possesses an inherent affinity to its mappings onto various multi-processor organizations. Therefore, a search into a wafer scale integration will be the next probable step in realizing data-driven supercomputing.

References

[1] H. Nishikawa, K. Asada, and H. Terada, "A Decentralized Controlled Multi-Processor System Based on the Data-Driven Scheme," *Proc. IEEE 3rd Int'l Conf. Distributed Computing Systems*, IEEE CS Press, Los Alamitos, Calif., 1982, pp. 639–644.

[2] H. Terada et al., "Design Philosophy of a Data-Driven Processor: Q-p," *J. Information Processing*, Vol. 10, No. 4, Mar. 1988, pp. 245–251.

[3] H. Nishikawa et al., "Architecture of a One-Chip Data-Driven Processor: Q-p," *Proc. 16th Int'l Conf. Parallel Processing*, Penn State Press, University Park, Penn., 1987, pp. 319–326.

[4] K. Asada et al., "Hardware Structure of a One-Chip Data-Driven Processor: Q-p," *Proc. 16th Int'l Conf. Parallel Processing*, Penn. State Press, University Park, Penn., 1987, pp. 327–343.

[5] T. Yamasaki et al., "VLSI Implementation of a Variable-Length Pipeline Scheme for Data-Driven Processors," *IEEE J. Solid-State Circuits*, Vol. 24, No. 4, Aug. 1989, pp. 933–937.

[6] F. Asai et al., "Self-Timed Clocking Design for a Data-Driven Microprocessor" *IEICE Trans.*, Vol. E-74, No. 11, Nov. 1991.

[7] S. Komori et al., "The Data-Driven Microprocessor," *IEEE MICRO*, Vol. 9, No. 3, June 1989, pp. 45–59.

[8] H. Nishikawa et al., "Architecture of a VLSI-Oriented Data-Driven Processor: The Q-v1," in *Advanced Topics in Data-Flow Computing*, Chap. 9, J.-L. Gaudiot and L. Bic, Eds., Prentice Hall, Englewood Cliffs, N.J., 1991, pp. 247–264.

[9] S. Komori et al., "A 40MFLOPS 32-bit Floating-Point Processor," *Proc. Int'l Solid State Circuits Conf.*, IEEE Press, New York, N.Y., 1989, pp. 46–47, 286.

[10] S. Komori et al., "A 40-MFLOPS 32-bit Floating Point Processor with Elastic Pipeline Scheme," *IEEE J. Solid-State Circuits*, Vol. 24, No. 5, Oct. 1989, pp. 1341–1347.

[11] S. Komori et al., "A 50MFLOPS Superpipelined Data-Driven Micro-processor," *Proc. IEEE Int'l Solid-State Circuits Conf.*, IEEE Press, New York, N.Y., 1991, pp. 284–286.

[12] H. Takata et al., "A 100-Mega-Access per Second Matching Memory for a Data-Driven Microprocessor," *IEEE J. Solid-State Circuits*, Vol. 25, No. 1, Feb. 1990, pp. 95–99.

[13] Y. Seguchi et al., "A Flexible Router Chip for Massively Parallel Data-Driven Computer," *Symp. VLSI Circuits, Dig. Tech. Papers*, 1991, pp. 27–28.

[14] T. Tamura et al., "A Data-Driven Architecture for Distributed Parallel Processing," *Proc. 1991 IEEE Int'l Conf. Computer Design (ICCD '91)*, IEEE CS Press, Los Alamitos, Calif., 1991, pp. 218–224.

[15] H. Tsubota, S. Komori, and H. Terada, "An Architectural Evaluation of Single Chip Data-Driven Processor," *Joint Symp. Parallel Processing 1992* (in Japanese), 1992.

Stream Data Types for Signal Processing

Jack B. Dennis
Associate Member, MIT Laboratory for Computer Science
Cambridge, Massachusetts

Streams of integers and streams of integer arrays are natural representations for the signals processed in speech analysis, image analysis, and seismic exploration, among other computer applications. In this paper we show how typical signal processing operations may be expressed in functional programming languages as tail-recursive functions using stream data types. Several programming styles are considered, with emphasis on illustrating the support for streams proposed for the SISAL 2 language. A signal processing application often decomposes as a set of modules that transform signals (data streams), where pairs of modules are connected by links and operate in producer/consumer mode. Such compositions of modules are readily expressed in a functional programming language as a composition of recursive functions operating on streams. One issue in compiling such programs into efficient machine code is the recognition of recursion schemes that may be transformed into non-recursive dataflow graphs. Another issue is recognizing when finite buffers may be used between processing modules without introducing the possibility of deadlock. These issues are treated for an important class of signal processing programs and it is suggested that multiprocessor computers with fine-grain scheduling capability will prove to be attractive for these computations.

1. Introduction

A *stream* is a sequence of values which may be infinite (unending); a stream of integers is a natural representation for a signal that has been converted into digital form. Interconnecting modules that process streams of data is a powerful means for combining program parts to build larger modules and is well matched to the needs of signal processing tasks. However, stream data types have seen little use in practical signal processing applications because programming languages generally do not provide support for streams, and because implementations of sufficiently high performance to meet the demands of applications are not available.

In this paper we illustrate the use of stream data types, as has been proposed for the SISAL 2 functional programming language, to express typical signal processing operations as recursive functions on streams. We show how the producer/consumer type of concurrency that occurs naturally in signal processing may be exposed and exploited by transforming the recursive schemes into (non-recursive) dataflow graphs. In this form, a multiprocessor computer built of multithreaded processing units is an attractive implementation vehicle.

SISAL 2 [18] is a proposed extension of the SISAL language [16] and is a functional programming language intended to support high performance execution of scientific codes on highly parallel computers. SISAL was developed at the Lawrence Livermore National Laboratory and has been used to express a variety of substantial scientific application codes. SISAL evolved from the Val language developed by the Computation Structures Group at the MIT Laboratory for Computer Science [2].

2. Stream Data Types and Operations

In SISAL, a stream data type T2 may be created for any type T1 by writing

```
type T2 = stream [ T1 ]
```

This means that values of type T2 are streams (sequences of indefinite length) of elements of type T1. Three basic operations are provided for stream data types. SISAL provides the operations **stream_first** and **stream_rest** for accessing the first element of a stream and for defining a stream consisting of the remaining elements (all but the first) of the given stream. The SISAL concatenate operation, denoted by | |, may be used to form a stream as a combination of given streams, for example

```
s2 := stream T [x] || s1;
```

in which

```
stream T [x]
```

defines a stream of a single element x of type T. The result s2 has x as its first element followed by the elements of stream s1. These operations are related by

```
s = stream T [ stream_first (s) ] || stream_rest (s)
```

Elements of a stream may also be accessed using subscript notation, as in the familiar syntax for array elements. The first element of a stream always has the index 1, so, for example

```
s[1] = stream_first (s)
```

and

```
s[2] = stream_first ( stream_first (s) )
```

3. Recursive Stream Processing Functions in SISAL

It is natural to write stream processing algorithms as recursive functions that define a result stream as the result of concatenating a new element with the stream produced by a recursive application of the function. The examples used below are based on simplified algorithms taken from a large-scale defense application studied by the Boeing Company. In a later section, we will show how the algorithms may be combined to define a complete process suitable for execution by a massively parallel computer.

3.1 Example: Averaging Samples of a Signal

The first example is the program in Figure 1. Each element of the result stream is the average value of two adjacent elements of the input stream. (It is a simple finite impulse response [FIR] filter.) This is a straightforward use of tail recursion to represent the incremental construction of a stream of integers from a given stream. The tail-recursive operator in this case is the concatenation of one element at the head of the result stream.

There is little difficulty in understanding that this function definition correctly defines the result sequence in terms of an input sequence. However, if this function were evaluated using conventional implementations of recursion, the execution would

```
type Signal = stream [integer];
function AveragePairs ( D: Signal returns Signal )
   stream integer [ (D[0] + D[1]) / 2 ]
         || AveragePairs ( stream_rest (D) )
end function
```

Figure 1: Stream function to average pairs of stream elements.

```
type Signal = stream [integer];
function FourForThree ( D: Signal returns Signal )
   let
      n1 := D[1];
      n2 := ( D[1] + 3 * D[2] ) / 4;
      n3 := ( D[2] + D[3] ) / 2;
      n4 := ( 3 * D[3] + D[4] ) / 4;
   in
      stream integer [ n1, n2, n3, n4 ]
            || FourForThree ( Tail (3, D) )
   end let
end function
```

Figure 2: The rate changer function written in SISAL.

perform an endless loop, generating a forever growing set of stack frames! On the other hand, this function is a special form of tail recursion that can be translated into a static dataflow graph that has a small, fixed storage requirement (see below).

This example has the property that (after an initial transient) one element is added to the output stream for each new element accessed in the input stream. The next example does not have this property.

3.2 Example: A Rate Changer

A frequent requirement in signal processing is to convert a signal to a different sampling rate. The stream function in Figure 2 produces four samples for each group of three samples in the input stream, thereby increasing the sampling rate by the factor 4/3. Each sample of the result is obtained by linear interpolation between the adjacent samples of the input stream. The function Tail (p, s) returns the stream obtained by removing p head elements from the stream s and may be implemented by p stream_rest operations.

3.3 Dataflow Graphs for Stream Processing Functions

The SISAL programs for stream processing functions do not indicate explicitly the concurrency that should be exploited; this is determined by the language implementation. Present compilers for SISAL have not emphasized high performance in stream processing because the kernels of scientific applications are mainly array-defining modules that make no use of stream data types.

The most general implementation to support stream data will require dynamic memory management, leading to considerable overhead cost on conventional computer

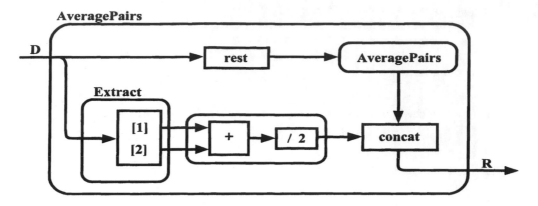

Figure 3: Recursive scheme of the averaging function.

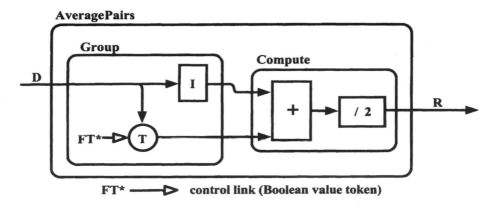

FT* ——▷ control link (Boolean value token)

Figure 4: Dataflow graph for the averaging function.

systems. However, many signal processing applications, including the examples in this paper, can be implemented using only statically allocated storage. We show this by converting the recursive stream functions into (static) dataflow graphs [7]. (Use of dataflow diagrams in signal processing goes back at least to [13] and has been studied extensively by Lee [12], [15]. Recent work includes [11].) We give a general transformation scheme in the next section.

The **AveragePairs** function may be described graphically as in Figure 3. The function body has three parts: one that extracts some head elements from the input stream; one that performs a computation on these element values; and one that is the concatenate operator that may be regarded as *affixing* the computed element at the head of the result stream and following it with the result stream from a recursive call of the function. The graphical scheme shown in Figure 3 is a form of recursive dataflow graph [7], [19].

Figure 4 shows an equivalent static dataflow graph. The identity and gate actors in the box labelled Group extract successive groups (pairs) of elements from the input stream and present them to the Compute component. The Compute component is exactly the same as its counterpart in the recursive scheme, except it must be able to

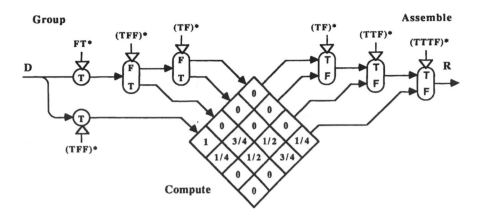

Figure 5: Dataflow graph for the rate changer function.

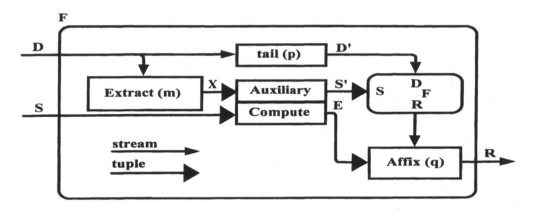

Figure 6: General form of recursive stream function.

process successive sets of data (by pipelining, perhaps). In this example, the output stream consists of the successive elements computed.

Figure 5 shows a dataflow graph for the rate changer stream function. Again, the switch actors on the left access groups of four elements from the input stream at positions separated by three elements. The merge actors on the right place the four computed values in the output stream. The control inputs to the gate, switch, and merge actors are specified by regular expressions on the alphabet {true, false} in lieu of showing configurations of dataflow actors that generate them. The figure shows the Compute box as a coefficient matrix. Each group (vector) of four input samples is multiplied by the matrix to yield the corresponding 4-vector of output samples.

4. Translation of Stream Functions into Dataflow Graphs

A general scheme for recursive stream processing functions is shown in Figure 6. We consider only tail-recursive functions in which the body, consisting of the Compute and Auxiliary boxes, is *well-behaved*, i.e., it produces a single set of output values for each set of input values, and the body is not history-sensitive. Besides the stream input D, the function may have a tuple S of additional inputs of arbitrary type. The pattern of operation of this general scheme is defined by three integers p, q, and m. At each

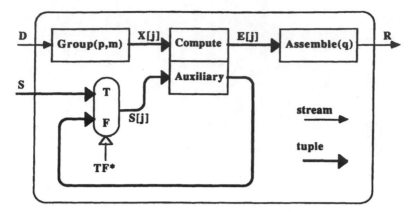

Figure 7: General form of the transformed stream function.

level of recursion, the function accesses m elements at the head of the input stream and emits q elements of the result stream R. The remainder of the result stream is the result of applying the stream function recursively to the input stream with p head elements removed. The function body contains an arbitrary function Compute with m inputs and q outputs, which defines elements of the result stream. The arbitrary function Auxiliary defines the tuple S$'$ of additional input values for the next deeper level of operation.

The transformed (dataflow) scheme is shown in Figure 7. The Group box corresponds to the Extract box in Figure 6. It forms groups of m elements from the input stream, starting at indices $1, 1 + p, 1 + 2p, \cdots$ and presents them to the Compute and Auxiliary boxes. The Assemble box takes successive groups of q elements defined by the Compute box and concatenates them to form the output stream. The additional inputs to the Compute and Auxiliary boxes are initially supplied from the additional schema inputs, but come from the outputs of the Auxiliary box on subsequent iterations.

The construction of the Group and Assemble modules is illustrated by the specific constructions shown for the rate changer in Figure 5. Proof of equivalence may be done by an induction, provided in the appendix, showing that the successive sets of values computed in the dataflow scheme are identical to the sequences of sets of values occurring at successive levels of recursion in the recursive scheme. The proof extends to stream processing modules that have several input and output data streams.

5. Composition of Stream Functions

Complete signal processing tasks often take the form of a set of processing modules, each generating a stream of values that is passed to other modules for further processing. Thus the overall computation may be described by an acyclic graph in which the nodes are stream processing modules such as those we have presented, and each link indicates a producer/consumer relationship between a pair of modules. It is well-known that such interconnections of modules may lead to deadlock if the temporary storage for stream elements in each link is bounded in capacity.

If each node in an acyclic composition of stream processing modules has the structure given in Figure 6, then each node may be characterized by a *gain* that is the ratio q/p of tokens produced to tokens consumed. The gain for a (directed) path in the graph is the product of the gains for each node in the path. A necessary and sufficient condition that an acyclic composition of such stream processing functions be free of deadlock is that for any pair of nodes *a* and *b*, all directed paths from *a* to *b* must have the same gain. A test of this condition may be incorporated into a SISAL compiler to warn the programmer if his program might deadlock.

6. Stream Computations in Other Languages

Functional programming languages are characterized by "referential transparency," a piece of program text has the same meaning regardless of the context in which it appears, and freedom from "side-effects," the notion that arguments and results of a program module are distinguished and argument values to a module instantiation do not change. These concepts provide functional programing languages with two advantages. The first is that programming is easier and more productive because programs are simpler, closer to mathematics, and easier to understand. The second is that functional programs are far easier for compilers to analyze into parts that may be executed concurrently on parallel computers.

The idea of programming with streams is old, having been described by Landin in 1965 [14]. However, most presentations of programming with streams are in the context of languages influenced by their implementations on conventional sequential computers.

In some languages the concept of stream is introduced as an application of lazy lists. A stream is represented by a linear list structure so that the CAR of the list is its first element and the CDR of the list represents the stream consisting of the remaining elements. The problem with the usual implementation of lists is that a stream represented as a list will not be accessible to a using program module until the list is completely constructed by the list generating module. This leads to needless memory demands and the impossibility of handling infinite streams, which are the usual form of data in signal processing.

A solution to this dilemma is to represent the remaining elements of a stream by an object variously called a "future" or a "promise to compute on demand." For example, the pair averaging function may be written in Scheme [1] as

```
(define (average-pairs D)
   (cons
      (divide (plus (car D) car (force (cdr D))))
      (delay (average-pairs (cdr D)))
   )
)
```

The delay operator defers the recursive call of average-pairs until access to the cdr of the list element is attempted by a consuming steam function. The force operator must be used to call for evaluation of a list component that may not have been computed yet. Treating all lists as composed of components to be evaluated on demand (the "lenient CONS") was suggested by Friedman and Wise [10]. The functional programming language Miranda [3] has embodied this concept of universal lazy evaluation so that use of special operators is not necessary to avoid waste of memory in stream processing. The pair averaging function may be written in Miranda as

```
average-pairs ( e1 : e2 : d ) =
       ( e1 + e ) / 2 : average-pairs ( e2 : d )
```

In this illustration, the colon stands for the associative list constructor (cons) and pattern matching is used to detect when sufficient elements of the input list are available to define more output.

A major drawback of Scheme and Miranda is the difficulty of exploiting the opportunities for parallelism offered by acyclic compositions of stream processing modules. Correct interpretation of Scheme programs calls for a co-routine-like execution which must be honored because Scheme (and Lisp) are not free of side-effects. Thus there is always a single locus of control. It seems that Miranda implementations are similar because this author is not aware of any efforts to develop parallel implementations of Miranda, and permitting "eager beaver" evaluation to achieve concurrent execution would alter Miranda semantics.

In contrast, SISAL is one of few languages that introduce streams as an explicit type generator, is free of side-effects, and is intended to support parallel implementations. The functional language Id [17] has similar goals, but does not include a stream type generator. Instead it provides support for lazy lists and eager evaluation. The operational mechanism to support streams by this combination of lazy and eager evaluation has been studied by Dennis and Weng [6], [5].

7. Image Processing: Streams of Arrays

The elements of the stream being processed need not be simple scalar values. The next two examples illustrate how operations on images may be represented in a way that allows massively parallel processing of image data. Typical image information takes the form of a sequence of frames or scans. It is often convenient to view the input data as an array of streams where each stream contains data for a particular line in successive frames or scans.

7.1 A Two-Dimension Filter

The function `TwoDimFilter` shown in Figure 8 represents a two-dimension filter by a single SISAL function. The filter is defined by a three-by-three array `Filter` which is applied at each position in the image data for which an output value is desired. The input is an array of streams indexed from 1 to w. The output is an array of streams indexed from 2 to $w - 1$. (The boundary elements are omitted from the result data to avoid applying the filter function to non-existing array positions.) As written, this function leads to duplicate computation of many intermediate values. This may be avoided, but requires more complex code [4] which would not suit the purposes of the present exposition.

7.2 A Peak Detector Algorithm

Figure 9 shows a `PeakDetect` function that identifies all elements of the (image) data that have a value that is at least equal to the values of all immediate neighbors and exceeds their average by a given threshold `Th`. The two conditions are tested separately and combined to determine the result. The input is an array of integer streams indexed from 2 to $w - 1$. The output stream is an array of Boolean streams indexed from 3 to $w - 2$. The peak detection function is similar in structure to the filter function; each element of the result is true if and only if the data surrounding the corresponding input pixel satisfies the specified conditions. As in the case of the two-dimension filter, a more complex code may be constructed that avoids recomputation of intermediate results.

```
type ImageStream = array [ stream [integer] ];

function TwoDimFilter (
     D: ImageStream, w: integer
     returns ImageStream )

  let
     Filter := array [-1:
        array [-1: 1, 2, 1 ],
        array [-1: 2, 3, 2 ],
        array [-1: 1, 2, 1 ],
        ];
     Dn := for i in 2, w-1
     return array of
        for g in -1, +1 cross h in -1, +1
        return value of sum Filter[g, h] * D[g+i, h+2]
        end for
     end for
     Dt := for i in 1, w
     return array of
        stream_rest ( D[i] )
     end for
     Dr := TwoDimFilter ( Dt, w );
  in
     for i in 2, w-1
     return array of
        stream integer [ Dn[i] ] || Dr[i]
     end for
  end let

end function
```

Figure 8: Two-dimension background filter in SISAL.

8. Composition of Stream Functions

The stream functions we have described may be combined as shown in Figure 10 to form a complete process, and may be written in SISAL as in Figure 11. This process may be partitioned advantageously for multiprocessing by dividing the streams into blocks allocated to each of several processors. This corresponds to slicing the diagram vertically and allocating each slice to a separate processing element.

9. Conclusions

The examples presented have shown how signal processing operations may be expressed elegantly using the stream data types of the SISAL functional programming language. A stream_tail operation that truncates the head of a stream by a specified number of elements would be a useful addition to the language. A transformation into

```
type ImageStream = array [ stream [integer] ];
type MarkStream = array [ stream [boolean] ];

function PeakDetect (
    D: ImageStream, w: integer
    returns MarkStream )

    let
        Pk := for i in 3, w-2
            P := D[i, 2]
            C := for g in -1, +1 cross h in -1, +1
            return value of product
                if (g = 0 & h = 0) then true
                else ( D[g+i, h+2] <= P )
                endif
            end for
            S := for g in -1, +1 cross h in -1, +1
            return value of sum
                if (g = 0 & h = 0) then 0
                else D[g+i, h+2]
                endif
            end for
            return array of C & ( 8 * P > S + 8 * Th )
        end for
        Dt := for i in 2, w-1
        return array of
            stream_rest ( D[i] )
        end for
        Pr := PeakDetect ( Dt, w );
    in
        for i in 3, w-2
        return array of
            stream boolean [ Pk[i] ] || Pr[i]
        end for
    end let

end function
```

Figure 9: The peak detector function in SISAL.

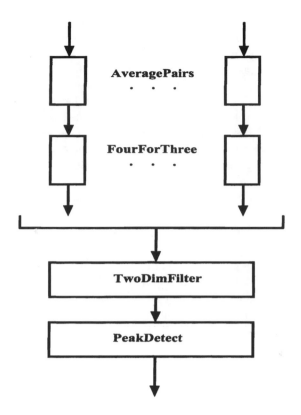

Figure 10: Diagram of the composition of stream functions.

```
type Signal = stream [integer];
type ImageStream = array [ stream [integer] ];
type MarkStream = array [ stream [boolean] ];

function Process (
   D: ImageStream, w: integer
   returns MarkStream )

   let
      R := for i in 1, w
      return array of
         FourForThree ( AveragePairs ( D[i] ) )
      end for
   in
      PeakDetect ( TwoDimFilter ( R, w ) )
   end let

end function
```

Figure 11: Composition of stream functions in SISAL.

dataflow graphs was given from which efficient implementations of compositions of stream functions may be derived. Dataflow computers and multithreaded processors capable of efficient fine-grain scheduling of threads would be attractive targets for this approach to high-performance signal processing [8], [9].

The work reported here applies the results of research conducted by the Computation Structures Group of the MIT Laboratory for Computer Science to practical signal processing algorithms. The algorithms are taken from a real surveillance task, but simplified to permit easier presentation in a brief paper. The complete original algorithms were expressed in a variant of the Val language [2] in a study performed by Dataflow Computer Corporation under contract to Boeing. The report of this work [4] included a suggested multithreaded processor design, manually derived machine code, and performance calculations for the Boeing application.

Appendix: Proof of the Transformation

We will show that the recursive scheme and the dataflow scheme implement the same function mapping input data into result data.

We assume that the Compute and Auxiliary boxes are functions that map vectors of scalars into vectors of scalars (Let the vector S have n elements.):

$$\text{Compute} : A^{m+n} \to A^q$$
$$\text{Auxiliary} : A^{m+n} \to A^n$$

The input and output streams are denoted by the (possibly infinite) sequences:

$$D = d_1, d_2, \cdots$$
$$R = r_1, r_2, \cdots$$

First we present the relationships among values imposed by each of the two schemes; a superscript r refers to the recursion scheme and a superscript d refers to the dataflow scheme. For the tail-recursion scheme, Figure 6, let the index $j \leq 0$ be the depth of recursion.

$$
\begin{aligned}
D_0^r &= D \\
D_{j+1}^r &= \text{Tail}\,(p, D_j^r) \\
X_j^r &= \text{Extract}\,(m, D_j^r) \\
S_0^r &= S \\
S_{j+1}^r &= \text{Auxiliary}\,(X_j^r, S_j^r) \\
E_j^r &= \text{Compute}\,(X_j^r, S_j^r) \\
R_j^r &= \text{Affix}\,(q, E_j^r, R_{j+1}^r)
\end{aligned}
$$

For the dataflow scheme, Figure 7, j indexes the successive values (tuples or stream elements) passed over links of the graph.

$$
\begin{aligned}
D_0^d &= D \\
D_{j+1}^d &= \text{Tail}\,(p, D_j^d) \\
X_j^d &= \text{Extract}\,(m, D_j^d) \\
S_j^d &= \textbf{if } j = 0 \textbf{ then } S \textbf{ else } \text{Auxiliary}\,(X_{j-1}^d, S_{j-1}^d) \\
E_j^d &= \text{Compute}\,(X_j^d, S_j^d) \\
R_j^d &= E_0^d \,\|\, E_1^d \,\|\, E_2^d \,\|\, E_3^d \,\|\, \cdots
\end{aligned}
$$

We show by induction that corresponding variables are equal for all $j \geq 0$. Basis $(j = 0)$:

$$
\begin{aligned}
X_0^r &= \text{Extract}\,(m, D_0^r) \\
&= \text{Extract}\,(m, D) \\
&= \text{Extract}\,(m, D_0^d) \\
&= X_0^d
\end{aligned}
$$

$$
S_0^r = S = S_0^d
$$

$$
\begin{aligned}
E_0^r &= \text{Compute}\,(X_0^r, S_0^r) \\
&= \text{Compute}\,(X_0^d, S_0^d) \\
&= E_0^d
\end{aligned}
$$

Induction $(j > 0)$:

$$
\begin{aligned}
D_j^r &= \text{Tail}\,(p, D_{j-1}^r) \\
&= \text{Tail}\,(p, D_{j-1}^d) \\
&= D_j^d
\end{aligned}
$$

$$
\begin{aligned}
X_j^r &= \text{Extract}\,(m, D_j^r) \\
&= \text{Extract}\,(m, D_j^d) \\
&= X_j^d
\end{aligned}
$$

$$
\begin{aligned}
S_j^r &= \text{Auxiliary}\,(r, X_{j-1}^r, S_{j-1}^r) \\
&= \text{Auxiliary}\,(r, X_{j-1}^d, S_{j-1}^d) \\
&= S_j^d
\end{aligned}
$$

$$
\begin{aligned}
E_j^r &= \text{Compute}\,(X_j^r, S_j^r) \\
&= \text{Compute}\,(X_j^d, S_j^d) \\
&= E_j^d
\end{aligned}
$$

It follows that

$$
\begin{aligned}
R^r &= \text{Affix}\,(q, E_0^r, \text{Affix}\,(q, E_1^r, \cdots)) \\
&= E_0^r \parallel E_1^r \parallel \cdots \\
&= E_0^d \parallel E_1^d \parallel \cdots \\
&= R^d
\end{aligned}
$$

References

[1] H. Abelson and G.J. Sussman, *Structure and Interpretation of Computer Programs*, MIT Press, Cambridge, Mass., 1985.

[2] W.B. Ackerman and J.B. Dennis, "VAL—A Value-Oriented Algorithmic Language," Technical Report 218, Laboratory for Computer Science, MIT, Cambridge, Mass., 1979.

[3] R. Bird and P. Wadler, "Introduction to Functional Programming," *Prentice-Hall International Series in Computer Science*, Prentice Hall, Englewood Cliffs, N.J., 1988.

[4] Dataflow Computer Corporation, "Time Dependent Signal Processing Algorithms for Optical Surveillance," Final Report for Contract HA4176 to Boeing Aerospace, Dataflow Computer Corporation, Belmont, Mass., Nov. 1988.

[5] J.B. Dennis, "An Operational Semantics for a Language with Early Completion Data Structures," in *Formalization of Programming Concepts*, Vol. 107, Lecture Notes in Computer Science, Springer-Verlag, Berlin, Germany, 1981, pp. 260–267.

[6] J.B. Dennis and K.S. Weng, "An Abstract Implementation for Concurrent Computations with Streams," *Proc. 1979 Int'l Conf. Parallel Processing*, IEEE CS Press, Los Alamitos, Calif., 1979, pp. 35–45.

[7] J.B. Dennis, "First Version of a Data-Flow Procedure Language," *Proc. Colloque sur la Programmation*, Vol. 19, Lecture Notes in Computer Science, Springer-Verlag, Berlin, Germany, 1975, pp. 362–376.

[8] J.B. Dennis, "The Evolution of 'Static' Data-Flow Architecture," in *Advanced Topics in Data-Flow Computing*, Chap. 2, J.-L. Gaudiot and L. Bic, Eds., Prentice-Hall, Englewood Cliffs, N.J., 1991.

[9] J.B. Dennis and G.R. Gao, "Multithreaded Architectures: Principles, Projects, and Issues," in *Advances in Multithreaded Computer Architecture*, R.A. Ianucci, Ed., Kluwer, Norwell, Mass., 1994.

[10] D.P. Friedman and D.S. Wise, "CONS Should Not Evaluate Its Arguments," in *Automata, Languages and Programming: 3rd Int'l Colloquium*, S. Michaelson and R. Milner, Eds., Edinburgh Univ. Press, 1976, pp. 257–284.

[11] G.R. Gao, R. Govindarajan, and P. Panangaden, "Well-Behaved Programs for DSP Computation," *Proc. Int'l Conf. Acoustics, Speech, and Signal Processing*, 1992, pp. V–561–564.

[12] W.H. Ho, E.A. Lee, and D.G. Messerschmitt, "High Level Data Flow Programming for Signal Processing," in *VLSI Signal Processing*, R.W. Broderson and H.S. Muscovitz, Eds., Vol. III, IEEE Press, New York, N.Y., 1988, pp. 385–395.

[13] J. Kelly, C. Lochbaum, and Victor Vyssotsky, "A Block Diagram Compiler," *Bell System Technical J.*, Vol. 40, No. 3, May 1961.

[14] P.J. Landin, "A Correspondence Between Algol 60 and Church's Lambda Notation: Part I," *Comm. ACM*, Vol. 8, No. 2, Feb. 1965, pp. 89–101.

[15] E.A. Lee, "Consistency in Dataflow Graphs," *IEEE Trans. Parallel and Distributed Systems*, Vol. 2, No. 2, Apr. 1991, pp. 223–235.

[16] J. McGraw et al., "SISAL: Streams and Iteration in a Single Assignment Language: Reference Manual Version 1.2," Technical Report M-146, Rev. 1, Lawrence Livermore Nat. Laboratory, Livermore, Calif., 1985.

[17] R.S. Nikhil and Arvind, "Id: A Language with Implicit Parallelism," Computation Structures Group Memo 305, Laboratory for Computer Science, MIT, Cambridge, Mass., 1990.

[18] R.R. Oldehoeft, et al., "SISAL Reference Manual: Language Version 2.0," Technical report, Lawrence Livermore Nat. Laboratory and Colorado State University, 1992.

[19] K.S. Weng, "Stream-Oriented Computation in Recursive Data Flow Schemes," Technical Report MAC/TM–68, MIT Laboratory for Computer Science, Cambridge, Mass., Oct. 1975.

Multilateral Diagrammatical Specification Environment Based on Data-Driven Paradigm

Makoto Iwata and Hiroaki Terada
Department of Information Systems Engineering
Faculty of Engineering, Osaka University
2-1 Yamadaoka, Suita 565 Japan

In this paper, we show how the principles of data-driven computation are suited to the development of well-structured software with high maintenance and validation capabilities. We demonstrate this through the implementation of a truly flexible software production environment in which a target program can be naturally represented as easily understandable specifications that can be directly transformed into a highly parallel and safe program executable on our dynamic data-driven multiprocessor system.

1. Introduction

Data-driven or dataflow paradigm is often adopted as a foundation in developing external specifications such as SA (Structured Analysis) and others [1], [2] since the structural relationship between process and data, both of which are essential information to model and specify a target system, can be directly and naturally represented as data-dependency within the framework of the data-driven paradigm.

However, in current programming environments for conventional processors, programmers are requested to go through an elaborate translation phase in which naturally described original specifications are forced to be restructured into a completely different processing structure conforming to an execution scheme based on a sequential control flow description. In other words, the original data-dependence descriptions are transformed into control-dependency structures in which true data dependency is obscured by remote data passing among assignment statements. Most of the current integrated CASE (Computer Aided Software Engineering) tools are, thus, unable to fill the semantic gap between the upper and the lower streams of software development processes and, as a result, leave the most laborious part of the job to the programmers.

If true data dependency could be handled directly by an executable object code, it would then become possible to eliminate the unnecessary painstaking transformation processes between the upper and the lower streams. This is due to the fact that the entire specification processes could be covered by homomorphic hierarchical descriptions based on the data-driven execution principle. It is expected, therefore, that the data-driven processors would bring a major paradigm change into the current software engineering field. This is the reason why AESOP (Advanced Environment for Software Production) [3] project was inaugurated along with a development project for the Qv series VLSI oriented data-driven processors [4]–[7].

Since the foundation of AESOP is the data-driven principle, a block-diagram-like graphical description representing data dependencies among functional blocks and a class of diagrammatical representation for data structures play central roles in describing processing structure of the target system. In order to improve readability, AESOP is designed to extensively employ diagrammatical representations. For example, an augmented sequence chart and a state transition diagram are introduced to describe system behavior, and a decision table is exclusively deployed for indicating conditional selection of operations.

Detailed specification described by these representations can be finally interpreted in a framework of the data-driven principle. However, the pure data-driven principle cannot incorporate history-sensitive processes. Thus, the data-driven processing model of AESOP was augmented to interpret history-sensitive processes.

In Section 2, a multilateral diagrammatical specification paradigm and an augmented dynamic data-driven scheme incorporating history sensitivity will be discussed as they relate to the design concept of AESOP. In Section 3, we present a prototype system of AESOP and argue why it is suited to the development of well-structured specifications with high maintenance and validation capabilities.

2. Data-Driven Software

Reusing and prototyping specifications enhance software productivity and maintainability. Data-driven schema offers a theoretical basis of software reusability through explicit data transfer between instructions. Partially ordered instructions can naturally represent the inherent parallelism of a given parallel algorithm. The dynamic data-driven execution principle in particular allows multiple data sets to be shared by an identical program, and mutually independent programs to be executed concurrently without any complex context-switching and scheduling processes.

By taking advantage of the data-driven scheme, detailed descriptions of the external specifications can be directly transformed into homomorphic internal specifications which, as a result, can be interpreted under the data-driven principle. We, therefore, introduced the following specification paradigm and a directly transformable data-driven schema incorporating history sensitivity.

2.1 Specification Paradigm

Specification paradigm must offer intuitively understandable and verifiable description, since the users' requirements are not necessarily clear at the beginning of defining specifications. By offering such a specification description, the paradigm enables users to easily translate ambiguous requirements into complete specifications, as well as to verify the correspondence between the requirements in the user's mind and the described specifications.

In order to improve understandability of specifications, AESOP allows customers to state their requirement by using semiformal diagrammatical representations along with their preferred viewpoint. AESOP also enables designers to define precise specifications by using various formal diagrammatical representations. Furthermore, in order to facilitate smooth communication between customers and designers, AESOP supports a mutual transformation function among formal and semiformal representations and offers a visual prototyping function of the specifications. (An implementation of these functions will be explained in the next section.)

In order to provide these functions, the AESOP system adopts three types of software expressions, i.e., specifications, an intermediate form, and target object programs, as shown in Figure 1. Since there are various ways by which different users describe their specifications as well as various target machines, even when realizing the same target requirement, AESOP adopted an intermediate form which represents essential process information for a variety of specifications and target machines.

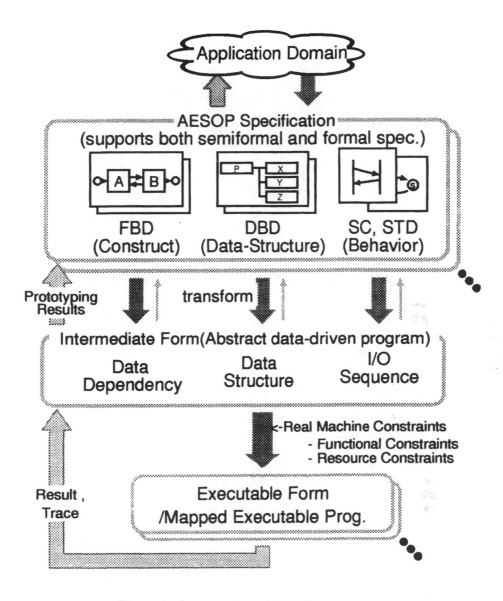

Figure 1: A conception of AESOP system.

- A given application domain is first analyzed by customers and designers.

- After analysis, the customers and designers define the application using the AESOP specifications from the viewpoint of process constructs, data structures, or behaviors.

- The AESOP system interactively transforms the described specifications into an intermediate form which can be interpreted on an *abstract* data-driven machine. The *abstract* machine has no resource constraints, e.g., a machine with infinite number of processors, zero communication latency, etc.

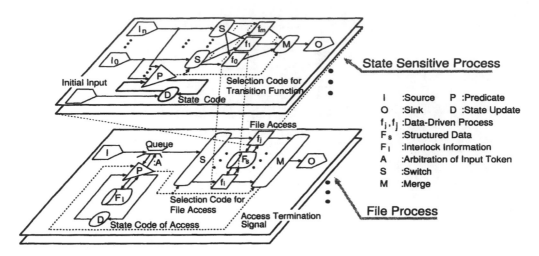

Figure 2: A Schematic of a data-driven processing model.

- If the intermediate abstract program is partially completed and interpreted, the interpreted subprogram is translated into executable forms which satisfy the functional and resource constraints of the target processor.

- The executable subprogram is partitioned and mapped onto the Qv series multiprocessors to be executed in parallel.

- Resultant and trace data from the multiprocessors are transformed back into either data-structure diagram at the specification level, or into domain-specific data forms at the application domain level (e.g., image, voice, etc.).

In this environment, if users define multilateral specifications revolving around the functional block diagram, which is a semiformal representation in a super class of data-driven schema, they can design internal specifications within the same framework of the computation model and directly execute their specifications to verify them.

2.2 Data-Driven Processing Model Incorporating History Sensitivity

Pure dynamic data-driven model cannot incorporate history-sensitive processes. Viewing from a different standpoint, the functionality of data-driven schema can be regarded as a feature which clarifies history sensitivity in the target specification. Thus, we have introduced an expanded dynamic data-driven processing model which can separate state-sensitive algorithms and history-sensitive data-structure processes (which is called file process), as shown in Figure 2. The state should be defined as a local memory to select a transition within an individual process, while the shared history-sensitive data-structures should be unified and managed to guarantee consistency among multiple queries.

(a) *State Sensitive Process (SSP)*

The selection of a desired transition, or a subalgorithm, in the upper part of Figure 2 depends on the input events and the present state. The figure further illustrates a state sensitive processing structure which is executed as following. An input token with process identifier drives a predicate function in which the input token is evaluated along with the state code token which has a corresponding process identifier. Then the destination node number of the input token is decided in a multiway branch function. The updated state code token becomes the next state in U.

Since the order of input tokens generated at an external demand source is guaranteed during the execution of an SSP, multiple sequences of input tokens can share the same SSP program and can be independently executed by adding only a sequence (process) identifier to each token. SSP minimizes state updating process to maximize acceptable input event rate and enhances concurrent execution of multiple instances within the same program.

(b) *File Process (FP)*

FP offers an abstract data access interface to application processes and manipulates history-sensitive data structures while keeping consistency among multiple queries coming from the processes running concurrently. In Figure 2, arbitration function *A* of the input queries which arrive non-deterministically into the file process interlocks data structures shared by multiple application processes. Since the arbitration function *A* dynamically creates a software pipeline structure which consists of query processes of the target shared data structure, a fine-grain interlocking is realized for each individual shared data structure. As for individual history-sensitive data structures in each application process, the FP allows concurrent access in order to efficiently supply resultant data to as many application processes as possible. Furthermore, the FP minimizes sending/receiving data of a query in order to maximize the effective bandwidth of the file process interface.

Since the FP program is transformed from the AESOP specification, it is individually tuned according to the features of each application-specific data structure and is executed efficiently and flexibly.

By introducing the above processing model as the foundation for AESOP's intermediate form, specifications are transformed into data-oriented software structure which enables users to realize higher maintainability of the specifications.

3. Multilateral Specification Environment: AESOP

A specification environment based on the expanded data-driven model was initially designed to allow the reuse of functional modules at the specification level, and was later realized as a prototype of the AESOP (Advanced Environment for Software Production) system [3].

3.1 Diagrammatical Specification and Its Interpretation

As mentioned in the previous section, we adopted a specification paradigm by which users may describe both external and internal specifications throughout their specification processes based upon the data-driven principle. One of the main notations adopted in the AESOP prototype is the functional block diagram (FBD) which enables the description of a data-driven computational graph including file access functions. Another one is the data block diagram (DBD) which represents data structures on arcs or files represented in the FBD.

Specifications based on the FBD do not strictly conform to the data-driven principle. In AESOP, specifications can be hierarchically described either in a top-down or a bottom-up fashion. The AESOP system interprets specifications according to the data-driven processing model. When it is possible to interpret them, the AESOP

Class/Formality	Semiformal	Formal
Process structure	FBD	DFG
Data structure	TBL	DBD
Process behavior	SC	DT, STD

FBD: Functional Block Diagram
TBL: Tabular form
SC : Sequence chart
DFG: Dataflow graph
DBD: Data Block Diagram
DT : Decision Table
STD: State Transition Diagram

Table 1: Diagrammatical notations employed in AESOP.

system regards users' description as a complete specification. If that is not possible, the AESOP system presents the incomplete information on other kinds of descriptions to interactively prompt users' definition.

In addition to the FBD and DBD notations, users can also use tabular form (TBL), sequence chart (SC), state transition diagram (STD) and decision table (DT) as listed in Table 1. The TBL semiformally represents tabular data forms such as sales slips and vouchers. The SC semiformally represents an input-output relationship of a function and its temporal ordering. The STD formally represents algorithm selection with an internal state and input events based on a finite state machine. The DT formally represents a selective function with some conditions based on predicate logic.

Such a multilateral diagrammatical description environment allows users to define their specification from their preferred viewpoint, and encourages interactive communication between users such as between customers and developers. Users can also utilize those notations through interactive functions, e.g., mutual transformation and prototyping function. These features allow users to describe their specifications without restricting their freedom of expression.

An example of the AESOP specification is illustrated in Figure 3, which is a screen image of the AESOP prototype. The figure shows the top level specification of the lift control process which is one of the benchmark problems proposed at the 4th international workshop on software specification and design [9]. This multilateral diagrammatical specification implicitly indicates that multiple lift control processes are concurrently executed in accordance with input *Stop_Request* events. Furthermore, a typical producer-consumer problem with *Stop_Request* can be naturally represented by the AESOP descriptions.

3.2 Direct Transformation Scheme of the AESOP Specification
Since the abstract data-driven program in the intermediate level is guaranteed to be executed without any side-effects, a global analysis of the program, which is needed for validating a conventional sequential program with global variables, is unnecessary. Therefore, the transformation scheme adopted in the AESOP system consists of a set of simple mapping rules of individual diagrammatic elements. By applying the appropriate rule from the set of rules to each operation conducted by the user, such as adding a module in an FBD description, his or her specification is interpreted

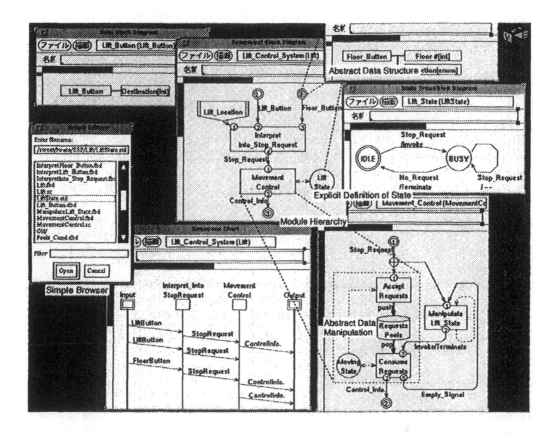

Figure 3: An example of the AESOP specifications (Lift control process).

and reflected onto the abstract data-driven program. By inversely applying the set of rules to the abstract data-driven program, mutual transformation among different description forms can be realized.

In AESOP, the following set of rules are implemented.

1. Functions and their connections represented by modules, terminals, and links of an FBD description are respectively transformed into nodes, ports, and arcs in a corresponding DFG.

2. A data set represented in a DBD description is transformed into a tagged token stream or a set of arcs in a corresponding DFG. In explicitly defining a file access, a DBD description is transformed into a history-sensitive data structure.

3. Behavioral information represented by an SC or STD description is transformed into an input-output sequence of a function node in a corresponding DFG. This transformation enables users to generate stub modules as an early stage proto-type.

Since those transformation rules define one-to-one mapping of each specification element, specifications are immediately transformed according to each descriptive operation conducted by the users. When a new description form is introduced or when the abstract data-driven machine is to accommodate expansion, one only has to add new transformation rules to the existing set.

3.3 Reusing Specification Components

Software reuse is a promising technology which improves software productivity and maintainability. Since both the input/output data and the invocation conditions of all function nodes are clearly defined in the framework of data-driven principle, safe software components are created and applied more easily. Furthermore, influences of an applied component are easily reflected onto other modules by analyzing the data dependencies among the components.

AESOP accumulates essential component information in an intermediate form based on the data-driven processing model and presents the component information to users in the form of multilateral specification diagrams so they can be easily understood. This kind of reusable environment allows users to extensively reuse specification components the users accumulated in the AESOP system throughout their design process.

As for the components database management, the differences among many components are easily managed because the data-driven program is invariant as far as their topology of dependencies is concerned. Therefore, a dedicated specification environment where users can specify their target systems simply by selecting the appropriate components becomes possible.

3.4 Prototyping Environment

By utilizing a prototyping function to verify the execution results, users can quickly detect the difference between described specifications and their intended requirements in testing a single module as well as combined modules. Simply by retaining the consistency of shared history-sensitive data structures, AESOP guarantees that unexpected side-effects will not occur in executing specifications in parallel. These verified specifications are not thrown away but can be used as "prototypes" from the initial step to the final step. For example, by using the stub generation function mentioned in Subsection 3.2, it is possible to utilize early prototyping function which can simulate the behavior due to typical data values and conduct symbolic execution.

In addition, since resultant data can be reflected back onto multilateral and hierarchical specifications, users can check the result at any laterals and at any levels. The prototyping function of AESOP also allows developers to evaluate the behavior and performance of our data-driven processor by animating the processor behavior through a visual user-interface.

3.5 A Prototype Implementation of AESOP

A prototype of AESOP was designed to be a well-structured system based upon the above-mentioned dynamic data-driven processing model incorporating history-sensitivity. As shown in Figure 4, AESOP consists of the following two main parts:

1. Sub-systems in the upper part of the figure select sub-algorithms decided by an input event and present state, and execute them in parallel. Editor provides editing functions and animating function for various AESOP specification diagrams. Browser and component manager support to register and browse

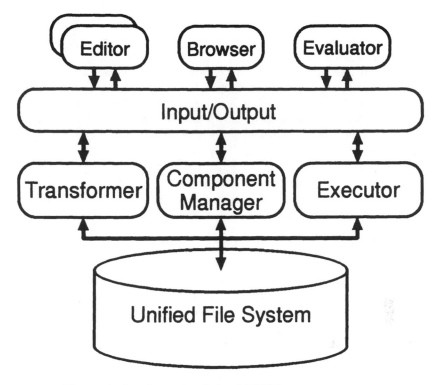

Figure 4: A schematic of the AESOP prototype.

the AESOP components. Input/output sub-system supports interactive protocol among GUI Tools, transformer, and executor. Transformer supports in generating intermediate form and conducting mutual transformation. Executor supports in translating intermediate program according to the target machine architecture and its configuration.

2. A unified file system (UF) in the bottom is implemented as FP in the proposed data-driven processing model and manipulates all history-sensitive data structures accessed by the above sub-systems in a consistent fashion. If various intelligent access schemes are implemented in the UF, AESOP will be able to support computer-supported cooperative work (CSCW) which is necessary for developing a software of practical scale.

Although the current prototype is implemented on a Von Neumann based workstation, it simulates a macro dataflow execution in which each subsystem in AESOP is represented as a unit of dataflow actors. Therefore, the prototype is expected to be easily transplanted onto our data-driven multiprocessor system.

4. Conclusion

An advanced specification environment based on a dynamic data-driven scheme incorporating history sensitivity has been designed for flexible software development and maintenance. Since the data-driven execution principle is one of the most promising models, with its natural representation capability of software systems as well as its fine-grain parallel execution capability, AESOP is expected to evolve into a software development environment for a massively parallel machine. Developing such a flexible software environment would also contribute to spreading the application area of our data-driven processor systems.

AESOP must also be sophisticated enough to apply to a practical software system. For example, supporting groupware and intelligent management of components are necessary issues for large-scale software development environment. Currently, the applicability and practicability of the AESOP environment are being investigated for real-time processing applications such as communication protocol software [9]. Further, AESOP is gradually being implemented on our data-driven processors to corroborate our approach.

Although AESOP has not been completely evaluated for practical problems, its design concept is expected to play an important role in data-driven software production.

Acknowledgments

Although it is impossible to give credit individually to all members of the AESOP project and Terada laboratory for their contributive discussions concerning this paper, the authors would like to express their sincere appreciation to all their colleagues.

The authors are very grateful to Mr. S. Yoshida of Sharp Corp. and Mrs. H. Tsubota of Mitsubishi Electric Corp. for their helpful advice and support concerning the software environment for Qv series VLSI data-driven processor systems.

The work described in this paper is partly supported by a grant from the Ministry of Education, Science and Culture (S-B2-05452363).

References

[1] D.T. Ross, "Structured Analysis (SA): A Language for Communicating Ideas," *IEEE Trans. Software Eng.*, Vol. SE-3, No. 1, Jan. 1977.

[2] P.T. Ward, "The Transformation Schema: An Extension of the Data Flow Diagram to Represent Control and Timing," *IEEE Trans. Software Eng.*, Vol. SE-12, No. 2, Jan. 1986, pp. 198–210.

[3] H. Nishikawa et al., "Design Philosophy of Advanced Environment for Software Production: AESOP," Tech. Report of IPSJ (in Japanese), 90-ARC-83-2, 1990-07, pp. 7–12.

[4] S. Komori et al., "The Data-Driven Microprocessor," *IEEE Micro*, Vol. 9, No. 3, June 1989, pp. 45–59.

[5] H. Nishikawa et al., "Architecture of a VLSI-Oriented Data-Driven Processor: The Q-v1," in *Advanced Topics in Dataflow Computing*, Chap. 9, Prentice Hall, Englewood Cliffs, N.J., Jan. 1991, pp. 247–264.

[6] S. Komori et al., "A 50 MFLOPS Superpipelined Data-Driven Microprocessor," *Proc. ISSCC '91*, Feb. 1991, pp. 92–93.

[7] H. Terada et al., "Superpipelined Dynamic Data-Driven VLSI Processors," in *Advanced Topics in Dataflow Computing and Multithreading*, IEEE CS Press, 1995.

[8] H. Nishikawa and H. Terada, "Advanced Software Technologies Implementing Intelligent and User-Friendly Services—Trends of Recent Research Activities," *Proc. Int'l Conf. Communication Systems*, 1990, pp. 11.1.1–11.2.5.

[9] "Problem Set for the Fourth International Workshop on Software Specification and Design," *Proc. 4th Int'l Workshop Software Specification and Design*, 1987.

Coarse-Grain Dataflow Programming of Conventional Parallel Computers

R. Jagannathan
Computer Science Laboratory
SRI International
Menlo Park, California 94025

Granular Lucid (or GLU) is a coarse-grain dataflow language for programming conventional parallel computers. It is based on Lucid (circa 1994) which is an implicitly parallel, multidimensional dataflow language. A GLU program is a Lucid program with imperatively defined data functions and data types.

In this paper, we briefly describe a system for coarse-grain parallel programming based on GLU. We discuss the expressiveness of GLU in composing different kinds of parallel programs. We also discuss the efficiency with which parallelism in GLU programs can be exploited on conventional parallel computers.

1. Introduction

One of the main advantages of dataflow computers is that they are easy to program since they directly support high-level dataflow languages. Conventional parallel computers, on the other hand, embody low-level programming models based on communicating sequential processes, thus forcing the programmer to deal with operational issues that have nothing to do with the application itself. What is desirable is a high-level language based on dataflow programming principles for programming conventional parallel computers. If such a language could be efficiently implemented, it would considerably alleviate the difficulties of programming such computers.

GLU (short for Granular Lucid) is a high-level dataflow language for programming conventional parallel computers. It is a coarse-grain version of the multidimensional dataflow programming language Lucid by extending Lucid in two simple ways: user-defined functions are specified in a foreign language (such as C) and values are of foreign types (such as C data types) [5], [3].

Programming a conventional parallel computer with GLU consists of three stages:

1. Develop a coarse-grain dataflow program using GLU in which parallelism is implicitly expressed.

2. Select an appropriate abstract architecture to which the program is automatically mapped.

3. Compile the abstract program architecture to a specific conventional parallel computer.

GLU programs are highly portable because architectural dependencies are hidden from the program itself and captured in Stages 2 and 3. GLU programs can largely be derived from existing sequential applications since user-defined functions can reuse procedural code with only nominal modifications.

In addition to describing the GLU system in this paper, we also discuss how well GLU addresses two important issues relating to coarse-grain dataflow programming of conventional parallel computers, namely, expressiveness and efficiency. Expressiveness of GLU is the extent to which diverse parallel programs can be easily expressed and the extent to which existing sequential code can be reused with only nominal modifications. Efficiency of GLU is measured by the extent to which inherent coarse-grain parallelism in GLU programs is exploited on conventional parallel computers. We address these issues by using well-understood application kernels (sorting, prime number generation, and matrix multiplication) and a small-scale yet ubiquitous parallel computer, namely, a workstation cluster.

2. GLU Model of Programming

GLU is a hybrid programming model that combines the multidimensional dataflow language Lucid and the procedural language C. A GLU program consists of two distinct parts: a Lucid part that specifies the program composition and a C part that defines various data types and data functions referred to in the Lucid part.

2.1 Lucid circa 1994

The language Lucid has evolved from a temporal dataflow language [10] to a multidimensional dataflow language [3]. It is the only dataflow language in which multidimensional data structures are implicit. This has significant consequences on its ability to express different kinds of parallelism as we shall see later in this chapter. We briefly review the essential aspects of Lucid circa 1994.

A Lucid program is a structured set of equations where each equation defines a variable. Associated with each set of equations is one or more user-defined dimensions. These orthogonal dimensions, which are infinite in extent, define a multidimensional space in which each variable denotes a scalar value at each point in the space. Thus, a Lucid program computes values of specific variables at specific points in the nested multidimensional space that it defines. Computation of each desired value requires the computation of other values at various points as specified by the equations of the Lucid program.

Let us briefly consider the syntax of Lucid. The left-hand-side (LHS) of an equation is a variable. The right-hand-side (RHS) of each equation is a term which can be a constant, a variable, an operation applied to other terms, or a user-defined function whose arguments are other terms.

If the RHS is a constant, the value of the LHS variable at all points in the enclosing multidimensional space is that constant.

If the RHS is a variable, the value of the LHS variable is the same as that of variable on the RHS at all points in the enclosing multidimensional space.

If the RHS is an operation applied to other terms, the value at each point of the LHS variable is given by the application of the operation to values of the operand terms at appropriate points in the enclosing multidimensional space.

If the operation is a data operation such as +, or <, the value of the LHS variable at a given point is the result of the operation applied to the appropriate values of the operand terms at the same point. For example, the equation `a = if p then b else c fi` defines `a` at each point to be either the value of `b` or `c` at that point depending on whether the value of `p` is `true` or `false` at that point. If the operation is a dimensional operation, then the value of the LHS variable at a given point is the result of the operation applied to values of the operand terms at points defined by the operation.

The two basic dimensional operations are @ and #. The expression a @.x n refers to the value of a at the nth point in dimension x. The expression #.x refers to the "current" implicit point of evaluation in the x dimension.

Other dimensional operations can be defined in terms of @ and #. For example, the dimensional operation fby.x (which should be read as "followed by in the x dimension"), as in a fby.x b, can be defined as follows:

```
if( #.x == 0 ) then a @.x 0 else b @.x (#.x - 1) fi;
```

In the equation, a = b fby.x c, for all points where the x dimension position is 0, the value of a is the same as the value of b at that point. For all other points, the value of a is the value of c at the preceding point (in the x dimension).

Also, dimensional operation asa.x (which should be read as "as soon as in the x dimension"), in expression e asa.x p, can be defined as follows:

```
e asa.x p = a
where
  a = if( p @.x #.x ) then e @.x #.x else next.x a fi
      where
        next.x a = a @.x (#.x + 1);
      end;
end
```

In the equation, a = e asa.x p, the value of a at all points in the x dimension is the value of e at a point in the x dimension such that the value of p at that point is true and the value of p at each of the preceding points in the x dimension is false.

If the RHS is a user-defined function, the value of the LHS variable is the same as the value of invoking the RHS function on its argument expressions using call-by-need semantics.

```
a = nxt( b, n )
where
  nxt( c, n ) = c @.x (#.x + n );
end
```

The value of a at a given point in the x dimension is the value of function nxt given arguments b and n at the same point. Function nxt is the value of b, n points from the current point in the x dimension.

In Lucid, user-defined functions like operations can be dimensionally abstract. For example, it is possible to define the function nxt such that it works in any dimension rather than just in the x dimension.

```
a = nxt.x( b, n )
where
  nxt.z( c, n ) =  c @.z (#.z + n );
end
```

Next, we shall see how dimensionally abstract functions can be used as "templates" for implicitly expressing parallelism.

2.2 Implicit Parallelism in Lucid Compositions

Almost all parallelism expressed in Lucid can be characterized as dimensional parallelism because they arise out of multidimensional Lucid compositions. (Since Lucid is also a first-order functional language, standard functional parallelism can be expressed orthogonal to dimensional parallelism.)

We illustrate various kinds of dimensional parallelism by way of simple examples.

2.2.1 Pipelined Parallelism

Pipelined parallelism arises when a stream of data is being processed by a "pipeline" of functions where each function of the pipeline is simultaneously processing a different part of the data stream. Also known as stream parallelism, pipelined parallelism is naturally expressible in dataflow languages. In Lucid, it is a simple instance of dimensional parallelism as the following example illustrates.

```
a where
    a = 0 fby.x f( b );
    b = 0 fby.x g( c );
    c = 0 fby.x h( d );
    d = 1 fby.x d + 1;
end
```

The computation of successive values of a in the x dimension has implicit parallelism due to pipelining. While c at some point i in dimension x is being computed, b at point $i - 1$ in dimension x is being computed and a at point $i - 2$ in dimension x is also being computed.

2.2.2 Data Parallelism

Simply speaking, data parallelism is the simultaneous processing of different data using the same function. Data parallelism is the principal source of massive parallelism in most scientific computations. Lucid, being a multidimensional language, is well suited to expressing such parallelism as the following example illustrates.

```
a = b fby.time if boundary
            then B
            else ( prev.x a + next.x a + prev.y a + next.y a ) / 4
            fi;
```

In this example, variable a can be thought of as a temporal stream of planes. Initially, the value of each element of a (as given by the implicit contexts x and y) is the value of the corresponding element of b. At each successive time step, the value of a is either the boundary value B if the point of the value is at a boundary or it is the average of the four neighboring values of a from the previous time. Note that the four neighbors can be accessed by manipulating the x and y contexts using operations **prev** and **next**.

2.2.3 Tournament Parallelism

Tournament parallelism arises in tree computations as logarithmically decreasing data parallelism at each level of the tree [2]. (It is closely related to parallelism found in "divide-and-conquer" algorithms.) In Lucid, tournament parallelism is an example of dimensional parallelism as illustrated by the following example.

```
c = b asa.t i == n
   where
      dimension t;
      i = 1 fby.t 2*i;
      b = a fby.t ( f( b, next.x b) @.x (2 * #.x) );
   end;
```

The variable c is defined to be the value of b at the point in the t dimension where the value of i equals n (which we assume to be a power of 2). Variable i is defined as 1 at t-dimension point 0, 2 at point 1, 4 at point 2, and so on. The point in the t-dimension when i will equal n is actually $\log_2(n)$.

Variable b is initially the same as a for all points in the x dimension. At each successive point in the t dimension, the value of b at a point k in the x-dimension if the value returned by function f applied to the value of b at points $2k$ and $2k + 1$ in the x-dimension and at the previous point in the t-dimension.

The following is an equivalent mathematical definition of b.

$$b_{x=k,t=l} = \begin{cases} a_{x=k} & \text{if t is 0} \\ f(b_{x=2k,t=l-1}, b_{x=2k+1,t=l-1}) & \text{otherwise} \end{cases}$$

Tree computations occur frequently enough that we can define a dimensionally abstract function linear_tree to express one-dimensional tree computations.

```
linear_tree.z( f, a, n ) = b asa.t i == n
   where
      dimension t;
      i = 1 fby.t 2*i;
      b = a fby.t ( f( b, next.z b) @.z (2 * #.z) );
   end;
```

Expression linear_tree.x(f, a, n) expresses precisely the same computation as given in the earlier example. And linear_tree.x(add, a, n) computes the sum of the first n values of a in the x dimension using a binary summation tree. At each level of binary tree, pairwise additions can occur simultaneously with the degree of data parallelism being $n/2$ initially and decreasing geometrically by 2 with each additional level.

Similarly, it is possible to define dimensionally abstract functions planar_tree and cubic_tree to express tree computations in two and three dimensions respectively. As an example of their use, expression planar_tree.x,y(max, a, n*n) computes the maximum of n^2 values (at points given in the plane defined by the first n points in dimension x and y) using a two-dimensional binary tree or pyramid. Each level of the pyramid, comparisons in four value groups can occur in parallel with the degree of data parallelism being $n * n/4$ initially and decreasing geometrically by four with each additional level.

2.3 Granulating Parallelism

Consider a Lucid program for sorting using the mergesort algorithm. In mergesort, a list of elements (initially, singletons) is merged into a list of pairs where each pair is in sorted order. At each successive stage, a list of sorted sublists is merged into a list of half-as-many but twice-as-large sorted sublists until the resultant sublist is the entire list.

```
mergesort.s( a, 1 ) = realign.aux,s b asa.t size >= 1
  where
    dimension t, aux;

    size = 1 fby.t 2*size;
    b = a fby.t merge.aux( lparent.s b, rparent.s b );
    merge.i( x, y ) = if xx <= yy then xx else yy fi
                      where
                        xx = x upon.i xx <= yy;
                        yy = x upon.i xx > yy;
                      end;
    lparent.z( c ) = c @.z (2 * #.z);
    rparent.z( c ) = c @.z (2 * #.z + 1);
  end;
```

The dimensionally abstract function **mergesort** takes a list **a** of 1 element in the
s dimension and returns a sorted list in the same dimension. The definition of **b**
initially is the unsorted list; at each successive stage (in the **t** dimension), it is the
result of merging pairs of elements of the list (which are really sublists). The merging
is done using function **merge** and the crucial point is that it accepts two sublists as
its arguments and returns a single sorted list that varies in the **aux** dimension which
is orthogonal to the **s** dimension. Thus at each stage, there are half as many elements
(or sublists) in the **s** dimension and twice as elements per sublist which is defined
over the **aux** dimension. Finally (when there is only one sublist with the same size as
the original unsorted list), the sorted list **b** which is defined over the **aux** dimension is
converted into a list that is defined over the **s** dimension using the **realign** operator.

This example illustrates the use of Lucid to express computation and therein parallelism. There are two points to observe:

1. The parallelism in the simultaneous merging of pairs of sublists is essentially fine
   grain (at the level of comparison of two elements).

2. The program makes use of the **aux** dimension to retain sorted sublists and of
   the **upon** operator to merge two sorted lists.

The fine-grain parallelism inherent in the above program cannot be readily and
effectively exploited on conventional parallel computers. Thus, it is important to gran-
ulate parallelism expressible by Lucid. This is precisely what GLU allows. Consider
the following GLU program.

```
LIST merge( LIST, LIST );

mergesort.s( a, 1 ) = b asa.t size >= 1
  where
    dimension t;

    size = 1 fby.t 2*size;
    b = a fby.t merge( lparent.s b, rparent.s b );
  end;
```

The main difference between this program and the Lucid version is that **merge** is an
externally specified function that accepts two arguments each of which are externally

defined lists and returns a sorted externally defined list. The function **merge** as far as the rest of the program is concerned is simply a pointwise function that operates on externally defined data structures (LIST) and returns an externally defined data structure (LIST). It is worth observing that while the Lucid program used the **aux** dimension to retain sorted sublists, the GLU program uses an external data structure to do so. Furthermore, the parallelism is coarse grain because it is at the level of merging two externally defined lists instead of being at the level of comparing elements of two lists (as it is with the Lucid program.)

Thus, a GLU program consists of a top-level Lucid composition that implicitly expresses different kinds of parallelism and a set of externally defined functions appealed to by the composition. By having computations expressed as imperative functions, it is possible to reuse the considerable amount of existing working software in various application domains written in languages like C and Fortran. For the purposes of this discussion, we will assume that the imperative language is C.

The above program can be further refined as follows.

```
// External data structure definitions
typedef int ELEMENT;
struct list { int length; ELEMENT elts[length]; }
typedef struct list *LIST;

// External imperative function prototype definitions
LIST merge( LIST, LIST );

// Lucid composition
mergesort.s( a, l ) = b asa.t size >= 1
  where
    dimension t;

    size = 1 fby.t 2*size;
    b = a fby.t merge( lparent.s b, rparent.s b );
  end;
```

Note that the GLU program has three parts: The first defines the external data structures, the second declares the function prototype description, and the last is the dependency specification that appeals to the external imperative function **merge**.

We can further refine this program by applying the **linear_tree** dimensionally-abstract function introduced earlier.

```
// External data structure definitions
typedef int ELEMENT;
struct list { int length; ELEMENT elts[length]; }
typedef struct list *LIST;

// External function prototype description
LIST merge( LIST, LIST );
int  listsize( LIST );

// Lucid composition
mergesort.s( a, l ) = linear_tree.s( merge, a, l )
```

The above is a compact expression of parallel mergesort in which the hardest-working part i.e., merge, is specified imperatively in function **merge**.

We have seen how coarse-grain dataflow programs can be developed using GLU. Next, we briefly discuss how such programs can be compiled to execute in parallel on conventional parallel computers.

3. Compiling to Conventional Parallel Computers

The process of generating parallel executables for conventional parallel computers from a GLU program consists of two distinct steps.

- *Step 1.* Mapping GLU program to an abstract program architecture.

- *Step 2.* Compiling the abstract program architecture to a specific conventional parallel computer.

The executables produced by Step 2 when executed on the appropriate parallel computer would exploit coarse-grain parallelism inherent in the program. We consider each of the steps below.

3.1 Generating Abstract Program Architectures

For each GLU program, there are several possible abstract program architectures each of which constitute virtual machines for executing the GLU program. Each program architecture embodies a model of computation that unravels implicit coarse-grain parallelism in the associated program.

Currently, the GLU programming system supports a particular abstract program architecture template that we refer to as the *generator/executor abstract architecture*. We describe this abstract architecture next, starting with the model of computation that it embodies.

3.1.1 Model of Computation

A GLU program can be given meaning mathematically without appealing to operational notions. While a GLU program does not prescribe a model of computation, its mathematical semantics has primacy over all possible models of computation that can be used to derive its meaning operationally.

The model of computation embodied by the generator/executor abstract architecture is called *eduction* [1]. Eduction corresponds to a lazy evaluation strategy for Lucid (and GLU) programs. The strategy is typically implemented using demand-driven execution, although it is also possible to use a combination of demand-driven and data-driven execution [6].

Using a lazy model of computation such as eduction means that there is no superfluous computation. However, exploitation of parallelism is more conservative when compared to its eager counterpart. Also, eduction, when implemented using demand-driven execution incurs the overhead of demand propagation in evaluating programs.

We illustrate a purely demand-driven implementation of eduction by evaluating the mergesort program described earlier (page 119). Consider a list of m elements in dimension **seq** denoted by L. When **mergesort.seq(L, m)** is invoked, it causes **linear_tree.seq(merge, L, m)** to be invoked.

From the definition of **linear_tree** (page 117), it causes **b asa.t i == m** to be demanded at point **seq=0**. Demand for the value of the expression proceeds as follows: first, **i** at point **t=0,seq=0** is demanded which from the definition of **i** is 1. If the **m** at point **seq=0** is 1, then the left hand side of the **asa** expression is demanded at that point, i.e., b at point t=0,seq=0. If not, i at point t=1,seq=0 is demanded which is the value of i at point t=0,seq=0 times 2. Again, the resulting value of i is compared to that of m at point seq=0. The process continues until the comparison succeeds which will be at point t = T where $T = \log_2 m$. This will cause b to be demanded at point t=T,seq=0.

The definition of b is such that this demand will result in merge(b, next.seq b) at point t=T-1,seq=0 which, in turn, will cause b to be demanded at points t=T-1,seq=0 and t=T-1,seq=1. These demands will result in further demands for b at points (t=T-2,seq=0), (t=T-2,seq=1), (t=T-2,seq=2), and (t=T-2,seq=3).

Eventually, demands for L at points seq=0, seq=1, ..., seq=m will be issued. Since these demands can be immediately satisfied, the results will be processed by function merge applied to pairs of elements of L producing a sorted list of pairs. When these list of pairs is produced, function merge will again be applied pairwise to produce a list of sorted lists of size 4. This process will continue until a single sorted list of size m is produced.

3.1.2 Generator/Executor Abstract Architecture

The generator/executor abstract architecture consists of a single generator and multiple executors. The generator is responsible for all aspects of eductive evaluation except for execution of certain imperative user-defined functions. This is done at the executors by sending them the names of functions and their arguments and receiving the results of function applications.

Coarse-grain parallelism is exploited by keeping several executors simultaneously busy. The extent to which parallelism can be exploited depends on how rapidly arguments to imperative functions can be generated by the generator and how rapidly these arguments can be transported to an executor relative to the time taken to execute the ripe functions at the executor.

Load balancing is dynamic. Each executor is capable of executing any imperative function, and no state is kept at any executor such that the result of executing an imperative function depends on that state. Each executor blocks on the generator pending the generation of a ripe function. When an executor is given a ripe function to execute, it unblocks, executes the function, returns the result to the generator, and blocks again.

For each GLU program, the generator/executor abstract architecture is instantiated, resulting in a specific program architecture whose generator evaluates the Lucid part of the program and executes certain imperative user-defined functions and whose executor applies certain other imperative user-defined functions to their arguments. For the mergesort program, all imperative functions except sort will be executed locally by the generator itself; only sort is granular enough to be executed by the executors.

3.2 Compiling Abstract Program Architectures

Once a GLU program has been mapped to an abstract architecture, the resulting abstract program architecture has to be realized on specific conventional parallel computers. Since most conventional parallel computers have a process-based operating system such as Unix augmented with some message-passing capability, the compilation to a particular target computer is fairly straightforward. Basically, the generator and executor manifest as separate executables. The generator process runs on one processor and several executor processes run on their own processors. While the executors do not communicate with each other, they all communicate and synchronize with the generator.

In the GLU system we have implemented, we use an asynchronous remote procedure call facility to support interactions between the generator and executors. The facility is at a sufficiently high level such that the nature of the underlying architecture (shared memory versus distributed memory) is hidden. It is also possible to use systems such as Linda [4] or PVM [8] or Active Messages [9] to provide this support.

4. Application Kernels in GLU

Having described the GLU programming system, we now illustrate the expressiveness of GLU in two ways: in being able to succinctly express granular parallelism and in being able to reuse existing sequential code. For this, we use two kernel applications: prime number generation and block matrix multiplication.

4.1 Prime Number Generation

The problem is to find all prime numbers between 1 and N. The solution is essentially iterative. Starting with an initial set of primes (which we will call p_0), generate the next set of primes between $\max(p_0) + 2$ and $\max(p_0)^2$. The target range is divided into fixed intervals and primes are simultaneously found in each of those intervals using a sequential algorithm using the current set of primes. The primes from each of these intervals are combined to form the new set of primes which are used to find more primes until all primes no greater than N are found.

```
struct list {
  int x;
  int v[x];
};
typedef struct list *LIST;

int display( LIST );
int max( LIST );
LIST initial_primes( int );
LIST seq_gen( LIST, int, int );
LIST catenate( LIST, LIST );

p asa.time ( max(p) >= N )
  where
    p = initial_primes( 2 ) fby.time
        catenate( p, rest_primes( p, low, high ) );
    low = max( p );
    high = low*low;
    rest_primes( p, lo, hi ) = linear_tree.s( catenate, segment, nsegment )
      where
        dimension s;
        segment = seq_gen( p, l, h );
        l = lo fby.s l + INTERVAL;
        h = if( l + INTERVAL > hi ) then hi else l + INTERVAL fi;
        nsegment = ( hi - lo ) / INTERVAL;
      end;
  end
```

The program above uses four imperative functions: **initial_primes**, **catenate**, **rest_primes**, and **seq_gen**. These functions can easily be derived from existing sequential code with minor stylistic modifications. (In fact, it is straightforward to compose a sequential prime generation application using these four functions.)

The evolving set of primes is denoted by variable **p** which initially has only the first two primes (returned by `initial_primes( 2 )`) and at each subsequent step combines the current set with the new set found using function `rest_primes( p, low, high )` where `low` is the maximum of the current set and `high` is its square.

Function `rest_primes` is a Lucid function that divides the range `lo` through `hi` into fixed intervals of size `INTERVAL`, finds primes in each of these intervals using `seq_gen`, and combines these primes into the result using `linear_tree`.

The main source of parallelism is the simultaneous invocation of `seq_gen` with **p**, the current set of primes, for the different intervals. This parallelism is implicit in the way the primes of each interval is combined using function `catenate` in `linear_tree`. Structurally, function `rest_primes` is similar to function `mergesort` that we saw earlier.

This application kernel shows how GLU can be used to express iteration and tournament parallelism within each iteration.

4.2 Matrix Multiplication

The matrix multiplication application kernel illustrates the use of the `cubic_tree` dimensionally abstract function to express three-dimensional tournament parallelism.

Given two matrices A of size p by q and B of size q by r, compute $C = AB$ where size of C is p by r such that

$$C_{i,j} = \sum_{k=1}^{q} A_{i,k} B_{k,j}.$$

The standard algorithm to compute matrix product has a complexity of $O(n^3)$ where n is the number of multiplications.

The standard algorithm can be expressed as follows. Let A and B be two n by n matrices where n is a power of two (without loss of generality). We can divide each of A and B into four $n/2$ by $n/2$ matrices and express the product of A and B in terms of these $n/2$ by $n/2$ matrices.

$$\begin{bmatrix} C_{11} & C_{12} \\ C_{21} & C_{22} \end{bmatrix} = \begin{bmatrix} A_{11} & A_{12} \\ A_{21} & A_{22} \end{bmatrix} \begin{bmatrix} B_{11} & B_{12} \\ B_{21} & B_{22} \end{bmatrix}$$

where

$$\begin{aligned}
C_{11} &= A_{11}B_{11} + A_{12}B_{21}, \\
C_{12} &= A_{11}B_{12} + A_{12}B_{22}, \\
C_{21} &= A_{21}B_{11} + A_{22}B_{21}, \\
C_{22} &= A_{21}B_{12} + A_{22}B_{22}.
\end{aligned}$$

Observe that the "divide-and-conquer" approach can be applied recursively to multiplication of the smaller matrices. Further observe that the computation of each of the eight products of the $n/2$ by $n/2$ matrices can occur simultaneously.

We present the GLU program for the solution which completely avoids division through recursion (and the associated overhead cost). Instead, it simply builds the product matrix by repeated addition and juxtaposition of products of submatrices.

The program is as follows:

```
// external data structure definition
struct matrix
    {
        double v[x][y];
    };
typedef struct matrix *MATRIX;

// external imperative function prototype definitions
MATRIX mult( MATRIX, MATRIX );
MATRIX juxtapose( MATRIX, MATRIX, MATRIX, MATRIX,
                  MATRIX, MATRIX, MATRIX, MATRIX
            );
MATRIX combine( MATRIX, MATRIX, MATRIX, MATRIX );
MATRIX add( MATRIX, MATRIX );
MATRIX extract( MATRIX, int, int, int );
MATRIX in( int, int );

// top-level Lucid composition of
// matrix multiplication of two matrices of order MATRIX_ORDER
// using blocks of order BLOCK_ORDER

matmult( A, B )
where
  A = in( 0, MATRIX_ORDER );
  B = in( 1, MATRIX_ORDER );
  nb = ( MATRIX_ORDER / BLOCK_ORDER );
  matmult( A, B ) = cubic_tree.i,j,k( juxtapose, p, nb^3 )
    where
      dimension i, j, k;
        p = mult( a @.j k, b @.i k );
        juxtapose( m000, m001, m010, m011, m100, m101, m110, m111 )
                 = combine( add( m000, m001 ), add( m010, m011 ),
                            add( m100, m101 ), add( m110, m111 )
                          );
      a = extract( A, i, j, BLOCK_ORDER );
      b = extract( B, i, j, BLOCK_ORDER );
    end;
end
```

The external imperative functions `mult`, `combine`, `add`, `extract` and in can be constructed with only nominal stylistic changes to existing sequential code. Variables A and B denote the names of the two matrices to be multiplied. Function `extract` selects the (i,j)th block (of size BLOCK_ORDER) from the argument matrix and returns it as the result. Variables a and b, which vary in both the i and j dimension, denote the extracted submatrices.

Figure 1 illustrates the computation specified by the above GLU program. It should be evident that at the initial stage, there is data parallelism in the simultaneous multiplications of each submatrix of A with each submatrix of B. In particular, assuming nb^2 submatrices per multiplicand matrix, nb^3 simultaneous submatrix mul-

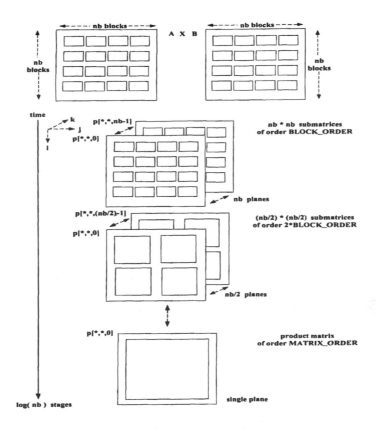

Figure 1: Block matrix multiplication using `cubic_tree` template.

tiplications can occur in parallel. The granularity of parallelism is relatively coarse since it corresponds to BLOCK_ORDER^3 multiplications. At each subsequent stage, there is geometrically decreasing data parallelism in the simultaneous addition and juxtaposition of submatrices which are in geometrically increasing order.

Let us consider the parallelism inherent in the program. The program is defined in terms of the `cubic_tree` template which corresponds to a three-dimensional tree computation. At the first stage of the tree computation, the inner product of rows of submatrices of A and columns of submatrices of B are computed. This results in a vector of planes where the Kth plane denotes the submatrices obtained by multiplying the Kth submatrix of each row of A with the Kth submatrix of each column of B. Another way of viewing this is as follows: the vector denoted by the $(I, J)^{th}$ submatrix of each plane corresponds to the product of the Ith row of submatrices of A with the Jth column of submatrices of B. At each subsequent stage, identically positioned submatrices of adjacent planes are added pointwise, thus reducing each adjacent pair of planes of submatrices to a single plane of submatrices. And quartets of adjacent submatrices are juxtaposed into a single submatrix, thus reducing the number of submatrices per plane by four, with each resulting submatrix having four times as many elements. Eventually, after $\lceil \log_2(\text{nb}) \rceil$ stages, this results in a single plane consisting of a single matrix of the same order as the multiplicand matrices **A** and **B**. This corresponds to the product of the two matrices.

In the application kernels that we have considered, we have seen repeated expression of tournament parallelism using `linear_tree` and `cubic_tree`. This is because tournament parallelism is inherent in several otherwise diverse applications [7].

5. Parallel Execution of GLU Programs

The principal objective of this section on performance is to show that GLU programs despite being expressed at a very high level of abstraction do not pay for this by being inefficient on conventional parallel computers. We show this by using a particular abstract architecture, namely the generator/executor architecture, which is inherently limited in the extent to which it can scale.

The most appropriate measure of performance of parallel execution of GLU programs is speedup efficiency. It is defined as the ratio of time taken by a sequential version of a program on a single processor divided by the product of the time taken of the GLU version on multiple processors and the number of processors. When speedup efficiency is close to 100%, program parallelism is being efficiently exploited. And when speedup efficiency is sustained with increasing number of processors, it means that the performance of the program is scalable.

We consider the three programs that we have described thus far: mergesort, prime number generation, and matrix multiplication. For a conventional parallel computer, we use a network of workstations on a local area network. Each workstation is a Sun SparcStation 2 with at least 16 megabytes of internal memory, sufficient swap space, and very little other user activity. The local area network is a 10 megabits per second ethernet.

5.1 Application Kernels Speedup

Figure 2 shows the speedup efficiencies of the three application kernels, mergesort, prime number generation, and matrix multiplication. The mergesort kernel sorts 2^{20} numbers using 16 initial subsequences with only the initial `sort` being executed remotely. The prime number generation kernel finds all primes no greater than 4 million with only `seq_gen` being executed remotely. And the matrix multiplication kernel multiplies two 800×800 real matrices decomposed into 200×200 submatrices with only `mult` being executed remotely.

The performance of all three application kernels is above 85% for up to four processors. While mergesort and prime number generation degrade to slightly over 70% with 16 processors, matrix multiplication shows a speedup efficiency of 60% with 16 processors.

5.2 Detailed Performance

Let us consider the performance of each of the application kernels in terms of granularity of parallelism, which is defined as the ratio of executor compute time to executor communication time, generator utilization which is the sum of the percentages of the total elapsed time used by the generator in communicating with executors, in eductive evaluation, and in executing "local" imperative functions, and executor utilization which is the fraction of the total elapsed time during which the executor is busy computing.

Table 1 shows the granularity, generator utilization, and executor utilization for the mergesort application kernel.

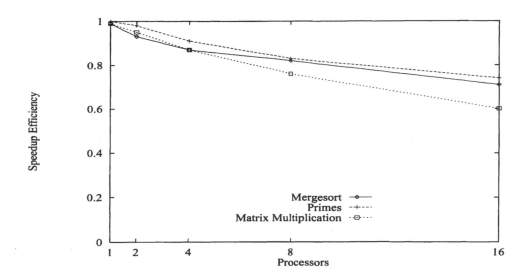

Figure 2: Performance of GLU application kernels on workstation cluster.

Processors	Granularity	Generator Utilization			Executor Utilization
		Communication	*Eduction*	*Local Function*	
1	84	1.2	0.0	1.2	98.1
2	102	1.9	0.0	2.8	94.9
4	93	4.0	0.6	4.3	91.8
8	91	7.9	0.1	8.7	89.3
16	93	13.2	0.1	15.2	77.1

Table 1: Mergesort performance.

The principal reason that the performance of mergesort degrades with increased number of processors despite having a high granularity of parallelism is because of increased generator utilization. Of the three components of generator utilization, only the overhead associated with eductive evaluation stays negligible. Both communication overhead and local function utilization increase with the number of processors. And, correspondingly, the average executor utilization decreases.

Table 2 shows the granularity and the utilizations of the generator and executors with varying number of processors for the prime number generation kernel.

This application kernel despite having even higher granularity than mergesort shows degradation in performance as the number of processors increase. As with mergesort, this is because the generator being busy results in the executors to idle between function applications as evidenced by lower average executor utilization with higher number of processors.

Table 3 shows the granularity and the utilizations of the generator and executors with varying number of processors for the matrix multiplication kernel.

Unlike mergesort and prime number generation, the granularity of parallelism is much lower. This causes the generator to be busier with both communication and

Processors	Granularity	Generator Utilization			Executor Utilization
		Communication	Eduction	Local Function	
1	127	0.8	0.1	1.2	98.2
2	182	1.1	0.1	1.8	97.8
4	128	2.9	0.3	3.8	92.5
8	168	4.1	0.4	6.1	86.7
16	150	8.2	2.0	11.5	77.2

Table 2: Prime number generation performance.

Processors	Granularity	Generator Utilization			Executor Utilization
		Communication	Eduction	Local Function	
1	17	5.5	0.1	3.9	91.5
2	18	10.0	0.2	6.8	88.9
4	18	18.7	0.2	12.8	84.7
8	18	32.6	0.3	22.6	74.1
16	18	53.4	1.3	34.3	59.8

Table 3: Matrix multiplication performance.

local function execution resulting in lower average executor utilization. Thus, the degradation in speedup efficiency is more pronounced as the number of processors increase.

5.3 Results Discussion

This performance study illustrates that coarser granularity of parallelism implies that performance can be scaled with increasing number of processors. While very good speedup efficiency can be achieved for small number of processors with relatively medium-grain parallelism, sustaining this efficiency on a large workstation cluster is only possible if remote computing time is at least two orders of magnitude larger than the associated communication time. This study also confirms the fairly obvious intuition that the generator is the bottleneck of the generator/executor abstract architecture. There are two aspects to the generator bottleneck: one is the cost of communicating with all the executors and the other is the time spent in local function execution (i.e., the serial part of the application). And importantly, the generator spends only nominal amount of its time on eductive evaluation of the application kernels that were studied.

6. Concluding Remarks

The main contribution of this chapter is the validation of a dataflow-based approach to programming conventional parallel computers by showing that standard parallel application kernels can be succinctly expressed while reusing existing sequential code and that these kernels exhibit parallel performance which are comparable to those of equivalent kernels developed in lower-level explicit parallel programming systems.

In particular, we have described a coarse-grain dataflow system for programming conventional parallel computers. The system is based on a hybrid model of programming (GLU) that consists of a multidimensional dataflow language Lucid for composing implicitly parallel programs using imperatively specified functions that specify computations.

We have shown how GLU can be used to succinctly compose applications with substantial inherent parallelism from existing sequential code with only nominal modifications.

We have shown how GLU programs can be mapped to abstract architectures which then can be compiled to specific target computers. Using the generator/executor abstract architecture, we have considered the efficiency of GLU programs executing in parallel on workstation networks. The speedup efficiency observed (speedup being relative to sequential execution on one processor) suggests that the generator eventually becomes the bottleneck mainly because communication cost and local function execution cost begin to dominate. We also observe that coarser granularity of parallelism means that better scaling of performance. Importantly, the performance study shows that GLU itself is not the source of any degradation since the cost of implementing demand-driven eduction in the generator is negligible.

Clearly, it is important to not only exercise the GLU programming model in expressing diverse applications, but also to develop abstract architectures that are inherently more scalable, thus effectively exploiting less coarse-grain parallelism.

References

[1] E.A. Ashcroft, "Dataflow and Eduction: Data-driven and Demand-driven Distributed Computation," in *Current Trends in Concurrenty*, Lecture Notes in Computer Science, Vol. 224, Springer-Verlag, Berlin, Germany, 1986.

[2] E.A. Ashcroft, "Tournament Computations," *Proc. 3rd Int'l Symp. Lucid and Intensional Programming*, Queen's Univ., Kingston, Ontario, Canada, 1990.

[3] E.A. Ashcroft et al., "Multidimensional Declarative Programming," Oxford Univ. Press, ISBN 0-19-507597-8, 1994.

[4] N. Carriero and D. Gelernter, "Linda in Context," *Comm. ACM*, Vol. 32, No. 4, Apr. 1989, pp. 444–458.

[5] A.A. Faustini and R. Jagannathan, "Multidimensional Programming in Lucid," Technical Report SRI-CSL-93-03, Computer Science Laboratory, SRI International, Menlo Park, Calif., Jan. 1993.

[6] R. Jagannathan, "A Descriptive and Prescriptive Model for Dataflow Semantics," Technical Report CSL-88-5, Computer Science Laboratory, SRI International, Menlo Park, Calif., May 1988.

[7] R. Jagannathan and A.A. Faustini, "Tournament Computations in GLU," *Proc. 4th Int'l Symp. Lucid and Intensional Programming*, Computer Science Laboratory, SRI International, Menlo Park, Calif., 1991.

[8] V. Sunderam, "PVM: A Framework for Parallel Distributed Computing," *Concurrency: Practice and Experience*, Vol. 2, No. 4, Dec. 1990.

[9] T. von Eicken et al., "Active Messages: A Mechanism for Integrated Communication and Computation," *Proc. 19th Annual Int'l Symp. Computer Architecture*, ACM Press, New York, N.Y., 1992, pp. 256–266.

[10] W.W. Wadge and E.A. Ashcroft, *Lucid, the Dataflow Programming Language*, Academic Press, New York, N.Y., 1985.

Distributed Data Structure in Thread-Based Programming for a Highly Parallel Dataflow Machine EM-4

Mitsuhisa Sato, Yuetsu Kodama, Shuichi Sakai,
Yoshinori Yamaguchi, and Satoshi Sekiguchi
Electrotechnical Laboratory
1-1-4 Umezono, Tsukuba, Ibaraki 305, Japan

From the viewpoint of an executing sequential thread, the EM-4 dataflow machine can be thought of as a distributed-memory processor. In this paper, we describe a distributed data structure shared by threads in different PEs. Threads may communicate and coordinate by leaving data in global address space. A new distributed data structure, called the Q-structure, is introduced. This can be used as a shared queue in the context of thread-based programming. Since the Q-structure is a restricted form of Linda's tuple space, it inherits the properties of Linda's generative communication. The dataflow mechanism allows very efficient remote operation invocation to access distributed data in different PEs.

1. Introduction

EM-4 is a highly parallel dataflow machine, that is designed to have more than 1,000 processing elements (PEs). The advantage of dataflow architecture is the integration of the processor into the network. The processing elements are designed to directly send and dispatch small fixed-size messages to and from the network. Those messages invoke the destination threads in other processors. The dataflow mechanism allows multiple threads of control to be created and interact efficiently.

In thread-based programming with a sequential imperative language on the EM-4 [6], parallelism and synchronization of threads of sequential execution are described explicitly by the programmer. As a multithreaded processor, each PE may have many sequential threads of control. This leads to an entirely different view of computation compared to dataflow computation model, and makes it easy to execute programs written in familiar imperative languages. Our approach is not to compile programs written in an imperative language directly into the dataflow machine, but to provide appropriate tools with which a programmer can write parallel application programs, based on threads of sequential execution. From the viewpoint of an executing sequential thread, the EM-4 can be thought of as a memory-distributed multiprocessor: each PE has its own local memory, and threads in the PE operate on the local memory. To express parallelism explicitly, a set of operations is provided to fork a new thread, send/receive messages between threads, and share data by remote memory access. We developed a "sequential" C compiler for EMC-R to write programs for threads. These operations are provided as built-in library functions in our C compiler.

In this paper, we present a distributed data structure called the Extended I-structure or Q-structure for thread-based programming in the EM-4, together with

131

its implementation. We use the term "distributed data structure" to refer to a data structure that is directly accessible by many threads. This term was introduced in the parallel language, Linda. Our distributed data structure provides a restricted form of Linda's tuple space. From the viewpoint of thread-based programming, the Q-structure is used as the communication channel between threads. The feature of the Q-structure is that it allows its elements to be exclusively accessed to its element by different threads. From the viewpoint of the dataflow architecture, the set of operations defined for the Q-structure is the same as the extended I-structure, formerly referred to a "the restricted I-structure" [7] proposed by the SIGMA-1 group at ETL, and implemented in SIGMA-1's structure elements (SE) unit. Of course, the I-structure and M-structure in the functional programming languages, Id, are regarded as being types of distributed data structure. We describe these structures in the context of thread-based programming, rather than in the context of functional programming.

EM-4 has the following advantages in supporting programming with a distributed data structure:

Efficient Remote Operation—Remote operations such as remote memory access and synchronized data access can be efficiently invoked from different PEs, using dataflow packets.

Efficient Creation/Scheduling of Threads—A new thread can be created efficiently. The hardware packet queue acts as a scheduler of threads.

Continuation in Packet—The state of an inactive thread is represented by a single word continuation. The packet can carry the continuation to a different PE, and it can be stored in memory.

In this paper, we demonstrate that EM-4 provides effective architectural support for the distributed data structure between PEs in thread-based programming. In Section 2, we first present the EM-4 architecture and how to execute the threads of an imperative language. Section 3 describes our distributed data structure and its implementation. Section 4 discusses programming with the distributed data structure. Section 5 concludes this paper.

2. The EM-4 Multiprocessor

2.1 Architecture

EM-4 consists of single chip processors, EMC-Rs, which are connected via a Circular Omega Network. EMC-R is a RISC-style processor suitable for fine-grain parallel processing. The pipeline of EMC-R is designed to integrate the register-based execution and the packet-based dataflow execution. All communication in the system is done with small-fixed size packets. As a dataflow machine, the design of the architecture of the EM-4 is based on a modified dataflow model called the *strongly connected arc model* [5]. Packets arrive from the network and are buffered in the packet queue. As a packet is read from the packet queue, a thread of computation, called the SCB (*strongly connected block*), specified by the address portion of the packet is instantiated along with the one word data. Execution of the SCB is controlled by the program counter, in exactly the same way as in a conventional von Neumann architecture, rather than by recirculating tokens in a circular pipeline. The thread then runs to its

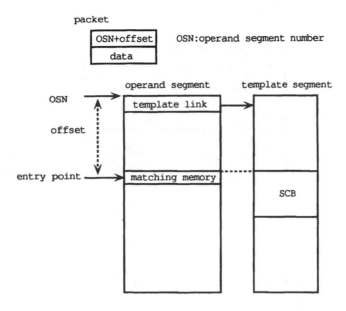

Figure 1: Entry point of SCB and direct matching.

completion, and the next packet is automatically dequeued and interpreted from the packet queue.

Network packets can be interpreted as dataflow tokens. Dataflow tokens have the option of matching with another token on arrival. Unless both tokens have arrived, the token will save itself in memory and cause the next packet to be processed.

The interpretation of packets can also be defined in software. The special packet has additional information, called *packet type*, to specify software-defined actions. On the arrival of a special packet, the associated system-defined handler is executed. For example, this mechanism is used to allocate resources in a different PE. The special packets are also used for remote memory access, as described in Section 3.

EM-4 prototype system with 80 PEs became fully operational in April 1990. The performance of EMC-R is 12.5 MIPS/chip. Interconnection network has 60.9 Mbytes/s/port transfer rate.

2.2 Runtime Structure

EM-4 recognizes two storage resources, namely, the template segments and the operand segments; An activation frame, called *the operand segment*, is dynamically allocated by the caller at invocation time. The compiled codes of the function are stored in another area called *the template segment*. The template segment number is stored into the first word of the operand segment to link the codes to its activation frame, as shown in Figure 1.

The format of a packet is shown in Figure 2. PE is the processing element number and OSN is the operand segment number for the activation frame. The offset is used to calculate the *entry address* of the SCB in the template segment linked from its operand segment. WCF is the waiting condition flag which specifies the *firing-rule* of the data token. For dyadic inputs, in order to reduce the overhead of operand matching, the EM-4 supports the direct matching scheme. Waiting token is stored in the entry points

address part

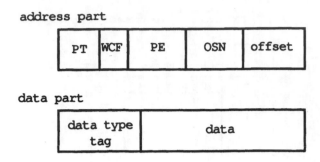

data part

Figure 2: Packet format.

in the operand segment, shown in Figure 1. PT is the packet type which indicates a special packet.

The first instruction of SCB operates on input tokens for the SCB, which are loaded into the *left operand register (r0)* and the *right operand register (r1)*. The address portion of the input packet is set in the operand segment register (seg).

The MKPKT instruction sends a packet directly into the network. The instruction mkpkt r0,r1 sends a packet containing the value of r0 to the address specified by r1, where the value of r1 has the same format as the address port of the packet. The GET instruction sends the continuation to an entry point in the current operand segment as data. It is used to send a continuation of a return point for a function call.

2.3 Executing Threads

A thread is an independent instruction stream that can execute a sequential program written in an imperative language such as C or FORTRAN. In the EM-4, a thread can be implemented by SCBs to execute those SCBs sequentially.[1]

To call a function in the same PE, the caller allocates an operand segment locally, and links to the template segment of the calling function code. The caller sets arguments in the callee's frame, and sends the continuation for its return point as a token to the entry point of the function. Upon calling the function, the SCB of the caller is terminated. Receiving a result token from the callee causes the execution of the caller to resume. In the function, local variables and temporaries are allocated in the activation frame.

As a multithreaded processor, each PE in the EM-4 can have many sequential threads of control. Threads in each PE interact with each other by communicating with messages or by accessing remote memory rather than by consuming tokens and firing instructions as in the dataflow computational model.

An SCB is a short sequential uninterrupted thread of control. During the execution of an SCB, each instruction operates on the register file as well as on local memory. At the end of an SCB, the live registers can be spilled out into its activation frame to pass variables to the next SCB. A packet transferred between SCBs can be thought of as the minimum state of a thread. It contains:

---

[1] For as long as the thread executes a sequential program correctly, it can be executed by more fine-grain threads as in a superscalar processor.

- The program counter.

- The activation frame (or the operand segment).

- One word of internal state.

The internal state may include a continuation for a function call. A packet is automatically dequeued from the packet queue to resume the execution of the associated thread whenever a processor requires work. The packet queue works as the process ready queue of a conventional operating system, but is scheduled efficiently by hardware, removing the need for a software kernel.

3. Distributed Data Structure With the EM-4

In this section, we describe a set of operations on our distributed data structure and its implementation with the EM-4. Threads in a program may communicate and coordinate by leaving and removing data in the distributed data structure. We describe these operations on the distributed data structure as C built-in functions, which are expanded in-line at compile time.

3.1 Global Address Space and Remote Memory Access

In C programs, the operation mem_write and mem_read are used explicitly to access memory in different PEs.

```
mem_write(global_addr,word)
word = mem_read(global_addr)
```

global_addr specifies the *global address* of memory that includes the PE number as well as its local address within the specified PE.

For remote memory access, we use the packet address as a global address rather than as the SCB entry point. When a special packet handler is executed, the SCB of the handler can receive the address part in the segment register as a argument as well as the data in the left operand register. For example, the handler MEM_READ for remote memory read fetches the word in the PE's local memory at the location in the segment register, and returns the word to the destination continuation in the left operand register. The code for the MEM_READ special packet handlers is as follows:

```
MEM_READ:   l seg,r1            ; fetch the word in local memory
            mkpkt r0,r1 :break   ; send it back to the continuation
```

The data portion of the received packet is loaded into r0. The segment register seg is set to the address portion that specifies the location to be fetched. LOAD instruction l loads the data into r1 to send it back to the continuation, then terminates the SCB. The mem_read is expanded in-line as follows:

```
        get r0,C.v :ptype=MEM_READ :break
        ; r0 is the global address to be fetched.  And suspend.
C:      op @v                  ; any instruction to use the fetched data.
```

The option ptype=MEM_READ specifies the packet type, and the option :break specifies the end of the SCB, suspending the current thread to await remote memory data.

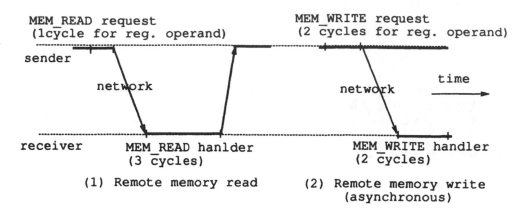

Figure 3: Timing of remote memory access operations.

Figure 3 shows the timing diagram for remote memory access. The average execution times for remote memory read and write are, respectively, 1.85 μs, 0.40 μs in unloaded network.

3.2 Extended I-Structure: Q-Structure
In the EM-4, I-structure memory is also implemented by using the special packet mechanism.

```
I_write(global_addr,word)
word = I_read(global_addr)
```

If a word has not yet been written by I_write at the specified location, I_read blocks the execution of the current thread. The subsequent I_write resumes the execution of the thread blocked by I_read. Different from the original I-structure [1], our I_read removes the data. We extend the I-structure to share data by several threads. The structure memory at g_addr may contain either multiple data or multiple continuations in the associated queue. Thus, we call this extended I-structure the *Q-structure*.

```
Q_out(g_addr,word)
word = Q_in(g_addr)
```

Q_in is blocked until data is written by Q_out. Multiple Q_in operations also block the calling threads. The continuations of these threads are stored in the queue. Q_out resumes the corresponding waiting threads. The data written by Q_out is returned to the caller of Q_in. If the memory already contains data, data written by multiple Q_out are buffered in the associated queue. This set of operations is similar to the operations on the M-structure of MIT. We developed these operations in the context of thread-based programming. For example, multiple Q_out operations allow structure memory to be used as a communication channel between threads.

```
word = Q_read(g_addr)
```

Q_read reads the data at g_addr, but does not get rid of the data. If the structure memory contains no data, Q_read blocks the calling thread as Q_in.

3.3 Q-Structure With Key

The Q-structure described above maps the distributed data structure to global address space. To support sparse distributed data structures, we introduce *Q-structure with key*, which associates data in the queue with a key.

```
Q_out_with_key(g_addr,key,word)
word=Q_in_with_key(g_addr,key)
word=Q_read_with_key(g_addr,key)
```

Q_out_with_key puts word with key **key** into the structure memory at **g_addr**. Q_in_with_key takes data associated with the given key from the queue. If such data is not found, Q_in_with_key blocks the calling thread, and its continuation is stored in the queue with the key. When data with the key is put by Q_out_with_key, the waiting thread is resumed, and returns with the data.

```
Q_out_with_any(g_addr,word)
word=Q_in_with_any(g_addr,&key)
word=Q_read_with_any(g_addr,&key)
```

These operations are the same as those of Q_out_with_key, Q_in_with_key and Q_read_with_key except that these operations match any key. For Q_in_with_key and Q_read_with_key, the key is returned with its data.

3.4 Forking a Thread

In C programs, a new thread is created by the operation `fork`.

```
void fork(pe_addr,func,n,arg1,...,argn)
```

where **pe_addr** is a global address that specifies the PE where the new thread is executed. The created thread starts executing a given function with the following arguments. When the main function is returned, the thread being executed disappears. A thread can notify its termination by leaving data in the distributed data structure rather than executing a "JOIN" instruction.

For a distributed data structure, the following fork operations create new threads that store the return value of the function into the structure memory.

```
I_fork(g_addr,func,narg,arg1,...)
Q_fork(g_addr,func,narg,arg1,...)
Q_fork_with_key(g_addr,key,func,arg1,...)
```

where **g_addr** specifies the structure memory address. The new thread is executed in the same PE as that where the structure memory is located, and terminated when the return value of `func` is "out"ed. These functions are useful for the live-data-structure program [3].

3.5 Implementation of Distributed Data Structure

The special packet mechanism plays an important role in implementing the distributed data structure. Operations for Q-structure and I-structure are implemented by using the special packet mechanism.

Q_read sends a special packet whose address part specifies the global address and whose data part specifies the current continuation. Then, the calling thread suspends (terminates the current SCB) until the packet from the special packet handler resumes

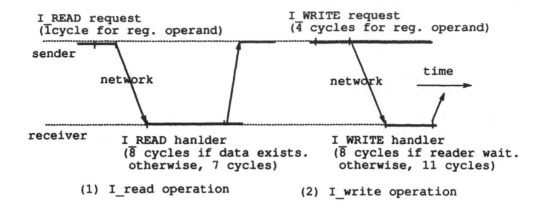

Figure 4: Timing of I_read and I_write.

the thread. The special packet handler of Q_read fetches the word at the location specified by the address part. If any data have not yet been stored, the continuation in the packet data part is stored in that location. Therefore, the calling thread is blocked. If other continuations have been already stored, the continuation is managed in a queue associated with that location. If data exist at the location, those data are taken from the location to send to the continuation.

Q_out sends its special packet whose address part specifies the global address and whose data part specifies the data. The calling threads continue to execute. The special packet handler of Q_out fetches the word at the location specified by address part. If any continuations have not yet been stored, the data in the packet are stored at that location. If other data have already been stored, those data are managed in a queue associated with that location. If a continuation exists at the location, the continuation is taken from the location to invoke the waiting thread along with data.

Figure 4 shows the timing diagram for I_read, I_write operations by current implementation. The Q-structure operations may take additional time to manage the queue if required.

The other way to implement the operation is by using the remote procedure call. To call the function in other PEs, it needs to allocate the operand segment before passing arguments. Since more than three arguments cannot be passed to the special packet handler by a packet and only one value is returned, some operations for the Q-structure with key are implemented by using the remote procedure call.

. Programming with Distributed Data Structure

4.1 Linda versus Q-Structure

Our Q-structure provides a restricted form of Linda's tuple space. As the computation environment "tuple space" (TS) provides the basis for Linda's communication model, the global address space is used as the communication environment of our computation model using distributed data structure. As in Linda, distributed data structure in global address space is equally accessible to all threads. Until it is explicitly withdrawn, the data generated by a thread has an independent existence, and is bounded to none. Data is exchanged in the form of a persistent object, not a transient message.

Linda's TS is more general than our distributed data structure. It is not concerned with processor allocation or data allocation for tuples. When using the Q-structure, the programmer needs to consider these issues explicitly to obtain high performance. Q-structures are simple enough to implement efficiently using the EM-4 dataflow mechanism. Linda is inherently a shared-memory model. Supporting it in the absence of physically shared memory requires a coherence mechanism. Although TS has been implemented in software on many conventional multiprocessors, the Linda kernel will spend large amounts of time for communication.

4.2 Examples

We demonstrate some examples of the Q-structure, as described in [4].

Remote Procedure Call—Clearly, the Q-structure can be used to implement message-passing. The following example implements the structure referred to as an "active procedure":

```
struct {
    g_addr_t ret_addr;
    word_t args[N_ARGS]
    } x,y;

g_addr_t me;
g_addr_t proc_port;

/* caller */
x.ret_addr = me;
x.args[0] = ...; /* set args */
Q_out_block(proc_port,&x,sizeof(x));
result = I_read(me);

/* callee */
Q_in_block(proc_port,&y,sizeof(y));
... body of ''proc'' ...
I_write(y.ret_addr,result);
```

in which proc_port and me are given a global address. Note that Q_out_block/ Q_in_block are different versions of Q_out/Q_in that communicate a memory block rather than a word.

Shared Variable and Semaphore—Since operations of the Q structure are performed atomically, a shared variable at the global address var_addr can be updated as follows:

```
Q_in(var_addr); /* discard old value */
Q_out(var_addr,new_value);
```

The value of the shared variable can be referenced by Q_read.

As in Linda, `Q_in` and `Q_out` are functionally equivalent to the semaphore operation P and V. The critical section can be implemented as follows:

```
g_addr_t sem; /* global address of semaphore */
Q_out(sem); /* initialize */
....
Q_in(sem); /* P operation */
... body of critical section ...
Q_out(sem); /* V operation */
```

Delayed Statement—This example of *delay statement* uses the Q-structure with keys. While the Q-structure maps data structure into a global address space, we have to use keys of the Q-structure when the data structure to be mapped is unknown or sparse.

The clock process (or thread) executes the following statement:

```
g_addr_t clock;

Q_in_with_any(clock,&now);
Q_out_with_key(clock,now+1);
```

To read the clock, any thread can execute:

```
Q_read_with_any(clock,&now);
```

The function `delay(d)` delays the calling threads for (at least **d**) time units.

```
delay(d){
    int now;

    Q_in_read_any(clock,&now);
    Q_read_with_key(clock,now+d);
}
```

Live Data Structure—The live data structure is one of Linda's programming methods [3]: each element of this data structure is implicitly a separate process, which becomes a data object upon terminating. To communicate, they simply "refer" to each other as elements of some data structure. The following example shows a live-data-structure program written using the Q-structure, which computes the fibonacci number:

```
main()
{
    int i;
    /* ... some initialization ... */
    for(i=i; i<=10; i++)
        Q_fork(fib_g_addr(i),fib,1,i);
    printf("fib(10)=%d\n",Q_read(fib_g_addr(10)));
}

fib(n)
```

```
{
    if(n <= 2) return(1);
    else {
      return(Q_read(fib_g_addr(n-1))+
             Q_read(fib_g_addr(n-2)));
    }
}
```

where the function `fib_g_addr` maps the data structure to global address space.

4.3 Distributed Data Structures in Dataflow Machines

In the dataflow computation model, many types of synchronized data structure were proposed. Many of these come in the context of functional programming languages. These structure memory data are assumed to be automatically reclaimed by the garbage collection in the language system. The I-structure [1] limits one writer to the same address. Multiple read operations can await the data written by the writer. The M-structure was originally designed for making histograms in parallel. The major difference from the I-structure is that the write operation resumes a suspended read operation. This structure is found as Mutex-structure in [2].

Compared with the M-structure, the Q-structure has a queue for written data. In addition to the functionality of the M-structure, this structure is also effective to implement the producer/consumer type synchronization mechanism, as discussed in this paper. This distributed structure is often used for the task bag structure for load balancing.

The Q-structure operations are the same as that of Extended I-structure on the SIGMA-1, and similar to the operations on M-structure. Also they do not suspend the write operation. A precise definition of the operation of this structure is given in [7] as the restricted I-structure. This gives a detailed definition of access operations at the viewpoint of the dataflow architecture.

5. Conclusion

In this paper, we have proposed a distributed data structure that can be shared by several threads. The dataflow mechanism of the EM-4 allows efficient implementation of the operations on the distributed data structure. Using the distributed data structure, a programmer can create and coordinate multiple threads in thread-based programming. As an example, we showed that our distributed data structure enables a programmer to easily incorporate Linda's programming model. Different from the structure memory proposed in functional programming language, it can be used as parallel data structures such as the communication channels between threads and the task bag for load balancing. It also allows a programmer to control parallelism and data distribution in the global address space of the EM-4.

Acknowledgments

We wish to thank Dr. Toshitsugu Yuba, ex-director of the Computer Science Division of ETL, and Mr. Toshio Shimada, ex-chief of the Computer Architecture Section for supporting this research, and also thank the staff of the Computer Architecture Section for their fruitful discussion.

References

[1] Arvind, R.S. Nikhil, and K.K. Pingali, "I-Structures: Data Structures for Parallel Computing," *ACM Trans. Programming Languages and Systems*, Vol. 11, No. 4, Oct. 1989, pp. 598–632.

[2] P. Barth, R.S. Nikhil, and Arvind, "M-structures: Extending a Parallel, Non-Strict, Functional Language with State," *Proc. Functional Programming and Computer Architecture*, Springer-Verlag LNCS 523, Berlin, Germany, 1991 pp. 538–568. Also: CSG Memo 327, MIT Laboratory for Computer Science, 545 Technology Square, Cambridge, Mass., Mar. 1991.

[3] N. Carriero and D. Gelernter, "How to Write Parallel Programs: A Guide to the Perplexed," *ACM Computing Surveys*, Vol. 21, No. 3, 1989, pp. 323–357.

[4] D. Gelernter, "Generative Communication in Linda," *ACM Trans. Programming Languages and Systems*, Vol. 7, No. 1, 1985, pp. 80–112.

[5] S. Sakai et al., "An Architecture of a Dataflow Single Chip Processor," *Proc. 16th Ann. Int'l Symp. Computer Architecture*, 1989, IEEE CS Press, Los Alamitos, Calif., pp. 46–53.

[6] M. Sato et al., "Thread-Based Programming for the EM-4 Hybrid Dataflow Machine," *Proc. 19th Ann. Int'l Symp. Computer Architecture*, ACM Press, New York, N.Y., 1992, pp. 146–155.

[7] Sekiguchi, Satoshi, Toshio Shimada, and Kei Hiraki, "Sequential Description and Parallel Execution Language DFC II for Dataflow Supercomputers," *Proc. 1991 Int'l Conf. Supercomputing*, IEEE CS Press, Los Alamitos, Calif., 1991, pp. 57–66.

Programmability and Performance Issues of Multiprocessors on Hard Nonnumeric Problems

Andrew Sohn[1] and Jean-Luc Gaudiot[2]

Nonnumeric problems are known to be difficult to parallelize due to their irregular behavior. This paper presents the results of experiments with parallel nonnumeric computations on two completely different types of multiprocessors and their programming environments. The first type of multiprocessor (Sequent Symmetry and Cray-2 shared-memory multiprocessors), uses the functional language SISAL and its automatic parallelizing compiler OSC. The second type of multiprocessor, the EM-4 multithreaded distributed-memory multiprocessor, uses the imperative language EM-C with manual parallelization. Three typical nonnumeric problems were selected for the experiments: two moderately sized search problems, the Eight Puzzle and the Towers of Hanoi, and a very large problem (Ops5, a production system interpreter). We take a three-step approach to compare the performance of the three machines and their programming environments: (1) parallelism profiling using SISAL, (2) algorithm level parallelization by parallel heuristic search and speculative computation, and (3) implementation level parallelization by multithreading and partial overlapping of loop iterations. All three problems were implemented on the three multiprocessors. Execution results indicate that the combination of shared-memory machines and of the functional language SISAL with its automatic parallelizing compiler OSC provide high programmability as they require little parallelization effort. On the other hand, the combination of a distributed-memory machine with an imperative language (C with explicit parallelization) yielded approximately twice the performance of the shared-memory combination, but low programmability.

1. Introduction

Parallel computation of scientific problems has been the main focus of supercomputing. Numerous scientific problems have been successfully implemented on various parallel computers. Regular runtime behavior and deterministic resource usage are among the reasons which have contributed to their successful parallel implementations. One of the most commonly used benchmarking problems, matrix multiplication, possesses an extremely regular and deterministic behavior: the total number of remote memory operations and the total number of instructions are both known in advance. Due to this type of deterministic behavior, the resource allocation becomes rather straightforward for this type of numeric problems. Although there are many other scientific problems that exhibit random or semi-deterministic behavior due to the runtime computation of array indices, the majority of numeric problems still possesses a large amount of deterministic behavior.

This work is supported in part by NJIT SBR No. 421820, Japanese Information Science Foundation 92-1-3-394, NSF CCR-9013965, and NSF INT-9310972.

[1] Dept. of Computer and Information Science, New Jersey Institute of Technology, Newark, NJ 07102.
[2] Dept. of Electrical Engineering-Systems, University of Southern California, Los Angeles, CA 90089.

Nonnumeric problems on the other hand have received little attention in terms of parallel implementation on multiprocessors. The main reasons that parallel nonnumeric computations have been less successful than numeric computations are the large amount of computational resource usage, their irregular runtime behavior, and often the unknown number of iterations. Typical nonnumeric problems such as search and expert systems are among those which are completely different than numeric problems. A search problem such as the Eight Puzzle has an unknown number of iterations and an unknown amount of runtime resource usage. Due to these unknown patterns, they are difficult to parallelize and implement on parallel machines. Even if they are successfully implemented, the resulting performance is often poor compared to that of numeric problems.

This paper presents our experiences in the parallel execution of hard nonnumeric problems. In particular, we present our findings of nonnumeric computations along the two important issues of programmability and performance [1], [10]. The programmability issue is addressed with the use of two dramatically different types of environments: automatic parallelizing compiler and explicit insertion of parallel constructs. The former uses the functional language SISAL [4], [11] with its automatic parallelizing compiler OSC [2] while the latter uses the imperative language EM-C with manual parallelization [15]. The performance issue is addressed by using two dramatically different types of multiprocessors: a shared-memory single address space multiprocessor, and a physically and logically distributed-memory multithreaded multiprocessor [14]. In particular, a Sequent Symmetry and Cray-2 are used as representatives of shared-memory platforms while the 80-processor EM-4 [14] is used as a representative of distributed-memory machines.

Three typical nonnumeric problems have been selected for the experiments: two moderately sized search problems; the Eight Puzzle and the Towers of Hanoi; and a very large problem, the Ops5 production system interpreter [6], [16]. We have taken three steps to parallelize and implement the problems on three platforms: (1) parallelism profiling, (2) algorithm level parallelization, and (3) implementation level parallelization and optimization. Parallelism profiles of all the problems have been constructed using SISAL to help identify potential parallelism. A study of the potential parallelism in the given algorithm is particularly helpful before and after parallelizing the given problem. Several parallelization techniques have been developed to parallelize the problems at the algorithm level, including parallel heuristic search and speculative computation of production systems. All these methods are architecture independent and have been designed to improve algorithmic performance. Implementation level parallelization techniques refer to partial overlapping of loop iterations technique (POLI) and multithreaded scheduling [3], [12], in particular explicit-switching multithreading [15], [17]. Multithreading applies only to the EM-4, where explicit thread switching is supported in hardware to a certain extent.

We begin our discussion in Section 2 by giving a brief introduction to the three nonnumeric problems. A generic sequential algorithm is outlined to illustrate necessary steps to implement the search problems and the Ops5 production system interpreter. Potential parallelism in the three problems is profiled in the section. Section 3 presents the parallelization process. To illustrate algorithm level parallelization, a parallel heuristic search is presented, followed by the speculative computation of Ops5. Partial overlapping of loop iterations and explicit-switching-based multithreading are described to illustrate implementation level parallelization. Section 4 lists actual execution results of the three problems on the three target multiprocessors. Section 5 discusses the performance of the three implementations on the three machines. We summarize our paper in the last section.

```
open = initial_state, closed=∅
Repeat
  1. selected_node ← SELECT(open)           ;Remove a node from open.
  2. succ ← EXPAND(selected_node)           ;Generate successors.
  3. succ ← FILTER(succ,open,closed)        ;Remove matching nodes from succ.
  4. open ← MERGE(succ,open)                ;Form a new open.
  5. closed ← MERGE(selected_node,closed)   ;Form a new closed.
Until (goal_state ∈ succ) or (open = ∅)     ;Test termination conditions.
```

Figure 1: A sequential search.

2. Three Nonnumeric Problems

The three nonnumeric problems are explained in this section. A brief description of each problem is presented, followed by a profile of potential parallelism. Parallelism profiles assume an infinite number of processors and are plotted in terms of instruction cycle. The generic algorithms are then compared with the parallelism profiles to identify the behavior of the algorithms.

2.1 Search Problems

The Tower of Hanoi and the Eight Puzzle are typical search problems. Given an initial state of each problem, the search process is to find a path which can lead to the goal state. While searching through the state space, a search strategy can be employed to guide the search process in an attempt to reduce the combinatorial explosion of the search effort. Figure 1 lists a generic and sequential search process. It involves two lists: open and closed. Open contains nodes to be examined, whereas closed has those nodes that are already examined.

The above algorithm is a generic search. Line 1 selects a *single* node from open. Line 2 generates successors of the selected node. Line 3 removes from succ those nodes that are either on open or closed. Line 4 merges two lists to form a new open. Line 5 forms a new closed. This algorithm is generic in that it uses no particular search strategy. A particular search strategy can be embedded by modifying the merge step of line 4. For example, depth first search can be readily implemented by inserting succ in front of open, provided that the selection step takes a node from in front of open. Breadth first search can be realized by inserting succ at the end of open. A guided heuristic search, A* search strategy [10], can also be easily implemented by inserting succ into open in ascending (or descending) order of heuristic values.

The above generic search is sequential in three aspects: First, the entire loop is sequential due to loop-carried dependencies between iterations. The central data structure is open. Iteration i uses open, which was *modified* at iteration $i - 1$. No two iterations can therefore be executed in parallel. The second sequentiality lies within the loop. Each iteration consists of five steps. Those five steps are again sequential due to their data dependencies. For example, lines 2 and 3 cannot be executed in parallel due to true data dependence. The third sequentiality stems from the fact that the selection step selects only *one* out of many nodes on open. The expansion step therefore works only on one node at a time in each iteration.

One would argue that the search process presented above has much parallelism to explore. Consider a search tree for the Eight Puzzle shown in Figure 2. Assume

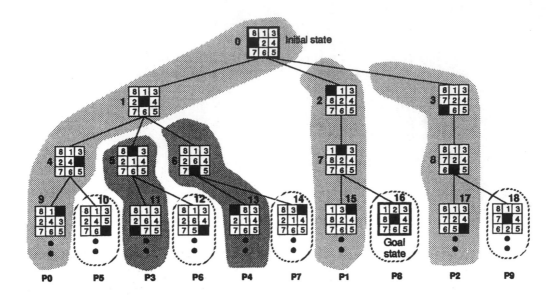

Figure 2: A simple parallelization method. As a new path is found, a new processor, if available, is assigned to the path. If every processor is working on a path, each processor will have to work on more than one path as the search tree grows. The above figure requires 10 processors, all of which are *independently* working to find the goal state in 3 iterations.

that nodes are generated in the following order: left, right, up, and down. A simple parallelization method assigns a processor to each path of the search tree as more paths are generated and to be explored.

Assume that 10 processors are available. The ten paths shown in Figure 2 can be searched by 10 processors simultaneously. Whichever processor finds the goal state will terminate the whole search process. This parallelization is simple and straightforward. And it would possibly give high speedup as the ten paths are explored *independently* and *simultaneously* by 10 processors. However, we reject this type of task-level parallelization because, (1) it is impractical, requiring a number of processors proportional to the number of paths in the search tree, (2) it has no global view of the search tree, and (3) it is not a true parallel search as no processors *cooperate* to solve a single problem. Parallel search methods which satisfy the above three criteria are discussed in [16]. Various issues in parallel search are beyond the scope of this paper and not considered further. Instead, we shall concentrate on how to utilize the potential parallelism present in the search problems.

2.2 Parallelism in the Eight Puzzle

Potential parallelism in the Eight Puzzle is constructed by using a dataflow graph generated from the SISAL functional language. Parallelism refers to a number of instructions (such as +, -, *, /, etc.), which can be executed simultaneously. Figure 3 shows a parallelism profile of the Eight Puzzle. The x-axis indicates the execution time while the y-axis is a number of instructions that can be executed in parallel, namely, parallelism. Note that the y-axis is plotted to logarithmic scale.

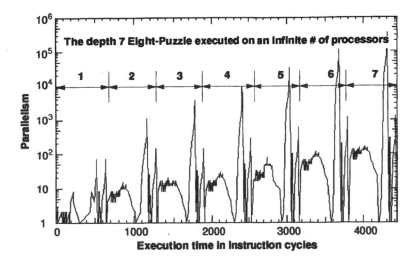

Figure 3: Parallelism profile of the Eight Puzzle. Note that the y-axis is plotted in logarithmic scale. The maximum parallelism for tree depth 7 of the Eight Puzzle is roughly 400,000!

Execution of the Eight Puzzle begins with an insertion of the initial state on open. Each iteration goes through the repeat loop of Figure 1. As we observe from the above figure, the amount of potential parallelism increases exponentially. Each iteration shows two typical peaks: the first peak is an expansion step (line 2 of Figure 1) while the second peak is a filter step (line 3 of Figure 1).

For example, consider iteration 4, which spans roughly 1900–2600. The first peak, spanning 1900–2300, is an expansion step which generates succ for all nodes on open. Parallelism is high at the beginning of the expansion step but quickly diminishes towards the end of the expansion step. One main reason for exhibiting such exponential decay is because it involves many data copying operations and memory (common data structure) access operations. At the very beginning, n expansion functions will be called in parallel for n nodes on open. However, instructions within each expansion function call are strictly sequential. In fact, most instructions engage in legality checking, i.e., check to see which tile can move to where. This legality checking involves heavy array operations to prepare a new array for next possible legal movements.

The second peak, spanning 2300–2500, is a filter step. It checks open and closed to see if any node on succ has already been on one of them. It is not surprising that the filter step exhibits a wide and relatively high peak because the step consists of three nested loops (one for each list) and is *completely* parallelized. Our SISAL implementation uses a 3×3 array to represent a node of 9 integers. Simple algebra can show that checking n nodes on succ, m nodes on open, and l nodes on closed will execute $9lmn$ comparison instructions. A small peak toward the end of the iteration shows the testing of termination condition.

2.3 Parallelism in the Tower of Hanoi

Figure 4 shows a potential parallelism profile for the Towers of Hanoi. Its parallelism behavior is essentially the same as that of the Eight Puzzle except that the amount of parallelism is smaller. And the rate at which the parallelism increases is smaller

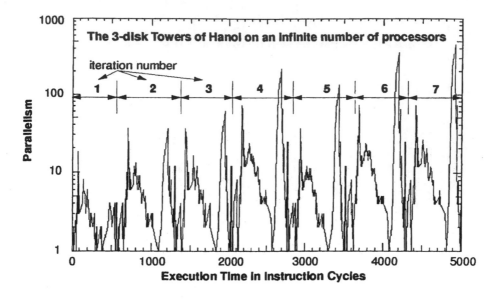

Figure 4: Parallelism profile of the Towers of Hanoi. An optimal number of iterations for the 3-disk Towers of Hanoi is seven.

than the Eight Puzzle due to a small branching factor. The Towers of Hanoi has a branching factor of two while the Eight Puzzle has three.

2.4 Production Systems

The second target nonnumeric problem for our experiments is production systems. The importance of production systems has been repeatedly demonstrated by a large number of expert systems. A production system consists of a production memory (PM), a working memory (WM), and an interpreter. The PM (or rulebase) is composed entirely of conditional statements called productions (or rules). These productions perform some predefined actions when all the necessary conditions are satisfied. The left-hand side (LHS) is the condition part of a production rule, while the right-hand side (RHS) is the action part. The LHS consists of one to many elements, called condition elements (CEs), while the RHS consists of one to many actions.

The productions operate on the WM, which is a database of assertions called working memory elements (wmes). Both condition elements and wmes have a list of elements, called attribute-value pairs (AVPs). The value to an attribute can be either constant or variable. Consider a toy Ops5 production system shown below in Figure 5 [6].

The production system shown above consists of one rule and four wmes. The rule above contains three conditions and two actions. The first condition element CE1 has two variables, $\langle x \rangle$ and $\langle y \rangle$, while the remaining two conditions have one each. The rule will perform action 1 and action 2 when all the conditions are verified in the working memory. The interpreter executes an infinite loop, which consists of the three steps shown in Figure 6 following:

Line 1 matches the LHSs of all the production rules against the current wmes. Wme1 in the above example can satisfy CE3 with the variable $\langle x \rangle$ instantiated to *. This step will eventually identify three wmes, 1, 2, and 4, which all satisfy the above rule with $\langle x \rangle$ and $\langle y \rangle$ instantiated, respectively, to * and +. If the set of

	Production Memory		*Working Memory*
Rule1:	(m (c $\langle$x$\rangle$) (d $\langle$y$\rangle$))	;CE1	wme1: (o (p 1) (q 2) (r *))
	(n (b $\langle$y$\rangle$))	;CE2	wme2: (m (c *) (d +))
	(o (p 1) (q 2) (r $\langle$x$\rangle$))	;CE3	wme3: (n (b 3))
	$\rightarrow$		wme4: (n (b +))
	(remove 2)	;Action 1	
	(make m (c $\langle$y$\rangle$)) (d $\langle$x$\rangle$)))	;Action 2	

Figure 5: A simple production system.

Repeat
1. conflict_set $\leftarrow$ MATCH(wm,pm)   ;Match rules and facts.
2. selected_rule $\leftarrow$ SELECT(conflict_set)   ;Select one from the matched rules.
3. wm $\leftarrow$ ACT(wm,pm,selected_rule)   ;Modify the wm
Until conflict_set = $\emptyset$;Test the termination condition.

Figure 6: A production system interpreter.

satisfied productions is non-empty, line 2 selects a rule for execution in the next step. Otherwise, the execution cycle halts because there are no satisfied productions. In the above example, only one rule is satisfied. It is therefore selected. Line 3 performs the actions specified in the RHS of the selected productions. In the above example, a new wme, (m (c +) (d *)), is added to the working memory and wme4, (n (b +)), is deleted from the working memory upon rule firing. The interpreter will halt the production system when there are no more satisfied productions.

2.5 Parallelism in the Ops5 Production System Interpreter

Various types of parallelism are known to be present in production systems [7], [8]. Figure 7 shows instruction level parallelism of Ops5 for the *Blocks World Problem*. The Blocks World Problem is a well-known toy problem which has four rules, *pick_up*, *holding*, *put_down*, and *switch*. The profile is a small window of the entire execution, which ran over 50,000 execution time units. Our purpose in showing the parallelism profile is that Ops5 also shows a parallelism behavior similar to the Towers of Hanoi and the Eight Puzzle. However, one difference between the search problems and Ops5 is that parallelism does not grow exponentially, as was the case for the search problems.

3. Parallelization of Three Problems

Several techniques are used to parallelize the three hard nonnumeric problems. The types of techniques are briefly presented in algorithm level and implementation level. Parallel heuristic search is used to parallelize search problems in algorithm level. Speculative computation is used to parallelize production systems in algorithm level. Multithreading and partial overlapping of loop iterations are used to parallelize the three problems in implementation level. We use the parallelism profiles constructed earlier to illustrate parallelization methods.

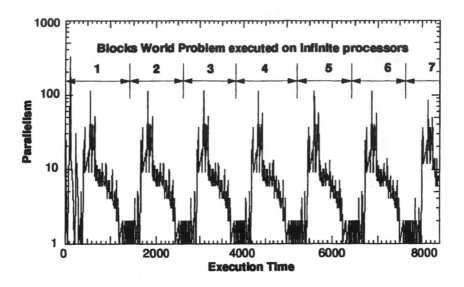

Figure 7: Parallelism profile of the Blocks World Problem.

3.1 Types of Parallelization

This paper attempts to present the effects of two different machine architectures, each of which uses a completely opposite programming environment. The shared-memory machines use the SISAL and OSC automatic parallclization environment, while the EM-4 distributed-memory machine uses the EM-C manual parallelization environment. The former is in pursuit of high programmability with acceptable performance, whereas the latter is mainly aimed at achieving high performance with little programmability. The SISAL and OSC environment, therefore, requires little effort for implementation level parallelization, while the EM-4 environment requires much effort to parallelize the three problems under consideration. To be more precise, parallelization can be classified into two different categories: *algorithm* level parallelization and *implementation* level parallelization.

The three problems are parallelized both in algorithm level and implementation level for two different environments. Parallel unidirectional heuristic search is used to parallelize search problems in algorithm level. This parallel search technique applies to both environments. Partial overlapping of loop iterations (POLI) is used to parallelize search problems in implementation level, which is applicable only to the EM-4 environment. The POLI technique is found to be difficult to realize in the SISAL+OSC environment since it requires low-level machine-dependent parallel constructs.

Ops5 interpreter has been parallelized mostly in implementation level. No particular technique is applied to parallelize Ops5 for SISAL+OSC, except parallel *for* loop constructs. However, two different algorithm level parallelization techniques are applied to Ops5 for the EM-4 environment: multiple-root node approach [7] and speculative computation approach. Implementation level parallelization of Ops5 for the EM-4 is done through multithreading, which will be explained shortly. Table 1 summarizes how the three problems are parallelized for two programming environments in algorithm level and implementation level.

	Search Problems		Production System Interpreter	
	Sisal+OSC	EM-4	Sisal+OSC	EM-4
Algorithm level	Parallel unidirectional heuristic search	Parallel unidirectional heuristic search	None	Speculative computation, multiple root node
Implementation level	Data parallelism with parallel *for* construct	Multithreading POLI	Data parallelism with parallel *for* construct	Multithreading

Table 1: Parallelization of three problems for two multiprocessor environments.

Iteration No.	At the Beginning of Iteration		Select & Expand		succ		At the End of Iteration	
	open	closed	P0	P1	P0	P1	open	closed
0	0		0		1, 2, 3		$1_{4,1,3}, 2_{4,1,3}, 3_{6,1,5}$	0
1	$1_{4,1,3}, 2_{4,1,3}, 3_{6,1,5}$	0	1	2	4, 5, 6	7	$7_{4,2,2}, 3_{6,1,5}, 5_{6,2,4}, 4_{7,2,5}, 6_{7,2,5}$	0, 1, 2
2	$7_{4,2,2}, 3_{6,1,5}, 5_{6,2,4}, 4_{7,2,5}, 6_{7,2,5}$	0, 1, 2	7	3	15, 16	8	$16_{3,3,0}, 15_{6,3,3}, 8_{6,2,4}, 5_{6,2,4}, 4_{7,2,5}, 6_{7,2,5}$	0, 1, 2, 7, 3

Figure 8: Parallel unidirectional heuristic search.

3.2 Algorithm Level Parallelization: Parallel Heuristic Search

Search problems are parallelized both at algorithm level and at implementation level. Algorithm level parallelization include parallel A* search [9]. A* search is a highly efficient search strategy [9]. It is a guided search based on the evaluation function $f = g + h$, where g is the cost of getting to the current state from the initial state, and h is the estimated cost to reach the goal from the current state. Given n nodes on open, it selects the most promising node, i.e., the node with the lowest (or highest) f value. Parallel heuristic search is similar to the A* search except now n nodes can be examined simultaneously by n processors. Figure 1 can be modified to accommodate parallel heuristic search as follows:

1. selected_nodes ← *select_n_best_nodes*(open)   ;Remove n best nodes from open.
2. succ ← *parallel_expand*(selected_nodes)   ;Generate successors in parallel.
3. succ ← *parallel_filter*(succ,open,closed)   ;Remove matching nodes from succ.
4. open ← *merge_sort*(succ,open)   ;Sort open in ascending order of f.

The main difference between the above and Figure 1 is the parallel expansion step and the sorting step. For our experiments, h for the Eight Puzzle is computed based on *the number of misplaced tiles* while g is simply set to 1 per arc. This heuristic function gives the goal state 0 for h value and, therefore, the most promising node is the one with the lowest f value. We use $N_{f,g,h}$ to denote a node with the three values. For example, $2_{4,1,3}$ denotes node 2 with $f = 4$, $g = 1$, and $h = 3$. Suppose we have *two* processors. Given open = (node 0), parallel heuristic search will go through the iterations shown in Figure 8 (see also Figure 2):

At the beginning of iteration 0, open=(0) and closed=( ). Now, processor 0 (or p_0) selects node 0 (there is only one on open) and generates three nodes, 1, 2, and

3. Attaching the three values (f,g,h) to each successor node and inserting them into open in ascending order of f, we now have open $= (1_{4,1,3}, 2_{4,1,3}, 3_{6,1,5})$ and closed $= (0)$. Note that open is kept at p_0 (master processor) while closed is evenly distributed to two processors. As we have stated earlier, the above parallelized version has a global view of the search process since open is kept at p_0 such that the processors will always select the best two nodes at each iteration. Parallel heuristic search takes three iterations to find the goal state (node 16) which is the optimal solution (or tree depth) for this particular initial state (node 0).

3.3 Algorithm Level Parallelization: Speculative Computation

The production system interpreter shown in Figure 6 has two types of dependencies: true data dependence *within* an iteration, and loop-carried dependence *between* iterations. Each iteration executes three steps in sequence due to true data dependence. Selection step can proceed only after the preceding match step completes. Conflict set will be computed only when the match step is finished. A similar dependence exists for the next function calls within an iteration. Due to all these true data dependencies, it is difficult to execute the three steps in parallel. One way to alleviate true data dependencies *within* an iteration is to execute each step in parallel, provided that each step has enough *data* parallelism to exploit.

Figure 6 clearly shows loop-carried dependence, where iteration i cannot start in theory until iteration $i-1$ completes. To be more precise, the match step of iteration i cannot start until the action step of iteration $i-1$ completes. There exists a dependence relationship between the two function calls, the act step of iteration $i-1$ and the match step of iteration i. It is this loop-carried dependence that forces the production system paradigm to execute in sequence, leaving very little parallelism across iterations. There are several ways to break or perhaps relax this loop boundary, such as loop unrolling or software pipelining. However, these methods are designed essentially for a uniprocessor environment. They are so designed to utilize parallelism in fine-grain instruction level that they are not suitable for multiprocessors due to communication overhead. We have therefore developed a *speculative* computation technique, which attempts to overlap two or more iterations by using speculative parallelism.

The idea of speculative computation is straightforward. Suppose that we have a multiprocessor with n processors. We split n processors into two or more groups such that each group performs its own action and possibly match step of the next cycle until it is instructed not to do so. To simplify our discussion, we shall use two groups, g_0 and g_1. Suppose that we have eight processors, $p_0, \cdots, p_7$, and 16 rules, $r_0, \cdots, r_{15}$. Assume that each processor has two rules allocated to it. Eight processors are divided into two groups, where the first group g_0 has $p_0, \cdots, p_3$, and the second group has $p_4, \cdots, p_7$. Figure 9 pictorially describes our approach to parallel speculative computation.

Note that the two processors, p_0 and p_4, are labeled GH, a group head processor. It is these group head processors that speculate on the selection, action, and possibly match step of the next cycle. At the very beginning, the eight processors perform a match step. Depending on the incoming working memory elements, some processors will take more or less time than others. Assume that all processors complete their match step. As soon as each processor finishes its own match step, it starts part of the selection step. Since we are assuming that each processor has two rules allocated to it, an individual processor can start part of the selection process, labeled *local select*. It is often true that a rule can have more than one instantiation. This local selection

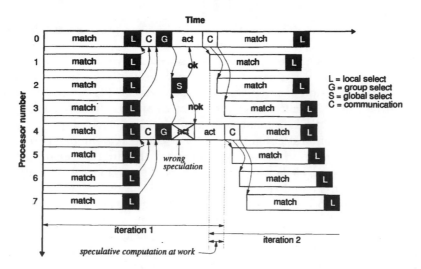

Figure 9: Speculative computation of production systems. Thin arrows out of processors p_1, p_2, p_3, p_5, p_6, and p_7 indicate that they send their processor number (PID) and the result of local selection step to their group head processors p_0 and p_4. Thin arrows out of p_0 and p_4 indicate the broadcasting of the newly generated wmes. Thick arrows indicate the interaction between group head processors for the group selection step. OK means the upper group's speculation is accepted while NOK indicates that the lower group's selection is rejected.

step can reduce much time in the overall selection step. For example, the Waltz Labeling algorithm can often have on the order of 1,000 instantiations for each rule. Local selection step performed within a processor will substantially reduce the overall selection time. In our implementation, the local selection step places the selected instantiation within a rule (or processor) at the last instantiation of the two input memory. This completes a local selection step.

The second step of the selection step is what we call *group select*, which selects one instantiation among processors within a group. As soon as the local selection step is complete, each processor sends its processor number (PID) and the result of local selection step to the head processor of a group. Figure 9 shows that processors p_1, $\cdots$, p_3 send their PIDs to their group head p_0 while processors p_5, $\cdots$, p_7 do so to their group head p_4.

Once a group head processor receives all the PIDs and their selection status, it immediately proceeds to the group selection step. The group selection step starts by remote reading selected instantiations from the other three processors. Remote memory reading is computationally expensive because it involves network usage. To avoid the possible congestion of the interconnection network, we read only wme numbers instead of entire wme contents. Reading of only wme numbers is made possible because newly generated wme contents are broadcast only once in each production cycle. We shall come back to this in greater detail in the next section where we demonstrate how interconnection topology is *effectively* used to eliminate an expensive broadcasting step. In any case, the two group-head processors (p_0 and p_4) read only a few integers from each processor, thereby making this group selection step feasible. The group selection process completes as a group-head processor selects a rule out of four processors (three and itself).

Upon finishing the group selection step, each group head processor sends a selected instantiation to the global head processor, where the final decision will be made. Figure 9 shows that the two GHs, p_0 and p_4, send their selected instantiation to p_2, where it decides which rule to fire. After each GH sends out a selected instantiation to p_2, it immediately starts an action step by generating new wmes. *This is where speculative computation takes place.* Note from the figure that p_0 and p_4 simultaneously perform their own action steps while p_2 is making the final decision.

When p_2 finishes its final decision, it sends the selected rule number to two GHs, each of which is performing an action step. Suppose the final decision made by p_2 follows the one made by p_0, as depicted in the figure. The action step currently being performed by p_0 is correct and requires no further attention. However, the action step currently being performed by p_4 is wrong and must be suspended immediately. Therefore, p_2 sends a NOK signal to p_4, where the current action step is halted and a new action step starts. The crossed action area of p_4 indicates the wrong speculation.

How does this speculative computation described above relax loop-carried dependence? Figure 9 also explains it. Note the dotted line which connects p_1 and p_4. It indicates that match and action steps are overlapped. Recall that the action step of p_4 belongs to iteration 1 while the match step of p_2 is the beginning of iteration 2. The amount of overlapping appears rather small compared to matching time or selection time. However, the issue here is not the amount of overlapping but is rather the fact that two iterations *can* be overlapped. If the total number of production cycles is on the order of tens, the effect of overlapping would be negligible. If however the cycles go over hundreds, thousands, or perhaps even more, then the effect of speculative computation will be substantial since a small amount will accumulate.

3.4 Implementation Level Parallelization: POLI

Implementation level parallelization refers to the explicit use of machine-dependent parallel constructs for the given machine architecture. We have seen from the three parallelism profiles shown in Figures 3, 4, and 7 that three problems do possess a reasonable amount of potential parallelism. However, the parallelisms are not very useful because they are inconsistent in time, consisting of many peaks and valleys. At times, parallelism comes down to merely 1 between iterations. If the parallelism is to be successfully exploited by a parallel machine, it is essential to have a consistent and less-fluctuating parallelism profile.

A possible way to fill the valleys between iterations is to break the iteration boundaries such that two or more iterations can be partially overlapped in execution, called *partial overlapping of loop iterations* (POLI). And an answer to the question of "what" is to cut the parallelism of peaks and fold them over to valleys. Figure 10 is a close-up version of Figure 3 for iterations 3 and 4. Region A (or C) is an expansion step of Figure 1 while Region B (or D) is a checking step. Again, the region A selects n nodes from open and generates their successors in the search tree while the region B checks to see if nodes generated by the expansion already exist on **open** or **closed**. The POLI technique comes in to fill the valleys by overlapping functions.

Consider the Towers of Hanoi with 3 disks, where an optimal number of iterations is 7. Suppose that the selection step has *four* nodes on open. Figure 11 shows how POLI works. When the master processor, p_0, starts executing the main program, it creates total of eight threads (four for EXPAND and four for MERGE) on four processors (p_0, p_1, p_2, and p_3). As soon as the threads are created on slave processors and the master processor, the rest is autonomous except when and only when the slave processors complete the given threads and there is no more left in the ready queue.

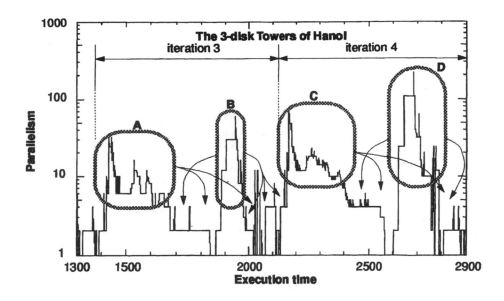

Figure 10: Folding parallelism over to valleys to fill the gap.

The thread creation on the master processor is not shown on the figure for the sake of clarity. When the first level thread, EXPAND, is created on each processor, it also creates the second level thread, FILTER, on other slave processors and the master. *This is where the valleys within an iteration are filled.* In other words, EXPAND and FILTER are heavily overlapped on all four processors.

For the running example shown in Figure 10, the valleys between A and B are filled with parallelism taken from A and B while the valleys between C and D are filled with parallelism taken from C and D. As each processor finishes the expansion step (this step includes check step, which is different from what we listed in Figure 1), it will return successor nodes to the master processor. If the master processor collects results from at least one slave processor, it can proceed to the *next* iteration while other slave processor are still working on expansion step or returning to the master processor. *This is where the overlapping of two iterations occurs.* The overlapped region is shaded in Figure 11. By overlapping two iterations, the valleys between iterations can be effectively filled with useful work while substantially reducing loop execution time. By remote thread creations and hiding remote accesses by context switch, the valleys are effectively filled with useful work, thereby reducing the sequentiality present in the sequential search problems.

The POLI method is possible in the EM-4 environment because the EM-4 provides an efficient context switch, fast remote read (2–3 μsec), fast thread invocation (6 μsec), and non-strict language support. It will be even more effective when there is enough consumer-producer parallelism present in the problem. The above example addresses just a few issues pertaining to multithreading. The current EM-4 implementation supports explicit thread switching, i.e., only one thread per activation frame. No register sharing for implicit switching is implemented, nor is instruction reordering performed at compile time. All these issues are currently being investigated toward implicit thread switching.

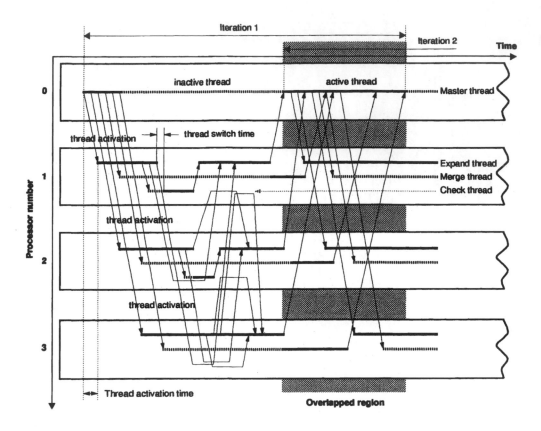

Figure 11: POLI with multithreading. Shaded area indicates the overlapping of two iterations. The figure is not drawn to exact time scale and check threads are not accurately depicted. The overlaps are done mostly on remote memory accesses. Processor 0 creates threads on slave processors and on itself, which is not shown. Thick solid lines indicate that the threads on the processor are being executed, while the thick dotted lines indicate the threads are suspended due to remote memory operations. Thin arrows indicate creations of threads and returns of results.

4. Experimental Results

Implementation details are presented in this section, followed by experimental results. Execution time of the three problems is listed to identify the relative performance of the platforms and their programming environments.

4.1 Eight Puzzle

The Eight Puzzle is implemented in SISAL for Symmetry and Cray, and in EM-C (superset of C) for the EM-4. We have executed four different problems of the Eight Puzzle as shown in Figure 12 (in fact, we have executed many more different and larger problem sizes but have listed a few sample problems only [16]). Each problem is defined in terms of the optimal number of iterations (or tree depth). A particular initial state uniquely defines the problem size of the Eight Puzzle since the optimal

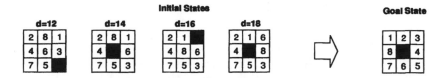

Figure 12: Four different initial states and a goal state for the Eight Puzzle.

No. of	Sequent Symmetry				Cray-2				EM-4			
PEs	12	14	16	18	12	14	16	18	12	14	16	18
1	1.73	14.46	63.64	727.55	0.294	2.344	9.371	75.222	0.175	1.125	4.005	37.058
2	1.23	9.03	38.13	435.50	0.208	1.503	5.874	49.568	0.195	0.384	2.785	25.265
3	0.99	7.22	29.98	388.05	0.167	1.171	4.583	39.595	0.258	0.496	1.941	17.415
4	0.86	6.66	26.25	298.30	0.146	1.083	3.999	34.984	0.259	0.500	1.421	12.681
8	0.91	5.80	20.86	222.69					0.056	0.431	0.900	7.404
10	1.18	4.29	19.76	208.85					0.064	0.513	0.754	6.664
20	3.16	6.34	20.50	187.12					0.099	0.984	0.744	5.589
30									0.127	0.210	0.699	5.393
40									0.134	0.223	0.641	5.301
50									0.157	0.304	0.469	5.006
60									0.183	0.319	0.468	4.662
70									0.918	0.364	0.512	4.346
80									0.218	0.385	0.656	3.864

Table 2: Execution time (in seconds).

number of iterations is fixed for the given initial state. For example, the left most initial state for Figure 12 (d = 12) indicates that the tree depth (or optimal number of iterations) is 12. Table 2 summarize execution time.

4.2 Towers of Hanoi

The Towers of Hanoi is implemented in SISAL for Symmetry and Cray, and in EM-C (superset of C) for the EM-4. Four different problems are used. Table 3 summarizes the execution time.

4.3 Ops5

Ops5 is a large nonnumeric program. We have implemented two versions: one for Symmetry and Cray using SISAL and the other for the EM-4 distributed-memory machine using C. The SISAL-Ops5 is one of the largest or perhaps the largest application program written in SISAL. The SISAL-Ops5 is approximately 10,000 lines of SISAL. It took over a year to implement by three people. It can run on many shared-memory machines where SISAL is ported.

Ops5 has also been implemented in EM-C on the EM-4. In fact, EM-Ops5 is the *first* full-scale implementation of Ops5 on distributed-memory multiprocessors. The program is approximately 6,000 lines of C code with various parallel constructs. Implementation took two summers (6 months) by one person. Its functionality is exactly the same as Ops5. The parallel version produces exactly the same rule firing sequence as the original Lisp version of Ops5. There are a few distinctions between the original Ops5 and EM-Ops5. The EM-Ops5 implementation presented in this paper is *character*-based implementation, i.e., all string comparison and pattern matching are done in characters, which is dramatically different from conventional symbol manipu-

No. of	Sequent Symmetry				Cray-2				EM-4			
PEs	4 disks	5 disks	6 disks	7 disks	4 disks	5 disks	6 disks	7 disks	4 disks	5 disks	6 disks	7 disks
1	0.33	3.99	22.58	326.53	0.034	0.238	1.889	8.188	0.129	0.670	4.216	30.330
2	0.27	2.79	15.69	313.73	0.023	0.127	0.946	6.099	0.071	0.506	3.523	28.165
3	0.21	2.02	14.72	181.04	0.018	0.094	0.600	4.726	0.053	0.305	2.114	16.554
4	0.17	2.32	4.16	194.00	0.016	0.069	0.456	3.196	0.035	0.188	1.291	11.613
8	0.21	1.18	8.19	80.53					0.036	0.138	0.775	5.391
10	0.21	1.24	8.46	95.56					0.035	0.144	0.707	4.624
20	0.23	1.41	10.46	84.85					0.039	0.148	0.726	3.959
30									0.046	0.156	0.840	4.523
40									0.052	0.165	0.763	4.253
50									0.059	0.176	0.776	4.475
60									0.065	0.186	0.789	4.380
70									0.072	0.197	0.807	4.478
80									0.078	0.209	0.824	4.491

Table 3: Execution time (in seconds).

lation. There are several reasons for that, and we will come back to this shortly. (At the time of writing this paper, the *integer*-based symbol manipulation has just been complete but experimental results are still under analysis. EM-Op5 is a very large nonnumeric application, and statistics gathering and their analysis require much time and effort. We intend to report in the near future the effects of multithreading on this large scale nonnumeric application as soon as analysis is complete.)

To test the functionality of both the SISAL-Ops5 and the EM-Ops5 with speculative computation, we have executed four production systems, ranging from a very small one (Monkey and Banana (MAB) and Blocks World Problem (BWP)) to a reasonably large one (Waltz). For OPS5 execution, four typical production systems are implemented. They are among those widely used for experiments. While more details can be found in [14], we briefly explain them below.

- *Blocks World Problem* (BWP) is a simple program for a robot to pick bricks from a pool of bricks and place them in ascending (or descending) size.

- *Monkey and Banana* (MAB) is a program where a hungry monkey grabs a banana hanging from the ceiling, given a couch and a ladder in the room.

- *n-Queen* is a classical problem which places n queens on an $n \times n$ board such that each row, column, and diagonal contains no more than one queen.

- *Waltz Labeling Algorithm* assigns a label (chosen from a finite set of possible labels) to each edge of a line drawing, where each label gives semantic information about the nature of the edge and the regions on each of its sides.

Several parameters characterize the complexity of a production system. Among them are a number of entries in the two-input memory of the last condition element of a rule. The Rete network used for pattern matching in Ops5 does propagate the effect of addition or deletion of wmes all the way to the two-input memory attached to the last condition element. This was a serious drawback of the Rete approach, which we indeed found was the case. We are planning to address this issue in the next version of EM-Ops5. Table 4 lists surface characteristics of the production system programs we have executed.

	BWP	MAB	8-Queen	Waltz
Number of rules	5	13	19	45
Number of condition elements in LHS	12	41	68	195
Number of actions in RHS	6	25	71	47
Maximum # of entries in α-memory/rule	16	9	48	141
Maximum # of entries in β-memory/rule	310	43	152	2527
Number of wmes generated	120	58	3866	292
Number of rules fired	41	16	1046	242

Table 4: Surface characteristics of the production system programs.

Number of Processors	BWP1	MAB	8-Queen	Waltz1
1	2.90	2.78	600.41	74.05
2	1.79	1.75	421.08	53.56
4	1.58	1.25	322.41	30.66
6	1.24	1.11	291.86	22.23
8	1.22	1.01	284.45	18.49
10	1.23	0.92	251.16	16.83
12	1.25	0.95	250.92	14.07
14	1.26	0.98	243.56	13.98
16	1.27	0.99	238.76	13.21
18	1.30	0.97	226.45	12.77
20	1.35	0.93	223.20	13.17

Table 5: SISAL-Ops5 execution time (in seconds) on a sequent symmetry.

The five production system programs listed in Table 4 were executed on the target machine. Table 5 summarizes the experimental results of SISAL-Ops5.

Table 6 lists experimental results of EM-Ops5.

Note that BWP1 and BWP2 are different; they are different problem instances with different amounts of data to begin with. BWP1 has approximately 10 times more data, i.e., initial working memory elements. The same applies to Waltz.

5. Discussion

Speedup curves are drawn from the execution results. Implications of the speedup curves for each problem are discussed to identify the scalability of each machine on

	BWP2	MAB	8-Queen	Waltz2
Sequential execution time (1 processor)	9.862	0.570	32.986	552.021
Number of processors used	10	20	80	80
Parallel execution time	5.617	0.208	5.320	150.151

Table 6: Execution time using character-based string matching on the EM-4.

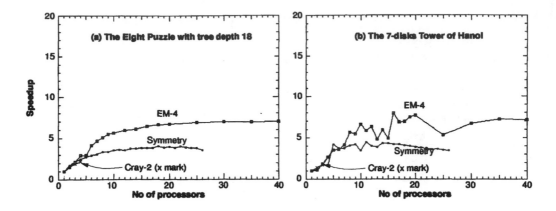

Figure 13: Comparison of the three implementations.

nonnumeric problems. Sequent results and EM-4 results are then compared to identify their respective merits. Programmability and performance are discussed based on the results of three nonnumeric problems.

5.1 Search Problems

Execution times shown in Tables 2 and 3 are converted to speedup factors. Speedup is defined as the execution time on a single processor over n processors for a given problem. For example, consider the problem size of 7 disks on a Symmetry. From Table 3, we find that the execution time for 7 disks on 1 processor is 326.53 seconds while it is 84.85 on 20 processors. Speedup is 326.53/84.85=3.8. Figure 13 illustrates various speedup curves for the largest problem sizes we executed on the three machines.

Figure 13 shows speedups for the two search problems on three parallel machines. We observe the following three facts from the curves:

- Speedup increases in general as the number of processors increases.

- The EM-4 speedup continuously increases while that of Symmetry saturates and falls back as the number of processors increases.

- The performance of EM-4 is approximately twice that of Symmetry.

The first observation verifies that the approach we have taken to parallelize the given problems works for the selected problems. The second observation indicates that automatic parallelization is not as effective as manual parallelization. It clearly shows that manual parallelization is twice as effective as automatic parallelization in terms of parallelism utilization. The EM-4 implementation used various parallelization techniques to exploit parallelism in several different levels. We have identified that POLI works well in the explicit-switching multithreaded architecture EM-4. However, it should also be noted that neither OSC nor SISAL require a substantial amount of parallelization efforts and customized techniques such as POLI. The only parallel construct SISAL requires is parallel *for* loops.

The absolute speedup is rather disappointing compared to the time and effort spent on parallelization. It appears reasonable for Symmetry and Cray-2 since no effort was expended on parallelization of nonnumeric problems. However, much effort was spent on parallelization for the EM-4 implementation, including POLI and multithreading, but the end result was the mere 7-fold speedup on 80 processors. This prompted us to look further into the two-search problem. We have implemented larger problem sizes of tree depth of up to 40 and found that the speedup reached over 40-fold [16]. These results were not included in this paper because we were unable to execute the large problem sizes on the Symmetry due to memory constraints. The three platforms can be compared fairly only when they can all execute the same problems sizes.

5.2 Ops5 Performance

Both the SISAL-Ops5 and the EM-Ops5 implementation took several years to complete by several people. Regardless of the efforts, the Ops5 performance on the three machines is disappointing. The maximum speedup obtained from Symmetry is 5.8 for Waltz. There are several reasons why the performance is poor. SISAL-Ops5 relies mostly on automatic parallelization through parallel *for* loops. Optimizing the SISAL compiler includes various stages of code optimization. Among them are IF2Mem and IF2Up, standing respectively for *build-in-place* and *update-in-place*. These two stages are designed to detect and resolve those program statements which introduce array copying. While the performance of the two analyzers is highly effective for those numeric problems such as partial differential equations, FFTs, etc. [5], it is not the case for nonnumeric problems.

The SISAL-Ops5 implementation contains a total of 406 array allocation/copy statements. Among them are 274 statements which may introduce array copying while the remaining 132 introduce array copying. This number is relatively large compared to the SISAL implementation of Eight Puzzle where there are only 4 runtime array allocation and 84 array copying. It is one of two important reasons that SISAL-Ops5 gives poor performance. One solution to array copying/updating would be to preallocate a large number of arrays at compile time and use them at runtime. This preallocation would solve problems when the size of arrays can be estimated. However, when there is no way of estimating the maximum number of nodes, the preallocation will be less effective. It would perhaps cause more trouble since it will unnecessarily hold a large amount of memory which cannot be used for other purposes.

The EM-Ops5 implementation was another valuable experience for the large-scale nonnumeric problem. The maximum speedup of the EM-Ops5 is 6.2 for 8-Queen, which is again a disappointing result. We had various problems in the course of implementation. One of the serious misconceptions we had at the very beginning was the decision to adopt the master-slave parallel programming paradigm. When we first started implementing the EM-Ops5 project, we figured data-parallelism present in the match step would be sufficient to obtain high performance for Ops5 in multiprocessor environments. It turned out not to be the case. By the time we found that the data-parallelism in match step does not adequately parallelize production systems, it had already taken some time. Following are reasons the data-parallelism utilization gave poor performance. First, the master processor was extremely busy handling various activities including matching, selection, action, distribution of wmes, collecting matched rules, etc. Second, the master-slave parallel programming paradigm required the master to have a great deal of memory since it kept almost all the information necessary to perform the "master" role. Third but not last was that the time taken by a master processor was relatively long compared to the slave processors. In a single processor environment, match step usually dominates the entire life cycle of production systems. However, when it becomes a multiprocessor implementation, especially over

50 processors, the match time becomes relatively small compared to the selection and action time. In fact, we often observed that the selection time takes longer than match time; so does the action time. This is one of the problems that we did not anticipate. Our primary target when we first started the EM-Ops5 project was to reduce match time by using many processors. The objective certainly has been achieved. However, as one problem was solved, another problem emerged, which was the long act time. This unbalanced execution time of each of the three steps led us to develop a different programming paradigm, speculative computation, which we eventually adopted after a time-consuming experience.

As we listed execution time above, the speedup is not as promising as we have stated throughout this paper. The most important reason is that all computations are *character*-based. Conventional Lisp processing systems use integers for string matching. However, we adopted character-based string matching because we wished to (1) have full control over all the information we were dealing with, and (2) identify how the 32-bit integer-based EM-4 machine handled character-based string manipulation. This character-based processing again turned out highly inadequate for production system processing. The EM-4 multiprocessor is a word-based machine where a word is 32 bits plus 6 more bits for dataflow synchronization mechanism. When an 8-bit character (or 1 byte) is to be read from memory, what is actually read from memory is a 32-bit word (or 4 bytes). After a word is read into a register, the desired character is accessed by breaking the word into four segments. Simple algebra shows that matching two strings, each of which is n characters, would require a minimum of *five* instructions: two for memory read, two for accessing individual characters stored now in registers, and one for comparison (not including shift and/or masking operations). To simplify our discussion, when a string matching operation is to be performed on a character basis, the machine executes at least *five* times more instructions than integer-based string matching. This discrepancy is a machine's built-in characteristic which has been verified by other integer benchmarking problems since the machine has been operational.

The five-times difference between character-based string matching and integer-based string matching directly translates to a minimum of five times speedup on what is listed in Table 6. Or, the difference would become even larger since the time to communicate to other processors will also decrease by a factor of five. To broadcast the newly generated wmes, the EM-Ops5 converts character-based wmes to integers. When wmes are received by a processor, they are converted back to character-based structures. This double conversion—character to integer and back to character—in fact, takes up most of the match and action time. Integer-based string matching eliminates all these unnecessary computations, which would give much more than five-times speedup. Our conservative estimate is also verified by benchmarking performed on the EM-4. At the time of writing this paper, we just finished converting the character-based string matching into an integer-based one. We are currently performing experiments and collecting statistics. The performance of the integer-based EM-Ops5 will be available in the near future.

5.3 Summary

Comparing the execution results of the EM-4 and a Symmetry is difficult and may mislead as they are two completely different implementations. To make a fair and reasonable comparison between the Symmetry and the EM-4, we have carefully selected data-structures and algorithms, whenever and wherever possible, such that they have many implementation details in common. Table 7 summarizes characteristics of our

	Symmetry and Cray-2	*EM-4*
Model of computation	von Neumann	multithreaded and data-flow
Total number of processors	4 to 20	80
Memory organization	shared single-address	distributed
Language	SISAL [11]	EM-C (superset of C) [15]
Algorithm complexity	same	
Typical data structures	1 or more dimension arrays	linked lists and arrays
Parallelizing compiler	yes: OSC [2]	none: manual
Parallelization method	loop slicing	POLI and speculative computation

Table 7: Surface characteristics of the two implementations.

implementations, which must be taken into consideration when comparing the results of the two machines.

The low speedup of the shared-memory implementation contradicts our earlier discussion on parallelism profiles. In Section 2, we predicted that the three problems would have a large amount of instruction-level parallelism. And in Section 3, we introduced various parallelization techniques to exploit such parallelism both in algorithm level and implementation level. However, actual experimental results show otherwise. It is obvious that the parallelism is apparently underutilized. There are two main reasons for the underutilization. First, there are numerous memory accesses. In fact, the three problems, like other true nonnumeric problems, spent more than half of the time accessing memory and handling structures. Considering that approximately 20%–30% of the total operations of semi-nonnumeric problems such as TeX or GCC (measured on Vax) is memory access (data transfer), this is substantially large. As we have stated above, the OSC performs rigorous memory optimization in terms of copy elimination and memory preallocation. We find that OSC was partially successful for search problems but not for Ops5. Our misconception in character-based implementation of Ops5 was the main cause of poor performance, since the EM-Ops5 spent more than half of the time accessing memories (local and remote) and structures.

Second, the two programming environments are two extremes: the Symmetry uses a *functional* language, SISAL, and its *automatic* parallelizing compiler, OSC, while the EM-4 uses an *imperative* language, EM-C, and *manual* parallelization. SISAL and OSC give relatively high programmability whereas EM-C gives very low programmability. OSC requires no effort by programmers while EM-C does require much effort to explicitly parallelize the programs by inserting various parallel constructs. We have identified that OSC parallelizes outer loops. Those inner loops with thin loop body are not parallelized. Search problems and Ops5 have many inner parallel loops but few instructions. Parallelism profiles shown in Section 2 include parallelism from all these inner parallel loops. However, these inner loops were not parallelized, resulting in poor performance.

EM-4 implementations include speculative computation and partial overlapping of sequential loop iterations. We have identified that the degree of overlapping for POLI was approximately 10% of each loop, which was not significant enough to show notable performance. The speculative computation technique used for Ops5 was effective in terms of overlapping two sequential loop iterations. However, we have also identified, through processor utilization plots, that the degree of overlapping was again less than 10%, which is indeed insignificant. At the time of writing this paper, we had collected limited statistics. We are currently fine-tuning the three problems to the machine architectures, and at the same time measuring various detailed statistics of the three problems. We expect that in the near future we will be able to provide detailed and quantitative numbers of the degree of overlapping of POLI and speculative computation. Upon completion of fine-tuning the three problems and collecting statistics, we will be able to explicate the performance of the three platforms. We believe that the current and forthcoming execution results on hard nonnumeric problems will clearly explain the two critical issues of programmability and performance toward general purpose parallel computing.

). Conclusions

Parallel computation of nonnumeric problems is a challenging task. The main reasons are the large amount of resource usage and the irregular behavior. This paper has presented parallel nonnumeric computations on two completely different types of multiprocessors and programming environments. We investigated two critical issues in parallel computing: *programmability* and *performance*, toward *general purpose* parallel computing. We have selected two drastically different types of multiprocessors: two shared-memory single-address space multiprocessors (a Sequent Symmetry and a Cray-2), and a multithreaded distributed-memory multiprocessor (EM-4). The programming environments for the three multiprocessors are at two extremes: the functional language SISAL and its automatic parallelizing compiler OSC for shared-memory machines and the imperative language EM-C with manual parallelization for the EM-4.

To demonstrate programmability and performance issues, three typical nonnumeric problems were selected for experiments: two moderately sized search problems, the Eight Puzzle and the Towers of Hanoi; and a very large problem, Ops5 production system interpreter. A three-step approach was taken to evaluate the performance of the three machines and their programming environments: parallelism profiling, algorithm level parallelization, and implementation level parallelization and optimization. Parallelism profiles of all the problems were constructed using the functional language SISAL. Parallel heuristic search and speculative computation were developed to parallelize the three problems in algorithm level. Multithreading and partial overlapping of loop iterations were used to break loop-carried dependencies and to tolerate remote memory latency for implementation level parallelization.

We encountered many practical difficulties implementing the three problems on the three machines (or at least in two programming environments). The main difficulty was the large resource usage of the three problems. Ops5 is a large program not only in terms of number of program lines but, more importantly, in terms of runtime memory usage. The Eight Puzzle and the Tower of Hanoi were moderately sized programs (depending on how one views them, one can implement the search problems in double recursion in Lisp, which would perhaps take only a page or less of Lisp code. However, our iterative implementation required various parallel activities, which made the program a few pages of EM-C codes). We attempted to run large problem sizes such as 100 disks of the Towers of Hanoi and tree depth of 100 (i.e., an optimal path to the goal is 100 steps) for the Eight Puzzle but were not successful because of the very large memory requirements. The memory size of a single processor has essentially limited the problem sizes which can be executed on the three multiprocessors. In any case, all the sequential and parallel versions of the three problems were successfully implemented on the three machines, with reasonably sized problem instances.

Our work showed that the combination of shared-memory machines and the functional language SISAL with its *automatic* parallelizing compiler OSC provides high programmability, as it requires *no* parallelization efforts. On the other hand, the combination of a distributed-memory machine and the imperative language EM-C with *explicit* parallelization gives approximately *twice* the performance of the shared-memory combination but *low* programmability. We have further found that the nonnumeric problems on the EM-4 yielded roughly a two-fold speedup over the shared-memory version, mainly because of manual parallelization and full control over potential parallelism. We have verified through analysis of processor utilization that explicit switching-based multithreading was effective in breaking loop-carried dependencies by overlapping computation and communication. We have also verified that speculative computation has worked well to overlap two iterations, thereby breaking loop-carried dependencies. Our experiments, however, were limited due to various implementation constraints such as large code size, memory capacity, etc. We are currently refining our implementations and measuring various detailed statistics of the three problems. In the near future, we expect to report detailed results of parameters which precisely characterize the machine platforms and their programming environments. All these results based on actual implementations will lead us to further explicate programmability and performance issues toward general purpose parallel computing.

Acknowledgments

We would like to thank the EM-4 group members (Mitsuhisa Sato, Shuichi Sakai, Yuetsu Kodama, and Yoshinori Yamaguchi) of the Electrotechnical Laboratory for providing access to the EM-4 multiprocessor. Andrew Sohn would like to thank Kenji Nishida of ETL for making practical arrangements during his stay at ETL. SISAL-Ops5 is a large program which took over a year to implement. Michel Guyot wrote the draft version, which Dominique Poudevigne further refined in order to be able to run it on a Cray-2 and a Sequent Symmetry, while Hung-Yu Tseng added various function capabilities and completed the large project SISAL-OPS5 for the Cray-2 and the Symmetry. Cray cycles were provided by the Lawrence Livermore Laboratory through the SISAL Scientific Computing Initiative. We would like to thank John Feo for providing access to Crays.

References

[1] D. Cann, "Retire Fortran: A Debate Rekindled," *Communications of the ACM*, Vol. 35, pp. 81–89, August 1992.

[2] D.C. Cann and R.R. Oldehoeft, "A Guide to Optimizing SISAL Compiler," Technical Report UCRL-MA-108369, Lawrence Livermore Laboratory, Livermore, CA, 1991.

[3] D.E. Culler, S.C. Goldstein, K.E. Schauser, and T. von Eicken, "TAM—A Compiler Controlled Threaded Abstract Machine," *Journal of Parallel and Distributed Computing*, Vol. 18, 1993, pp. 347–370.

[4] J.T. Feo, D.C. Cann, and R.R. Oldehoeft, "A Report on the SISAL Language Project," *Journal of Parallel and Distributed Computing*, 10, December 1990, pp. 349–365.

[5] J.T. Feo (Ed.), *Third SISAL Conference*, Lawrence Livermore National Laboratory, October 1993.

[6] C.L. Forgy, OPS5 User's Manual, Technical Report, CMU-CS-81-135, Carnegie Mellon University, July 1981.

[7] J-L. Gaudiot, and A. Sohn, "Data-Driven Parallel Production Systems," *IEEE Transactions on Software Engineering*, March 1990, pp. 281–293.

[8] A. Gupta, Parallelisms in Production Systems, Morgan Kaufmann Publishers, Inc., Los Altos, California, 1987.

[9] P.E. Hart, N.J. Nilson, and B. Raphael, "A Formal Basis for the Heuristic Determination of Minimum Cost Paths," *IEEE Transactions on SMC*, Vol. 4, No. 2, pp. 100–107, 1968.

[10] J. Hicks, D. Chiou, B.S. Ang, and Arvind, "Performance Studies of Id on the Monsoon Dataflow Systems," *Journal of Parallel and Distributed Computing 18*, 1993, pp. 273–300.

[11] J.R. McGraw, S.K. Skedzielewski, S.J. Allan, R.R. Oldehoeft, J. Glauert, C. Kirkham, W. Noyce, and R. Thomas, "SISAL: Streams and Iteration in a Single Assignment Language: Reference Manual version 1.2," Manual M-146, Rev. 1, Lawrence Livermore Laboratory, Livermore, CA, 1985.

[12] R.S. Nikhil, G.M. Papadopoulous, and Arvind, "*T: A Multithreaded Massively Parallel Architecture," *Proc. of ACM International Symposium on Computer Architecture*, Gold Coast, Australia, May 1992, pp. 156–167

[13] G.M. Papadopoulous and D. Culler, "Monsoon: an Explicit Token-Store Architecture," *Proc. of ACM International Symposium on Computer Architecture*, Seattle, Washington, May 1990.

[14] S. Sakai, Y. Yamaguchi, K. Hiraki, and T. Yuba, "An Architecture of a Data-flow Single Chip Processor," *Proc. of ACM International Symposium on Computer Architecture*, Jerusalem, Israel, May 1989, pp. 46–53.

[15] M. Sato, Y. Kodama, S. Sakai, Y. Yamaguchi, and Y. Koumura, "Thread-based Programming for the EM-4 Hybrid Data-flow Machine," *Proc. of ACM International Symposium on Computer Architecture*, Gold Coast, Australia, May 1992, pp. 146–155.

[16] A. Sohn, M. Sato, S. Sakai, Y. Kodama, and Y. Yamaguchi, "Nonnumeric Search Results on the EM-4 Distributed-Memory Multiprocessor," *Proc. of Supercomputing 94*, Washington, D.C., November 1994.

[17] A. Sohn, C. Kim, M. Sato, and S. Sakai, "Multithreading with the EM-4 Distributed-Memory Multiprocessor," Technical Report, NJIT-CIS-31-94, April 1994.

Exploiting Iteration-Level Parallelism in Dataflow Programs

Lubomir Bic, John M.A. Roy, and Mark Nagel
Department of Information and Computer Science
University of California, Irvine, CA 92717

The term "dataflow" generally encompasses three distinct aspects of computation—a data-driven model of computation, a functional/declarative programming language, and a special-purpose multiprocessor architecture. In this paper we decouple the language and architecture issues by demonstrating that declarative programming is a suitable vehicle for the programming of conventional distributed-memory multiprocessors.

This is achieved by applying several transformations to the compiled declarative program to achieve iteration-level (rather than instruction-level) parallelism. The transformations first group individual instructions into sequential lightweight processes, and then insert primitives to: (1) cause array allocation to be distributed over multiple processors, and (2) cause computation to follow the data distribution by inserting an index filtering mechanism into a given loop and spawning a copy of it on all PEs; the filter causes each instance of that loop to operate on a different subrange of the index variable.

The underlying model of computation is a dataflow/von Neumann hybrid in that execution within a process is control-driven while the creation, blocking, and activation of processes is data-driven.

The performance of this process-oriented dataflow system (PODS) is demonstrated using the hydrodynamics simulation benchmark called SIMPLE, where a 19-fold speedup on a 32-processor architecture has been achieved.

1. Introduction

The programming of parallel computer systems is a difficult and highly error-prone task. This is due primarily to the lack of adequate facilities to describe a problem to a parallel machine at a high level, without sacrificing performance. The current state of the art in programming parallel machines efficiently is to let the programmer explicitly partition the program into processes and insert the necessary synchronization and communication primitives.

There are several schools of thought on how to make parallel processing more accessible and more effective, as shown graphically in Figure 1. The most common (and least revolutionary) approach is to rely on existing sequential languages. These are either extended to allow the programmer to express parallelism explicitly, or they employ sophisticated compilers capable of extracting parallelism from a given program automatically.

At the opposite end of the spectrum are approaches which completely abandon conventional von Neumann systems in favor of radically new languages and architectures. Perhaps the best known representatives of this approach are dataflow systems, which start with a data-driven model of computation, employ a functional/declarative style of high-level programming, and design special-purpose architectures targeted specifically to the execution of dataflow programs.

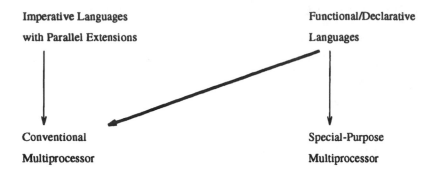

Figure 1: Approaches to parallel processing.

Our approach is intermediate to the above two extremes. We concentrate on conventional multiprocessors and investigate how to effectively program them using new languages. Specifically, our goal is to demonstrate that a declarative language, intended primarily for the programming of special-purpose dataflow architectures, is a highly suitable vehicle for the programming of commercially available multiprocessors.

The paper is organized as follows. Section 2 motivates the use of declarative programming. Sections 3 and 4 describe the principles of PODS—the Processes-Oriented Dataflow System. Specifically, Section 3 describes how dataflow programs are transformed into communicating processes, while Section 4 presents the mechanisms for distributing their execution over multiple processors. Section 5 then presents the results of the simulations. Finally, conclusions and comparisons to other approaches are given in Section 6.

2. Declarative Programming

Most programming languages today are based on the imperative style of programming, where data is viewed as passive elements in storage, which are accessed and manipulated by a stream of instructions under the control of a program counter. Alternative programming styles, including functional, logic, or object-oriented, have been developed in the past, with the objective of facilitating the task of program development. Specifically, functional programming has been studied extensively in the context of parallel machines, due to their clean mathematical properties and the lack of side-effects. Unfortunately, the syntax of pure functional languages, such as FP [7], where programs are essentially compositions of nested functions, is considered too "user-unfriendly" for the development of large scientific or commercial programs. They also lack the support for large data structures, such as arrays and matrices, which are considered essential for scientific programming.

In the context of dataflow systems, several functional languages, which overcome the above problems, have been developed. The best known such languages are VAL [1], SISAL [19], and Id [21], which all support the common control and data-manipulation constructs found in imperative languages, including if-then-else statements, for- and while-loops, procedure calls, and various facilities to manipulate data structures and streams. This makes the development of large programs using these languages not only possible but even easier than using conventional languages, such as C or Fortran [5].

In our research we use Id, which is a functional language augmented with a parallel data-structuring mechanism called I-structures [6]. I-structures may be viewed as arrays that obey the principle of *single assignment*, which is at the core of all functional languages. This principle states that any element of the array may be written into only once. After it has been written, it may be read any number times. The necessary synchronization, which delays all read requests until a value has been written and which also reports any attempts to rewrite a value as a single-assignment violation, is enforced automatically by the I-structure memory.

A *declarative* style of programming is defined as functional programming, augmented with the concept of single-assignment arrays, as embodied in the latest version of Id, called Id Nouveau [20], [4]. The main difference that sets declarative programming apart from pure functional programming is that *referential transparency* is given up. That is, values returned by two calls to the same function with the same arguments will not necessarily be indistinguishable. The advantage is that one can alter a data structure once it has been created, instead of having to specify the contents of all its elements at creation time, as is demanded by a purely functional language. This allows a style of programming which is more in tune with the way programmers think about a problem. Specifically, an I-structure may be defined initially as an empty set of slots, which may be filled (and consumed) later by subsequent computations. This is very similar to using arrays in conventional languages, except for the single-assignment property.

Note, however, that the *Church-Rosser property* [18], also called the confluence property, is preserved by declarative programs. This requires that the answer computed by an expression be unaffected by the choice of which subexpressions are evaluated first. Since I-structures enqueue all early reads until the element is written, and each element preserves single assignment, I-structures preserve the Church-Rosser property. No matter how one interleaves the execution of reads and writes, every fetch to a given I-structures element always returns the same value. Hence the overall program determinacy is guaranteed even if the machine exhibits non-determinacy in instruction scheduling.

3. Subcompact Processes

For the purposes of this paper, it is not necessary to understand the exact syntax or semantics of Id. (The interested reader is referred to [20], [4], [21].) It is, however, important to point out that the underlying clean semantics of Id (and other functional/declarative languages) make it possible to translate high-level language programs into dataflow graphs, which precisely capture the data dependencies among all operators.

The following is a simple Id program which fills a 2-dimensional array A by computing a value for each of its elements.

```
A = matrix(50,10);
for i = 1 to 50
  for j = 1 to 10
    A[i,j] = f(i,j);
```

Figure 2 shows the essential parts of the corresponding dataflow graph. There are three separate scopes (code blocks), each entered through L operators (or, initially, a function call) which create a new context for the corresponding scope. The outer-most scope causes the space for the array A to be allocated, given the array bounds. The array ID is passed into the inner-most loop where it is used by the write operator.

The middle scope contains the code to generate the index sequence for i. The initial value for i (1, in this case) is circulated through the switch, increment, and D operators until it reaches the value 50. A copy of each i is passed into the inner context, where the index sequences for j are generated in a similar manner and, together with each i, are used to compute the function f and to write the value into the appropriate element of A. (The meaning of the dashed arrows labeled "RF" will be explained later.)

The dataflow graph captures the underlying data-driven semantics of the high-level program. There is no program counter. Instead, each node of the dataflow graph is an autonomous instruction, capable of executing whenever it receives all its operands along the graph arcs. In principle, each node may be viewed as an independent "process," which is instantiated when the necessary operands arrive, performs the prescribed operation, and sends the resulting values to other such "processes" that need the data as their inputs.

One way to exploit this highly asynchronous model of computation is to build special-purpose dataflow architectures, capable of tolerating the resulting overhead of instruction-level parallelism. Another approach, the one taken in our project, is to increase the level of granularity from a single instruction to a group of instructions, thus permitting them to execute as threads or lightweight processes. In our case, the objective is to execute such processes on a conventional multiprocessor. Due to the minimal state associated with each such processes, we refer to them as Subcompact Processes (SPs).[1]

The idea of forming sequential threads of computation out of dataflow programs is the essence of dataflow/von Neumann hybrids, a number of which have been proposed in recent years [12], [14]–[17], [22], [24], [25]. One of the main issues, which differentiates the various approaches, is how to create processes, i.e., how to subdivide the original dataflow graph or program into sequential code segments. Our initial approach [9] was to divide the graph into paths according to their data-dependencies using a depth-first coloring scheme. Unfortunately, the resulting SPs were too small to execute efficiently on conventional distributed memory multiprocessors. The current approach is to make each function a new SP and, within each function, make each loop iteration level a separate SP. This coincides with the subdivision of the code generated by the Id Nouveau compiler. Hence each code block, when invoked, becomes a separate SP.

Consider again the dataflow graph in Figure 2. Each of the three scopes would be instantiated as an SP. In particular, SP1 performs the array allocation and then invokes SP2, which generates the 50 index values for i. For each i, it invokes SP3, which generates the 10 j-indices and performs the corresponding computation for each. In addition, each individual SP can be distributed over all PEs where each copy operates over a distinct subrange of the array.

While the execution within a given SP is control-driven, the instantiation and activation of SPs is triggered by the arrival of operands (i.e., still data-driven). An SP is passive as long as its first instruction is disabled. When all operands for the first instruction have arrived, the SP becomes active. This is accomplished by loading the SP into execution memory and creating a simple process control block (PCB) for it, consisting essentially of the starting address of the SP in execution memory, a program

---

[1] We have borrowed the term "subcompact" from the automobile industry to mean having the smallest possible state to still justify calling it a process.

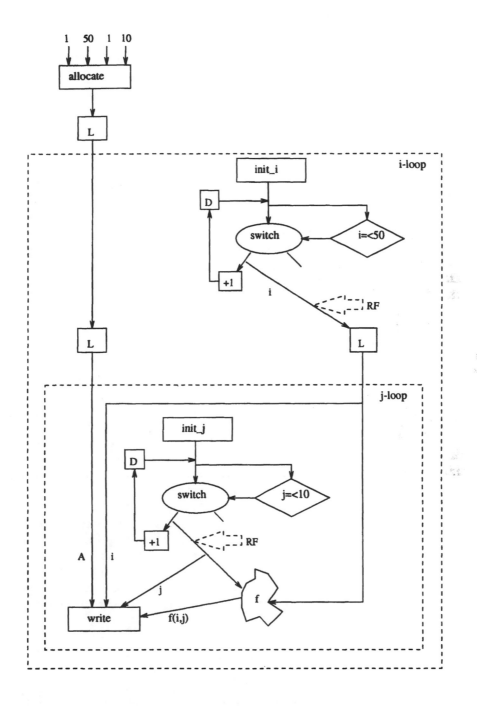

Figure 2: Example of a dataflow graph.

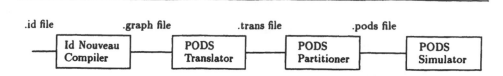

Figure 3: Organization of PODS.

counter pointing to the current instruction, and a status field indicating whether the process is running, ready, or blocked.

The three states are analogous to those found in most operating systems. An SP is running until it reaches the end of the SP (at which time it is destroyed) or until it encounters an instruction that does not yet have all its operands present. In the latter case, the SP is blocked and the PE switches to another ready SP. The blocked SP changes its status to ready as soon as the last operand for the current instruction arrives. This process-oriented viewpoint permits us to execute a dataflow program as a collection of communicating SPs. Hence we refer to our system as PODS—a *Process-Oriented Dataflow System*.

The overall organization of PODS is depicted in Figure 3. At the top level is the Id Nouveau compiler developed at MIT, which translates Id source programs into dataflow graphs. These are then translated in two steps into code executable on the PODS simulator. The first step, performed by the PODS Translator, converts code blocks into SPs. This consists primarily of (1) eliminating synchronization instructions used to implement k-bounded loops [2], [11], and (2) ordering instructions within each code block according to dataflow arcs such that no instruction depends on data generated by an instruction lower in the sequence. An important implicit change in semantics also takes place. The instructions within a code block are now viewed as a single sequential SP. This implies that every instruction, in addition to generating data values for subsequent instructions, must also modify a program counter. In most cases, the program counter is simply incremented. In the case of a switch operator, the program counter is either incremented, thus pointing to the true branch of the statement, or set to a new value to skip over to the false branch.

The next step, performed by the PODS Partitioner, is to modify the SPs to achieve distribution. This is accomplished by inserting three types of primitive into the SP code: a *distributing allocate operator*, which causes arrays to be spread over different PEs, a *distributing L operator*, which causes a given SP to be spawned on multiple PEs concurrently, and a *range filter*, which guarantees that each of the replicated SPs operates on a different index range. These primitives form the core of PODS and are the major focus of the next section.

4. Distributed Execution

PODS supports both functional and data parallelism. The main focus of this paper, however, is on data-parallelism. Specifically, we are interested in iteration-level parallelism (rather than instruction-level parallelism), which plays a prominent role in most scientific computations. The goal is to distribute the iteration space of a loop and the corresponding data over multiple PEs such that each would operate on a different subrange of the index space.

PODS has been targeted to a distributed memory MIMD architecture with a *non-uniform* access to memory, such as the Intel iPSC/2, the N-cube, or the cosmic cube. This means that access to non-local memory is much slower (involving the cooperation of the remote PE) than access to local memory.[2] For that reason we implement read requests to remote memory in a "split-phase" manner, where issuing the read request is separated from actually consuming the data [3]. This allows an SP to issue the request and to continue executing the current SP until the requested data are actually needed, or to perform a context switch in the meantime. Presence bits are used to indicate whether a given memory location contains a valid data item.

Under these architectural assumptions, it is necessary to decide how to distribute both data and the corresponding computation. Since arrays are the most important data structures in scientific computation, we concentrate on distributing *for-loops* operating over *arrays*. The main objective is to distribute computation evenly while keeping the number of remote data accesses to a minimum. PODS employs two techniques to achieve that. First, it uses the distribution of arrays to control the distribution of loop execution. This is called *Data-Distributed Execution*, and is accomplished in the following two conceptual steps:

1. Using a simple global algorithm, divide a given array into equal-size partitions and allocate each partition to a different PE.

2. Attempt to execute the loop iteration that *writes* a particular array element (there is only one under single assignment) on the same PE that holds that element.

The second technique is that of remote data *caching*. When a PE needs to read a remote data element, it send a message to the PE holding that element. This PE extracts the entire page containing that element and returns it to the requesting PE, where it is saved in a software cache. Due to locality of reference, this reduces the need for future remote requests to elements on the same page. The need is not completely eliminated because not all elements will, in general, be present at the time the page is transmitted. Hence the same page may be copied multiple times in the future as references to previously empty elements are being made. Note, however, that due to single assignment, there are no cache coherence problems and hence a cached page will never have to be invalidated or sent back to the original owner.

The following sections present the data and program distribution mechanisms in detail.

4.1 Array Partitioning and Distribution

The ability of code execution to follow the distribution of data (step 2 above) depends greatly on how well the direction in which a matrix is accessed by the code (e.g., row-major vs. column-major) matches the direction in which the matrix is cut up and distributed. This suggests that, instead of using a simple global algorithm for distributing all arrays, the compiler might attempt to distribute a given array based on an analysis of the code that accesses the array. Unfortunately, problems with aliasing (parameter binding) make a compile-time analysis very difficult. Furthermore, the same array may be used multiple times under different access patterns. Hence, instead of attempting to determine the best distribution pattern a priori, a better

---

[2]Note that a system with a uniform memory access time would only simplify the problem since the distribution of data would be of much less concern.

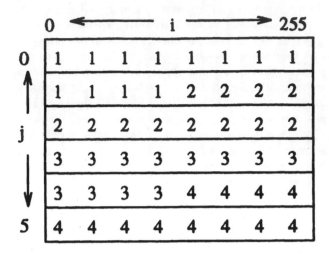

Figure 4: Partitioning of a 6 × 256 array over 4 PEs.

approach is to use the same pattern at all times, letting the programmer know which pattern is preferable. This is the approach used by many popular languages today. For example, "C" uses row-major and Fortran uses column-major storage for two-dimensional arrays. PODS uses row-major storage. The algorithm for distributing a given array is then as follows:

1. The array is cut-up row-major into pages of a fixed size, where the size is determined by the hardware architecture. For the iPSC/2, the best page size has been determined to be 32 elements or approximately 2 kilobytes. (Previous studies have shown that this is not a critical parameter [8].)

2. Pages are grouped into segments of approximately equal size, which are assigned to PEs sequentially. The number of segments corresponds to the number of PEs.

To illustrate this partitioning, consider the following example. A two-dimensional 6 × 256 array is to be partitioned and distributed over 4 PEs. There are 1536 elements in the array, resulting in 48 pages, i.e., 12 pages per PE. The diagram in Figure 4 illustrates which pages are mapped onto which PE, where each of the digits (1, 2, 3, 4) represents one page. That is, PE1 holds the first 12 pages, PE2 holds the next 12 pages, and so on.

Each PE keeps track of its area of responsibility using an array header, built at the time the array is allocated. This contains the array dimensions and, for each dimension, the starting and ending indices. As will be explained in Section 4.2.2, this information is used by the range filter at run time to determine whether a given computation is to be performed locally.

The distribution of each array is performed at run-time. It is implemented using a special *distributing allocate* operator, which functions as follows:

1. The operator requests a new array ID from the local Array Manager (see Section 5.1).

2. When the Array Manger receives the allocate request, it allocates the necessary space, builds the array header, returns the array ID to the requesting SP, and then sends a remote allocation request to all other PEs with the array ID attached. In this way all PEs receive the same ID for the same array.

3. Each of the remote PEs receiving the allocate request builds the corresponding header and allocates the appropriate space.

Note that the SP initiating the allocation is not blocked while the allocate operation is in progress. Instead, it continues executing until it encounters an instruction that actually needs the array's ID as an operand. If the Array Manager has not yet responded by filling in that operand, the SP will block, causing a context switch; otherwise it continues executing.

4.2 Distributing Execution

As mentioned earlier, computation in PODS is distributed by following the Data Distributed Execution principle, which tries to map the calculation of an array element to the same PE that owns that element. This is achieved using the distributing L operator and the Range Filter, as described next.

4.2.1 The Distributing L Operator

The original Id dataflow graphs use the L operator to enter each new loop nest. The operator's function is to create a new context, thus distinguishing all data tokens belonging to the same loop instance.

In PODS, each loop nest corresponds to a separate SP. Hence each L operator transmits data tokens to a new SP, which is instantiated when its first instruction receives its operands.

To allow process distribution, we distinguish two forms of the L operator—the regular (local) L, and the new distributing L, called L^D. Both operate as stated above, i.e., they transmit tokens to another SP. The main distinction, however, is the location of the new SP. In the case of the local L operator, the values remain within the same PE and hence a *single* instance of the new SP is created locally. In the case of L^D, the same data value is replicated and routed to *all* PEs, thus causing an instance of an identical SP to be spawned on every PE. To cause each of the SPs to operate on a different data set, Range Filters are inserted into the SPs, as is described next.

4.2.2 Range Filters

The objective of the Range Filter construct is to control which iterations of a distributed loop are to be executed by a given PE. Conceptually, the Range Filter (RF) may be viewed as a predicate inserted into the dataflow graph. Its function is to discard index tokens that are not within the PE's range of responsibility.

The dashed arrows labeled "RF" in Figure 2 indicate the location where a Range Filter would be placed. In the case of the outer index, i, the RF simply discards all values that are outside its PE's area of responsibility, which is determined from the header of the array written by this loop. The RF for the inner loop performs a similar function for the j index. Note, however, that the legal ranges for j depend on i, which must be made available to the RF. For example, the RF in PE1 (see Figure 4) produces the j range 0 : 255 when i is 0 but only 0:127 when i is 1.

The RFs as explained so far are only conceptual. There is no need to produce the entire index range in each PE and then discard all of it except for a small local subrange. A more efficient way is to replace the entire index generation subgraph by a modified version, which generates *only* the desired subranges in each PE. For an ascending loop, these modifications are shown in Figure 5. The initial index value, init-i, is replaced by the *maximum* of init-i and the starting index of the PE's area of responsibility. Similarly, the test for the ending value, n, is replaced by the *minimum* of n and the ending index of the PE's area of responsibility. (In the case of a descending loop, the minimum and maximum operators are simply interchanged.)

For the inner loop, the initial and final values for j are extended in an analogous fashion. The only difference is that these values also depend on the current i. Hence the i-values must be fed into the maximum/minimum computations, as shown in the graph. The L^D operators are placed in front of the outermost loop that contains a RF. In the above example, this would result in the SP corresponding to the i-loop to be replicated on all PEs, each operating on a different i subrange. For each iteration of this SP (i.e., for each i), a new SP corresponding to the j-loop is created and executed locally; each of these SPs operates on the j range corresponding to the given i.

4.2.3 RF Placement

In the previous discussion, we have assumed that each level of a nested loop would get its own RF. This section discusses two enhancements which have been implemented in order to reduce the number of RFs in nested loops. In the simulations described in Section 5, only one RF was used in any given loop, regardless of the level of nesting.

Consider an n-dimensional index space, where the dimensions are ordered by the levels of nesting. Say this multiple nested loop has index levels i_1, i_2, $\cdots$, i_n, with the SPs numbered correspondingly SP1, SP2, $\cdots$, SPn. It is possible to eliminate the RF at level i_1 by running only one instance of SP1. That is achieved by placing the L^D operator one level below the outer scope, i.e., into SP1 instead of its parent. Since there is only one instance of SP1, there is no need for a RF in that SP. However, all indices i_1 must now be broadcast to all PEs, where the RFs in the next-level SP2's check both i_1 and i_2 for the range boundaries. Eliminating the RF in SP1 is particularly appropriate when there is a loop-carried dependency at that level. In this case, the individual iterations within SP1 cannot proceed in parallel; at best, they will run in a staggered (doacross-like) manner. Hence distributing them over multiple PEs is not likely to improve performance.

This principle can be generalized to more than one level. That is, we can eliminate the RFs for all levels from i_1 to some level i_k by placing the L^D operator into SPk, thus causing SPk+1 to be distributed while SP1 through SPk remain centralized. Again, we use the presence of loop-carried dependencies as a guide to select the level i_k.

A different technique can be used to eliminate RFs *below* a certain level i_k. In this case, the RFs for SPk+1 through SPn are simply not included. This, however, does not come for free. The problem is that segment boundaries, in general, do not fall on array boundaries, as was illustrated for example in Figure 4. The consequence is that more than one PE may be responsible for the same index value. In the above example, both PE1 and PE2 own a portion of the row i = 1 and hence both must receive the value 1 for i. If there is no RF at the level j to discriminate between the different subranges at that level, both PEs would generate all values for j and hence the same row i = 1 would be computed twice.

One possible solutions to this problem is to assign the conflicting row to only one PE. We have implemented a simple rule to decide on the responsibility: the PE holding the *first* element of any given row is responsible for the entire row. The necessary consequence is that some number of remote writes will occur, since the index space partitioning does not exactly follow the partitioning of the array.

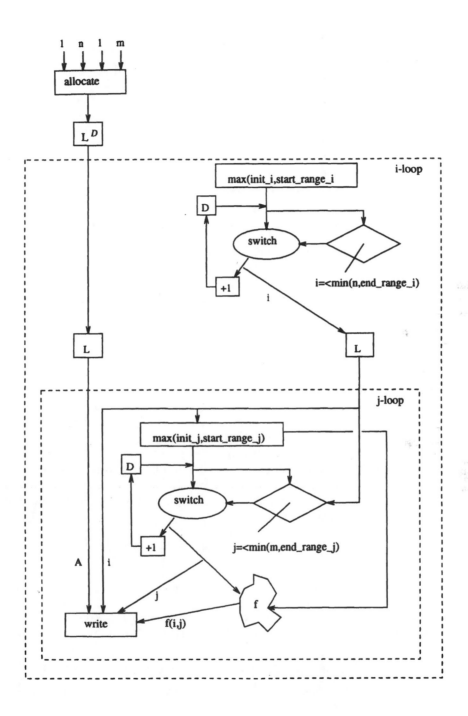

Figure 5: Modified range filters.

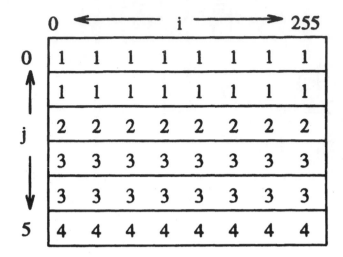

Figure 6: Index space partitioning.

To visualize this approach, consider the diagram in Figure 6. This shows the distribution of the iteration space for a nested loop operating on the array in Figure 4. In particular, PE1 is responsible for the first two rows, even though it only holds the first half of the second row in its local memory. PE2, on the other hand, computes only row 2; the values for the second half of row 1 are sent to it by PE1.

Note that once the RF below a given level i_k is eliminated, the RFs at all lower levels become superfluous. This is because the RF at level i_k partitions the index space along the i_k dimension into disjoint subranges (they are disjoint because of the first-element-ownership rule discussed above). For all levels below i_k the index ranges are then needed in their entirety (for every element of i_k).

4.2.4 For-Loop Distribution Algorithm By combining the two techniques described in Section 4.2.3, we can eliminate all but one RFs for any given nested loop of any depth. The following is the actual distribution algorithm used currently by PODS to distribute data and program execution:

1. Given an array A, partition and distribute it as described in Section 4.1.

2. Starting with the outer-most code block, repeat the following until all sets of nested loops are marked (depth-first traversal) as either distributed or local.

   a. Consider the next inner code block. If this code block does not have a loop-carried dependency (LCD), then mark it; all descendent SPs will be local.
   b. If this inner SP has an LCD, then goto step a.
   c. If this is the innermost SP, then consider the next unmarked SP (depth-first) and goto step a.

3. In each marked SP replace the predicate with a Range Filter.

4. In the parent of each marked SP change the L operators into L^D operators.

It is important to point out that the detection of LCDs in a declarative language is considerably simplified due to its side-effect-free semantics and the lack of general pointers to do aliasing. Furthermore, the only possible form of dependency is flow dependency. Despite these favorable characteristics, there are always cases where the presence or absence of LCDs cannot be determined at compile time. This, however, is not a significant limitation in our case. If the compiler fails to detect an existing dependency, the single assignment principle still guarantees a deterministic program behavior irrespective of timing issues. Hence, contrary to conventional language compilers, the detection of LCDs is only a useful heuristic and not a necessity to determine whether a loop can be distributed.

5. Simulation

5.1 The Target Architecture

The target architecture for PODS is a MIMD architecture with distributed memory. Within each PE, there are multiple functional units, each dedicated to a specific function. Even though the ultimate goal of the project is to implement PODS on an iPSC hypercube, where each PE consists of an Execution Unit (ALU), local memory, and a routing unit, we have simulated all functional units as if they were separate hardware units operating concurrently. The main reason for this was to find out which functional unit would be the most critical and thus would need the most efficient implementation. As will be discussed shortly, most of the units other than the actual execution unit were only lightly loaded most of the time and hence can easily be implemented within the existing iPSC node.

Figure 7 shows the overall organization of a PE. This architecture was simulated at the instruction level. In order to compare the results of PODS simulations to the outside world, the Simulator is set-up as if it were executing on Intel 386 microprocessors in a hypercube configuration. These are Intel 80386/80387 CPU's at 16 MHz with Direct-Connect Modules for communication. Each of the tasks and the timing assumptions of the functional units is explained below.

Matching Unit

When an input token arrives (via the Routing Unit), it is run through the Matching Unit. If the corresponding SP is already active, the token is passed to it immediately. Otherwise it is enqueued at the SP's entry in the Matching Unit. This is implemented as a hash table lookup based upon the SP ID, and the frame pointer. It takes 15 μseconds.

Note that only a small percentage of all tokens generated during a computation actually pass through the Matching Unit. Most tokens are produced and consumed internally within the same SP and hence are stored directly into the appropriate operand slots. Only tokens exchanged between different SPs go through the Matching Unit.

Memory Manager

The Memory Manager maintains two separate memory areas: a Program Memory, where the code for all SPs is kept, and an Execution Memory, containing all currently active SPs. The Memory Manager loads an SP from Program Memory into Execution Memory when the first instruction of that SP is enabled, and it releases the space when the SP terminates. To perform these tasks, it must allocate/deallocate execution memory frames from free memory, which are maintained as linked lists. We assume that each add or delete operation from the linked list takes approximately 3 memory references or 0.9 μseconds.

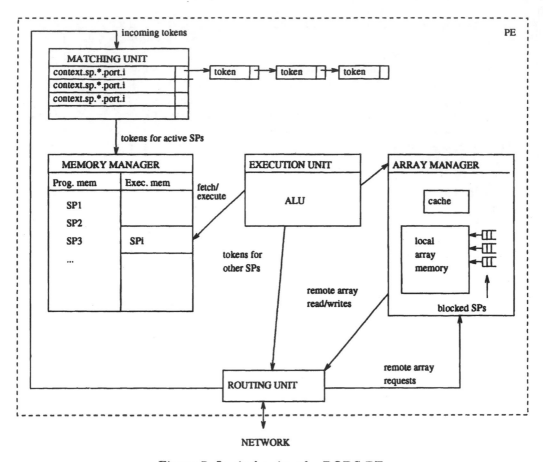

Figure 7: Logical units of a PODS PE.

Execution Unit

The Execution Unit is a conventional von Neumann ALU which executes the current SP in a control-driven manner, using a simple program counter. A context switch occurs when a disabled instruction is encountered. Most of the time, data tokens are produced and consumed within the current SP, i.e., they are written into and read from appropriate slots in Execution Memory. The only exceptions are array accesses, which are passed on to the Array Manager, and tokens destined for other SPs, which are passed on to the Routing Unit.

The timing of the Execution Unit is based upon three calculations: (1) the time of each normal (local) operation; (2) the time it takes to perform a fast context switch; and (3) the time to perform a local array read. (The time for remote accesses and for token routing is accounted for by the Array Manager and the Routing Unit, respectively.)

Routing Unit

This unit is responsible for taking a token, forming a message, and sending it over the network to the correct PE and SP. It is also responsible for receiving array read/write requests from other PEs, which it passes on to the Array Manager. Dunigan [13] has done extensive testing of the iPSC/2 and found that the communication can effectively be expressed using the following equations:

if (message_length $\leq$ 100 bytes) then 390 μsec

if (message_length > 100 bytes) then 697 + 0.4 * message_length μsec

When the Routing Unit receives a token to route, a simple table look-up is used to find the destination SPs. This is then used in a hash function to find the destination PE. Since tokens are less than 100 bytes, and they are batched together in groups of 20, the simulation uses an estimate of 19.5 μseconds for each token added to a batch.

Array Manager

The Array Manager handles all array allocations and array accesses. To allocate an array, the Array Manager on the PE where the allocate operator is initiated assigns the array a unique ID and broadcasts the request to all PEs as described in Section 4.1.

To perform a local array read, the Array Manager determines whether the element is present or absent. In the first case, the value is simply read and returned to the Execution Unit. In the second case, the request is enqueued by setting a flag in the memory location of the cell to indicate that there are requests which will need to be serviced when the cell is written. This is much like the implementation of I-structures [6], [3].

To perform a remote array read, the Array Manager first examines the cache. If the element is present, it is read just like a local element. Otherwise, a request is sent via the Routing Unit to the appropriate PE. If the value is present in the target PE then the entire page is returned and cached in the requesting PE; if it is absent, the request is queued in the target PE.

To perform a write, the Array Manager also distinguishes between a local and a remote location. (Due to single assignment, the value cannot yet exist in the cache.) If the location is local, the value is written into that location and the SPs blocked on that location are reactivated. For a remote location, the value is sent to the target PE, which writes it into the appropriate array slot and also reactivates all PEs blocked on that location.

As mentioned earlier, single assignment guarantees that there are no cache coherence problems. Hence a write operation need not be propagated to other PEs, since that element cannot exist in any PE's cache.

Network

Since the Routing Unit handles all of the transmission setup, the Network models only the physical propagation time. The iPSC/2 has a theoretical 100 Mbyte per second bandwidth. Assuming each message is approximately 100 bytes, the time for 1 hop is 1 μsecond. The network time is set to 2.5 μseconds, simulating an average of 2.5 hops.

5.2 SIMPLE

In addition to running a few generic examples, such as matrix multiply, we have concentrated on the SIMPLE benchmark [10], developed by Lawrence Livermore Laboratory. This code is a hydrodynamics and heat conduction simulation and is indicative of the large-scale scientific code which is executed on supercomputers today. It simulates the behavior of a fluid in a sphere, using a Lagrangian formulation and equations.

SIMPLE consists of three major routines: velocity_position, hydrodynamics, and conduction. All of the other procedures are either run only once or are called by one of the above. Each routine is essentially a set of deeply nested loops operating on multidimensional arrays. The most important routine is conduction; both velocity_position,

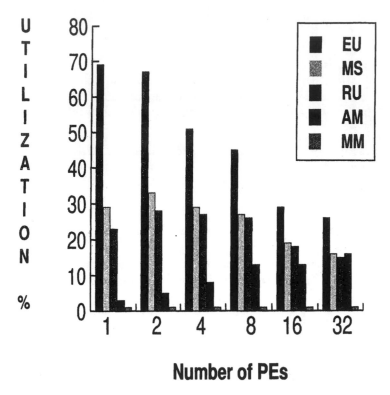

Figure 8: Average utilization of each functional unit.

and hydrodynamics are much easier to parallelize. Velocity_position has no LCDs and no function calls, and thus runs very well in parallel. Hydrodynamics has only 5 SPs and is basically one big nested loop. Conduction is the most difficult to parallelize because of: (1) the sweep phases where every element is recalculated twice, based upon its neighbors; (2) the complexity of the resulting 15 SPs plus multiple function calls; and (3) the large number of LCDs with both ascending and descending for-loops. These LCD's make iteration level parallelism a challenging task.

The following sections give the results of executing SIMPLE under the conditions described in Section 5.1. The program, written in ID Nouveau, was first translated by the MIT compiler. The resulting dataflow graphs were then transformed automatically into distributed SPs, as indicated in Figure 3. No optimization techniques, except for standard scalar expansion, were applied.

5.3 Results

5.3.1 Functional Unit Balance This addresses the question of balance among the various functional units within a PE and is measured as the fraction of the time a given facility is busy. Figure 8 summarizes the results for a 16 × 16 problem size. This shows clearly that the Execution Unit (EU) is the most heavily utilized. The most important implication of these measurements is that, while specialized hardware units would be beneficial to performance, these supporting tasks do not dominate the execution and hence the corresponding functional units can all be implemented in software, running on the same iPSC processor as the Execution Unit.

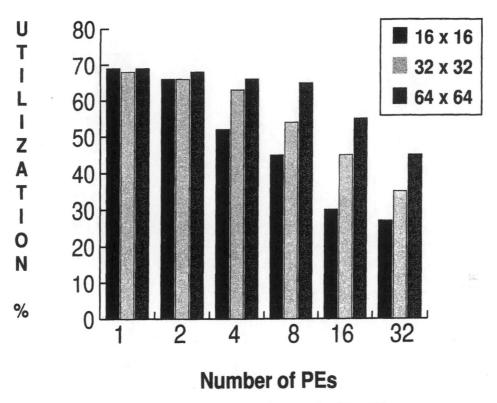

Figure 9: Execution unit utilization for SIMPLE.

5.3.2 Average Execution Unit Utilization Having established that the Execution Unit is the most critical unit in the system, we now investigate its utilization in more detail.

Figure 9 shows the results for different problem sizes. For a 64×64 SIMPLE the utilization starts out at approximately 70% for 1 PE and goes down to 50% for 32 PEs. On smaller problems (16×16) the Execution Unit utilization is lower than on large problems, especially when the number of PEs is large. It is, however, interesting to note that SIMPLE continues to speedup even when the Execution Units are 50% idle (see Figure 10).

5.3.3 Scalability This measures how much a problem speeds up as the number of PEs is increased, and is perhaps the single most important characteristic of a multiprocessor system. *Speedup* is defined to be the time of a single PE run divided by the time of the multiple PE run. Figure 10 shows the speedup for different problem sizes. The 45° curve represents ideal speedup (100%). For comparison the speedup obtained by Pingali and Rogers [23] for a 64×64 run is also plotted (P&R).

For the small 16×16 case, PODS tops out at a speedup of 8.1. For the 32×32 case, speedup tops out at 12.4, i.e., more than an order of magnitude. The 64×64 problem size is much more typical of a "real" hydrodynamics simulation and is thus a better gauge for the success of PODS in parallelizing scientific code. For the 64×64

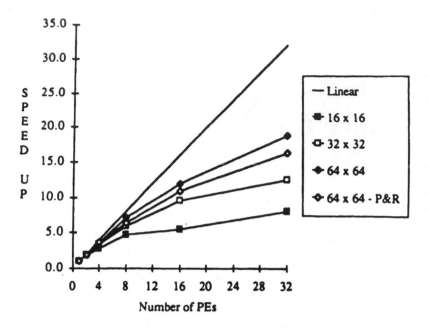

Figure 10: Speedup of SIMPLE.

case, PODS is able to spread the work efficiently across all of the PEs, achieving a speedup of 18.9 on 32 PEs.

5.3.4 Efficiency Comparison   When studying speedup, it is important to consider the efficiency of the parallel version running on a single PE as compared to the most efficient sequential version (written in a conventional language). Typically, the parallel version will be less efficient because of the additional tasks that must be performed for multiple PEs even though there is only one operating. Also, commercial systems provide a variety of additional optimizations which research systems may not offer. Only if this comparison shows that the parallel system running on one PE is within some reasonable percentage of the sequential version, can the scalability results be considered to have a valid base time.

We have compiled a sequential version of SIMPLE, written in C, using the Intel-supplied compiler, and timed its execution on the iPSC/2 host. A 32 × 32 input conduction takes 0.9 seconds on a single iPSC/2 PE. The PODS Simulator estimated that the program would run in 1.72 seconds. This is approximately twice the time of the commercial version, and shows that PODS, when running sequentially, is not grossly inefficient. This has been found to be true of all the test cases, thus giving credence to the scalability results presented in Section 5.3.3.

. **Conclusions and Comparison with Related Work**

The objective of this project is to demonstrate that declarative programming is a suitable approach to the programming of conventional coarse-grain multiprocessors. This objective is similar to that of Pingali and Rogers [23], [24]; the approaches, however are quite different. Their approach is based on compiling Id programs into

C for execution on the iPSC/2. Once the programs are compiled into native code, processes are statically scheduled onto processor nodes and execution proceeds in a completely control-driven manner. With PODS, execution is still driven by the production and availability of data. First, an SP is instantiated by the arrival of its operands; furthermore, while its progress is governed by a program counter, the availability of operands governs the state transitions between the ready, blocked, and running states. As shown in Figure 10, PODS outperformed the pure compilation approach using the SIMPLE benchmark when the problem size was sufficiently large.

While PODS is closest to the above compilation approach in its *objective*, namely to utilize a commercially available conventional multiprocessor, in its *approach* it is closest to a dataflow hybrid, a number of which have been developed in the recent past [12], [14]–[17], [22], [24], [25]. What these approaches have in common is the idea of creating sequential processes or threads out of dataflow programs. In most cases, the threads are very short, comprising at most a few dozens of instructions. To compensate for the overhead associated with the frequent context switching, special-purpose architectures (processors) are necessary. Hence the term "hybrid" refers to the fact that the underlying architecture combines the features of both von Neumann and dataflow computers.

The objective in PODS, on the other hand, is to use standard von Neumann processors interconnected into a multicomputer or multiprocessor architecture with long remote memory latencies. Consequently, the process granularity is much larger, comprising entire ranges of loop iterations and function invocations. As has been demonstrated with the SIMPLE benchmark, there are sufficient amounts of iteration-level parallelism in scientific code to adequately exploit the hardware parallelism of medium-scale multiprocessors, without having to expose parallelism at a finer level.

The basic mechanisms that work together to achieve iteration-level parallelism in PODS are the distributing allocate operator for subdividing arrays over multiple PEs, the distributing L operator for spawning multiple instances of the same process on multiple PEs, and the Range Filter, which divides the index space of a loop such that each process operates on a different subrange. We wish to point out that these mechanisms, while developed and presented in the context of Id, are not restricted to Id or to a declarative language in general. They rely primarily on the single-assignment principle to guarantee deterministic program execution, and thus could be incorporated into any language that supports this style of programming.

References

[1] W.B. Ackerman and D.J. Val, "A Value-Oriented Algorithmic Language," Technical Report MIT/LCS/TM-218, Laboratory for Computer Science, MIT, June 1979.

[2] Arvind and D.E. Culler, "Dataflow Architectures," Technical Report MIT/LCS/TM-294, Laboratory for Computer Science, MIT, February 1986.

[3] Arvind and R.S. Nikhil, "Executing a Program on the MIT Tagged-Token Dataflow Architecture," Computation Structures Group Memo 271, Laboratory for Computer Science, MIT, Cambridge, Mass., march 1987.

[4] Arvind, R.S. Nikhil, K.K. Pingali, "ID Nouveau Reference manual Part II: Operational Semantics," Technical Report, Laboratory for Computer Science, MIT, April 1987.

[5] Arvind and K. Ekanadham, "Future Scientific Programming on Parallel Machines," *J. Parallel Dist. Comp.*, Vol. 5, No. 5, 1988, pp. 460–493.

[6] Arvind, R.S. Nikhil, K.K. Pingali, "I-Structures: Data Structures for Parallel Computing," *ACM TOPLAS*, Vol. 11, No. 4, October 1989, pp. 598–632.

[7] J. Backus, "Can Programming Be Liberated from the von Neumann Style? A Functional Style and Its Algebra of Programs," *Communications of the ACM*, Vol. 21, August 1978, pp. 613–640.

[8] L. Bic, M.D. Nagel, J.M.A. Roy, "Automatic Data/Program Partitioning Using the Single Assignment Principle," *Supercomputing '89*, 1989, pp. 551–556.

[9] L. Bic, "A Process-Oriented Model for Efficient Execution of Dataflow Programs," *J. Parallel and Distributed Computing*, Vol. 8, No. 1, January 1990, pp. 42–51.

[10] W.P. Crowley, C.P. Henderson, T.E. Rudy, "The SIMPLE Code," UCID 17715, Lawrence Livermore Laboratory, February 1978.

[11] D.E. Culler, "Managing Parallelism and Resources in Scientific Dataflow Programs," Ph.D. thesis, Laboratory for Computer Science, MIT, Cambridge, Mass., 1989.

[12] D.E. Culler et al., "Fine-Grain Parallelism with Minimal Hardware Support: A Compiler-Controlled Threaded Abstract Machine," *Proc. ASPLOS-IV*, Santa Clara, Calif., April 1991.

[13] T.H. Dunigan, "Performance of a Second Generation Hypercube," Technical Report ORNL/TM-10881, Oak Ridge National Laboratory, November 1988.

[14] J.L. Gaudiot, P. Evripidou, "The USC Decoupled Multilevel Data-Flow Execution Model," in *Advanced Topics in Data-Flow Computing*, J-L. Gaudiot and L. Bic, Eds, Prentice-Hall, 1991.

[15] G.R. Gao, "A Flexible Architecture Model for Hybrid Dataflow and Control-Flow Evaluation," in *Advanced Topics in Data-Flow Computing*, J-L. Gaudiot and L. Bic, Eds, Prentice-Hall, 1991.

[16] V.G. Grafe, G.S. Davidson, J.E. Hoch, V.P. Holmes, "The Epsilon Dataflow Processor," *Proc. 16th Annual Int'l Symp. on Computer Arch.*, 1989.

[17] Robert A. Iannucci, "Toward a Dataflow/von Neumann Hybrid Architecture," *Proc. 15th Int'l Symp. on Computer Architecture*, 1988.

[18] P.J. Landin, "A Correspondence Between ALGOL 60 and Church's Lambda-Notation: Part I," *Comm. ACM*, Vol. 8, No. 2, 1965, pp. 89–101.

[19] J.R. McGraw, S. Skedzielewski, A. Allan, D. Grit, R. Oldehoeft, J.R.W. Glauert, I. Dobes, P. Hohensee, "SISAL—Streams and Iterations in a Single-Assignment Language," Language Reference Manual, TR M-146, Lawrence Livermore Lab., March 1985.

[20] R.S. Nikhil, "ID Nouveau Reference Manual Part I: Syntax," MIT Technical Report, Laboratory for Computer Science, MIT, April 1987.

[21] R.S. Nikhil, Computation Structures Group Memo 284, ID Reference Manual, ver. 88.1, Laboratory for Computer Science, MIT, Cambridge, Mass., August 1988.

[22] R.S. Nikhil and Arvind, "Can Dataflow Subsume von Neumann Computing?," *16th Int'l Computer Architecture Conference*, Jerusalem, 1989, pp. 262–272.

[23] K. Pingali and A. Rogers, "Compiler Parallelization of SIMPLE for a Distributed Memory Machine," TR 90-1084, Department of Computer Science, Cornell University, January 1990.

[24] A. Rogers and K. Pingali, "Compiling Programs for Distributed Memory Architectures," *4th Hypercube Concurrent Computers and Applications Conference*, 1989, pp. 529–542.

[25] S. Sakai, Y. Yamaguchi, K. Hiraki, Y. Kodama, T. Tuba, "An Architecture of a Dataflow Chip Processor," *Proc. 16th Annual Int'l Symp. on Computer Arch.*, Jerusalem, June 1989.

Empirical Study of a Dataflow Language on the CM-5

David E. Culler, Seth Copen Goldstein, Klaus Erik Schauser,
and Thorsten von Eicken
Computer Science Division
Department of Electrical Engineering and Computer Sciences
College of Engineering
University of California, Berkeley

This paper presents empirical data on the behavior of large dataflow programs on a distributed memory multiprocessor. The programs, written in the dataflow language Id90, are compiled via a Threaded Abstract Machine (TAM) for the CM-5. TAM refines dataflow execution models by addressing critical constraints that modern parallel architectures place on the compilation of general-purpose parallel programming languages. It exposes synchronization, scheduling, and network access so that the compiler can optimize against the cost of these operations.

The data presented in this paper evaluate the TAM approach in compiling dataflow languages on stock hardware. We present data on the instruction mix, speedup, scheduling behavior, and locality of large Id90 programs. It is shown that the TAM scheduling hierarchy is able to tolerate long communication latencies, especially when some degree of I-structure locality is present. We investigate how frame allocation strategies, k-bounded loops, and I-structure caching and distribution together affect the overall efficiency. Finally, we document some scheduling anomalies.

1. Introduction

The goals of dataflow models of computation are to exploit irregular or unstructured parallelism arising in general purpose programs and to enable development of high-level parallel languages in which the programmer need not manage every detail of the mapping of program and data onto the machine. It has been demonstrated that direct execution of dataflow graphs is not essential to attain these goals, as dataflow graphs are equivalent to threaded instruction sets with very weak addressing modes [9], [18]. Dataflow graphs are, however, very useful in the compilation process [4], [22], [23], [25], [28]. At the machine level, the essential aspect of dataflow is efficient dynamic scheduling. Dynamic scheduling provides tolerance to communication latency, since the processor picks up other useful work rather than waiting for each response. It avoids synchronization waits in the same manner, and further reduces the impact of transient load imbalance, since a processor remains busy as long as *any* local work is available. Dynamic scheduling supports powerful parallel languages with synchronizing data access [3] or non-strict order of evaluation [7], [27]. Dataflow processors operate greedily, grabbing hold of any available useful work, rather than sitting idle. The general belief in the dataflow research community is that if such an eager processor can be built with a reasonable cost/performance ratio, the remaining systems

---

This paper was presented at the ISCA '92 Dataflow Workshop. The results are based on the 1992 version of our compiler and runtime system.

issues involved in actually mapping the computation and data to the machine could be solved.

Even though the research area is several years old, today we have almost no solid empirical data to substantiate this belief. There are plenty of novel ideas for implementing dynamic scheduling, but little evidence that it actually simplifies the task of managing resources or scheduling computation, or that it translates into performance on a large scale. Simulations of paper designs and small prototypes provide only limited data, since they cannot model the behavior of large programs in-the-large. The Manchester dataflow machine is correctly considered a single processor, as the multiple bit-slice-ALUs are a technological artifact. Monsoon [17] is only available in very small configurations. At the time the machine was designed, the characteristics of the per-processor storage hierarchy were not understood, so the issue was intentionally avoided by using fast static RAM for all the memory in the processor. The network operates at five times the processor clock rate, so there is little communication latency. Sigma-1 and EM-4 are available in large configurations, but the only programs that have been run are small, regular, and hand tuned. Static dataflow machines have been applied primarily to regular, structured problems [10], [11], [24]. Dataflow languages, including SISAL and a restricted form of Id, have been implemented on conventional architectures, by exploiting the regular structure in traditional Fortran-like applications [5], [19].

Our work attempts to fill some of this empirical vacuum by implementing Id90 on large parallel machines in a manner that retains the efficient dynamic scheduling of dataflow models. The approach we have taken is to define a threaded abstract machine (TAM) that remedies some basic shortcomings in previous dataflow models and is closer to conventional architectures. TAM exposes synchronization, scheduling, and network access so that the compiler can optimize against the cost of these operations. The Id90 compiler has been substantially rewritten to target TL0, the TAM assembly language, rather than a dataflow instruction set. A key step in the compilation process is partitioning the dataflow program graph into threads [22], [28]. The other new aspects of the compilation process involve management of registers and local storage in the context of dynamic scheduling and code generation for threads. A separate compilation step translates the TL0 code to native machine code for a variety of platforms, including large network-based multiprocessors (Thinking Machines CM-5 and the nCUBE/2), small shared-memory multiprocessors (Sequent Balance and Motorola Delta), and conventional workstations. The TL0-to-machine step focuses on specifics of the target instruction set and processor/network interface.[1] One virtue of this two-step compilation approach is that TL0 execution statistics can be collected efficiently by compiling the data collection directly into the machine code.

In this paper we provide preliminary empirical data on the behavior of large Id90 programs compiled via TAM for the CM-5. This is the first commercial machine to provide a sufficiently accessible and efficient processor/network interface to allow a meaningful study of this kind. Our active message layer on the machine [29] imposes a per-message overhead that is an order of magnitude less than that of commercial message passing systems and approaches current hardware implementations of shared-memory and message-driven models. Nevertheless, there is considerable improvement possible through hardware support, and we intend this paper to provide grist for the design of the next generation of machines supporting dataflow languages, e.g., *T and EM-5.

---

[1] A generic back-end translates up to C and uses the local C compiler as an assembler.

The paper is organized as follows. Section 2 explains the TAM model and briefly outlines how Id90 programs are compiled to TAM and then to the CM-5. Section 3 provides crude program performance data, such as speedup and program behavior, including TL0-level instruction mixes, scheduling behavior, and locality. Section 4 discusses the effects of resource management policies including the effects of a variety of frame allocation policies, efforts to reduce contention, including I-structure spreading and caching, and the impact of k-bounded loops. Section 5 documents some disturbing scheduling anomalies.

Briefly, the main observations of the study are as follows. It is possible to implement a dataflow language on stock hardware and provide fast dynamic scheduling, although current processor network interfaces are inadequate. The TAM scheduling hierarchy appears to work even under significant latency, especially when some degree of I-structure locality is obtained. Simple frame allocation policies appear to do a reasonable job of balancing the computational load while preserving a significant degree of locality. However, I-structure load can be extremely unbalanced, resulting in significant contention. Dynamic scheduling of work on a per-processor basis does little to mediate the effects of persistent load imbalance or contention. This must be addressed in the way work and data are assigned to processors. Replication of I-structure data can significantly reduce contention, at a cost. Finally, in a dataflow implementation a host of factors interact in complex ways: scheduling, assignment of work, allocation of I-structures, and I-structure reference patterns. The absence of a high-level program execution strategy makes these interactions difficult to understand or control.

2. Threaded Abstract Machine

In this section, we describe TAM [8], a threaded abstract machine that serves as an intermediate step in compiling the dataflow language Id90 for conventional parallel (and sequential) architectures. Historically, Id90 was developed in close connection with dynamic dataflow architectures, especially the MIT Tagged Token Dataflow Architecture. It demands the dynamic scheduling and tagged heap storage that these designs offer. However, the extent to which these capabilities need to be supported directly in hardware remains an open question. The evolution of the MIT dataflow architectures has been driven primarily by advancement in compiler technology; each step in understanding how to compile the language resulted in a simplification of the architecture. TAM represents an effort to simplify the architecture even further, relying heavily on sophisticated compilation techniques. Traub's "compilation as partitioning" framework [26] and Iannucci's thread generation for the hybrid architecture [14] demonstrated that it was possible to reduce the amount of dynamic scheduling required. TAM builds directly on this work, but it addresses three other issues as well. First, there is no hardware management of storage resources. More precisely, there is no implicit storage allocation in the machine model.[2] Storage is explicitly allocated in large chunks, namely activation frames and heap data structures, and the compiler is responsible for storage management. Second, the low-level scheduling of computation is focused to enhance the locality of reference within each processor, and allows efficient dynamic scheduling on conventional processors. Third, the high level scheduling of computation is exposed so that a global strategy can be "compiled in"

---

[2]Our current implementation of deferred reads backs off from this requirement slightly for performance reasons, but this deviation is not fundamental.

the program. (Our TAM implementation provides this level of control to the Id90 compiler, but we have not fully exercised it.) These goals are quite compatible and can be addressed within a simple run-time program structure, described below.

2.1 Activation Frames

The key to understanding TAM and its relationship to dataflow models is to examine the requirements of a function invocation. In a conventional sequential language, a function is invoked by allocating storage for local variables on the stack (the activation frame), pushing arguments onto the stack, and transferring control to the entry point of the function. The key difference in a parallel language is that the caller does not suspend on every invocation, so it may invoke many other functions to run concurrently. Thus, the dynamic call structure at any point in time forms a tree, rather than a stack, which grows and shrinks over time. Dynamic dataflow architectures implicitly allocate storage for the invocation tree, since the matching store allocates storage on a token-by-token basis. However, if we examine the language implementations on the TTDA [1] or Manchester machine [13] more carefully, we see that the function invocation involves allocating a "context" or portion of the tag space. In effect, this allocates an entire region of addresses to the function invocation; the matching store is simply a means of representing a sparsely populated address space. Of course, the other novelty in the dataflow approach is that each argument transfers control to an entry point of the function. Thus, we may think of each argument as initiating a thread of control within the function invocation. Threads are implicitly synchronized and forked in the dataflow graph representation.

The Explicit Token Store [9] model returns to the conventional idea of allocating storage for local variables with each invocation. It makes the further assumption that the entire invocation will execute on the processor to which the activation frame belongs. Monsoon [17] associates a presence-bit with each frame slot to support the dataflow view which associates a thread of control with every element of local data. Hybrid [14] adopted a complementary view, providing explicit threads of control which suspend upon access to a frame slot that is marked not-present. P-Risc [16] observed that presence-bits can be kept in the frame like local data, rather than as special tags, and that matching could be simulated by toggling the tag bit atomically and suspending on the result.

What none of these models provide is a way of referring to the set threads associated with a particular function invocation. They all rely on a scheduling queue that is outside the run-time program structure; this is the token queue in dataflow machines and Monsoon. As a result, there is no way of articulating what executes next after a thread stops or suspends. Hence, the locus of computation on each processor hops around arbitrarily from thread to thread. This prevents effective use of a modern processor storage hierarchy, including a large processor register set, sRAM cache, and dRAM main store.[3] Moreover, this queue may grow arbitrarily large (as can the activation tree), since it must represent all the parallel threads in the program. The novel contribution in TAM is to maintain the scheduling queue within the collection of activation frames, as suggested by Figure 1. A portion of each frame is used to hold a stack of instructions pointers, called the *continuation vector* (CV), representing the enabled threads for the corresponding function invocation. The compiler can determine the maximum size of this region in a manner much like register allocation.

---

[3]This was precisely why the initial design of Monsoon relied on a large static RAM, rather than more cost-effective cache structure.

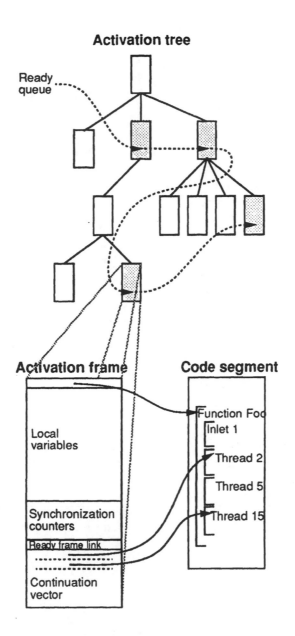

Figure 1: TAM activation tree and embedded scheduling queue. For each function call, an activation frame is allocated. Each frame, in addition to holding all local variables, contains counters used to synchronize threads and inlets, and provides space for the *continuation vector*—the addresses of all currently enabled threads of the activation. On each processor, all frames holding enabled threads are linked into a ready queue. Maintaining the scheduling queue within the activation keeps costs low: enabling a thread simply consists of pushing its instruction address into the continuation vector and sometimes linking the frame into the ready queue. Scheduling the next thread within the same activation is simply a pop-jump.

The scheduling queue on each processor is formed by simply linking together frames containing enabled threads.[4] This simple scheme addresses our goals, as follows:

- The scheduling queue is no longer a specialized resource. There is a single resource that can grow arbitrarily, the activation tree, and it may occupy all of memory, just like the stack in a conventional language.[5] It is allocated only upon function invocation.

- The TAM representation dictates a natural scheduling hierarchy which enhances the locality of reference within the processor. When a frame is scheduled, threads are executed from that frame until none remain in the CV. We call this dynamic "chunk" of work a *quantum*. Focusing on the work for a frame should improve the effectiveness of the processor cache. More importantly, the processor registers are valid across threads within a quantum. We expect that in practice quanta will include several points of potential suspension, since often multiple arguments to a function arrive close together in time or multiple remote fetches will complete together.

- Dynamic scheduling among threads within the same function is extremely inexpensive. To fork a new thread, the address of the thread is simply pushed onto the CV. When a thread stops, the next thread is popped off the CV. Coordination among threads is implemented by using frame slots as thread entry counts. The fork to a synchronizing thread involves decrementing a counter. The thread is only enabled when the counter reaches zero. These counters are explicitly maintained by the program.

- The global scheduling structure is simply a data structure built out of frames, i.e., a list or priority queue. The links in this structure are accessible to the executing program, much like local variables. By generating code to access the frame queue, the compiler can build global scheduling policies into the program. At the very least, the frame swap itself is handled explicitly as part of code generation. The thread at the bottom of the CV performs the swap to the enter thread of the next ready frame. This means that the compiler may speculate that threads will execute in the same quantum and carry values in registers between threads.

2.2 Program Representation

An Id90 program is a collection of *code-blocks*, corresponding roughly to user defined functions in the Id90 program. Each code-block is a collection of threads and inlets. TAM threads are straight-line code, with synchronization occurring only at thread entry. Thus, the basic control operation is to fork a thread. The fork may be conditional or unconditional and the thread may be synchronizing (i.e., require multiple forks) or not. Each TAM processor contains a frame-pointer register that refers to the currently active frame on the processor and an instruction-pointer register that refers to the current instruction of the current thread of the code-block associated with the current frame. In addition, there is a set of general purpose registers. Distinguishing registers from frame slots allows the compiler to exercise greater control over the

---

[4] Observe that the instruction pointer in the frame is a full continuation, since the frame pointer portion is determined upon traversing the link to the frame.

[5] As with conventional languages, there is also a heap for arrays and non-local data.

local processor storage hierarchy, which is central to our research. Registers are not implicitly saved or invalidated when a thread switch or frame swap occurs; they are explicitly managed by the compiler. TL0 instructions are generally of three-address form, with operands drawn from frame slots, processor registers, or immediates.

Long latency operations, such as I-Fetch or Send, implicitly fork a thread when the request completes. This allows the processor to continue with useful work while the remote access is outstanding. The destination of an I-fetch operation is an *inlet*. An inlet is a compiler-generated instruction sequence, much like a thread, that receives data from the network interface and stores it into the frame for the invocation that issued the I-fetch. It will also post a thread into that frame if the entry count is satisfied. If the frame is idle when the post occurs, it is placed on the frame queue. If it is ready, i.e., already on the queue, it simply accumulates another thread in the CV. If the frame is currently running, the inlet may take some special action to put the data directly in registers, or it may simply post the thread. The key difference between inlets and threads is that inlets preempt threads in response to message arrival. Inlets must service the network quickly and terminate. They are atomic with respect to each other. To minimize the interaction between the two priority levels, the CV is split into two parts, a remote continuation vector (RCV) in the frame and a local continuation vector (LCV) that is part of the processor.[6] Forks push thread pointers onto the LCV, whereas posts in inlets push thread pointers onto the RCV. Similarly, the destination of a SEND instruction is an inlet in another frame; this is the child frame for argument passing and the parent frame for return values. Access to I-structure elements is performed by a standard inlet on the processor that is local to the accessed element. It reads the element and its presence bits, performs the state transition, and replies to the program inlet.

2.3 Translating Id90 to TAM

In this section, we briefly address partitioning Id90 programs into TAM threads. Both synchronizing data structures and non-strict evaluation enhance parallelism by allowing producers and consumers to overlap. It is possible to construct cases where this makes a tremendous difference in the available parallelism. Consider, for example, a tree traversal using accumulation lists. Under non-strict evaluation the two subtrees of a node can be processed in parallel, even though the result of processing one subtree will be used in processing the other [15]. Parallelism aside, if non-strict evaluation is provided to the programmer as part of the language semantics, the expressive power of the language is enhanced. For example, it is possible to define circular data structures in a non-strict functional language. Basically, it is permissible to use portions of the result of a function call as arguments to the call, relying on non-strictness to make the result available before all arguments are provided. For example, the Id90 binding a = (1,a) defines a to be a pair with itself as its second element. Recursive data structures arise quite reasonably in practice [2]. The expressive power of non-strictness and synchronizing data access makes compiling into threads tricky, because static scheduling decisions can potentially introduce deadlock. While compiling a function it may be impossible to determine a static ordering of the operations, even in the absence of conditionals. The best we can do is to identify collections of instructions (threads) that can be statically ordered and schedule these threads dynamically.

---

[6]Alternatively, inlets may execute on a separate processor that is closely coupled to the thread processor. Still it is valuable to minimize the interactions between the two.

In general, any input to a function—arguments, heap access responses, and results returned from subordinate calls—can potentially depend in some manner upon any output of the function. For example, any operation that has an effect outside the function, including returning results, storing to heap locations, and passing arguments to subordinate calls, can affect the inputs to the function. Somewhere outside the function body, some output may be used in deriving an input to the function. These dependencies may go through any number of levels of indirection and cannot always be identified at compile time. Thus, the task of the compiler in partitioning the dataflow graph into threads is to prove where such external dependencies cannot exist. The basic analysis techniques for partitioning are described in [8], [22], [23]. In addition [28] shows how this analysis can be carried out globally.

2.4 Translation from TAM

The second compilation step translates the TAM program to an executable for a specific parallel machine and addresses specifics of the target, such as the particular network interface, addressing modes, etc. In particular, TAM defines a set of primitive data types but does not specify the size of these types. For example, global addresses may be 64 bits on a large parallel machine and only 32 bits on a workstation. TAM registers are partitioned by type and must be mapped to physical registers or spill areas by the final translator. A generic TL0 translator maps the TL0 instructions into C and compiles the resulting C code for the machine [12]. Data collection code can be inserted while translating the TL0 code to facilitate experimentation at the TL0 level. For dynamically scheduled programs any attempt to record program behavior can possibly modify the behavior. We attempt to minimize the distortion by compiling limited data collection in-line. All the data presented in this paper was collected in this manner.

3. Program Measurements

In this section we report on the performance and characteristics observed for Id programs on a CM-5 multiprocessor. This motivates a more detailed analysis of various aspects of program behavior in later sections. The machine consists of 64 Sparc processors running at 33MHz, each with a 8 MByte memory, a 64 KByte cache, and a floating-point co-processor. The processors are connected as an incomplete fat-tree of degree four, so the maximum distance between processors is 6 hops and the average distance is 5.4 hops. Communication is supported by active messages [29] driving a custom network interface via the memory bus. Sending or receiving a message takes approximately 50 cycles.

We focus on two application benchmark programs written in Id90. These were developed by other researchers in the context of other platforms, especially the GITA dataflow graph interpreter and the Monsoon machine. We have not modified the source programs to tune for our environment, although such tuning is certainly possible (and desirable). We focus on two application kernels: Gamteb and Simple.

Gamteb is a Monte Carlo simulation of neutron transport. The basic structure consists of a loop over a collection of initial particles, where each iteration traces a particle through the geometry from a random initial state. The work associated with a particle is unpredictable, since particles may be absorbed or scattered due to collisions with various materials, or may split into multiple particles. Splitting is handled by recursive calls to the trace particle routine. Particles are independent, but statistics from each of the particle traces are combined into a global result, including a set

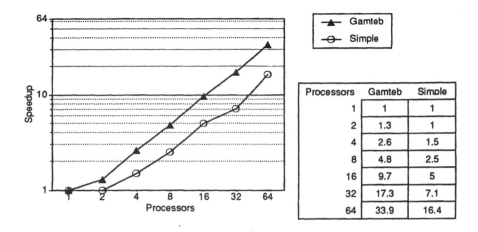

Figure 2: Speedup for Gamteb and Simple from 1 to 64 processors on the CM-5.

of histograms represented as M-structures. In addition, event counts represented as tuples are combined as the recursion unwinds. The geometry in Gamteb is small and could be replicated on each node, however, we do not exploit this possibility since production codes of this ilk, such as MCNP, require large geometries, too big to fit on a node. The problem size for Gamteb is specified by the number of initial particles.

Simple is a hydrodynamics and heat conduction simulation. The basic structure is a loop that integrates the solution to several partial differential equations forward in time over a collection of roughly 25 large rectangular grids. Each iteration consists of several distinct phases that address various aspects of the hydrodynamics and heat conduction. The irregularity arises partly from the relationship between the phases, which traverse the data structures in different ways. In addition, table look-ups are performed inside of the grid-point calculation and boundaries are handled specially. The problem size is specified by the size of the (square) grid in one dimension.

3.1 Speedup

Figure 2 shows the speedup obtained on the CM-5 for the two applications benchmarks (the numeric data is displayed in the table to the right). Before commenting on the data, we must state the fairly large set of conditions under which it is collected, including problem scaling, parallelism scaling (k-bounds), frame allocation policy, and I-structure management policy. In the following sections we will study these in more detail. For Gamteb, the problem size is scaled to maintain a constant number of initial particles per processor ($N = 128 * P$). The parallelism is scaled by adjusting the k-bound on the outer-most loop in proportion to the number of processors ($k = 32 * P$). The frame allocation policy wraps k-bounded loop frames around the processors (i.e., processor p allocates the next frame on processor $(p + 1)$ mod P) and function call frames are allocated in a local neighborhood (policy S33N3, described below). I-structures of size 32 or more are allocated horizontally across processors (interleaved), while smaller ones are allocated on the processor that requests the allocation. No caching is employed. For Simple the problem size is fixed ($N = 128$ for one timestep) and the parallelism is scaled by adjusting the k-bound for the outer loop of several loop nests that iterate the grids ($k = 2 * P$). The frame allocation policy is essentially the same as in Gamteb, except the function call frame policy is a little more "selfish"

	Gamteb 8096	*Simple 128*
Avg. TL0 Insts. per Thread	4.5	6.4
% Non-synchronizing Threads	39.1	45.3
Average entry for synchronizing Thread	2.6	3.8
Avg. TL0 Insts. per Inlet	5.1	3.4
Inlets per Threads	0.4	1.1
Threads per Quanta	12.4	12.6
CV Size when Scheduled	1.7	1.8
Threads forked during Quantum	9.6	7.6
Threads posted during Quantum	1.1	3.2
Quanta per Invocation	3.3	3.0

Table 1: Dynamic scheduling characteristics under TAM
for two programs on a 64-processor CM-5

(S50N3). The I-structure allocation policy only differs from Gamteb in that caching is employed.

In both applications we observe a linear speedup beyond a small number of processors. At 64 processors the performance is comparable to that on a 16-node Monsoon configuration (8 processor nodes and 8 I-structure nodes). Going from one processor to two we see the effect of message handling overhead. Roughly half the processor is lost to message handling overhead in Gamteb and three-quarters in Simple. The difference is attributable to the remote reference rates in the two programs, as discussed below.

3.2 TL0 Behavior

We now consider the effectiveness of the TAM approach, focusing on the behavior of our two applications on 64 processors. The top half of Table 1 gives the characteristics of threads, while the bottom half gives dynamic scheduling characteristics. The first row of Table 1 shows the average thread length. This is roughly the length of a typical basic block, which is not surprising given that fork is the only form of control transfer in TL0.[7] A looser definition of thread would allow control transfer within a thread and treat synchronization events as defining the thread boundaries. The second row shows the fraction of non-synchronizing threads. This would seem to indicate that threads are much larger when branching is permitted. However, more than half of the non-synchronizing threads are posted from inlets, and these would remain distinct threads even under the looser definition.

The third row shows the average entry count for synchronizing threads. Under traditional dataflow execution mechanisms the entry count would be two. Grouping together the nodes that depend on a single matching event to form a thread, as on Monsoon or EM-4 [21], does not change the entry count. Our partitioning algorithm is more aggressive and will group larger collections of nodes together to form a thread with a higher entry count. However, it will also eliminate redundant forks, thereby reducing the entry count. The combination of entry count and thread length influences the cost of each scheduling event and the amount of work per event.

---

[7]Recall, TL0 allows frame relative addressing and single instruction network access. On current RISC architectures the average TL0 instruction expands into multiple instructions. A detailed cost analysis on the CM-5 shows the average TL0 instruction to require a little more than ten cycles on a Sparc. The SEND, receive, and post contribute most to the cycle count.

Instruction Class	Gamteb 8092	Simple 128
Control	34.1%	21.9%
Stop	19.3%	14.4%
Swap	0.5%	0.4%
Move	3.7%	4.5%
Init	13.5%	8.6%
Int Arith	3.9%	16.3%
Float Arith	9.2%	13.5%
Split-Phase	12.9%	20.0%

Table 2: Dynamic instruction mix for major classes of instructions.

The fourth and fifth rows indicate the division of work between message handling and thread processing. A simple inlet contains three instructions: receive, post, and stop. However, inlets also initialize thread entry counts, accounting for the remaining portion of the instructions per inlet.

The bottom half of Table 1 provides data on the effectiveness of the two-level scheduling hierarchy under long remote access latency and parallel execution. For these programs, on average more than twelve threads are executed per quantum. Thus, if register allocation is performed across threads, there are roughly seventy instructions to work with, rather than five to ten. The cost of posting and swapping the frame is amortized over this amount of work, as well. The origin of the threads constituting a quantum is given in the next three rows of the table. We see that when a frame becomes active, it has usually accumulated multiple threads. Each thread requires multiple posts, so a sizable amount of data has accumulated in the frame. As a result, several potential synchronization events are passed without suspension and many threads are forked while the frame is running. Typically, more than one message response arrives during the quantum in which it was issued, triggering further activity. Note that I-fetches that are serviced locally will complete during the issuing quantum. Viewed another way, a typical frame experiences about three periods of activity (last row) during its lifetime. This is comparable in a sequential to a function language that makes two calls.

3.3 Instruction Mix

The following provides a breakdown of TAM threads based on the two benchmarks. Table 2 gives the dynamic instruction frequency for major classes of instructions. The control class includes all forms of fork: conditional, unconditional, synchronizing, and non-synchronizing. Split-phase operations include accesses to the global heap, denoted by I-fetches and I-stores, and sends of argument and result values.

The TL0 translator specializes the control transfer to use the simplest form on the target machine. A detailed breakdown of the control instructions and their frequencies is given in Table 3. Where possible the translator will pull a non-synchronizing fork to the end of the thread and replace it by a simple fall-through, an unconditional jump, or conditional branch. Other non-synchronizing forks involve a push onto the LCV. If there are only synchronizing forks in a thread, the last one is specialized to a sequence of instructions that decrement the counter and branch to the target thread. Other synchronizing forks remain a test and push. The conditional fork instruction, switch, forks one of two threads based on a Boolean input. Either target

Fork Type	Gamteb 8092	Simple 128
Fall-through	3.9%	1.2%
Jump	3.1%	2.5%
Branch	8.6%	2.7%
Push	0.2%	0.0%
Sync jump	30.3%	38.7%
Sync branch	20.0%	4.2%
Sync push	30.1%	47.9%
Other	3.9%	2.7%

Table 3: Break-down of control transfer operations in threads. The TL0-to-machine translator specializes forks and conditional forks, where possible, into simple jumps and branches. A decrement and test is required if the target thread is synchronizing.

Split-Phase Type	Gamteb 8092	Simple 128
I-Fetch	33.3	66.3
Local	26.4	2.1
Remote	73.6	99.9
I-Store	20.1	9.1
Local	99.1	15.2
Remote	0.9	84.8
Send	33.7	19.1
Other	12.9	5.5

Table 4: Breakdown of split-phase operations into instruction types and locality. In Gamteb local allocation of small structures allows most of the stores and many of the fetches to be serviced without network access. Localization in Simple is much less successful, since the data structures are large and no correlation is established between program and data mapping.

thread may be synchronizing. The row labeled "other" reflects switch operations that are synchronizing on one side and not on the other. The most common control transfers are synchronizing, unconditional forks. Roughly half the pushes are simplified in favor of jumps or branches.

Table 4 shows the breakdown of split-phase operations for the two programs. For heap accesses, fetch and store operations are divided further to show the fraction of accesses to an element that is local to the processor issuing the access. The I-structure allocation policy recognizes two I-structure mappings. I-structures that are smaller than some threshold are allocated within a single processor, while those larger than the threshold are interleaved across processors. Small structures are allocated on the processor that requests the allocation. We see that in Gamteb almost all the I-stores are local under this policy, as are one quarter of the fetches. Gamteb allocates many small tuples dynamically as particles are traced through the geometry. Under this policy (and frame allocation policy s33n3, described below) they are created and filled in one place, but only a quarter of the I-fetches are local. Simple, on the other hand, operates mostly on large grids interleaved over the machine. No correspondence is established between the data structures and the computations that access them.

Below we discuss I-structure caching, which localizes 38% of the otherwise remote accesses in Gamteb and 79% in Simple. The other important statistic is that 64% of the I-fetches in Gamteb are deferred, as are 23% of the I-fetches in Simple.

4. Resource Management Policies

In this section we report the effect of different resource management policies on the efficiency and scalability of the Id programs. We begin by parameterizing the space of frame allocation policies. We find that the frame allocation policies, which dictate how work is distributed among the processors, interact greatly with the data distribution on the processors. To reduce this dependency we introduce I-structure caching which improves the overall utilization of the processors. Finally, we discuss the use of k-bounded loops to increase the available parallelism and thus the scalability of the programs.

4.1 Frame Allocation Policies

The primary vehicle for storage management and distribution of work in a TAM-based implementation of Id90 is the allocation of activation frames. In this section, we examine a range of frame allocation policies and report on their performance and characteristics. We assume that frames for the iterations of k-bounded loops are wrapped around the machine. This section concerns itself with the allocation of frames for function calls. For example, each frame could be randomly allocated on any processor in the machine or the frame could always be allocated locally, i.e., on the processor that performs the call. To examine the space of policies between these two extremes, we consider the policies as representing points in a two dimensional space. One axis is the probability that a frame will be allocated locally. We call this the *selfishness* of the policy. The other axis is the size of the neighborhood into which a frame is allocated. We use the notation sXXnYY to denote a policy, where XX is the percent of selfishness and YY is the size of neighborhood. Thus, the local policy is s100n1 and the completely random policy on 64 processors is s03n64. (In other words, there is a 3% chance the frame will be allocated on a single processor and the other 97% of the time the frame will be allocated on one of the other 63 processors.) The policy represented by s50n3 alternates as "one for me, one to the left, one for me, one to the right." Random allocation of a neighborhood of eight processors containing the calling processor is s12n8.

Figure 3 shows the execution time for Gamteb with and without statistics for several policies on 64 processors. We see that the simple alternating policies over a small neighborhood perform better than either the extreme local or extreme random policies.

To better understand the performance difference of these policies, Figure 4 shows how the time is spent on each of the processors using the local (s100n1), alternating (s33n3), and random (s03n64) policies. To account for processor time, we consider the number of threads it executes, the number of I-fetches or I-stores it services, and the number of idle events it experiences. We see that the computational load (number of threads) is very even with the random policy but uneven with the local policy. This phenomenon is due to the variations in the amount of computation required per source particle. As a result, the local policy experiences a large number of idle events. On the other hand, when combined with an I-structure policy that allocates small objects locally, the local frame policy results in a much lower fraction of remote message sends. The simple alternating policy achieves reasonably good load balance while still achieving a significant amount of localization. Examining the distribution

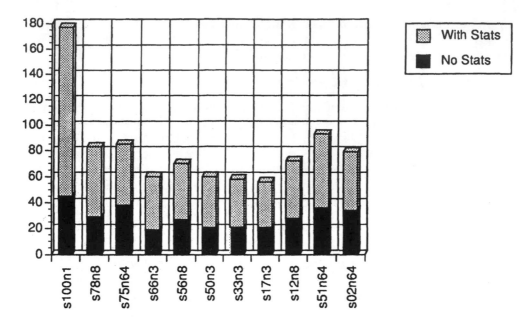

Figure 3: Execution time for Gamteb using a range of policies.

of I-structures serviced we see that one processor is serving an inordinate number of accesses. This processor limits the rate of the entire system.

In Gamteb there are many small structures representing particles, a few M-structure arrays of thirty-five elements that represent the energy bins, and some constant structures. Reducing the threshold for the size of interleaved structures causes the energy bins and some of the constant structures to be spread across the machine. This results in a more uniform I-structure service load (see Figure 5), although there is still significant imbalance. Figure 5 shows the profiles for the three basic policies with I-structures and M-structures larger than 32 spread across the machine. There is little change in the remote message rate. All of the policies are improved, but the local policies show the largest improvement. The number of idle events is roughly halved.

4.2 I-Structure Caching

To further smooth the load and reduce the number of remote messages, we have implemented I-structure caching. Each processor maintains an I-structure cache in software. The cache is a table organized very much like a normal I-structure. The global address is hashed to obtain an index into a table of 32K elements. The address is checked against the address in the table. On a hit, the data entry in the table is accessed. On a miss, the request is placed in the table entry and the entry is marked deferred. A request is sent to the actual I-structure, but the return address specifies the table entry rather than a frame. This request may be deferred at the I-structure until the I-store completes. Eventually, the cache table entry will be updated and the original request serviced. Whenever an additional request for the same element occurs while the global access is outstanding, it is deferred locally. If a request with a different key hashes into a table entry that is deferred, the request is serviced as a standard I-fetch, bypassing the cache. To avoid coherence issues, only I-structures are

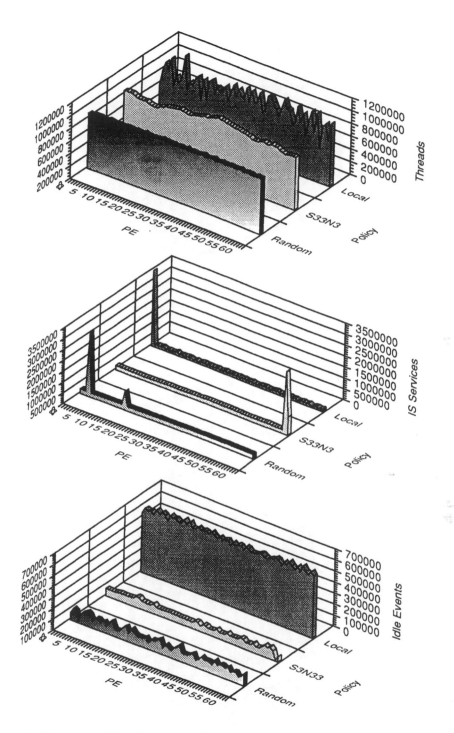

Figure 4: Thread profile, idle events, I-structure service, and fraction of remote messages for three frame allocation policies on Gamteb.

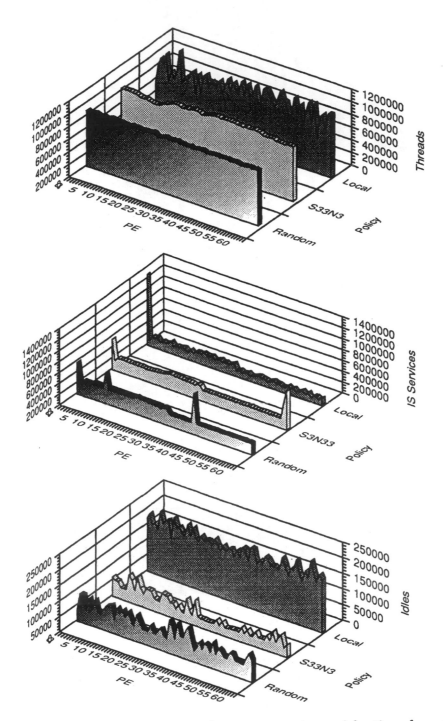

Figure 5: Thread profile, idle events, I-structure service, and fraction of remote messages for three frame allocation policies on Gamteb with I-structure spreading.

cached, not M-structures. Since I-structures are write-once data structures, the only coherence operation is for using a previously deallocated I-structure. To address this, deallocates are buffered until the system runs low on storage. Then all the caches are flushed and the deallocates serviced. I-structure caching yields the processor profiles shown in Figure 6. We see that most of the I-structure load imbalance is successfully eliminated by caching, even though the miss rate is 60 to 70% for the non-local policies.

I-structure caching makes a more significant difference in Simple, as shown in Figure 7 for the frame allocation policy s50n3. It eliminates an extremely serious imbalance in I-structure services and localizes 50% of the accesses. Observe that the computational load is quite even with this policy. Caching results in a five-fold speedup.

4.3 K-bounds

Several techniques have been proposed in the literature for controlling parallelism, including k-bounded loops [6] and activation tree throttling [20]. For the most part, these approaches have been validated through idealized simulations and execution on a small number of processors. Here we present data on the effects of k-bounded loops on 64 processors. In this case, we study Gamteb under a fixed problem size (8092 particles) on a fixed number of processors (64) using the fixed allocation policies described above. The k-bound for the outer-most loop is varied from $k = 2P$ to $k = 32P$, giving the execution times shown in Figure 8. The execution time decreases as the k-bound is increased, but the improvement diminishes. The execution time for $k = 16P$ and $k = 32P$ are essentially equal. Increasing the number of simultaneously active particles per processor increases the amount of available parallelism that can be used in tolerating latency and also decreases the likelihood that a quickly serviced particle will leave the processor idle.

To better understand the effects of changes in the k-bound, we run a version of the program with instrumentation code compiled in-line to record the depth of the queue of enabled frames on each processor. Each processor maintains a histogram of frame queue depths. Whenever a frame is put onto the queue, the bin corresponding to the current depth is incremented. At the end of the program the local histograms are summed into a single global histogram and normalized to obtain a probability distribution. Figure 9 shows the probability distributions for the various k-bounds discussed above. As the k-bound increases, the mean frame queue depth increases. In particular, the queue is empty a much smaller fraction of the time. However, the resulting distribution is somewhat surprising. One might expect the program to operate at a certain average queue depth, with variations above and below resulting in a tailing off away from the mean. Instead, we observe something close to a geometric distribution falling off from zero. This might occur if the frame queue depth were oscillating wildly and always returns to zero before building again. Increasing the k-bound increases the depth to which it grows, but does not prevent it from returning to empty.

To verify this theory we examine the utilization of the processors as the program executes. Figure 10 shows the percent of the time each processor is busy over time for each of 64 processors. We see that most of the processors are indeed alternating between periods of full utilization and idleness. We do not yet have a complete explanation of this behavior.

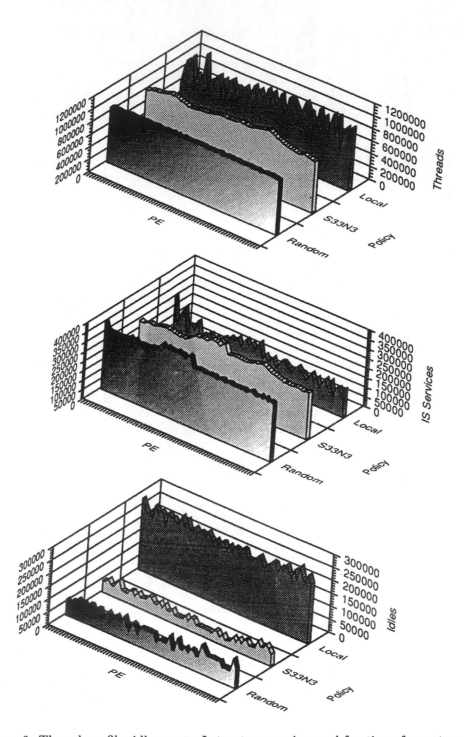

Figure 6: Thread profile, idle events, I-structure service, and fraction of remote messages for three frame allocation policies on Gamteb with I-structure spreading and caching.

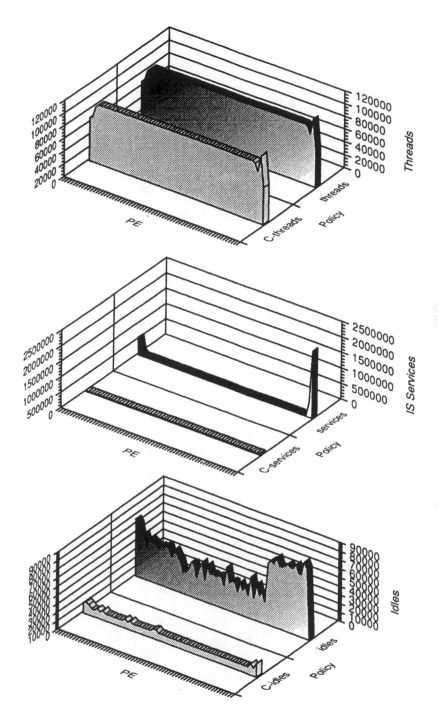

Figure 7: Thread profile, idle events, I-structure service, and fraction of remote messages for s50n3 frame allocation policy on Simple with and without caching.

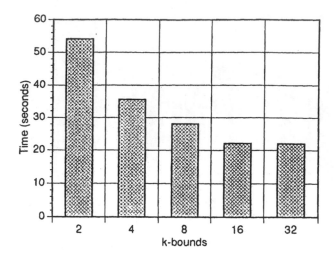

Figure 8: Effect of k-bound on execution time for Gamteb with
$N = 8092$ on 64 processors.

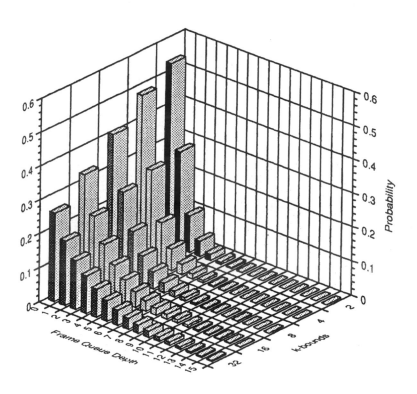

Figure 9: Frame queue depth probability distribution for various k-bounds
on Gamteb with $N = 8092$ on 64 processors.

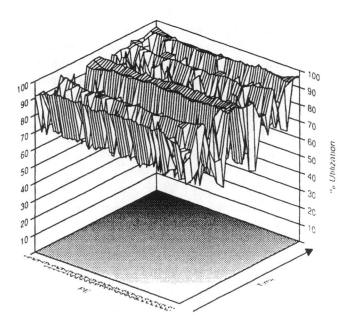

Figure 10: Average processor utilization over time for each of 64 processors on Gamteb with $N = 8192$ and $k = 32 * P$.

5. Scheduling Anomalies

Although automatic scheduling and management of resources in Id90 programs appear to be successful for large programs on a sizable number of processors, we have also observed serious scheduling pathologies. An extreme example is demonstrated by the following silly Id90 program that computes n*m as a parallel loop containing a sequential loop.

```
def foo n m k =
  {osum = 0;
  in {for o <- 1 to n bound k do
    next osum = osum + {isum = 0;
                in {for i <- 1 to m sequential do
                  next isum = isum + 1;
                  finally isum}};
    finally osum}};
```

The outer loop is a parallel loop, limited only by the data dependencies on **osum** and whatever k-bounds are imposed. Each iteration of the outer loop has two tasks to perform. It starts the next iteration (passing it $o + 1$) and it performs one instance of the inner loop. Since the inner loop is sequential, it can either be split out into a separate frame or retained in the frame of the associated iteration of the outer loop. The Berkeley compiler provides an option to do either one, but we will assume it is executed in-place. There is no dependence between these two tasks, so they may be performed in either order. However, if the processor starts working on the inner loop

207

before initiating the next iteration of the outer loop, only one processor will be busy in the entire system. Under TAM the processor will execute the entire inner loop without suspension, while the thread that starts the next iteration sits on the bottom of the CV. All other dataflow machines can manifest the same pathology, although with very fine grain scheduling it may be harder to produce an example. K-bounded loops do not help the problem in any way, nor are they the root cause. The real issue is that the program is self-scheduled at a very low level. And thus, independent of the scheduling policy, important events may become delayed arbitrarily.

6. Summary

We have shown that dataflow languages can be implemented on conventional architectures and obtain reasonable performance. However, current processor/network interfaces present far too much overhead for programs that operate in a global address space with little locality. We saw that the performance improvement was negligible on a small number of processors, but that once the remote reference frequency flattened out, the speedup was quite good. This suggests that the performance of the program is determined primarily by the frequency of remote access, rather than the latency in transmitting the request to a remote processor. So the compiler controlled multithreading approach appears to be successful in tolerating latency. Nonetheless, it is clear that all levels of the storage hierarchy must be addressed in implementing a parallel language. The characteristics of the local storage hierarchy cannot be ignored in attempting to optimize for the inter-processor level, as they are on traditional dataflow machines.

In spite of the performance impact of network access overhead, we can utilize the large multiprocessor systems that exist today to study the system level issues that will be critical to the success of the next generation of dataflow architectures and cannot be studied on small prototypes or under simulation. The two-level scheduling policy in TAM appears to be successful in enhancing the computational locality far beyond what static analysis of the program alone would provide. This motivates us to study techniques for register management under asynchronous scheduling and to examine how to implement the TAM model more efficiently through hardware support. Simple frame allocation policies appear to yield a reasonably balanced computational load. Allocation of small structures locally is often beneficial in localizing access, given such a frame allocation policy. However, without some form of replication, contention for I-structure elements can be very severe. Dynamic scheduling does not overcome the impact of persistent load imbalance or contention. Simple caching techniques and compiler controlled replication may go a long ways toward alleviating this problem.

Finally, it appears unlikely that microscopic dynamic scheduling, whether it be under the TAM model or traditional dataflow, will be adequate for large programs. With any predetermined local scheduling policy, some important event is likely to get buried and compromise the useful parallelism. There needs to be a global strategy for executing the program as a whole, not just local greedy scheduling. TAM provides a means of representing such a strategy by allowing specialized scheduling data structures to be constructed at the frame level. It remains an open question whether global analysis of the program can yield an overall strategy that can be represented in this fashion.

Acknowledgments

We are grateful to the anonymous referees for their valuable comments. Computational support at Berkeley was provided by the NSF Infrastructure Grant number CDA-8722788. David Culler is supported by an NSF Presidential Faculty Fellowship CCR-9253705 and LLNL Grant UCB-ERL-92/172. Seth Copen Goldstein is supported by an AT&T Graduate Fellowship. Klaus Erik Schauser is supported by an IBM Graduate Fellowship. Thorsten von Eicken is supported by the Semiconductor Research Corporation.

References

[1] Arvind and D. E. Culler, "Dataflow Architectures," in *Annual Reviews in Computer Science*, Annual Reviews Inc., Palo Alto, Calif., Vol. 1. 1986, pp. 225–253. Reprinted in *Dataflow and Reduction Architectures*, S.S. Thakkar, Ed., IEEE Computer Society Press, 1987.

[2] Arvind and K. Ekanadham, "Future Scientific Programming on Parallel Machines," *Journal of Parallel and Distributed Computing*, Vol. 5, No. 5, October 1988, pp. 460–493.

[3] Arvind, R.S. Nikhil, and K.K. Pingali, "I-Structures: Data Structures for Parallel Computing," Technical Report CSG Memo 269, MIT Lab for Comp. Sci., 545 Tech. Square, Cambridge, MA, February, 1987. (Also in *Proc. of the Graph Reduction Workshop*, Santa Fe, NM, October 1986).

[4] M. Beck and K. Pingali, "From Control Flow to Dataflow," Technical Report TR 89-1050, Cornell Univ., Dept. of Computer Science, October 1989.

[5] David Cann, "Retire Fortran? A Debate Rekindled," *Proc. of Supercomputing '91*, Alb., NM, November 1991, pp. 264–272.

[6] D.E. Culler, "Managing Parallelism and Resources in Scientific Dataflow Programs," Technical Report 446, MIT Lab for Comp. Sci., March 1990.

[7] D.E. Culler, "Multithreading: Fundamental Limits, Potential Gains, and Alternatives," *Proc. of the Supercomputing '91 Workshop on Multithreading*, 1992.

[8] D.E. Culler, S.C. Goldstein, K.E. Schauser, and T. von Eicken, "TAM—A Compiler Controlled Threaded Abstract Machine," *Journal of Parallel and Distributed Computing*, July 1993, pp. 347–370. (Special Issue on Dataflow).

[9] D.E. Culler and G.M. Papadopoulos, "The Explicit Token Store," *Journal of Parallel and Distributed Computing*, January 1990, pp. 289–308.

[10] J.B. Dennis, G. Gao, and K.W. Todd, "Modeling the Weather with a Data Flow Supercomputer," *IEEE Transactions on Computers*, Vol. C-33, No. 7, July 1984, pp. 592–603.

[11] J. Gaudiot, R.W. Vedder, G.K. Tucker, D. Finn, and M.L. Campbell, "A Distributed VLSI Architecture for Efficient Signal Processing," *IEEE Transactions on Computers*, Vol. C-34, No. 12, December 1985, pp. 1072–1087.

[12] S.C. Goldsteain, "Implementation of a Threaded Abstract Machine on Sequential and Multiprocessors," Master's thesis, Computer Science Division—EECS, Univ. of California, Berkeley, 1994. (In preparation, to appear as UCB/CSD Technical Report).

[13] J. Gurd, C.C. Kirkham, and I. Watson, "The Manchester Prototype Dataflow Computer," *Communications of the Association for Computing Machinery*, Vol. 28, No. 1, January 1985, pp. 34–52.

[14] R.A. Inannucci, "Toward A Dataflow/von Neumann Hybrid Architecture," *Proc. 15th Int. Symp. on Comp. Arch.*, Hawaii, May 1988, pp. 131–140.

[15] R.S. Nikhil, "The Parallel Programming Language Id and its Compilation for Parallel Machines," *Proc. Workshop on Massive Parallelism*, Amalfi, Italy, October 1989, Academic Press, 1991. Also: CSG Memo 313, MIT Laboratory for Computer Science, 545 Technology Square, Cambridge, MA 02139, USA.

[16] R.S. Nikhil and Arvind, "Can Dataflow Subsume von Neumann Computing?" *Proc. of the 16th Annual Int. Symp. on Comp. Arch.*, Jerusalem, Israel, May 1989.

[17] G.M. Papadopoulos and D.E. Culler, "Monsoon: An Explicit Token-Store Architecture," *Proc. of the 17th Annual Int. Symp. on Comp. Arch.*, Seattle, Washington, May 1990.

[18] G.M. Papadopoulos and K.R. Traub, "A Revisionist View of Dataflow Architectures," *Proc. of the 18th Int'l Symp. on Computer Architecture*, Toronto, Canada, May 1991, pp. 342–351.

[19] A. Rogers and K. Pingali, "Compiling Programs for Distributed Memory Architectures," *Proc. of the 4th Hypercube Computers and Applications Conference*, Monterey, CA, March 1989.

[20] C.A. Ruggiero, "Throttle Mechanisms for the Manchester Dataflow Machine," Ph.D. thesis, University of Manchester, Manchester M13 9PL, England, July 1987.

[21] S. Sakai et al., "An Architecture of a Dataflow Single Chip Processor," *Proc. of the 16th Annual Int. Symp. on Comp. Arch.*, Jerusalem, Israel, June 1989, pp. 46–53.

[22] K.E. Schauser, D. Culler, and T. von Eicken, "Compiler-controlled Multithreading for Lenient Parallel Languages," *Proceedings of the 1991 Conference on Functional Programming Languages and Computer Architecture*, Cambridge, MA, August 1991. (Also available as Technical Report UCB/CSD 91/640, CS Div., University of California at Berkeley).

[23] Klaus Erik Schauser, "Compiling Dataflows into Threads," Master's thesis, Computer Science Div., Report No. UCB/CSD 91/644, University of California, Berkeley, July 1991.

[24] T. Temma, S. Hasegawa, and S. Hanaki, "Dataflow Processor for Image Processing," *Proc. of 11 Int'l Symp. on Mini and Microcomputers*, 1980, pp. 52–56.

[25] K.R. Traub, "A Compiler for the MIT Tagged-Token Dataflow Architecture," MS thesis, Dept. of EECS, MIT Technical Report TR-370, MIT Lab for Comp. Sci., 545 Tech. Square, Cambridge, MA, August 1986.

[26] K.R. Traub, "Compilation as Partitioning: A New Approach to Compiling Non-strict Functional Languages," *Proc. of the Apenas Workshop on the Implementation of Lazy Functional Languages*, Chalmers Univ., Goteborg, Sweden, September 1988. (Also CSG Group Memo 291, MIT Lab. for Computer Science).

[27] K.R. Traub, "Sequential Implementation of Lenient Programming Languages," Ph.D. thesis, Dept. of EECS, MIT. Technical Report TR-417, MIT Lab. for Comp. Sci., 545 Tech. Square, Cambridge, MA, September 1988.

[28] K.R. Traub, D.E. Culler, and K.E. Schauser, "Global Analysis for Partitioning Non-Strict Programs into Sequential Threads," *Proc. of the ACM Conf. on LISP and Functional Programming*, San Francisco, CA, June 1992.

[29] T. von Eicken, D.E. Culler, S.C. Goldstein, and K.E. Schauser, "Active Messages: A Mechanism for Integrated Communication and Computation," *Proc. of the 19th Int'l Symposium on Computer Architecture*, Gold Coast, Australia, May 1992. (Also available as Technical Report UCB/CSD 92/675, CS Div., University of California, Berkeley, CA).

Programming the ADAM Architecture with SISAL

Srdjan Mitrović[1]
Computer Engineering and Networks Laboratory
Swiss Federal Institute of Technology
Zürich, Switzerland

The ADAM parallel machine is based on the multithreading architecture design. It is available in the form of a simulator named Metamachine. Verifying the significance of the proposed ADAM architecture consists of implementing a code generator for an existing parallel language and analyzing its programmability.

We choose the single-assignment language SISAL for generating code for the Metamachine. Code generated from the optimizing SISAL compiler (OSC) is efficient and fast and runs on various parallel machines. An implementation of a SISAL code generator, which should approach the quality of OSC, must use most of existing optimizations. Therefore, the code generator replaces only the last phase of the OSC. The feasibility of such an approach and the quality of the generated code are investigated.

1. Introduction

Project ADAM[2] emerged from the earlier project EMPRESS [1] in which a 16 processor machine had been realized in hardware. Learning from those experiences, the project group developed a new von Neumann/dataflow hybrid architecture concurrently with code generators for programming languages SISAL [9] and MFL [13]. The goal of the project ADAM is to investigate the feasibility of a programmable and scalable multiprocessor. The programmability issue was investigated by using existing and new functional languages. In an iterative process, after various hardware implementation studies, the architecture evolved to a form that is realizable in hardware up to a scale of 256 processors. It provides a good speedup for parallel problems and a small semantic gap between the machine instruction set and the targeted high-level languages. The early stages of the architecture and the code generator for SISAL have been described in [2] and [11], respectively. The ADAM architecture is realized in the form of a register level simulator named Metamachine [8].

This paper describes the code generator for the functional language SISAL and the performance obtained when running SISAL programs on the Metamachine. The advantage of SISAL is that it has been designed with no specific parallel architecture in mind. This means that the user is not forced to program with the knowledge of the computer architecture, thus slowing the problem formulation process. Instead, the same program can be run without changes on different parallel and sequential architectures. ITH [12], a code generator tool for executing SISAL programs on the Metamachine, investigates the usefulness of SISAL for programming a multithreading architecture like Metamachine, and the quality of various architecture design issues in the ADAM architecture.

---

[1]Current address: Computing Research Group, L-419, Lawrence Livermore National Laboratory, Livermore, CA 94551.
[2]ADAM is the abbreviation for Advanced Dataflow Machine.

The section about the Metamachine describes the ADAM architecture from the programmers' view. Dynamic load-flow, the throttling issue, and other architecture relevant problems and solutions are not described in this work. They can be found in [7]. The optimizations done by the ITH code generator have been selected after experimenting with many different benchmarks. All parallel benchmarks described in the last section are being run with the same OSC and ITH settings. There is no parameter tuning for benchmarks, as the measured gains where too small compared to the inconvenience to the user.

2. Tools

This section explains shortly some software tools used. The target machine for running programs is the ADAM simulator named Metamachine. Metamachine reads object files containing code and debugging information. Various views of the inner parts of the Metamachine provide monitoring facilities. A browser allows stepwise source-level debugging. The resource view gathers simulation data into a log-file that is analyzed by a commercial statistics tool. Most of the architecture parameters are variable through preference windows. The simulation speed of the Metamachine is up to 50,000 cycles[3] per second.

HLA,[4] an assembler for the Metamachine, is a one-pass assembler extended with high level constructs and a syntax closely related to the instruction set of the Metamachine. An HLA program consists of constant, type, and block definitions. Blocks are execution units that contain the instruction sequence. There is no mechanism for automatic deadlock prevention in HLA. Section 4 describes the syntax of this language. A disassembler allows the analysis of code generated from other compilers. Figure 1 shows the matrix multiplication written in HLA and a part of the corresponding disassembled code.

The current SISAL compiler is a set of compilation phases named OSC.[5] It is a sophisticated optimizing tool for the applicative language SISAL. OSC parses a SISAL 1.2 source file and generates an IF2 file. IF2 contains acyclic dataflow graphs. The last phase of OSC translates the dataflow graphs into C-code. The IF2-to-HLA (ITH) code generator replaces that last phase and produces an HLA file. The following sections will give a more detailed description of this tool.

The necessity of a dataflow graph browser emerges from the fact that the documentation of IF2 is neither complete nor stable. An interactive graph-display program offers the possibility of the detailed analysis of each edge and node, mapping the graph elements to corresponding source lines. A detailed description of this display tool is given in [10].

SISAL programs can be debugged directly with the Metamachine because all line and name informations are propagated through the IF1 and IF2 files.

3. SISAL and OSC

The language SISAL [9] and the compiler system OSC[6] have been developed by Colorado State University and Lawrence Livermore National Laboratory. SISAL is designed for scientific computation and belongs to the family of functional languages. Its syntax and semantics make no assumptions about the target architecture [3] [5].

---

[3]This has been measured for 256 processor configuration running on a 32 Transputer cluster.
[4]High-level assembler.
[5]OSC V12.7 has been used at the time of the writing.
[6]OSC stands for Optimizing SISAL Compiler.

```
HLA Code                              Disassembled code

BLOCK MatMul(a,b:Matrix;OUT c: Matrix);   CODE:
                                            BLOCK MatMul
VAR i, j, k, sum, t1, t2: INTEGER;        00000:: $3B020082 b[2]  := LD([0], 2)
                                          00001:: $3B030081 a[3]  := LD([0], 1)
BEGIN                                      00002:: $4204FF00 c[4]  := NEWOBJ(4097
  NEW (c);                                           $00001001
  FOR i := 0 TO n - 1 DO                   00004:: $40058080 i[5]  := MOVE(0)
    t1 := (i * n) + 1;                     00005:: $071E05BF [30]  := LTE(i[5], 63)
    FOR j := 0 TO n - 1 DO                 00006:: $4C00FF1E JUMPFN(47, [30])
      sum := 0;                                    $0000002F
      t2 := j + 1;                         00008:: $0D1E05FF [30]  := MUL(i[5], 64)
      FOR k := 0 TO n - 1 DO                        $00000040
        sum := sum+(a[t1+k]*               00010:: $0B061E81 1[6]  := ADD([30], 1)
               b[(k*n)+t2]);               00011:: $40078080 j[7]  := MOVE(0)
      END;                                 00012:: $071D07BF [29]  := LTE(j[7], 63)
      c [t1 + j] := sum;                   00013:: $4C00FF1D JUMPFN(45, [29])
    END;                                           $0000002D
  END;                                     00015:: $40088080 sum[8]  := MOVE(0)
END MatMul;                                00016:: $0B090781 t2[9]  := ADD(j[7], 1)
                                           00017:: $400A8080 k[10]  := MOVE(0)
                                           00018:: $071C0ABF [28]  := LTE(k[10],63)
                                           00019:: $4C00FF1C JUMPFN(37, [28])
                                                   $00000025
                                           00021:: $0B1B060A [27]:=ADD(t1[6],k[10])
                                           00022:: $569B1B81 [27]:=CHECK([27] ...
```

Figure 1: HLA program and its disassembled code.

SISAL follows the single assignment convention, allowing the compiler to detect implicit parallelism. The SISAL front-end generates an IF1 file [16]—a list of acyclic dataflow graphs. The OSC system consists of the SISAL 1.2 front-end, several optimization passes, and a C-code generator. These passes optimize the IF1 to the IF2 form. The IF2 file includes operations for direct manipulation of memory, reference count informations, and other pragma marks. A detailed description of OSC is given in [4] and [6].

While IF1 syntax is stable and well documented, it is far from being optimal as input for code generators because of the memory efficiency issues. Its superset, IF2 form, is better for feeding a code generator, but the definition of IF2 is not stable and only partially documented. With the help of an IF2 graph-browser, it is possible to understand and use most of the undocumented features of IF2. Furthermore, the comparison of the IF2 graphs with the generated C-code is a complete although cumbersome way to analyze and understand IF2.

OSC has several parameters of interest for a multithreading architecture: a threshold parameter specifies and determines at what size a forall node should be marked for parallelization and the selective inlining prevents excessive needs for value holders like registers or activation frames (the inlining options allow either an automatic inlining of all functions or a manual specification of functions to inline). A threshold for specifying a maximum size for a graph to be inlined is missing. The ADAM architecture, with the fixed frame size of 32 registers and the function level parallelism may not execute well a program that is completely inlined. The full constant propagation, i.e., propagation into the called functions, is done only through inlining. This optimization enhances the performance of programs significantly, as fewer parameters must be calculated or passed between functions. The propagation of constants into functions without full inlining would be desirable. The OSC graph partitioner takes the number

```
MODULE ExplMod;

BLOCK explosion (level: INTEGER; OUT result: INTEGER);
    VAR abs1, abs2[4], tmp1, tmp2: INTEGER;
BEGIN
    IF level = 0 THEN
        result := 1
    ELSE
        (* with assembler commands *)
        tmp1 := ABSI(level); abs1 := SUB(tmp1, 1);
        (* ...or expressions *)
        abs2 := 1 - ABS(level);
        explosion (abs1, tmp1);
        explosion (abs2, tmp2);
        res := abs1+abs2;
    END;
END explosion;

BLOCK MAIN (OUT explosionResult: INTEGER)
    res := explosion (12);
END MAIN;

END ExplMod.
```

Figure 2: An HLA program.

of processors and the partitioning threshold as parameters. The first parameter of the partitioner is set to maximum, as we do not compile programs for a specific number of processors. Additionally, the needed number of parallel codeblocks in the ADAM architecture is greater than the number of available processors by a varying factor. The slice threshold is set at 1000, a number that has been defined by experiments.

4. HLA

The development of code generators for MFL and SISAL occurred in parallel with the realization of the Metamachine. At that time, when the ITH code generator was not yet able to produce code, we needed a simple low-level programming language. The assembler HLA has been designed for programming simple programs and to be used as an intermediate form for the code generator. An HLA file contains one module. The module may contain type, constant, and block definitions. A block is a sequential unit containing a sequence of instructions. Variables can be defined and referenced only inside a codeblock. Apart from all assembler mnemonics, HLA can also translate expressions and complex instructions. The assembler has been influenced by the syntax of Modula-2, the main programming language in project ADAM, and by the architecture of the Metamachine. Figure 2 shows an example of an HLA program.

When passing an argument list, HLA assembler generates code for building and filling the argument and the result object. It inserts the deallocate operations for parameter objects at appropriate places automatically. A couple of frame registers are reserved, but others can be used for local variables. A variable number of registers are used for expression evaluation (i.e., stack), while other registers are reserved for passing parameters. The assembler allocates the free registers to the declared variables if they do not have a register specified in the declaration. The variable in the example of Figure 2 declares that variable **abs2** is allocated to the register number 4 while the variable **abs1** is allocated in any other free register. Furthermore, the value of **abs1** is defined with assembler operations and the value of **abs2** with an expression.

5. Metamachine

The Metamachine, a software tool, implements the ADAM architecture in the form of a register level simulator. The simulator kernel is running either on a 32 Transputer cluster or on a Macintosh computer. Metamachine allows simulations of various kinds of networks and operation delays. It allows the definition of machines with up to 256 processors, with six different network configurations[7] and variable cycle times for every instruction and delay.

The ADAM parallel processor is a homogeneous distributed memory machine with global address space. Every processing element has a local memory that is part of the global address space. A processing element connects through a fast packet-switched network with up to 255 other processing elements. One processing element consists of several functional units. Because of the complexity of a processing element, the complete execution time of an operation cannot be specified; it depends on the current state of the machine. The preference file defines the delay times for atomic operations. The standard setting assumes that Boolean operations execute in one cycle and that an integer multiplication executes in 3 cycles. These are not the complete execution time, which may also include the operation and instruction fetching, cache misses, or request-building and -forwarding delays. A context switch needs about 6 cycles to complete.

5.1 The Programming Model of the Metamachine

The code-file consists of the following information blocks: the code, the jump-table, and the debugging references. The code consists of at least one codeblock, which is a sequence of instructions.

Codeblocks are execution threads that execute in parallel and synchronize through data. They are the scheduling quanta of the ADAM architecture and correspond to the functions in the SISAL program. The instruction-list of a codeblock executes sequentially. An instruction suspends its execution when its input is missing. Particularly, this leads to the suspension of the codeblock itself. The operation CALL and its derivatives generate codeblock tokens. The distributed dynamic load-flow mechanism is responsible for keeping a codeblock in the form of a token and expanding it only where there is too little work. An initiated, i.e., called, codeblock exists either as a token, or in the expanded form. An expanded codeblock owns a frame and a context. The codeblock can be in one of the three states after the expansion: ready, active, or waiting. Active codeblocks execute, the waiting codeblocks wait for data to be returned and the ready codeblocks can become active at the next context-switch. The codeblocks are assigned to a processor only after the expansion and then they execute on that processor until they terminate.

The frames build the synchronization space of the Metamachine. A frame consists of a fixed number of registers. The disassembled code in Figure 3 dumps every referenced register number in square brackets. A register holds data and three additional bits: wait, present, and valid. The valid bit propagates errors, the present bit marks the availability of data, and the wait bit marks a suspended access. The current design

---

[7]The following network topologies are implemented: ring, chordal ring, shuffle, torus, hypercube, and fully connected.

```
        BLOCK MAIN;                    BLOCK MAIN
                                       00101:: $4F82FE85    a[2]  := CALL(MODREF, 5, 0)
                                               $80000000
        VAR a, b, c: Matrix;           00103:: $4F83FE85    b[3]  := CALL(MODREF, 5, 0)
        BEGIN                                  $80000000
          Sample (a);                  00105:: $421F8300    [31]  := NEWOBJ(3)
          Sample (b);                  00106:: $3D9F1F81    [31]  := STO([31], 1, a[2])
          MatMul (a, b, c);                    $02000000
          RETURN (c);                  00108:: $3D9F1F82    [31]  := STO([31], 2, b[3])
        END MAIN;                              $03000000
                                       00110:: $4F84FE83    c[4]  := CALL(MODREF, 3, [31])
                                               $1F000000
                                       00112:: $3F000104    STF([1], c[4])
                                       00113:: $53000000    ENDCB()
```

Figure 3: HLA and the disassembled code of a codeblock
calling three other codeblocks.

```
(* 1 *) BANOBJ := NEWOBJ (9);
(* ........ *)
(* 17 *) s_42 := s_33.BASE;
BANOBJ := STO(BANOBJ, 7, s_42);
(* 18 *) s_43 := s_34.BASE;
(* 19 *) s_44 := s_35.BASE;
(* 20 *) s_45 := s_33.BASE;
BANOBJ := STO(BANOBJ, 8, s_45);
(* 21 *) s_46 := s_33.BASE;
(* 22 *) FOR s_50 := startCount TO endCount DO
    s_42 := LD(BANOBJ, 7);
    (* 23 *) s_51 := s_42[s_50];   (*AElement*)
    (* 24 *) s_52 := s_43[s_50];   (*AElement*)
    (* 25 *) s_53 := s_44[s_50];   (*AElement*)
```

Figure 4: HLA code for spilling variables from frame.

implements the frames with the fixed number of 32 registers with every register being 35-bit wide. In cases where the local variables of a codeblock need more registers than available in the frame, the codeblock must allocate a structure that holds those values in the main memory. The code must fetch those values before consumption from the main memory and into registers or save them back after the change. Figure 4 is an excerpt from the code of the eighth Livermore Loop. Variables that must be swapped are called spilled and the memory structure to swap into is a local object is named BANOBJ.

The frame holds atomic values like integers, real numbers, and structure references. The content of structures, e.g., arrays and records, resides in the main memory that is part of the global address space. The code must synchronize access to structures with barriers separating the write from the read accesses to the structures.[8]

The instruction-set consists of n-address operations with direct access to registers. Every instruction checks the present-state of all input registers and sets the present bit of the result register. We can classify the instructions in the synchronous (S)

---

[8]The advantage of this design is that there are no queues of deferred reads; only the owner of the frame must be awakened when data arrive.

and asynchronous (A) class. The S-instructions write into the registers. Arithmetic and logic operations belong to this group. The A-instructions trigger a request and clear the present bit of the destination register, without writing results into it. The structure-access instructions, i.e., the split transactions, belong to this group. Instructions can suspend execution only when fetching data from the frame. In Figure 5, a load instruction executes at address 547, clearing the present bit of the temporary s_21 at register [20]. The result of this split transaction is written later at register [20] so that the codeblock can continue its execution. The result is needed only at address 557. A cleared present bit in register [20] will lead to the suspension of the MULR operation and of the codeblock itself.

The structures are kept in main or structure memory and are accessed through an object reference and an index. An illegal access to an object will clear the valid bit in the frame-register. Every object has a reference count at index zero; the first available element starts at index one. Execution of the DISPOSE operation will either decrement the reference-count or free the allocated memory of the specified object. The objects are allocated with one of the three available allocation operations. Each one produces a different kind of object. The local object is allocated on the same processor where the allocation instruction is issued. This kind of object is used for local and small structures. Local objects are easy to deallocate and use little memory but can produce a request bottleneck if accessed by multiple code-blocks from different processors. Parameter and result objects are usually allocated as local objects. The interleaved objects are used mainly for homogeneous aggregates consumed or produced by parallel code-blocks. The content of such objects is evenly distributed on all processors, thus removing request bottlenecks. Due to the distribution strategy and the address translation mechanism, an element of any interleaved object with a fixed index n is always allocated on the same processor. Therefore, those types of objects are only suitable for homogeneous structures with proportionate access frequency on all elements. The third class of object is the replicated object. Constant objects like program code are of this type. Every processing element holds the complete copy of this object.

5.2 The Parallelism in the ADAM Architecture

In ADAM architecture, the parallelism of a problem is used to hide access latencies and increase the speedup of computation by keeping processors busy. The first characteristic is necessary for realizing scalable multiprocessors while the second one accelerates the execution of the program.

On the one hand, the structure and the kind of the problem, respectively the algorithm, limits the available parallelism. On the other hand, the size of the scheduling quanta constrains the amount of exploitable parallelism on a machine. The sensible size of the scheduling quanta depends on the machine design.

The ADAM architecture supports three kinds of parallelisms, namely the instruction, the function, and the loop level parallelism. The instruction level parallelism is used for hiding access latency. While computing the results from the split-instructions, other code from the same codeblock can execute in parallel. A suitable instruction sorting algorithm improves the execution time. The sorting separates the consuming instruction from the producing A-instructions, thus allowing the request sometimes to complete before its result is needed. Figure 5 shows a sorted program where results of load instructions are consumed as late as possible.

A codeblock can execute in parallel with the caller's codeblock. All codeblock calls are non-blocking calls. The caller continues its execution after calling a codeblock. It is

```
00543:: $40131180    s_11[19] := MOVE(startCount[17])
00544:: $071E1312    [30]   := LTE(s_11[19], endCount[18])
00545:: $4C00FF1E    JUMPFN(567, [30])
        $00000237
00547:: $3B140B13    s_21[20] := LD(s_8[11], s_11[19])
00548:: $0B15138A    s_20[21] := ADD(s_11[19], 10)
00549:: $3B160C15    s_18[22] := LD(s_9[12], s_20[21])
00550:: $0B15138B    s_20[21] := ADD(s_11[19], 11)
00551:: $3B170D15    s_19[23] := LD(s_10[13], s_20[21])
00552:: $1C15FF16    s_20[21] := MULR(0.01000, s_18[22])
        $3C23D1CC
00554:: $1C16FF17    s_18[22] := MULR(0.01000, s_19[23])
        $3C23D1CC
00556:: $1A171516    s_19[23] := ADDR(s_20[21], s_18[22])
00557:: $1C151714    s_20[21] := MULR(s_19[23], s_21[20])
00558:: $1A1415FF    s_21[20] := ADDR(s_20[21], 0.01000)
        $3C23D1DD
00560:: $3B1E0981    [30]   := LD(s_6[9], 1)
00561:: $3D9E1E0A    [30]   := STO([30], s_7[10], s_21[20])
        $14000000
00563:: $0B0A810A    s_7[10] := ADD(1, s_7[10])
00564:: $0B138113    s_11[19] := ADD(1, s_11[19])
00565:: $4A00FF00    JUMP(544)
        $00000220
```

Figure 5: Disassembled body of the first Livermore loop.

not predictable if the called codeblock will really execute in parallel on other processors because this depends on the current state of the machine. The called codeblock can be expanded on the same processor where the caller codeblock is running if the load distribution mechanism decides so. The access latency can then be hidden through the fast context-switch between both codeblocks. Figure 3 shows a codeblock issuing three **CALL** instructions. Both calls for **Sample** blocks can be executed in parallel as they are not data dependent. The third **CALL** needs data of the first two and must wait until the results are written in the register [2] and [3].

A modified call instruction supports the product-form loops. The parallel call (PCALL) generates a specified number of parallel codeblocks. Every parallel codeblock works on a distinct loop-slice of a fixed size. The number of codeblocks is calculated before the PCALL instruction is issued.

The work-load, in form of codeblock tokens, is spread dynamically on the entire machine through the token network. A simple but efficient mechanism is responsible for balancing the workload while throttling the parallelism [7].

5.3 The Call Mechanism

The parameter list of a call instruction consists of the block number, the parameter object, and the result address. The result address can be any of the registers of the caller's frame. The present bit of the result register is cleared by the callers **CALL** instruction and set by the called codeblock (CB) when he returns results. The called CB receives the parameter object in the register [0] and the return address in the register [1]. The called CB synchronizes through this global return address with the

```
SISAL code:                          Disassembled:

if abs(LTrap+HTrap-Trap)<0.0001      00535::$421F8600 [31]:=NEWOBJ(6)
  then LTrap + HTrap                 00536::$3D9F1F81 [31]:=STO([31],1,s_7[10])
else                                          $0A000000
  Quad(Low,FLow,Mid,FMid,LTrap)+     00538::$3D9F1F82 [31]:=STO([31],2,s_10[12])
  Quad(Mid,FMid,High,FHigh,HTrap)             $0C000000
end if                               00540::$3D9F1F83 [31]:=STO([31],3,s_4[7])
                                              $07000000
                                     00542::$3D9F1F84 [31]:=STO([31],4,s_3[6])
                                              $06000000
                                     00544::$3D9F1F85 [31]:=STO([31],5,s_17[11])
                                              $0B000000
                                     00546::$4F90FE96 s_24[16]:=CALL(MODREF,22,[31])
                                              $1F000000
                                     00548::$1A040F10 s_22[4]:=ADDR(s_23[15],s_24[16])
                                     00549::$3F000104 STF([1],s_22[4])
```

Figure 6: Example of a call instruction as translated from SISAL code.

caller and writes the result into it. The caller is responsible for building the argument object and for disposing the result object after the result has been extracted. The called CB builds the result object and frees the argument object. Of course, blocks receiving only one argument or returning one result do not need to build objects. Those blocks have a significantly lower communication overhead. The dynamic image of a program is not a call stack but a call tree with all leaves executing in parallel as long as data is available. Figures 6 and 3 show examples of call instructions with multiple and single arguments.

The parallel call, in contrast to the CALL instructions, generates a variable number of tokens. The PCALL receives as arguments a parameter object and the number of tokens to generate. Every such codeblock token represents a slice of the product-form loop and differs only in a counter. This counter determines the subrange of the loop slice. Every parallel block signals through the parameter object its completion. The caller block synchronizes by waiting until all parallel blocks have finished.

An example of a parallel call written in HLA is given in Figure 7. After allocation, the parameter object is filled with all data that the parallel loop needs. The result object must also be allocated outside the parallel block. Note that the block MatMulRow is itself a parallel block. All instances of that block receive the same parameter reference in register zero but a unique count in register one. When calling PCALL with last parameter set at n, then n parallel codeblocks will be generated. Every parallel codeblock signals its termination with SIGNAL instruction. The caller waits for n signals with the SWAIT instruction.

The number of iterations per slice is calculated at compile time. The calculations are based on the range of the parallel loop and the size of the one iteration. The number of parallel codeblocks is calculated either at run time or at compile time if the bounds of the parallel loops are constant. Figure 8 shows the corresponding formulas.

6. The Code Generator ITH

The C-code generator, named "if2gen," is the only machine dependent pass of the compiler system OSC. ITH, the IF2 to HLA translator, replaces that pass. This section describes ITH, the code generator for the multithreading architecture ADAM as it has been implemented at the time of the writing. The parser of ITH reads the IF2

```
BLOCK MatMulRow (parms: MatMulRowParms);
VAR i [1]: INTEGER; (* i specifies loop slice to calculate *)
    a, b, c: Matrix;
    eparms: MatMulElemParms;
BEGIN   (* parms is assigned to register 0  and
            contains all data neded  for the outer loop*)
    NEW (eparms);
    a := parms.a; b := parms.b; c := parms.c;
    eparms.COUNT := 0; eparms.t1 := (i * n) + 1;
    eparms.i := i;
    eparms.a := a; eparms.b := b; eparms.c := c;
    PCALL (MODREF, MatMulElem, eparms, n);
    eparms := SWAIT (eparms, n);
    DISPOSE (eparms,1);
    SIGNAL (parms);
END MatMulRow;
```

Figure 7: Issuing a parallel call in assembler version of matrix multiplication.

$$SliceSz := (propFactor * initCosts)/execCostOfOneIter \; //$$
$$NrOfCodeblocks := (upBound - lowBound + SliceSz)/SliceSz$$

Figure 8: Formulas for parallel codeblocks.

file and builds an acyclic hierarchic dataflow graph. This structure defines a partial order of nodes through data and dependency edges. The sequentialization of the graph determines a total order of the nodes. A depth-first ordering offers an efficient use of available resources because the lifetime of edges is as short as possible and the number of needed registers is minimal. Because the performance of a codeblock decreases if variables must be spilled in and out of frame, the depth-first order should be the base for any other ordering scheme. On the other side, the split transactions and their consumers should be separated from each other so that an unnecessary context switch is avoided. The operations that read results from a call instruction should be separated from the call operation or they would insert unnecessary synchronization barriers inside the codeblock. The sorting algorithm of ITH advances all call and asynchronous instructions to the top of a codeblock and delays the execution of all instructions that read results of A-instructions. Figure 5 in Section 5 shows the sorted code for the first Livermore Loop. All LD instructions are asynchronous load operations and are executed early. The consumption of results is delayed with the effect that the number of context switches decreases and that the latency is better hidden.

The IF2 file maps the names of SISAL values to the corresponding edges. The code generator tries to propagate those names as long as they do not generate inconsistencies in HLA programs. The goal is to enable debugging of the executable code directly on the target architecture. A SISAL program can be debugged on the Metamachine as all names are preserved. The source window of the browser contains at this stage of the code generator the intermediate HLA file but it will be replaced by the SISAL source file as the line information is provided in the IF2 files. Inlining of functions and loop unrolling can produce inconsistent name assignment to edges and are replaced by the code generator with new names. The difference of scope definitions in HLA and

SISAL is another source of name conflicts. The naming algorithm allocates registers to identifiers, too. If the number of needed registers exceeds the available number, then some identifiers must be spilled to main memory. Those identifiers are called spilled variables and are kept in a structure allocated in the local structure memory. They are fetched from the spill structure when they are needed and are saved back after a modification or generation. The variables assigned to legal registers and with lowest access frequency will be spilled first. The access frequency of a variable is the ratio of the number of accesses to the life time. The variables with register-assignment outside legal frame register range and the highest access frequency will be assigned first to a free register. The needed additional spill code degrades the performance of a codeblock. Any optimizations leading to an excessive need for registers should be avoided as their benefits may be lower than the penalty of longer code.

Figure 9 displays the register allocation of Livermore Loop 10. Provided an unlimited number of registers, this loop would need more than 70 registers. The restriction of 32 registers per frame can easily be changed to a larger number by modifying Metamachine and the HLA assembler. Nonetheless, the frame has a fixed and limited size. The need of code may always exceed the available number of registers. The solution is not to stretch the available number of registers but to provide a spilling mechanism.

The spilling phase of ITH selects and declares some variables as spilled from frame, i.e., they have no permanent residence in a register but must reside outside the frame in the spill object. The example in Figure 4 shows the code for swapping the variables to and from the frame. The spilling phase selects which variables assigned to the legal register range to spill and reassigns the free registers to variables outside the legal range. Every access to a spilled variable is either preceded by a load or followed by a store to spill object. Before inserting those instructions, unnecessary reads and writes are removed allowing some spilled variables to be in a register for longer than the execution time of one operation. Figure 10 shows the allocation statistics for Livermore loop 10 after 38 variables have been spilled from the frame.

Using a threshold cost parameter, OSC analyzes parallel loops or the forall compound nodes at IF2 level respectively. The OSC pass "if2part" compares the cost of the compound nodes with a threshold and marks them if sliceable. Such loops, i.e., compound nodes, are transformed into a PCALL instruction and a new parallel codeblock. In all other cases a codeblock corresponds to a top-scope graph in IF2 that is a transformation of a SISAL function.

A distinct property of SISAL is the versatile array manipulation possibility. The bounds and size of an array are variable at execution time. The array type is mapped to HLA in the form of a descriptor and a data container. The descriptor is a record holding the size, the lower bound, the dimension of the object, and a reference to the data container. The data container is an array of atomic values. In case of a multidimensional array it contains structure references. The descriptor is allocated as a replicated object and the data container as an interleaved object. The unoptimized access to array includes two load operations: fetching the reference from the descriptor and fetching data from the container. Access inside loops is optimized by prefetching the container reference from loop invariant descriptors outside the loop. C-code generated with OSC uses a similar but more complex and more efficient organization of arrays. It has a pointer to the physically allocated memory and an access pointer. The access pointer cannot be implemented in the current Metamachine architecture because a legal object reference exists only in increments of four. The two lowest bits in an object reference define the type of the object and cannot be used to address directly an element. Arrays with a fixed lower bound have a better performance

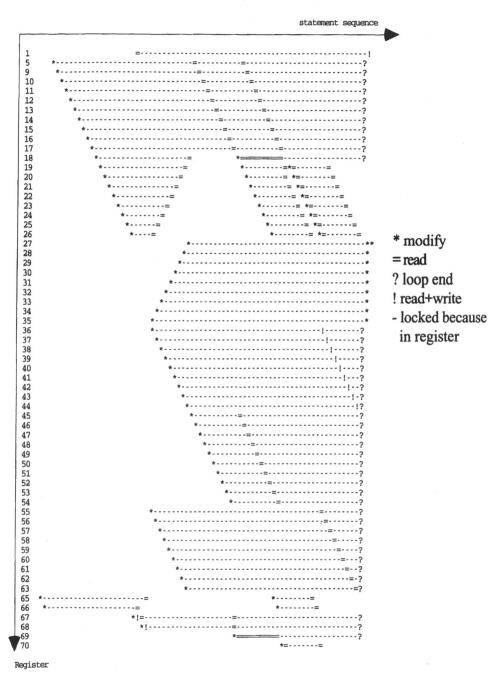

Figure 9: Register allocation for the loop 10 without spilling.

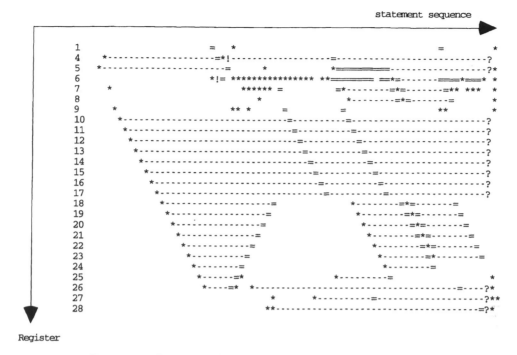

Figure 10: Register allocation for the loop 10 with spilling.

than arrays in which the access pointer is shifted, because the offset must always be recalculated. Various other array access optimizations are under investigation as an optimal access to arrays is very important in SISAL programs. Streams have not been implemented at this stage of ITH mainly because the benchmarks of interest are not using them. Other work described run time support for streams that may also be feasible approaches for the Metamachine [6] and [15]. The run time system needed consists mainly of a set of input and output routines and some array manipulation codeblocks.

7. Results

The following benchmarks analyze the quality of the code generator ITH in combination with the ADAM architecture. All programs have been written in SISAL and run on the Metamachine. The data network is a hypercube and the token network has a chordal ring topology. The delays are set to 16 cycles. All benchmark execution times are given in Metamachine cycles and do not include the time for generating benchmark data, i.e., the initialization of the benchmark. Every benchmark is briefly introduced and its kind and size are described. The slice size, i.e., the number of iterations in one parallel codeblock as calculated by the ITH, is given together with the corresponding speedup. All parameters of ITH and OSC are kept unchanged for all benchmarks. The speedup is calculated as the ratio between the execution time of parallel code on one processor and the time when run on a configuration with n processors. A linear speedup always yields a value of n. The SISAL programs have been compiled with OSC V12. The selected parameters include the inlining of the benchmark functions, prohibiting the loop unrolling and setting the slice threshold at

1000. All other parameters are the defaults of OSC V12. All SISAL programs are compiled once for any number of processors. Such code has additional instructions that parallelize the execution of the programs with no information about the machine configuration. The code generator ITH can produce sequential code by setting the slice threshold of OSC so high that no product loops are marked as sliceable. Such code has no overhead of parallelization control instructions. The comparison of such sequential code with the parallel code running on one processor measures the losses of the parallelization. All benchmarks, except for the modified Livermore loop and the Conway's life program, are compiled as they are available from the FTP server at Lawrence Livermore National Laboratory. The program calculating Mandelbrot sets has been written by O. Maquelin. The data containers of arrays are allocated as interleaved objects and the array descriptors as replicated objects. The parameters for the parallel codeblocks are allocated as replicated objects, too. A more dedicated selection of object-class would improve the execution of programs and is a matter of further investigation.

8. The Benchmarks

Livermore loops are among the most popular benchmarks in the parallel computation community (see Figure 11). They are 24 short programs extracted from production code used at Lawrence Livermore National Laboratory. Only one iteration is run for every loop. Benchmark LOOP1 is the first Livermore loop and contains a one-dimensional parallel loop working on a one-dimensional array in range of 103. With the slice size of 23 iterations per parallel codeblock, this benchmark has a small amount of parallelism. This means that only around 40 parallel codeblocks can be created. The LOOP1L program is the same code with the problem size in range of $3 * 104$. LOOP1L program has a slice size of 1. Program LOOP8P is the eighth Livermore loop working with three-dimensional arrays with the dimension of $15 * 2 * 101$. The benchmark LOOP8pU has been generated by compiling the eighth loop with the unrolling option. The unrolled benchmark has spilled variables that degrade the performance. The Livermore loops with the provided input data are problems too small to measure large processor configurations. Another suite of loop measurements working with much larger data structure will be realized later.

Matrix multiplication is a two-dimensional problem working on a rectangular matrix in the form of two one-dimensional arrays. The name of the benchmark defines the size of the matrix. MM40 means a multiplication of two $40 * 40$ matrices. The benchmarks are translated into nested parallel calls. The outer call always has the slice size of 1 while the inner call has a slice size of 6 for MM8 and 1 for MM40 (see Figure 12). The speedup of both benchmarks is not impressive mainly because of the small problem sizes.

The MANDEL program calculates points of the Mandelbrot sets in a $64 * 64$ space. The slice sizes for the inner and outer loops are 1. The body of this benchmark has variable execution time. The speedup reached is excellent thanks to dynamic load-flow (see Figure 13). The program LIFE is John Conway's game of life. The algorithm works on a grid with every cell of the grid being one or zero. A new grid cell is calculated by analyzing the neighborhood of the cell. The grid is treated as a torus, i.e., the top cells are neighbors of bottom cells. The size of the grid is $100 * 100$. The inner loop has a slice size of 22 and the outer loop has one iteration per parallel codeblock. The speedup for larger numbers of processors is worsened by the fact that the problem size is too small and that, especially the inner loop with

	Processors			
	1	4	16	64
cycles	139846	41164	21903	
speedup	1	3.4	6.3	

LOOP1

	Processors			
	1	4	16	64
cycles	4504254	1221763	335661	168481
speedup	1	3.7	13.4	26.7

LOOP1l

	Processors			
	1	4	16	64
cycles	112447	36305	16992	
speedup	1	3	6.6	

LOOP8p

	Processors			
	1	4	16	64
cycles	147139	44648	21993	
speedup	1	3.3	6.7	

LOOP8pU

Figure 11: Speedup table for some Livermore Loops.

only 5 parallel codeblocks, should work with the local instead of replicated objects. Replicated objects can be costly in larger numbers of processors.

The recursive integration program QUAD (see Figure 14) is integrating the function $X * X + 10.0$ in the range of 1.0 to 100.0 with an epsilon of 0.0001. The main recursive function cannot be inline expanded. This means that no constant propagation is done as it can be completed only on inlined functions. This is a deficiency as such an optimization would improve the speedup because fewer parameters would be passed. This would mean less call overhead as the main recursive routine uses four variables as arguments, two of them being constant.

Two of the mentioned benchmarks have been realized in assembler as first benchmark programs for the Metamachine and have been used in [14]. The matrix multiplication written in HLA, has been implemented with an algorithm working on one-dimensional arrays with fixed size instead of two-dimensional arrays with dynamic size as done in MM40. The Mandelbrot program in HLA is working with two-dimensional arrays of size 64. The slice size is the same on all versions. The assembler programs do not need to access array descriptors. Although the access to the arrays, especially in loops, is optimized by prefetching invariant array descriptors, the penalty for additional allocation of descriptors is not insignificant and is the main source of performance loss (see Figure 15).

	Processors			
	1	4	16	64
cycles	50808	22222		
speedup	1	2.3		

MM8

	Processors			
	1	4	16	64
cycles	5963926	1723802	476056	187589
speedup	1	3.5	12.5	31.8

MM40

Figure 12: Speedups for matrix multiplication with varying matrix size.

	Processors				
	1	4	16	64	128
cycles	3636238	971170	271271	96321	86498
speedup	1	3.7	13.4	37.7	42

LIFE

	Processors				
	1	4	16	64	128
cycles	11837559	2978253	764168	213950	130333
speedup	1	4	15.5	55.3	90.8

MANDEL

Figure 13: Speedup for LIFE and MANDEL.

Following benchmarks show that the additional code, that makes a program executable on any number of processors, is not significant. A one-dimensional parallel loop (LOOP1) and two two-dimensional loops of varying sizes (MM8, MM40) are compiled into a sequential and a parallel code. The sequential versions have no parallel calls, no synchronization instructions, and no context switches (access to local memory is not a split-transaction). The parallel versions of benchmark have every dimension spread through parallel calls. No information about processor configuration is used either at compilation or at execution of benchmarks. Both versions of each SISAL program are run on one-processor configurations. Figure 16 depicts that the smaller benchmarks produce higher losses through parallel code although it is always below 10%. For example, the MM8 has only 2 parallel blocks for the inner loop, one block working in

	Processors			
	1	4	16	64
cycles	1288868	328631	90942	32932
speedup	1	3.9	14.7	39

QUAD

Figure 14: Speedup of QUAD.

	HLA (Assembler)	SISAL	Loss in Percent
Mandelbrot	168025	213950	22
Matrix multiplication	124858	144989	14

Figure 15: Assembler vs. SISAL versions on 64 processors.

	Sequential	Parallel	Loss in Percent
LOOP1	131856	139857	8
MM8	46282	50797	9
MM40	5813033	5963926	2.6

Figure 16: Execution times of sequential and parallel code.

range of 1 to 6, the second in range 7 to 8. Large problems have negligible losses of parallelization. Note that Metamachine has been designed to execute efficiently also in 1 processor configuration although many of its features are not used in such a situation.

9. Conclusion

The results show that it is possible to generate efficient code for the Metamachine from existing SISAL programs. SISAL is a very strong candidate for programming the family of von Neumann/dataflow hybrid or multithreading architectures. The array allocation and access strategies and the simple partitioning formulas showed good results for various problem sizes. The ADAM architecture proves to be able to execute sequential and parallel programs efficiently. To strengthen those statements, the presented benchmarks should be supplemented by larger SISAL benchmarks like Weather forecast or SIMPLE. It is yet to be seen if the needed optimizations can be implemented by extending OSC or by implementing them in ITH. The missing optimizations include the extension of automatic inlining with a threshold parameter and the propagation of constants into the graphs. The format of the intermediate file IF2 is easily understandable although the documentation is not complete.

Acknowledgments

The author thanks all members of the ADAM research group for their various contributions to the project and the students who helped in the realization of the tools. Part of this work has been supported by grant No. 2.309-0.86 of the *Schweizerische Nationalfonds*.

References

[1] R.E. Buehrer et al., "The ETH-Multiprocessor EMPRESS: A Dynamically Configurable MIMS System," *IEEE Trans. on Computers*, Vol. C-31, No. 11, November 1982, pp. 1035–1044.

[2] R.E. Buehrer et al., "The ETH Codeblock-Dataflow Project ADAM," Institute of Electronics, ETH Zürich, November 1991.

[3] David Cann, "Retire Fortran? A Debate Rekindled," *Proceedings of Supercomputing '91*, November 1991.

[4] David Cann, "The Optimizing SISAL Compiler: Version 12.0," Lawrence Livermore National Laboratories.

[5] D.C. Cann and J. Feo, "SISAL versus FORTRAN: A Comparision Using the Livermore Loops," Lawrence Livermore National Laboratory Report, 1990.

[6] J. Feo, D. Cann, and R. Oldehoeft, "A Report on the SISAL Language Project," *Journal of Parallel and Distributed Computing*, December 1990.

[7] O. Maquelin, "ADAM: A Coarse-Grain Dataflow Architecture that Addresses the Load Balancing and Throttling Problems," *Proceedings of CONPAR '90*, Springer, 1990.

[8] O. Maquelin, "The ADAM Architecture and its Simulation," Ph.D. thesis, Computer Engineering and Networks Laboratory, ETH Zürich ISBN 3 7281 2113 4, 1994.

[9] J.R. McGraw et al., "SISAL: Streams and Iteration in a Single Assignment Language: Reference Manual Version 1.2," Lawrence Livermore National Laboratories, Livermore CA, March 1985.

[10] S. Mitrovic, S. Murer, "A Tool to Display Hierarchical Acyclic Dataflow Graphs," *Proceedings of the International Conference on Parallel Computing Technologies*, Novosibirsk USSR, World Scientific Publishing, September 1991, pp. 304–315.

[11] S. Mitrovic et al., "A Distributed Memory Multiprocessor Based on the Dataflow Synchronization," *Proceedings of International Phoenix Conference on Computers and Communication*, 1990.

[12] S. Mitrovic, "Compiling SISAL for the ADAM Architecture," Ph.D. thesis, Computer Engineering and Networks Laboratory, ETH Zürich. ISBN 3 7281 2051 0, 1993.

[13] S. Murer, "A Latency Tolerant Code Generation Algorithm for a Coarse Grain Dataflow Machine," *Proceedings of CONPAR '90*, Springer, 1990.

[14] S. Murer and Philipp Färber, "A Scalable Distributed Shared Memory," TIK Report, ETH Zuerich, 1992.

[15] R.R. Oldehoeft and S.J. Allan, "Execution Support For HEP SISAL," *Parallel MIMD Computation, The HEP Supercomputer and its Applications*, MIT Press, 1985.

[16] S. Skedzielewski and J. Glauert, "An Intermediate Form for Applicative Languages," Lawrence Livermore National Laboratory Report, 1984.

Can Dataflow Machines be Programmed With an Imperative Language?

Simon F. Wail

IBM—Science and Technology Development
South Melbourne, Victoria, Australia

David Abramson

Griffith University—School of Computing and Information Technology
Nathan, Queensland, Australia

1. Introduction

Traditionally, dataflow machines have been programmed in dataflow languages. These languages differ from imperative ones in that they usually utilize functional semantics, which makes the translation onto the underlying machine relatively simple. It also allows quite high levels of concurrency to be revealed. However, dataflow languages suffer because their syntax and semantics are different from the more popular programming languages like C, Fortran, and Pascal. Consequently, they have been slow to gain acceptance by the programming community.

Another option that has only been explored by a few people is the possibility of using an established imperative language to program dataflow machines. In the past it has been believed that the side-effects in imperative languages would be too difficult to implement in a functional environment, and would also reduce concurrency. It was also presumed that programs written in imperative languages for sequential execution would contain little inherent parallelism. The approach has the advantage that the base language is well know. It has the disadvantage that the generation of good parallel code can be extremely difficult.

This project is concerned with the translation of an imperative language (in this case Pascal [30]) for execution on a dataflow machine. No programmer specification is required to inform the compiler as to which code should be parallelized; maximum parallelism is achieved in several ways. First, it is achieved through the inherent concurrent evaluation available in the dataflow model. Second, analysis and transformations of the source code are performed to determine data dependencies and to allow the parallelization of loops. Specific emphasis is given to those features of Pascal and other imperative languages that are omitted from parallel functional languages for dataflow architectures, such as global variables, function side-effects, variable aliasing, and pointers. Several methods to implement these features in a dataflow environment are presented, but the use of these facilities in the language will reduce possible concurrency by introducing data dependencies. The compiler generates a functional intermediate code form (IF1). This code is portable and allows the IF1 back-end translators to produce parallel code best suited to the architecture involved. Performance results of parallel Pascal execution are presented which highlight the extent of parallelism available in an imperative language. These results compare favorably with equivalent code written in Streams and Iteration in a Single-Assignment Language (SISAL) as well as hand-parallelized C code executing on a shared memory multiprocessor.

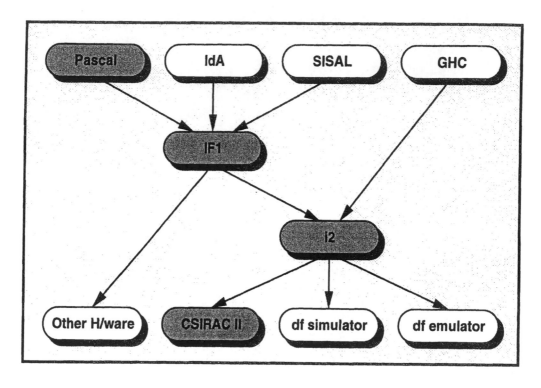

Figure 1: Software hierarchy for the CSIRAC II architecture.

1.1 RMIT/CSIRO Parallel Systems Architecture Project

This research began in February 1988 as part of the Joint Royal Melbourne Institute of Technology (RMIT) and Commonwealth Scientific Industrial Research Organisation (CSIRO) Parallel Systems Architecture project (PSAP). This project commenced in May 1986 and its purpose was to investigate parallel algorithms, methodologies, languages, and architectures. Given the resources, the project concentrated on the dataflow model of computation The variant of dataflow being used was based on an architecture which was first designed in 1976 by Egan at Manchester University, UK [16] and subsequently developed at RMIT [1] and now Swinburne Institute of Technology [17]. A multiprocessor emulation facility is available for high-speed interpretation of the programs as well as a conventional discrete-event simulation of the architecture.

Compilers for a number of languages were developed as part of the project. These include IdA [32] (a version of the near functional language Id Nouveau [22]), GHC (Guarded Horn Clauses, a logic programming variant with explicit parallelism and committed choice [24]), SISAL, and of course Pascal [14], [30], [33], which is the imperative language that is the topic of this paper.

Figure 1 reflects the software environment for the architecture designed as part of the project—CSIRAC II. All of the high-level languages have been designed and developed over the years by different people for different purposes. Compilers for these languages, excluding SISAL, have been written as part of PSAP in order to investigate parallel languages.

2. Dataflow Programming

Much research has concentrated on the manner with which to program dataflow machines in order to obtain the maximum benefit of the parallel execution model. To program a parallel computer to achieve an acceptable level of performance requires a well-designed algorithm and an appropriate implementation of the programming language. There are two main strategies to facilitate the construction of parallel programs. The first involves modifying a *programming language* with constructs that can be translated into parallel code, and removing constructs that tend to degrade performance and cause sequential execution. The most radical approach is to develop a new language specifically designed for a particular machine or model of execution. The second approach is to construct a *compiler* that performs sufficiently sophisticated analysis to generate parallel code. The patterns that such a compiler recognizes need to cover broad categories in order to receive the most benefit from automatic parallelization.

The following sections introduce and compare these two different approaches in the context of dataflow programming. As the dataflow model is fundamentally distinct from traditional computing models, much emphasis has been in the development of new languages. Some studies have involved the second approach and have found merits in the construction of sophisticated compilers to translate the traditional imperative languages.

2.1 Functional Languages

Functional languages are programming languages that closely follow the mathematical definition of a function. In such a language a series of functions are applied to a group of values returning a result. There are no side-effects of the functions as there is no hidden communication between functions. A consequence of this is the lack of *history sensitivity* in programs, as the result of a function is independent of any previous call to the same function. Thus, constructs that can maintain global state, such as global variables, are not allowed. Functions are defined with a name and perform operations on the incoming values. The operations may be simple mathematical operations, such as add or subtract, or more complex operations like function selection. In order to produce a usable language, the syntax often allows the binding of names to values. This does not allude to the storage of the value in memory, as in imperative languages, but allows the value to be referred to by the name. This concept is called the *single assignment rule* as names can only be bound to a value once. The single assignment rule, together with the lack of side-effects, allows functional programs to not require any particular ordering of operations as execution is strictly based on the data dependencies between operations.

Dataflow languages are descended from functional languages but much of their syntax is gained from imperative languages. These languages were developed as the functional semantics allowed simple translation into dataflow graphs, while attaining a more practical and higher level of programming than possible with graphs alone. Some examples of dataflow languages are VAL [2], SISAL [19], Id [8], Lapse [18], and valid [7].

The features of dataflow languages can be summarized, as appear in [3], as follows:

1. freedom from side-effects;
2. locality of effect;
3. equivalence of instruction scheduling constraints with data dependencies;
4. single assignment semantics;
5. unusual notation for iteration, necessitated by (1) and (4); and
6. a lack of history sensitivity.

2.2 Imperative Languages

High-level imperative languages have been around since the early days of computing and most are based on the von Neumann control flow model of computation. Over the decades, many have evolved into powerful languages with huge application bases. The imperative nature of these languages, such as multiple assignment, pointers, and global variables, facilitate the use of side-effects where all the inputs and outputs of a statement are not always explicitly indicated. For example, the evaluation of an expression may call a function that modifies a global variable. The features in the languages that make side-effects attractive are generally the same that make the translation of an imperative program into a dataflow graph problematic.

Early in dataflow research, the advantage of imperative language compilation was recognized and led to several compiler projects, but these often excluded solutions for the side-effects of the language. Whitelock [31] constructed a compiler for the Manchester Dataflow Machine that accepted a quite restricted subset of Pascal. Among the restrictions was the exclusion of jumps, aliasing, indirect recursion, pointers, and data structures. At the same time Allan et al. were defining a new language based again on Pascal, but omitting all "features incompatible with the notion of functionality" [23], [6]. More recently, two independent research groups have developed compilers for the C programming language for different dataflow architectures. The RC (Restricted C) compiler for the DTN Dataflow Computer [29] and the DFC II (DataFlowCII) compiler for the SIGMA-1 Dataflow Computer [25]. The RC compiler is based on preliminary work performed by Veen which found that the complications due to side-effects are over-estimated [28]. Currently the language conforms to the ANSI C standard but has a number of restrictions, the most serious being the lack of the address operator (&), recursion, and the goto statement. The most important feature of the DFC II compiler is that side-effects are controlled by the programmer. Synchronization statements are an addition to the standard C language to allow the user to write code that will provide deterministic results.

The project described in this paper involves the implementation of the Pascal programming language [33] for the CSIRAC II Dataflow Computer [30]. The rationale of this project is to produce a compiler for the Pascal language that can generate parallel code without any specification by the programmer. The compiler must be sufficiently sophisticated to extract as much parallelism as possible from a seemingly sequential list of statements. This involves determining the data dependencies between statements, and resolving all the side-effects in a program. The code generated by the compiler is IF1 [26], an intermediate graph form used by SISAL compilers. This code is functional and completely machine independent and therefore allows Pascal programs, compiled to IF1, to execute on any machine that has an IF1 translator. Currently there are IF1 compilers for a wide range of computers including commercial workstations and multiprocessors, supercomputers such as CrayS and Connection Machines, as well as various dataflow computers. This portability of IF1 code was one of the main reasons for choosing IF1 as the target code for the Pascal compiler. Unlike other conventional compilers for parallel computers, which are designed and optimized for a particular machine, Pascal programs compiled by this Pascal compiler can be executed efficiently on many different computers with absolutely no changes to the Pascal source code or the compiler. Another reason for using IF1 is that most SISAL compilers generate IF1 code and this allows a direct comparison of Pascal programs to functional SISAL programs. This is used to highlight the extent of parallelism available in an imperative language, and the success of the Pascal compiler in exposing such parallelism. There are also many programs that manipulate IF1 code to perform such optimizations as common sub-expression elimination, loop invariant removal, constant folding, and dead code removal [11], [27]. With this wide range of back-end processing available, the Pascal compiler is concerned only with the fundamental problems of compiling an imperative language for a dataflow architecture.

2.3 Side-Effects in Imperative Languages

It is generally agreed that the implementation of an imperative language on a dataflow architecture would be of great value, due to the extensive software already available in most imperative languages, but first, solutions are required for the side-effects of the languages, as outlined by Veen [28]:

- *Jumps*—the regular control flow implied by structured statements may be disturbed by escapes or *goto*s;

- *Aliasing*—one memory location can be addressed and modified through different access paths. The multiple paths can be created by pointers, call-by-reference parameters, explicit aliasing (*equivalence* statement in Fortran), or through array indexing (a[i] may address the same location as a[j]);

- *Multiple Assignment*—a variable can appear as the target of several assignments;

- *Global Objects*—through global objects, a nested procedure invocation may exchange information with another one without this being immediately visible at intermediate levels; and

- *Selective Modification of Data Structures*—a selective update operation may replace a single element of a large data structure.

Imperative programs are often seen as a list of statements to be executed sequentially which affect the computational state of the program. This computational state refers directly to the memory in a conventional computer. The side-effects of a program can be eliminated by replacing jumps with a conditional or loop, and adding the computational state to the interface (all inputs and outputs) of each statement. If such a transformed program was then translated into a dataflow graph an almost linear graph would result as each statement would be dependent on its predecessor and there would be little parallelism. With the aid of *dataflow analysis* (Section 3.1) which determines the real interface, a subset of the computational state can be added to the statements, thus removing some data dependencies between statements and increasing parallelism.

The Pascal programming language was chosen over other imperative languages, such as Fortran or C, because of the increased complexities of the side-effects in these other languages and the restriction to parallelism that they exhibit. Specifically Fortran was dismissed because of the following:

- No recursion—the lack of this feature reduces potential concurrency as recursion can be a major contributor to parallel execution in a dataflow architecture;

- *Goto* statements are the dominant control flow statement in Fortran and require extensive analysis and high execution overhead to implement;

- Parameter interface—in Fortran all parameters are passed by reference and this may introduce superfluous dependencies between the subroutine calls and other statements, if some parameters are actually only required as value parameters;

- *Common statements* establish global objects into programs and enable simple introduction of variable aliasing; and

- *Equivalence* statements are explicit activations of variable aliasing.

The greatest problem with C is pointers. C makes the assumption that variables are stored in memory somewhere and this enables the use of pointers to reference any variable by the simple use of the address operator (&). As this object, in the dataflow model, would not be stored in memory, but exist as a token passed between nodes, the concept of its address and a pointer to it, is meaningless. The use of the address operator also introduces an alias between the variable itself, and the pointer assigned to the address of the variable. The value stored in memory may be accessed and modified directly via the variable name, or indirectly by the pointer. These features pose complications in a dataflow architecture, and would demand complex analysis of the code to determine the dependencies between variables to enable the generation of instructions to retain the semantics of the original source code. The analysis could be too conservative in its investigation of the code and increase the data dependencies between statements, which could in turn greatly deteriorate execution performance.

C defines a special storage class called *static* that causes problems in the dataflow model. Internal static variables in a function retain their value between function calls, providing private, permanent storage for the function. In the dataflow model, as no storage is available, it is not possible to retain such values as there is no where to store them. One possible solution would be to transfer the values between function calls via the parameter interface. This would introduce a data dependency between the calls and thus reduce possible concurrency.

Outlined above are the reasons why Pascal is preferred over the more common imperative languages, Fortran and C. Pascal exhibits similar complications to the other languages but in Pascal these same problems are constrained by the syntax and semantics of the language, and are easier to detect, analyze, and overcome. Global variables in Pascal are explicitly declared in the source file and there are no external definitions. The variable scoping rules in Pascal enable clear resolution as to whether global or local variables are being accessed at any time. With these rules the global variable problem can be solved by passing them as parameters for the required procedures and functions. This also limits the variable aliasing analysis to reference parameters. Pascal pointers are strictly controlled by type and variable declarations. For a variable to be a pointer it must be explicitly declared as a pointer to a particular object. To assign a value to a pointer, a call to the *new* procedure is required to allocate a new object and a pointer to it, or it must be assigned the value of a previously defined pointer. There is no address operator, and no interaction between pointers and normal variables that are not declared as pointer objects. This limits the pointer problem to a well-defined set of variables and objects. Unfortunately gotos are not implemented in this Pascal compiler. It is very difficult, in terms of the data required, to determine the full effect of a jump to another point in a program. Due to the powerful high-level statement and function structures available in Pascal, gotos are very rarely used by programmers, and strongly discouraged by supporters of structured programming.

3. The Compiler

The compilation of Pascal is divided into three distinct passes. The first is a standard recursive descent parser with type checking [4]. In this phase an abstract syntax tree of the program is built to enable the second and third stages of the compiler to make multiple passes of the code. The second pass, outlined in the following sections, performs several examinations of the code, while the third and final pass is the code generation phase (Section 4).

The analysis phase of the compiler is required to gain information about the program being compiled and enable correct and deterministic code to be generated. There are three stages of this analysis and each is required to help solve the problems of compiling Pascal for a dataflow architecture, as outlined in Section 2.3. These stages are as follows:

1. Dataflow Analysis;
2. Global Variable Transformation; and
3. Variable Aliasing Analysis.

The information obtained about the program by this analysis phase is used by the only optimization performed by this compiler. Loop optimization (Section 3.4) is required to facilitate the generation of parallel loops which enable a great increase in concurrent execution. Most other methods of code optimization are not required as they are accomplished by various programs that manipulate the IF1 code generated by the compiler.

3.1 Dataflow Analysis

This section describes the dataflow analysis that is performed by the compiler based on the work of Allan [5]. Dataflow analysis is a technique used to collect information about a program as a whole. Dataflow analysis can detect where global variables are used and modified, as well as dependencies within loops to facilitate in the generation of parallel loop code. The information collected also determines which variables are required and modified for every statement, statement block, and function. This is required to enable the correct generation of some of the IF1 nodes, especially compound nodes. Once dataflow analysis is completed the program need not be referred to as a static sequence of instructions, but rather a collection of computations partially ordered by the data dependencies between the instructions.

The initial phase of the dataflow analysis generates two lists associated with every statement entry in the syntax tree—an input list and an output list. The input list for a statement contains the names of all the variables that are referenced by the statement before possibly being redefined by the statement. The output list for a statement contains the names of all the variables that are defined by the statement.

Once the input and output lists have been constructed for the whole program, the use and definition information can be collected. For all statements in the syntax tree where variables are modified, a list for each variable is maintained showing all statements where that variable is used. For all statements requiring a variable, an ordered list for each variable is maintained containing the statement where that variable is defined. For structured statements more information is required. The definition list for each variable consists of multiple links to the statement where the variable was defined before the structured statement, as well as the last statement where the variable is redefined in the enclosed statement block(s). The use list for each variable provides links to every use of the variable within the block, as well as the uses outside the block.

Live variable analysis is the final phase of the dataflow analysis implemented by the compiler. This analysis is used to determine when the computation for a variable is not required by any subsequent statements and therefore need not be executed. A variable is said to be *live* at a given point in a program if the variable is used by a subsequent statement or is used by the enclosing block. The Boolean *live* value, associated with every variable in an output list, is calculated simply by examining the use list for the variable. An empty list implies a dead (false) variable, otherwise the variable is live (true).

3.2 Global Variable Analysis

This phase of the compiler solves the problem of non-determinism due to the side-effects in functions caused by global or non-local variables. In a sequential architecture global variables are stored in one location and always accessed through this location. As execution is sequential the effect of modifications to global variables is deterministic as the order of computation is explicitly specified in the program. In the parallel execution environment of a dataflow architecture, concurrent references and modifications of global variables are non-deterministic as no data dependency exists between the different values.

The compiler solves the global variable problem by passing required global variables as parameters to functions where side-effects occur. This introduces a data dependency between different uses and definitions of the global variables, and enables the correct code to be generated. Unfortunately, the data dependency can reduce available concurrency, but this is necessary to retain the semantics of the code.

Pascal is a highly structured language, which allows the scope of variables and functions to be controlled by the programmer. Another feature of Pascal is the ability for functions to call any other functions that are *visible* within their scope. This can lead to quite complex execution paths [9], and is further complicated by variables that are defined and used in different function blocks. As part of the dataflow analysis described in Section 3.1, a list is maintained for each function which specifies all the other functions called by the current function being studied. Another list is associated with every function which after further analysis contains every function that can be reached, by any number of intermediate calls, from the current function. These lists are used to determine all the non-local variables that are required for each function, including those variables that pass through intermediate calls before being accessed.

Once all the variable information is known for each function, the syntax tree is modified to reflect the code changes. The formal parameter lists are changed by adding the required non-local variables and each call is changed so that the actual parameter lists match the new formal parameter lists. One of the important features of these changes is that only variables that are output from a function are passed as variable parameters. This reduces the data dependencies between function calls and can increase potential concurrency as execution is not delayed while waiting for a function to return a value. The final stage of the global variable transformation is to change all references to global and non-local variables to their local equivalent parameter variables. Figure 2 lists on the left-hand side an example Pascal program comprising variables and functions with different scoping levels and a complicated execution path, while the listing on the right-hand side is the same program after the global variable analysis and code modifications described above are performed. The code changes and additions are shown in italics.

3.3 Variable Alias Analysis

The Pascal compiler must handle potential aliases involving formal parameters passed as reference parameters. In sequential architectures, variable parameters are implemented by binding the formal parameter name to the address of the memory location used to store the actual parameter variable. Aliasing occurs where multiple formal

```
 1 program p;                            1 program p;
 2                                       2
 3 var x,y,z: integer;                   3 var x,y,z: integer;
 4                                       4
 5 procedure p3 (var x3,y3: integer);    5 procedure p3 (var p3'x,p3'y,x3,y3:
 6                                       6                   integer);
 7 begin                                 7 begin
 8  if x = y then                        8  if p3'x = p3'y then
 9    x3 := 5                            9    x3 := 5
10  else                               10  else
11    y3 := 5;                         11    y3 := 5;
12  x := y3;                           12  p3'x := y3;
13 end;                                13 end;
14                                      14
15 procedure p1 (var y1: integer);     15 procedure p1 (var p1'y,p1'z,p1'x,
16                                      16              y1: integer);
17 var x1,z1: integer;                 17 var x1,z1: integer;
18                                      18
19  procedure p2 (var x2: integer);    19  procedure p2 (p2'z1: integer;
20                                      20              var p2'z,p2'y1,
21                                      21              p2'y,p2'x1,p2'x,x2:
22                                      22              integer);
23  var y2: integer;                   23  var y2: integer;
24                                      24
25  begin                              25  begin
26    if z1 = z then                   26    if p2'z1 = p2'z then
27     p1(x2)                          27     p1(p2'y,p2'z,p2'x,x2)
28    else                             28    else
29     p1(z);                          29     p1(p2'y,p2'z,p2'x,p2'z);
30    y2 := x1;                        30    y2 := p2'x1;
31   end;                              31   end;
32                                      32
33 begin                               33 begin
34  if x1 = 5 then                     34  if x1 = 5 then
35    p2(z)                            35    p2(z1,p1'z,y1,p1'y,x1,p1'x,p1'z)
36  else                               36  else
37    if x1 > 5 then                   37    if x1 > 5 then
38     p2(y1);                         38     p2(z1,p1'z,y1,p1'y,x1,p1'x,y1);
39  p3(y1,y);                          39  p3(p1'x,p1'y,y1,p1'y);
40  x1 := y1;                          40  x1 := y1;
41 end;                                41 end;
42                                      42
43 begin                               43 begin
44  p1(y);                             44  p1(y,z,x,y);
45  p1(x);                             45  p1(y,z,x,x);
46  p3(y,z);                           46  p3(x,y,y,z);
47 end.                                47 end.
```

Figure 2: Global variable transformation example code.

parameters, in a particular function, are bound to the same storage location. This leads to a situation where references and modifications of one formal parameter can affect other formal parameters. Therefore the order of execution is vital in order to obtain deterministic results, and this is a problem for dataflow architectures, where the concept of control flow does not exist. This section describes how all possible aliases are detected in a particular function, while Section 5.2 outlines the implementation of a solution to this problem.

The aim of variable alias analysis is to annotate each function with a list of all aliases which can hold on entry to the function. Each entry in the list represents a potential alias pair of the two variables that are aliased. The presence of a particular pair does not imply that in every invocation of the function the variables in the pair are aliased, but that the function can be called with the variables aliased.

The analysis of aliases can be broken into two distinct tasks [15]. First, the *introduction* of aliases, where a variable globally visible is passed as an actual parameter, and second, the *propagation* of aliases, where a variable that is already involved in an alias pair is used as an actual parameter. Alias introduction occurs at call sites, where name to location mapping can be modified. An alias is created when the called function is given multiple names for a single memory location. Due to global variable transformation, outlined previously in Section 3.2, where all global variables are replaced by local parameters, the only way of introducing aliases is when a single actual parameter is passed in more than one parameter position. This binds the corresponding formal parameters of the called function to a single memory location, making them potential aliases. When this situation is found an entry is added to the called function's alias list that contains the pair of formal parameters that are potential aliases.

Once an alias has been introduced at a call site, that alias can hold on entry to the called function. All call sites within the called function may then propagate the alias pair to another function simply by giving the second called function a name for each element of the alias pair. Again, due to global variable transformation, the only way to propagate aliases is where both elements of an alias pair, which are formal parameters of the calling function, appear in the actual parameter list of the called function. If the corresponding formal parameters are variable parameters then the alias is propagated to the called function and another alias pair is added to the called function's alias list that contains these formal parameters.

It may seem that the addition of the global variables as parameters (Section 3.2) has exacerbated the alias situation, but it can actually reduce the problem. Global variables are only passed as parameters if they are required in the code, thus alias analysis of the original code would calculate similar alias lists due to the scoping of global variables within functions. In fact some aliases are removed due to the extensive code analysis performed in the previous passes of the compiler.

3.4 Loop Optimizations

As yet all the code analysis and transformations described previously have not involved any optimizations to improve execution performance or increase concurrency. Many programs spend a high proportion of execution time performing loop iterations, and if these loop iterations could be computed in parallel, total execution time could be greatly reduced. Unfortunately one optimization that is not available in any of the IF1 optimizers is where sequential loops are translated into parallel loops. Therefore this must be performed by compilers that generate IF1 by using the parallel loop construct included in the language. This section outlines the analysis required to determine if

```
1 program beforeinduction;          1 program afterinduction;
2                                    2
3 var a, b : array [1..100] of      3 var a, b : array [1..100] of
4            integer;                4            integer;
5     i, k : integer;               5     i, k : integer;
6                                    6
7 begin                             7 begin
8     k := 101;                     8
9     for i := 1 to 100 do begin    9       for i := 1 to 100 do
10        k := k - 1;               10
11        a[i] := b[k];             11            a[i] := b[101 - i];
12    end;                          12
13 end.                             13 end.
```

Figure 3: Induction variable removal example code.

loops iterations can execute in parallel. The dataflow information, gained from the dataflow analysis described in Section 3.1, is used by algorithms based on the work of Allan [5].

3.4.1 Induction Value Removal Induction variables are variables that appear in a loop and are incremented or decremented by a constant amount in each iteration of the loop. Examples of the ways these variables may be modified in a loop take the form of: i := i + 1 or i := j - 3, where j is another induction variable. The statements where induction variables are modified, introduce data dependencies between loop iterations and inhibit the generation of a parallel loop. This is because the new value of the induction variable is dependent on the previous value of the same variable, or of some other induction variable. In many cases, an induction variable may be replaced by some function of other variables, and thus allows the elimination of the induction variable. The removal of an induction variable removes the data dependencies it establishes and may allow a parallel loop to be produced.

The process to remove induction variables involves the searching of all the assignment statements in a loop, and checking if the variable assigned a new value meets the criteria of an induction variable outlined above. Once all the induction variables of a loop are detected, they may then be removed and replaced with their appropriate function. All these functions are expressions containing the loop control variable to calculate the correct value. Where an induction variable is removed the dataflow information for that particular statement is modified to reflect the change in the code. Now when the data dependence analysis is performed on the loop, the induction variables removed will no longer restrict the parallelization of the loop.

Figure 3 shows an example loop program before and after the induction variable k is removed. The code analysis identifies k as an induction variable in the loop and then modifications are made to the program to remove all occurrences of k within the loop and replace it with the function 101 - i. Further loop analysis will now be able to parallelize the new loop code.

3.4.2 Reduction Analysis Some loops calculate the sum or product of certain values and these operations are usually performed by modifying a scalar variable in the body of the loop. These variables are similar to induction variables except that they may be modified by any arbitrary, non-constant expression. As with induction

```
1 program matrixmul;            1 program matrixmul;
2                               2
3 var i,j,k: integer;           3 var i,j,k: integer;
4     a,b,c: array[1..10, 1..10] of   4     a,b,c: array[1..10, 1..10] of
5               real;            5               real;
6                               6
7 begin                         7 begin
8  for i := 1 to 10 do          8  for i := 1 to 10 do
9    for j := 1 to 10 do begin  9    for j := 1 to 10 do begin
10    a[i,j] := 0;              10    a[i,j] := 0;
11    for k := 1 to 10 do       11    for k := 1 to 10 do
12    a[i,j] := a[i,j]+         12    a[i,j] := sum of
13            b[i,k]*c[k,j];    13            0.0+b[i,k]*c[k,j];
14    end;                      14    end;
15 end.                         15 end.
```

Figure 4: Matrix multiply—Example of reduction operation.

variables, these variables introduce a data dependency between loop iterations and prevent parallel loop generation.

IF1 has a feature, available in all its loop constructs, that will perform such a sum or product reduction without the need to calculate intermediate results. Boolean **or** and **and** reduction operations may also be represented as sum or product reductions respectively. Each body of the loop can independently evaluate the expression to be used in the reduction, and when all these values have been determined, at the conclusion of all loop bodies, the values are reduced by summation or product operations to a single value.

In order to use the IF1 reduction features, the loop body must be analyzed in a way similar to the search for induction variables. Each assignment statement is checked to ascertain whether the assignment is actually performing a reduction operation and when such a statement is found, the reduction variable on the right-hand side of the assignment operator is removed from the expression. With the removal of the reduction variable from the right-hand side of the assignment operator, the dataflow information is updated to reflect this change. Therefore the reduction variable is no longer an input variable to the statement, it is only output by the assignment statement. This removes a data dependency that would otherwise prevent the loop executing in parallel.

A common example of a reduction operation is the algorithm for matrix multiplication shown in Figure 4 on the left-hand side. Each element in the result matrix is calculated as a sum of the multiplication of the row elements of one matrix, with the column elements of the other matrix. The assignment that performs this operation appears on line 12 in Figure 4. This assignment is detected by the compiler as a sum reduction and replaces the reduction variable on the right-hand side with 0.0. The statement in the abstract syntax tree is annotated as a reduction operation to allow the generation of appropriate IF1 reduction code. The conceptual modification to the source code is shown in Figure 4 on the right-hand side.

Another loop optimization that is performed at the same time as the reduction analysis, is the search for array initializations. The Pascal language does not allow a single value to be placed in every element of an array without the use of a loop to assign the value to each element in the array. When the value placed in the array is constant throughout the loop, the operation may be implemented by a single IF1 node that places a value into every element of an array. In some cases where a loop contains only array initializations, the whole loop may be discarded. To find array initialization statements requires analyzing each assignment statement in a similar way used to detect reduction operations. The variable on the left-hand side of the assignment operator must be an array indexed by the current loop control variable, and the expression on the right-hand side must be constant in the loop. This does not exclude variables appearing on the right-hand side, but they must be constant values in the loop.

3.4.3 Dependence Analysis In order for the Pascal compiler to generate code for a parallel loop, the loop must be analyzed to check for loop-carried data dependencies. A loop-carried dependency is where two or more statements are dependent on each other for their data values and the dependencies cross the interface between loop iterations. When this occurs, the loop iterations are not independent of each other and therefore cannot execute concurrently without some sort of loop transformation. If no loop-carried dependencies exist in a particular loop, code to produce a parallel loop can be generated by the compiler.

The analysis process to find loop-carried dependencies involves creating an *order* matrix [5] for the body of the loop, which indicates the order in which two statements must be executed. The ordering of statements is determined by the data dependencies between the statements. For each statement in a loop, the output list (Section 3.1) is parsed, and the dependence relation between where the current variable from the list is defined, and where that value is used, is analyzed. The dependence analysis for array structures that contain the loop control variable in their index expressions, requires examination of these index expressions in order to determine the correct ordering of the loop statements. Modifying and accessing array elements in different ways can introduce interference between loop iterations, as an element that is defined in a previous or future loop iteration can be accessed by the current iteration. In this situation, if the loop iterations are executed independently of each other, and each array is shared between all iterations as in a conventional architecture, there is no guarantee that the accessed value is correct. This problem is detected by analysis of the array subscript expressions, and the ordering of the statements is determined in order to ensure that access to original values occurs before they are modified, and access to modified values occurs after their definition. In fact the only array dependence that limits the parallelization of loops in a dataflow architecture is when an array element defined in a previous iteration is accessed. This is because arrays are not stored in memory in a dataflow computer and the original unmodified arrays are always accessible by every iteration of the loop.

Once the order matrix is constructed, it is analyzed for cycles which represent loop-carried dependencies. When a cycle is found, the data dependence relations in the cycle are examined to ascertain whether the cycle can be broken. The only cycles that cannot currently be broken are those in which an array element is defined and then accessed by a subsequent iteration, or in which a scalar variable is conditionally defined in the loop. If no cycles remain after this analysis, then the loop iterations are independent of each other and the loop is designated as being able to be executed in parallel. Otherwise the loop requires sequential execution. When a loop is deemed parallel it is converted into a *for* loop even if it appears as a *repeat* or *while* loop in the original source code.

4. Code Generation

The code generation phase of the compiler traverses the entire abstract syntax tree producing code for each statement. This code, as mentioned in Section 2.2 is IF1 [26], an intermediate graph form used by SISAL compilers. IF1 is based on acyclic graphs. There are four components to a graph—nodes, edges, types, and graph boundaries. There is a wide variety of nodes defined in IF1 to perform many operations, from simple arithmetic operators, to reduction operations, and array and record manipulation. Edges specify the interconnection of nodes in a graph which allows the output(s) of one node to become the input(s) of other nodes. Each edge is annotated with a type specification as IF1 is a strongly typed language. Graph boundaries are used to separate graphs in the code. Each function is a single graph and edges connected to the graph boundary specify the interface for the function. To perform complex operations, such as iteration and selection, requires the use of IF1 compound nodes that contain a number of subgraphs. Each subgraph consists of nodes to carry out a different fragment of the operation, such as a loop test, or the body of a loop.

Most of the generation of IF1 code for Pascal is straightforward as IF1 contain nodes and type structures that allow the implementation of many of the high-level features of Pascal. In this section, only those features of Pascal that require special consideration when generating code are described. In most cases these features are related to side-effects in the code, or the more complex data structures such as files, strings, and sets.

4.1 Expressions and Simple Statements

Simple arithmetic expressions are represented in IF1 by a number of nodes and edges that carry the intermediate results between the nodes. Usually the number of nodes required for such an expression is a 1:1 mapping with the number of operators in the given expression. An access to a variable in an expression generates an edge from the expression that previously defined the variable, via an assignment, and the node that requires the variable in the current expression. Access to arrays and records in an expression involve using nodes to extract the required value from the structure (**AElement** and **RElements** nodes). Function calls in an expression are covered later in this section, and pointer variables are discussed in detail in Section 5.1.

Assignments allow the result of a particular expression to be remembered and accessed for a finite period of time after which the assignment variable is given a new value or becomes inactive. When the assignment variable on the left-hand side of the assignment operator is a complete variable, i.e., it does not access array, record, or pointer fields, the code for the assignment is only that which is necessary for the expression on the right-hand side. The output edge of the expression is stored and this edge is used to access the assignment variable by any subsequent statements. To allow multiple assignments to variables, a new output edge is stored for each assignment of a particular variable and used until another assignment of that variable occurs.

The assignment of array elements and record fields involves the use of nodes to replace a new value into a structure (**AReplace** and **RReplace** nodes). According to the Pascal Standard [33] the order of evaluation of expressions on the left-hand side of the assignment operator, and those on the right-hand side are implementation-dependent. In this compiler the right-hand side of an assignment is *always* evaluated before the left-hand side. Also index expressions appearing on the left-hand side that are needed to update an array element are evaluated, from left to right, before the array structure is accessed to perform this update. This is because an index expression may contain

Pascal Statement	IF1 Compound Node
If...then...[else]	Select
Case	Select or TagCase (Variant Records)
Repeat	LoopA
While	LoopB
For	LoopB or Forall (Parallel)

Table 1: Mapping of Pascal Statements to IF1 Compound Nodes.

a function call that modifies the array variable, and the assignment of the array is to use the new array returned from the function call. Therefore in this compiler a function call that appears in an assignment that modifies the assignment variable on the left-hand side could produce unexpected results.

Function and procedure calls are implemented in IF1 by use of the Call node. Due to the static nature of the Call node it is not possible to allow procedures or functions to be used as parameters. The Call node requires a static literal string and explicit function type to specify which function to call and therefore it is not possible to use a passed parameter to identify the function to call.

4.2 Structured Statements

Pascal structured statements are implemented using IF1 compound nodes. The compound nodes have very similar operational semantics to the high-level Pascal statements that are to be executed. Table 1 shows each Pascal structured statement and the compound node used to implement those statements.

4.2.1 Parallel Loops As described in Section 3.4, loops with independent iteration can execute in parallel, with each loop body evaluated concurrently. To implement such a loop in IF1 requires the use of a special compound node called ForAll. This node consists of three subgraphs—Generate, Body, and Returns, and the semantics of the loop are very different to the sequential LoopA and LoopB nodes. The generate subgraph contains nodes that produce a stream of multiple values from their inputs. The only nodes permitted inside the generate subgraph are RangeGenerate or AScatter nodes. The RangeGenerate node takes two integer inputs and outputs a list of integers that are in the inclusive range between the inputs. The AScatter node takes an array and outputs all its elements and their respective indexes. Each element of these multiple value lists is sent to a distinct instance of the loop body subgraph on a multiple value port; they are not broadcast to all instances of the body. Therefore the number of parallel loop bodies that are executed is determined by the maximum number of elements in any of the multiple value streams. The body subgraph contains the code for the loop body which may consist of any IF1 nodes. The returns subgraph is invoked when all the loop iterations have been executed and it takes all the outputs of the body subgraph and reduces them according to a specified operation to a single value. These values are then the results of the loop.

Figure 5 show the template for a parallel loop in IF1. As mentioned in Section 3.4, all parallel loops are represented as Pascal *for* loops, and therefore the initial and final values for a loop variable are calculated outside the loop and remain constant throughout the execution of the loop. These values together with any other variable values required for the loop can be seen entering the ForAll node in the top left section of Figure 5. The remaining sections of Figure 5 show the details of each of the three subgraphs of the `ForAll` node.

The generator subgraph shown in the top right section of Figure 5 provides the multiple values for the loop bodies. The `RangeGenerate` node takes the loop boundary values and generates a list of integers which are used as the loop control variable (V). The `AScatter` nodes take each input array (K ports) that is modified by the loop and produces a list of elements and indexes that are placed on consecutive multiple value ports (M ports).

The body subgraph (bottom left section of Figure 5) is generated in much the same way as for sequential loops but some important differences need to be explained. First, any arrays modified by the body, and therefore scattered by the generator subgraph, do not require the usual `AElement` or `AReplace` nodes, as the current element is available from a multiple value port, and all the new elements of an array are output on a different result port (T ports) and built into new arrays in the returns subgraph. Second, the arrays scattered by the generator subgraph can be accessed as a complete unmodified array from their original input port. Therefore any element of a modified array can be used in any loop body. Obviously it has already been determined that there are no data dependencies between the elements accessed and the current loop iteration. The returns subgraph (bottom right section of Figure 5) may contain various nodes which can reduce multiple values into single values in different ways. The `Finalvalue` node returns the last value from the input stream. As the result is the value from the last loop body, it is the result of the last definition of the variable. The `Reduce` node performs the reduction operations described in Section 3.4.2. Each expression from the loop bodies passes through the node and the result is the sum or product of all these values. The `AGather` node performs the opposite operation to the `AScatter` node, and therefore for each `AScatter` node in the generator subgraph of a `ForAll` node, there is a matching `AGather` node in the returns subgraph of the compound node. The `AGather` node takes a list of multiple values and places them into consecutive elements of a new array.

The last part of the code generated for a parallel *for* loop appears outside the compound node. If a segment of an array is modified by the loop, then a merge of the old and new values of the array is required. This involves extracting the parts of the array not modified by the loop from the old array, and concatenating them on either side of the new array. This is shown pictorially in Figure 6.

4.3 Library Functions

The Pascal Standard [33] specifies quite a number of required procedures and functions that must be available in all implementations of the language. The complexity of implementing these procedures and functions varies. For example, it is possible to plant inline code consisting of simple or compound nodes, or to actually write the code in SISAL, and allow the back-end translators to link the various IF1 files together. In this section, most of the standard Pascal procedures or functions are explained. Only *new* and *dispose* are detailed in Section 5.1.

4.3.1 File Operators

In order to explain the Pascal I/O routines a description of how the file structures are implemented in IF1 is necessary. Files are represented in IF1 as an array[1] for each file containing the file elements, where these elements are

---

[1]It would be preferable to implement a text file or other files as an IF1 stream, but this feature is not yet available in the CSIRAC II IF1 translator.

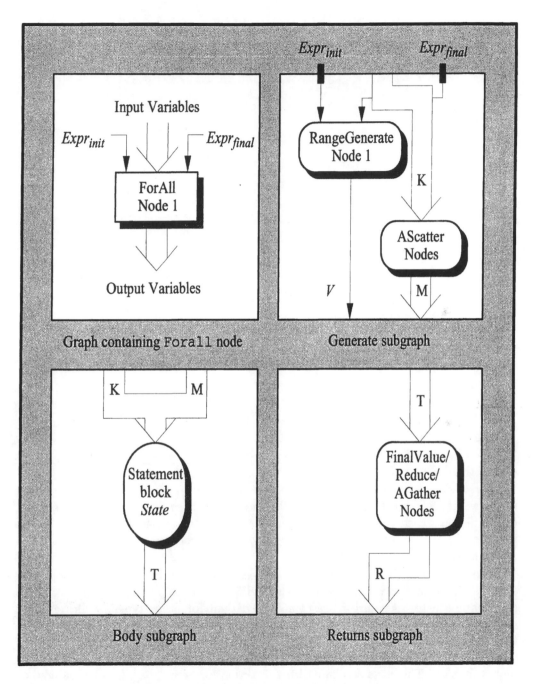

Figure 5: Template for parallel *For* statement.

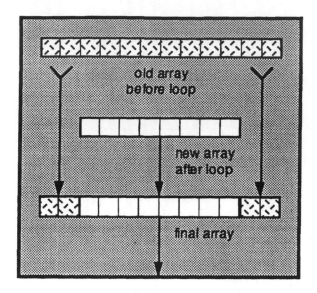

Figure 6: Array merge at the conclusion of a parallel loop.

read (f, V)	$\equiv$	**begin** $V := f \uparrow$; get (f) **end**
write $(f, Expr)$	$\equiv$	**begin** $f \uparrow := Expr$; put (f) **end**

Figure 7: Translation of *read* and *write*.

homogeneous. Using this structure the basic file functions can be easily seen. The *get* procedure removes the first element of the file array (**ARemL** node), and then updates the file buffer variable ($f \uparrow$). This is performed by using an **AElement** node to extract the file element. The *put* procedure takes the file buffer value and appends it to the end of the file array (**AAddH** node).

A *read* call is equivalent to an assignment of the given variable to the current file buffer value, followed by a *get* call, while a *write* call is equivalent to an assignment of the file buffer variable, followed by a *put* call. This code is shown in Figure 7. The IF1 code for *read* and *write* calls is a translation of this code using the nodes described above for the *get* and *put* functions.

The remaining input and output routines, *readln, writeln, eoln,* and *page,* are only valid for text files and are written in SISAL. The input and output routines to manipulate text files are more complicated than for other types of files as they require a translation between character sequences and scalar values. This is because text files consist of characters while the routines access scalar values, and therefore there must be some conversion between a string of characters and the required scalar representation. There is a separate SISAL function for each type that may be read or written, as well as some utility routines to convert integers to strings (`itoa`) and vice versa (`atoi`).

4.3.2 String and Set Operators Character strings are implemented as arrays of characters and behave the same as any other arrays with one very important exception, strings may be compared to each other. Two strings can appear on opposing sides of any of the six standard relational operators $(=, \neq, <, <=, >, >=)$ and a single Boolean value is returned from the expression. The strings must be of the same size and the comparisons are according to the ASCII ordering of the characters. Strings are equal if they are identical in every way (size, contents, and ordering).

To implement these comparisons in IF1 necessitates the use of a parallel loop. The ForAll node contains a body subgraph that compares the scattered string elements with an Equal and/or NotEqual node, and then the results of this comparison are reduced to a single Boolean value in the returns subgraph using a combination of a Reduce and/or Firstvalue node depending on the relational operator.

The implementation of Pascal sets can be placed into two independent categories, integer sets and non-integer sets. The description of the different implementation for integer sets can be found later in this section. Sets can only contain ordinal values so the non-integer sets available consist of Boolean, character, or enumerated values. The maximum set size of these types is static and known at compile time, and an array of Boolean, where the set items are used as the indexes to access the array, can be utilized to implement any set of these types. A true element in the array specifies that the set item (index) associated to that array element currently exists in the set, while a false element indicates that the set item is omitted from the set.

The complexity of performing the different operations on sets varies from single IF1 nodes to access elements of the set array, to using parallel loops to do relational $(=, \neq, <=, >=)$ or combinational (union, intersection, or difference) operations. To add a single item to the set involves setting the appropriate array element to true, and to check if an item is currently in the set (*in* operation) can be accomplished with a single AElement node, which will return the correct Boolean value.

The set relational operators are implemented in a similar way to the string equal and not equal tests. A ForAll node is used, where the generator subgraph scatters both set arrays, the body subgraph performs some Boolean test, and the returns subgraph uses a Reduce node to determine the final result. The less than or equal, or greater than or equal operators when concerned with sets are interpreted as the complete inclusion of one set in the other. This test can be accomplished by performing a set intersection and then testing for equality against one of the original sets. The combination operators, union (+), intersection (*), and difference (-), all return a new set array. Therefore the body of the ForAll node determines if each set item will appear in the new array, and the returns subgraph gathers all the Boolean values into a new set array.

Integer sets cannot be implemented in the same way as non-integer sets. This is because it is not practical to have an array with index values ranging from -maxint...maxint. Even if the size was limited to a smaller value, like many Pascal implementations impose, it would still have to be quite a large array to allow integer sets to be useful. Therefore the solution in this implementation of Pascal is to store integer sets as arrays of integer values. If a value appears in the array it is currently in the set, while if it is not in the array it is not part of the set. This implementation complicates all the available set operations as each set item cannot be accessed by a single array operation as it is not known where each set item appears in the array. This is why all set operations for integer sets are performed by calls to different SISAL functions.

5. Resolving Side-Effects

Sections 2.3 and 3.3 introduced the problems of pointers and aliasing in a parallel execution environment, and this section describes the solutions implemented by the Pascal compiler to overcome these obstacles. In a conventional architecture a pointer is an address into the memory space of the program. The address is normally allocated by some sort of memory management routine which sets aside enough memory to store the object that the pointer will reference. In Pascal this operation is performed by a call to the standard procedure, *new*, with a pointer variable as a parameter. The call apportions the required memory, and then assigns the parameter to the address of the allocated memory, to allow the placement of values into the memory by de-referencing the pointer variable.

When reference parameters are passed to functions on conventional architectures, usually the memory address of the parameter is placed on the stack, rather than the parameter's actual value. This then allows the called function to access the parameter's value, as well as modify the value, by de-referencing the memory address on the stack. In fact reference parameters can be thought of as pointers to the memory where the data are actually stored. From this it can be seen that there is a close relationship between pointers and variable parameters. Therefore the solution to pointers and aliasing, in the presence of variable parameters, is implemented in a similar fashion.

The flexibility offered by IF1 array structures is used as the basis for the pointer and aliasing solution. Unlike Pascal, arrays in IF1 may vary their size throughout the execution of a program. They can be created empty with elements then added or removed when required, or whole arrays can be concatenated together. By using these arrays to store pointer objects and aliased variables, a memory address, that would be used in a conventional architecture, effectively becomes an index to the appropriate element in an array.

5.1 Pointer Implementation

Since IF1 arrays can only contain homogeneous elements, a different array is required to store the various pointer objects that appear in a single program. This has the advantage that accesses to different typed objects are independent and allow more concurrency than they would if all the objects were in one array. There are also two alternative array definitions implemented for pointers. The alternative used is controlled by a compiler argument that specifies which pointer implementation is generated. One implementation is optimized for high speed and efficiency, while ignoring the size to which each pointer array might grow. The other implementation tries to keep the array size to a minimum but this is generally slower. The two different array structures are shown in Figure 8. The top array displays a section of an array used when optimal execution time is requested. The array contains some valid objects as well as some disposed elements displayed as crosses (x). Whenever a new pointer object is required, an element is appended to the end of the array ignoring any previously disposed elements. When minimum array size is requested the array structure displayed in the bottom of the figure is used. Each element of the array is a record containing a tag field and the actual pointer object. The tag field is used to maintain a list of free elements in the array for use when a new pointer object is required. The time optimized method executes in less time than the space optimized method as no extra code is needed to provide the free list, while the space optimized method keeps the array size to a minimum by allowing the re-allocation of disposed objects. The advantage of a smaller array is that less bandwidth is needed to transmit the pointer array between nodes, and less elements are copied when the array is modified.

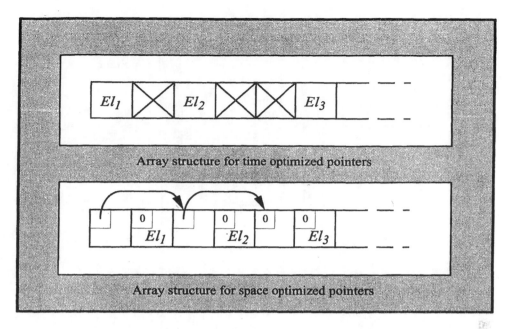

Figure 8: Array structure used for pointers.

The dataflow analysis, described in Section 3.1, determines the use and definition of all pointer variables in a program. From this information it can be established which statements affect particular pointers and therefore the arrays that store the objects that the pointers access. These arrays can then be passed to the appropriate nodes where the pointer variables are used. Multiple accesses without modification of pointer objects can occur concurrently, while an update requires the array to be passed to the node that changes the array, and then the modified array is passed to subsequent accesses or updates.

When a pointer object is addressed via a pointer variable, an access to the appropriate pointer array is required using the pointer value as an index. This is displayed in Figure 9 and shows the difference between the two implementations possible for pointer structures. The middle diagram reveals that only a single **AElement** node is required to access a pointer object in the fast implementation, as the pointer array only contains pointer objects. The **AElement** node takes the pointer array, which is obtained from its last modification, and outputs the element indexed by the pointer variable. The space optimized method, reflected in the right-hand side diagram, requires an extra **RElements** node to extract the object. The additional node is needed to separate the record containing the tag field and the actual object field.

The code required to modify a pointer object is similar to that used to access such an object. In the fast version, a single **AReplace** node is needed to place the new pointer object in the pointer array. The node outputs a new copy of the pointer array, and this value is used for subsequent pointer object accesses and updates. For the space optimized implementation, two additional nodes are necessary to change a pointer object. First the record containing the pointer object is extracted from the array, using an **AElement** node, then the object field is updated by a **RReplace** node, and finally the new record is replaced in the pointer array with an **AReplace** node.

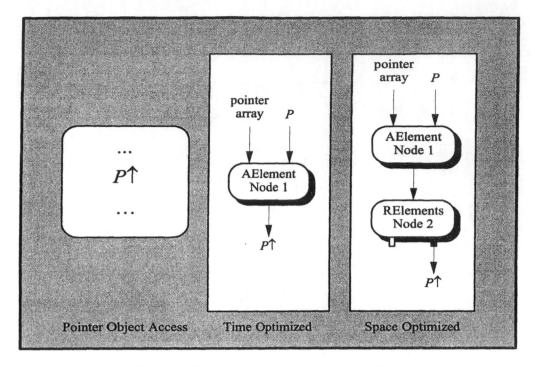

Figure 9: Template to access a pointer object.

One of the major problems of pointers in a parallel execution environment is obtaining correct results is the presence of pointer aliasing, i.e., when two or more pointers refer to the same object. This occurs when a pointer variable is given the same value as another pointer variable by an assignment statement, or due to the name binding by a function call. Pointer aliasing is a problem when code executes concurrently as the order of evaluation can affect the final result. Execution must proceed in the order specified by the textual ordering of the statements. In this implementation this problem is solved by the data dependency forced on the code by the pointer array. Even if two pointer variables are equal, any modification to their object will occur in the order that the statements appear in the original source, as the pointer array is passed from one update to the next. Any accesses to the object are extracted from the most recent modification of the pointer array.

Figure 10 shows an example of possible pointer aliasing. The code segment on the left-hand side of the figure demonstrates two pointer variables, p and q, that are equal, and then includes some accesses and modifications to each of their objects, which are the same element in the pointer array. The diagram on the right-hand side shows the flow of the pointer array between the accesses and updates. Even though the pointer variables are equal, no special code is required to retain the original semantics of the code, as the dependency on the pointer array ensures the code is executed in the correct order. It should also be noted that an access can execute concurrently with an update as evidenced by the diagram.

The standard routines which dynamically allocate (*new*), and de-allocate (*dispose*) space for pointer objects are achieved by generating inline IF1 nodes. The implementation of the *new* and *dispose* procedures for the time optimized method is very simple. For the *new* procedure a pointer object is added to the end of the appropriate pointer array (**AAddH** node), and the index is determined by an **ALimH** node, which returns

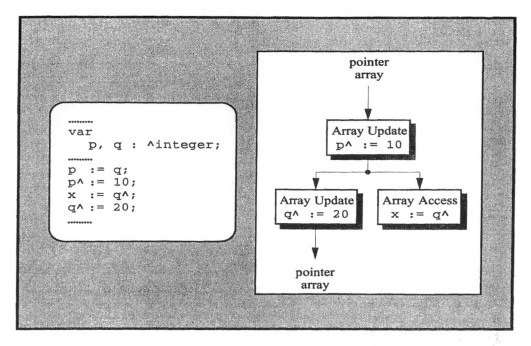

Figure 10: Example of pointer aliasing.

the high bound index of an array. This value is returned by the *new* procedure as the value for the pointer variable provided as a parameter to the procedure. The only change that takes place when an object is disposed is that the pointer variable is set to zero which represents a *nil* pointer. Any other pointer that happens to reference the same object can still do so but according to the Pascal Standard [33] this is an error. As it is not possible to trace all pointer variables that may point to a disposed object, this error is undetected as provisioned by the Standard.[2]

Figure 11 displays the pseudo-code for the *new* procedure where array size is considered and kept to a minimum. From this figure it can be seen that the code is more complicated than the time optimized method and takes longer to execute. The first step of the *new* procedure is a check of the free list to determine if any elements of the array are available for re-allocation. The head of the free list is always contained in the first (1) element of the array, and a zero in the tag field represents a *nil* pointer. If no free elements are found a new element is added to the end of the array in the same way as described for the time optimized implementation. If a free element is found the pointer variable is assigned its index, and the head of the list is updated to the next element in the free list. Also the tag field of the element being re-used is reset to zero as it is now "in-use."

In the space optimized implementation of pointers, a disposed object must be added to the free list to allow it to be re-allocated by a future *new* call. The pseudo-code to perform this operation is shown in Figure 12. The tag field of the element being disposed, indexed by the pointer, P, is updated to point to the current head of the free list. Then the tag of the first element of the array, which always points to the head of the free list is changed to point to the element being disposed. Finally the pointer variable is returned with a value of zero, similar to the time optimized version

---

[2]An error is defined as a violation by a program of the requirements of the Standard that a processor is permitted to leave undetected.

```
begin
        if pointer array[1].tag = 0 then begin
                Empty Free List
                pointer array := AAddH(pointer array)
                P := ALimH(pointer array)
                end
        else begin
                P := pointer array[1].tag
                pointer array[1].tag := pointer array[P].tag
                pointer array[P].tag := 0
                end
end
```

Figure 11: Pseudo-code for *new* procedure.

```
begin
        pointer array[P].tag := pointer array[1].tag
        pointer array[1].tag := P
        P := 0
end
```

Figure 12: Pseudo-code for *dispose* procedure.

of the *dispose* procedure. Again any erroneous "dangling" references by different pointer variables to a disposed element are possible, and such a reference may return unexpected values as the element may be re-allocated and modified in the meantime.

5.2 Variable Alias Implementation

Discussed in the introduction of Section 5, there is a close relationship between reference parameters and pointers. This is important as variable aliasing can only occur in the presence of reference parameters, and therefore an array implementation similar to that for pointers can be used to solve the alias problem. In Section 3.3 a method to detect all possible aliases is described, while in this section a technique is outlined to produce deterministic code whenever an alias might exist. As the definite occurrence of a particular alias can often not be determined statically at compile-time, and as routines in which aliasing can occur might be invoked without an alias, it is necessary that the code generated is correct for the situations where an alias is valid as well as where it is invalid.

In general terms the solution to variable aliasing is to place the possibly aliased variables into an array, and then use an index value to access each variable. When two variables are actually aliased, their index values are the same and therefore access the same element in the array. This is identical to the form of pointer aliasing described previously and the correct deterministic results are guaranteed in the same way. However, if two variables are not aliased at a particular point in time, their index values are different and thus they access their own independent values in the array. Therefore the same code can be used to access variables whether or not they are aliased at a particular time.

Different arrays are required for aliased variables of different types. Aliasing can only occur between variables of the same type except when structured variables are involved in a particular way. Currently this implementation of the compiler cannot handle the case where a base structure and any of its items are passed as variable parameters within the one call. This is because within a called function, where the alias occurs, the base structure and its items have completely different names and it is impossible at compile-time to determine if an access to the base structure will access one of the items passed separately to the function.

Every function is annotated by the alias analysis code (Section 3.3) with a list of possible aliases that are valid within the function. Whenever a function with a non-empty alias list is called, special code must be produced to implement the array solution to aliasing. As there are two ways aliases are transmitted to functions, whether they be introduced or propagated, so there are two ways the aliased variables must be placed into the arrays and passed to a called function. Also when the code for the function that contains an alias is generated, it must include nodes to access the aliased variables from the arrays. These methods are described below.

For an alias to be active it must first be "introduced" to a function. As Section 3.3 described, an alias is introduced when an actual parameter appears more than once in a parameter list. For every formal parameter that may be aliased in the function, the corresponding actual parameter must be added to the alias array. This action is performed by an **AAddH** node, which adds the supplied value to the end of an array. Once an actual parameter value is added to the array, the index value to be used to access the value is obtained from an **ALimH** node which returns the high bound of the array. The index value is remembered for each actual parameter, and if the same variable appears again in the parameter list, thus introducing a definite alias, any previously saved index value is forgotten. Finally the alias array and the index values for each possibly aliased parameter are connected to a **Call** node which transfers execution to the called function. Figure 13 demonstrates the previously described operations with an introduced alias of the variable, V.

After the called function has completed execution, the aliased values must be accessed and removed from the alias array. Each parameter retrieves its value from the array, using the previously saved index value. The value returned is then assigned to the actual parameter. To keep the alias array size to the minimum required at any time, each introduced alias value is removed from the array when it is no longer necessary for it to be in the array. This operation is performed by an **ARemH** node which removes the high bound element of an array.

An alias is propagated to a function only if both elements of an alias pair in the calling function's alias list are passed as reference parameters to the called function. As an alias that is propagated must first be introduced to a function, the function must have been passed an alias array, as well as the index values for access to the aliased formal parameters. To propagate this alias to another function all that is required is to pass the alias array and the index values to the called function. This is shown in Figure 14. $Form_1$ and $Form_2$ refer to the index values for the possibly aliased formal parameters that entered the calling function through its interface, and are now being propagated to function, $func_2$. A single function call may introduce and propagate different aliases simultaneously. In this situation a combination of the code for introduced and propagated aliases is generated.

The code to access possibly aliased variables is identical to that for the time optimized pointer implementation shown in Figure 9. The pointer array is replaced with the appropriate alias array, and the value of P is the variable's index value passed into

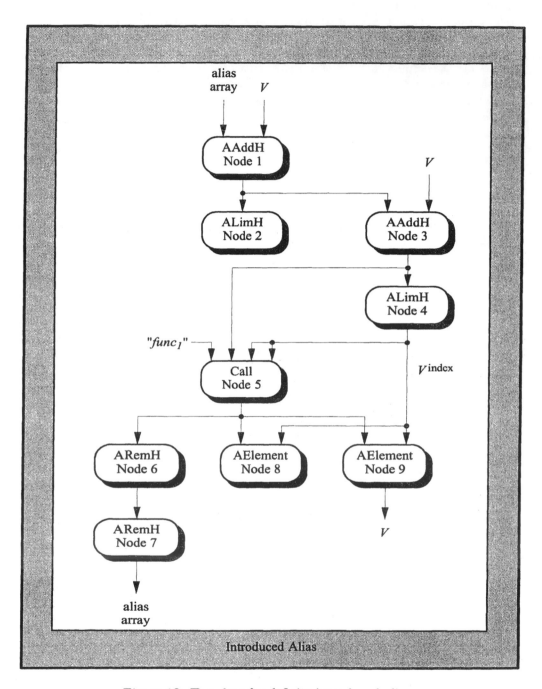

Figure 13: Template for definite introduced alias.

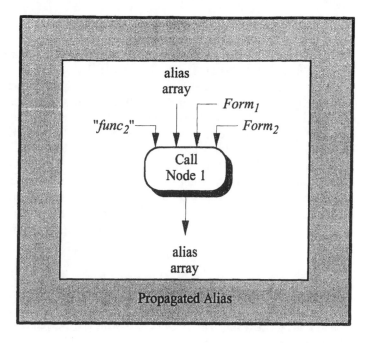

Figure 14: Template for propagated alias.

the current function. From this explanation it can be seen that pointer and reference parameter implementations are closely related. Aliased variables can be modified by using an **AReplace** node instead of the **AElement** node shown in the figure.

To obtain the correct deterministic results in the presence of aliasing, the access and modification of aliased variables must occur in the order presented in the source code, and a change to one aliased variable must also alter the other variable in the alias pair. The method to solve aliasing that has been presented achieves this goal in two ways. First, the order of the code execution is controlled by the data dependency imposed on the nodes by the alias array. This is similar to the pointer alias situation presented previously and shown diagrammatically in Figure 10. Second, using the same index value to access and update the same element of the alias array allows two variables of different names to refer to the one value.

One form of aliasing that has been omitted from all previous discussion is when multiple items of a single structure are passed as variable parameters, possibly introducing an alias. This occurs when array elements of the same array are used as parameters, and the run time value of the index expressions that access the elements determine whether an alias actually exists. Another possibility is when pointer objects of the same type are passed. In this situation the value of the pointers determine if an alias becomes active. Two equal pointer variables that refer to the same object will introduce an alias. The code previously presented for introduced aliases is not sufficient to solve this problem. It is not known until run-time whether the objects are aliased, so it is also not known whether one index should be used for multiple parameters, or different indexes are required. This leads to the need to generate additional code that at run-time determines which index values to pass as parameters. The extra code required is a series of **Select** nodes, which check all the index expressions and pointer variables to see if they are equal to each other. If it is found that more than one parameter refers to the same item of data, then an alias is introduced and the

255

same index value is passed for each of the aliased parameters. The number of `Select` nodes required to check all the expressions is proportional to the square of the number of expressions ($O(n^2)$), therefore the run-time code for this implementation can have a high overhead. Aliases of this type can be propagated to other functions without any additional code. Once the alias introduction code has determined if the objects are aliased, then propagating the alias only requires the index values and the alias array to be passed to any other functions. As described earlier, the base structure of the items aliased cannot be accessed within the function where the alias occurs. Therefore, further alias complications, of the nature where additional array elements, or pointer objects are passed together with the already aliased variables, are not possible. To avoid this alias problem completely the Pascal source code can be modified to either pass the whole array and the necessary indexes, or pass the pointer variables by themselves. This removes the possible alias between the structure elements, but requires code in the called function to de-reference the appropriate structures.

6. Results

The results presented below have all been obtained using the SISAL compilation system on the Cray Y-MP/864 at the National Energy Research Supercomputer Centre (NERSC). For the Pascal programs, the IF1 output from the Pascal compiler was processed by the back-end optimizers and translators of the Optimizing SISAL Compiler (OSC Version 12.7) [11]. The SISAL equivalent programs were completely compiled by OSC. The tables show a comparison of execution time and speedups between Pascal and SISAL of several different benchmark programs. The percentage figures displayed in the tables are a ratio of the SISAL execution time versus the Pascal execution time. A figure of less than 100% implies that the SISAL program executes faster than the Pascal program, while a figure greater than 100% means that the Pascal program is faster. Where more than one version of a particular program is presented, the best time is used in the calculation of the ratio. Most programs were compiled for both concurrent and vector execution and it was left to the OSC defaults to determine if was worth recommending such execution for each parallel loop it encountered in the IF1 code.

6.1 Lawrence Livermore Loops

The Lawrence Livermore Loops are a collection of 24 scientific kernels taken from production codes at the Lawrence Livermore National Laboratory [21]. For many years, scientists have used these loops to benchmark high performance computers. The timings presented in Tables 2a and 2b are for 4000 repetitions of each kernel. Each loop was transliterated from the original Fortran code into Pascal, with the only change being that of changing column major arrays used in Fortran into row major arrays for Pascal. For loops 16 and 17, the SISAL code was used to aid the translation as the Fortran versions contained many gotos to implement the kernel. As discussed in Section 4.2.1, some arrays are merged at the completion of a parallel loop. Merging occurs because the compiler has determined that a loop does not iterate across a complete array, or it cannot conclusively calculate if the bounds of a loop match the array size. This merging introduces array copying that cannot be removed by the IF1 optimizers [11]. Array copying increases execution time, so for those loops where this occurs, the Pascal code was altered to try to eliminate this problem, and the results are shown in the amended columns of Tables 2a and 2b. In most cases the only change was the adjustment of the declared size of the resultant array of the kernel to be the

| Cray Y-MP/864 | Concurrent-Vector | | Seconds |
| | One CPU | | |
Loop #	Pascal	Pascal Amended	SISAL	$\frac{SISAL}{Pascal}$
1	0.2445	0.1121	0.1051	93.76%
2	0.1369		0.1357	99.12%
3	0.0495	0.0389	0.0371	95.37%
4	0.0334		0.0335	100.30%
5	0.1773		0.1155	65.14%
6	2.0854	0.6596	0.6722	101.91%
7	0.3857	0.2533	0.2404	94.91%
8	6.7522	2.4175	0.9972	41.25%
9	0.5079	0.0743	0.0774	104.17%
10	1.8054	0.5342	0.4646	86.97%
11	0.1749		0.1126	64.38%
12	0.1962	0.0594	0.0515	86.70%
13	1.5251	1.0127	1.3686	135.14%
14	2.8157		2.8050	99.62%
15	13.4990	3.4767	2.3455	67.46%
16	0.7868		2.4169	307.18%
17	0.3771		0.3295	87.38%
18	7.1728	3.3576	1.8602	55.40%
19	0.3521	0.2073	0.2496	120.41%
20	0.7697		0.6674	86.71%
21	5.7370	0.7959	0.8642	108.58%
22	0.3949	0.2003	0.0893	44.58%
23	2.3889		1.9595	82.03%
24	1.3711		0.1145	8.35%

Table 2a: Execution times for Lawrence Livermore Loops.

same as the bounds of the loop. If a change of array size was not possible due to the kernel algorithm, the loop bounds were expanded to include the whole array, and the body of the loop was protected by an *if* statement.

Table 2a presents the performance data, in seconds, for each loop running on a single processor. The data show that for many of the benchmarks, the best Pascal times are almost identical to the SISAL times. For those loops where there is a relatively large difference in the times, the reasons can be explained. The SISAL code for loops 5, 11, and 24 are all recognized by OSC as a special vectorized Fortran routines (Tridiagonal, First sum, and First minimum or maximum respectively). Unfortunately as the IF1 code output by the Pascal compiler is slightly different than that produced by OSC, the Pascal code is not vectorized and takes longer to execute. For loop 8 not all the array copying could be removed from the amended version, and in loops 15 and 18 the Pascal code has to execute extra iterations of the kernel loop to remove the array copying. This is because the size of the arrays cannot be adjusted to remove the copying, so therefore the loop bounds are increased.

Cray Y-MP/864		Concurrent-Vector			Seconds
Loop #	# CPUs	Pascal	Pascal Amended	SISAL	SISAL / Pascal
	1	0.3857	0.2533	0.2404	94.91%
7	4	0.2335	0.1110	0.2405	216.67%
	8	0.3624	0.2497	0.2398	96.04%
	1	13.4990	3.4767	2.3455	67.46%
15	4	13.2573	2.0309	1.0723	52.80%
	8	13.2391	3.7670	1.0811	28.70%
	1	0.7868		2.4169	307.18%
16	4	0.7871		0.7214	91.65%
	8	0.7961		0.4179	52.49%
	1	7.1728	3.3576	1.8602	55.40%
18	4	3.7159	1.9310	1.1609	60.12%
	8	2.7740	1.8507	0.9267	50.07%
	1	5.7370	0.7959	0.8642	108.58%
21	4	1.9785	0.2909	0.3347	115.06%
	8	1.5679	0.2391	0.2183	91.30%

Table 2b: Speedup times for Lawrence Livermore Loops.

All the Lawrence Livermore loops were executed on the Cray using up to eight processors to determine the speedup available for each kernel. It was discovered that with the default settings for OSC, most of the parallel loops were vectorized but concurrentization was not recommended. Therefore only a few loops demonstrated any speedup, and these results are shown in Table 2b. The results for loop 16 require an explanation. The Pascal version only generates a sequential loop as the least reduction operation contained in the loop is not recognized by the compiler, while the SISAL code uses a parallel loop. From the run times it can be seen there is quite a code overhead for parallel loop execution, but as the number of processors increases this overhead is minimized.

6.2 Ricard

Ricard is a simulation of experimentally observed elution patterns of proteins and ligands in a column of gel. It is a production code developed at the University of Colorado Medical Centre [10]. For the comparisons presented in Table 3, the production code was run for 4000 time steps for a simulation involving 5 proteins and a column of 1315 levels. As with the Lawrence Livermore Loops, the Pascal code is a transliteration of the original Fortran code and the amended Pascal code has eliminated array copying wherever possible.

A comparison of the original Pascal times and the amended Pascal times, in Table 3, demonstrate the problem of array copying in the SISAL compilation system. Both the amended Pascal and SISAL codes show comparable speedups even though the Pascal is slower. It is believed this is because all the array copying could not be removed from the Pascal version. These speedups are also comparable to those presented by Cann [12] for the same production code.

Cray Y-MP/864			Concurrent-Vector				Seconds
			Pascal				SISAL
CPUs	Pascal	Speedup	Amended	Speedup	SISAL	Speedup	Pascal
1	589.6180	1.000	6.8093	1.000	4.2680	1.000	62.68%
2	374.0274	1.576	4.0885	1.665	2.4235	1.761	59.28%
3	300.3422	1.963	3.0482	2.234	1.7302	2.467	56.76%
4	263.8192	2.235	2.6687	2.552	1.4090	3.029	52.80%
5	244.3406	2.413	2.1716	3.136	1.2235	3.488	56.34%
6	306.5018	1.924	2.0176	3.375	1.1404	3.743	56.52%
7	398.3413	1.480	1.8611	3.659	1.0744	3.972	57.73%
8	398.3413	1.480	2.4049	2.831	1.0397	4.105	43.23%

Table 3: Speedup times for Ricard.

Cray Y-MP/864			Concurrent				Seconds
			SISAL		SISAL		SISAL
CPUs	Pascal	Speedup	If	Speedup	Catenate	Speedup	Pacal
1	198.7148	1.000	220.0444	1.000	217.3989	1.000	109.40%
2	108.6633	1.829	119.7435	1.838	120.8982	1.798	110.20%
3	85.2369	2.331	87.2376	2.522	86.1999	2.522	101.13%
4	68.1746	2.915	68.6664	3.205	70.7396	3.073	100.72%
5	63.4550	3.132	62.6607	3.512	59.9301	3.628	94.45%
6	76.6121	2.594	54.8101	4.015	65.8235	3.303	71.54%
7	92.8941	2.139	85.9136	2.561	73.2022	2.970	78.80%
8	110.4700	1.799	195.4341	2.087	111.1489	1.956	100.61%

Table 4: Speedup times for Shallow Grid Model.

6.3 Shallow

The shallow codes are a model for numerical weather prediction. There are two possible implementations for this code where the representation of space is different. The grid model represents the area of study as a series of grid points in space, while the spectral model uses spatial basis functions.

6.3.1 Grid Model The grid model was originally written by Snelling et al., and Egan converted it into SISAL. From this program the code was then translated into Pascal. The problem size for the results presented in Table 4 are for a 64 by 64 grid space and executed for 9600 time steps. The two SISAL versions differ in the way the boundaries of the grid are calculated, either by using an *if* statement to treat the boundaries as special, or by a concatenation of the boundaries to the main array.

The results of the concurrent execution of the Shallow grid programs on the Cray are displayed in Table 4. The execution times and speedups are very similar between the different programs. Vectorization of the programs was disabled for these results in order to highlight the speedups possible with parallel loop execution. When vectorization is enabled negligible speedups are obtained for all the Shallow grid programs. This is because with a small grid size of 64, all of the inner loops are performed as single vector operations and only the outer loops are executed concurrently.

| Cray Y-MP/864 | | Concurrent-Vector | | Seconds |
CPUs	Pascal	Speedup	Amended	Speedup
1	51.1452	1.000	50.5170	1.000
2	40.7856	1.254	26.3547	1.917
3	38.1396	1.341	18.2724	2.765
4	36.2989	1.409	14.1054	3.581
5	35.8411	1.427	11.3271	4.460
6	35.6910	1.433	10.0793	5.012
7	35.0790	1.458	10.9718	4.604
8	35.4437	1.443	16.0327	3.151

Table 5: Speedup times for Shallow Spectral Model.

6.3.2 Spectral Model The spectral model written in Pascal was transliterated from a C version adapted by Martin Dix from the CSIRO Division of Atmospheric Research. No exact SISAL equivalent is available although this Shallow spectral code is a simplified version of the same algorithm used by Pau Chang to write a SISAL version of the program [13]. In this case simplified does not necessarily imply fewer calculations or better performance. The version of the Fortran code, on which the SISAL program is based, contains a more efficient Fast Fourier Transform algorithm than the C and Pascal programs. Some elaborate array manipulation schemes are also included in the Fortran code to improve performance. The C program was simplified in such a way as to clarify some of the more complex operations, at the cost of possibly degrading performance. The C and Pascal Shallow spectral codes also read the initial state from a file rather than calculating it as part of the program as in the SISAL version. The parameters for the results presented in Table 5 are a resolution of 30 with the number of latitudinal and longitudinal points being 128 and 80, respectively. The code was executed for 24 time steps.

The performance results of concurrent vectorized execution of the Shallow spectral model on the Cray are displayed in Table 5. Once again there is a Pascal amended version of the program where array copying is eliminated if possible, and in this case some of the code is changed slightly to allow the loop optimizations to parallelize some of the loops. As many of the data items in this program are complex numbers, they are stored as records containing two fields—the real part and the imaginary part of the complex number. Most of these complex numbers are stored in arrays that are modified in loops. Some of these loops perform summations of the complex number fields and should be able to execute concurrently. Unfortunately the loop optimizations, described in Section 3.4, are not refined enough to allow multiple fields of a record to be involved in sum reductions in a parallel loop. Therefore the code is changed to separate the record field changes into two loops, one where the real part of the complex numbers are updated, and the other to modify the imaginary parts. With these code changes the speedups obtained for the amended program are quite encouraging.

Cray Y-MP/864		Concurrent-Vector			Seconds
CPUs	Pascal	Speedup	SISAL	Speedup	$\frac{SISAL}{Pascal}$
1	1.2424	1.000	1.3225	1.000	106.45%
2	0.6301	1.972	0.6620	1.998	105.06%
3	0.5814	2.137	0.4602	2.874	79.15%
4	0.3682	3.374	0.3383	3.909	91.88%
5	0.5665	2.193	0.4102	3.224	72.41%
6	0.2440	5.092	0.2369	5.583	97.09%
7	0.2083	5.964	0.2752	4.806	132.12%
8	0.3121	3.981	0.2062	6.414	66.07%

Table 6: Speedup times for Average operator.

Cray Y-MP/864		Concurrent-Vector			Seconds
CPUs	Pascal	Speedup	SISAL	Speedup	$\frac{SISAL}{Pascal}$
1	0.0220	1.000	0.0257	1.000	116.82%
2	0.0178	1.236	0.0157	1.637	88.20%
3	0.0184	1.196	0.0130	1.977	70.65%
4	0.0121	1.818	0.0155	1.658	128.10%
5	0.0140	1.571	0.0181	1.420	129.29%
6	0.0120	1.833	0.0123	2.089	102.50%
7	0.0105	2.095	0.0198	1.298	188.57%
8	0.0120	1.833	0.0130	1.977	108.33%

Table 7: Speedup times for Threshold operator.

6.4 Image Processing

Image processing software typically has a small number of simple operators applied to very large amounts of data. The operations is this case are: average, threshold, median, and thinning. These operations are applied to a standard image called the Abingdon Cross Benchmark. This image is of a solid cross imbedded in white Gaussian noise, and the aim of the image processing operations is to extract a clear image of the cross. The image is 512 pixels by 512 pixels with a depth of 8 bits. SISAL and C versions for the above operators were written by McKay [20]. The C version was then transliterated into Pascal for the comparative results shown in the tables below.

The result for the image processing operations are very encouraging as most operations have good speedup for both the Pascal and SISAL code, and the Pascal times are comparative to the SISAL times (see Tables 8–10). The reason for the disappointing SISAL result for the thinning operation, shown in Table 9, is that SISAL does not allow the use of a least reduction of Boolean values in a loop. This feature is available in IF1 and used by the Pascal compiler. A summary of all the image processing results can be found in Table 11.

Cray Y-MP/864		Concurrent-Vector			Seconds
CPUs	Pascal	Speedup	SISAL	Speedup	$\frac{SISAL}{Pascal}$
1	7.0170	1.000	7.3162	1.000	104.26%
2	5.4529	1.287	3.6638	1.997	67.19%
3	2.9181	2.405	2.4299	3.011	83.27%
4	2.0606	3.405	1.8469	3.961	89.63%
5	1.9566	3.586	1.4785	4.948	75.56%
6	2.8920	2.426	2.4393	2.999	84.35%
7	3.0026	2.337	1.5027	4.869	50.05%
8	2.7017	2.597	0.9685	7.554	35.85%

Table 8: Speedup times for Median operator.

Cray Y-MP/864		Concurrent-Vector			Seconds
CPUs	Pascal	Speedup	SISAL	Speedup	$\frac{SISAL}{Pascal}$
1	9.1009	1.000	18.5337	1.000	203.65%
2	4.6918	1.940	9.7374	1.903	207.54%
3	3.6744	2.477	6.9617	2.662	189.46%
4	2.6929	3.380	5.0299	3.685	186.78%
5	2.6474	3.438	4.7903	3.869	180.94%
6	2.1220	4.289	5.1663	3.587	243.46%
7	4.2252	2.154	8.9661	2.067	212.21%
8	4.1870	2.174	7.5762	2.446	180.95%

Table 9: Speedup times for Thinning operator.

Cray Y-MP/864		Concurrent-Vector			Seconds
CPUs	Pascal	Speedup	SISAL	Speedup	$\frac{SISAL}{Pascal}$
1	18.8893	1.000	28.4508	1.000	150.62%
2	10.0030	1.888	14.4629	1.967	144.59%
3	6.8474	2.759	10.4933	2.711	153.25%
4	6.3372	2.981	7.5733	3.757	119.51%
5	4.5853	4.120	6.4823	4.389	141.37%
6	3.8596	4.894	5.1733	5.500	134.04%
7	3.5386	5.338	5.0420	5.643	142.49%
8	2.9368	6.432	4.8508	5.865	165.17%

Table 10: Speedup times for all operations.

| Cray Y-MP/864 | | Concurrent-Vector | | Seconds |
| | | | | $\frac{SISAL}{Pascal}$ |
Program	# CPUs	Pascal	SISAL	
	1	1.2424	1.3225	106.45%
Average	4	0.3682	0.3383	91.88%
	8	0.3121	0.2062	66.07%
	1	0.0220	0.0257	116.82%
Threshold	4	0.0121	0.0155	128.10%
	8	0.0120	0.0130	108.33%
	1	7.0170	7.3162	104.26%
Median	4	2.0606	1.8469	89.63%
	8	2.7017	0.9685	35.85%
	1	9.1009	18.5337	203.65%
Thinning	4	2.6929	5.0299	186.78%
	8	4.1870	7.5762	180.95%
	1	18.8893	28.4508	150.62%
All	4	6.3372	7.5733	119.51%
	8	2.9368	4.8508	165.17%

Table 11: Summary of image processing results.

7. Conclusion

This paper has discussed issues in the design and implementation of an imperative programming language for a dataflow architecture. Several issues of significance have been introduced especially in the area of code analysis and transformations required to maximize parallelism. The intermediate form, IF1, has been described as a portable standard intermediate parallel language, and is the code that is generated by the compiler to be later translated into machine code for the particular architecture being used. Some of the specific code generation issues have been outlined like loop optimizations and the implementation of pointers.

There have been no explicit changes to the syntax or semantics of the Pascal programming language, and so programmers need only concern themselves with algorithm design in order to maximize the parallelism that can be extracted. Therefore programs should be written that reduce the use of global variables and variable parameters, contain loops that are easily parallelized, especially *for* loops. Pointers also need to be handled efficiently. This research has also shown that *smart* compilers for conventional languages, which perform extensive code analysis and optimization, can produce parallel code comparable with that of parallel functional languages.

Acknowledgments

This research was conducted as part of the joint High Performance Computation Program within the CSIRO—Division of Information Technology and the Royal Melbourne Institute of Technology. The authors would like to express their thanks for all the help and support provided by the CSIRO and all its research and administrative staff. Thanks must especially go to Paul Whiting, Mark Rawling, Ian Mathieson, and Rhys Francis. A special thanks to Adam McKay for producing the SISAL Image processing results in time. Also Greg Egan, Neil Webb, and Robert Pascoe helped in the early stages of this project.

References

[1] D. Abramson and G.K. Egan, "Design of a High-Performance Dataflow Multiprocessor," in *Advanced Topics in Dataflow Computing*, J.L. Gaudiot and L. Bic, Eds., Prentice-Hall, New Jersey, 1991. Reproduced from RMIT TR 112-73 R, chap. 4, pp. 121–141.

[2] W.B. Ackerman and J.B. Dennis, *VAL—A value-Oriented Algorithmic Language: Preliminary Reference Manual*, Laboratory for Computer Science, Massachusetts Institute of Technology, June 1979, MIT/LCS/TR 218.

[3] W.B. Ackerman, "Dataflow Languages," *IEEE Computer*, vol. 15, no. 2, February 1982, pp. 50–69.

[4] A.V. Aho, R. Sethi, and J.D. Ullman, *Compilers—Principles, Techniques, and Tools*, K. Guardino, Ed., Addison-Wesley, 1986.

[5] S.J. Allan, *The Reduction of Data Dependencies in High Level Programs*, Ph.D. dissertation, Department of Computer Science, Iowa State University, 1979.

[6] S.J. Allan and A.E. Oldehoeft, "A Flow Analysis Procedure for the Translation of High-Level Languages to a Dataflow Language," *IEEE Transactions on Computers*, Vol. C-29, No. 9, September 1980, pp. 826–831.

[7] M. Amamiya et al., "A List-Processing-Oriented Dataflow Machine Architecture," *AFIPS National Computer Conference*, June 1982, pp. 143–151.

[8] Arvind, K.P. Gostelow, and W. Plouffe, "An Asynchronous Programming Language and Computing Machine," Tech. Rept. 114a, Department of Information and Computer Science, University of California, Irvine, December 1978.

[9] J.P. Banning, "An Efficient Way to Find the Side Effects of Procedure Calls and the Aliases of Variables," *Conference Record of the Sixth Annual ACM Symposium on Principles of Programming Languages*, Association for Computing Machinery, ACM Press, January 1979, pp. 29–41.

[10] J.R. Cann et al., "Small Zone Gel Chromatography of Interacting Systems: Theoretical and Experimental Evaluation of Elution Profiles for Kinetically Controlled Macromolecule-Ligand Reations," *Analytical Biochemistry*, No. 175, December 1988.

[11] D.C. Cann, "Compilation Techniques for High Performance Applicative Computation," Tech. Rept. TR CS-89-108, Colorado State University, 1989.

[12] D.C. Cann, "Retire Fortran: A Debate Rekindled," in *Proceedings of the Sixth International Conference on Supercomputing*, International Supercomputing Institute, Albuquerque, New Mexico. (Appeared in Communications of the ACM, August 1992), November 1991.

[13] P. Chang and G.K. Egan, "An Implementation of a Barotropic Numerical Weather Prediction Model in the Functional Language SISAL," *Proceedings of the SIGPLAN 1990 Symposium on Principles and Practice of Parallel Programming*, March 1990.

[14] D. Cooper, *Standard Pascal User Reference Manual*, W.W. Norton & Company, New York 1983.

[15] K.D. Cooper, "Analyzing Aliases of Reference Formal Parameters," *Conference Record of the Twelfth Annual ACM Symposium on Principles of Programming Languages*, Association for Computing Machinery, ACM Press, January 1985, pp. 281–290.

[16] G.K. Egan, *Dataflow: Its Application to Decentralised Control*, Ph.D. dissertation, Department of Computer Science, University of Manchester, 1979.

[17] G.K. Egan, N.J. Webb, and A.P.W. Böhm, "Some Architectural Features of the CSIRAC II dataflow Computer," in *Advanced Topics in dataflow Computing*, J.L. Gaudiot and L. Bic, Eds., Prentice-Hall, New Jersey 1991, reproduced from Swinburne Institute of Technology Tech. Rept. 31-007, Chap. 5, pp. 143–173.

[18] J.L.R.W. Glauert, *A Single Assignment Language for Dataflow Computing*, Master's thesis, Department of Computer Science, University of Manchester, January 1978.

[19] J. McGraw et al., *SISAL: Streams and Iteration in a Single Assignment Language, Language Reference Manual*, Manual M-146, Lawrence Livermore National Laboratories, Ver. 1.2, March, 1985.

[20] A. McKay and D. Abramson, "Using SISAL to Implement the Abingdon Cross Image Processing Benchmark," *Proceedings of the Fourth Australian Supercomputing Conference*, Gold Coast, Queensland, December 1991, pp. 107–116.

[21] F.H. McMahon, "Livermore Fortran Kernels: A Computer Test of the Numerical Performance Range," Tech. Rept. UCRL-53475, Lawrence Livermore National Laboratory, December 1986.

[22] R.S. Nikhil, K. Pingali, and Arvind, "Id Nouveau," Tech. Rept. 265, Computational Structures Group Memo, Laboratory for Computer Science, Massachusetts Institute of Technology, July 1986.

[23] A.E. Oldehoeft et al., "Translation of High Level Programs to Dataflow and their Execution on a Feedback Interpreter," Tech. Rept. 78-2, Department of Computer Science, Iowa State University, 1978.

[24] M.W. Rawling, "GHC on the CSIRAC II Dataflow Computer," Tech. Rept. TR118-90R, Department of Communication and Electrical Engineering, Royal Melbourne Institute of Technology, 1989.

[25] S. Sekiguchi, T. Shimada, and K. Hiraki, "Sequential Description and Parallel Execution Language DFC II for Dataflow Supercomputers," Tech. Rept. TR-91-25, Electrotechnical Laboratory, August 1991.

[26] S.K. Skedzielewski and J. Glauert, *IF1, An Intermediate Form for Applicative Languages*, Lawrence Livermore National Laboratory, Ver. 1.0, Manual M-170, July, 1985.

[27] S.K. Skedzielewski and M.L. Welcome, "Dataflow Graph Optimization in IF1," in *Functional Programming Languages and Computer Architecture*, J.P. Jouannaud Ed., Springer-Verlag, New York, September 1985, pp. 17–34.

[28] A.H. Veen, *The Misconstrued Semicolon: Reconciling Imperative Languages and Dataflow Machines*, Centre for Mathematics and Computer Science, CWI Tract 26, July 1986.

[29] A.H. Veen and R. van den Born, "The RC Compiler for the DTN Dataflow Computer," *Journal of Parallel and Distributed Computing*, Vol. 10, No. 4, December 1990, pp. 319–332.

[30] S.F. Wail, *Implementing an Imperative Language for the CSIRAC II Dataflow Computer*, Ph.D. dissertation, Department of Computer Systems Engineering, Royal Melbourne Institute of Technology, 1992.

[31] P.J. Whitelock, *A Conventional Language for Dataflow Computing*, Master's thesis, Department of Computer Science, University of Manchester, 1978.

[32] P.G. Whiting, *Compilation of a Functional Programming Language for the CSIRAC II Dataflow Computer*, Master's thesis, reproduced in CSIRO TR-DB-91-11, Department of Computer Science, Royal Melbourne Institute of Technology, 1991.

[33] *Programming Language—PASCAL*, Standards Association of Australia, Standards House, 80 Arthur Street, North Sydney 2060, AS 2580 (1983), is identical to British Standard BS6192:1982 and ISO 7185 will refer to the text of BS 6192 for the whole of the technical content.

The Token Flow Model

Joseph Buck[1] and Edward A. Lee[2]
Dept. of Electrical Engineering and Computer Science
University of California
Berkeley, CA 94720

This paper reviews and extends an analytical model for the behavior of dataflow graphs with data-dependent control flow. The number of tokens produced or consumed by each actor is given as a symbolic function of the Boolean values in the system. Long-term averages can be analyzed to determine consistency of token flow rates. Short-term behavior can be analyzed to construct an annotated schedule, or a static schedule that annotates each firing of an actor with the Boolean conditions under which that firing occurs. Necessary and sufficient conditions for bounded-length schedules, as well as sufficient conditions for determining that a dataflow graph can be scheduled in bounded memory are given. Annotated schedules can be used to generate efficient implementations of the algorithms described by the dataflow graphs.

1. Introduction

The principal strength of dataflow graphs is that they do not over-specify an algorithm by imposing unnecessary sequencing constraints between operators. Instead, they specify a partial order, where sequencing constraints are imposed only by data precedences. Since the representation does not over-constrain the order of operations, a scheduler has the freedom it needs to adequately exploit deep pipelines, to maximize re-use of limited hardware resources, or to exploit parallel processing units. To get these benefits, compilers for pipelined or parallel machines often heavily rely on dataflow analysis. The most successful compilers either address only the modest parallelism in pipelined and superscalar machines or restrict themselves to domain-specific areas such as signal processing. For the most part, only dataflow graphs with deterministic control flow have been handled (though there are interesting hybrid representations that handle dynamic control as well, e.g., [3]). The general class of such graphs is called *synchronous dataflow* (SDF) [18]. However, the class of applications that fit this model is too restricted. In compilers, the SDF model constrains the dataflow analysis to lie within so-called "basic blocks," regions of code delimited by branches or branch destinations. In parallelizing schedulers, it limits the use of dataflow techniques to overly specialized domains with restricted run-time decision making. The model must be broadened.

A dataflow graph is a directed graph with actors at the nodes. The arcs represent the flow of data. Although there are many variations in implementation, conceptually arcs behave as FIFO queues, sometimes with limited capacity, sometimes not. While tagged tokens [1] achieve behavior equivalent to a FIFO queue, they do not require that tokens be produced or consumed in order. Tokens are tagged with context information so that their conceptual position in the queue is maintained independent of the order in

---

[1]Dr. Buck is now a research engineer with Synopsys, Inc., 700 E. Middlefield Rd., Mountain View, CA 94087.
[2]The authors gratefully acknowledge the support of DARPA (J-FBI 90-073), NSF (MIP-8657523), Semiconductor Research Corp. (93-DC-008), and The Sony Corporation.

which they are processed. We will assume in this paper that FIFO behavior is enforced on the arcs. This can lead to simpler run-time implementation than a tagged-token schema.

Dataflow graphs can be considered to have data-driven or demand-driven semantics. It is the availability of operands that enables an operator; alternatively, the need for an operand can cause the execution of an actor. Hence, sequencing constraints follow only from data availability or the need for data. Although this feature is useful, it has its limitations. Virtually all programming languages provide primitives for directly specifying control flow, such as the familiar if-then-else, do-while, goto, and for loops. A purely data-driven language provides no such primitives, relying instead on actors that direct the flow of tokens. We are so familiar with these control flow constructs that expressing equivalent functionality using dataflow semantics can be awkward. If this awkwardness stems primarily from lack of experience, however, then there is much to be gained by exploring languages that have purely dataflow semantics at the source code level.

Such languages are rare. Even so called "dataflow" languages, such as Val [22] and ID [23], and functional languages such as DFL (Silage) [14] contain familiar "for" loops and "if-then-else" constructs. These are sometimes translated into a purely data-driven internal representation, such as the machine code for a dataflow machine. In signal processing, however, purely data-driven semantics are attractive. Signal processing is special in that dataflow graphs are a natural representation for algorithms *even in the absence of other practical motivations.*

The intent of this paper is not to propose a particular language design, nor to advocate a particular choice of actors on which to base dataflow graphs. It is instead to develop an analytical technique that applies to a class of languages in which operators are described in terms of consumption and production of tokens. The key property of these languages is that operators and functions operate on streams of tokens. Although we will use a graphical syntax to illustrate example programs, the method is not restricted to graphical languages. For some applications, particularly signal processing, graphical syntax has proven attractive (see [8] for one example and references to dozens of others). For others it has not, and textual functional languages are more attractive. To date, however, very few experiments have been done with graphical syntax of the type discussed in this paper. A textual syntax with the same or related semantics could easily be created, but it would demand more of the reader without adding materially to the exposition in this paper.

The method in this paper is inspired by the algebraic techniques of Benveniste et al. [4], [5], [6], [21], which can accomplish some of the same objectives for a different class of languages. Fortunately, for dataflow semantics our method is usually simpler than an adaptation to dataflow of that in [4].

This paper begins with a brief review of SDF, emphasizing the analytical properties that can be used for static scheduling. The analysis and scheduling methodology for dynamic dataflow will follow the same pattern, but computations will be symbolic rather than numeric. The token flow model as presented in [20] is reviewed and then extended to model cyclic firings, rather than just long term averages. Consistency and strong consistency are defined and analytical methods are given for checking for them. "Complete cycles" are then defined, enabling the systematic construction of "annotated schedules," or static schedules annotated with the Boolean conditions under which actors fire.

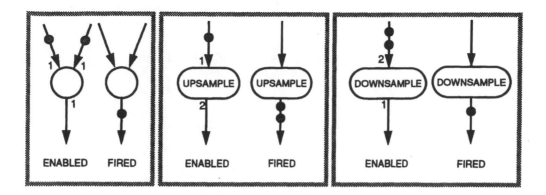

Figure 1: Synchronous dataflow actors consume and produce fixed numbers of tokens.

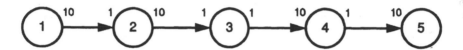

Figure 2: A nested iteration expressed as an SDF graph.

2. Synchronous Dataflow

Synchronous dataflow (SDF) is a special case of dataflow where the number of tokens consumed or produced by a given actor when it fires is fixed and known at compile time. In repeated firing of the same actor, the same behavior will be repeated. Figure 1 shows some SDF actors. In the left-most box, the actor has two operands, and the presence of one token on each input enables the firing of the actor. When it fires, it produces one token on its output. In the middle, a single token enables the firing, but multiple tokens (two shown) are produced. The right-most actor is enabled by multiple tokens, and produces a single token when it fires.

2.1 Manifest Iteration

Consider the dataflow graph in Figure 2. The numbers adjacent to the inputs and outputs of the actors indicate how many tokens are consumed and produced each time the actor fires. Consequently, the third actor fires ten times for every firing of the second, which in turn fires ten times for every firing of the first. There is nothing in this model to prevent simultaneous firing of successive invocations of the same actor, so this schema solves the first open problem listed by Dennis in [12], providing the semantics of a "parallel for" in dataflow. The iteration is specified in a truly data-driven way. Of course, if we restrict the dataflow actors to be SDF, then the iteration can only be manifest, where the number of cycles of the iteration is known at compile-time.

Figure 3: A unit delay represents an initial token on an arc.

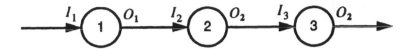

Figure 4: Three actors annotated with the number of tokens consumed
and produced on each firing.

2.2 Delays

A dataflow graph may contain initial tokens on an arc. These will be indicated in this
paper with a diamond, as shown in Figure 3.

These tokens can be viewed as causing an offset between the tokens produced and
the tokens consumed on the arc. Hence, such an initial token is called a unit delay. A
delay can enable the firing a downstream actor. For instance, at the start of execution,
actor 2 in Figure 3 is enabled.

2.3 Topology Matrix and Repetitions Vector

Because of the predictable production and consumption of tokens, SDF graphs can
be scheduled statically, at compile time. When the graph is going to be repeatedly
executed, this can result in considerable speedup or simpler hardware, compared to
run-time scheduling. For signal processing applications the graph is typically repeatedly executed a very large number of times on a continuous stream of input data. If
the application has real-time constraints, then the speedup achieved by scheduling at
compile time can be critical.

When an SDF graph is to be executed repeatedly, the compiler should construct
just one cycle of a periodic schedule. The first step is to determine how many invocations of each actor should be included in each cycle. This can be determined
using information about the number of samples consumed and produced. Consider
the connection of three actors shown in Figure 4. Let I_i denote the number of tokens
consumed by the ith actor, and O_i denote the number of tokens produced by the
i^{th} actor, as shown in the figure. Let r_i denote the number of times the ith actor is
repeated in the each cycle of the iterated schedule. Then it must be true that

$$r_1 O_1 = r_2 I_2 \qquad (1)$$
$$r_2 O_2 = r_3 I_3 \qquad (2)$$

These two equations ensure that the number of tokens produced on each arc is
equal to the number consumed on that arc in each cycle of the iterated schedule.
Indeed, the first step in finding a schedule for an SDF graph is to solve a set of such
equations, one for each arc in the graph, for the unknowns r_i.

These equations can be written concisely by constructing a *topology matrix* Γ that contains the integer O_i in position (j, i) if the ith actor produces O_i tokens on the jth arc. It also contains the integer $-I_i$ in position (j, i) if the ith actor consumes I_i tokens from the jth arc. For example, the nested iteration shown in Figure 2 has the following topology matrix

$$\Gamma = \begin{bmatrix} 10 & -1 & 0 & 0 & 0 \\ 0 & 10 & -1 & 0 & 0 \\ 0 & 0 & 1 & -10 & 0 \\ 0 & 0 & 0 & 1 & -10 \end{bmatrix}. \tag{3}$$

Then the system of equations to be solved is

$$\Gamma \vec{r} = \vec{o} \tag{4}$$

where $\vec{o}$ is a vector full of zeros, and $\vec{r}$ is the repetition vector containing the r_i for each actor. Printz calls (4) the "balance equations" [25]. For the topology matrix in (9), one solution is

$$\vec{r} = \begin{vmatrix} 1 \\ 10 \\ 100 \\ 10 \\ 1 \end{vmatrix}. \tag{5}$$

In fact, this solution is the smallest one with integer entries. For a connected SDF graph, it is shown in [18] that a necessary condition to be able to construct an admissible periodic schedule is that the rank of Γ be equal to one less than the number of actors in the graph. This means that the null space of Γ has dimension one. From (4) we see that $\vec{r}$ must lie in the null space of Γ. It is also shown in [18] that when the rank is correct, there always exists a vector that contains only integers and lies in this null space. Solving for the smallest such vector is a simple procedure that involves finding a fractional solution and applying Euclid's algorithm to find the least common multiple of all the denominators. This technique has been implemented in the Gabriel [8] and Ptolemy [9] systems, and it is simple and fast. Furthermore, the technique can be re-targeted to a wide variety of architectures, including arrays of processors.

In order to construct a periodic schedule we must rule out the possibility of deadlock [18]. In this paper, we will simply assume the graphs we work with do not deadlock.

2.4 Inconsistency

For some SDF graphs, (4) has no solution. An example is shown in Figure 5. The error here is that actor 3 expects two streams with the same rate of token flow, and it is getting two streams with different rates of flow. There is no schedule that can repeatedly run this graph with bounded memory.

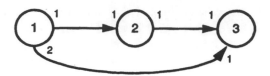

Figure 5: An inconsistent SDF graph.

2.5 Disconnected Graphs

For disconnected graphs, if each graph is itself consistent, then the null space of Γ has dimension equal to the number of disconnected graphs. In this case, the scheduling problem is easily partitioned into smaller problems each of which involves only a connected subgraph.

2.6 Static Scheduling

Scheduling an SDF graph begins with solving for the smallest integer vector $\vec{r}$ in the null space of the topology matrix. This vector, as illustrated in (5), indicates how many times each actor should be invoked in one cycle of a periodic schedule. Given this set of numbers, the required invocations can be assembled into an acyclic precedence graph (APG). The procedure for doing this is straightforward; it consists of simulating a dynamically scheduled run until each actor has been added to the APG r_i times. When an actor becomes enabled, an invocation of that actor is added to the precedence graph, and precedence arc connections are made to previous actors whose firings supplied the enabling data. Initially, only source actors (which have no input paths) and actors that have enough delays on their input paths are enabled. But once an invocation is added to the precedence graph, a data structure is updated to indicate the data that would be produced by a firing of that actor. This extra data, in turn, enables other actors.

The method for constructing the APG can be described precisely. Let $\vec{b}(n)$ be a vector denoting the number of tokens in each arc at step n of the procedure. Hence $\vec{b}(0)$ denotes the initial state of the graph, indicating which arcs contain how many delays. Suppose that at the initial state a certain actor i is enabled. Then an invocation of that actor can be put in the APG with no ancestors, indicating that there are no precedents to be honored. The state of the system is then updated by constructing a vector $\vec{q}(n)$ with a 1 in the ith position, and zeros everywhere else, and writing

$$\vec{b}(n+1) = \vec{b}(n) + \Gamma\vec{q}(n). \tag{6}$$

By only letting $\vec{q}(n)$ indicate enabled actors, $\vec{b}(n)$ is guaranteed to always have non-negative entries.

The process is repeated with the new system state. Whenever a new actor is added to the APG, arcs are created to indicate precedences. No actor i will be added to the APG more than r_i times, and the graph will be declared complete when

$$\sum_{n=0}^{N} \vec{q}(n) = \vec{r}. \tag{7}$$

Notice that

$$\vec{b}(N) = \vec{b}(0) + \Gamma\vec{r} = \vec{b}(0), \tag{8}$$

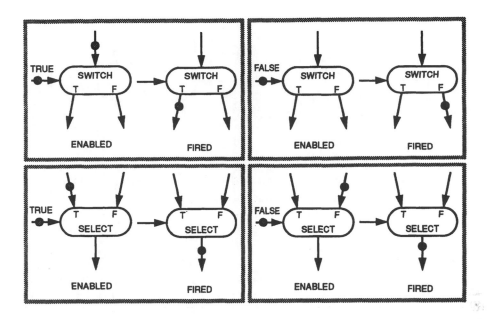

Figure 6: Dynamic dataflow actors consume and produce tokens depending on Booleans in the system.

indicating that the state of the arcs after performing all invocations in the APG will be the same as it was before.

Once the APG is constructed, there are many scheduling alternatives. For single processor targets, some reasonable scheduling objectives might include minimization of data or program memory requirements. For multiprocessor targets, minimizing makespan, or maximizing flowtime are more likely objectives. For some examples of scheduling heuristics that have been applied, see [26].

3. Dynamic Dataflow

Although SDF is adequate for representing large parts of many algorithms, it is rarely sufficient for expressing an entire program. A more general dataflow model is needed in order to express data-dependent iteration, conditionals, and recursion. The addition of two actors, SWITCH and SELECT, enables all of these except recursion (for a discussion of recursion see [20]). The behavior of these actors is shown in Figure 6. These are minor variations of the original Dennis actors [12], also used in [28], [27], and [24], and are the same as the distributor and selector in [11]. Neither actor is SDF because the number of tokens consumed or produced is not fixed. It depends on the Boolean control input. In the case of the SWITCH, the firing of downstream actors will be data-dependent. In the case of the SELECT actor, the firing of upstream actors will be data-dependent. In both cases, run-time control is required.

The characterization of actors for SDF graphs can be extended to graphs containing SWITCH and SELECT actors. The number of inputs consumed and produced must now be represented as a function of Booleans in the system.

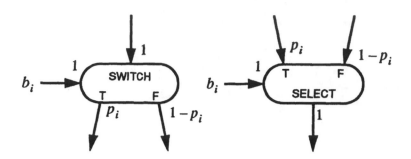

Figure 7: Dynamic dataflow actors annotated with the expected number of tokens produced or consumed per firing as a function of p_i, the probability that a token from the stream b_i is TRUE.

3.1 The Token Flow Model

Loosely speaking, the balance equations require that in the long run, the number of tokens produced on an arc must equal the number of tokens consumed. This can be checked by relating the average number of tokens consumed and produced to the average number of TRUEs in the Boolean streams in the system. This is shown for the SWITCH and SELECT actors in Figure 7. Loosely, p_i is the long term proportion of TRUEs in the Boolean stream b_i, which supplies the control inputs.

Several rigorous interpretations of p_i in Figure 7 are possible. The most general interpretation of p_i is that it is a formal placeholder for an unknown quantity that determines number of tokens produced or consumed. In a probabilistic formulation, we model the Boolean stream b_i as a random process, and p_i is the marginal probability that a token from b_i is TRUE. This interpretation requires that the marginal probability be constant across firings. Equivalently, b_i is stationary in the mean. For practical dataflow graphs, this requirement is overly restrictive. Fortunately, for most dataflow graphs, p_i can be interpreted as the proportion of TRUE tokens in a well-defined finite subsequence (called a *complete cycle*) of the infinite stream b_i. Furthermore, we will see that we never need to know or estimate the numerical value of p_i. All manipulations that use it can use it symbolically. For the initial development, for clarity and intuition, we will assume the probabilistic interpretation. The complete cycle interpretation will follow.

Non-SDF actors other than SWITCH and SELECT can be modeled as well, as long as they have representations like that in Figure 7. This even includes non-determinate actors as in [17] (see [20]). In this paper, however, we will use only SWITCH and SELECT in our examples because they are traditional and familiar in the dataflow literature.

Consider the if-then-else program shown in Figure 8. The SWITCH directs the incoming token to one of two subsystems, 3 or 4, depending on the Boolean supplied by actor 7. Since the Boolean is supplied to two actors, it is implicitly forked into two Boolean streams labeled b_1 and b_2. It will be important to recognize these as two Boolean streams. In this figure, the numbers adjacent to the arcs will be used only to identify them.

Assuming that all unmarked actors produce and consume a single token when they fire, the topology matrix for this system is given by:

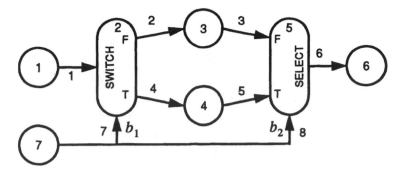

Figure 8: An if-then-else dataflow graph.
The numbers adjacent to the arcs merely identify them.

$$\Gamma(\vec{p}) = \begin{vmatrix} 1 & -1 & 0 & 0 & 0 & 0 & 0 \\ 0 & (1-p_1) & -1 & 0 & 0 & 0 & 0 \\ 0 & 0 & 1 & 0 & (p_2-1) & 0 & 0 \\ 0 & p_1 & 0 & -1 & 0 & 0 & 0 \\ 0 & 0 & 0 & 1 & -p_2 & 0 & 0 \\ 0 & 0 & 0 & 0 & 1 & -1 & 0 \\ 0 & -1 & 0 & 0 & 0 & 0 & 1 \\ 0 & 0 & 0 & 0 & -1 & 0 & 1 \end{vmatrix}. \tag{9}$$

Here, $\vec{p}$ is a vector with all Boolean probabilities. Analogous to (4), we need to find a vector $\vec{r}(\vec{p})$ such that

$$\Gamma(\vec{p})\vec{r}(\vec{p}) = \vec{o} \tag{10}$$

$\Gamma(\vec{p})$ must have rank 6 (or equivalently, its null space must have rank 1). It is easy to verify that it has rank 6 if and only if

$$p_1 = p_2, \tag{11}$$

which fortunately is true trivially, since b_1 and b_2 emanate from the same actor. A suitable vector in the nullspace of $\Gamma(\vec{p})$ is given by

$$\vec{r}(\vec{p}) = [1 \quad 1 \quad (1-p_1) \quad p_1 \quad 1 \quad 1 \quad 1]^T. \tag{12}$$

Notice that this vector works for any numerical value of p_1 and p_2. One interpretation for this is that, on average, for every firing of actor 1, actor 3 will fire $(1-p_1)$ times, and actor 4 will fire p_1 times. This is intuitive. Since p_1 is not an integer, in general, it makes little sense to talk of finding the smallest integer vector in the null-space of $\Gamma(\vec{p})$. However, the information gained from any solution to (10) is useful. It tells us (a) that a solution exists, and (b) in what proportion the actors in the actors in the system should fire as functions of the Boolean proportions in the system. We will strive for a schedule such that $\vec{r}(\vec{p})/\|\vec{r}(\vec{p})\|$ is a vector giving the probability that each actor will fire given that one actor fires. Furthermore, we will extend this model below in such a way that for most graphs we can find a similar vector that always has integer values and can be used to construct compile-time schedules.

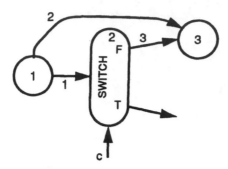

Figure 9: A dataflow graph that is consistent if and only if c is always false.

3.2 Consistency

In [20], the above *token-flow* model is used to define *consistency* for dynamic dataflow graphs. Two kinds of consistency are identified, *strong* and *weak*. Strong consistency means that there exists a vector $\vec{r}(\vec{p})$ such that (10) is satisfied for any allowed value of the Boolean proportions $\vec{p}$ in the system. Weak consistency means that (10) is satisfied only for certain values of the Boolean proportions $\vec{p}$. The if-then-else of Figure 8 is consistent subject to the condition in (11). Since this condition is always satisfied, the dataflow graph is strongly consistent.

However, not all dataflow graphs are strongly consistent. Consider the example in Figure 9. The topology matrix for this system is

$$\Gamma(p_c) = \begin{bmatrix} 1 & -1 & 0 \\ 1 & 0 & -1 \\ 0 & (1-p_c) & -1 \end{bmatrix}. \tag{13}$$

This assumes that actors 1 and 3 consume and produce only single tokens when they fire. Unless

$$p_c = 0, \tag{14}$$

meaning that c is always false, this matrix has full rank. Since given the information we have, there is no reason to believe that $p_c = 0$, the graph is not strongly consistent.

Intuitively, each time actor 1 fires, it supplies a token to both the SWITCH (actor 2) and actor 3. However, actor 3 can only consume that token if the SWITCH also provides it with a token, which occurs only if the Boolean c is false. Hence, each time c is true, another token accumulates on arc 2. These tokens will accumulate indefinitely, requiring unbounded memory.

Some additional notation will help to make the ideas below precise. Let $\vec{p}$ be a vector containing the Boolean probabilities in a system. Then define an *indicator* function $C(\vec{p})$ that has value "true" if $\Gamma(\vec{p})$ has the appropriate rank for this particular $\vec{p}$. Otherwise, it has value "false." Hence, a particular graph will be said to be consistent subject to $C(\vec{p})$. It is strongly consistent if $C(\vec{p})$ is always true, and inconsistent if $C(\vec{p})$ is always false. For the system in Figure 9, (14) is equivalent to

$$C(\vec{p}) = \begin{cases} \text{TRUE;} & p_c = 0 \\ \text{FALSE;} & \text{otherwise} \end{cases}. \tag{15}$$

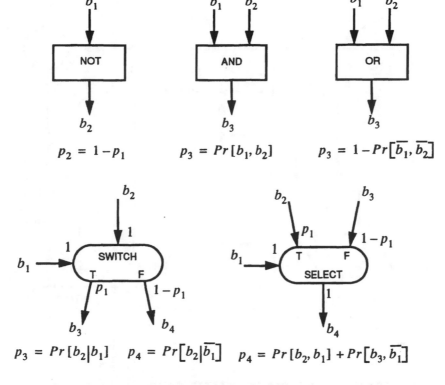

$$p_2 = 1 - p_1 \qquad p_3 = Pr\,[b_1, b_2] \qquad p_3 = 1 - Pr\big[\overline{b_1}, \overline{b_2}\big]$$

$$p_3 = Pr\,[b_2|b_1] \qquad p_4 = Pr\big[b_2|\overline{b_1}\big] \qquad p_4 = Pr\,[b_2, b_1] + Pr\big[b_3, \overline{b_1}\big]$$

Figure 10: Actors that operate on Boolean Streams may produce new Boolean streams that are interrelated as shown in these examples.

3.3 Mutually Dependent Booleans

The if-then-else of Figure 8 is consistent subject to condition (11), which we know to be trivially true, so the graph is strongly consistent. In general, however, there may be dependencies between Boolean streams that are harder to discern. In particular, when Boolean streams are interrelated, a graph that appears to be only conditionally consistent may in fact be strongly consistent. The interrelationships between Boolean streams can come about from logical operators, such as those in Figure 10. In that figure, $Pr\,[b_1, b_2]$ means the probability that two *simultaneously consumed* tokens from the streams b_1 and b_2 are true. Similarly, $Pr\,[\overline{b_1}, \overline{b_2}]$ means the probability that they are both false, and $Pr\,[b_2|b_1]$ means the probability that a token b_2 is true given that the *simultaneously consumed* token b_1 is true. These relationships must be applied with care because they are only valid for tokens that are simultaneously consumed. However, even with this restriction, they can be used sometimes to determine that conditionally consistent graphs are in fact strongly consistent.

Consider the example in Figure 11. This dataflow graph can be shown to be consistent if and only if

$$p_3 = p_2 p_4. \tag{16}$$

In other words,

$$C(\vec{p}) = \begin{cases} \text{TRUE;} & p_3 = p_2 p_4. \\ \text{FALSE;} & \text{otherwise} \end{cases} \tag{17}$$

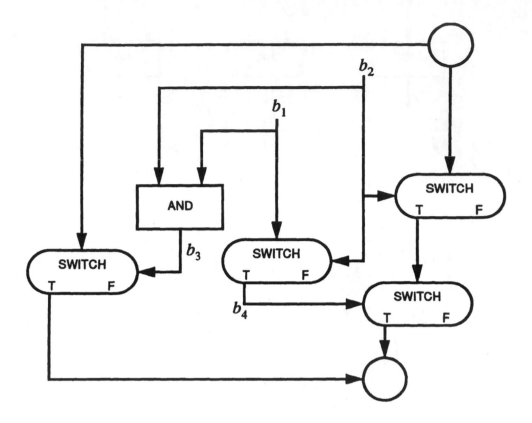

Figure 11: An example of a graph that appears at first glance to be only conditionally consistent, but on further analysis proves to be strongly consistent.

From the relationships in Figure 10,

$$p_3 = Pr[b_1, b_2] \tag{18}$$
$$p_4 = Pr[b_1|b_2]. \tag{19}$$

Hence condition (16) is equivalent to

$$Pr[b_1, b_2] = p_2 Pr[b_1|b_2], \tag{20}$$

which is always true by the multiplication rule in probability. Consequently, this graph is strongly consistent.

The above analysis must be performed carefully, ensuring that when probabilities are combined at a logical operator, they are combined for tokens that are simultaneously consumed. If, for example, a delay were introduced in the path of one of the Boolean streams in Figure 11, the analysis might require information about the joint statistics of successive tokens in a Boolean stream. This knowledge may not be available to a compiler, or even to the programmer. Similarly, Booleans that are generated by testing non-Boolean streams may have joint statistics that are difficult or impossible for a compiler to discern. In principle, a compiler that does elaborate semantic analysis of the program and has complete information about the inputs might be able to use this type of analysis to verify consistency, but such a compiler is not practical. A practical compiler will alert the programmer with a warning when a conditionally consistent dataflow graph is encountered, and the conditions cannot be proven to be satisfied.

3.4 The Limitations of Consistency

In all cases above, inconsistency indicates a peculiar graph that is probably erroneous. This suggests, at minimum, defining languages that do not admit inconsistent graphs. Conditionally consistent graphs could be admitted with a warning, because a compiler cannot always determine the relationships between separate Boolean streams.

The question arises, then, of whether consistency can be used in compilation of dataflow graphs. Synchronous dataflow graphs, for example, can be statically scheduled onto multiple processors [18]. Moreover, memory can be statically allocated for each arc, leading to particularly simple implementations on ordinary processors [19]. We wish to determine when these properties extend to more general dataflow graphs. For a given graph, we wish to answer the following questions:

1. Can we define a schedule at compile time for execution of the graph?

2. Can we find an upper bound on the memory required to execute the graph?

We wish to answer both questions in finite time for an infinite execution of the graph. Not surprisingly, we will find that we cannot always answer these questions definitively. However, for a large class of dataflow graphs, we can answer quickly in the affirmative and synthesize a lean implementation. Dataflow graphs for which the answer to both questions is yes have most, if not all the desirable properties of the clean dataflow graphs of Davis [11], the well-behaved dataflow graphs of Arvind [1] and Gao [13], and k-bounded loops of Arvind and Culler [2].

Strong consistency is necessary, but not sufficient, to ensure that a graph will execute in bounded memory. Perfectly correct (and strongly consistent) programs exist that cannot be executed indefinitely in bounded memory. Consider the example in Figure 12, given by Gao et al. [13]. A solution to the balance equations for this system is where $p = p_1 = p_2$. If a FIFO schema on the arcs is enforced, the memory required to execute this graph is not bounded. Suppose for example the Boolean streams b_1 and b_2 consist of a single TRUE token followed by an unbounded number of FALSE tokens. The SELECT actor cannot fire until actor 4 has fired, and actor 4 cannot fire until a second TRUE token arrives. Hence, the arc between actor 3 and the SELECT will require unbounded memory. A related example, devised independently of [13], is shown in Figure 13. As in Figure 8, this graph is consistent if $p_1 = p_2$. In the probabilistic interpretation of p_i, the initial token implied by the delay has no effect on p_2, so $p_1 = p_2$, and the graph is strongly consistent. Suppose, however, that the value of the initial token is TRUE, and b_1 consists of an infinite sequence of FALSE tokens. Then the SELECT can never fire.

$$\vec{r}(\vec{p}) = [2 \quad 2 \quad (1-p) \quad p \quad 2 \quad 2 \quad 2]^T, \tag{21}$$

Note that the examples in Figures 12 and 13 have bounded memory requirements under a tagged-token schema, which does not require that actors process tokens in order. A variant of Figure 12, shown in Figure 14, has unbounded memory requirements under any dataflow schema. The feedback loop effectively enforces serial execution of actors 6 and 7, so that tokens into 6 must be processed in order.

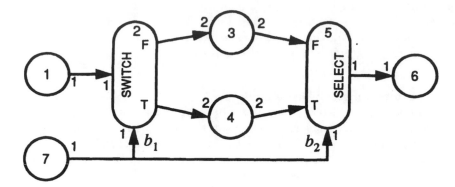

Figure 12: An example of a strongly consistent system that cannot execute in bounded memory if a FIFO protocol is enforced on the arcs.

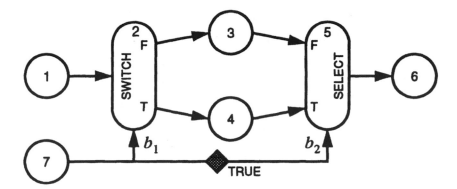

Figure 13: A graph that is strongly consistent but cannot execute in bounded memory if a FIFO schema is enforced on the arcs.

We recognize, however, that perfectly correct programs can have unbounded memory requirements (consider a program that recognizes a context-free grammar, for example). Such programs fundamentally require dynamic memory allocation and at least some measure of dynamic scheduling. However, we wish to isolate the particular dataflow arcs and actors that require this, and incur the additional runtime cost *only where needed*. The vast majority of arcs and actors in a typical program have no such requirement, and can be implemented with much lower run-time cost on routine hardware.

4. Scheduling

To construct a static schedule, we need to consider not probabilistic behavior of the dynamic dataflow actors, but rather the behavior over short, well-defined firing sequences. To do this, we modify the token flow model to consider not the probability p_i, but rather the proportion of TRUE tokens in a finite firing sequence S. For a particular firing sequence S, let $t_i(S)$ denote the number of TRUE tokens consumed from stream within the sequence. Let $n_i(S)$ denote the total number of tokens consumed from b_i in S. This is an unknown that we will only manipulate symbolically. Define

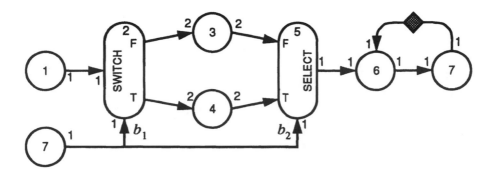

Figure 14: A variant of Figure 12 that cannot execute in bounded memory even under a tagged-token schema.

the vector

$$\overrightarrow{p}(S) = \begin{bmatrix} t_1(S)/n_1(S) \\ t_2(S)/n_2(S) \\ \cdots \end{bmatrix}, \tag{22}$$

where the size of the vector equals the number of Boolean streams in the graph. We wish to find a bounded-length S such that $C(\overrightarrow{p}(S))$ is true for any possible outcomes of the Boolean proportions $t_i(S)/n_i(S)$. Let $\overrightarrow{r}(S)$ denote the number of firings of each actor in S. Note that $\overrightarrow{r}(S)$ must evaluate to an integer vector (actors can't fire a fractional number of times) regardless of the outcomes of the Boolean proportions $t_i(S)/n_i(S)$. Furthermore, we require that all arcs in the graph have the same number of tokens after executing S as before, or equivalently, that

$$\Gamma(\overrightarrow{p}(S))\overrightarrow{r}(S) = \overrightarrow{o}. \tag{23}$$

We elaborate these requirements below, first showing how they are all satisfied for an appropriately chosen S for the if-then-else example.

4.1 Annotated Firing Sequence
In the if-then-else example in Figure 8, consider the following annotated firing sequence:

$$S = \{1, 7, 2, (1 - t_1(S))\, 3, (t_1(S))\, 4, 5, 6\}. \tag{24}$$

The parenthesized expressions give the conditions under which the corresponding actor should fire. In this case, actor 3 will fire if $t_1(S)$ is unity, and otherwise 4 will fire. Exactly one token is consumed in S from each Boolean stream, so $n_1(S) = n_2(S) = 1$. Furthermore, $t_1(S) = t_2(S)$.

The firing sequence in (24) can be repeated indefinitely, and hence constitutes an admissible periodic annotated schedule. For this example, the number of firings of each actor in S is given by

$$\vec{r}(S) = \begin{vmatrix} 1 \\ 1 \\ t_1(S) \\ 1 - t_1(S) \\ 1 \\ 1 \\ 1 \end{vmatrix}. \tag{25}$$

Since $t_1(S)$ can only take on values zero or one, $\vec{r}(S)$ is a vector of integers for any realization of S. Further, defining

$$\vec{p}(S) = \begin{bmatrix} t_1(S) \\ t_1(S) \end{bmatrix} \tag{26}$$

$C(\vec{p}(S))$ is always true, and using the topology matrix in (9), we get,

$$\Gamma(\vec{p}(S))\vec{r}(S) = \vec{o}, \tag{27}$$

where again $\vec{o}$ is the vector of zeros.

4.2 Complete Cycles

A *complete cycle* is a sequence of (possibly annotated) firings where the number of tokens on each arc after the sequence is equal to the number before, and any Boolean control tokens have the same values as before. Fractional firings are not allowed, of course. It is similar to the "firing cycle" of Kavi, et al. [16], but applies to more general dataflow graphs. Any S satisfying (27) for all possible outcomes of all Boolean proportions $t_i(S)/n_i(S)$ is a complete cycle. Mathematically, for any annotated sequence S, the state of the FIFO buffers after the sequence fires is given by

$$\vec{b}(S) = \vec{b}(0) + \Gamma(\vec{p}(S))\vec{r}(S), \tag{28}$$

analogous to (8).

The problem of scheduling a dynamic dataflow graph at compile time is one of devising a complete cycle. We wish to find a complete cycle that can be expressed as a bounded-length annotated firing sequence. Since such a sequence returns the number of tokens on each arc to its original value, it can be repeated indefinitely. Furthermore, since the annotated sequence consists of a bounded number of firings of each actor, then the total memory requirements for indefinite execution of the graph can be bounded.

It is immediate that any graph possessing a bounded-length complete cycle can be executed in bounded memory. Since the state of the graph after the cycle is the same as before, then memory requirements on arcs cannot accumulate over multiple cycles. Within a cycle, every actor fires a finite number of times with an easily derived upper bound, so there is no possibility of unbounded storage requirements.

Unfortunately, a bounded-length complete cycle does not exist for some strongly consistent graphs. Consider again the example in Figure 13. This graph is consistent under the condition $p_1 = p_2$, in which case a solution to the balance equations is given by (12). This condition is satisfied under the probabilistic formulation of the token-flow model, but will not be satisfied for any finite firing sequence in general. From (12) we can see that if a complete sequence exists for this graph, it must contain the same number of firings of actors 1, 2, 5, 6, and 7. Let that number be N. Hence $n_1(S) = n_2(S) = N$. Then the repetition vector for is given by

$$\vec{r}(\vec{p}(S)) = [N \quad N \quad [N - t_1(S)] \quad [t_2(S)] \quad N \quad N \quad N]^T. \tag{29}$$

But this repetition vector will not satisfy the balance equations unless $t_1(S) = t_2(S)$. Furthermore, this latter condition cannot be satisfied unless the last Boolean produced by actor 7 in the sequence S has value TRUE, returning the Boolean arc to its original state.

The example in Figure 12 has a different problem with the same net effect. Let S be any firing sequence that contains N firings of actors 1, 2, 5, 6, and 7. From (21), it is clear that any complete cycle S must fire these actors the same number of times. N, therefore, gives the number of Boolean values consumed in S on both b_1 and b_2. Hence the repetition vector is

$$\vec{r}(\vec{p}(S)) = \left[N \quad N \quad \frac{N - t_1(S)}{2} \quad \frac{t_1(S)}{2} \quad N \quad N \quad N\right]^T. \tag{30}$$

Since $t_1(S)$ can take on any integer value between zero and N, there is no assurance for any N that the third and fourth entry will be integers. Since no firing sequence can fire any actor a non-integer number of times, there is no bounded-length complete cycle for this graph.

Dataflow graphs that require bounded memory may nevertheless have complete cycles that are unbounded in length. Graphs corresponding to data-dependent iteration, where the number of times an actor is executed depends on the data itself and cannot be bounded at compile time, fall into this category.

We will develop below two methods, called *clustering* and *state enumeration*, that can identify infinite complete cycles that can be scheduled in bounded memory for some types of graphs. However, even with these methods, some perfectly correct graphs will elude our analysis. Our strategy will be to identify subgraphs for which we can find a complete cycle, construct a static schedule, and if possible statically allocate memory for the arcs. Graphs for which we cannot find a complete cycle, but which are consistent, will require dynamic memory allocation and probably dynamic scheduling. In many cases, this extra overhead is fundamentally required by the program. Although it is certainly possible to schedule the graph in Figure 13, no scheduling policy can guarantee finite memory requirements. Buffers will have to be dynamically allocated, greatly increasing the cost of implementation compared to static allocation.

4.3 Constructing Annotated Schedules when a Bounded-Length Firing Sequence Exists

Assume we have a dataflow graph with no delays on Boolean arcs and with an integer solution to the balance equations. A procedure similar to that of the SDF case can be applied to this dynamic dataflow case to construct annotated schedules. In this paper, we can only briefly describe this procedure, and only for a single processor schedule. For multiple processors, the procedure must be modified to construct an annotated precedence graph, which in turn can be used (in principle) to construct multiprocessor schedules (the procedure for doing so is described in [10]). The annotated precedence graph can also be used to check for deadlock conditions, although in this paper we simply assume deadlock does not occur.

Constructing a single processor annotated schedule requires successively adding actors to a schedule list S, together with the annotations that enable them, until the number of invocations of the actors $\vec{r}(S)$ forms a vector in the nullspace of the appropriate matrix $\Gamma(\overline{p}(S))$, where $\overline{p}(S)$ is a vector of Boolean proportions for the Boolean tokens consumed in S. Note that $\overline{p}(S)$ is not well-defined for streams that have no Booleans consumed yet in S, but these undefined entries also cannot affect the system state, and hence can be ignored.

Define the state of the system to be the number of tokens on each arc (there are no delays on Boolean arcs, recall). The initial state reflects the initial tokens on arcs with delays. We must also uniquely label every Boolean token that is consumed in S. In general, the number of tokens on an arc may be a symbolic function of $\overline{p}(S)$. With a given system state, some actors are conditionally enabled. An actor is conditionally enabled if for some Boolean condition B the number of tokens on its input arcs is greater than or equal to the number of tokens it requires to fire. If B is a function that maps Boolean outcomes onto $\{0, 1\}$, then the number of tokens the actor puts on its output arcs is B times the number of tokens it produces on each output when it fires. This symbolic function is used to update the state of the system after conditionally scheduling the enabled actor. The number of firings of the actor is incremented by the symbolic function B. Scheduling is completed when the vector $\overline{r}(S)$ is in the null-space of $\Gamma(\overline{p}(S))$. Except for the increased complication of having to manipulate symbolic expressions, the scheduling procedure is not much more complicated than for the SDF case.

4.4 Conditions for Bounded Cycle Length

Elsewhere in this paper we assume that graphs do not deadlock; however, if deadlock actually occurs, this fact will be detected during the process of building the annotated precedence graph (if will be impossible to complete its construction). The existence of a bounded integer solution to the balance equations, together with the successful construction of the annotated precedence graph, are necessary and sufficient conditions for bounded cycle length. In addition to guaranteeing bounded memory requirements, this condition can be important in scheduling the graph with a hard real-time constraint, as it may permit a proof that the constraint is always met regardless of the Boolean outcomes.

4.5 Clustering

Some graphs do not have bounded cycle length, but nonetheless can be scheduled with bounded memory. Consider the example in Figure 15. This graph is strongly consistent, with

$$\overline{r}(\overline{p}) = \begin{bmatrix} 1 & 1 & 1 & p_1 & \dfrac{(1 - p_1)}{2} \end{bmatrix}^T \tag{31}$$

offering one solution to the balance equations. However, this graph has no bounded-length complete cycle. To see this, let N be the number of repetitions in any S of actors 1, 2, and 3. Any complete cycle S must have an equal number of firings of these three actors, as can be seen from (31). If t_1 is the number of TRUE tokens consumed by actor 2 in S, then

$$\overline{r}(\overline{p}(S)) = \begin{bmatrix} N & N & N & t_1 & \dfrac{N - t_1}{2} \end{bmatrix}^T \tag{32}$$

For any N, the last entry may not be an integer.

Consider clustering the graph as shown in Figure 15. Actors 1, 2, 3, and 4 are collected into a cluster that internally has a complete cycle and an easily derived

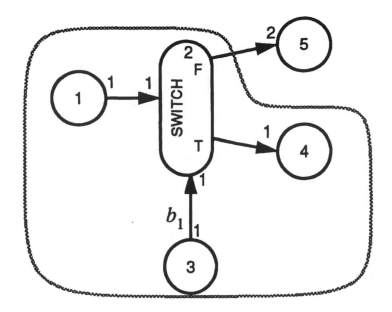

Figure 15: A graph that can be executed in bounded memory, but has no finite complete cycle. Actors 1 to 4 considered alone, however, do have a complete cycle; we can treat them as a cluster and execute the cluster until actors 5's requirements are met.

annotated schedule. Moreover, a bounded memory schedule can be constructed as follows:

```
repeat_forever {
        n=0;
        do {
                fire 1;
                fire 3;
                fire 2;
                if (t) fire 4;
                n += t;
        } while (n < 2);
}
```

In this pseudo-code notation, we use "t" to denote the Boolean value of the token produced by actor 3. It takes on value 0 or 1.

We have developed systematic methods for constructing clusters like that in Figure 15. The method is related to the loop-scheduling of Bhattacharyya and Lee [7], but generalized beyond SDF graphs. Briefly, these methods begin a cluster with a single actor, and augment the cluster with a new actor when

1. the new actor has the same "repetition rate" as the cluster (on the connecting arc, the source actor always writes the same number of tokens that the destination actor reads);

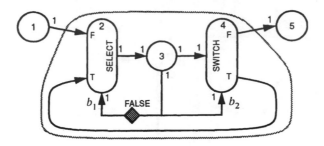

Figure 16: A do-while construct. This graph is strongly consistent, and can execute in bounded memory, but it has no finite complete cycle. Constructing a static schedule requires both clustering and state enumeration.

2. the augmented cluster has a finite complete cycle, and

3. when the augmented cluster is treated as an atomic actor, the graph does not deadlock.

The final test passes if no actor external to the newly formed cluster is a predecessor of one of the actors to be merged and at the same time a successor of the other. When a cluster can no longer be augmented, it is treated as an atomic unit and invoked however many times are required to match the "repetition rates" of its neighbors. In this repeated invocation of the cluster, we allow an unbounded number of invocations, implemented by embedding the schedule for the cluster inside a while loop. We can still guarantee bounded memory requirements because the cluster internally repeats a complete cycle, and hence has bounded memory requirements. Repetition for a fixed number of cycles and conditional execution are also permitted. The algorithm is described in detail in [10].

Once a cluster is repeated so that it matches its neighbors, more merging is possible; the process of merging actors into clusters, and of looping the clusters, is repeated until no more changes are possible. The resulting hierarchical structure of clusters reflects the loop structure of the dataflow graph, with loops, *if-then*, and *do-while* constructs.

This procedure is precisely the reverse of the "well-behaved dataflow graph" approach of [13]; instead of building up the dataflow graph out of bounded subunits, the clustering algorithm finds the well-behaved subunits. Consequently, it also permits constructs that are not "well-behaved" but nevertheless correspond to useful and correct programs.

4.6 State Enumeration

A more difficult example is shown in Figure 16. This graph is strongly consistent, with

$$\vec{r}(\overline{p}) = [(1 - p_1) \quad 1 \quad 1 \quad 1 \quad (p_2)]^T \tag{33}$$

satisfying the balance equations, assuming $p_1 = p_2$. The difficulty arises when we try to construct a finite complete cycle, and we discover that we cannot assure that $t_1 = t_2$. Hence, a schedule with repetition vector

$$\vec{r}(\overline{p}(S)) = [(N - t_1) \quad N \quad N \quad N \quad (t_2)]^T \tag{34}$$

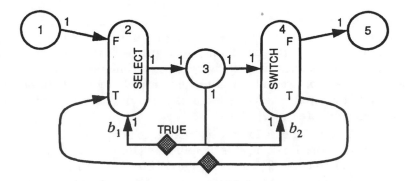

Figure 17: One of two possible ending states for the graph in Figure 16 after executing a schedule with repetition vector given by (34).

may not satisfy the balance equations. The solution is two-fold. First, we cluster the graph as shown in Figure 16. The cluster is internally SDF and can be cyclically scheduled using the firing sequence $S_1 = \{2, 3, 4\}$. Then we construct a schedule S_2 that returns the cluster to its original state:

```
do {
        fire S1;
} while (b1 = TRUE);
```

Treated as a unit, the cluster always consumes and produces exactly one token, so the resulting schedule is

$$S = \{1, S_2, 5\}. \tag{35}$$

For this purpose, the "state" of a dataflow graph has two components, the number of tokens on each arc, and the value of any Boolean tokens on Boolean arcs.

An alternative approach is to construct a schedule with the repetition vector given by (34) with $N = 1$, and observe that two possible states can result from executing this schedule. One of these states is the original state, denoted Σ_1. The second is a new state, Σ_2, shown in Figure 17. If a schedule with repetition vector (34) is applied to the starting state Σ_2, then exactly two ending states are possible, Σ_1 and Σ_2. Consequently, a schedule with repetition vector (34) can be repeated indefinitely with no difficulty.

Yet a third alternative approach is to construct a *preamble*, or initial schedule that transforms the graph into one that has no delays on Boolean arcs. For the graph in Figure 16, firing actors 1 and 2 constitute such a preamble. After the preamble has executed, then ordinary scheduling methods can be applied.

4.7 Scheduling Graphs That Require Unbounded Memory
All three methods fail, however, for the graph in Figure 13. The number of states that would need to be considered is unbounded. For this graph, we offer no alternative to dynamic scheduling with dynamic memory allocation. However, the clustering algorithm still finds well-behaved substructures in the graph; by clustering the graph as much as possible, we reduce the amount of dynamic memory allocation and scheduling that is required.

Some complex and irregular graphs will not be successfully clustered by our algorithm, and state enumeration requires a heuristic to avoid exploring the (possibly infinite) state space forever. Because of this, some graphs that have bounded-memory schedules may not be handled successfully by these techniques. If so, some dynamic memory allocation will be used although it is not actually required. However, graphs composed only of the "well-behaved" structures appearing in the dataflow literature are handled successfully (e.g., [12], [13]).

We have not given techniques for proving that graphs require unbounded memory in this paper. A technique for doing so is described in [10]; it is a generalization of the reachability tree construction algorithm for Petri nets that was first given by Karp and Miller [15]. In the cases of the graphs of Figure 12 and Figure 13, this algorithm proves that certain arcs of the graph must grow without bound. In both cases, it can be shown that a repeated sequence of actor executions that steadily increases the number of tokens on certain arcs must occur given certain Boolean outcomes.

Unfortunately, this algorithm is not guaranteed to terminate (so that it is not a true algorithm unless a heuristic cutoff is added to terminate the state space search). In fact, no algorithm that decides whether a dynamic dataflow graph including SWITCH, SELECT, and actors that perform arithmetic on the integers requires bounded memory is possible, because this is equivalent to the halting problem for Turing machines (see [10] for a proof). Nevertheless, the practical consequence of this is that dynamic memory allocation may be used unnecessarily in some cases for irregular graphs.

5. Conclusions

Dataflow graphs that are strongly consistent and have finite complete cycles can always be scheduled statically and executed in bounded memory. Some strongly consistent graphs without finite complete cycles can also be executed in bounded memory. We have described a clustering technique that can identify such graphs and construct their schedules. However, some perfectly correct graphs may not fit the models described. To execute these, we must resort to the much more costly methods of dynamic scheduling and memory allocation. Nonetheless, even within such uncooperative graphs, large subgraphs are likely to be consistent and have finite complete cycles. These subgraphs should be statically scheduled and memory should be statically allocated. The cost of dynamic scheduling and memory allocation should be incurred only where absolutely necessary.

References

[1] Arvind and K.P. Gostelow, "The U-Interpreter," *Computer*, Vol. 15, No. 2, February 1982.

[2] Arvind and D.E. Culler, "Managing Resources in a Parallel Machine," in *Fifth Generation Computer Architectures*, Elsevier Science Publishers, 1986, pp. 103–121.

[3] R.A. Ballance, A.B. Maccabe, and K.J. Ottenstein, "The Program Dependence Web: A Representation Supporting Control-, Data-, and Demand-Driven Interpretation of Imperative Languages," *Proc. ACM SIGPLAN '90 Conf. on Programming Language Design and Implementation*, June 1990, pp. 257–271.

[4] A. Benveniste, B. Le Goff, and P. Le Guernic, "Hybrid Dynamical Systems Theory and the Language SIGNAL," Research Report No. 838, Institut National de Recherche en Informatique et en Automatique (INRIA), Domain de Voluceau, Rocquencourt, B.P. 105, 78153 Le Chesnay Cedex, France, April 1988.

[5] A. Benveniste and P. Le Guernic, "Hybrid Dynamical Systems Theory and the SIGNAL Language," *IEEE Trans. on Automatic Control*, Vol. 35, No. 5, pp. 525–546, May 1990.

[6] A. Benveniste, P. Le Guernic, Y. Sorel, and M. Sorine, "A Denotational Theory of Synchronous Reactive Systems," *Information and Computating*, Vol. 99, No. 2, pp. 192–230, 1992.

[7] S. Bhattacharyya and E.A. Lee, "Scheduling Synchronous Dataflow Graphs for Efficient Looping," *J. of VLSI Signal Processing* Vol. 6, No. 3, pp. 271–288, December 1993.

[8] J. Bier et al., "Gabriel: A Design Environment for DSP," *IEEE Micro Magazine*, Vol. 10, No. 5, October 1990, pp. 28–45.

[9] J. Buck, S. Ha, E.A. Lee, and D.G. Messerschmitt, "Ptolemy: A Platform for Heterogeneous Simulation and Prototyping," *Proc. 1991 European Simulation Conference*, Copenhagen, Denmark, June 17–19, 1991.

[10] J. Buck, *Scheduling Dynamic Dataflow Graphs With Bounded Memory Using the Token Flow Model*, Memorandum No. UCB/ERL M93/69 Ph.D. thesis, EECS Dept., University of California, Berkeley, CA 94720, September 1993.

[11] A.L. Davis and R.M. Keller, "Data Flow Program Graphs," *Computer*, Vol. 15, No. 2, February 1982.

[12] J.B. Dennis, "First Version Data Flow Procedure Language," Technical Memo MAC TM61, MIT Laboratory for Computer Science, Cambridge, MA 02139, May 1975.

[13] G.R. Gao, R. Govindarajan, P. Panangaden, "Well-Behaved Programs for DSP Computation," *Proc. ICASSp 1992*, San Francisco, March 1992.

[14] P.N. Hilfinger, "Silage Reference Manual, DRAFT Release 2.0," Computer Science Division, EECS Dept., University of California, Berkeley, CA 94720, July 8, 1989.

[15] R.M. Karp and R.E. Miller, "Parallel Programming Schemata," *Journal of Computer and System Sciences*, Vol. 3, No. 2, May 1969, pp. 147–195.

[16] K. Kavi, B.P. Buckles, U.N. Bhat, "A Formal Definition of Data Flow Graph Models," *IEEE Trans. on Computers*, Vol. C-35, No. 11, November 1986.

[17] P.R. Kosinski, "A Straightforward Denotational Semantics for Non-Determinate Data Flow Programs," *Conf. Record of the 5th Ann. ACM Symp. on Principles of Programming Languages*, Tuscon, AZ, 1978.

[18] E.A. Lee and D.G. Messerschmitt, "Static Scheduling of Synchronous Data Flow Programs for Digital Signal Processing," *IEEE Trans. on Computers*, January 1987.

[19] E.A. Lee and D.G. Messerschmitt, "Synchronous Data Flow," *IEEE Proceedings*, September 1987.

[20] E.A. Lee, "Consistency in Dataflow Graphs," *IEEE Transactions on Parallel and Distributed Systems*, Vol. 2, No. 2, April 1991.

[21] P. Le Guernic and T. Gautier, "Data-flow to Von Neumann: the SIGNAL approach," in *Advanced Topics in Data-Flow Computing*, J.-L. Gaudiot and L. Bic, Eds., Prentice-Hall, 1991.

[22] J.R. McGraw, "The VAL Language: Description and Analysis," *ACM Trans. on Programming Languages and Systems*, Vol. 4, No. 1, January 1982, pp. 44–82.

[23] R.S. Nikhil, "ID Reference Manual," Computation Structures Group Memo 284, Massachusetts Institute of Technology, 545 Technology Square, Cambridge, MA 02139, August 29, 1988.

[24] K. Pingali and Arvind, "Efficient Demand-Driven Evaluation. Part I," *ACM Trans. on Programming Languages and Systems*, Vol. 7, No. 2, April 1985, pp. 311–333.

[25] H. Printz, *Automatic Mapping of Large Signal Processing Systems to a Parallel Machine*, Memorandum CMU-CS-91-101, Ph.D. thesis, School of Computer Science, Carnegie Mellon University, May 15, 1991.

[26] Gilbert C. Sih, *Multiprocessor Scheduling to Account for Inter-processor Communication*, Memorandum No. UCB/ERL M91/29, Ph.D. thesis, University of California, Berkeley, CA 94720, April 22, 1991.

[27] D.A. Turner, "The Semantic Elegance of Applicative Languages," *Proc. of the ACM Conf. on Functional Programming Languages and Computer Architecture*, Portsmouth, NH, 1981, pp. 85–92.

[28] K.-S. Weng, "Stream-Oriented Computation in Recursive Data Flow Schemas," Laboratory for Computer Science (TM-68), MIT, Cambridge, MA 02139, Oct. 1975.

Distributed Task Management in SISAL

Matthew Haines and A.P. Wim Böhm
Computer Science Department
Colorado State University, Fort Collins, CO 80523

In this paper we present the design of a flexible task management system for executing SISAL tasks on a distributed memory multiprocessor. The design focuses on the ability to execute both large and small numbers of tasks on both a large and a small number of processors. We describe the role and scope of a SISAL task and its shared memory implementation. We then describe the distributed memory design and implementation, and provide the performance and analysis of two simple programs on an nCUBE/2 distributed memory multiprocessor.

1. Introduction

Due to the inability of shared memory multiprocessors to scale past a relatively small number of processors, today's most powerful computers are *distributed memory multiprocessors* [20], [12], [16]. This gives rise to two issues that are becoming increasingly important:

- *Detecting* enough parallelism in an application to keep the machine resources busy. As the number of processors in these systems increases into the thousands, the amount of parallelism needed to obtain thousand-fold speedups increases proportionally. Applicative (or functional) languages have demonstrated their ability to expose parallelism in an application as well as simplify the task of parallel programming [17], [9].

- *Managing* the parallelism for efficient execution. Once the parallelism in an application has been revealed, it is up to the compiler, runtime system, and hardware to manage the parallelism for efficient utilization of the machine resources, and hence efficient execution. Since most of these large distributed memory multiprocessors have an order of magnitude difference in the time to access local memory versus the time to access remote memory, managing this latency is tantamount to efficient execution. Latency can either be *avoided* by ensuring that memory accesses are local, or *tolerated* if the memory access is remote and there is other useful work that can be done in the time it takes to satisfy the remote reference (i.e., *multithreading*). Latency avoidance requires that the data used by a code segment (or *thread*) be mapped to the same node as the code segment, and that the code segment exhibits some degree of locality. Latency tolerance requires a fast context switching mechanism (i.e., lightweight threads), and an abundance of parallelism so that there is more than enough work to keep all of the processors busy.

SISAL (Streams and Iterations in a Single Assignment Language) is a functional language that supports data types and operations for scientific computation [14]. Cur-

---

This work was supported in part by NSF Grant MIP-9113268 and by grants AE-1214 and 87-4763 from Sandia National Laboratory.

rent implementations of SISAL exist for sequential machines and a variety of multiprocessor architectures, including shared memory [5], vector [4], [13], hierarchical memory [21], and dataflow [2]. We will focus on the non dataflow implementations, which map SISAL onto a parallel machine using C as an intermediate code. The SISAL compiler consists of three parts: a frontend, a backend, and a run time system, taking a SISAL program and generating a C program which is then compiled using the native C compiler and linked with the SISAL runtime library to produce machine-dependent code [3]. The current compiler[1] assumes that all user data structures exist in a flat, shared addressing space. Also, the runtime structures, such as task queues, are shared and protected with locks. While this has provided efficient implementations of SISAL on a variety of multiprocessor architectures [6], [9], it has precluded an efficient implementation of SISAL on a distributed memory multiprocessor.

The runtime system is responsible for providing the SISAL compiler with two main abstractions: task management and memory management. The task management abstraction [10] supports lightweight tasks. SISAL tasks correspond roughly to loop or function bodies in the SISAL text, and thus fall between dataflow threads and program modules in the spectrum of parallelism granularity. For shared memory multiprocessors, tasks are placed in a shared queue. While this provides inherent load balancing, it creates contention for accessing the shared queue, and is not a feasible option for a scalable implementation of a distributed memory platform. Thus the runtime system must now concern itself with the issue of task distribution.

This paper describes the design and implementation of a flexible task management system for executing SISAL tasks on a distributed memory multiprocessor. In Section 2 we discuss SISAL tasks and their shared memory implementation. In Section 3 we introduce our distributed memory task management system for both flat and nested loops. In Section 4 we show performance numbers for two sample programs that highlight both flat and nested parallel loops. We conclude and provide future directions in Section 5.

2. SISAL Tasks and Shared Memory

2.1 SISAL Parallelism

The functional language semantics of SISAL ensures that only "true" data dependence constrains the parallelism of a program. Thus *independence* is defined in this context as having no data dependence between functions, loops, or expressions. SISAL allows for the extraction of parallelism at three levels:

- *Function-level parallelism* exists when two functions are independent of each other, and thus may be executed in parallel. Functional language semantics ensure that if functions are independent of one another (in terms of input and result values), the order of evaluation will not affect the outcome of the program (*Church-Rosser property*).

- *Loop-level parallelism* exists when the iterations of a loop are partially independent of each other, and thus may be executed in parallel. SISAL provides two forms of an iterative construct, though the task of determining which loop construct to use is left to the programmer.

---

[1]The current SISAL compiler is *osc* version 12.0.

> - **for initial**, used for specifying loops which must be executed sequentially or in pipeline fashion.[2]
> - **for**, used for specifying loops in which the loop bodies may execute in parallel, which corresponds to the concept of *data parallelism*.

- *Instruction-level parallelism* exists when two instructions are independent of each other, and thus may be executed in parallel. SISAL programs can be represented by a dataflow graph, which exposes the instruction-level dependencies. Several dataflow architectures, including the Manchester Dataflow Machine [2], the RMIT/CSIRO Dataflow Machine (CSIRAC) [1], and the ADAM dataflow architecture [15], have used these dataflow graphs to exploit instruction-level parallelism.

The current multiprocessor-based SISAL implementation is optimized for efficient execution of scientific applications. Therefore, although SISAL language semantics allow for the extraction of all three levels of parallelism, the current multiprocessor-based compiler and runtime system support only *loop-level parallelism*, as this is the dominant form of parallelism in many scientific applications.

2.2 The Master-Slave Model

The current SISAL runtime system employs a *master-slave* model of parallel execution, in which the roles of each process type are defined as follows:

- The **master** process executes all sequential portions of the code, including I/O, initialization, and synchronization. Additionally, the master process is responsible for setting up and initiating parallel execution of a loop, in which the following actions are performed:

  1. The parallel loop is divided into a set of independent *tasks*, where each task represents a contiguous set of loop bodies.
  2. The tasks are distributed among the participating slave processes for parallel execution.
  3. A *barrier* is established, which prevents the master from continuing until all of the slave processes have completed their tasks.

  Once the barrier has been completed, the master continues with the execution of the program.

- The **slave** processes are responsible for executing the parallel *tasks* that are distributed by the master as follows:

  1. Each slave continues to check a *ready queue* for the appearance of a task that needs to be executed.
  2. Tasks are removed from the ready queue and executed by the slave processes in parallel.
  3. The result of the task is either a partial value that needs to be combined with the global value held by the master (i.e., *reduction*), or is a set of array elements representing a portion of a newly formed array.

---

[2]However, the current SISAL compiler does not support pipeline parallelism in the **for initial** construct.

4. After reporting the results, the slave indicates that it has completed this task.

Nested parallel loops imply that the tasks representing the outer parallel loop will contain parallel loops themselves, and thus every slave process must be capable of initiating (or becoming) a master process to facilitate the parallel execution of the inner loop. Therefore, it is more convenient to think of masters and slaves as *processes* rather than *processors*, since at any given time, a single processor may be playing the role of either the master of slave.

2.3 Slices and Activation Records

Whereas a *task* in SISAL is the general term used for parallel work, a *slice* is, specifically, a contiguous set of parallel loop bodies. The *thickness* of a slice is defined as the number of contiguous iterations it contains, and is determined by the loop bounds, the number of slave processes executing the loop, and the loop distribution strategy. The runtime data structure for a slice is an *activation record*, containing the following minimal set of information:

- A range of execution. Since SISAL slices are defined as a *contiguous* set of loop bodies, a range *(lo, hi)* is sufficient for defining the scope of parallel execution for a task.

- A code pointer, representing the function that the slave will execute. This function consists of a parameterized version of the parallel loop, where the parameters represent the range of execution.

- An argument list. Besides the range of execution, each task may require additional inputs, such as the location of a global array to be operated on, or the values of some global variables. Additionally, an output argument is specified which denotes the location of a global value or pointer to an array that is to be filled. These arguments are packed into a single record by the compiler and included in the activation record as a single argument.

- A unique loop identifier, which will be used in the case of nested parallel loops to identify which barrier counter is to be updated upon receipt of a slice-completion message.

In general, the terms *task*, *slice*, and *activation record* all represent the concept of parallel work in SISAL as a contiguous set of loop bodies and, although the terms are often interchanged, the concept remains clear.

2.4 Shared Memory Task Management

Now that we have defined the unit of parallel work in SISAL, the task, and the method of performing parallel work, the master-slave model, we will describe task management as it exists in the shared memory implementations of SISAL.

At the heart of the shared memory implementation is the *shared ready queue*, in which the master enqueues each of the activation records (or slices) and from which the slaves receive them, as depicted in Figure 1. The ready queue is allocated from shared memory, and thus is accessible to the slave processes on all processors. Barrier synchronization is performed by having the slaves set a *done* flag in the activation record on the shared ready queue, and the master counts the number of activations

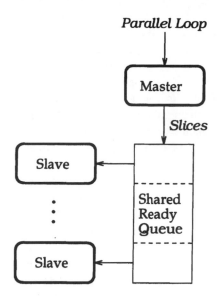

Figure 1: Shared memory task organization.

that have completed. When the count equals the number of activations enqueued, the activations are removed from the queue and the barrier is complete.

The advantage of this approach is that *load balancing* techniques, such as *guided self-scheduling* [18], are possible due to the shared nature of the queue. Load balancing is the problem of ensuring that each processor in a parallel machine performs roughly the same amount of parallel work, so that minimal time is lost on barrier synchronization. Since all of the activation records are placed in a single location, a slave simply gets the next slice from the queue, executes the slice, and returns for more. Slaves continue to execute the slices until none remain, at which time the slaves will wait for more work.

The disadvantage of this approach is that since multiple processors have access to this queue, the queue becomes a *shared resource* that must be accessed using a critical section. The SISAL runtime system uses a lock-based protocol for ensuring mutually exclusive access to the queue. This means that before any master or slave process may access the queue, a lock must be successfully acquired, and if the lock is not available, then the process must wait. Therefore, *contention* for the shared resource creates a runtime overhead, which is minimally the time required to execute the lock protocol, but can be extended when the process must wait for the lock. Since this overhead due to contention grows with the number of processors in the system, we say that the design does not *scale*. Still, this shared memory design has resulted in efficient implementations for shared memory multiprocessors that can quickly and efficiently access shared data structures [7], as the number of processors for these systems is relatively low.

3. Distributed Task Management

Executing the SISAL master-slave model of parallel execution in a distributed memory environment implies that a shared ready queue is not available. Therefore, a new method for distributing the tasks to the slaves, and a new method for performing a barrier synchronization is required.

3.1 Task Distribution and Barrier Synchronization

Since shared data structures are not supported by hardware in a distributed memory multiprocessor, we give each slave process its own *private* ready queue. The master then sends the activation records to the nodes containing the slave processes using the native message passing mechanisms, where the message is received (asynchronously) and placed onto the private ready queue of the local slave process. The slave monitors its own private ready list, which can now be done without having to obtain exclusive access, and executes any slice that arrives. Resulting values and a completion message are sent back to the master upon completion of each slice.

Barrier synchronization is now performed by having the master process count each of the slice-completion messages, and when the count is equal to the number of slices distributed, the barrier is complete. However, in the case of nested parallel loops, it is not sufficient for a single counter to keep track of the slice-completion messages, since a single processor may receive slice completion messages for both a parallel outer and parallel inner loop, for which it is the master. Thus it is necessary to distinguish among the slice completion records, and this is done by assigning a unique loop identifier to each parallel loop. An identifier is removed from a pool of identifiers that is local to each processor, and is replaced when the barrier for a loop is complete. Also, each processor maintains an array of barrier counters, corresponding to the loop identifiers, so that when a slice-completion message is received, the proper barrier counter can be incremented.

This distributed design has removed the need for obtaining critical section locks to access the ready queue, thus eliminating the overhead for contention and allowing for a scalable number of slaves to be employed. However, the implicit load balancing capabilities of the shared queue have been lost, and thus it is now possible for the system load to become imbalanced. Although various dynamic load balancing schemes could be employed to ensure that the load remains balanced [8], we have chosen not to implement any of these schemes for two main reasons:

1. Dynamic load balancing strategies work by migrating work from an over-utilized node to an under-utilized node, either because the under-utilized node asked for the work (*active load balancing*) or because the over-utilized node decided to give some work away (*passive load balancing*). Either way, parallel work, in our case slices, would migrate from one node to another, disrupting the original distribution pattern. Since our system is designed to minimize the number of remote references by closely tying the distribution of tasks with the distribution of data, a dynamic load balancing technique would disrupt this alignment, possibly creating excessive remote references and causing an increase in the total execution time rather than a decrease.

2. Dynamic load balancing algorithms require updated information about their surrounding processors, resulting in a runtime overhead for exchanging this information. Also, task migration results in even more message passing. Dynamic load balancing is an expensive operation, and will not be undertaken until it is determined that the loads are imbalanced, and that this imbalance could benefit from a load balancing strategy. Thus, there is not enough analysis at this point to justify the added expense of a dynamic load balancing strategy.

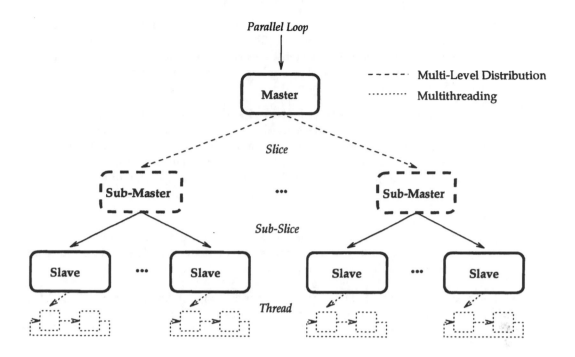

Figure 2: Distributed memory task organization.

3.2 Extending the Master-Slave Model of Parallel Execution

Our distributed memory task management system is intended to execute on a wide variety of distributed memory machines, with sizes ranging from tens to thousands of processors. As previously defined in Section 2, SISAL parallelism is expressed in terms of a *task*, which represents a contiguous set of loop bodies that can be executed in parallel, and implemented dynamically as a *slice*, which is defined by an *activation record*. Because distributing these slices over a large number of processors can create a sequential bottleneck, and because the ability to mask latency requires the parallel execution of tasks within a single processor, we have augmented the single-level definition of SISAL parallelism to create a flexible multi-level parallelism hierarchy, as depicted in Figure 2. To maintain the high level of execution efficiency that is achieved by *slices* in the single-level design, each level of the hierarchy still corresponds to a contiguous set of loop bodies, where *slices* are "thicker" than *sub-slices*, and sub-slices are thicker than *threads*. Since we have changed the definition of parallel work in the SISAL system, we must also modify the master-slave execution model to account for the various levels of parallelism. Thus we augment the master-slave model with two new models of parallel execution: *multi-level distribution* and *multithreading*.

3.3 The Multi-Level Distribution Model of Parallel Execution

The multi-level distribution (MLD) model of execution is designed to parallelize the distribution of tasks from master to slaves, and parallelize the reduction of values from slaves to master. This becomes necessary when the number of slave processes gets large enough that the sequential distribution and reduction times start to lower the efficiency of the parallel execution time. The MLD model works as follows (refer to Figure 2):

- The **master** process divides the parallel loop into a number of *slices*, where the number is called the *fan-out degree*. These slices are then sent to **sub-master** processes, and a barrier is initiated to wait for the completion of the sub-master processes. After the barrier is complete, the master returns execution at the point following the parallel loop.

- Each **sub-master** process will divide its slice into *sub-slices*, and distribute these sub-slices among a subset of the **slave** processes *in parallel*, where the degree of parallelism is equal to the fan-out degree. Each sub-master process then performs a barrier synchronization for the sub-slices it has distributed, and collects the reduction values from the slaves. Upon completion of the barrier, the sub-masters will report their values to the master and indicate that the assigned slice has been completed.

- The **slave** processes execute the sub-slices obtained from the sub-master, and report back to the sub-master with the results of the sub-slice and an indication that the sub-slice has been completed.

The main goal of our MLD design was to enable parallel distribution and reduction without requiring the compiler to re-structure the loop slices, thus remaining independent of the compiler and allowing MLD to be enabled or disabled without having to re-compile.

For MLD execution, the runtime system divides a parallel loop into *fan-out* slices, rather than p slices, where p is the number of participating processors. The slices are then distributed to the *fan-out* sub-master processes, who will further subdivide the slices and distribute them among $p/fan-out$ slave processes in parallel. If the loop results in a reduction, then each of the sub-master processes will allocate a local value to accumulate the reduction values from the slaves it controls. When the slave processes complete their slices, they will send their completion message and reduction value back to their sub-master process. When a sub-master completes the barrier for the slaves it initiated, it will report back to the master with the accumulated reduction value and a completion message. When the master completes the barrier for all of the sub-master processes, the loop has terminated.

The only new structures required for this design are MLD barriers and intermediate reduction values for the sub-master processes. Since we utilize the same loop slice method of parallelism, and loop slices are controlled by the runtime system, we meet our design goal of isolating the compiler from the operation of MLD.

As we will see in Section 4, the distribution of slices can create a significant sequential bottleneck when the number of processors is in the hundreds. By creating this extra level of sub-masters and sub-slices, MLD serves to parallelize this sequential bottleneck, effectively boosting the parallel efficiency.

3.4 Control Parameters for Parallel Loops

Flat, or single-level, parallel loops offer few choices for parallelization and distribution: if the loop is parallelized, then it is typically distributed among all participating nodes, using either the single-level distribution or multi-level distribution strategy. Nested parallel loops, on the other hand, provide a wide range of distribution options, such as distributing the outer loop for parallel execution and executing the inner loop sequentially (called *sequential inner loop*), distributing both outer and inner loops for parallel execution (called *fully distributed inner loop*), and fully distributing the outer loop while only partially distributing the inner loop (called *partially distributed*

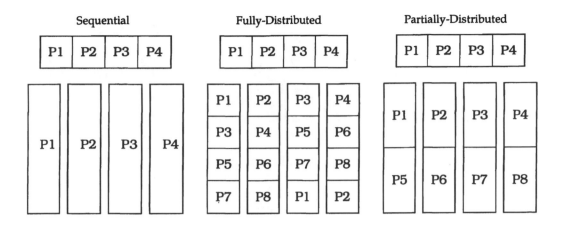

Figure 3: Distribution options for nested parallel loops.

inner loop). These nested loop distribution schemes are depicted in Figure 3, where the outer loop is fully-distributed over the first four processors, and the inner loop is distributed over some set of the 8 available processors.

The first distribution scheme (*sequential inner loop*) minimizes the overhead of the inner loop by executing the loop sequentially, but limits the amount of available parallelism to the size of the outer loop. Any machine parallelism in excess of the outer loop parallelism would be wasted. The second distribution scheme (*fully distributed inner loop*) allows us to exploit the combined parallelism of both outer and inner loops, and instead of wasting machine parallelism, this strategy often over-saturates the machine resources, causing unnecessary overheads. Therefore, the third scheme (*partially distributed inner loop*) was created as a hybrid of the first two. When the outer loop parallelism (n) is larger than the number of processors (p), the inner loop is run sequentially, but when p exceeds n, we will distribute the inner loop in a controlled fashion for parallel execution. For example, suppose we are executing a nested parallel loop with 4 outer loop iterations ($n = 4$) and 4 inner loop iterations ($m = 4$) on 8 processors ($p = 8$). Since the outer loop parallelism will not cover the machine parallelism, we will distribute the outer loop to 4 of the processors (P_0, P_1, P_2, P_3) and each of these processors, P_i, will distribute the inner loop to P_i and $P_{i+(p/m)}$. This distribution scheme will utilize all the processors while minimizing the overhead of distributing the inner loop.

Since the decision of which distribution scheme to use can only be made after runtime parameters have been established (i.e., size of loops, number of processors), we have equipped our runtime system with the ability to handle the three nested loop distribution schemes discussed, and the flexibility to create others. The actual decision can then be made by a compiler using runtime profiles or other analysis, or by the programmer. This is accomplished by associating three control parameters to each parallel loop: *blocksize, start node,* and *stride.* The *blocksize* specifies the thickness of the loop slices, i.e., the number of contiguous loop iterations for each slice, thereby creating $n/blocksize$ slices of the loop to be distributed. By default, *blocksize* is set to n/p so that p slices are created, one per processor, minimizing overhead. The slices are then distributed among the processors, starting with *start node* and continuing

Distribution Scheme	Blocksize		Start Node		Stride	
	Outer	Inner	Outer	Inner	Outer	Inner
Sequential Inner Loop	n/p	m	P_{id}	P_{id}	1	1
Fully-Distributed Inner Loop	n/p	m/p	P_{id}	P_{id}	1	1
Partially-Distributed Inner Loop	1	mn/p	P_{id}	P_{id}	p/n	1

Table 1: Control parameter settings for nested loop distribution schemes.

at an increment of *stride* until all slices have been distributed. Slices are wrapped in modulo fashion when their number exceeds the number of processors divided by the stride ($n/blocksize > p/stride$). Table 1 gives the parameter settings for the three nested loop distribution schemes discussed earlier, where n is the number of outer loop iterations, m is the number of inner loop iterations, p is the number of processors, and P_{id} is the designator for each processor $id = 0 \cdots p - 1$.

4. Performance and Analysis

4.1 Task Management for Flat Loops

We compare the single-level and multi-level loop distribution schemes for a large un-nested (flat) loop by measuring the performance of Purdue Parallel Benchmark #1 [19], which approximates the value of the integral of $f(x)$ in the interval [a, b] using the trapezoidal rule:

$$T_N = h * \left(\frac{f(a) + f(b)}{2} + \sum_{i=1}^{N-1} f(a + i * h) \right)$$

where N is the number of intervals in the estimate and, $h = (b - a)/N$. For our implementation, we compute $\int_0^\pi \sin(x)$, where $\sin(x)$ is computed using a Taylor series of fourteen terms ($\frac{x^1}{1!} - \frac{x^3}{3!} + \cdots - \frac{x^{27}}{27!}$), resulting in 55 floating-point operations per invocation and matching the precision of the nCUBE/2 system sin function.

Table 2 displays the execution times for this program, which ran for 10^7 iterations, where Sp represents the parallel speedup (T_1/T_n) and *Eff* represents the parallel efficiency (Sp/n). These execution times compare favorably to the single processor sequential C program that performs the same computation in 414.96 seconds. The disparity in single processor execution time between SISAL and C results from the fact that the SISAL compiler generates very efficient C code that is often easier for the native C compiler to optimize than hand-coded C programs.

Fan-out corresponds to the number of *sub-master* processes used in multi-level distribution, and *OFO* in Table 2 represents the optimal fan-out degree for each machine configuration. Fan-out provides a means to control the amount of *overhead* for multi-level distribution (exemplified by the sequential loop in the master process that distributes the sub-tasks), versus the *gain* of having the sub-masters distribute the slices in parallel. Figure 4 depicts this tradeoff for all possible fan-out degrees on 512 processors, where a fan-out degree of 1 represents single-level distribution. In the fan-out region $[1 \cdots 8]$ there is not enough sub-master parallelism, whereas in the fan-out region $[128 \cdots 512]$ there is too much overhead. A fan-out degree about equal to the square root of the number of processors appears to be most effective for most applications, and is currently the default in our system.

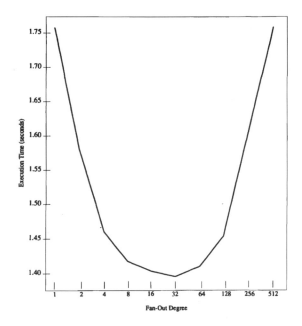

Figure 4: Performance of Purdue #1 on 512 processors, various fan-out degrees.

Table 2 shows that the efficiency of this application using both single-level distribution and multi-level distribution is 100% up to 32 processors. For higher numbers of
processors, the efficiency starts to decrease, getting much worse for 256 and 512 processors, especially for single-level-distribution. Thus, for this program, 64 processors
is the point at which the overhead for sequentially distributing the loop slices starts
to have a noticeable detrimental effect on the performance, and multi-level distribution is able to recapture some of the lost performance by parallelizing the distribution
phase. For 256 and 512 processors, the gain is substantial: 5% and 10% efficiency,
respectively.

Table 2 also reflects the effect that the ratio of *computation time to communica-*

	Single-level Distribution			Multi-level Distribution			
PEs	*Time(s)*	*Sp.*	*Eff. (%)*	*OFO*	*Time(s)*	*Sp.*	*Eff. (%)*
1	355.8472	1.00	100				
2	177.9336	2.00	100	2	177.9343	2.00	100
4	88.9698	4.00	100	2	88.9701	4.00	100
8	44.4940	8.00	100	2	44.4932	8.00	100
16	22.2639	15.98	100	4	22.2601	15.99	100
32	11.1649	31.87	100	4	11.1538	31.90	100
64	5.6461	63.03	98	8	5.6207	63.31	99
128	2.9484	120.69	94	8	2.8936	122.98	96
256	1.7236	206.46	81	16	1.6084	221.24	86
512	1.7582	202.39	40	32	1.3961	254.89	50

Table 2: Performance of Purdue #1, single and multi-level distribution.

	Single-Level Distribution			Multi-Level Distribution			
PEs	Time(s)	Sp.	Eff. (%)	OFO	Time(s)	Sp.	Eff. (%)
1	149.8411	1.00	100				
2	74.9305	2.00	100	2	74.9309	2.00	100
4	37.4680	4.00	100	2	37.4684	4.00	100
8	18.7430	7.99	100	2	18.7424	7.99	100
16	9.3885	15.96	100	4	9.3846	15.97	100
32	4.7272	31.70	99	4	4.7161	31.77	99
64	2.4273	61.73	96	8	2.4017	62.39	97
128	1.3394	111.87	87	8	1.2842	116.68	91
256	0.9194	162.98	64	16	0.8029	186.83	73
512	1.3551	110.58	22	16	0.9155	163.67	32

Table 3: Performance of Purdue #1, 1/2 Taylor series.

tion time can have on the performance of the program. As we double the number of processors, the computation time of each parallel slice is *halved*, since the same number of loop bodies are now distributed over twice the number of loop slices, and the communication time is *doubled*, since there are now twice the number of loop slices to be distributed and twice the number of intermediate values to be reduced. Thus the ratio of computation time to communication time, which determines the efficiency of an application, is reduced by a factor of four each time the number of processors is doubled. We can see the effect of this diminishing ratio in the efficiency for 256 and 512 processors. Multi-level distribution reduces the rate at which the communication time increases, thus decreasing the rate at which efficiency is lost. If the initial loop-body computation time were reduced, the ratio would be more dependent on the communication time increase rather than the computation time decrease, and thus the effect of multi-level distribution on slowing the declining efficiency would be greater. To see this effect, we reduce the Taylor series from 14 terms to 7 terms, effectively halving the computation time for each loop iteration. The results of this experiment are displayed in Table 3. Comparing the gain in efficiency for multi-level distribution with the first experiment (Table 2), we see that the gain is increased. Given this performance gain, and the ability to employ multi-level distribution along with the other runtime options (such as multithreading), we will typically employ multi-level distribution for most of our sample programs, particularly in the last processor configuration grouping ($16 \cdots 128$ processors).

4.2 Task Management for Nested Loops
We now examine the effects of the nested loop distribution schemes, as defined in Table 1, on the performance of Purdue Parallel Benchmark #2, which computes e^* by:

$$e^* = \sum_{i=1}^{n} \prod_{j=1}^{m} (1 + e^{(-|i-j|)}).$$

Table 4 gives the performance numbers for inputs $n = 64$ and $m = 524288$ (2^{19}), where *Sequential*, *Fully Distributed*, and *Partially Distributed* describe the inner loop distribution scheme, *Sp* is the parallel speedup, and *Eff* is the parallel efficiency (%).

PEs	Sequential			Fully-Distributed			Partially-Distributed		
	Time(s)	Sp.	Eff. (%)	Time(s)	Sp.	Eff. (%)	Time(s)	Sp.	Eff. (%)
1	296.6874	1.00	100						
2	148.3511	2.00	100	147.9001	2.00	100	148.3511	2.00	100
4	74.1801	4.00	100	74.0986	2.00	100	74.1801	2.00	100
8	37.0962	8.00	100	37.2061	7.97	100	37.0962	8.00	100
16	18.5605	15.98	100	18.9324	15.67	98	18.5605	15.98	100
32	9.3051	31.58	100	9.9582	29.79	93	9.3051	31.58	100
64	4.7005	63.12	99	5.8988	50.30	79	4.7005	63.12	99
128	4.7090	63.00	49	4.0136	73.92	58	3.5198	84.29	66
256	4.7261	62.78	25	4.1539	71.42	28	3.5128	84.46	33
512	4.7601	62.33	12	6.9894	42.45	8	5.1946	57.11	11

Table 4: Performance of Purdue #2, various inner loop distribution schemes.

We intentionally select a value of n less than the total machine parallelism of the nCUBE/2 so that the effects of the *fully distributed inner loop* and *partially distributed inner loop* distribution schemes can be observed. The results in Table 1 confirm the following assumptions about these nested task distribution schemes:

- When the outer loop is sufficiently large to cover the available machine parallelism, the inner loop should be run sequentially to minimize the overhead for parallelism, since more parallelism is not needed.

- When the machine parallelism exceeds the outer loop parallelism, both the *Fully Distributed* and the *Partially Distributed* inner loop distribution techniques are effective at utilizing the excess machine parallelism, and the latter method is more efficient than the former method since the overhead of distribution and reduction have been minimized for the amount of parallelism needed to cover the available machine parallelism.

- For large numbers of processors (e.g., 512), the overhead for distributing the inner loop of this program defeats the purpose of utilizing the excess machine parallelism, and the *Sequential* inner loop distribution mechanism provides the best performance, even though many of the processors are not utilized.

- For this program, the inner loop body performs few computations so, as we increase the number of processors, the increase in communication time dwarfs the computation time. Thus this program, with these inputs, should not be executed on more than 128 processors, which provides the highest performance in terms of execution time (3.5128 s) using the *Partially Distributed* inner loop distribution scheme.

5. Conclusion

In this paper we have outlined the design and implementation of distributed task management for SISAL, which is part of a larger system to provide both task and data management for a distributed memory implementation of SISAL [11].

We have outlined the design of a flexible task distribution hierarchy that can take advantage of parallel distribution to reduce the overhead in distributing work to a large number of processors. We have demonstrated that for large flat loops, the multi-level distribution scheme is effective at reducing overhead, thereby reducing the rate at which efficiency is lost. We have also outlined the design of task distribution and barrier synchronization for nested loops, and the use of control parameters to specify the distribution of each nesting level. We have demonstrated that the ability to fully control the distribution level of each parallel loop allows for enough work to keep all of the processors busy while minimizing the overhead that results from over-distributing tasks in a nested parallel loop.

This study represents only a first step towards a distributed memory implementation of SISAL. We have designed a system that provides both task and data management primitives for a distributed memory implementation of SISAL, yet a key component is still missing, namely the compiler. Compiler modifications are still necessary to perform analysis that will help to determine the proper partitioning and distribution for both tasks and data, and generate the appropriate runtime service calls for operations that cannot be predicted at compile time. However, until this step is taken, our runtime-based implementation of distributed SISAL allows for continued testing and experimentation that will hopefully shed light on the issues of most importance to a high performance implementation of SISAL on distributed memory multiprocessors.

References

[1] D. Abramson and G.K. Egan, "Implementation of the RMIT/CSIRO Dataflow Machine—CSIRAC," *Proc. Data-flow Computing: A Status Report*, 1989.

[2] A.P.W. Böhm and J. Sargeant, "Code Optimization for Tagged-Token Dataflow Machines," *IEEE Transactions on Computers*, January 1989, pp. 4–14.

[3] D.C. Cann, *Compilation Techniques for High Performance Applicative Computation*, Ph.D. thesis, Colorado State University, Computer Science Department, Fort Collins, CO, 1989.

[4] D.C. Cann, "Vectorization of an Applicative Language: Currents Results and Future Directions," *Compcon 91*, February 1991, pp. 396–402.

[5] D.C. Cann and R.R. Oldehoeft, "Porting Multiprocessor SISAL Software," Technical Report CS-88-104, Computer Science Department, Colorado State University, Fort Collins, CO, May 1988.

[6] D.C. Cann, Richard Wolski, and John Feo, "Parallel Functional Computation: Current Results and Observations," Technical report, Lawrence Livermore National Laboratory, February 1991.

[7] David Cann, "Retire Fortran? A Debate Rekindled," *Communications of the ACM*, Vol. 35, No. 8, August 1992, pp. 81–89.

[8] Shyamal Chowdhury, "The Greedy Load Sharing Algorithm," *Journal of Parallel and Distributed Computing*, Vol. 9, 1990, pp. 93–99.

[9] J.T. Feo, D.C. Cann, and R.R. Oldehoeft, "A Report on the SISAL Language Project," *Journal of Parallel and Distributed Computing*, Vol. 10, No. 4, December 1990, pp. 349–366.

[10] Matthew Haines and Wim Böhm, "Towards a Distributed Memory Implementation of SISAL," in *Scalable High Performance Computing Conference*, IEEE, pp. 385–392. Also appears as Technical Report CS-91-123, Computer Science Department, Colorado State University, April 1992.

[11] Matthew Haines and Wim Böhm, "On the Design of Distributed Memory SISAL," *Journal of Programming Languages*, Vol. 1, 1993, pp. 209–240.

[12] Interl Corporation, Beaverton, OR, *Paragon OSF/1 User's Guide*, April 1993.

[13] C. Lee, S. Skedzielewski, and J. Feo, "On the Implementation of Applicative Languages on Shared-Memory, MIMD Multiprocessors," *Proceedings of the Symposium on Parallel Programming: Experience with Applications, Languages and Systems*, Hew Haven, CT, pp. 188–197. Available in SIGPLAN Notices 23, 9, September 1988.

[14] J.R. McGraw et al., *SISAL: Streams and Iteration in a Single Assignment Language: Reference Manual Version 1.2*, Manual M-146, Rev. 1, Lawrence Livermore National Laboratory, Livermore, CA, March 1985.

[15] S. Mitrovic, "An IF2 Code Generator for ADAM Architecture," *Proceedings of the Second SISAL User's Conference*, J.T. Feo, C. Frerkling, and P.J. Miller, Eds., San Diego, CA, October 1992, pp. 93–109.

[16] nCUBE, Beaverton, OR, *nCUBE/2 Technical Overview, SYSTEMS* 1990.

[17] R.S. Nikhil, "Id (Version 90.0) Reference Manual," Technical Report CSG Memo 284-1, MIT Laboratory for Computer Science, 545 Technology Square, Cambridge, MA 02139, July 1990. Supercedes: Id/83s (July 1985) Id Nouveau (July 1986), Id 88.0 (March 1988), Id 88.1 (August 1988).

[18] C.D. Polychronopoulos and D.J. Kuck, "Guided Self-Scheduling: A Practical Scheduling Scheme for Parallel Supercomputers," *IEEE Transactions on Computers*, Vol. C- 36, No. 12, December 1987, pp. 1425–1439.

[19] John R. Rice, "Problems to Test Parallel and Vector Languages," Technical Report CSD-TR-516, Purdue University Computer Science Department, May 1985.

[20] Thinking Machines Corporation, Cambridge, Massachusetts, *CM5 Technical Summary*, October 1991.

[21] R. Wolski, J. Feo, and D.C. Cann, "A Prototype Functional Language Implementation for Hierarchical-Memory Architectures," Technical Report UCRL-JC-107437, Lawrence Livermore National Laboratory, June 1991.

Load Balancing and Resource Management in the ADAM Machine

Olivier C. Maquelin
Laboratory of Computer Engineering and Networks
Swiss Federal Institute of Technology, CH-8092 Zurich

The dataflow architectures are well-known for their ability to expose large amounts of parallelism. However, when running highly parallel programs this property can become a serious drawback. Due to the aggressive exposure of parallelism, a large amount of storage may be needed to hold intermediate results of the computation. Diverse throttling mechanisms have been proposed so far, both in hardware and in software, but none of them seems to offer a definitive solution. For such a mechanism to work, it should not only be able to limit the exploitation of further parallelism depending on the load of the machine, but it should also be able to guess with sufficient accuracy which portions of the code should be executed next. This goal can be very difficult to achieve, especially in conjunction with a non-strict execution model.

Load balancing mechanisms were incorporated from the beginning into the ADAM architecture. In contrast to most other dataflow designs, this machine has a strict execution model, which may restrict the exploitable parallelism in some cases, but makes resource management much easier. The ADAM architecture is actually a von Neumann/dataflow hybrid, which uses blocks of code as scheduling quanta instead of individual instructions. Codeblocks behave like small processes, which can be started and stopped with just a few instructions. Split-phase transactions are used to access remote data and implicit synchronization mechanisms are used to stop the execution of codeblocks trying to access results which are not yet available.

This paper will first describe briefly the execution model of the ADAM machine and then explain the algorithms and heuristics used for load management. The resources needed to run several example programs exhibiting widely different execution patterns will be shown, based on simulation results. The total storage requirements during program execution will be shown, as well as other interesting quantities, like the number of executable codeblocks, the number of codeblock tokens, i.e. the number of codeblocks which have not yet been scheduled for execution, and the ratio of local calls versus external calls, which shows how well locality is being exploited.

1. Introduction

Dataflow architectures represent a radical departure from conventional architectures, because they use dataflow graphs as their machine language. These graphs specify only a partial order for the execution of instructions and thus provide opportunities for parallel and pipelined execution at the level of individual instructions. Because even instruction-level parallelism can be exploited, such machines are able theoretically to exploit all the available program parallelism. On the other hand, scheduling each instruction separately and synchronizing on each data value leads to a large amount of overhead. As an example, in the Manchester dataflow computer [2] the data tokens sent through the main switch are 96 bits wide for 37 bits of actual data. The remaining 59 bits are used to identify the destination address and the context to which the data belongs.

In order to do all the matching, buffering and scheduling work for each instruction and still keep a high throughput, dataflow architectures are usually organized as a pipelined ring structure. However, this organization cannot reduce the time needed for a single token to go through the different execution stages. The length of the pipeline limits the performance of the machine in the case of sequential code and sets a lower limit on the amount of parallelism needed to keep even a single processor busy. Due to these limitations, the focus of research shifted in recent years to architectures which schedule whole blocks of code at a time instead of individual instruction [8], [3], [9]. Besides reducing the scheduling and synchronization overhead, this makes it possible to exploit some locality. Intermediate results can be kept in some fast storage instead of being written to the main store every time.

The strength of dataflow architectures lies in their ability to expose large amounts of all sorts of parallelism. However, when running highly parallel programs this aggressive exposure of parallelism can become a serious drawback. Depending on the particular order of execution, a large number of intermediate results may be generated. This causes excessive memory usage, and in extreme cases a deadlock of the machine due to lack of free memory. For example, in the case of a parallel loop with a million iterations it would be very inefficient to first start all iterations before beginning execution of the first loop body. If such programs are to be executed, it is crucial to be able to restrict the amount of parallelism that is being exploited.

Different solutions for the control of parallelism have been proposed [10], [11], one of which is the idea of k-bounded loops [1]. Code is planted by the compiler, which allows only k cycles to execute in parallel, where k is determined at run-time. Some problems remain unsolved by this method, however. With non-strict languages, dependencies may exist between loop itcrations, making it difficult for the compiler to determine in which order to execute the code. Failing to detect a dependency may result in a deadlock, while on the other hand failing to insert a bounding construct may result in excessive resource consumption. A complex analysis has to be done in order to determine the storage and computation requirements at compile-time. This approach may work for simple programs, but in the general case it is not possible to reliably determine the value of k. More importantly, this approach is limited to parallel loops and does not work with recursion or higher-order functions.

Load balancing mechanisms were incorporated from the beginning into the ADAM architecture. In contrast to most other dataflow designs, this machine has a strict execution model. Functions are called and loop iterations are started only when all parameters are available. This may somewhat restrict the exploitable parallelism, but the lack of dependencies between threads makes it easier to build deadlock-free and efficient throttling mechanisms.

The execution model of the ADAM architecture is based on blocks of code as the scheduling quanta. The dataflow graphs are partitioned and sequentialized at compile-time. The granularity of the codeblocks should be such that the calling overhead is kept low without unnecessarily restricting the parallelism. At run-time, the codeblocks are used as load units by the scheduler as they are distributed among the processors. The scheduler is built into the hardware and maintains information on the number of active threads and on the load of the neighbor processors. It uses this information to decide when to begin executing a new thread and which one to execute. The goal of the load management strategy being used is to maximize the amount of parallelism as long as some processors are idle, but to otherwise keep the resource consumption as low as possible.

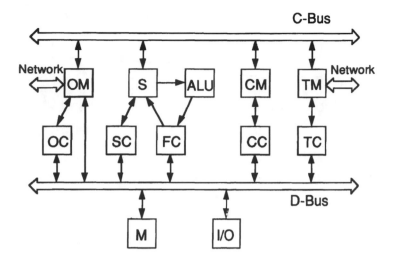

Figure 1: Overview of an ADAM processor.

2. Machine Overview

The ADAM machine is a homogeneous, distributed-memory multiprocessor. Each processing element consists of several functional units communicating either directly or via buses (see Figure 1). These functional units are grouped in four blocks, which work asynchronously. The first block contains the sequencer (S) and ALU. It fetches and executes the sequential code generated by the compiler and sends requests to the other blocks when encountering certain special instructions. The object manager (OM) forms the second block, responsible for external data accesses and for memory management. The next block contains the context manager (CM), which is responsible for process management. The last block contains the token manager (TM) and its links to the neighbor processors. It is responsible for load management. Communication between the four blocks and with the local memory and I/O ports is done through the C-bus or D-bus. Accesses to the local memory are done through five caches (OC, SC, FC, CC, TC) in order to improve response time and reduce the load on the D-bus.

2.1 Codeblocks

At compile-time, the dataflow graph is first partitioned into codeblocks and then the sequential code for each codeblock is generated. Codeblocks are the scheduling quanta of the ADAM architecture. They behave like small processes, which can be created, started, suspended, reactivated, or terminated dynamically at run-time with a few simple instructions. Each codeblock is executed sequentially, but can run concurrently with other codeblocks (see Figure 2). Each codeblock instance has its own frame memory where local variables are stored. A main source of parallelism is the fact that codeblock calls are nonblocking. The caller continues to execute, making it possible for the called function to be executed concurrently on an other processor. Only when the results are accessed is it necessary to check if they are present. If they have not yet been produced, the running codeblock is automatically suspended and other codeblocks are executed until the data are available.

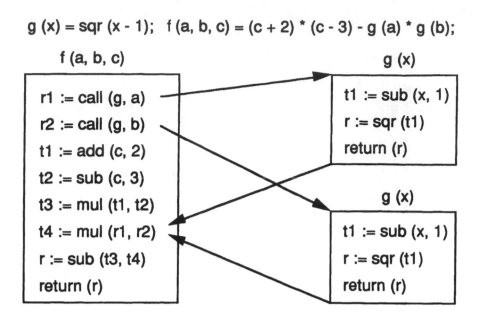

Figure 2: Sample codeblocks.

In Figure 2, two codeblocks have been generated by the compiler, one for each function. At the beginning of function $f()$, two calls are made, which start two instances of the function $g()$. The results of these two function calls are used by the multiplication instruction near the end of function $f()$. Depending on the load of the machine, these three codeblocks will be executed either sequentially on the same processor or concurrently on different processors. The synchronization and load balancing mechanisms are described below.

2.2 Synchronization

Accesses to non-local memory are implemented as split-phase transactions. When the sequencer executes a load instruction referencing some external data, it sends a load request to the object manager, marks the memory cell where the result is expected as empty, and then continues executing the code. The object manager then fetches the data, communicating with the other processors through the network. The non-blocking nature of external loads makes it possible to overlap data fetches and computations and thus to hide network latencies. Of course, if the data is needed before it has arrived, execution of the codeblock will have to be suspended. It is usually possible to send several external requests before accessing some of the results, increasing the amount of concurrency and reducing the number of context switches. In fact, reordering the code in order to optimize this behavior is an important aspect of code generation [5].

The same synchronization mechanism is used for split-phase transactions and for function calls. Presence and wait bits in the frame memory are used to keep track of the state of the transaction. The frame of a codeblock is a block of memory which contains local variables and corresponds to the register set of a conventional processor. Frames are allocated from the local memory, with a cache being used to reduce bus traffic and to speed up accesses.

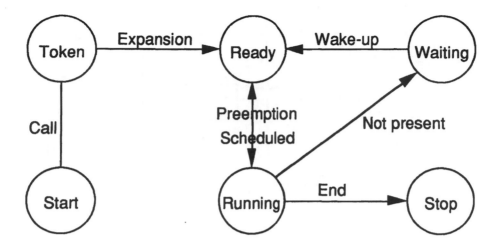

Figure 3: Codeblock states.

When a function is called or an external access is made, the presence bit is cleared at the address where the results are expected and the execution of the codeblock continues. In the meantime, the request is sent through the network and the data is fetched. Two situations can arise: either the data arrives before it is needed, or it arrives later. If the data arrives first, it is written in the frame and the presence bit is set. The data can then be accessed normally by the codeblock. If the data is accessed before it has arrived, the execution of the codeblock is suspended and the wait bit is set. Upon arrival of the data, it written into the frame, the presence bit is set, and because the wait bit was set the codeblock is also waken up.

When more than one result is returned by a function, the address of a block of memory containing all the results is returned instead. As with external memory accesses, the compiler will try to reorder the code in order to call more than one function before the results are accessed. This makes it possible for all these functions to execute in parallel and is one of the main sources of parallelism in the ADAM machine.

2.3 Codeblock States

Codeblocks can be in one of four states, as shown in Figure 3. As the result of a function call, a codeblock token is created that contains in a compact form all informations needed to execute the function. However, the codeblock is not directly started as a result of the call instruction. Instead, it stays in token form until the context manager expands it, i.e. allocates a frame for it and inserts it in the list of ready codeblocks. This happens only when the load on one of the processor has become too low and additional work is needed to keep it.

Tokens play a crucial role in load management, as they represent work units. Load can be exchanged between processors simply by exchanging tokens. Because the information they contain is globally valid, they can be expanded on any processor. If a codeblock executes on a different processor than its caller, it can still access all necessary data because data accesses work transparently across the machine.

After it has been expanded, a codeblock can be executed and will switch between the states ready, running and waiting as appropriate. Expanded codeblocks stay on

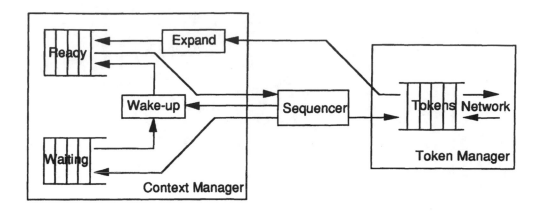

Figure 4: Flow of codeblock information.

the same processor until they terminate. They cannot be moved to an other processor and thus play no active role in the load distribution.

2.4 Load Management

Load management is done by the context manager and the token manager, each one being responsible for specific tasks. The context manager maintains the ready and waiting lists and supervises context switches. It is responsible for keeping the processor busy. As soon as there are no more ready contexts, the context manager fetches a token from the token manager and expands it.

The task of the token manager is to distribute the tokens within the machine. Tokens are sent based on load information received from the neighbor processors. If a token manager has some tokens in its buffer and a neighbor processor informs it that it has no more tokens, a token will be sent to the requesting processor. The token managers only keep track of the state of their neighbors. Trying to maintain a consistent view of the whole machine would be too costly. Instead, load is exchanged among neighbors, propagating eventually to all processors.

Figure 4 shows how information related to codeblocks flow through the machine. Tokens are created by the sequencer and sent to the token manager. From there, they can either go to an other processor or be expanded by the context manager. After the expansion, the relevant information may be sent to the sequencer as a codeblock context.

Tokens are sent only when needed, i.e., only when a token manager has no more tokens in its buffer. The amount of work represented by a token is variable and tokens are constantly created and destroyed, so averaging the tokens across the machine would not necessarily lead to an even work distribution. Moreover, this would lead to a much higher traffic through the network. Even if one processor has many more tokens than the others, this does not mean that the other processors work less. Rather, as long as each processor has at least one token it is a sign that it is busy and does not need more work. Sending tokens only when necessary also helps to keep related activities together. This is important if the locality inherent in most programs is to be exploited.

Besides deciding when to send tokens, the token manager has also to decide which token to send. The importance of this decision can best be shown with an example.

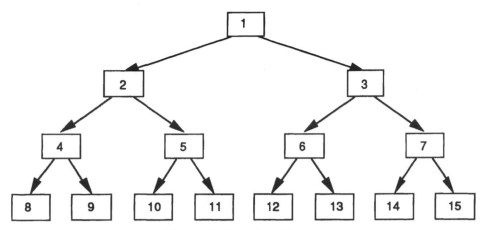

Figure 5: Sample call tree.

Figure 5 shows the call tree of a simple doubly recursive function. Obviously, different orders of execution are possible. For example, the order 1, 2, 3, 4, 5, 6, 7, 8, 9, 10, 11, 12, 13, 14, 15 would correspond to a breadth-first execution. This would lead to a maximum parallelism of 8, but up to 8 codeblocks would be executing at the same time, taking up memory space. If the order 1, 2, 4, 8, 9, 5, 10, 11, 3, 6, 12, 13, 7, 14, 15 is chosen instead, this would correspond to a depth-first execution. In that case, the maximum parallelism is 1, but only up to 4 codeblocks are in memory at any time. For this trivial example the difference is small, but with deeper recursions it can become quite significant. Depending on the size of the machine and on its load, either a depth-first or a breadth-first strategy may give best results. For best results, it will usually be necessary to choose an intermediate strategy, where parallelism is only exploited up to a certain point.

When designing the token manager, the goal was to find a strategy which allows maximum parallelism to be exploited as long as the load is low, but which minimizes resources when all processors are busy. The actual strategy consists of using a ring buffer, which is accessed from both sides, depending on the source or destination of the token (see Figure 6). New tokens originating from the sequencer or meant for the context manager are inserted and removed from the left side, while tokens exchanged through the network are taken from the right side. The token buffer behaves therefore like a stack for local accesses. The tokens which were generated last are the first to be executed. This leads to a depth-first execution of the code, at least as long as tokens are only created and consumed locally. On the other hand, when exchanging tokens with other processors the buffer behaves as a FIFO. The tokens which were generated first are also sent first. This causes breadth-first execution of the code, leading to maximum exploitation of parallelism. The token buffer does not behave as a stack for exchanges with other processors, because tokens are only sent when the buffer is empty.

With this distribution strategy, the execution order becomes dependant on the load of the machine. As long the machine is busy, the code will be executed mostly in a depth-first manner, using minimum resources. As soon as a processor needs some more work, some more parallelism will be exploited. Usually, the execution order is not perfectly depth-first, however, even on a single processor. The context manager makes sure that there are always at least two active codeblocks, one being executed and the other one being ready. In addition, when accesses to external data are made

Figure 6: Access to the token list.

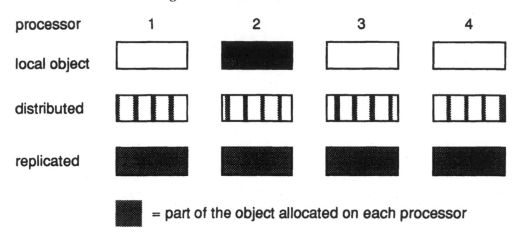

Figure 7: Allocation strategies.

it may be necessary to start even more codeblocks in order to keep the processor busy. The tokens generated by these concurrent activities are mixed in the token buffer, leading to an execution strategy which is not strictly depth-first. This is not a serious problem, however, as practical experiments demonstrate. Depending on the number of concurrent codeblocks needed to keep the processor busy, the number of expanded codeblocks is usually larger than in the ideal case by a factor of only two to ten.

2.5 Accessing Data

Accesses to remote data are not performed by the sequencer itself, but by the object manager. The object manager also manages the local memory, allocating and deallocating blocks of memory at the request of the sequencer and handles data access requests coming from other processors. All object manager requests are implemented as split-phase transactions, thus permitting the object manager to work concurrently with the sequencer.

A very important aspect of memory allocation in a distributed-memory machine is the prevention of hot spots. If all processors try to access data residing on the same processor, the performance of the machine degrades rapidly, especially with large numbers of processors. Unfortunately, such situations can arise very easily. Data produced during one part of the computation, maybe only on one processor, may be needed for a large parallel loop occupying the whole machine. As an attempt to solve this problem, three allocation strategies for blocks of memory, called data objects in the ADAM architecture, are supported. Data objects can be either local, distributed or replicated [7]. Figure 7 illustrates how memory would be allocated in each case.

Local objects are the simplest case. They are allocated on only one processor. For replicated objects, a complete copy exists on each processor. These objects are costly, because a broadcast is necessary for each modification of the data. On the other hand, read accesses can be made by all processors without causing network traffic. These objects are ideal for code and constants and may be used for data which is read very often during the computation. For distributed objects, each processor contains only part of the object. In the case of 4 processors, processor 1 would contain the 1st, 5th, 9th, etc. word of the object, while processor 2 would contain the 2nd, 6th, 10th word etc.

It is the task of the compiler to decide which allocation strategy to use. As a general rule, arrays, especially large ones, are usually best allocated as distributed objects. Most accesses to such objects will have to be sent through the network, but this is not a serious problem as it is usually possible to hide the network latency by having multiple codeblocks executing concurrently. Different distribution strategies could be devised which would attempt to store data where it will be most needed. However, because of the dynamic load distribution it is usually impossible to determine in advance where data structures should be allocated. In practice, the simple distribution strategy used in the ADAM architecture works fairly well. Problems occur only when the size of the objects is smaller than the number of processors. Because network latency can be easily hidden, it is much more important to distribute the data access load across the machine than to achieve a good locality.

Another possibility to reduce the number of accesses across the network would be to use caches. However, caches can only prevent repeated accesses to the same data from occurring and introduce new problems of their own. Even with caches, all processors need to access the data at least once. Each cache will initiate a separate read, which may already cause too much traffic for the target processor to handle. In addition, the problem of cache coherence is not easy to solve for large, loosely coupled multiprocessors. By using replicated objects, on the other hand, all copies can be updated with a single broadcast, making this method of distributing data costly but scalable.

2.6 Programming Environment

Three different languages have been implemented for the ADAM architecture: SISAL (Streams and Iteration in a Single-Assignment Language), HLA (High-Level Assembler), and FOOL (Functional Object-Oriented Language). SISAL [4] is used mainly for benchmarks, as a means to compare our architecture with other efforts.

HLA is used for testing purposes and as an intermediate language for the SISAL compiler. This is a low-level language which supports some high-level constructs, but also allows direct specification of any sequence of machine instructions. Examples of language constructs supported by the HLA compiler are simple types, if-then-else, for-loops, expressions, etc. FOOL [6] is our own programming language and environment. It is a hybrid language, composed of a single-assignment kernel language, extended with a sequential, object-oriented framework. The reason for the hybrid approach was that functional languages are not suitable for all types of programs. Especially event-driven applications and nondeterminism are difficult to express with such languages.

The ADAM architecture is the result of an iterative design process. When we started designing the architecture, it was clear that neither hardware technology nor our ideas were ready for a hardware implementation. Therefore, we built a simulator which enabled us to test our ideas and allowed quick changes to the design. The architecture was totally redesigned twice, leading in the end to the model presented here. Having working versions of the simulator early also allowed us to jointly develop the architecture and the software environment, enabling them to fit well together.

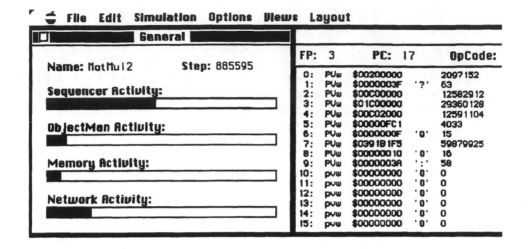

Figure 8: The ADAM simulator.

The current version of the simulator is an interactive tool which allows us to explore the architecture and to test the code generated by the compilers. Simulations are made at register transfer level, allowing a precise modeling of the communication processes inside the machine. The simulator runs on Apple Macintosh computers, taking advantage of the graphical user interface to display the machine state (Figure 8). A source-level debugger is built into the simulator, which allows the complete state of a program to be displayed and breakpoints on code and data to be set. For large simulations, a cluster of 32 Transputers is used, speeding up computations by a factor of up to ten. All results presented in this paper were obtained with this simulator.

3. Simulation Results

The behavior of the load balancing mechanisms is best shown with some examples. The SISAL program in Figure 9 contains a simple, doubly recursive function. The function explosion() computes the value 2^{level} in exponential time, generating $2^{(level+1)-1}$ function calls. The call tree generated by this function is a binary tree of depth 17, similar to the example shown in Figure 5. This program was compiled with our SISAL compiler and then run on the simulator.

3.1 Codeblock Expansion

Figure 10 shows the number of codeblocks in the machine during the starting phase of the program. This is the total number of codeblocks, including codeblocks which are executing, ready or waiting for some results. Because no large data structures are allocated, the storage requirements for the computation are proportional to this number.

```
function explosion (level: integer returns integer)
    if level = 0 then
        1
    else
        explosion (abs (level) - 1) + explosion (1 - abs (level))
    end if
end function

function main (returns integer)
    explosion (16)
end function
```

Figure 9: Doubly recursive function.

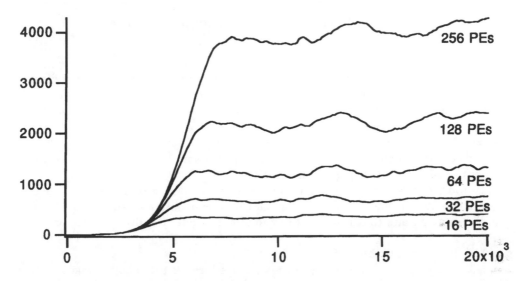

Figure 10: Number of expanded codeblocks.

The effects of the load balancing are easily visible. During the starting phase, the number of codeblocks increases roughly exponentially until every processor is busy. Then the load stays constant for the rest of the execution. The number of codeblocks during the main part of the computation is roughly proportional to the number of processors. Please note that the same program was run on all machine configurations. Because the load balancing is built into the hardware, it is not necessary to recompile the program in order to take advantage of a larger number of processors.

This behavior is the result of the combined breadth-first/depth-first execution order. At the beginning and as long as processors are available, tokens are expanded breadth-first, resulting in a fast increase in parallelism. Then, it becomes unnecessary to exchange tokens among the processors and the normal execution order becomes depth-first, resulting in a low resource consumption. Processors being available means not only processors being physically available in the machine, but means also that they have no work of their own to do. If an instance of this program were started on each processor, each program would behave as if it were run on a single-processor machine.

Processors	1	2	4	8	16	32	64	128	256
Memory	9	18	38	79	146	279	540	1018	1904
Max frames	47	83	173	330	607	1122	2056	3622	6168
Avg. mem	9	9	9.5	9.8	9.1	8.7	8.4	7.9	7.4
Avg. frames	47	41.5	43.2	41.2	37.9	35.1	32.1	28.3	24.1

Figure 11: Memory usage for different machine sizes.

Level	12	13	14	15	16	17	18
Memory	419	452	479	507	540	559	584
Max frames	1094	1340	1560	1814	2056	2235	2427
Avg. mem	6.5	7.1	7.5	7.9	8.4	8.7	9.1
Avg. frames	17.1	20.9	24.4	28.3	32.1	34.9	37.9

Figure 12: Memory usage for different problem sizes.

Figure 11 shows the amount of memory in kilobytes and the total number of frames needed to execute this program. The memory requirements are computed from the number of memory pages allocated on each processor and include some management overhead for the memory management unit and the token manager, but do not take the size of the code into account. The total number of frames is computed as the sum of the maximum number of codeblocks on each processor. It is an upper bound to the number of codeblocks existing at any one time.

The average memory requirements and the average number of frames are relatively constant for all machine sizes. As a comparison, a conventional sequential processor would need 17 frames to execute this program in a strictly depth-first manner.

3.2 Influence of Problem Size

Instead of varying the number of processors, the effects of the load management can also be demonstrated by varying the problem size. Figure 12 shows the same numbers as Figure 11, but for different values of level and for a fixed machine size of 64 processors. The total number of function calls executed in each case is proportional to 2^{level}.

The results are similar to those in the table above. Large variations of the problem size only cause relatively small differences in the memory requirements.

3.3 Program Execution

Figure 13 shows the execution profile of this program on a 256-processor machine. The three curves show the total number of codeblocks, the number of active codeblocks and the number of tokens respectively. Active codeblocks are codeblocks which are either being executed or which are ready for execution. As can be seen from the graphs, the number of active codeblocks is kept very constant during the whole program execution. About 500 codeblocks are active on average, which corresponds to two codeblocks per processor. This is due to the context manager, which tries to always have at least one ready codeblock. The number of tokens is very low during the start and end phases. During these two phases, all tokens are being expanded as soon as they are produced because the load of some of the processors is too low. The total number of

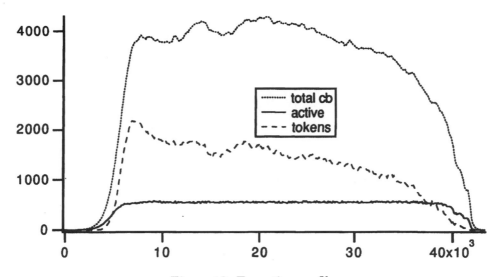

Figure 13: Execution profile.

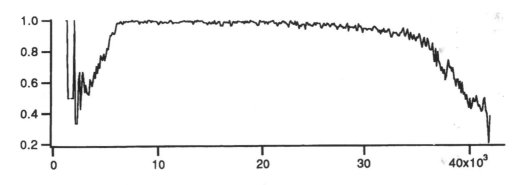

Figure 14: Locality.

codeblocks also stays relatively constant during the whole execution. This number is not restricted directly by the load balancing mechanisms, but is due to the execution order dictated by the token manager.

3.4 Locality

Another interesting measurement is the amount of locality that is being exploited. A function call is local if it is executed on the same processor as its parent. Local calls are desirable because parameters and results can be accessed locally. Figure 14 shows the percentage of local calls during the execution of the program. This is the same program, with a level of 16 and running on a machine with 256 processors.

The locality is low during the start and end phases. This is because during these phases a large number of tokens are exchanged between the processors. During the rest of the execution, however, the locality is very good. Of the 131072 function calls made by this program, 119630 (91.2%) were local. The amount of locality normally decreases with larger numbers of processors. When the same program is run on only 16 processors, 130602 calls (99.6%) are local.

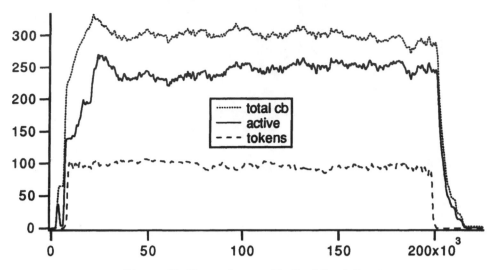

Figure 15: Execution profile for Mandelbrot.

3.5 Mandelbrot

Parallel loops are a very common source of parallelism. A classic example for this kind of parallelism is the calculation of the Mandelbrot set. Each point can be calculated separately, making this benchmark well suited for distributed-memory machines. An interesting property of this algorithm is that the time needed to compute each point varies widely. Furthermore, points belonging to the Mandelbrot set (and thus taking longer to compute) tend to be clustered together. Without dynamic load balancing, it would be difficult to achieve a good speedup. When running on the ADAM machine, each point is computed with a separate codeblock. This makes it possible to distribute the load very evenly among the processors. Figure 15 shows the execution profile for a SISAL implementation of Mandelbrot. This program computes a 64 * 64 picture on 64 processors.

The code generated by the SISAL compiler consists of a two-dimensional parallel loop, with a dimension of 64 for both the outer and the inner loop. In comparison to the previous example, the total number of codeblocks existing at any time is much smaller, while the number of active codeblocks is higher. The small number of codeblocks is due to the fact that the maximum depth of the call tree is only 3 instead of 17 as in the previous example. On the other hand, much less locality can be exploited. The calls made by the 64 codeblocks of the outer loop are spread over many processors, resulting in only 368 of the 4161 calls (8.8%) being local. Because of the lower locality, additional parallelism has to be used to mask the network delays. Delays can occur at the start of the codeblock, when fetching parameters, and at the end, when writing back the results. The context manager expands more codeblocks in order to mask these delays, which has the effect of increasing the average number of codeblocks being active to a value of about 4 per processor.

For this program, increasing the size of the problem does not cause a significant increase in memory usage, except for the larger picture. With larger problem sizes, however, the locality is much better, at least during the first part of the execution. Because more codeblocks of the outer loop are available, codeblocks of the inner loops are less often exchanged among the processors. The amount of locality has no significant influence on the execution time, however, because the data access delays can be easily hidden by using up some parallelism.

3.6 Matrix Multiplication

In the previous examples, the amount of data exchanged through the network was small. This is not always the case, however. A very good example for this is the matrix multiplication. In order to compute an element of the resulting matrix, two data accesses have to be done for each multiplication and addition. This would not be a problem if the data were available on all processors, i.e., if the source matrices were replicated objects, but this is normally not the case, as the creation of such objects is expensive. Usually, large arrays are allocated as distributed objects. This makes it possible to spread the load of the accesses over the whole machine. Even though most accesses must go through the network, the large overall network bandwidth makes it possible to achieve good speedups nevertheless. Because the bandwidth of the network increases with the number of processors, it is possible to execute memory intensive programs even on large machines.

Figure 16 shows the resource requirements for the multiplication of two 64 * 64 matrices on a 64-processor machine. At the start of the program, the input matrices are initialized, causing a first burst of activity. As can be easily seen from the graphs, the number of active codeblocks is higher than in the previous examples. About 400 codeblocks are active at all times, which corresponds to about 6 codeblocks per processor. Because codeblocks are often waiting for external data, more are expanded by the context manager to keep the processor busy. Due to the randomness of the network traffic, the number of ready codeblocks varies widely, giving a large average value. Still, the resource requirements are quite reasonable and the speedup is good, even though the network is used to its maximum capacity.

With large numbers of processors, a weakness of the simple allocation strategy used for distributed objects becomes visible. For each distributed array, the data at index 1 is stored in processor 1, the data at index 2 in processor 2, etc. This works well as long as the size of the arrays is smaller than the number of processors. However, in the case of the matrix multiplication the SISAL compiler allocates the matrices as arrays of arrays. Because each one of these arrays contains only 64 elements, this results in all three matrices being stored on the first 64 processors. Because the network bandwidth is being fully utilized even when the data is spread evenly over the machine, the performance does not increase significantly for more than 64 processors.

Figure 17 shows the speedup curves for three different versions of the matrix multiplication. The size of the input and output matrices is 64 * 64 in all three cases. The lowest curve shows what happens when the data is stored locally on one of the processors. The maximum speedup in this case is 8.3. The middle curve shows the code generated by the SISAL compiler. For up to 64 processors the performance is good, but it does not increase significantly for 256 processors. The best results were obtained by allocating the matrices as single distributed arrays. A speedup of 194.4 was obtained for 256 processors.

Conclusions and Project Status

The ADAM project shows the feasibility of a family of computers with scalable performance from a single-processor machine to high-performance computers with hundreds of processors. Due to the built-in support for load balancing, the same program can be run on machines of any size without need for recompilation. The goals of the load management are twofold. On one hand it tries to exploit enough parallelism to keep all processors busy, while on the other hand it tries to limit the amount of memory needed to execute the program. The results shown in this paper show that these goals can be

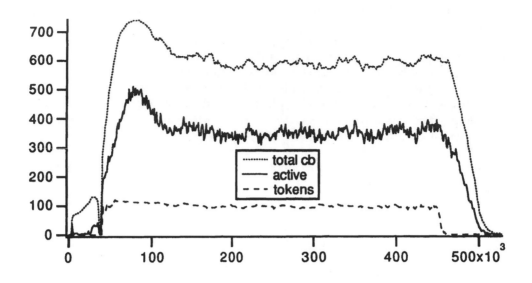

Figure 16: Execution profile for matrix multiplication.

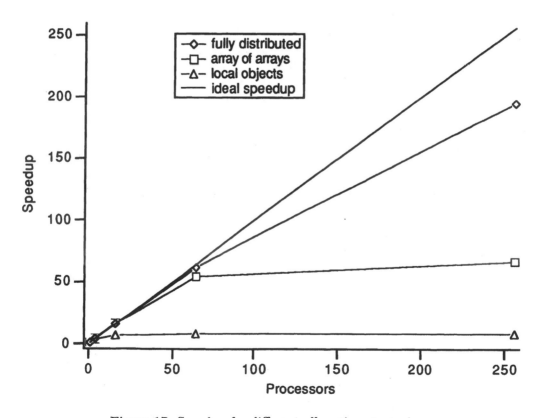

Figure 17: Speedup for different allocation strategies.

met in practice, although some room for improvement remains, especially regarding data access strategies.

Currently, work is being done on the SISAL and FOOL compilers in order to take full advantage of the different object allocation strategies. Further developments include a run-time kernel implementing our architecture in software on an existing distributed-memory machine. In addition to these software efforts, a first hardware prototype of the ADAM architecture is being implemented. This prototype should enable us to test the validity of our approach on real-world programs.

Acknowledgments

I would like to thank the other members of the ADAM group: P. Faerber, R. Marti, S. Mitrovic, S. Murer, P. Schibli, and M. Tadjan for their diverse contributions, and Professor A. Kuendig for providing the research facilities.

Part of the ADAM project has been supported by grant no. 2.309-0.86 of the Schweizerischer Nationalfonds.

References

[1] D.E. Culler, "Effective Dataflow Execution of Scientific Applications," Ph.D. thesis, Laboratory for Computer Science, Massachusetts Institute of Technology, June 1989.

[2] J.R. Gurd, C.C. Kirkham and I. Watson, "The Manchester Prototype Dataflow Computer," *Communications of the ACM*, Vol. 28, January 1985, pp. 34–52.

[3] R.A. Iannucci, "A Dataflow/von Neumann Hybrid Architecture," Ph.D. thesis, Laboratory for Computer Science, Massachusetts Institute of Technology, May 1988.

[4] J.R. McGraw et al., "SISAL-Streams and Iterations in a Single Assignment Language, Language Reference Manual, version 1.2," Technical Report TR M-146, University of California, Lawrence Livermore Laboratory, March 1985.

[5] S. Murer, "A Latency Tolerant Code Generation Algorithm for a Coarse Grain Dataflow Machine," *Proceedings of CONPAR 90*, VAPP IV, Zurich, Springer LNCS 457, September 1990.

[6] S. Murer and R. Marti, "The FOOL Programming Language: Integrating Single-Assignment and Object-Oriented Paradigms," *Proceedings of the European Workshop on Parallel Computing 1992*, IOS Press, Amsterdam, 1992.

[7] S. Murer and P. Faerber, "A Scalable Distributed Shared Memory," TIK Report, Swiss Federal Institute of Technology, Zurich, 1992.

[8] G.M. Papadopoulos and K.R. Traub, "Multithreading: A Revisionist View of Dataflow Architectures," *Proceedings of the 18th Annual International Symposium on Computer Architecture*, May 1991, pp. 342–351.

[9] S. Sakai et al., "An Architecture of a Dataflow Single Chip Processor," *Proceedings of the 16th Annual International Symposium on Computer Architecture*, May 1989, pp. 46–53.

[10] J. Sargeant, "Load Balancing, Locality and Parallelism Control in Fine-Grain Parallel Machines," Technical Report Series, University of Manchester, 1987.

[11] Y. Teo and W. Bohm, "Resource Management and Iterative Instructions," in *Advanced Topics in Data-Flow Computing*, J.-L. Gaudiot, L. Bic, Eds., Prentice Hall, 1991.

Workload Management in Massively Parallel Computers: Some Dataflow Experiences

David F. Snelling and John R. Gurd
Centre for Novel Computing
Department of Computer Science
University of Manchester
Oxford Road, Manchester M13 9PL

Many of the problems encountered recently in parallel computing research are already familiar to the dataflow research community. This is a direct result of the fine-grain nature of dataflow computation, which has caused researchers to face the problems of "massive" parallelism earlier than has proved necessary in the more coarse-grain, thread-based systems.

Over the past five years, dataflow research groups have been using a number of techniques to manage workload, and its associated resources, in their machines. In particular, they have addressed the problem of scheduling, and allocating memory for, many thousands of independent computational tasks. Thread-based parallel computing is moving towards the need to manage thousands of parallel threads, and we believe that the experience of dataflow research is relevant to the successful future development of such systems.

This paper reviews the issues of workload management, in both dataflow and thread-based parallel computing, and draws parallels between the two styles. The history of workload management in dataflow systems, in general, and in the Manchester Dataflow Machine (MDFM), in particular, is surveyed. The effectiveness of several management techniques is analyzed, in terms of their ability to control the instantaneous amount of memory required versus the induced decrease in performance. This is attempted for both the shared memory style MDFM and a distributed memory style system known as the Stateless Dataflow Architecture (SDFA).

1. Introduction

High-performance parallel programs are generally acknowledged to require additional memory, compared with sequential programs. Indeed, performance seems to "trade-off" against memory use. The dataflow research community was the first to encounter this phenomenon, and begin to consider ways to *control* the trade-off in a fashion appropriate to the execution environment.

However, these problems are not exclusive to dataflow and, although the problems in thread-based systems are not yet as acute, this paper explores the implications of results from the dataflow world for the future development of both kinds of system.

1.1 The Problem

The general problem is to exercise control over the generation of new "work" during execution of a computation, so as to limit the amount of additional memory called for, while maximizing performance. This can be thought of as a process of "workload management."

Grain Size	Type of System		
	Thread-Based (1)	*Dataflow*	*Thread-Based (2)*
Large	Job	Multiple Job	Multiple Job
Medium	Process	Program	Job
Small	Thread	Activation	Process
Fine	Instruction	Instruction	Thread

Table 1: Views of the hierarchy of parallel grain structure.

We can draw an analogy here with the management of certain forms of human workload: For example, effective management of a large-scale factory requires hierarchy, together with effective management of resources, especially people. Effective management of people requires both explicit direction (to define what needs to be done) and *laissez-faire* (to allow freedom for the individual to choose how to achieve goals). The art of good management lies in defining a workable hierarchy and in achieving an appropriate balance between the conflicting needs of the two styles of managing people. This paper advocates an analogous approach to management of massively parallel computations.

Since *de facto* hierarchies (which we assume to have arisen because they are appropriate) already exist for parallel computations, the key need is to identify the structure of these hierarchies, and to demonstrate how the management of parallel computing resources can be made to strike an acceptable balance between explicit direction and *laissez-faire*.

1.2 The Context

Our presentation draws parallels between dataflow and thread-based models of parallel computation. Each model has a well-defined "natural" hierarchy, and systems based on both models have employed both resource management strategies, with varying degrees of success.

Table 1 shows three possible views that can be taken of the hierarchical structure of parallel computations. Each level in the hierarchy is associated with a relative grain size. The highest (lowest, respectively) level of the hierarchy is associated with the largest (smallest, respectively) grain size. The names used for grain sizes are arbitrary, but intended to be indicative.

The first column shows a conventional view of thread-based multiprocessing, where the finest grain elements are *Instructions* (which in this case must be issued in sequence). At the highest level, programs are jobs made up of multiple parallel *Processes* containing multiple parallel *Threads* of multiple sequential Instructions.

The second column shows the view taken in dataflow, where the finest grain element is also the Instruction. In this case, *Programs* are constructed from multiple parallel calls to functions and loop bodies (collectively called *Activations*) which contain multiple parallel Instructions. Multiple Jobs can be constructed by executing multiple parallel Programs simultaneously.

The final column shows what happens to the conventional view of thread-based multiprocessing if sequential elements are excluded from the hierarchy. Now the Thread becomes the finest grain element, effectively shifting the column down the hierarchy.

Abstraction	Type of System	
	Dataflow	Thread-Based (2)
Unit of Computation	Instruction	Thread
Task	Activation	Process
Unit of memory	Token	Page
Maximum address space	"Tag space"	Virtual memory allocated
Scheduling priority	Call-tree depth	Nice Numbers etc.
Explicit management	—	Processor Domains
Quotas	Maximum Activations	Maximum swap space etc.
Measure of current load	Number of "active" Activations	Number of running threads
Measure of load surplus	Length of Token Queues	Number of waiting threads

Table 2: Comparison between dataflow and (type 2) thread-based multiprocessing.

For the purposes of this paper, we take the views illustrated in the second and third columns of Table 1. The workload (see below) is thus consistently associated with the finest parallel grain size of the hierarchy.

For those who understand either or both of these views more fully, it is helpful to take this analogy further, as shown in Table 2, which illustrates how the different terms, used to describe facets of the two types of system, correspond to one another.

1.3 Terminology

The terms used to describe massively parallel computation are not well established. Hence, we first define terms that we wish to use unambiguously in this paper. We apologize for the use of any non-standard terms, but hope that the definitions appeal to the reader's intuition. The terms fall into two main categories: *computation* and *workload*.

1.4 Computation

- **Unit of Computation**—*The smallest executable computational action in a computer system*—By *executable*, in the parallel context, we mean that these Units of Computation must be capable of being executed simultaneously and asynchronously at the hardware level. The Units of Computation may be of any size, and the two cases that are of special interest in this paper are defined as follows:

    - **Dataflow Systems**—Units of Computation are *Instructions* (as commonly understood).

    - **Thread-Based Systems**—Units of Computation are *Threads* (i.e., chains of Instructions which will be executed in sequence).

- **Massively Parallel Computer**—*A computer that is capable of executing a massive number of Units of Computation simultaneously*—Elsewhere [20], we have defined a *massive number* to be 10^4 or more.

- **Task**—*The smallest schedulable computational action in a Massively Parallel Computer*—By *schedulable*, we mean that, once the Task has been created, it becomes eligible for "selection to be executed" and that, once so selected, it will execute to completion without interruption.[1] Tasks usually, but not necessarily, contain multiple Units of Computation. In the two cases of special interest, Tasks are defined as follows:

- **Dataflow Systems**—Tasks are *Activations* [16], [28] containing multiple parallel Instructions.

- **Thread-Based Systems**—Tasks are *Processes* [24], [26] containing multiple parallel Threads.

- **Job**—*A closely linked group of Tasks that are executed on a Massively Parallel Computer*—By *closely linked*, we mean that the Tasks depend on one another for input and output data.

- **Multi-Job**—*A set of independent Jobs executing together on a Massively Parallel Computer*—By *independent*, we mean that the Tasks in any one Job do not depend on Tasks in any other Job for input or output data.

- **Massively Parallel Computation**—*Any Job or Multi-Job that can potentially saturate a Massively Parallel Computer*—By *saturate* we mean that the Job or Multi-Job is capable of creating at some time during its execution a greater number of Units of Computation than the hardware of the Massively Parallel Computer is capable of executing simultaneously.

1.4.1 Workload

- **Workload**—*The instantaneously active Units of Computation*—By *active* we mean that they are attributable to the Tasks that have been created but have not yet terminated (i.e., Tasks that are either scheduled-and-executing, or scheduled-and-waiting-to-be-executed, or created-but-not-yet-scheduled).

- **Workload Management**—*The process of controlling the creation, scheduling and execution of individual Tasks.*

- **Workload Manager**—*A device or mechanism for achieving Workload Management*—Workload Managers are designed to control the dynamic Workload of their systems by regulating the use of memory via the systematic release of new Tasks. The design of a Workload Manager is an exercise in control engineering; it involves identification of suitable *control variables* in Massively Parallel Computers, plus schemes for their *measurement* and *regulation*.

1.5 Summary

The choice of grain size for parallel computing is arbitrary: One person's coarse-grain is another person's fine-grain. However, the problems associated with containing memory use while achieving high performance are universal to Massively Parallel Computers. Designers of Thread-Based systems will undoubtedly benefit from a better understanding of Dataflow Workload Managers, provided that reliable methods for evaluating competing designs can be devised. Some proposals for evaluation criteria

---

[1]It may be "time-sliced" or "swapped out" by the operating system, but it will not need to be re-scheduled.

are presented in the next section, and are used to analyze the experimental results presented towards the end of the paper.

The remainder of the paper restricts itself mostly to the state-of-the-art in Dataflow Workload Management. First, we give a survey of the techniques that have been tried. Then we look at a selection of specific approaches, and show the results of using these in practical situations. We use the Manchester Dataflow Machine (MDFM) [16], [18] and the Stateless Dataflow Architecture (SDFA) [32] as illustrative case studies. Finally, we try to explicate the relevance of the accumulated Dataflow experience to the design of future Thread-Based systems.

2. Background

2.1 Dataflow Systems

2.1.1 Architectural Organization Dataflow multiprocessors are like any other multiprocessors in the sense that they comprise interconnected hardware components that communicate by passing *packets* of data (i.e., electronic messages) between one another. A hardware component is either a *Processing Element*, which executes specialized Dataflow Instructions, a *Memory Element*, which acts as a conventional passive memory, or an *Interconnection Switch*, which facilitates the passing of the data packets between the other kinds of components.

Two main Dataflow multiprocessor configurations are possible, akin to conventional *shared memory* and *distributed memory* organizations [22]. The former has separate Processing Elements and Memory Elements with an Interconnection Switch sitting between them; the latter has each Processing Element attached to a Memory Element to form a *Processing/Memory Element*, with the Processing/Memory Elements connected together via an Interconnection Switch. The data packets passed between the hardware components represent *tokens* passing through Dataflow *program graphs* [1], [18], and will be referred to henceforth as *Tokens*. Specialized Dataflow Instructions, executed in the Processing Elements, represent the activities to be performed at each *node* of the program graph.

The internal structure of hardware components is uniform across many different Dataflow computers. First, each component is "uni-directional" (i.e., it comprises an *input port*, through which it receives input Tokens, and an *output port*, through which it produces output Tokens). All components have a *buffer* for data packets, known as the *Token Queue*. Processing Elements contain a *Waiting/Matching Area*, where pairs of Tokens that are destined to be processed by one particular Instruction are *matched* together prior to execution (any Tokens that arrive early are stored here until their partners arrive). Tokens that do not require matching with a partner simply *by-pass* the Waiting/Matching Area.

Dataflow object-code is normally "re-entrant" (i.e., the same Instruction is allowed to be executed repeatedly and simultaneously). Different instances of execution are distinguished by means of a unique *Tag* which is attached to each Token. Special Instructions are used to manipulate the Tag.

2.1.2 Execution of Programs Dataflow programs are usually written in a *functional* or *single-assignment* programming language [1], [18]. Such languages provide facilities for structuring re-entrant programs hierarchically, by means of function definitions/calls, "for-all" loops, and other code-blocks. The *static call graph* of the program [3] indicates the calling structure of the component functions, loops, and code-blocks.

At compile-time, each such component is converted into the form of Dataflow subgraph known as an *Activation*. At run-time, the actual calling behavior of these components generates a dynamic structure of *currently active Activations*, each one of which is given a unique *Activation Name* for the duration of its execution. Due to the functional nature of the programs, the structure of the currently active Activations is at all times a *tree*, known as the (dynamic) *call-tree*.

2.1.3 Experience of Workload Management Because of their inherently fine grain size, Dataflow systems [13], [18], [28], [31] have been the first to execute truly Massively Parallel Computations. As a result, they have experienced an early need to manage the Workload so that it "matches" the available hardware parallelism. This has led to detailed studies of the problems of measuring and managing parallelism in such systems [2], [14], [30]. Two main problems have emerged:

- Badly managed systems are vulnerable to "mushrooming" calls on memory space [17]. This is due to sections of a program that greatly increase the amount of parallel activity in the hardware system, resulting in the build-up of large numbers of Tokens in the Token Queues and Waiting/Matching Areas. We call this condition *memory overload*. In extreme cases, it will lead to deadlock.

- Attempts to ameliorate memory overload can affect performance adversely. For example, where memory utilization is traded for performance [17], "miserly" memory management causes systems to perform badly. Consequently, the decision *when* to allow execution of a scheduled Task to start is as important as restricting its consumption of resources once it has started.

Hence, the aim of Dataflow Workload Management has been to maintain a usefully high degree of parallelism, yet prevent memory overload and avoid deadlock. A number of Dataflow Workload Managers[2] that try to achieve this have been described [2], [6], [14].

2.2 Thread-Based Systems

2.2.1 Architectural Organization Viewed from a distance, Thread-Based multiprocessors are identical in structure to the Dataflow multiprocessors described in Section 2.1.1.

Modern Thread-Based Massively Parallel Computers tend to use the *distributed memory* organization, in which each Processing Element is closely coupled with a Memory Element to form a Processing/Memory Element, in order to achieve *scalability*. Some earlier systems were based on the *shared memory* approach, but these were found to have only limited scalability. Each Processing Element executes a conventional stream of Instructions, governed by a *program counter*.

2.2.2 Execution of Programs In general, Thread-Based parallel programs are written using explicitly parallel, imperative programming languages. These allow Processes and Threads to be invoked at run-time, under programmer control, often by means of "parallelizing" certain forms of program loop executing across *array*

---

[2]The first Workload Managers in Dataflow systems were given the name "throttle" [6], [29]. This is an unfortunate choice of term, since it could be confused with an accelerator of speed, rather than a controller of Workload. Except when describing a specific piece of Dataflow hardware, we shall use the term "Workload Manager."

data structures. Processes communicate with one another by using the primitive *message-passing* commands, *send* and *receive*. Threads (sometimes called "lightweight processes") communicate by sharing access to common variables.

The compiler simply translates the explicit parallel commands into corresponding object-code, including calls to the run-time system, where appropriate, to invoke, terminate, or communicate between Processes and/or Threads. At run-time, dynamic calling structures will be created, relating the Processes and Threads to one another: these are akin to the call-tree of an executing Dataflow program (as described in Section 2.1.2).

2.2.3 Experience of Workload Management It is anticipated that the problems mentioned in Section 2.1.3 will be universal in Massively Parallel Computers, and that mechanisms similar to the Workload Managers of Dataflow machines will need to be developed for future Thread-Based systems. However, most prior attempts at Thread-Based Workload Management have relied on the existence of a relatively small number of Processing Elements (maximum of 10s) which are managed centrally, usually in a *shared memory* configuration.[3]

Early work of this nature resulted in the UPX operating system, delivered with HEP-1 systems from Denelcor [11]. More recently, these early concepts have been developed towards being operating system extensions, such as the IEEE POSIX standard [24]. In systems like the HEP-1, perhaps several hundred (parallel) Threads are scheduled simultaneously. However, the need for distributed management of many thousands of Threads, executing over hundreds, or even thousands, of (Processing Element, Memory Element) pairs is rapidly approaching, with the new generation of scalable Massively Parallel Computers [10], [25], [26], [33].

2.3 Common Ground

For the purposes of Workload Management, there are more similarities than differences in the structure and operation of Dataflow and Thread-Based systems. Both require careful *scheduling* of the Tasks (i.e., determining at which time each Task should be allowed to execute) and adequate *allocation of resources* to Tasks that have already been scheduled (so that they are able to execute to completion).

Since both systems basically consist of processing and memory components, this is tantamount to (1) allocating some memory space in which the Task might execute, and (2) finding a "time" when it can occupy a processing component. Such a separation of concerns has already been found useful in conventional operating systems [21].

The major complicating factor in achieving this for a Massively Parallel Computer is the likelihood of memory overload. Hence, Workload Management, in both cases, boils down to limiting the instantaneous amount of memory used to the maximum extent possible without overly impairing performance.

2.3.1 Reference Case A particularly important concept is that of the *Reference Case*, against which the effectiveness of a specific Workload Management scheme can be assessed.

In any kind of system, the "worst" form of management is unconstrained *laissez-faire*. In a Massively Parallel Computer, such a policy is *anarchic* in the sense that,

---

[3]Most contemporary Thread-Based systems allow the Workload Management software to execute in any available Processing Element although, in most cases, only one instance of this software is allowed to be active at any time.

any time a Process or Activation becomes eligible for selection, it is immediately scheduled and allowed to execute, and the consequences of subsequent memory demands are ignored. This is the approach taken by workstations in which access to the processing resource is *time-sliced*. Any dire consequences are avoided by the use of virtual memory, but there are many occasions when such a system "thrashes," often fatally. The anarchic case in a Dataflow system is "natural" (unmanaged) execution, where the memory overload manifests itself in the Waiting/Matching Area [17]. A similar situation can arise in a Thread-Based system when a handful of Processing Elements are given a Job comprising many thousands of Processes. Each Process is allocated stack-space and started on a given Processing Element which it will time-share with many other Processes; the same memory overload is experienced as in the Dataflow case, but the additional overhead of time-slicing must be borne.

For any form of Massively Parallel Computation, *laissez-faire* alone is a disastrous policy, leading almost immediately to an unsupportable memory overload.

2.4 Evaluation Criteria

In order to analyze the relative effectiveness of different techniques for Workload Management of different systems, suitable evaluation criteria are required. Two main criteria apply, namely *reduction of memory use*, and *achieved performance*, compared to the (anarchic) Reference Case. A secondary issue, desirable in Multi-Job execution, is *fairness*.

2.4.1 Reduction of Memory Use
A good Workload Manager should be capable of applying differing degrees of control over the instantaneous amount of memory used by a Job, so as to allow a user to make an explicit choice between high performance and profligate memory use. We measure the extent of this control, for a particular combination of program and hardware configuration, by the ratio between the amount of memory used in the Reference Case, and that used for a particular set of Workload Management parameters. We call this ratio the *Memory Reduction Factor*: the larger the value, the more "miserly" the control that is being exercised.

2.4.2 Achieved Performance
In principle, achieved performance applies both to the whole system performance, under a particular management strategy, and to the Workload Manager performance in implementing the management strategy. Prior work has tended to assume that the Workload Manager implements all strategies perfectly, and has therefore concentrated on the impact of each strategy on the performance of the whole system. A common technique is to report performance in terms of the inverse of (simulated) execution times.

In general, "miserly" control of memory use will impair whole system performance. The extent to which this is happening can be readily assessed by calculating the proportion of performance "lost" (compared with the Reference Case). We call this proportion the *Performance Loss*.

2.4.3 Fairness
Fairness is important when the system is executing a Multi-Job. A good Workload Manager should ensure that no one Job is made to suffer poor performance, or run short of memory, as a result of another Job achieving better performance, or more favorable memory allocation.

It is difficult to reduce a measurement of fairness to a single value. Hence, where results are presented later for Multi-Job experiments, we ensure that all Jobs start simultaneously, and we report the termination time for each Job individually: This helps us to develop a qualitative discussion of fairness issues.

2.5 Summary

Dataflow and Thread-Based systems have much in common when it comes to Workload Management. We expect the existing experience of managing Massively Parallel Computations in Dataflow systems to contribute to the emerging need for such management in Thread-Based systems. We have identified some evaluation criteria that will be helpful in comparing the effectiveness of different management techniques applied in fundamentally different kinds of systems. In particular, we expect to be interested in the variation of the Memory Reduction Factor as a function of the Performance Loss: one Workload Manager is superior to another if it consistently produces either a higher Memory Reduction Factor for a similar Performance Loss or less Performance Loss for the same Memory Reduction Factor.

3. Workload Management in Dataflow Systems

3.1 Introduction

Although there exist at least two thorough surveys of Dataflow Workload Management [7], [30], we include a brief survey here, in order that the reader can understand the nature of the case studies presented at the end of this section.

In general terms, the objective of Dataflow Workload Management is systematically to increase the Workload when it is relatively light, and decrease it when it is relatively heavy, thus tending to maintain equilibrium around a median level. Historically speaking, Dataflow Workload Management has involved two main techniques, namely *fine-grain* and *small-grain* [29], [30].

3.2 Fine-Grain Techniques

Fine-grain techniques attempt to direct control at all levels of a computation by operating solely at the level of the finest grain size shown in Table 1. This is too low a level for software to influence, and so fine-grain Workload Management is achieved in the hardware.

3.2.1 Manipulation of the Waiting/Matching Behavior

The first experiment in fine-grain Dataflow Workload Management was undertaken for the Manchester Dataflow Machine (MDFM) [29], and was based on the following reasoning. First, we note that a Token which matches with a partner in a Waiting/Matching Area cannot increase the Workload, except in the relatively rare case of a PROliferate Instruction [4]. Conversely, we note that a Token which by-passes a Waiting/Matching Area cannot decrease the Workload, except in the rare cases of either a KILl Instruction or a BRAnch Instruction which happens to produce no output Token.

Hence, favoring matching pairs of Tokens under heavy Workload, and by-pass Tokens under light Workload, should achieve the required Workload Management objective. Unfortunately, this technique was not found to be effective in the MDFM [29], due to the over-simplistic nature of the above reasoning.[4]

3.2.2 Stacking Tokens versus Queuing Tokens

A related fine-grain technique, also investigated for the MDFM, is the Token Stack.[5] This is based on the assumption that the Tokens most recently created will be most rapidly needed. This technique was partially successful for some applications, but, for others, the fundamentally unfair

---

[4]This has nothing to do with the rare exceptions mentioned above: other Instructions turn out to have more influence on the generation and termination of parallel activity.

[5]A technique originally suggested by Ian Watson.

nature of the Token Stack resulted in slower execution times and memory overload (full details are given in Chapter 3 of [29]).

3.3 Small-Grain Techniques

Small-grain Workload Management techniques operate at the next largest grain size in Table 1, leaving activity at the fine-grain level uncontrolled. This represents a hybrid approach, with explicit direction at the higher level, and *laissez-faire* at the fine-grain level. The latter provides the fine-grain parallelism needed both to fill the pipelines and to mask the memory access latency. There are both software and hardware variants of small-grain Workload Managers, employing both static and dynamic mechanisms.

3.3.1 Static Software Techniques

In static, software-based techniques, code is modified in such a way that unwanted side-effects, such as memory overload, are avoided. These techniques usually cause a reduction in the available parallelism.

The simplest of these techniques is based on the observation that sequential code requires less memory than parallel code.[6] By forcing sequentiality at the outer-most and/or inner-most levels of a computation, the total amount of parallelism (and hence memory) can be reduced. Unfortunately, this reduction can adversely affect the ability of the system to balance the Workload, and the serialization of the outer-most loop can cause a significant loss of parallelism, see [2].

Another static software technique is to insist that *all* the parameters required as input to an Activation be present before it is scheduled: this technique is known as "being *strict* in the parameters" of the Activation.[7] The scheme acts at all levels of the program, more-or-less uniformly, reducing the degree of parallelism and increasing the grain size. Because it is uniform, the technique is more effective than serialization. However, additional instructions must be executed to enforce the strictness on the input parameters.

The major problem with static techniques is that they must be "tuned" to a specific combination of program and machine *at compile-time*. Hence, if either the problem or the machine size changes, re-tuning and re-compilation are necessary.

3.3.2 Dynamic Hardware/Software Techniques

Dynamic techniques involve a mixture of hardware and software, and have the natural advantage of being able to respond to the *current* Workload in the machine. The best known of these techniques, employed in the MIT Tagged Token Dataflow Architecture (TTDA) [1], is known as K-bounded loops [2]. This allows K instances of a given "loop" Activation to execute in the usual non-strict Dataflow fashion. Through the use of pragmas, either the compiler or the programmer specifies a "guideline" value of K for each Activation. At run-time, the machine uses the "guideline" value, plus information on the current Workload, to make a final selection of a value of K for that Activation. As each instance completes, all results are synchronized, and then another instance is allowed to start. Not only does this technique reduce memory overload, it also allows explicit management of memory [28]. However, the approach fails to support call-trees in which the order of evaluation is not fully pre-determined.

Other designs which use the K-bounded loop approach are the Extended Token Store architecture [28], the EMPIRE system [23], and the ϵ machine [15].

---

[6]Dataflow compilers generate sequential code by planting synchronization Instructions which, for example, force one iteration of a loop to wait for the completion of the prior iteration before starting.
[7]This should not be confused with "being strict in assembling the elements" of an array.

A less well known, but straightforward, dynamic technique is to have the compiler generate both sequential and parallel code for selected Activations. When such an Activation is ready to be scheduled at run-time, the Workload is checked, and the code appropriate to the conditions is selected for execution [8]. This requires both extra memory, for the additional object-code, and the execution of additional Instructions, to select the required code "branch."

The Intelligent Token Queue[8] (ITQ) is a dynamic, hardware-based scheme which enhances the "locality" of a computation by moving Tokens in the Token Queues so that they are *adjacent* to others from the same Activation (e.g., clustered by Activation Name). The first ITQ design for the MDFM [29] identifies a preferred "current" Activation Name, and gives priority to Tokens with Tags containing this Activation Name. The "current" Activation Name remains selected until there are no more Tokens carrying it in the Token Queue, at which point a new "current" Activation Name is chosen. The two selection methods studied in [29], namely *Lowest-Activation-Name-First* and *Highest-Activation-Name-First*, work best for iterative and multi-way recursive programs, respectively. It is, therefore, necessary to decide what kind of program the machine is executing *before* choosing the next "current" Activation Name. There are obvious problems associated with Multi-Jobs that contain fundamentally different kinds of Jobs, or Jobs containing fundamentally different kinds of Activation. The scheme also relies on the hardware system to issue Activation Names in ascending order, something that cannot be guaranteed by systems which *recycle* Activation Names [6].

There have been several approaches to Workload Management by restricting the release of Activation Names. The simplest of these is known as *T*-leaf, and is based on the following simple set of rules:

1. The hierarchy of requests to create Activations is maintained in an *Activation Tree*.

2. In the evolution of the Activation Tree, a request to create a *new child* Activation is *always* granted, and a count of the number of active Activations is incremented.

3. A request to create an *additional child* Activation is granted *if and only if* the count of the number of active Activations is less than a set maximum, *T*. Otherwise, the request is *suspended*, together with any other "sibling" requests from the same "parent."

4. When an Activation terminates, a suspended "sibling" request, if there is one, is *released*: Otherwise, the count of the number of active Activations is decremented.

This scheme works well, once an optimum value for *T* has been determined. However, the optimum value is a function of the machine configuration, the structure of the program, and the sizes of the individual Activations in the program. Hence, the scheme requires "tuning" for each program and machine.

This final weakness can be redressed by taking a dynamic measurement of the Workload, for example, by measuring the length of the input Token Queues in the Processing Elements and the Memory Elements. As the Workload increases, these queues grow longer. This information can be used to determine when to release additional Activations. Workload Managers for the latest design of the MDFM use this technique, as described in Section 3.4.1.

---

[8]A technique originally suggested by John Sargeant.

3.3.3 Related Approaches SIGMA-1 [31] is a Tagged-Token Dataflow machine built from interconnected *clusters* of Processing Elements and Memory Elements. Like the MDFM, SIGMA-1 controls the level of the Workload by managing the invocation of functions and loop bodies. Activations are distinguished by "link numbers," similar to Activation Names, and the number of these that are in use within a cluster of the machine determines the loading on that cluster. Since there are only a finite number of "link numbers" available, requests for them are occasionally suspended. However, suspended requests may be released to some other cluster which is relatively lightly loaded. The Delta Workload Manager in the CISRAC II operates on similar principles [14].

3.4 Case Studies

The two systems chosen for analysis as case studies are the Manchester Dataflow Machine (MDFM) [18], [16], [19] and the Stateless Dataflow Architecture (SDFA) [32]. These have been selected as being representative of the state-of-the-art in the small-grain and fine-grain approaches, respectively. The MDFM has a shared memory style of architecture, while the SDFA has a distributed memory style of architecture. Evolution of the MDFM Workload Manager is the more advanced of the two.

3.4.1 The Manchester Dataflow Machine The Intelligent Token Queue study [29] isolated the Activation level as the most promising for Workload Management in the MDFM system, and recent work, focused on small-grain techniques which treat an Activation as a Task, has confirmed this promise [19].

Since Activation Names must be unique, they are allocated globally, by a hardware *Throttle Unit*.[9] Based on information received about the Workload from other parts of the system, the Throttle Unit manages the release of new work by holding up the issuance of new Activation Names, according to its view of the current Workload. When it receives requests for Activation Names and the system is too busy, the requests are queued in a pseudo-tree data structure, known as the *Suspended Activation Name Request Queue*. When a reduction in the system workload permits, the "deepest, left-most" suspended request is released[10] [6].

In the earliest version of this Workload Manager, the queue length information was received in the form of special *activity Tokens*, sent through the Interconnection Switch whenever the number of entries in a Token Queue rose above or fell below set levels.[11] A major reason for adopting this scheme was a belief that the use of activity Tokens provides a *scalable* mechanism (i.e., a mechanism that can grow, along with the configuration size, without the need for additional hardware) for measuring system-wide activity. However, it has proven to be ineffective, mainly due to the following sources of "pure time delay" in the control loop:

1. The activity Tokens have to travel through the Interconnection Switch;

2. In larger systems, serious congestion is observed at the entrance to the Throttle Unit;

3. The original Throttle Unit algorithm is slow, requiring 16 non-pipelined machine cycles for each operation;

---

[9] We use the name Throttle Unit here solely because of its longstanding use in the literature: we re-emphasize the comment, made earlier, about this being a bad choice of name.

[10] The MDFM approximates this by releasing suspended requests in "deepest, first-to-arrive" order.

[11] The activity Tokens have value "up" when the Token Queue is increasing in size, and "down" when it is shrinking. If desired, an element of hysteresis can be built into this mechanism [6].

4. The subsequent rise in Workload occurs a relatively long time after the release of the Activation Name that generates it.

In addition, the associated control function (i.e., the algorithm for deciding whether or not to release an Activation Name) [6] was adopted for *ad hoc* reasons, and has been found to be unstable and overly sensitive to changes in system size and application type.

Recently, significant changes have been made to the simulated MDFM architecture [19] (significant enough to warrant a change of name, to the NMDFM (for "New MDFM")) and to its Workload Manager, in particular, in order to address these problems. Although nothing can be done about the fourth source of delay, mentioned above, the other three delays have been substantially reduced:

- The measure of activity in the Processing Elements and Memory Elements has been refined to include active pipeline stages, function units and switch modules. The activity Tokens have been replaced by a small number of hardwired signals, direct from each Processing Element and Memory Element to the Throttle Unit, each indicating whether the associated activity has grown, shrunk, or remained steady since the last clock cycle. This provides the Throttle Unit with immediate feedback of the Workload, thus removing the first source of delay. It also removes the second source of delay, since it reduces the number of Tokens traversing the Interconnection Switch, in general, and at the entrance to the Throttle Unit, in particular.

- The third source of delay is reduced by changes in the hardware technology and improvements to the algorithms for suspending and subsequently releasing Activation Name requests [19].

The new Throttle Unit also employs a different approach for deciding when to release a suspended Activation Name request. It aims to achieve a specified *Target Workload*, expressed as a percentage of the total *Capacity* of the system pipelines [20], employing a "bang-bang" control mechanism. Bang-bang control is binary in nature: the Workload Manager is either releasing requests at its maximum rate, or not releasing them at all. Every clock cycle, the Throttle Unit measures its *Current Workload* (i.e., the number of entries in the Token Queues, plus the number of active pipeline stages, function units and switch modules). If this is less than the Target Workload, a suspended Activation Name request (if there is one) is released. This is a classical "proportional" control function and it has been used to generate the results presented in Section 4.2.1.

3.4.2 The Stateless Dataflow Architecture The Stateless Dataflow Architecture (SDFA) [32] is an experimental system of the *distributed memory* architecture style. It is based on a dynamic, Tagged-Token Dataflow model of computation, and the Instruction-set is simple—the Dataflow equivalent of RISC. Unlike the MDFM, SDFA has no explicit Activation Names. Loop bodies and function invocations are distinguished by Tag fields, called the *Recursive Tag* and the *Recursive Tag Stack*. These are set by the Processing/Memory Elements using special Instructions which "re-tag" all Tokens entering a function or loop body. There is no need for an equivalent of the MDFM Throttle Unit since the re-tagging process is controlled entirely by software.

Because the system has only fine-grain activity (i.e., there are no small-grain Activations), the Workload Management techniques are hardware-based and static. Three schemes have been used to generate the experimental results presented in Section 4.2.2. In the first scheme, the Token Queue acts as a *first-in-first-out* queue, implementing the (anarchic) Reference Case. In the second scheme, the Token Queue implements a Token Stack, as described in Section 3.2.2. In the third scheme, Tokens waiting in the Token Queue are *sorted* by Tag. The Tag sorting function is designed to favor Tokens from "deeper" in the call-tree and with larger *index* values (as used to select array elements). Possible implementation strategies for this mechanism are discussed in [32]. Note that these schemes are only distinguishable from one another when the Token Queue contains more than one Token.

The advantages of these schemes are their conceptual simplicity and the fact that their software implementation can be easily distributed evenly among the Processing/Memory Elements. Their major weakness is that they act only locally.

3.5 Summary

Dataflow Workload Management has a long history, and much relevant experience has been gained. State-of-the-art Dataflow Workload Managers are sophisticated control devices working at various levels of the grain size hierarchy.

4. Experimental Work

The main hypothesis governing the experimental work is that use of memory can be controlled at the expense of some loss in performance. The experiments associated with this main hypothesis are designed to demonstrate that there is a controllable trade-off between memory use and performance.

A secondary hypothesis is that *fair* behavior can be enforced in Multi-Job executions. The experiments associated with this secondary hypothesis are designed to illustrate that mechanisms exist which can change the relative priorities of Jobs in a Multi-Job.

4.1 Method

A group of synthetic Job and Multi-Job benchmarks is used to investigate the run-time behavior of various Workload Managers. For simplicity, the Multi-Job benchmarks contain only two *component Jobs*, namely a matrix multiplication (MM) and a divide-and-conquer solution to the "N-queens on an $N \times N$ chessboard" problem (NQ). These particular component Jobs have been chosen because of their fundamentally different natures, MM being iterative, while NQ is highly recursive.

The component Jobs (MM and NQ) are carefully matched so that, executed in isolation, they have nearly equal execution times. There are two versions of each component Job: one (known as the *large* version) is designed to *saturate* the test system configuration; the other (the *small* version) is designed so as to not saturate the test system on its own, but to do so when executed alongside another *small* component Job. The design "tuning" is specific to one particular NMDFM configuration, namely the "balanced" 64 Processing Element and 64 Memory Element machine, known as 64×64. The main benchmarks are used in exactly the same form for the SDFA experiments.[12]

---

[12]In particular, the sizes are the same, and the saturation and "balance" qualities that they possess for the NMDFM do not necessarily apply to the SDFA.

Acronym	Multi-Job Description	Characteristics for the 64 × 64 NMDFM
SMX	small MM alone	32 × 32 matrix multiplication
SQX	small NQ alone	6-queens on a 6 × 6 chessboard
SMQ	small MM with small NQ	
SCQ	modified version of SMQ	gives priority to small MM
SMC	modified version of SMQ	gives priority to small NQ
LMX	large MM alone	2 simultaneous 64 × 64 matrix multiplications
LQX	large NQ alone	8-queens on a 8 × 8 chessboard
LMQ	large MM with large NQ	
LCQ	modified version of LMQ	gives priority to large MM
LMC	modified version of LMQ	gives priority to large NQ

Table 3: Benchmark Jobs and Multi-Jobs "tuned" for the 64 × 64 NMDFM.

The names and relevant characteristics of each benchmark are shown in Table 3. Benchmarks SCQ, SMC, LCQ and LMC are special versions of the Multi-Jobs SMQ and LMQ which are used to demonstrate control of *fairness* in the NMDFM Workload Manager (see Section 4.2.1).

For the NMDFM system, these benchmarks are compiled from the high level programming language SISAL[13] [5], [27]. For the SDFA system, they are written in assembler.

4.2 Results

4.2.1 Manchester Dataflow Machine
Memory Control versus Performance— We take the two individual large Jobs, LQX and LMX, and execute them on the (simulated) 64 × 64 NMDFM configuration for a range of specified Target Workloads. We record the (simulated) execution time and the approximate instantaneous maximum amount of data memory used.[14] The Reference Case is when the Target Workload tends to infinity: in practice, a value of 10^6 suffices.[15]

From the measured values for each Job, we derive the Memory Reduction Factor and (Percentage) Performance Loss, as described in Section 2.4, and plot the one against the other. The results are shown in Figures 1 (for Job LQX) and 2 (for Job LMX).

These diagrams show that a considerable amount of control can be exercised over the use of memory in the NMDFM, by varying the Target Workload being aimed for by the Throttle Unit. The two different kinds of Jobs behave similarly, and the attendant Performance Loss varies in a regular and readily controllable fashion. Miserly control of memory use can result in extreme loss of performance. These observations support

---

[13] Because the matrices being multiplied together contain elements of the same value, the SISAL compiler uses an optimization that reduces the amount of memory required to store them from $O(n^2)$ to $O(n)$. This affects the measurements of memory use presented in Section 4.2.1, although its effects have been compensated for in Section 4.3.

[14] The exact instantaneous maximum amount is not readily available, so we use an (over-)estimate which is produced by summing the instantaneous maxima in each of the component Processing Elements and Memory Elements.

[15] For Job LMX, it is not possible to simulate the Reference Case, due to the excessive memory overload caused by anarchic scheduling. Hence, we have estimated values for the Reference Case execution time and maximum memory used, based on extrapolation from smaller cases that can be simulated.

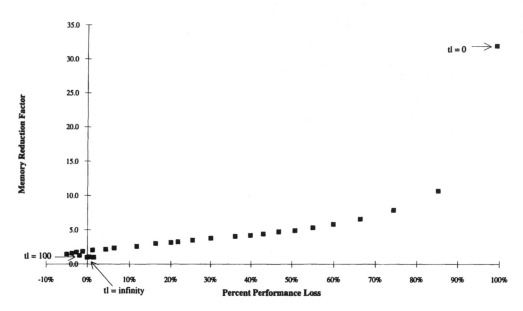

Figure 1: Memory reduction versus performance loss for job LQX.

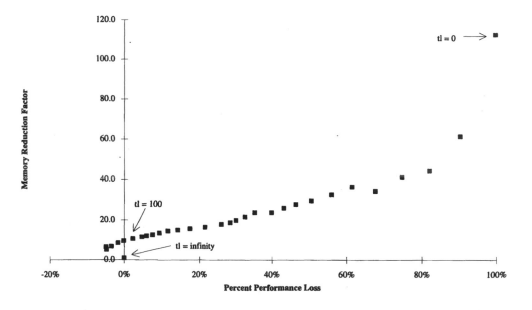

Figure 2: Memory reduction versus performance loss for job LMX.

Benchmark	MM Finish Time	NQ Finish Time	Maximum Data Memory
SMX	0.71 ms	—	50911 Tokens
SQX	—	0.78 ms	4394 Tokens
SMQ	0.68 ms	1.00 ms	51026 Tokens
SCQ	0.82 ms	1.04 ms	52209 Tokens
SMC	0.68 ms	1.13 ms	52708 Tokens
LMX	4.85 ms	—	135421 Tokens
LQX	—	4.84 ms	41995 Tokens
LMQ	8.71 ms	8.81 ms	148591 Tokens
LCQ	4.97 ms	9.31 ms	141303 Tokens
LMC	8.75 ms	8.95 ms	146124 Tokens

Table 4: Execution summary for benchmark Jobs and
Multi-Jobs on a 64 × 64 NMDFM.

the main hypothesis, that use of memory can be controlled at the expense of some loss of performance.

Note that, as has been observed elsewhere [17], a small degree of control over memory use actually improves performance, compared with the anarchic Reference Case.

For the remainder of the NMDFM experiments, the Target Workload has been set to 100%, this being a reasonable compromise value, as can be seen from Figures 1 and 2.

Fairness—We execute *all* the benchmarks on the (simulated) 64 × 64 NMDFM configuration, and record the *Finish Time* for each (individual and component) Job. We also record the approximate instantaneous maximum amount of data memory used, as described above. These results are shown in Table 4.

As expected, the time to execute the two small Jobs together is significantly less than the sum of their execution times when executed in isolation, since neither alone saturates the system. The time to execute the two large Jobs is nearly the same as the sum of their individual execution times, since each in isolation almost saturates the system. The maximum memory use for the Multi-Jobs is consistently significantly less than that for the individual Jobs.

In all the Multi-Job benchmarks, the MM component Job finishes prior to the NQ component Job. Indeed, this effect can be heightened by exploiting the built-in bias of the NMDFM Throttle Unit, which tends to favor Activations lying "deeper" in the pseudo-tree structure of the Suspended Activation Name Request Queue. To this end, benchmarks SCQ and LCQ are modified versions of SMQ and LMQ, respectively, in which the component Job MM "cheats" the Workload Manager, by making several recursive calls to itself before doing its "real" work. This artificially places the innermost loops of MM "deeper" than those of NQ in the Suspended Activation Name Request Queue. In the *large* case, this approach gives MM almost exclusive access to the system until it has completed.

One might expect that the balance between the component Jobs could be reversed by allowing NQ to "cheat" in the same way. However, using this particular Workload Manager, NQ operates in bursts of activity and, between bursts, MM has the opportunity to swamp the system with new Activations. This appears to suppress the natural tendency of NQ to exploit the Throttle Unit bias, as well as its effort to "cheat." In

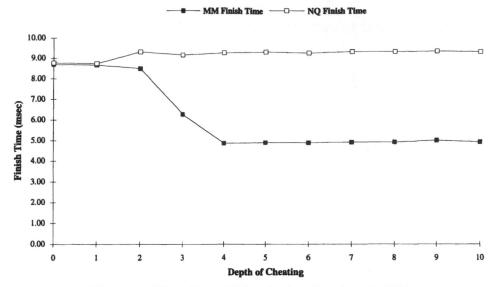

Figure 3: The effect of "cheating" in benchmark LCQ.

fact, the end result of NQ trying to "cheat," as it does in benchmarks SMC and LMC, is that both Jobs run more slowly. A more sophisticated Workload Manager might be able to detect the bursty nature of NQ and compensate for it.

For the *small* benchmarks, the low ambient Workload ensures that the bias of the Throttle Unit remains hidden.

Figure 3 explores the effect of a gradual increase in the "depth" of "cheating" in benchmark LCQ. This certainly demonstrates the existence of a mechanism for increasing the priority of a Job. It thereby at least partially supports the secondary hypothesis, in that one can imagine that fair behavior might be enforceable in Multi-Job executions, provided a more sophisticated Workload Manager could be developed.

4.2.2 Stateless Dataflow Architecture *Memory Control versus Performance—* We take the main *large* benchmarks, LQX, LMX and LMQ, and execute them on the (simulated) 64 Processing/Memory Element SDFA configuration using the three different Token Queuing techniques described in Section 3.4.2. We record the (simulated) execution time and the instantaneous maximum amount of data memory used. The Reference Case is the *first-in-first-out Queuing* system. Results are missing for benchmarks LMX and LMQ on the *Stacking* system due to the induced memory overload.

From the measured values for each benchmark, we derive the Memory Reduction Factor and (Percentage) Performance Loss, as described in Section 2.4, for each of the *Stacking* and *Sorting* schemes. There is no means of varying the degree of control being exercised in either scheme. The results are presented in Table 5.

A small degree of control is being exercised over memory use, with some impact on performance (including cases where performance is improved). However, these results are disappointing, compared to those obtained for the NMDFM. There is no means of gradually introducing more control, as required by our definition of a "good Workload Manager" (see Section 2.4). As a result, the scheme is, at best, *pseudo-dynamic*: that is, its effect varies with the number of entries in the Token Queues, but its extent cannot be modified. We conclude that these fine-grain techniques, and

Benchmark	Token Queue	Memory Reduction Factor	Performance Loss
LMX	*Stacking*	—	—
LMX	*Sorting*	1.9	11.6%
LQX	*Stacking*	1.6	−8.9%
LQX	*Sorting*	1.8	−8.2%
LMQ	*Stacking*	—	—
LMQ	*Sorting*	1.5	−2.1%

Table 5: Memory reduction and performance loss for two SDFA Workload Managers.

Benchmark	Sequential	*64 Processing/ Memory Element Thread-Based*	*64 × 64 NMDFM*	*64 Processing/ Memory Element "Sorting" SDFA*
SMX	3073 values	17408 values	46117 Tokens	24320 Tokens
LMX	24576 values	139264 values	136035 Tokens	220452 Tokens

Table 6: Approximate memory use in Dataflow and Thread-Based systems.

especially Token Sorting, are not convincingly effective, even when the "richer" form of Tag found in the SDFA is available.[16]

To date, there exists no mechanism for selectively controlling the priority of different Jobs in a Multi-Job. Multiple Jobs in the system are distinguished by part of the Tag—the Process Tag. However, in light of the above results for Token Sorting, it is unlikely that sorting by Process Tag would alter the priority significantly.

4.3 Comparison with Thread-Based Systems

Efforts to compare memory use in Dataflow machines to that of Thread-Based parallel machines are fraught with difficulty; however, there are some simple conclusions that can be drawn. We discuss only MM, since analysis of the memory behavior of NQ would require more space than we have available.

Consider two cases of matrix multiply in conventional computing, a "standard" sequential version, with three nested loops, and a *blocked parallel* version [12]. The amount of memory needed in the sequential version is assumed to be that required to store the source and destination matrices. In the blocked parallel version, it includes the copies of rows and columns of the source matrices that are needed to support the blocked algorithm, plus the destination matrices. These values are minima, as they do not take into account any bookkeeping memory or additional memory needed to support parallelism on the individual Processing/Memory Elements.[17] Table 6 contains the results of these comparisons.

Two points are worth noting. First, these two Dataflow systems are not excessively memory hungry, when compared to a typical parallel system. Second, dynamic, small-grain Workload Management techniques are more effective than static, fine-grain ones. These effects are more pronounced for larger problems.

---

[16]SDFA Tokens may be sorted according to the Recursive Tag, the Recursive Tag Stack, and up to three index fields, independently, or in combination.

[17]The number of values per matrix multiply is $n^2 + 2n^2\sqrt{p}$, where n is the size of the matrix, and p is the number of Processing/Memory Elements.

4.4 Summary

The Workload Manager developed for the NMDFM provides effective control of memory use without undue loss of performance, compared to the unmanaged Reference Case. For execution times within a few percent of the best possible, the maximum memory size can be reduced by a significant factor. Fair behavior potentially can be affected by manipulating the "depth" of key Activations in the call-tree.

Only preliminary work has been done on Workload Management for the SDFA system, but it is enough for us to believe that static, fine-grain techniques will not prove robust enough for general-purpose computation. From the above results, they seem to provide a slight reduction in memory use, but at an unpredictable cost in performance. However, such *laissez-faire* approaches, used in conjunction with global dynamic techniques, might provide an effective mechanism for controlling the local Workload. There is, to date, no indication that fairness can be enforced in a SDFA system.

Both systems compare acceptably well with Thread-Based competitors, given the prevailing view of memory use in Dataflow systems.

5. Conclusions

5.1 Lessons from Dataflow Systems

As we have pointed out, Dataflow systems are growing to Massively Parallel proportions in advance of Thread-Based systems. Having tackled the universal problems of Workload Management, with varying degrees of success, Dataflow research is in a position to help the future development of Thread-Based systems.

The main lessons learned from Dataflow fall into three categories.

First, there are common concerns, namely allocation of resources (principally the control of memory overload) and scheduling of computational tasks (a closely associated issue, that must work well in harness with the chosen scheme for memory control). Every Massively Parallel Computer has these twin problems and, while it helps to understand systems by pretending to separate these concerns, they cannot really be separated because they inevitably trade off one against the other.

Second, the large plurality of mechanisms for Workload Management requires painstaking and systematic study. Only a few of the possible schemes for Dataflow have been investigated thoroughly, and methods for evaluating schemes against one another are poorly developed. In particular, we are not aware of any studies of Workload Management schemes at the medium-grain and large-grain levels of the grain size hierarchy. Also, investigation of the balance between *laissez-faire* and directed Workload Management is in its infancy.

Finally, there are several important grain size issues. First, there are distinct grain sizes associated with the Units of Computation (let's call this the *computation grain*) and the managed Tasks (let's call this the *management grain*). In spite of many attempts at fine-grain Dataflow Workload Management, none have been wholly effective. This implies that the management grain should be (perhaps considerably) coarser than the computation grain. On the other hand, it has been found that finer management grains lead to more stable control, due to the "smoothing" effects of large quantities of discrete activities. It is also the case that, in order to be manageable, Jobs must consist of large numbers of Tasks.

5.2 Lessons for Thread-Based Systems

If, as we suspect, the above lessons apply also to Thread-Based systems (as suggested by Tables 1 and 2), then two conclusions can be drawn:

- Thread-Based systems will need to have their Workload managed at the small-grain (i.e., Process) level, or above;

- Manageable jobs will have to consist of large numbers of potentially parallel Processes, each comprising large numbers of parallel Threads.

There are also implications for the architecture of Thread-Based Massively Parallel Computers. If there are (at least) three important levels of the Workload Management hierarchy, then hardware structures will probably need to reflect this. In particular, hardware will need to support many simultaneously active Threads using some form of *laissez-faire* technique and without losing control of memory use.

5.3 Other Observations

We are searching for a framework for comparison of "whole systems." The measures developed in Section 2.4 are a helpful step towards a usable evaluation scheme, but they are still primitive.

In many ways, Dataflow and Thread-Based systems are analogs of one another. For example, consider the comparison between the two types of systems, presented in Table 2. In neither case is the actual size, in time or memory requirements, of a Task known exactly. This is reminiscent of early multiprocessing batch systems, where the appropriate Job memory and CPU time requirements had to be entered on a "job card." Indeed, in the K-bounded loop Dataflow Workload Management strategy [2], an analog of the "job card" is attached to each section of code in the form of a "guideline" value for K.

Some Thread-Based systems allow parts of the Workload to be redistributed, dynamically, to other Processing/Memory Elements which are less heavily loaded. This has also been investigated to a small extent in Dataflow systems. For example, Tokens by-passing the Waiting/Matching Area in the NMDFM can be executed in any Processing Element [19].

5.4 Future Work

The introduction of a "derivative" term into the NMDFM Throttle Unit control function would turn it into a classical "proportional-plus-derivative" controller, which would be expected to provide more effective control of memory use for the same Performance Loss. This can be implemented by adding a "lookahead" factor to the measurement of the Current Workload (in effect, computing an Expected Workload for some future time, to compare against the Target Workload). Preliminary experiments along these lines are already showing improved results. In particular, it appears that control over fairness is facilitated.

Development of the Dataflow Workload Managers described above will continue, particularly pursuing scalable, hybrid static/dynamic, approaches. Any further problems solved in the Dataflow environment will provide insight into, if not immediate solutions to, related problems in Thread-Based Massively Parallel Computers.

It is tempting for us to apply the above lessons to the development of a Workload Manager for some Thread-Based Massively Parallel Computer. In particular, our group has access to a Thread-Based KSR1 parallel supercomputer [26] which can be used for experimental work. We intend to commence such a project in the near future.

Acknowledgments

Financial support for this work was originally offered by the Science and Engineering Research Council (SERC) of Great Britain, under grant reference number GR/F/04292, but, in the event, payment was not forthcoming, for procedural reasons. The authors are grateful for the resulting emergency support given by the Department of Computer Science at the University of Manchester. SERC supported construction of the prototype Manchester Dataflow Machine. The authors gratefully acknowledge the contributions of their colleagues in the Centre for Novel Computing at the University of Manchester.

References

[1] Arvind, S.A. Brobst, and G.K. Maa, "Evaluation of the MIT Tagged-Token Dataflow Project," CSG Memo 281, Laboratory for Computer Science, MIT, December 1985.

[2] Arvind and D.E. Culler, "Managing Resources in a Parallel Machine," in *Fifth Generation Computer Architectures*, J. V. Woods, Ed., North Holland, 1986, pp. 103–121.

[3] A.P.W. Böhm and J.R. Gurd, "Tools for Performance Evaluation of Parallel Machines," Lecture Notes in Computer Science, Vol. 297, 1987, pp. 212–228.

[4] A.P.W. Böhm and J.R. Gurd, "Iterative Instructions in the Manchester Dataflow Computer," *IEEE Transactions on Parallel and Distributed Systems*, Vol. 1/2, 1990, pp. 129–139.

[5] A.P.W. Böhm and J. Sargeant, "Code Optimization for Tagged-Token Dataflow Machines," *IEEE Transactions on Computers*, Vol. 38/1, 1989, pp. 4–14.

[6] A.P.W. Böhm and Y.M. Teo, "Resource Management in a Multi-Ring Dataflow Machine," *CONPAR 88*, C.R. Jesshope and K.D. Reinartz, Eds., Cambridge University Press, 1989, pp. 566–577.

[7] A.P.W. Böhm and Y.M. Teo, "Resource Management and Iterative Instructions," in *Advanced Topics in Dataflow Computing*, J.L. Gaudiot and L. Bic, Eds., Prentice Hall, 1991, pp. 481–500.

[8] V.J. Bush and J.R. Gurd, "Transforming Recursive Programs for Execution on Parallel Machines," Lecture Notes in Computer Science, Vol. 201, 1985, pp. 350–367.

[9] Cray Research Corporation, T3D, Cray Research Inc., 655A Lone Oak Drive, Eagan, MN, 1993.

[10] Denelcor, "HEP System Software," Technical Data Sheet, Denelcor, 16000 E. Ohio Place, Aurora, CO, November 1982.

[11] J.J. Dongarra et al., "A Set of Level 3 Basic Linear Algebra Subprograms," Technical Report ANL-MCS-P1-0888, Argonne National Laboratory, August 1988.

[12] G.K. Egan, "The CSIRC II Dataflow Computer: Token and Node Definitions," Technical Report 31-001, Laboratory for Concurrent Computer Systems, School of Electrical Engineering, Swinburne Institute of Technology, 1990.

[13] G.K. Egan, "The Delta Throttle," Technical Report 31-009, Laboratory for Concurrent Computer Systems, School of Electrical Engineering, Swinburne Institute of Technology, 1990.

[14] V. Grafe et al., "The Epsilon Project," in *Advanced Topics in Dataflow Computing*, J.L. Gaudiot and L. Bic, Eds., Prentice-Hall, 1991, pp. 175–205.

[15] J.R. Gurd, A.P.W. Böhm, and C.C. Kirkham, "The Manchester Dataflow Computing System," in *Experimental Parallel Computing Architectures*, J.J. Dongarra, Ed., North Holland, 1987, pp. 177–219.

[16] J.R. Gurd, A.P.W. Böhm, and Y.M. Teo, "Performance Issues in Dataflow Machines," *Fifth Generation Computer Systems*, Vol. 3/4, 1987, pp. 285–297.

[17] J.R. Gurd, C.C. Kirkham, and I. Watson, "The Manchester Prototype Dataflow Computer," *Communications of the ACM*, Vol. 28/1, 1985, pp. 34–52.

[18] J.R. Gurd and D.F. Snelling, "Manchester Dataflow: A Progress Report," *Proceedings 6th ACM International Conference on Supercomputing*, July 1992, pp. 216–225.

[19] J.R. Gurd and D.F. Snelling, "A Terminology for (Parallel) Supercomputing," in *Abstract Machine Models for Highly Parallel Computers*, J.R. Davy and P.E. Dew, Eds., to be published by O.U.P., 1994.

[20] P. Brinch Hansen, *Operating Systems Principles*, Prentice-Hall, 1973.

[21] R.W. Hockney and C.R. Jesshope, *Parallel Computers 2*, Adam Hilger, 1988.

[22] R.A. Iannucci, "A Dataflow/von Neumann Architecture," Technical Report TR-418, Laboratory for Computer Science, MIT, May 1988.

[23] IEEE, "Threads Extension for Portable Operating System: POSIX," Draft Standard P1003.4a. IEEE, 1991.

[24] Intel Corporation, *Paragon*, Intel Corporation, Scientific Computers Division, 15201, NW Greenbriar Parkway, Beaverton, OR, 1993.

[25] Kendall Square Research Corporation, *KSR1 Principles of Operation*, Kendall Square Research Corporation, 170 Tracer Lane, Waltham, MA, October 1991.

[26] J.R. McGraw et al., "SISAL: Streams and Iteration in a Single-Assignment Language," *Language Reference Manual*, Version 1.2, Lawrence Livermore National Laboratory, Livermore, CA, January 1985.

[27] G. Papadopoulos, *Implementation of a General-Purpose Dataflow Multiprocessor*, Pitman, 1991.

[28] C.A. Ruggiero, *Throttle Mechanisms for the Manchester Dataflow Machine*, Ph.D. thesis UMCS-87-8-1, Department of Computer Science, University of Manchester, August 1987.

[29] C.A. Ruggiero, and J. Sargeant, "Control of Parallelism in the Manchester Dataflow Computer," Lecture Notes in Computer Science, Vol. 274, 1987, pp. 1–15.

[30] T. Shimada et al., "Evaluation of a Prototype Dataflow Processor of the SIGMA-1 for Scientific Computations," *ACM Computer Architecture News*, Vol. 14/2, 1986, pp. 226–234.

[31] D.F. Snelling, "The Stateless Dataflow Architecture," Ph.D. thesis UMCS-93-7-2, Department of Computer Science, University of Manchester, July 1993.

[32] Thinking Machines Corporation, *Connection Machine CM-5*, Thinking Machines Corporation, 245 First Street, Cambridge, MA, 1993.

Studies on Optimal Task Granularity and Random Mapping

Thomas Sterling
USRA Center for Excellence in Space Data and Information Sciences

James Kuehn and Mark Thistle
IDA Supercomputing Research Center

Tom Anastasio
University of Maryland, Baltimore County

The operating space of near-fine-grain dataflow architecture was investigated through analysis and simulation of the Anida abstract architecture. Analytical expressions for a robust upper bound and approximate predictor of peak performance gain are provided as a function of program average parallelism, architecture execution path latency, and average overhead. These models are verified through simulation studies. The use of the random mapping strategy for operation assignment is explored in the context of fine-grain dataflow architecture and found to be a good method for achieving near-best performance without requiring detailed compile time analysis. The trade-off space for multithreading is investigated to determine the range of thread granularity that achieves the best balance between reductions of overhead and latency on the one hand, and the loss of available parallelism on the other. Simulations suggest a non-monotonic curve for performance versus thread size with a well-defined domain of optimal behavior.

1. Introduction

As dataflow evolves, both as a computing model and as a basis for parallel computer architecture [1], optimality is sought in performance gain, efficiency, and programmability. Dataflow architecture [2], [3], more than any other paradigm, endeavors to exploit the diverse and abundant forms of program parallelism in order to achieve greatest performance through scalability governed by a natural parallel programming model [4]. Yet the relationship between the abstract execution model and the efficient application of the underlying computing resources is not so simple as was once optimistically envisioned. Factors that influence system behavior such as finite program parallelism, execution path latency, and synchronization and communication overhead, complicate the task of achieving an optimal operating point. This paper presents a study that explores several aspects of this complex trade-off space. Through analysis and simulation we have investigated the general properties of performance gain through parallelism as a function of latency and overhead. Then, an empirical study of the viability of random mapping as a method of load balancing [5] is described along with the implications of its results. Finally, we have explored the question of task granularity as it relates to optimal performance and will present key findings along with our conclusions drawn from them. This last work is of particular relevance to hybrid dataflow concepts and multithreaded architecture. Together, these investigations begin to reveal some of the bounding conditions that constrain the domain of effective operation for dataflow architectures.

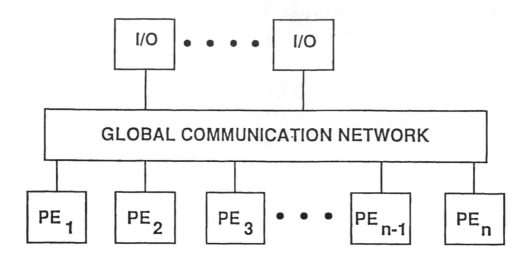

Figure 1: The Anida system block diagram.

2. Anida Abstract Architecture

These studies were conducted using a detailed simulation of an abstract hybrid dataflow [6] architecture. Anida (A Non-Interesting Dataflow Architecture) is a processor structure devised as a vehicle for exploring efficiency issues in dataflow computation. The Anida architecture is incomplete in that elements not directly germane to the intent of the planned experiments were excluded for simplicity of design and ease (and speed) of simulation. To this end, Anida is a variant of the static dataflow family [7] of architectures and there is currently no structure store [8] included. Nonetheless, although Anida was not intended itself as a target for implementation, a detailed RTL design was developed for all critical processor elements so that only realizable mechanisms were incorporated and all timing data reflects a high fidelity execution model.

The global block diagram for Anida as shown in Figure 1 is the canonical picture used to illustrate most distributed computer structures at the top level. Processing Elements (PEs) along the bottom of the figure are interconnected among themselves and with special I/O processors by means of a token package switched network. Anida was conceived with the expectation of using H-net, a desperation or "hot-potato" routed small-packet network developed for the Horizon architecture [9], a precursor to the Tera Computer [10] under development by Burton Smith. A prototype of H-net has been implemented and is undergoing extensive testing under varying network traffic loads. The H-net can accept and deliver one token packet per system clock cycle at each PE. The I/O processors interface with conventional file systems and user interaction to produce and consume token streams from the distributed PEs. All I/O operation templates are executed by these resource management oriented processors.

While prosaic in many respects, Anida incorporates certain features that distinguish it from some other dataflow architectures that have been studied. A concern driving the evolution of the Anida architecture was minimizing critical path time. Fine-grain dataflow is exceptional at hiding system latency. But a cost is incurred in terms of scalability; parallelism is traded for utilization, limiting potential peak per-

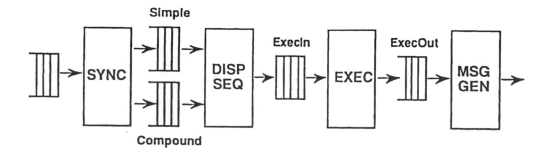

Figure 2: Anida processing element execution path.

formance gain for a given parallel application program. As with other architectures, mechanisms that perform single cycle token synchronization were devised. N-way result token fanout was implemented (in simulation) as well. But for the purposes of studying thread granularity, the most interesting aspect of the Anida architecture is its ability to exploit near-fine-grain threads. Short sequences of operations can be performed, with intra-thread inter-operation synchronization controlled by an incrementing instruction counter. Intra-thread intermediate results are exchanged via dedicated registers. Because threads are initially synchronized by dataflow control semantics all argument values required are provided prior to thread scheduling, precluding the need to suspend threads once activated. This also precludes values being exchanged between active threads.

It was hypothesized that the principal efficiency improvements from instruction aggregation would be achieved within the regime of near-fine-grain threads. For simplicity, threads were defined to preclude branching operations. As will be discussed, this proved to be an unfortunate choice, but the experiments performed still reflect the trade-off space of interest. The operations performed as part of individual threads are interleaved with simple fine-grain (single) operations through each PEs execution pipeline. This ameliorates the effects of "hogging," separates register read and write cycles of successive intra-thread operations, and encourages averaging of token output packet cycles to avoid execution pipeline blocking.

The execution path of a PE is represented in Figure 2 as a pipeline schematic. The token input stream enters the PE from the left, one token being assimilated per cycle when available. Synchronization is performed in one cycle. If the token satisfied the synchronization constraints of either a simple operation or a thread, an activation pointer is put on the respective work pending queue. During every other cycle a fine-grain operation is performed. If a thread is active, its operations are performed in the intervening cycle. In the case of no active thread, simple operations are performed continuously, demand permitting. The multi-stage ALU pipeline produces result values which are queued in a finite buffer, ready to be transmitted via token packets to PE token inputs. The token generation stage includes a lookup table of destinations for each operation and sends tokens to all required destinations, one token per cycle.

3. Test Programs

Two programming languages [11] were used to represent the application test programs. A low level Algol-like single-assignment language called SRCAL-1 (SRC Assembly

Language), pronounced "circle one," was used directly and as the target for a translator from a high-level language. SRCAL provides constructs for representing dataflow graph segments directly, user-defined macros for instantiating previously defined graph segments, and replication constructs for building high-order graphs from templates. SRCAL also permitted optional annotation for asserting mapping directives.

A prototype of a Lisp [12] derived language was developed for exploiting the power of the Lisp program development environment. An extended subset of "pure" (i.e., functional) Lisp, referred to as LST (Lisp to SRCAL-1 Translation), was devised and a translator from LST to SRCAL was implemented. The objective was neither to convert all of Lisp into dataflow graphs, nor to represent all well formed dataflow graphs in LST. Rather, the intent was to create a restrictive but useful formalism incorporating a set of suitable constructs capable of representing user level application programs. Key to the success of this endeavor was compatibility between the Common Lisp and the dataflow graph translator. All correct programs in LST should be executable on Anida or within the Lisp program development environment. Thus, all the tools available for code development within the Common Lisp framework can be brought to bear for Anida application programming.

Experiments to be described used a collection of seven application program kernels. While these test kernels were simpler than full application programs, they were much more than toy programs and reflect the demands of real-world user problems. Two integer application codes, X1 and Score, are examples of combinatoric problems. CrossCor performs a standard cross correlation. Two linear algebra routines, SparseLU and SparseQR, perform matrix operations on sparse arrays. The second of these two was driven by an electric power grid simulation data set. CircuitSim is an LSI simulator, used here to model a ring oscillator. The final kernel is an FFT.

While we refrain from giving details of the specific codes, Table 1 provides a table of the three important execution profile parameters for each example program. These were derived from the Anida simulator which includes an operational mode for generating *ideal computing profiles*, also known as *parallelism profiles*. All the idealizations are assumed when operating in this mode: no synchronization overhead, single-cycle operation execution, zero communication latency, and infinite processors. For each test program, the table presents the total number of operations performed (W), the number of cycles to execute (T_c), and the average parallelism (P_a) which is the ratio of the first two parameters. This execution level characterization of the test programs reveals much about their scaling behavior as will be shown in the following section. However, it does not give an adequate representation of the dataflow graph topology which in turn impacts opportunities for aggregation.

4. Modeling Peak Performance Gain

While empirical data are the test of truth, models are the means to understanding. Here, we consider the important question of scalability by focusing on peak performance gain. Peak performance gain is the maximum speedup with respect to single-processor execution that can be expected to be achieved, assuming sufficient processors are available. Our objective is to derive a robust upper bound of peak performance for a given program and a reasonable estimate as well. This work benefits from several earlier studies performed by other workers in the field.

Peak performance gain is a metric that measures the maximum attainable speedup for a fixed-size application program given an unbounded number of parallel processing elements. It reflects operational factors that impose an upper bound on potential

Program	# Instructions	W	T_c	P_a
X1	2775	1380360	3778	365
Cross Correlation	977	616586	17751	35
Score	2848	258917	968	267
Sparse LU	13246	13246	224	59
Sparse QR	5085	208965	1299	161
Circuit Simulation	1540	1581756	41020	39
FFT	1952	4530	20	226

Table 1: Table of program characteristics.

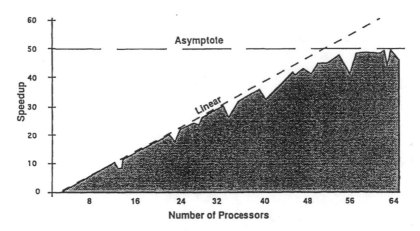

Figure 3: Score program speedup curve.

speedup. Peak performance gain is illustrated in Figure 3 which presents the speedup curve for the Score test program across a range of 64 processors. This curve was empirically derived from the Anida simulator and includes all of the complexities of the architecture and its intrinsic computing policies. The curve is bounded by two asymptotes: the linear bound of unity slope and a flat bound representing the maximum gain. We identify three regions within this curve that reflect three separate scaling behaviors. The linear region, the balanced (or intermediate) region, and the saturation region. The first implies approximately uniform performance gain with respect to applied processing resources. The last recognizes the point beyond which essentially no performance gain can be achieved, independent of additional applied resources. And the balanced region, which is centered at the intercept of the two asymptotes, reflects an intermediate point where one might expect the best compromise to occur.

For the ideal case (as described above), it can be shown that the asymptote bounding the saturation region is equal to the average parallelism, P_a. For more realistic scenarios, machine dependent characteristics impact the peak performance gain. We consider two: execution path latency and an important type of overhead. The latency is the minimum number of time steps required for a single token to enter a processor, cause an operation to be initiated, execute, and deliver a result data token packet to the input of the receiving processor. For the Anida architecture assuming a full interconnect network, this has been shown to be 7 cycles. The network is simplified

Program	$\overline{G}_\infty$	1000 Processors	Difference (%)
X1	143	113	26
Sparse Matrix	14	11	24
QR	76	57	33
Circuit Simulation	16	12	31
Cross Correlation	15	11	46

Table 2: Peak performance gain upper bound.

to permit processor oriented studies. Network driven behavior is reflected in other studies. The overhead is the cycles required to generate result tokens for a given operation performed. This adds potential blocking to the execution flow. In other studies, processor imbalance between ALU utilization and token I/O port utilization has been shown to be approximated by the average overhead as just defined.

To derive an upper bound on peak performance gain, an upper bound on the uniprocessor execution time, $\overline{T}_1$, and a lower bound on the infinite processor execution time, $\underline{T}_\infty$, are sought.

$$\overline{G}_\infty = \frac{\overline{T}_1}{\underline{T}_\infty}$$

We state without detailed derivation that these can be shown to be,

$$\overline{T}_1 = LT_c + V$$
$$\underline{T}_\infty = (L + 1)T_c$$

where L is the processor latency and V is the total program overhead, the total number of tokens generated during test program execution. After some manipulation, an upper bound for peak performance gain is found to be

$$\overline{G}_\infty = \frac{L + P_a v_a}{L + 1}$$

where v_a is the average overhead per operation. The quantity v_a has a lower bound of one because each operation must generate at least one result token.

To validate this measure, the predicted upper bound is compared to performance gain measured running on one thousand processors for some of the test programs. These results are captured in Table 2 which presents a table of measured gains and upper bounds. For convenience, the percentage difference of the upper bound to the measured gains is also given. Two observations can be made. Most importantly, the differences are all positive so that the putative upper bound is indeed biased on the high side, as it should be. The other observation is that it is a useful bound; the differences are well within a factor of 2 rather than being orders of magnitude.

Even with this reasonable upper bound, a predictor relationship would be useful. This is one that would usually be closer to the actual value of peak performance gain but with the sign of the error not guaranteed. The upper bound was derived by assuming the extreme cases on the overhead measure. Here, an average of the per-operation overhead is employed instead. The resulting relation for this estimate of peak performance gain, $\tilde{G}_\infty$ is then found to be,

Program	$\overline{G}_{\infty}$	1000 Processors	Difference (%)
X1	105	114	−7.5
Sparse Matrix	10	11	−5.3
QR	56	57	−2.7
Circuit Simulation	11	12	−11.2
Cross Correlation	11.3	10.5	+7.3

Table 3: Peak performance gain estimate.

$$\tilde{G}_{\infty} = \frac{P_a}{1 + \dfrac{L}{v_a}}$$

Again, a check is made against empirical data. Table 3, like the previous figure, presents a table of simulation gains for some of the test programs and compares the results with estimated gains according to the relation above. Focusing on the percentage difference column, it can be seen that the fit is much tighter than the upper bound and that the difference can be of either sign.

The implication of this analysis is that the peak performance gain is a function of three parameters: average parallelism which is purely determined by the application program (assuming fine-grain tasks), the execution path latency which is purely determined by the processor architecture, and the average (per-operation) serial overhead which is determined both by the program (which tokens go between what templates) and the architecture (number of cycles per token generated). However, perhaps counter-intuitively, if valid, it says that peak performance gain is not an absolute figure of merit. It is seen that this predictor increases in value with increased overhead. It is presumed that overhead is bad or at least neutral and therefore a measure of improved system behavior should not respond positively to increases in overhead.

5. Load Balancing by Random Mapping

Effective use of parallel computing relies in part on a viable strategy of program mapping, i.e., the assignment of program activities and data to the processors and memory [13] comprising the physical parallel computing systems. Many strategies have been considered for diverse architectures. For dataflow architectures, it has been speculated that one of the most simple strategies, that of random assignment, should be sufficient for most purposes to provide reasonable load balancing within constraints of program parallelism. There are factors contributing to this intuition. Because of the dynamic synchronization and instantaneous context switching that are the hallmark of dataflow architectures, they should be much less sensitive to vagaries of mapping. This study was conducted to determine the degree of variation that should be experienced when mapping randomly. Specifically we focus on the relative spread of the execution time distribution known as the coefficient of variance which is the ratio of the standard deviation and the mean of the execution times.

It is not unreasonable to anticipate a relatively small spread under favorable conditions. A gedanken experiment imagines each operation performed in the parallelism profile to be mapped randomly among the available processors. For any one processor, the Bernoulli distribution describes the number of operations to be performed by a

Program	$S_r\%$
X1	1.6
Cross Correlation	0.8
Score	3.2
Sparse Matrix	6.7
QR	2.8
Circuit Simulation	0.5

Table 4: Table of predicted coefficient of variance for random mapping.

given processor for a given time step. The mean and variance of the sum of all the operations across the time steps for a given processor can be computed as well. It can be shown that the relative spread for a given program is:

$$S_r = \sqrt{\frac{N}{W}}$$

where N is the number of processors used in the computation. For a given number of processors, the relative spread becomes small as the problem achieves sufficient size. An interesting reference point is to consider a balanced system scale with respect to problem size such that the number of processors employed is equal to the average parallelism, P_a. In this case,

$$S_r = \frac{1}{\sqrt{T_c}}$$

which indicates that as the critical path of the problem increases, the relative spread should decrease and random mapping should scale well for large systems and problems. As an example, we calculate what relative spread we might anticipate for our test programs. Assuming that $N = P_a$ in each case, Table 4 presents a table of expected relative spreads for some of our examples. From this data, we might expect to see a change of 5% or less for most programs.

A number of complicating factors have been swept under the rug for simplicity. Determining whether this intuition is generally valid is the object of the following experiments. The approach is straightforward, a large number of runs of some of the test programs are performed. Each run of a given program employs a unique mapping chosen randomly. A histogram of the execution times is derived and the relevant statistics calculated. Three different system sizes were employed for each test program to reflect the linear, balanced, and saturation regimes of problem scaling. An example of such an experiment is shown in Figure 4 where a histogram of the execution times for the Score test program is presented where close to one thousand runs were performed. The histogram reveals that the relative band of execution times is very narrow with the longest times observed being only about 5% longer than the shortest. Moreover, the maximum likelihood execution duration is less than 3% greater than the shortest observed execution times. Similar results were observed for the other test programs.

It is expected that the coefficient of variance will be sensitive to machine size so, as indicated above, three different machine sizes were selected for each problem, reflecting the linear, balanced, and saturation operational regimes. Figure 5 demonstrates the

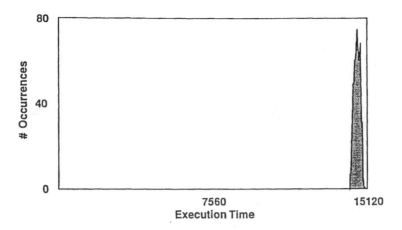

Figure 4: Histogram of execution times for Score program.

effect of machine size on the coefficient of variance. While some anomalies may be observed, in general the balanced regime shows the greatest spread while the saturation and linear regimes are usually significantly less, although again usually within a factor of two. But in all cases, the spread is very narrow and random mapping seems to provide near-best performance, at least within the framework of dataflow architecture.

Slight modifications to the pure random mapping strategy were investigated with mixed results. Forced balancing was one such modification. In this case, random mapping is adjusted to ensure that an equal number (plus or minus one) of work units are allocated to each processor. These units may be either instructions or token packets. Figure 6 presents the results of statically enforcing this level of load balancing for the set of test programs.

The results show that for many cases, both instruction and token balancing provide performance improvement, but not always. In almost all cases, token message balancing provided better performance than instruction balancing, even when both performed worse than pure random mapping. We can not yet explain why the balanced method should produce worse performance than pure random. But in all cases, the performance variations range within 20% of the pure random method.

Finally, with some embarrassment, we reveal the results of one last mapping experiment. As a poor man's version of a control to the previous empirical work, a mapping method we refer to as *uniform scattering* was applied. This is simply a round-robin technique of going through the textual list of instructions and distributing them in order to the processors. Thus the allocation is entirely determined by the order in which the instructions happened to be encoded in the program source file. Table 5 provides a table of results that compare the execution times of the test programs mapped using this uniform scattering method to the random mapping method. In more than half the cases, the uniform scattering performed almost twice as well as random mapping. At a minimum, this experience indicates the need for a stronger control case against which to evaluate the random mapping strategy. But also, it implies that there are certain subtle effects at work here that have yet to be understood.

This study into mapping strategies has provided a strong indication that as anticipated by many in the dataflow community, random mapping of fine-grain computation is a reasonable approach to resource allocation. Most of the available performance can

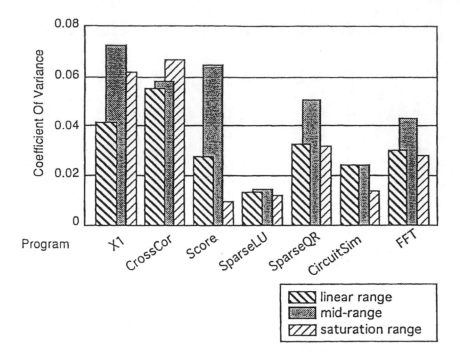

Figure 5: Bar chart of effect of machine size.

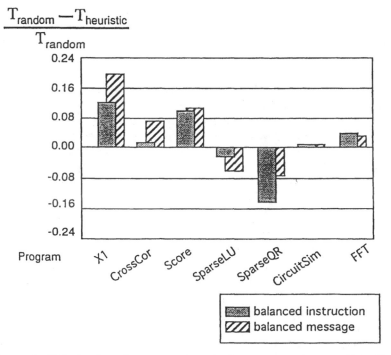

Figure 6: Effect of random mapping strategy on mean execution time.

	Scattered Mapping Execution Time	Random Mapping Execution Time	
Program	*Scattered Mapping Execution Time*	*Minimum*	*Mean*
X1	70332	73835	86796
Cross Correlation	328121	265575	318492
Score	13619	14774	16322
SparseLU	3322	3111	3262
SparseQR	23028	24230	26625
Circuit Simulation	608303	625274	659821
FFT	393	404	445

Table 5: Table of scattered mapping.

be expected to be delivered through this method. The small amount of performance degradation that may occur is probably out-weighed by the convenience and simplicity of the method. While the experiments discussed here focused exclusively on processor load balancing and did not include network considerations such as contention and variable latency, more recent experiments have shown these effects to be marginal and the original conclusions to be still valid.

6. Performance Versus Task Granularity

Investigations with the Anida abstract architecture operating strictly in fine-grain mode (without multi-instruction threads) have revealed sources of performance degradation observed by other research groups as well. Foremost among these are the critical path latency for single operations and the overhead of token assimilation and generation. Multithreading architectures may alleviate these effects through aggregation of operations into threads. Threads may also be formed from higher level source code tasks. Either way, the per-operation overhead is reduced by employing registers for intra-thread value passing and sequential instruction issuing for intra-thread flow control. The number of per-operation message packets is lessened as a consequence. The average inter-operation critical path length is reduced because a preceding operation need not propagate through the entire execution pipeline including the message communication path before an immediately succeeding operation can be scheduled. The combination of these two effects may in many cases enhance performance with respect to that of a pure fine-grain execution model.

Countering the positive effects of aggregation is the potential loss of parallelism caused by going to coarser-grained threads. According to the previous analysis, peak performance gain is roughly proportional to the application program's average parallelism. As that parallelism is lost to aggregation, the opportunity to apply more processing resources is diminished. Therefore, in seeking the optimal operating point in terms of thread granularity, there is a tension between overhead and critical path length on the one hand and available parallelism on the other. The objective of the study (to be described) is to expose this trade-off space and reveal its characteristics. The motivation is to understand how best to design compilers and processor architectures to achieve optimal system operation.

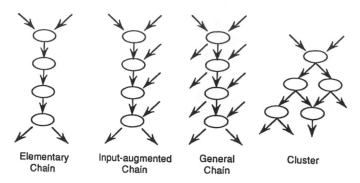

Figure 7: Graph segment thread topology classes.

The Anida abstract architecture was devised to exploit near-fine-grain thread aggregation as it was anticipated that it was in this regime that best system behavior would be realized. Control and sequencing were intentionally kept simple consistent with the needs of this mode of operation. Threads were limited to strict operations without conditionals. In retrospect this proved to be a poor choice, as it required all branching operations to be performed as simple, i.e., fine-grain, operations. Thus opportunities for thread aggregation were limited in some application programs.

Application programs were developed as fine-grain dataflow graphs. Threads were aggregated from graph segments. Several different topology classes were identified and are shown in Figure 7. Aggregation of elementary chains reduce overhead and latency without loss of parallelism. Input-augmented chains and general chains sacrifice some parallelism because they skew scheduling of external operations dependent on them. Aggregation of these chains has the strongest latency reduction because the distance between the beginning and end operations is the longest. Clusters give up more parallelism and retrieve less in terms of critical path latency. However, the opportunity within a program is highest for clusters and lowest for elementary chains. Thus the overall impact in program performance improvement may come from the general chains and clusters simply because there are more of them within the program dataflow graph. The ultimate extent of an atomic thread is usually bounded by a conditional operator.

Within the constraints described above, aggregation is performed incrementally: first for elementary chains, then for input-augmented chains which subsume elementary chains, and so on up through clusters. Figure 8 presents the relative performance gain achieved with respect to pure fine-grain operation across a range of processors for the Score test program. Roughly speaking, there was a 20% to 25% performance improvement over the experimental range.

However, a very different behavior is observed in Figure 9 which presents the results for the same experiment performed on the X1 test program. The elementary and input augmented chains show similar behavior to the previous experiment. But the exploitation of general chains shows a radically different scaling behavior. While the performance gain is the same for small number of processors, as the number of processors exceed about 16, the advantages achieved are lost and beyond that point, performance degradation is experienced with respect to pure fine-grain operation. Small clusters were tried and as the plot demonstrates, within the bounds of their size, performance gain was retained, although not to the degree achieved by the input-augmented chains. When large clusters were attempted, similar degradation was observed as the general chains but of a slightly less degree.

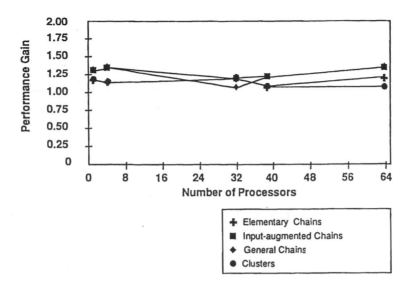

Figure 8: Graph of performance gain versus number of processors for Score.

To understand the implications of these results, some more detailed experimental data is provided in Table 6 for the X1 test program. It is observed that the number of operations aggregated varies among the methods tried. The general chains and elementary/input-augmented chains subsume about the same number of operations but the general chains do it in fewer threads. The average overhead is about the same with the general chains achieving somewhat less. Although there are fewer general chains than the simpler chains, more operations are subsumed. This is explained by the slightly greater length of the general chain.

The clusters are interesting because of how they behave compared to the different kinds of chains. Far fewer operations were incorporated in the smaller clusters but the large clusters included almost as many operations as the general chains. The small clusters had the smallest granularity of all while the large clusters had the largest granularity of all. Yet the small clusters provided some performance gain across the processor range and the large clusters did not experience the same level of degradation as that of the general chains.

While these results are multifaceted and even a little confusing, Figure 10 presents a somewhat simplified picture of what is being observed to clarify the trade-offs. This abstracted qualitative diagram shows execution time on the ordinate axis and average thread granularity on the abscissa for an application of fixed workload. The parallelism of the application varies as the grain size of the threads is varied by means of instruction aggregation. The intersection of the curve with the left side of the graph is the execution time of the program with no aggregation, that is with independently scheduled fine-grain operations. If the right side of the graph were to be permitted to extend to its ultimate point, the end would represent the pure sequential uniprocessor execution time. The performance versus thread granularity trade-off space has been broken up into three domains for convenience of discussion and because each represents a region in which a different factor dominates.

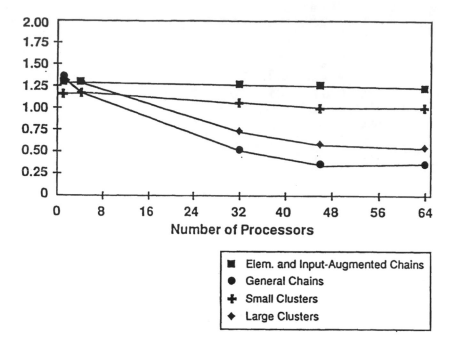

Figure 9: Graph of performance gain versus number of processors for X1.

Type of Aggregate	Average Size	Number of Aggregates	Operations Aggregated	Message Overhead	Number of Processors				
					1	4	32	46	64
					Execution Cycles				
Base Case				3.5	49	13.0	1.9	1.5	1.1×10^5
Elem. & Input- Aug. Chains	2.8 ± 0.6	652	1844	2.7	37	9.7	1.5	1.2	0.9×10^5
Small Clusters	2.3 ± 0.6	504	1174	3.1	42	11.0	1.8	1.5	1.2×10^5
Large Clusters	3.5 ± 1.98	506	1774	2.7	37	10.0	2.6	2.6	2.1×10^5
General Chains	3.0 ± 1.0	600	1856	2.6	36	11.0	3.7	4.3	3.1×10^5

N=2754
Avg. Par=321

Results of Compounding for the X1 Program

Table 6: Table of results of aggregation for X1.

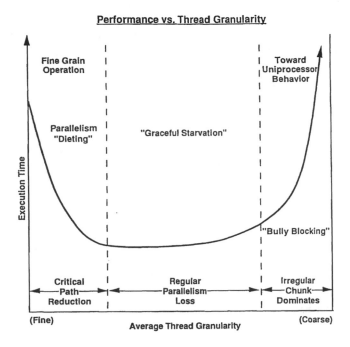

Figure 10: Summary graph of granularity optimization curve.

In the left-hand region, aggregation clearly improves system performance for a given number of processors. Here, reduced critical path latency and overhead contribute to decreasing execution time, while program parallelism is still sufficient to drive the majority of processors most of the time. But as threads increase in length, the degree of performance advantage slows. In this region, which we dub "parallelism dieting," excessive parallelism is being sacrificed for critical path reduction.

The central region begins at the point where a dramatic slope change occurs and the rapid performance improvement with increased average thread length terminates abruptly. The relatively small incremental gain in performance through continued overhead reduction is offset by the loss of available parallelism. Processors begin to experience more frequent idle cycles because of starvation. The threads are of sufficiently uniform chunkiness that overall flow control is not drastically skewed, but the decreasing work availability causes execution time to gradually rise. This region is labeled "graceful starvation."

The last and right-most of the three regions identified is another exhibiting pronounced performance change, but this time showing rapid increase in execution time. One would expect that this must ultimately converge to the uniprocessor execution time. However, the factors that dominate are not simply gradually increasing starvation due to decreasing available parallelism. One is that the variance in granularity of threads becomes more pronounced and the longest one at any point in the execution may determine the critical path time of that segment of the program execution. But in some sense more insidious is the forced skewing of synchronization events. A thread can not be scheduled until all of the external arguments to all of its operations are available. Thus, early operations of a thread which might have been performed are deferred until operand requirements of following operations within the thread are also satisfied. These, in turn delay the results of the next thread and its contribution to synchronizing further computation. Thus, past a certain point, individual threads have a much more constraining effect on the flow of execution than would be anticipated. We call this regime "bully blocking" because individual chunks can inhibit many others from executing.

7. Conclusions

A number of conclusions can be drawn about methods of organizing computation on a multithreaded dataflow system from the studies presented in this paper. Our data supports a model of scalability that relates peak performance gain to average parallelism, execution path latency, and serial overhead. For sufficiently large and parallel programs, peak gain is approximately proportional to average program parallelism and approximately inversely proportional to latency. But we also recognize that increased overhead will cause peak gain to be increased as well. Therefore, peak performance gain is not a perfect metric of quality for system operation since gain can increase while performance decreases. Random mapping, as many have suspected, is an acceptable and useful strategy for allocating resources to fine-grain dataflow operations. Its utility for the multithreading context has yet to be verified. Some simple enhancements to pure random mapping will frequently yield small improvements to overall performance. Of these, avoidance of I/O bottlenecks (not discussed in the paper) and forced equalizing of token packets among processors appear to have the most favorable impact overall. Reduction in average overhead and apparent execution latency through aggregation of operations into sequential threads can yield performance gains. But loss of parallelism and skewing of synchronization events can result in performance degradation when employing higher numbers of processors. For many problems, an optimal region with respect to average thread granularity exists and defines the locus of best operating point for multithreaded dataflow architectures. Understanding of these factors contributing to ultimate system performance is essential to architecture development and compiler design.

References

[1] Arvind, R.A. Iannucci, "Two Fundamental Issues in Multiprocessing," *Proceedings of DFVLR—Conference 1987 on Parallel Processing in Science and Engineering*, Bonn-Bad Godesberg, W. Germany, Springer-Verlag LNCS 295, June 1987.

[2] J.A. Sharp, *Dataflow Computing Theory and Practice*, Ablex Publishing Corporation, 1992.

[3] J.L. Gaudiot and L. Bic, *Advanced Topics in Data-Flow Computing*, Prentice Hall, 1991.

[4] Arvind, D.E. Culler, K.A. Maa, "Assessing the Benefits of Fine-grained Parallelism in Dataflow Programs," *International Journal of Supercomputer Applications*, Vol. 2, No. 3, 1988.

[5] D.E. Culler and Arvind, "Resource Requirements of Dataflow Programs," *Proceedings of the 15th Annual International Symposium on Computer Architecture*, May 1988.

[6] R.A. Iannucci, "Toward a Dataflow/von Neumann Hybrid Architecture," *Proceedings of the 15th Annual International Symposium on Computer Architecture*, May 1988.

[7] J.B. Dennis, "Data Flow Supercomputers," *IEEE Computer*, Nov. 1980.

[8] Arvind, R.S. Nikhil, and K.K. Pingali, "I-Structures: Data Structures for Parallel Computing," *ACM Transactions on Programming Languages and Systems*, Vol. 11, No. 4, Oct. 1989.

[9] J.T. Kuehn and B.J. Smith, "The Horizon Supercomputing System: Architecture and Software," *Proceedings of the 1st IEEE Supercomputing Conference*, Nov. 1988.

[10] R. Alverson et al., "The Tera Computer System," *Proceedings of the International Conference on Supercomputing*, June 1990.

[11] W.B. Ackerman, "Data Flow Languages," *IEEE Computer*, Feb. 1982.

[12] G.L. Steele, *Common LISP: the Language*, Digital Press, 1984.

[13] S.H. Bokhari, *Assignment Problems in Parallel and Distributed Computing*, Kluwer Academic Publishers, 1987.

The Effects of Resource Limitations on Program Parallelism

Kevin B. Theobald, Guang R. Gao, and Laurie J. Hendren
Advanced Compilers, Architectures, and Parallel Systems
McGill University School of Computer Science
3480 University St., Montréal, Québec, Canada H3A 2A7

Many of the studies of the "limits of instruction parallelism" in application programs made use of machine models with unlimited or ideal resources. In this study, we impose certain limitations on machine resources and measure the effects of those limitations. Beginning with an ideal "oracle" model, we selectively remove the ideal branch-prediction capability, and the ability to rename variables in the heap and stack, to measure the impact of control dependencies and memory reuse on potential parallelism.

Next, we study what happens when the number of processors is limited, which forces some operations to be deferred to a later time. We introduce and define "smoothability," which quantifies how much the parallelism and processor utilization are affected by such deferment. Finally, a memory latency model is added to measure the effects of non-local memory accesses. Our experiments show that programs with a large amount of intrinsic parallelism are quite "smoothable," even when memory latency is included. This suggests that real multiprocessor designs should be able to run these programs with a high level of processor utilization.

1. Introduction

At the current rate of progress in VLSI technology, it will be possible by the turn of the century to produce a single chip with tens to hundreds of millions of transistors. This level of integration can be used to implement a high-density, high-performance processor on a single chip, perhaps one based on advanced architectural ideas such as dataflow or multithreaded architectures [1], [4], [5], [7], [9], [15], [17]. Such processors can then become the building blocks of an advanced, massively parallel computer.

Those contemplating the design of highly parallel machines must ask two fundamental questions:

Limits of Parallelism: How much parallelism exists in the target applications?
Resource Limits: How is the available parallelism affected by limitations in machine resources? In particular, is it "smooth" enough to be effectively exploited when the number of processors is limited, and when non-local memory accesses have high latency?

In order to justify having machines supporting extensive parallelism, there must be enough useful work to do at any point in time to keep most of the processors usefully busy. This means that not only must there be enough parallelism in the application to be exploited by these processors, but the parallelism must also be smoothable; it must be possible to distribute the operations evenly over time. Otherwise, Amdahl's Law will take effect and prevent the computer from achieving a good speedup.

There have been many experiments, involving a wide variety of machine models and target applications, to measure the limits of parallelism that may be exploited in a program [2], [3], [11]–[14], [23], [24]. Most studies measured the limits of parallelism under ideal conditions (e.g., where parallelism is only limited by true flow dependencies), and then measured the drop in parallelism when specific architectural limitations were introduced into the model. Our experimental methods are similar, but we study different kinds of limitations:

1. Our "idealized" model includes the ability to rename memory objects in the stack and the heap, which eliminates false data dependencies. By selectively removing this ability from the heap and the stack, we can observe the impact on parallelism of the reuse of memory.

2. We consider what happens when the number of processors is limited. For instance, we measure the speedup (average parallelism) attainable from an unlimited number of processors, then limit the number of processors to that speedup value. In such an experiment, an operation occurring during a period of peak parallelism may have to be deferred to a later time when fewer operations are being performed. We introduce *smoothability* as a measure to characterize program parallelism. Smoothability is measured quantitatively and compared for our test programs. Our results indicate that the parallelism obtained has a relatively smooth temporal profile.

3. Finally, we consider the effects of non-uniform memory access latencies, to model what would be expected on a large-scale multiprocessor with either distributed memory or cached shared memory. We find that while memory latency can reduce the upper limits of parallelism, the parallelism is still quite smoothable, and it is possible for processors to tolerate non-local memory latencies by performing other operations while waiting for the accesses to complete.

To search for the limits of parallelism and measure its smoothability under different architectural ideas, we have developed an experimental testbed called SITA (Sequential Instruction Trace Analyzer) [19]–[22]. This testbed is based on a trace simulation method similar to previous experiments [2], [3], [13], [24]. The tool allows us to analyze the execution of real code and calculates, under a chosen architecture model, how much parallelism could potentially be attained for that model. Using this tool, we began with a true "Omniscient Oracle" machine model and measured the idealized limit of parallelism. We then examined the degradation in performance as we selectively added constraints to the resources of the Omniscient Oracle and moved it towards more realistic machine models at different levels. We ran a total of 405 experiments, whose results are presented in this paper.

Our oracle machine models, like oracles in other studies [13], [14], ignore control dependencies entirely. While the results obtained from an oracle are an upper bound, and may be unrealistically high, we believe that suitably designed programs with appropriate parallel algorithms can get parallelism results which are reasonably close to an oracle. (One shortcoming common to most of the cited parallelism studies is that they look for parallelism in code that had been originally written for uniprocessors.)

It is not the goal of this research to design a machine which can execute the benchmarks in a manner corresponding to the analysis in our experiments. Instead, we are interested in studying the upper bounds of potential parallelism inherent in the application. Our objective in this paper is not to provide a recipe for the design of specific architectures and then measure the achievable parallelism, but rather to study which effects of the limitations of each architecture model make it *impossible* to achieve the parallelism limits.

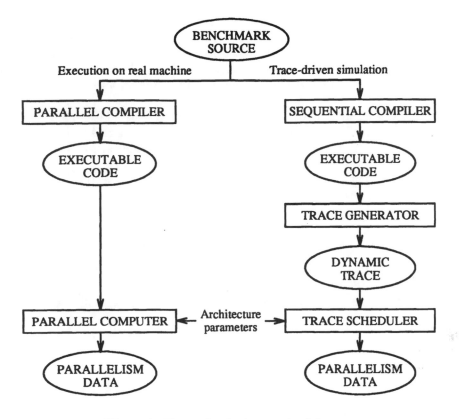

Figure 1: Trace simulation methodology.

In the next section, we describe how trace analysis works and develop the models used in our study. Section 3 presents the results from the basic studies, in which all memory accesses are fast and there are infinitely many processors. Smoothability is defined and discussed in Section 4. The latency model is added in Section 5. In Section 6, we compare our work to previous studies. The final section summarizes the paper, discusses the conclusions that may be drawn from this study, and describes how we plan to extend SITA in the future. We briefly describe the implementation of SITA in an appendix.

2. Methodology

This section describes the trace simulation techniques used in our study. First, we show conceptually how our trace analysis reveals parallelism in a program, and how various features added to a model affect potential parallelism. These effects are illustrated using a simple loop. Next, we describe the tool used to analyze the traces, and the benchmarks used in the experiments.

2.1 Trace Simulation

Figure 1 shows the basic methodology used in our study. We would like to determine how a benchmark program might be executed on an idealized machine with a given set of architectural characteristics, as shown in the left fork in the flowchart. Lacking such a machine, we model it using trace simulation, as shown in the right fork.

First, a benchmark program is compiled into an executable file using a conventional sequential compiler. Then the executable code is run through a trace generator, which produces a program trace. This trace consists of a stream of operations representing the actual sequence of instructions executed (*not* the static object code). For each executed operation, the trace gives the opcode, PC address, and load or store address (if any).

The trace scheduler reads the operations from the stream and packs them into *parallel instructions* (PIs) componentwise on a Sparc processor. As the scheduler reads each operation in the trace, it inserts the operation into the earliest PI possible, while simultaneously respecting the dependencies between that operation and all previous operations. The following types of dependencies between operation S_1, inserted into PI_i, and a later operation S_2 may exist:

- *Flow dependence:* if S_2 reads a storage location (register or memory cell) which was most recently written by S_1, then S_2 can be scheduled no earlier than PI_{i+1}.

- *Anti-dependence:* if S_2 writes a storage location which was most recently read by S_1, then S_2 can be scheduled no earlier than PI_i. (It is assumed that the write and read can occur simultaneously, and S_1 will read the proper value.)

- *Output dependence:* if S_2 writes a storage location which was most recently written by S_1, then S_2 can be scheduled no earlier than PI_{i+1}.

- *Control dependence:* if S_1 is the most recent conditional branch in the trace whose outcome must be decided before it is known whether or not S_2 will be executed, then S_2 can be scheduled no earlier than PI_{i+1}.

For the initial experiments, we assume that all operations (including memory references) take a single cycle to execute. Memory is global with unlimited access, and there are no caches. Infinitely many functional units are available to execute all operations which can be packed into one PI. (In later sections, we limit the number of processors and add latency to the memory accesses.) Operations arbitrarily far apart in the dynamic trace can be packed into the same PI, so long as all other dependence constraints are obeyed. Real machines may not be so generous, but this study aims to determine how much parallelism is truly inherent in a program, independent of any particular hardware limitations.

To illustrate the basic principle, consider this simple loop fragment for multiplying two vectors componentwise on a Sparc processor:

```
S1 :    ld  [%o2 + %o1], %f0
S2 :    ld  [%o3 + %o1], %f1
S3 :    fmuls %f0, %f1, %f2
S4 :    st  %f2, [%o4 + %o1]
S5 :    subcc %o1, 4, %o1
S6 :    bg S1
S7 :    nop
```

In a dynamic trace, the sequence S1–S7 may be repeated many times. The left half of Figure 2 shows how our trace analyzer would pack these operations into PIs if all four dependence types listed above were obeyed. Plain arcs are drawn to show the

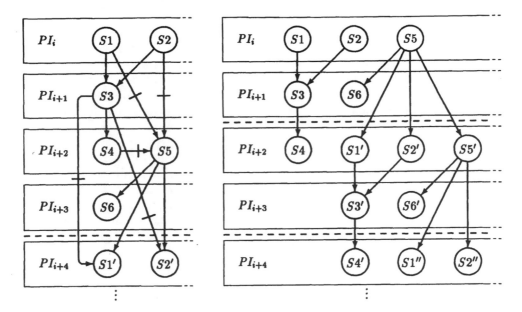

Figure 2: Packing parallelizable instructions: An example.

flow dependencies between operations. The arcs with small marks (e.g., from S4 to S5) indicate anti-dependencies. The dashed line represents a barrier caused by the conditional branch at S6, which may prevent future operations from being scheduled before that barrier.[1] One iteration of the loop can be initiated every 4 cycles, so the parallelism is 1.5. (Parallelism is defined as the total number of sequential operations divided by the total number of PIs required by the scheduler.) The right half of Figure 2 shows how the operations would be packed if anti- and output dependencies were ignored.

Other models, described later, relax the dependence constraints; some also tighten the resource limitations. The next three subsections describe how these constraints may be modified, through such means as register renaming and branch prediction, and the effects such changes will have on overall parallelism.

2.1.1 Memory Disambiguation Memory references can't always be determined at compile-time, due to indirect addressing. A conservative analysis would assume that any two memory references *could* refer to the same memory location, in which case a dependence would exist between them. Thus, for instance, a conservative scheduler would have to assume that a flow dependence might exist between S4 in iteration j and S1 in iteration $j + 1$, making it harder to overlap separate iterations of the loop.

However, since the actual addresses of memory accesses appear in the trace, a trace analyzer can determine at run-time whether two memory references really conflict. This would model the potential effects of perfect compiler alias-analysis and/or special hardware to check for memory conflicts at run-time. With our tool, the user can choose whether or not run-time memory disambiguation is performed.

2.1.2 Register and Memory Renaming A false dependence (anti- or output) exists between two operations when one must follow the other, *not* because the latter

---

[1]For operations S1–S3 and S5, there are also output dependencies between corresponding operations in different iterations; these have been left out of Figure 2 for clarity.

requires data produced by the former, but merely because the latter needs to reuse a storage location (register or memory cell) used by the former. An example of this in the code sample is the use of register %o1 for the loop index, which cannot be updated (by S5) before being used to construct a memory address (by S4). Thus, overlapping the iterations of the loop body, as in software pipelining, is impossible.

False dependencies may also exist in references to main memory. This can reduce parallelism in two ways:

1. Many sequential programs reuse data structures (such as arrays) to conserve memory. Such optimization may be a good idea in programs with a single thread of control. In parallel machines, however, reusing memory in this way means that available processors cannot start operating on an updated version of a data structure while other processors continue to read the old version, because the update must wait until all processors are finished with the old copy.

2. Under the conventional stack architecture, procedure calls at the same level in a program reuse the same portion of the stack, leading to contention for that part of the stack. For instance, when executing object code corresponding to

$$x = sin(y) + cos(z);$$

the processor cannot push z onto the stack and call cos until it has popped the return value of sin(y) off the stack, even though these two function calls are independent and could run in parallel.

The inhibiting effects of false dependencies can be eliminated by ensuring that each register or memory location is written only once. In a real processor, false dependencies can be reduced by creating a sufficiently large register file, coupled with other techniques such as *register renaming*. The architecture provides additional registers that are not programmer-visible, and dynamically allocates them to store each new value generated. This will enforce a *single-assignment* rule and hence resolve the anti- and output dependencies.[2]

False dependencies in the heap can, in principle, be eliminated by adhering to the single-assignment rule, either explicitly in the programming language (e.g., Streams and Iteration in a Single-Assignment Language (SISAL) [6]), or by using *memory renaming*. Conventional architectures do not presently perform memory renaming, although dynamic dataflow machines with "colored tokens" [1] employ a form of re-naming.

False dependencies in the stack can be caused by the linear stack model, the standard runtime memory organization for supporting nested procedure invocations on sequential machines. Such false dependencies can be eliminated, for example, by organizing the memory frames for procedure invocation in a tree-like structure, as proposed in several dataflow and multithreaded architecture models [4], [15], [17].

Infinite renaming, in which a register or memory location can be renamed any number of times, is equivalent to ignoring all false dependencies between objects of a particular type. For instance, if register renaming is applied to the dependence graph in Figure 2, then S5 can be executed in parallel with S1 and S2 of the same iteration, as the anti-dependence with S4 no longer exists. This moves operation S6 up as well,

---

[2]For instance, the IBM RISC 6000 superscalar machine implements a form of register renaming in its floating point unit [16].

so the conditional-branch barrier has moved up by 2 PIs. If perfect disambiguation is also used, then the iteration issue rate increases to once every other cycle, raising parallelism to 3, as the right half of Figure 2 shows.[3]

2.1.3 Control Barrier Elimination

Previous parallelism experiments in which conditional branches were barriers to upward motion of all operations generally had low parallelism, especially in non-numerical programs. This is because conditional branches occur quite frequently in most programs, which confines the search for parallelism to small "basic blocks" in the code. To get better parallelism results, one must consider models representing possible architectures which reduce the deleterious effects of conditional branches.

The *oracle*, introduced in [14], makes the most optimistic assumptions by ignoring control dependencies entirely. Our oracles, like most others, also ignore output and anti-dependencies, so that parallelism is only limited by true flow dependencies in the program.

It is possible to use more conservative models between the extremes of having an oracle and forcing barriers at every conditional branch. One way to reduce the serializing effects of conditional branches is to analyze the code to determine which parts of the code are really control-dependent on a given branch. For instance, while the then-clause and else-clause of an if-statement are control-dependent on the if-expression, the statements *following* the if-statement often are not. Similarly, two consecutive but independent for-loops should be able to run concurrently. Also, the barriers produced by branches in one procedure usually do not affect the scheduling of operations within other procedures.

These examples show why we have adopted the definition of control dependence in Section 2.1 rather than making a branch block the upward motion of *all* succeeding instructions in the trace. We assume that a compiler can analyze the source code to determine the true control dependencies, so that operations on a parallel architecture can be scheduled accordingly. For some scientific code with regular control structures, this analysis is sufficient to yield high levels of parallelism close to an oracle [13], [22].

If this is not enough, then *speculative execution* can be used to get more parallelism. The processor tries to decide which branch is most likely to be taken, and takes that branch. When a predicted branch is taken, and it later turns out that that branch should not have been taken, then all instructions executed after the incorrect branch must be aborted and their side-effects reversed. There can be more branches in between the time when a mispredicted branch is taken and the time at which this error is discovered, which means that at any time there may be multiple active machine states, only one of which is valid.

Branch prediction is modeled by the trace analyzer by ignoring all relevant barriers created by correctly predicted branches, and keeping barriers created by incorrectly predicted branches (see the appendix). We used a method of dynamic branch prediction in which the prediction of which way to branch comes from a 2-bit count which is based on the history of previous executions of that particular branch instruction [18], [22], [24]. Jump prediction is done simply by predicting that the processor will jump to the same destination as the previous occurrence of that particular jump instruction.

2.2 Experimental Tool and Benchmarks

To measure the parallelism available under the various models, the SITA (Sequential Instruction Trace Analyzer) testbed was developed. Since programs can show sig-

---

[3]This assumes the input and output arrays do not overlap in such a way as to create flow dependencies.

				Useful	*Call*	*% of Ops.*		
Source	*Program*	*Description*	*Test Case*	*Ops* $\times 10^6$	*Depth*	*FP*	*Ld.*	*St.*
DLX suite	tex	Text formatting	draft (11 p.)	109	23	.04	15	8.0
Industry	speech	Speech recognit.	recognize "he"	551	12	4.5	14	2.8
SPEC89	li	Lisp interpreter	(queens 7)	205	75103	0	22	8.6
Test	eqntott	Truth-table gen.	int_pri_3.eqn	1,770	18	0	33	0.7
Suite	fpppp	Quantum	NATOMS=4	277	14	19	43	10
		chemistry	NATOMS=6	1,258	14	19	43	10

Table 1: Benchmarks and test cases used.

nificant differences in behavior when run on short inputs and on larger inputs, we designed SITA to handle traces for realistic input sizes. Also, we stipulated that all programs tested should run to completion, giving the analyzer enough opportunity to extract parallelism from all parts of the code. Implementation details are provided in the appendix.

We decided to base the analysis on traces of programs executed on Sun SparcStations. The Sparc architecture was chosen for the testbed because it is representative of present-day RISC processors. Also, the Sparc processor has a special feature facilitating procedure calls: the partitioning of registers into sets which are selectively visible to the processor via "register windows." The mundane task of saving and restoring local registers and passing parameters is much more efficient. This avoids inflating the parallelism numbers with the pushes and pops which the analyzer would schedule in parallel. Finally, some of the recent trace-driven experiments have used MIPS workstations, and we decided to confirm the generality of the results by using a different RISC processor.

In this study, we ran our analysis tool on five benchmarks under nine basic models (described in the next section), with additional tests done after limiting the processor resources and adding memory latency. We chose problems that we feel are representative of the types of computations that are likely to be performed on future high-performance architectures. We looked for programs large enough to give figures suggestive of what can be achieved with "grand challenge" problems, without being so large as to overwhelm our analyzer.

The benchmarks consist of a regular FP-intensive scientific program, written in Fortran, and four symbolic applications written in C. All are from standard benchmark test suites, except for a speech-recognition program taken from an actual industrial application. We used standard input cases, except that we reduced the size of the queens problem run on the Lisp interpreter (li) from nine queens to seven. Also, we tried two different sizes for the scientific benchmark. The tests are summarized in Table 1.

One of the goals of our study was to analyze complete program executions, rather than stopping at some point as in some previous studies. Our experiments confirmed the wisdom of this choice, as some of the programs showed long-term changes in parallelism over time. By programming SITA to print intermediate results at regular intervals, we found, for instance, that total parallelism of eqntott under one of the models dropped by half between the checkpoints at 100 million operations and half a billion operations.

Model Name	Memory Disamb.	Rename Regs.	Rename Memory	Control Barriers
Ominiscient Oracle	yes	yes	all	none
Speculative Dataflow	yes	yes	all	all relevant; prediction
Fine Dataflow	yes	yes	all	all relevant
Coarse Dataflow	yes	yes	all	all in same procedure
Smart Superscalar	yes	yes	all	all
Tree Oracle	yes	yes	stack	none
Linear Oracle	yes	yes	heap	none
Frugal Oracle	yes	yes	none	none
Stupid Superscalar	no	no	none	all

Table 2: Basic machine models.

3. Basic Experiments

This section presents the results of our "basic" experiments, involving models with infinitely many processors and uniform memory latency. These experiments were intended to find the upper bounds of parallelism in a program, and to measure how these limits are affected by control dependencies and the reuse of memory. In the two sections that follow this one, we limit the number of processors and add memory latency.

In general, we chose a top-down approach. From the discussion in the previous section, it is clear that the most ideal oracle model, which we call the *Omniscient Oracle*, should have the following features:

- Perfect memory disambiguation

- Infinite register renaming

- Infinite memory renaming

- No barriers due to control dependencies

We then created models in which one or more features are restricted, to measure their importance. We ran a total of 54 experiments. All the basic models used are summarized in Table 2 and described in the individual subsections that follow.

3.1 Effects of Branch and Jump Prediction

The first five models in our study are the *Omniscient Oracle, Speculative Dataflow, Fine Dataflow, Coarse Dataflow*, and *Smart Superscalar* models. All of these models have perfect memory disambiguation (see Section 2.1.1) and infinite memory/register renaming (see Section 2.1.2). The only difference among them is how much they are affected by control dependencies.

The Omniscient Oracle has perfect foreknowledge of every jump and branch outcome, while the other four do not. Therefore, the latter are constrained by control dependencies. These four models reflect different levels of optimism about how much can be done to determine true control dependencies and to predict branches. In the most pessimistic model, the Smart Superscalar, if a conditional branch is scheduled

Benchmark	Omniscient Oracle	Speculative Dataflow	Fine Dataflow	Coarse Dataflow	Smart Superscalar
tex	192	36.3	5.31	3.04	2.08
speech	8,105	1,192	45.4	6.30	1.80
li	1,570	59.4	9.71	3.91	1.69
eqntott	43,298	675	2.24	1.66	1.46
fpppp (4)	4,978	4,166	1,179	52.7	30.1
fpppp (6)	11,296	10,720	3,023	54.1	32.6

Table 3: Results on five basic models.

in PI_i, then *all* instructions that follow it in the trace must be scheduled no earlier than PI_{i+1}, whether or not they are control-dependent on that branch (as defined in Section 2.1). In the Coarse Dataflow model, a conditional branch only impacts the scheduling of a future instruction if both are within the same procedure invocation (we call this rule *procedure separation*). The Fine Dataflow machine is even more lenient; any two instructions may be scheduled concurrently if they are not directly or indirectly control-dependent (as defined in Section 2.1) even if there are conditional branches between them in the trace. This model's name comes from the fact that its behavior models what might occur on an idealized dataflow machine (with infinite renaming) executing a sequential benchmark without the algorithm modifications that would be necessary to approach the oracles' levels of performance. The Speculative Dataflow model attempts to predict branches so that control-dependent instructions may be speculatively executed before the branch outcomes are known, but unlike an oracle, it sometimes makes mistakes.

Examining Table 3, we note that the results vary from surprisingly high parallelism results for the Omniscient Oracle to generally poor parallelism results for the Smart Superscalar model. In the case of the Omniscient Oracle, we find impressive parallelism for speech (8,105), eqntott (43,298), and fpppp (4,978–11,296). Reasonable parallelism was measured for li (1,570), and moderate parallelism was measured for tex (192).

From Table 3 we can make the following observations:

- For some programs like li and eqntott, the power to predict jumps and branches *perfectly* is extremely important. As expected, for scientific programs that have regular, data-independent behavior like fpppp, branch prediction is much less of an issue, as shown by the relatively high performance of the Fine Dataflow model.

- There is a substantial parallelism loss between the Speculative Dataflow model and the Fine Dataflow model, especially for the symbolic benchmarks. This result indicates that for programs with irregular control flow, speculative execution may be very important.

- In most cases, the performance of the Coarse Dataflow machine is near the geometric mean of the Fine Dataflow and Smart Superscalar machines. This shows that it is important to avoid false control dependencies both *between* procedures (by using procedure separation) and *within* procedures (by performing control-dependence analysis). The latter is clearly more important for numerical

Benchmark	Omni. Oracle	Tree Oracle	% of O.O.	Linear Oracle	% of O.O.	Frugal Oracle	% of O.O.	Smart Super.	Stupid Super.	% of Smart
tex	192	75.8	39.4	167	86.9	71.5	37.2	2.08	1.66	80.8
speech	8,105	136	1.68	57.1	0.70	53.6	0.66	1.80	1.62	89.9
li	1,570	59.5	3.79	343	21.8	59.3	3.78	1.69	1.44	85.2
eqntott	43,298	1,742	4.02	1,314	3.03	1,314	3.03	1.46	1.43	98.2
fpppp (4)	4,978	4,978	100	71.0	1.43	70.9	1.42	30.1	2.88	9.56
fpppp (6)	11,296	11,296	100	73.7	0.65	73.6	0.65	32.6	2.91	8.94

Table 4: The effects of frugal use of memory.

programs like fpppp, since procedures in these programs tend to be larger and less frequent.

3.2 Effects of Memory Reuse

Having seen the effects of control dependencies on parallelism, we wanted to measure how the reuse of memory in conventional programs can affect parallelism. Therefore, our next experiments were with "frugal oracles." These oracles are just like the Omniscient Oracle, but they don't have full memory-renaming capability. The *Tree Oracle* allows renaming of stack variables, to measure the limits of parallelism exploitable by a machine using a tree of stacks or some equivalent implementation, but does not allow renaming in the heap.[4] The *Linear Oracle* retains the linear stack model, by not allowing stack elements to be renamed, but allows renaming in the heap. The *Frugal Oracle* has no memory renaming.

The results of these experiments are shown in Table 4. In this table, we list the parallelism measurements for the Tree Oracle, the Linear Oracle, and the truly Frugal Oracle. For each result, we give the percentage of parallelism relative to the Omniscient Oracle. Studying these results, we can make the following observations:

- Stack renaming is very important for numeric programs, and for symbolic programs like speech and eqntott. This is probably due to overlapping of successive iterations that call the same procedure in numeric programs, and concurrent execution of separate procedure calls in symbolic programs.

- Heap renaming is extremely important for li, speech, and eqntott. This reflects the fact that the programs are computing with large dynamically allocated data structures. Heap renaming is irrelevant to fpppp, mostly due to the lack of heap-allocated data structures in Fortran programs (only global variables are affected by this renaming capability).

- Every program shows marked loss of parallelism with the Frugal Oracle. Thus, it appears that renaming of both stack-allocated data structures and heap-allocated data structures is an important characteristic of the Omniscient Oracle. Usually, one or the other is the limiting case for a given application. In every case, the Frugal Oracle performs as well or almost as well as the slower of the Tree Oracle and Linear Oracle.

---

[4]In this study, "heap" includes both dynamically allocated and global (static) variables.

We ran one final model, the *Stupid Superscalar*, to test the benefits of renaming and disambiguation at the "low" end of the scale. The Stupid Superscalar is like the Smart Superscalar, but has neither memory disambiguation nor register/memory renaming.[5] Results for this model are given in the right-most two columns of Table 4.

Both superscalar models have the property that a conditional branch affects the scheduling of all future instructions. Thus, these machines can generally only find parallelism within basic blocks. Indeed, the right-most column of Table 4, which gives the performance of the Stupid Superscalar relative to the Smart Superscalar, shows that for irregular code, renaming and disambiguation by themselves produce little benefit. Only fpppp shows a big gain when renaming and disambiguation are added, probably due to its large basic blocks and regular code structure. For codes with frequent branches, we must go to more aggressive models, such as the Fine Dataflow and Speculative Dataflow models.

4. Smoothability

As highlighted in the introduction, an important question to ask about programs with high degrees of parallelism is: how evenly can this parallelism be distributed? If a program's parallelism is concentrated in short bursts of massive parallelism separated by long sequential sections, then Amdahl's Law will take over and the machine will need many more processors than the average to achieve the theoretical parallelism limits. Furthermore, the utilization of these processors will be poor during the sequential sections of the execution. If the number of processors is limited, then some operations will be delayed, but this delay will add to the total execution time only if the delayed operations are in critical paths. In this section, we describe how our analyzer can measure this effect, and we define a value called *smoothability* which quantifies this property.

SITA has the ability to limit the number of operations which can be packed into one PI. This limitation puts an upper bound on the maximum attainable parallelism, and may cause some operations to be delayed (scheduled into later PIs) because the PIs into which they first could be packed are already full. Because SITA's scheduler processes operations in the order in which they appear in the dynamic trace, it is always the later instructions which will be delayed.

For a given architectural model, and a given benchmark program, we can define $P(n)$, the "parallelism" function, which gives the average parallelism when the width of each PI is limited to n operations (i.e., there are n processors). We use $P(\infty)$ to denote the parallelism when the number of processors is infinite. A plot of $P(n)$ will look something like Figure 3.

This curve is bounded above by two factors. For small values of n, $P(n)$ is bounded by n, since we can't have greater than linear speedup. This is represented by the diagonal dashed line in Figure 3. Once n reaches $P(\infty)$, that value becomes the new bound, since $P(n)$ can never be greater than $P(\infty)$; this is shown by a horizontal dashed line. $P(n)$ is guaranteed to reach $P(\infty)$ if n equals or exceeds n_{peak}, the largest number of operations packed into any single PI, i.e., the peak instantaneous parallelism, because above that point, all operations are executed immediately and

---

[5]The Stupid Superscalar is similar to Wall's "Stupid" model [24], except that Wall's model was limited to 64 processors, and could only schedule operations from within a window of 2,048 instructions. These limitations, however, had almost no additional impact on the Stupid model, since register and memory reuse, control dependencies, and lack of memory disambiguation generally removed almost all available parallelism except that within basic blocks.

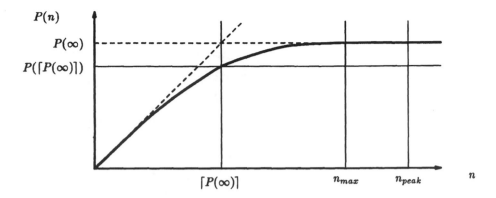

Figure 3: Standard smoothability profile.

there are no delays. Under the more optimistic models, n_{peak} may be quite high, since many operations not dependent on previous operations will be packed into the first PI. Usually, $P(n)$ will reach $P(\infty)$ at some lower value of n, called n_{max}. When n is between n_{max} and n_{peak}, some operations are delayed, but the delays do not affect critical paths, so the total number of PIs doesn't increase.

If a program is perfectly "smooth" (evenly distributed over time), then the number of operations performed in every cycle is either $\lfloor P(\infty) \rfloor$ or $\lceil P(\infty) \rceil$ (since $P(\infty)$ may be non-integral, and each PI has an integral number of operations). Thus, $\lceil P(\infty) \rceil$ processors are sufficient to guarantee that every operation in the trace is executed as early as possible. A program that is not as smooth, however, will have (with infinite processors) some PIs with more than $\lceil P(\infty) \rceil$ operations. With only $\lceil P(\infty) \rceil$ processors, some of these operations will need to be deferred until a later PI in which not so many operations are packed. If the deferred operation is not on a critical path, and its results are not immediately needed, then this delay won't increase the total number of PIs needed to execute the program. However, if the operation is in a critical path, and it is delayed by k cycles, it is possible that every future operation dependent on that operation will be delayed by k cycles, increasing the total number of PIs by k.

Since $P(n)$ is bounded above in the manner previously described, we can normalize $P(n)$ with respect to that upper bound, to measure how well the processors are utilized compared to the ideal case:

$$P'(n) = \begin{cases} \dfrac{P(n)}{n} & \text{if } n \le P(\infty) \\[2mm] \dfrac{P(n)}{P(\infty)} & \text{if } n > P(\infty) \end{cases}$$

A normalized curve corresponding to the curve in Figure 3 is shown in Figure 4.

We define *smoothability* to be the processor utilization at the critical value $n = \lceil P(\infty) \rceil$, i.e.,

$$S = P'(\lceil P(\infty) \rceil) = \frac{(\lceil P(\infty) \rceil)}{P(\infty)}$$

SITA can keep a record of how many operations are in each PI, and can delay operations whenever a PI becomes full. To measure the smoothability for a given

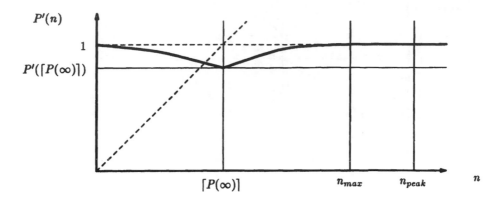

Figure 4: Normalized smoothability profile.

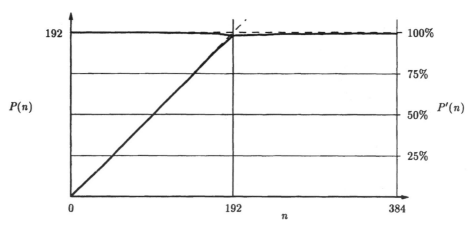

Figure 5: Smoothability profile for **tex** ($S = 98.3\%$).

model, we first compute $P(\infty)$ for that model, round it to the next integer, and rerun the program with the resulting value as the PI width limit.

The next six figures (5–10) show parallelism curves for the six benchmarks used in our experiments, under the Omniscient Oracle model. To generate each curve, we ran the benchmark 20 times, limiting the number of processors to $\lceil kP(\infty) \rceil$, where k ranged from 0.10 to 2.00 by increments of 0.10, and $P(\infty)$ came from the Omniscient Oracle column of Table 3. Therefore, each graph shows n (the number of processors) between 0 and $2P(\infty)$. A total of 120 experiments were run.

The curve splits into two parts to the left of $n = P(\infty)$. The lower curve represents $P(n)$, corresponding to Figure 3, and measures absolute parallelism, as shown on the scale at the left of each graph. The upper curve represents $P'(n)$, corresponding to Figure 4, and measures the percentage of parallelism achievable compared to the ideal case, as shown on the scale at the right of each graph. With these scales, both curves coincide to the right of $n = P(\infty)$.

From the six curves shown, the following observations can be made:

- The most smoothable application is **fpppp**. This program performs physical simulation, and the computation load is fairly evenly distributed over time.

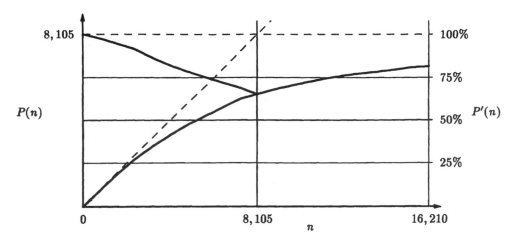

Figure 6: Smoothability profile for speech $(S = 65.3\%)$.

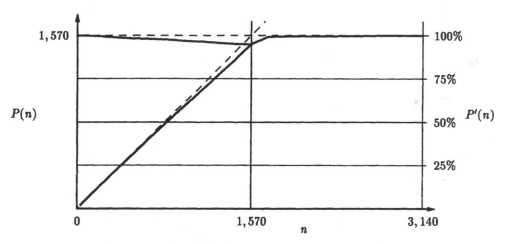

Figure 7: Smoothability profile for li $(S = 94.9\%)$.

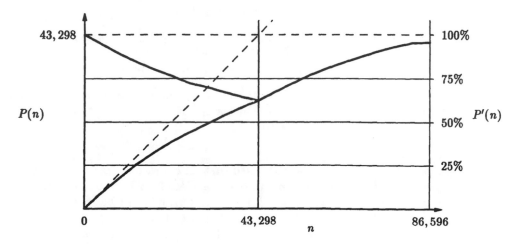

Figure 8: Smoothability profile for eqntott $(S = 62.6\%)$.

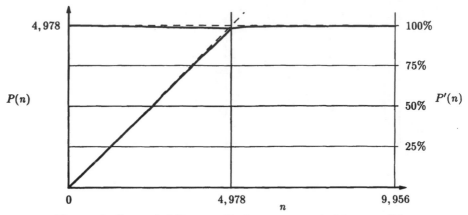

Figure 9: Smoothability profile for **fpppp** (4) ($S = 98.2\%$).

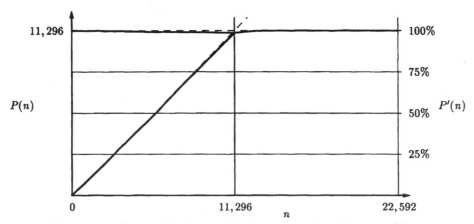

Figure 10: Smoothability profile for **fpppp** (6) ($S = 98.7\%$).

Thus, there is not much peak parallelism, and limiting the processor count only reduces parallelism significantly when the count drops below $P(\infty)$.

- The symbolic applications **tex** and **li** are only slightly less smoothable than **fpppp**.[6] This may be due to their relatively low values of $P(\infty)$. It is easier to achieve maximum parallelism when the maximum is lower.

- The other two programs are less smoothable. Even so, in both cases the processor utilization below $n = P(\infty)$ is always at least 60%.

5. Latency

Up to this point, all experiments have assumed that all operations, including memory accesses, take the same amount of time to execute. While it may be acceptable to include local memory operations within this assumption, it won't be true for remote memory operations. Physical constraints will always ensure that operations requiring transmissions over long distances will take longer than operations that can be

---

[6]While the smoothability (S) is slightly higher for **tex** than for **fpppp** (4), note that $P(n)$ rises more slowly for $n > P(\infty)$.

performed entirely within a processor. Parallel machines will require some kind of communication between processors, and this communication will take longer than a single clock cycle.

Therefore, we wish to measure the effects such latencies will have on parallelism. First, we propose a latency model to be used in our experiments. We then present the results of these experiments involving both latency and finite processors.

5.1 Latency Model

Ordinarily, when a load instruction appears in the instruction trace, SITA schedules the instruction into the earliest possible PI, subject to dependencies and constraints, and the register(s) loaded can be read as early as the following PI. Similarly, when a store occurs, the memory location(s) written to can be read as early as the following PI. In our extended model, we compute the latency l for a given load or store operation. If a load or store is scheduled in PI_i, then any operation reading the register or memory location written by the load/store can't be scheduled any earlier than PI_{i+l}.

In a distributed-memory machine, some memory accesses will refer to local items or items in a local cache, and we assume these will only take 1 cycle, like the other instructions. Some fraction of the accesses will refer to items in other processors, and will have a higher latency. Determining which references are local and which are remote is problematic, because it depends on having exact information about how memory objects are distributed among the processors. Since partitioning is beyond the scope of this project, we have chosen a probabilistic model for determining misses. A "miss rate" is chosen prior to running an experiment, and then the analyzer chooses random loads and stores from the instruction stream to be "misses," so that the average miss rate equals the chosen parameter.[7]

When a miss occurs, the analyzer assigns a latency greater than 1 to the memory access. Since both hypercubes and multistage interconnection networks, two popular networks for parallel processors, have average routing distance proportional to log n, we assume in most cases that the latency is $\lceil \log_2 n \rceil$ cycles. For instance, if there are 1,024 processors, the latency for any remote access is 10 cycles. Because the network may not be able to attain this high speed, we assume a higher latency of $10\lceil \log_2 n \rceil$ cycles in some experiments.

5.2 Latency Experiments

For the final 231 experiments, we added both the latency model (described in the previous subsection) and limits on processor count to the Omniscient Oracle model. Each of the six test cases was run with various processor counts, latencies, and miss rates. For each case, five to seven processor counts were chosen; all were powers of 2 in the vicinity of $P(\infty)$ (see the Omniscient Oracle results in Table 3).

For each chosen processor count, seven tests were run. For the first six, the (miss) memory latency was equal to the log of the processor count, and the miss rates were 0%, 10%, 20%, 30%, 60%, 100%. A seventh test was run in which latency was increased by a factor of 10 (i.e., equal to $10\log_2 n$) and a miss rate of 10% was assumed. We expected the results to be similar to the results for the shorter-latency network with a 100% miss rate, since the average latency per memory access would be the same.

---

[7]The term "miss" implies a shared-memory model. It is not entirely an accurate term for a message-passing model, but the choice of memory model is too specific a detail for this study. Therefore, in this section, a "miss" means either a remote memory access or the sending of a value to another processor via a message.

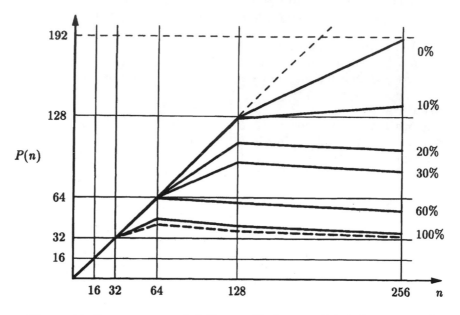

Figure 11: Latency-smoothability profile for **tex** (16–256 processors).

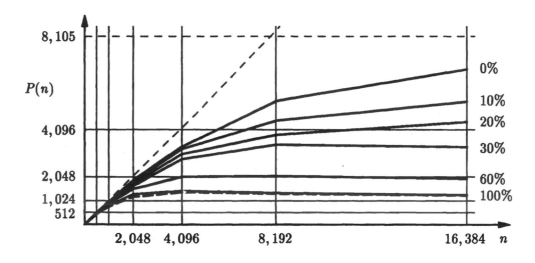

Figure 12: Latency-smoothability profile for **speech** (512–16K processors).

Figures 11–16 show the results of the experiments. Each graph shows the parallelism curves for the six miss rates with short latency (labeled with the miss rates) and the single long-latency experiment (thick dashed line). Thin dashed lines show the upper bounds $P(n) = n$ and $P(n) = P(\infty)$.

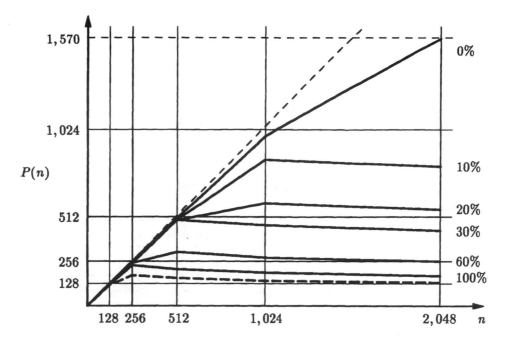

Figure 13: Latency-smoothability profile for 1i (128–2K processors).

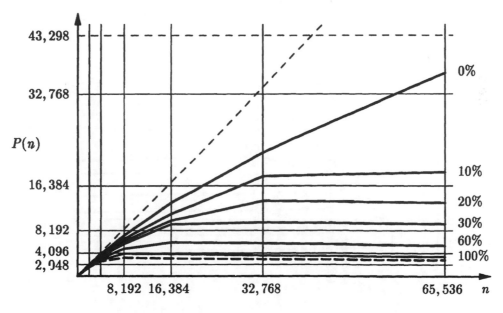

Figure 14: Latency-smoothability profile for eqntott (1K–64K processors).

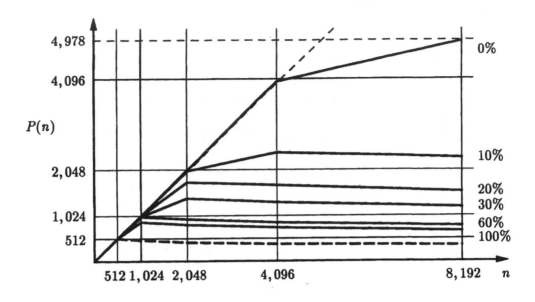

Figure 15: Latency-smoothability profile for **fpppp (4)** (512–8K processors).

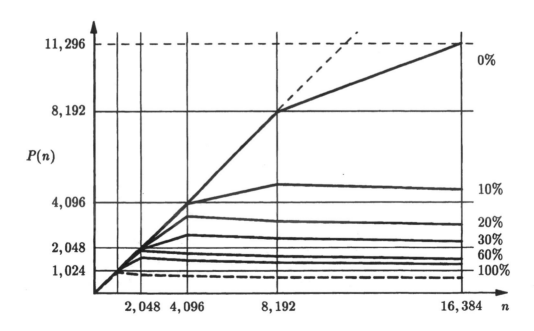

Figure 16: Latency-smoothability profile for **fpppp (6)** (1K–16K processors).

What can be seen from all the graphs is that for a given miss rate, the parallelism curve looks similar to the parallelism curves shown in Section 4. Parallelism initially increases linearly, then tapers off as it approaches an asymptotic value. This is the point where adding more processors doesn't decrease execution time significantly, because the limit of program parallelism has been reached. In the experiments with non-zero miss rates, it can be seen that parallelism slowly declines after reaching a maximum. This is an effect of the latency model: miss latency increases by 1 cycle every time the number of processors is doubled.

In all cases, the long-latency model with a 10% miss rate was worse than the short-latency, 100%-miss model, and the relative difference depended on the application. There was almost no difference with **speech**, while **fpppp** showed a significant difference.

The asymptote (maximum parallelism) decreases as the miss rate increases, which shows that increasing memory latency will cause the critical path(s) to lengthen. This is to be expected. When a processor has to wait for a remote access, it can fill in the gap by executing other instructions. However, these other instructions can be executed on a separate processor on a machine without long-latency accesses. Thus, filling in latency gaps by executing other instructions will decrease the overall parallelism. As the widths of the gaps increase, more instructions must be diverted from other processors to fill in the gaps, which decreases available parallelism still further.

What is encouraging, however, is the behavior of each parallelism curve near its "knee" where it first approaches its asymptote. Below the knee, the experiments show that the processors could achieve good utilization. This shows that the execution of different instructions (i.e., a context switch) to hide memory latencies can be an effective means of improving overall processor utilization.

6. Previous Studies

Most previous studies on the limits of program parallelism have taken one of two approaches. One approach is to analyze the selected benchmark at either the source-code or object-code level, usually with a special interpreter that is based on a certain parallel machine model. The other approach, used in our study, is to schedule machine instructions from a trace generated by an actual execution of the object code. The following presents some of the previous work along both paths.

An early experimental tool, designed by Kuck, Muraoka, and Chen [11], compiled small Fortran programs to run on an abstract parallel machine. By recognizing parallelism at the source code level (e.g., parallel iterations of DO-loops) and by aggressively reordering complex expressions, they were able to speed up most programs by a factor of 2–7, and speed up some by as much as 25. Tjaden and Flynn built a simulator based on the superscalar model [23]. Their simulator could execute ordinary IBM 7094 machine code, but attempted to reschedule operations dynamically using a look-ahead window of between 2 and 10 operations. They obtained speedups of up to 3 on a suite of 31 library routines. Both studies got modest results because they only looked for parallelism within small blocks, and could not execute independent instructions from separate blocks. These blocks are typically separated by conditional branches, and if the decision whether to execute one block is controlled by the outcome of a conditional branch in another block, the first block can't begin execution until the branch has been resolved.

Nicolau and Fisher wrote an interpreter for intermediate code generated by a compiler front-end, and a tool to analyze the instruction trace generated by the interpreter

[14]. They addressed the shortcomings of the previous studies by allowing operations from many parts of the program to execute concurrently. They introduced the oracle model, which they added to their analysis tool. The analyzer also ignored any dependence which was not a "true" data dependence. They were able to obtain respectable speedups from small scientific routines.

Kumar [12] developed a tool that automatically added statistics-gathering statements to Fortran source-code. By running the modified Fortran programs, he was able to measure parallelism figures for scientific applications. The tool also performed control-dependence analysis, so that independent Fortran statements separated by barriers could still run concurrently. Kumar found the potential for high levels of parallelism in regular numerical code.

Wall [24] analyzed benchmarks (SPEC89 programs, system utilities, and toy benchmarks) in which the number of executed operations ranged from 1 million to 2 billion. He developed a series of models representing various levels of optimism about what the hardware and compiler could do. He then ran the benchmarks on a MIPS R3000 processor, and analyzed the instruction traces in a manner similar to Tjaden and Flynn, and Nicolau and Fisher. Even under his "perfect" model, with oracle-like branch prediction, parallelism rarely exceeded 40. This is because his scheduler used only 64 processors, a finite (2K) input window from which to fill parallel instructions, and no memory renaming (register renaming only).

Two recent studies measured the effects of limiting the size of the scheduling window, which determines how broad the search for parallelism in the sequential trace can be, on the parallelism available in SPEC89 benchmarks. Butler et al. [3], ran each trace for 10 million instructions on an M88000 processor, while Austin and Sohi [2] ran each trace for up to 100 million instructions on a MIPS processor. Both assumed perfect (oracular) branch prediction, but limited how far apart two instructions could be in the sequential trace and still be scheduled in the same parallel instruction. They both concluded that instructions must be drawn from regions far apart in order to achieve significant amounts of parallelism.

Wilson and Lam studied the way control flow limits parallelism [13]. They demonstrated that substantially higher parallelism can be achieved by relaxing the constraints imposed by control flow on parallelism using control-dependence analysis, executing multiple flows of control simultaneously, and performing speculative execution. They tested six SPEC89 programs and 4 other programs, running each program on a MIPS R3000 for up to 100 million instructions.

7. Conclusions

In this paper, we have presented a study of program parallelism and provided some answers to questions regarding the limits of parallelism and its smoothability.

We have reported on the construction of SITA, a testbed that was used to work with a wide variety of architecture models. SITA was designed to be able to perform experiments on complete traces for reasonably large benchmarks. This allowed us to experiment with both standard benchmark programs and a real speech application.

By examining an Omniscient Oracle and specializations of this oracle, we were able to study key features that are important in finding large amounts of fine-grain parallelism. These results showed that the power of branch and jump prediction is very important, especially for programs with irregular control flow. This confirms the results of previous experiments. In particular, we found disappointingly low amounts of parallelism for some of the irregular programs under the Fine Dataflow model. Other studies have seen similar results. However, some applications, like `tex`, intuitively seem to have much more potential parallelism than found by our Fine Dataflow model (5.31) or Lam and Wilson's similar Multithreaded model with control-dependence analysis (6.18).

This has important implications for future directions in architecture. It is sometimes believed that to exploit maximum parallelism, we only need to rewrite existing algorithms in a better language, such as a functional language, so that an efficient compiler can extract all the available parallelism without being burdened by such sequential artifacts as memory reuse. But the Fine Dataflow model gets poor results, even though it eliminates false data dependencies and represents what could be achieved by an efficient dataflow machine running well-compiled programs.

This would suggest that in many cases, large-scale parallelism will not be achieved merely by rewriting existing imperative-language programs in different languages. They must be redesigned completely, starting at the algorithmic level. Whether this will require the programmer to write programs with an explicit parallel machine model in mind, or to use a more abstract programming paradigm, is an interesting, but entirely different, area of research.

If such changes are impractical, then one should consider some sort of speculation for programs with irregular control flow. We showed that this can significantly improve program performance.

Our experiments also showed that restricting the Oracle by making it frugal (no memory renaming) resulted in reducing the parallelism dramatically. As part of this set of tests, we looked at the effect of allowing only stack renaming, and showed that this is a useful feature for many programs. For other programs, however, stack renaming is not enough, and heap renaming is also required. This indicates that further work at both the compiler and architecture level must be undertaken to remove the memory reuse bottleneck.

Smoothability has been demonstrated to be an interesting characteristic of a program's parallelism. We reported the observation that all programs under test demonstrated smoothability better than 60%. We also found that while adding memory latency reduces the upper bound on parallelism, the parallelism obtained is still quite smoothable. Thus, there is good hope for mapping the available parallelism onto finite resources, and that multithreading or dataflow scheduling of operations can be used to tolerate the latencies of remote memory accesses.

Our analyzer has proven to be a valuable experimental tool, and many useful extensions are possible. For future work, we plan to extend SITA in several ways. We plan to add ordering constraints to the scheduler, so that we can measure the effects of various multithreading scheduling strategies. Also, we want to connect the testbed to our McCAT compiler [8] so that we can add parameters relating to the real alias analyses that can be performed by a parallelizing compiler.

Appendix: An Experimental Testbed

The SITA analyzer consists of two parts. The first part, the decoder, takes the stream output generated by the Spy trace generator [10], decodes the opcode and other information, performs basic block flow analysis, and derives the relevant dependence data. The second part, the scheduler, packs the operations into PIs based on this data. The scheduler can run multiple models simultaneously, provided there is enough memory.

Section 2.1 talks about building a dependence graph for the entire program. Such an undertaking would be out of the question for benchmarks involving billions of

Register	Read	Write
⋮	⋮	⋮
Int. register 73	$i + 3$	$i + 3$
Int. register 74	$i - 3$	i
Int. register 75	$i - 3$	i
Int. register 76	$i - 1$	$i + 2$
⋮	⋮	⋮
Int. cond. codes	$i + 3$	$i + 3$
FP register 0	$i + 1$	$i + 1$
FP register 1	$i + 1$	$i + 1$
FP register 2	$i + 2$	$i + 2$
⋮	⋮	⋮

Figure 17: Example state of SITA scheduler.

operations. Fortunately, since the trace is generated by a sequential thread of control, it is only necessary to store the dependence information relative to the last access of each storage location. Thus, the amount of memory needed to record and compute dependencies is proportional to the total number of locations used, *not* the total number of *times* they are used.

A table records the earliest PI in which a given storage location can be read and written. Figure 17 shows what the table would look like after the first iteration of the loop in Section 2.1, assuming it is scheduled as shown in the left half of Figure 2. The Sparc processor has multiple register windows, so SITA has an entry for each *physical* register and performs the mapping at run time. (The number of physical register windows can be selected by the user.) In this example, window registers 9–12 (%o1--%o4) are mapped to physical registers 73–76. Furthermore, it is assumed in this example that the array base addresses (%o2--%o4) are created in PI_{i-1}.

When the second occurrence of S1 is encountered in the trace, the decoder will see that it is dependent on writing FP register 0, and reading physical registers 73 and 74 and the memory location read by the load. The maximum of all the corresponding entries in the table is $i + 3$. If the branch were predicted correctly, then the operation could be packed into PI_{i+3}. However, since there is no branch prediction with this example, the operation must go into PI_{i+4}, because the scheduler also keeps track of the most recent barrier. Once the operation has been packed, the read and write columns for FP register 0 are updated with $i + 5$, and the write columns for physical registers 73 and 74 are changed to $i + 4$.

If there is no memory disambiguation, then a single entry in the table represents all memory accesses. Otherwise, there must be a separate entry for each unit of memory. This is done using a complex dynamic data structure consisting of a hash table of linked lists of tables corresponding to individual pages of memory. The lower bits of the page number are used to hash the entries. Renaming, for both register and memory use, is done by ignoring the write component of the table entries. For models with partial memory renaming (e.g., the Tree Oracle), the decoder uses the memory address to determine if it is in the stack or the heap.

If one of the dataflow models is used, then barriers corresponding to conditional branches are kept on a stack. As conditional branches are scheduled, barriers are added to the stack and remain there until all dependent blocks have been executed, after which they are removed. A stack is sufficient to keep all live barrier information [21]. If branch prediction is used, the 2-bit count for that branch is used to derive the *predicted* branch outcome, which is compared to the *actual* outcome revealed in the trace. If prediction is correct, the barrier is marked as such. When an instruction is to be scheduled, the stack is searched top-down for the first barrier, which corresponds to a mispredicted branch on which it is control-dependent.

A finite processor count requires a table of how many operations are packed into each PI. Two-level paging is used to organize the table. For very long runs, the page table can become huge, so SITA performs optimizations such as freeing up the storage whenever all the PIs on a page are filled to their limits.

Acknowledgment

This research was supported by Micronet and the Natural Science and Engineering Research Council (NSERC), both funded by the Government of Canada. The authors would also like to thank Gordon Irlam for making his SPA (Sparc Performance Analyzer) tools [10] publicly available, and for giving technical assistance. The Spy trace generator, part of the SPA package, was an essential link in our experimental testbed.

References

[1] Arvind and K.P. Gostelow, "The U-Interpreter," *Computer*, Vol. 15, No. 2, February 1982, pp. 42–49.

[2] T.M. Austin and G.S. Sohi, "Dynamic Dependence Analysis of Ordinary Programs," *Proceedings of the 19th Annual International Symposium on Computer Architecture*, Gold Coast, Australia, May 1992, pp. 342–351.

[3] M. Butler et al., "Single Instruction Stream Parallelism Is Greater than Two," *Proceedings of the 18th Annual International Symposium on Computer Architecture*, Toronto, Ontario, May 1991, pp. 276–286.

[4] D.E. Culler, A. Sah, K.E. Schauser, T. von Eicken, and J. Wawrzynek, "Fine-grain Parallelism with Minimal Hardware Support: A Compiler-Controlled Threaded Abstract Machine," *Proceedings of the Fourth International Conference on Architectural Support for Programming Languages and Operating Systems*, Santa Clara, California, April 1991, pp. 164–175.

[5] J.B. Dennis and G.R. Gao, "An Efficient Pipelined Dataflow Processor Architecture," *Proceedings of Supercomputing '88*, Orlando, Florida, November 1988, pp. 368–373.

[6] J.T. Feo, D.C. Cann, and R.R. Oldehoeft, "A Report on the SISAL Language Project," *Journal of Parallel and Distributed Computing*, Vol. 10, No. 4, December 1990, pp. 349–366.

[7] J.-L. Gaudiot and L. Bic, Eds., *Advanced Topics in Data-Flow Computing*, Englewood Cliffs, New Jersey: Prentice-Hall, 1991. Book contains papers presented at the First Workshop on Data-Flow Computing, Eilat, Israel, May 1989.

[8] L. Hendren et al., "Designing the McCAT Compiler Based on a Family of Structured Intermediate Representations," *Proceedings of the 5th International Workshop on Languages and Compilers for Parallel Computing*, New Haven, Connecticut, August 1992, pp. 406–420, Berlin: Springer-Verlag, No. 757 in Lecture Notes in Computer Science. Published in 1993.

[9] R.A. Iannucci, G.R. Gao, R.H. Halstead, Jr., and B. Smith, Eds., *Multithreaded Computer Architecture: A Summary of the State of the Art*, Norwell, Massachusetts: Kluwer Academic Publishers, 1994. Book contains papers presented at the Workshop on Multithreaded Computers, Albuquerque, New Mexico, November 1991.

[10] G. Irlam, "Spa," World-Wide Web page URL: http://www.base.com/gordoni/spa.html.

[11] D.J. Kuck, Y. Muraoka, and S.-C. Chen, "On the Number of Operations Simultaneously Executable in Fortran-Like Programs and Their Resulting Speedup," *IEEE Transactions on Computers*, Vol. 21, No. 12, December 1972, pp. 1293–1310.

[12] M. Kumar, "Measuring Parallelism in Computation-Intensive Scientific/Engineering Applications," *IEEE Transactions on Computers*, Vol. 37, No. 9, September 1988, pp. 1088–1098.

[13] M.S. Lam and R.P. Wilson, "Limits of Control Flow on Parallelism," *Proceedings of the 19th Annual International Symposium on Computer Architecture*, Gold Coast, Australia, May 1992, pp. 46–57.

[14] A. Nicolau and J.A. Fisher, "Measuring the Parallelism Available for Very Long Instruction Word Architectures," *IEEE Transactions on Computers*, Vol. 33, No. 11, November 1984, pp. 968–976.

[15] R.S. Nikhil and Arvind, "Can Dataflow Subsume Von Neumann Computing?" *Proceedings of the 16th Annual International Symposium on Computer Architecture*, Jerusalem, Israel, May–June 1989, pp. 262–272.

[16] B. Olsson, R. Montoye, P. Markstein, and M. NguyunPhu, "RISC System/6000 Floating-Point Unit," *IBM RISC System/6000 Technology*, Mamata Misra, Ed. International Business Machines Corporation, Order No. SA23-2619, 1990, pp. 34–42.

[17] J. Rumbaugh, "A Data Flow Multiprocessor," *IEEE Transactions on Computers*, Vol. 26, No. 2, February 1977, pp. 138–146.

[18] J.E. Smith, "A Study of Branch Prediction Strategies," *Proceedings of the 8th Annual Symposium on Computer Architecture*, Minneapolis, Minnesota, May 1981, pp. 135–148.

[19] K.B. Theobald, G.R. Gao, and L.J. Hendren, "On the Limits of Program Parallelism and its Smoothability," ACAPS Technical Memo 40, School of Computer Science, McGill University, Montréal, Québec, June 1992. FTP from ftp-acaps.cs.mcgill.ca: /pub/doc/memos.

[20] K.B. Theobald, G.R. Gao, and L.J. Hendren, "On the Limits of Program Parallelism and its Smoothability," *Proceedings of the 25th Annual International Symposium on Microarchitecture*, Portland, Oregon, December 1992, pp. 10–19.

[21] K.B. Theobald, G.R. Gao, and L.J. Hendren, "Speculative Execution and Branch Prediction on Parallel Machines," ACAPS Technical Memo 57, School of Computer Science, McGill University, Montréal, Québec, December 1992. FTP from ftp-acaps.cs.mcgill.ca: /pub/doc/memos.

[22] K.B. Theobald, G.R. Gao, and L.J. Hendren, "Speculative Execution and Branch Prediction on Parallel Machines," *Conference Proceedings, 1993 International Conference on Supercomputing*, Tokyo, Japan, July 1993, pp. 77–86.

[23] G.S. Tjaden and M.J. Flynn, "Detection and Parallel Execution of Independent Instructions," *IEEE Transactions on Computers*, Vol. 19, No. 10, October 1970, pp. 889–895.

[24] D.W. Wall, "Limits of Instruction-Level Parallelism," *Proceedings of the Fourth International Conference on Architectural Support for Programming Languages and Operating Systems*, Santa Clara, California, April 1991, pp. 176–188.

The Dataflow Parallelism of FFT

A.P.W. Böhm
Computer Science Department
Colorado State University

R.E. Hiromoto
Division of Mathematics, Computer Science and Statistics
The University of Texas at San Antonio

1. Introduction

The notion of a high-level parallel programming language that automatically extracts the available parallelism of a program has been of research interest to a number of functional language groups around the world. The development and study of functional languages have been justified not only as a means to increase productivity by freeing the programmer from complex, machine dependent, explicitly parallel constructs thereby eliminating the bugs and booby traps of synchronization errors, but also to increase computational performance by the exploitation of fine-grain parallelism. Significant developments within the last few years may now allow us to realistically examine the claims made by the functional language community. Functional language and compilation research has resulted in several powerful, inherently parallel programming languages. Notable among these is Id, the work of Arvind's Computation Structures Group at MIT [11]. Based on the dataflow computational model, Id has a functional and deterministic subset, yet is a completely general purpose language supporting synchronizing data structures, and side-effects.

Few fine-grain dataflow computer systems have been developed in the past. One of the first research prototypes was designed and built at the University of Manchester [5]. This project resulted in identifying many important architectural issues in the design of support hardware for the dataflow execution model. The Manchester group used the purely functional Streams and Iteration in a Single-Assignment Language (SISAL) [9] and produced a SISAL compiler generating efficient dataflow code [4]. A more ambitious purely fine-grain dataflow project has resulted in the Sigma-1, a large dataflow system with 128 processing elements built at the Electro-Technical Laboratory (ETL) in Tsukuba, Japan [16]. From this and other dataflow experiences, a somewhat coarser-grain dataflow model has emerged and has many researchers very hopeful of its success. Today, several research groups are seriously involved with building prototypes of these multithreaded architectures such as ETL's EM-4 [14] and EM-5 [15], and Motorola and MIT's Monsoon [18] and *T [12].

With dataflow languages, compiler technology, and hardware maturing and becoming available for use, the opportunity to critically evaluate the advantages claimed by functional language and dataflow advocates has now become feasible.

In this paper we develop and analyze the simulated performance of codes for the Fast Fourier Transform (FFT) written in Id. The FFT application is of interest because of its computational parallelism, its requirement for global communication, and its array element data dependencies. We use the parallel profiling simulator Id World

This work was supported in part by NSF Grant MIP-9113268 and grant YCM002 from Motorola Inc.

to study the dataflow performance of various implementations. Our approach is *comparative*. We study two approaches, a recursive and an iterative one, and examine the effect of a variety of implementations. We contend that only through such comparative evaluations can significant insight be gained in the computational and structural details of functional algorithms.

2. Measures of Parallelism

The attractiveness of the dataflow model of computation is that all forms of parallelism can be expressed in it, which makes dataflow a suitable environment for the analysis of parallel algorithms, their sequential threads, and their resource requirements [8], [17]. Initial evaluation of a dataflow program is performed using the *Id World* simulator, which collects statistics while it executes the code [10]. Id World simulates the behavior of the "Tagged Token Dataflow Architecture" [2].

Simulation proceeds in discrete *time steps*, during which all instructions for which all data is available are executed. It is assumed that every instruction executes and sends its resulting data to its successor instructions in exactly one time step. Important machine level phenomena such as the effect of global communication time on the computation are not addressed when executing programs on the simulator. This mode of simulation is called *idealized execution*. Two time-related measurements are recorded: the *total work* S_1 is the total number of instructions executed; and the *critical path length* S_∞ is the total number of time steps required. The parallelism of the program is displayed in an *(ideal) parallelism profile* by plotting the number of executed instructions at each time step. In *limited parallelism mode* the simulator produces profiles where the number of instructions that can execute in one time step is bounded by a parameter p. The simulator just picks the first p-enabled instructions off its ready queue. Notice that the behavior of the simulation may vary depending on the choice of the enabled instructions. The related measure S_p gives the total number of time steps in this execution mode.

Given an input array size of n, the time complexity of the FFT algorithm is, as is well known, $O(n.\log(n))$. Any real parallel machine provides a fixed amount of parallelism, and will therefore not incur an order of magnitude speedup, and, thus, execute the FFT algorithm at best in $O(n.\log(n))$ time. In our idealized execution model, we allow all enabled instructions to execute in parallel and thus assume that there is always enough "machine" parallelism available. So where the measure S_1 coincides with the sequential time measure, the S_∞ measure gives an upper bound on the best possible execution time on a sufficiently parallel machine.

In the recursive FFT algorithm, the input array is shuffled into two arrays containing the odd and even elements. FFT is recursively applied to the two arrays, and the resulting arrays are recombined into the final result. $O(n)$ arrays are allocated, 2 of size n, 4 of size $n/2$, etc. The total size of the allocated arrays is $O(n.\log(n))$, because there are $O(\log(n))$ stages each allocating k arrays of size n/k. For each array element that is allocated, there is a constant amount of work to calculate its value, so there is $O(n.\log(n))$ total work. In a parallel implementation with sufficient machine parallelism, one would expect a critical path length of $O(\log(n))$ and no sequential stretches, as all elements of the array can be shuffled into place in parallel, and in the recombination two elements of the resulting array data depend on two elements of arrays from a previous stage.

```
def shuffle V =
 {(_,SizeV) = bounds V ; Mid = SizeV / 2 in
   ({ array(1, Mid) | [i] = V[(i*2)-1] || i <- 1 to Mid };
    { array(1, Mid) | [i] = V[(i*2)] || i <- 1 to Mid })
 };

def fft v =
 {(_,SizeV) = bounds V in
  if (SizeV == 1) then V else
  {(OddV,EvenV) = shuffle V ;
   fftO = fft OddV; fftE = fft EvenV;
   Mid = SizeV / 2; X = TwoPi / SizeV;
   Coeff = {array(1, Mid)
    | [i] = Cmplx(cos(X*(i-1))) (-sin(X*(i-1))) || i <- 1 to Mid};
   Prod = { array(1, Mid)
    | [i] = Cmplx_Mul Coeff[i] fftE[i] || i <- 1 to Mid}
   in
    {array(1,SizeV)
      | [i] = Cmplx_Add fftO[i] Prod[i] || i <- 1 to Mid
      | [Mid+i] = Cmplx_Sub fftO[i] Prod[i] || i <- 1 to Mid
    }
  }
 };
```

Figure 1: Recursive FFT.

We use the complexity of the algorithm, and the potential speedup derived from the data dependencies in the algorithm, as a yardstick for the performance of the language, compiler, and simulated machine architecture. As we will see in the next section, the straightforward recursive FFT algorithm written in Id and compiled for the TTDA has an S_∞ measure that is far from the expected $O(\log(n))$.

3. Recursive FFT

Figure 1 shows a first version of a recursive formulation of FFT in Id, straight from the mathematical definition.

In the *fft* function, recursive invocations are applied to the odd and even elements of *V* until the size of *V* is one. The data dependencies occurring in the recombination of smaller arrays into larger ones form "butterfly" patterns. In the program text in Figure 1, the definitions of the arrays *Coeff*, *Prod* , and the result of *fft* implement this recombination. The only Id language feature that needs some explanation is *array comprehension*:

$$\{array\langle bounds\rangle(|\langle target\rangle = \langle expression\rangle||\langle generator\rangle)*\}$$

In *bounds* the dimension and size of the resulting array are declared. Each *target*, *expression*, *generator* triple creates a loop: *for generator array[target] = expression*.

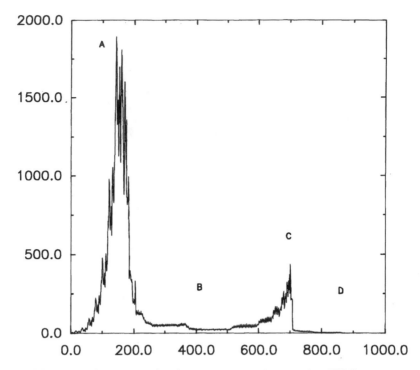

Figure 2: Ideal parallelism profile for unoptimized recursive FFT, $SizeV = 128$.

The parallelism profile in Figure 2 is the result of running the program in Figure 1 ($SizeV = 128$) on the Id world simulator, and is far from what is expected from the complexity and speedup measures discussed above. Observe that first there is explosive divide and conquer parallelism (A) peaking at 1900, followed by (B) a stretch of low parallelism of about 20. A second less significant burst of parallelism (C) follows, which dies down to an almost sequential tail (D). For larger problems, the two sequential stretches B and D are observed to dominate more and more. This is clearly disappointing given the available computational parallelism. We know that the FFT program takes $O(\log(SizeV))$ parallel steps to unfold all *fft* and *shuffle* functions, which accounts for the first burst (A) of the divide and conquer parallelism. Once the functions have been unfolded, the loops in the array comprehensions dictate the parallelism and consequently the speed of the computation.

4. Analysis of Loops and Double Recursion

In order to understand and improve the behavior of the recursive *fft* function, we need to study the dynamics of loops and double recursion. We, therefore, create four simple functions that can be analyzed thoroughly. Consider the following functions and their performance found in Table 1. The function *singleloop* is a while loop with a serial data dependence from one loop body to the next; *doubleloop* is a doubly nested loop. The function *createarray* creates an array using an array comprehension; the function *divco* is a divide and conquer type recursive function.

Function	m	n	S_1	S_∞
Singleloop		1	27	16
		2	34	21
		3	41	26
Doubleloop	1	10	140	80
	2	10	251	85
	3	10	362	90
	1	20	210	130
	2	20	391	135
	3	20	572	140
Createarray		16	223	101
		32	399	181
		64	751	342
		256	2,863	1,301
Divco		1	13	7
		2	56	19
		4	142	31
		8	314	43
		16	658	55

Table 1: Behavior of loops and recursion.

```
def singleloop n =
 {s=0 in {while s < n do next s=s+1; finally s}};

def doubleloop m n =
 {s=0; r=0 in
  {while s < m do next s = s + 1; next r = r + singleloop n;
   finally r}
};

def createarray n =
 { array (1,n) | [i] = i || i <- 1 to n };

def divco n =
 if (n == 1) then 1 else divco (n/2) + divco (n/2);
```

Analysis of S_1 and S_∞ for these programs brings us to the following observation. In the mapping from Id to Tagged Token Dataflow Code, it takes five steps along the critical path to spawn a loop, no matter whether it is an inner loop, an outer loop, or a loop in an array comprehension. We call the number of steps along the critical path to spawn a loop the *loop rate*. The loop rate plays an important role in the parallelism of a program: a high loop rate decreases parallelism. Take the function *doubleloop* as an example. The inner loop is almost sequential and its critical path length can be varied by varying n. The outer loop spawns inner loops every *loop rate* time steps, so the inner loops are skewed on top of each other as in Figure 3. The number of inner loops that run in parallel is $S_\infty(inner\ loop)/loop\ rate$. Note that this is independent of the total number of inner loops.

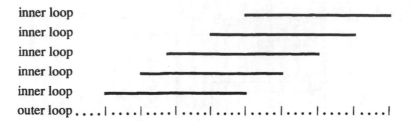

Figure 3: Effect of loop rate on parallelism.

Divide and conquer programs do not suffer from this skewing effect, as exemplified by the function *divco*, where S_1 grows linearly and S_∞ grows logarithmically with n.

We are now in a position to explain the parallelism profile in Figure 2. While the dynamic call tree unrolls in $O(\log(SizeV))$ time steps (phase A), the *shuffles* in the first *fft* produce one element every *loop rate* time steps. This results in a producer/consumer timing mismatch. The array elements are not all available at the moment the dynamic call tree is ready to manipulate them. The elements are put in place during the $O(\log(SizeV))$ shuffle stages without data dependence problems. In the $O(\log(SizeV))$ butterfly stages, the elements must wait to be combined with their corresponding elements that are not yet available. Phase B starts after the call tree is unrolled, and the program behaves very much like the *doubleloop* function with an inner loop of length $O(\log(SizeV))$. In this case the "inner loop" is spread over a number of butterfly stages. The parallelism in phase B is therefore $O(\log(SizeV))$ instead of the expected $O(SizeV)$. Phase B ends when the last array element has been shuffled into place. The remaining butterfly recombination stages can now execute in divide and conquer fashion (phase C). The sequential tail (phase D) is caused by the array comprehension in *fft* that generates the final array.

The solution to the problem is to spawn loops fast enough so that they do not cause unnecessary delay. This has been recognized by a number of dataflow groups who invented special instructions, very similar to vector instructions, to rapidly create parallel workload, especially in loops. Examples of these instructions are iterative instructions in the Manchester Dataflow Machine [3] and the CSIRAC-II Dataflow Machine [6], and the repeat mechanism in the Epsilon-2 machine [7]. Neither the tagged token dataflow machine nor the Monsoon machine [18] have this type of instruction. This was a design decision based on the RISC argument that these instructions cause pipeline bubbles [3].

```
def chunkarray n chunk =
{array(1,n) | [i] = i || j ← 1 to n by chunk &
 i ← j to j +(chunk-1)};
```

The loop delay problem can be addressed by optimizing compilation, such as loop unrolling. Therefore, it is still possible, although at a higher cost in terms of instruction counts, to create array elements at a higher rate. As stated, this should and can best be done by an optimizing compiler. However, as this optimization is not available in the current Id compiler, we resort to a rather inelegant programming trick similar to *strip-mining* [19] in a vector context. As an example, compare the function *createarray* in Table1 to a strip-mined version *chunkarray* in Table 2 where the depth of the loop unrolling is defined by $chunk = 16$.

Function	n	S_1	S_∞
Chunkarray	16	277	118
	32	504	123
	64	958	133
	256	3,682	198

Table 2: S_1 and S_∞ of a strip-mined loop.

```
def fft V RofU =
    (_,SizeV) = bounds V; (_,OrgSize) = bounds RofU in
    if (SizeV == 1) then V else
    {(OddV,EvenV) = shuffle V ;
     fftO = fft OddV ; fftE = fft EvenV ;
     m = SizeV / 2 ; X = TwoPi / SizeV ; step = OrgSize / m;
     R = 1D_I_array (1, SizeV)
    in if m > 16 then
        {for j <- 1 to m by 16 do {for i <- j to j+15 do
         prod = Cmplx_Mul RofU[((i-1)*step)+1] fftE[i];
         R[i] = Cmplx_Add fftO[i] prod;
         R[m+i] = Cmplx_Sub fftO[i] prod}
         finally R}
        else
        {for i <- 1 to m do
         prod = Cmplx_Mul RofU[((i-1)*step)+1] fftE[i];
         R[i] = Cmplx_Add fftO[i] prod;
         R[m+i] = Cmplx_Sub fftO[i] prod
         finally R} } }
```

Figure 4: Optimized recursive FFT.

Where in function *createarray* defined above the array elements are created at the loop rate, *chunk* array elements are created per *loop rate* in function *chunkarray*. Because we have strip-mined by hand, this comes at the cost of a higher S_1 value.

Although the array comprehensions in *fft* and *shuffle* (Figure 1) make for an elegant and functional programming style, they lack expressive power: it is impossible to derive two or more values in the expression part of the comprehension and assign these to two or more targets in the array. This is exactly what we would like to do in the butterfly part of the *fft* function. In order to avoid recomputation of the operands of the butterfly combine operation, we are forced to put intermediate results in array *Prod*. We can avoid doing this extra work by rewriting the butterfly part of *fft* using a loop instead of an array comprehension. It is standard in the FFT algorithm to table the roots of unity once in the main function calling *fft*. The version of *fft* in Figure 4 is strip-mined with a chunk size 16; it performs the recombination in a loop instead of an array comprehension, and retrieves the roots of unity from a table *RofU*.

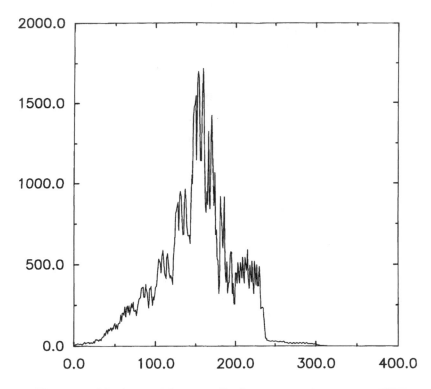

Figure 5: Ideal parallelism profile for optimized recursive FFT.

5. Strip-Mining and Operator Strength Reduction

In terms of total work, there are often two extreme ways to compute a certain function: *parallel but costly* versus *sequential but cheap*. An example is the computation of the roots of unity. The parallel way is to compute each root independently using sin and cos functions. The sequential way is to derive a recurrence relation, expressing the $(n + 1)$-th root as a function of the n-th root, a technique called *operator strength reduction*. A data dependence is introduced, but the resulting implementation is more efficient in terms of S_1. Ideally, we would like to be able to balance the amount of parallelism against S_1. This can be achieved by strip-mining: the outer loop uses the parallel data-independent method to start off inner loops using the recurrence relation. The code in Figure 6 computes the roots of unity in this manner. Figure 5 shows the resulting parallelism profile for FFT with $SizeV = 128$. The critical path length is now logarithmic, and the two sequential stretches B and D have disappeared.

6. Limited Machine Parallelism

The ideal parallelism profiles in both Figures 1 and 5 show a peak parallelism much higher than the parallelism available in say a four processor dataflow machine. Some of this excess parallelism is needed to hide latencies caused by remote memory references. Still, one could ask whether it is necessary to enhance the parallelism in these programs. We claim that this is the case because the *stretches of low, not high, parallelism govern the machine behavior*. This is nothing more than Amdahl's law. To

```
h = n/2;
theta = -TwoPi/ n;
RofU = 1D_I_array (1, h);
seed = cmplx(-2.0*((sin(0.5*theta))^2)) ( sin theta);
 {for j <- 1 to h by chunk do
  { RofU[j] = cmplx (cos (-theta*(j-1))) (-sin (-theta*(j-1))) in
    {for i <- j+1 to j+chunk-1 do
       RofU[i] = Cmplx_Add (Cmplx_Mul seed RofU[i-1]) RofU[i-1]
 }} }
```

Figure 6: Balancing efficiency and parallelism.

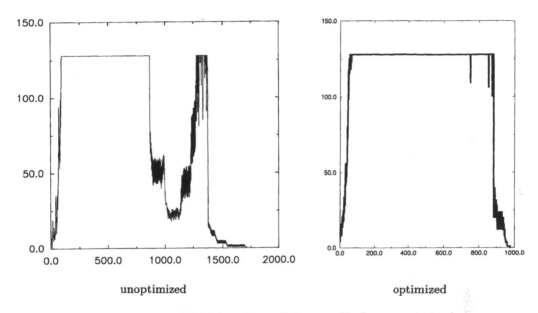

unoptimized   optimized

Figure 7: 128-fold limited parallelism profile for unoptimized
and optimized recursive FFT, $SizeV = 128$.

exemplify this, Figure 7 shows the limited parallelism profiles of the original recursive FFT algorithm (left) and the optimized version (right) for $SizeV = 128$ and $p = 128$. Notice that the critical path in the improved version is much (30%) shorter than the unoptimized version. Of course, both critical path lengths do increase as the available parallelism is decreased. Also notice the serious dent in parallelism in the profile, which has all but disappeared in the profile of the improved program.

7. Iterative FFT

In the iterative FFT algorithm, bit reversal of the index, instead of repeated shuffling, puts the array elements in the required place. Again we balance efficiency and parallelism by creating a nested loop, where the outer loop provides the parallelism and the inner loop the efficiency. The outer loop starts a sequence by just reversing the bits of the index: $B[bitrevJ] = A[J]$ and the inner loop uses a recurrence:

Method	Recursive (unoptimized)		Recursive		Iterative	
SizeV	S_1	S_∞	S_1	S_∞	S_1	S_∞
16	10,800	226	10,038	202	9,072	251
32	25,588	310	22,613	262	20,159	293
64	59,060	557	50,046	298	44,070	352
128	133,796	1,044	109,716	330	96,066	502

Table 3: S_1 and S_∞ of FFT algorithms.

$bitrev(J + 1) = (bitrev J) +' 1$, where $+'$ increments a bit pattern going from left to right [13], as in the following function *itershuffle*.

```
def iter_shuffle A = {
    (_,n) = bounds A; j = 1; B = 1D_I_Array (1,n) in
    {for k <- 1 to n by chunk do {
    j = bitrev k n in
    {for i <- k to (k+chunk-1) do
      B[i] = A[j];
      next j = { m = div n 2 in
                  if ((m>=2) and (j>m))
                  then { while ((m >=2 ) and ( j>m )) do
                        next j = j-m; next m = div m 2
                      finally j+m }
                  else j+m }
    }}
    finally B}
}
```

The iterative FFT differs from the recursive one in another aspect: the intermediate values are kept in $\log(SizeV)$ equal sized arrays. The iterative program is, apart from the strip-mining, an Id translation of the code in [13].

Table 3 gives S_1 and S_∞ values of the recursive and iterative FFT algorithms. The first column shows the figures for the initial recursive algorithm, the second and third columns show the results of the optimized recursive and iterative versions of the algorithm where the chunk sizes for strip-mining have been optimally chosen. Interestingly, there is no clear winner between the optimized cases. The optimized recursive algorithm has the shortest critical path, whereas the optimized iterative algorithm executes the smallest number of instructions. The instruction counts in this paper are those of the MIT Tagged Token Dataflow Architecture, the relative efficiency of which has been reported in [1].

8. Conclusion

We have used the notions of complexity and expected speedup of a parallel algorithm to evaluate the simulated behavior of two FFT algorithms. By applying this analysis, we were led to transform our initial FFT algorithms using well-understood conventional techniques such as strip-mining and operator strength reductions. Amdahl's law states that the speedup behavior of a parallel program is governed by its *sequential* parts, not its parallel parts. This means that even if there is a lot of parallelism in a program, or if it is "intuitively clear" how to parallelize a program, as is the case in FFT, we need to analyze it, study its sequential threads, and learn how to remove these. The Id World tools make it possible to identify and measure the sequential threads of a program. The results presented in this paper indicate that important improvements in the parallelism and total work efficiency can be achieved by striving for an actual parallelism profile that is in accordance with the complexity and expected speedup of the parallel algorithm.

The strengths of functional languages include their machine independence and their implicit expression of parallelism. This provides for portable parallel code. However, the development of *efficient parallel code* is as intellectually challenging for the functional programming paradigm as it is for the imperative paradigm. Implicit parallel programming does not replace the intelligent design and implementation of algorithms. An advantage of the functional, hence implicit, parallel programming approach is that even the optimizations are independent of the number of processors. Another advantage is that the non-sequential nature of the language provides a better starting point from which to tune codes for execution on parallel hardware.

References

[1] Arvind, D.E. Culler, and K. Ekanadham, *The Price of Asynchronous Parallelism: An Analysis of Dataflow Architectures*, C.R. Jesshope and K.D. Reinartz, Eds., CONPAR 88, Cambridge University Press, 1989, pp. 541–555.

[2] Arvind and R.A. Ianucci, *Instruction Set Definition for a Tagged Token Dataflow Machine*, LCS, MIT, 1983.

[3] A.P.W. Böhm and J.R. Gurd, "Iterative Instructions in the Manchester Dataflow Computer," *IEEE Transactions on Parallel and Distributed Systems*, Vol. 1, No. 2, April 1990, pp. 129–139.

[4] A.P.W. Böhm and J. Sargeant, "Code Optimisation for Tagged Token Dataflow Machines," *IEEE Transactions on Computers*, Vol. 38, No. 1, January 1989.

[5] A.P.W. Böhm, J.R. Gurd, and C.C. Kirkham, "The Manchester Dataflow Computing System," in *Experimental Parallel Computing Architectures*, J. Dongarra Ed., North Holland, 1987, pp. 177–219.

[6] G.K. Egan, N.J. Webb, and A.P.W. Böhm, "Some Architectural Features of the CSIRAC II Dataflow Computer," in *Advanced Topics in Data-Flow Computing*, J.L. Gaudiot and L. Bic, Eds., Prentice Hall, 1990.

[7] V. Grafe et al., "The Epsilon Project," in *Advanced Topics in Data-Flow Computing*, J.L. Gaudiot and L. Bic, Eds., Prentice Hall, 1990.

[8] J.R. Gurd, A.P.W. Böhm, and Y.M. Teo, "Performance Issues in Dataflow Machines," *Future Generation Computer Systems*, Vol. 3, 1987, pp. 285–297.

[9] J.R. McGraw et al., *SISAL—Streams and Iteration in a Single-Assignment Language*, Lawrence Livermore National Laboratory, M-146, 93, January 1985.

[10] D.R. Morais, *ID World: An Environment for the Development of Dataflow Programs Written in ID*, MIT LCS TR-365, May 1986.

[11] R.S. Nikhil, *Id (version 90.0) Reference Manual*, TR CSG Memo 284-1, MIT LCS, 1990.

[12] R.S. Nikhil, G.M. Papadopolous, and Arvind, **T: a Killer Micro for a Brave New World*, Computational Structures Group Memo 325, MIT, 1991.

[13] W.H. Press et al., *Numerical Recipes, the Art of Scientific Programming*, Cambridge University Press.

[14] S. Sakai et al., "An Architecture of a Dataflow Single Chip Processor," *Proceedings of the 1989 International Symposium on Computer Architecture*, Eilat, ACM, 1989, pp. 46–53.

[15] S. Sakai, Y. Kodoma, and Y. Yamaguchi, *Architectural Design of a Parallel Supercomputer EM-5*, JSPP91, May 1991.

[16] T. Shimada et al., "Evaluation of a Prototype Data Flow Processor of the SIGMA-1 for Scientific Computations," *Proceedings 13th International Symposium on Computer Architecture*, June 1986, pp. 226–234.

[17] Y.M. Teo and A.P.W. Böhm, "Resource Management in Dataflow Computers with Iterative Instructions," in *Advanced Topics in Data-Flow Computing*, J.L. Gaudiot and L. Bic, Eds., Prentice Hall, 1990.

[18] K.R. Traub, G.M. Papadopoulos, M.J. Beckerle, J.E. Hicks, and J. Young, "Overview of the Monsoon Project," *ICCD91*, IEEE, Oct. 1991, pp. 150–155.

[19] M. Wolfe, *Optimizing Supercompilers for Supercomputers*, MIT Press, 1989.

Locality in the Dataflow Paradigm

Israel Gottlieb and Liel Biran
Department of Mathematics and Computer Science
Bar Ilan University
Ramat Gan, Israel 52100

Current Dataflow and Hybrid multiprocessor designs employ specialized hardware to support efficient switching between large numbers of activities. The performance of such machines however, to the extent that they have been realized, remains less than cost effective. Much of the problem has been attributed to a lack of locality among the activities being held at readiness in the processor. However, the notion of locality, as it is used in connection with uniprocessor memory reference behavior, does not readily apply to the parallel execution of programs.

This paper investigates the issue of locality under the assumptions of a multithreaded machine. In particular, we develop an applicable definition of locality and then define a model of thread execution which is intended to expose what potential for locality exists in a given execution. Our model is derived from the Dynamically Partitioned Dataflow (DPDF) architecture proposal, in which a special lookahead mechanism allows a processor to determine, on the fly, which successors of the current instruction are enabled.

We present results from simulations of the model and discuss their implications for performance improvements in current designs.

1. Introduction

Multithreaded processor designs (e.g., [1], [2], [4], [5]) are prescribed for multiprocessors as a way to achieve better processor utilization in an environment characterized by frequent remote operations. If multiple contexts can achieve close to full processor utilization, the assumption is that such multiple processors can hope to achieve effective speedup. These architectures have dedicated mechanisms for supporting heavy context switch traffic.

There are basically two types of events which typically would limit full utilization and for which context switching is prescribed:

1. Pipeline latency of the execution unit within the processor—a locally determined delay.

2. Remote access to common structure store—a globally determined delay.

In this paper, we examine these two levels in detail and consider the limiting effect of locality on the expectable increase in utilization. To this end, we first develop a model designed to reflect the engineerable limits of multithreading. In particular, the model

- will assume that sufficient contexts are maintained to tolerate all latency—including that of context switching itself.

- will employ a reasonably optimal knowledge of how execution should progress in order to maximize thread life. "Reasonably optimal" will be defined in the sequel.

Finally, we present data obtained from simulations of the model and discuss their implications.

2. Background

A basic model for assessing the effectiveness of multithreaded architectures was presented in [6]. The thrust of the model is that, for a remote access latency R, time between such accesses I and new Context Initiation time CI, one can achieve a utilization of

$$\frac{I}{I + CI} \tag{1}$$

by providing a *saturation* level of switchable threads. Saturation is achieved when the number of threads is

$$\left\lfloor \frac{R}{I + CI} \right\rfloor + 1. \tag{2}$$

This model however, does not consider the effect of having multiple contexts readily executable—on the *local cycle time*. Many active contexts means a larger local processor state and hence a slower machine cycle. We try to solve the problem of remote latency by bringing more of the execution space into the local processor—in effect taking the problem that was remote and bringing it home.

Culler et al. have begun to address this problem in the TAM model [1], by distinguishing resident, as opposed to non-resident frames and using the compiler to (hopefully) stay with execution of threads from the resident frame as long as possible.

In what follows, we examine more closely the cost of "bringing the problem home," i.e., the increase in local processor state to support multiple contexts. This issue has been referred to in the literature in different ways, most commonly as the need for "greater locality" in multithreaded execution. Many perceived ills associated with dataflow and related machines are often blamed on a lack of locality. The large number of readily accessible contexts is the obvious example. A related problem is the small number of registers usable by a thread, where the popular superscalar designs tout effective utilization of large register sets. To get at the bottom of this issue, we posed the question: assuming ideal conditions, *how much locality exists in parallel program behavior to exploit?*

The term "ideal conditions" needs to be made more precise, and we do so shortly. The thrust of the question, however, is straightforward. In the well-developed memory technology used in uniprocessors, locality is an empirical fact of program behavior which can be measured. For a typical reference window in uniprocessor execution, the number of distinct data items in that window is a small fraction of the size of the window; we need only insert a cache to trap those references and reap the benefits. This phenomena is essentially a feature of the way human beings write programs—at least von Neumann programs. In a non-von Neumann execution of a dataflow program, we have in any case eliminated a good deal of the correspondence between the way a program is written and the way it executes. How do we know locality is a fact of execution behavior under these circumstances? Indeed, what exactly do we mean by locality in a multithreaded execution. Consider that if our policy is to schedule as many parallel threads as are required to hide long and unpredictable latencies, then, since parallel processes necessarily operate on independent data, our policy is counter to locality by definition.

3. The Model

In current machines, a context is generally the group of instructions in a compiler generated partition; one, two, or three instructions in a Monsoon type machine, three to ten or more in a TAM-like partition. The instructions in a context may be data dependent, data independent, or any combination of the two. Our interest is to determine the inherent locality achievable in multithreaded execution; a closely related goal is to obtain the maximum possible number of switchable contexts for a given level of locality. To clarify these matters, we need clear definitions for three things: a *process space*, the number of switchable *threads* in a process space, and a measure of the *locality* of the threads in that space. The notion of process space we wish to use is similar to an execution instance of a code block. The instructions in a TAM frame are a good example of a process space. Code block type processes are fairly well understood and we shall not belabor their meaning. For the notions *thread* and *locality*, we shall give a more careful definition.

When a thread stalls for lack of operand, the instructions which we know are certain to be non-executable until that operand arrives, are precisely those on the *data dependent path* of the current instruction. To squeeze the maximum number of switchable contexts from a given process space therefore, we define.

Definition 3.1 *The number of threads in a given process space is equal to the number of instances of distinct paths in the dataflow graph for which execution has been initiated in that process space. The datum being transformed along the path of a thread is called the* Home datum *of that thread.*

Thus in our model, a thread is synonymous with a *path process*, the latter being understood to progress only along a data dependent path.

By locality, we shall mean a measure of the *state space* required to maintain a given set of switchable contexts. Again, we want an optimistic measure reflecting the maximum potential, so we ignore costs associated with communicating data between contexts, replication of operands etc., and define.

Definition 3.2 *The size of the locality for a given number of path processes is equal to the number of distinct data items required by those processes.*

The size of the locality required to maintain a set of threads can be thought of as related to the required size of the processor state, since we wish to have the processor switching between those threads. In the original dataflow architectures, the matching store corresponds directly to our definition of locality, but the large size of the store makes it incongruous to consider it as reflecting the processor state. The poor performance of these designs can be viewed as indicative that their processor state actually did include the matching store!

There is a natural relationship between definitions 3.1 and 3.2; generally, there is one datum associated with each path—the Home datum. Hence we denote the number of data in the state per path by H. This correspondence may not be exact, however, because the results of an instruction may be held in state for use by other threads even while the producing thread may have gone on to successor instructions and hence transformed its Home datum. These instances may be counted however (as we do in our simulation), and an exact value obtained for H.

For a given local state space, we want to know how much useful execution is supported by that space. So we define the *locality strength L*.

Definition 3.3

$$L = \frac{l}{H}$$

where l is the mean number of execution cycles per context initiation and H is the mean number of distinct data items maintained per path.

The value l can be thought of as the number of instructions a path process manages to execute before being switched out for lack of operand.[1] The metric L says that l instruction executions were obtained for a cost of H data space; stronger locality means more instructions executed per datum.

We can define a "hit rate"—similar to the measure used for uniprocessor caches

$$h_P = 1 - \frac{H}{l(b+1)}$$

where b is the fraction of instructions which are binary. The number of data required to execute l instructions is $l(b+1)$ and on average H must be brought into state to permit the l executions, so the rest are a "hit" to data already in state. More accurately, not all the H data are brought into state from the backing store—some are produced internal to the state. In what follows, however, we shall be concerned more directly with the total state space required in the processor. Rather than refine the hit rate metric, we shall take as a working assumption that the number of paths (threads) being held in processor state is exactly CI/l, i.e., enough to completely mask the latency of bringing a new thread into state from the backing store. This situation would be realized where a new context switch is initiated every l instructions—when a thread stalls for lack of operand, and that context becomes ready to execute in state CI instruction cycles after it is initiated. Thus our model assumes a pipeline of contexts in the process of being made active—from backing store into processor state, much like the execution pipeline or network pipeline for remote loads. Under these assumptions, the metric of interest is L. The relationship between L and the cost effectiveness of multithreading is developed more fully in Section 4.

To assess the full potential for locality, we should arrange for operations to proceed according to some optimal or near optimal ordering. This would tell us what is theoretically possible; computer architects/compiler designers could then apply their ingenuity to try and approach that limit. Finding the true optimal ordering however is NP complete [3]. A simulator based on such knowledge is therefore impractical, but any real machine is unlikely to make use of optimal knowledge for the same reason. Instead, we shall investigate a model which assumes a version of global knowledge, which could conceivably be achieved by an actual machine. Although necessarily speculative, the notion we have in mind is intended to closely reflect current understanding of the complexity limits for digital hardware. Specifically, *given a particular current state*, the model will optimally maximize locality, but it will not have such perfect knowledge of *how to change the state* where such change is required—the latter being equivalent to the NP complete scheduling problem. We describe these two levels of scheduling in more detail.

---

[1] This is not exact because more than one thread, as we have defined them, can be initiated within the processor state, for a single context switch. This will occur when an instruction has multiple successors which are unary or for which the second argument is also in state. Thus our notion of executions per CI is intended to subsume the potential for partitions such as dependence sets used in [2] and [1]. At the same time we count the data dependent paths deriving from the CI separately, reflecting the theoretical potential of switching between them on e.g., remote call.

Definition 3.4 *The* local processor state, *or simply "state" where otherwise clear, is defined by a set of paths for which execution has been initiated but not terminated, and a parameter δ. The value δ specifies the* lifetime *of instruction results, i.e., the number of machine cycles from the point of creation, for which the result is held in state.*

During the lifetime δ of a result, other threads may consume it as an operand. This behavior is reflected in the value of l, the mean number of executions per thread. Presumably, if paths make their results available to all other paths in state, this will further the cause of longer thread execution. More specifically, the policy adopted in the model is as follows:

Policy 1

1. At each machine cycle, one instruction—if possible—is executed. The result is maintained in state for δ additional cycles.

2. During each cycle of δ that a datum d is maintained, any path waiting at instruction I for the operand d, may *capture* it. Once captured, it is maintained by the capturing path even after the period δ.

3. The capturing path looks ahead to all successors of I, and may capture an input operand for one of the successor instructions. In general, paths may lookahead for an arbitrary number of instructions, to the extent that the operands are found available in the δ pool. If operands are found for more than one successor at a given instruction, lookahead chooses one of them arbitrarily, but only one path is taken.

4. All paths may advance their lookahead by one instruction at each cycle.

5. A path which has more than one unary successor to the currently executed instruction will continue with one of them, but will initiate new threads within the processor state for the rest.

6. A result which has been captured by all consumers which will require it, is eliminated from the pool.

7. The model assumes a *backing store* for each local processor. A datum which has not been captured by all consumers which will require it, is written to the backing store after δ cycles.

8. When a second, matching operand is written to the backing store, the pair becomes a new enabled thread, to be brought into state at the discretion of the state change policy (below). A thread brought into state from the backing store is charged as a context initiation (CI).

9. The execution scheduler runs through the paths in round-robin fashion, executing an instruction from any path that has one enabled. At paths for which lookahead has created a sequence of enabled instructions, the scheduler executes all of them on successive cycles before going to the next path.

Lemma: *For a given state, the marginal change in locality strength L, effected by Policy 1, is optimal.*

Proof sketch: The factors in L are l and H. By Policy 1(2), all instructions which could be scheduled next along any path—based on the data currently in the state, will capture their operand and hence are guaranteed to be scheduled for execution in finite time. Hence the value $\Delta l / \Delta t$ where t is the cycle tick, contributed by the current cycle, is maximal. With regard to H, Policy 1(6) implies that, for the given δ, all data which can be removed from the pool based on the current state, will in fact be removed. Let the set of data which can be deleted from the pool in the current cycle be denoted $D(\delta)$. Let the set of paths whose Home datum is an element of $D(\delta)$ be denoted $P(\delta)$. Let the set of new paths created from backing store matches—during the current cycle, be denoted $N(\delta)$. Then the total state size changes in the current cycle by an amount $-|D(\delta)| + |P(\delta) \cap D(\delta)| + |N(\delta)|$. The only remaining degree of freedom is the choice of which among those paths with enabled instruction should be executed. However, the value $\Delta(l/H)/\Delta t$ contributed by the current tick is clearly not affected by this choice. ∎

We now address the issue of what policy to employ for changing the state. Adjustment of the parameter δ, in principle, also amounts to a change in the state, after a time δ. We chose to fix δ for a given execution in order to limit the degrees of freedom to a tractable level; the effect of different values of δ will be seen across different runs. Even so, many variations are possible; the number of choices for adding to, or removing from the state is exponential in the number of enabled instructions, i.e., the prevailing level of parallelism at that cycle. We suggest two approaches which in some sense represent the extreme points of the spectrum of possibilities:

Policy 2(a): Any path in state which is stalled for lack of operand will be swapped out in favor of an enabled path from backing store.

Policy 2(b): No path in state will be swapped out in favor of new paths unless there are no executable paths remaining in state.

The first favors as many active paths as possible; the second tries to give paths the longest opportunity to find an operand and become enabled for execution. In both policies, the path(s) removed will be the one(s) idling for the longest time.

4. Theoretical Bounds

Earlier we considered only the remote access delay R, the inter-access time I, and a context initiation cost CI. The utilization for a single context is $I/(I + R)$, that for multiple contexts to saturation is $I/(I + CI)$, so the performance improvement due to increased utilization, or effective speedup is

$$S_{sat} = \frac{I + R}{I + CI}.$$

(3)

However, we wish to obtain an expression for S_{sat} which reflects the latency due to three distinct types of events: execution pipeline latency, remote calls, and the latency due to context switch itself. Having masked all latency with thread switching, we shall make the cost explicit by considering the effect of the increased processor state space on the local cycle time. Consider first the events local to a single processor—execution pipeline delay and the delay of context switching.

A T stage execution pipeline requires as many ready contexts, if we are to keep the pipe full. After l instructions on average an operand is found missing from data in the local state, we are short one context out of the initial T and so we must bring one in from the backing store. This repeats every l instructions until the first CI completes and adds a new context, so the total number of contexts we must have at readiness is

$$P \geq T + \left\lfloor \frac{CI}{l} \right\rfloor + 1.$$

Define H_{min} as the average minimum state space for which the program will run. H_{min} is empirically observed to be between one and two; this is also what intuition would expect. Denote by l_{min} the average path length, i.e., instructions per CI, observed for H_{min}. The utilization at H_{min} is

$$\frac{l_{min}}{l_{min} + CI}$$

and the effective speedup we can expect from saturated multiple contexts is the inverse of this value. Given a function $t_c(H)$, the cycle time required for H space, the effective speedup may be expressed

$$S_{sat} = \left(\frac{t_c(H_{min})}{t_c(H \cdot P)} \right) \left(\frac{l_{min} + CI}{l_{min}} \right) \tag{4}$$

where $H \cdot P$ is minimized subject to $P \geq T + \lfloor CI/l \rfloor + 1$; P is the number of paths (contexts) and H is the average state space required per path. This relation assumes a given CI cost and will vary P—the number of contexts maintained in state—to achieve the smallest state space for which the CI latency is completely masked.

If we add remote access to the equation, the number of contexts required to tolerate both types of latency is increased by $\lfloor R/I \rfloor + 1$ for R remote access latency and I inter-access time. Note that we do not include the CI time in calculating the number of threads in saturation or the utilization—as is done in [6], because we assume instead that this time cost has been reduced to near zero by including the requisite number of threads in local state. Denote by $H_1 \cdot P_1$ the value $H \cdot P$ minimized above for multiple contexts in a single processor. Then the speedup obtainable by context saturation for multiple processors doing remote access is

$$S_{sat} = \left(\frac{l_{min} + CI}{l_{min}} \cdot \frac{t_c(H_{min})}{t_c(H_1 \cdot P_1)} \right) \left(\frac{I + R}{I} \cdot \frac{t_c(H_1 \cdot P_1)}{t_c(H \cdot P)} \right) \tag{5}$$

where $H \cdot P$ is minimized subject to

$$P \geq T + \left\lfloor \frac{CI}{l} \right\rfloor + \left\lfloor \frac{R}{I} \right\rfloor + 2. \tag{6}$$

We now consider $t_c(H)$. For a given technology, the access time for RAM memory is at least logarithmic in the square root of its size. However, we are dealing here with the processor state space, where operands are to be exchanged between frequently switched threads in a tightly coupled manner. This is basically a fully connected configuration and it is reasonable to take as a rule of thumb for the minimum cycle time a function which is logarithmic in the total state space. Further, we cannot use direct access to the data in local state; the parallel execution of threads draws from arbitrary places in the code and we require a method to identify their place in the program context. A hash function, for example, requires applying a calculation that depends on all the bits in an identifier and therefore takes time logarithmic in the state space. More recent machines use a direct access scheme based on frames, where every datum in the state has a unique offset from the frame base. However, for a level of parallelism $\approx P$, the number of paths in state, the total program process space which must be addressable will be many times P. An optimistic guess for this value might be P^2.[2] Either method gives a slowdown factor of $2 \log (H \cdot P)$ and we shall use this as our guide in what follows.

Interestingly, if only remote latency is considered, and using the relationships given here, the cost effectiveness of multithreading is less than satisfying. As an example, if we take a typical value of $R/I = 4$ (Network delays are usually $k \log N$ for N processors with $k \le 10$ in instruction cycles. For 2^{10} processors with $k = 6, I = 16; R/I = 4$), the above gives a speedup at saturation $S_{sat} = ((60 + 15/15))/(2 \log 4) = 5/4$, at a cost of four times the processor state space. While the cost of processor state may not be linear in its size, we can see that the values are not in a region of effective cost/performance.[3]

But where R/I is basically fixed by the program and the given network and hence dictates the number of threads required to mask remote access latency, this may not be true of the number of threads required to mask CI latency. Recalling (6), we see that although the speedup attributable to saturation of the CI term is always $(l_{min} + CI/l_{min})$, the number of threads required to achieve this speedup may be reduced from CI by the value of l. If we add to the previous example the necessary threads to mask the context switch latency, and $l = 10$ could be achieved, the picture changes dramatically. Taking $CI = 50$ (remember, CI is the cost of initiating a context from the backing store), $l_{min} = 1.4$,[4] we obtain $S_{sat} = (5 \times 36.7)/(2 \log (4 + 5)) \approx 30$ at the cost of a nine times increase in processor state size. The value of l corresponds fairly directly to the measure of locality strength L, defined earlier, and the above discussion shows the significance of such locality on cost effective speedup.

To see how this factor scales with an increase in the number of processors, consider that

$$S_{sat} = \frac{t_c(H_{min})}{t_c(H \cdot P)} \left(\frac{l_{min} + CI}{l_{min}} \right) \left(\frac{I + R}{I} \right) \le \frac{\rho^2}{2 \log \left(\frac{CI}{l} + \frac{R}{I} \right)} \tag{7}$$

where

$$\rho = \frac{1}{2} \left[\frac{l_{min} + CI}{l_{min}} + \frac{R + I}{I} \right] ; H \cdot P \ge \frac{CI}{l} + \frac{R}{I} \tag{8}$$

and again we take the access time function $t_c(statesize)$ to be $2 \log (statesize)$. As $(R + I/I)$ increases toward equality with CI, the above expression will approach its maximum value, hence scaling will have a positive effect on the net cost/performance figure. However, the effect of the multiplicative factor $(R + I)/I$ is extremely sensitive to the locality level achieved. For example, if we scale to $R/I = 10$, then if locality is minimal, i.e., $l = l_{min}$, we obtain $S_{sat} = (11 \times 36.7)/(2 \log (10+38)) \approx 38$ at a cost of 48 times the state, while if locality is $l = 10$ we get $S_{sat} = (11 \times 36.7)/(2 \log (10+5)) \approx 53$ at a cost of 15 times the state.

---

[2] Less than P^2 addressable space would imply more parallelism (and hence more speedup) than the square root of the number of dynamic instruction executions in the program—over the entire execution space.

[3] These estimates must be considered optimistic in that simple averages are used where the behavior considered is actually probabilistic. Variance from the averages will reduce the performance improvement further.

[4] A typically observed value.

5. Simulation Results

Preliminary data are given in the graphs on the following pages for eight Livermore loops. For each graph, the horizontal scale indicates P, the number of parallel threads, the vertical scale indicates L, the locality achieved, and the different curves correspond to different values of δ. An encouraging trend observable throughout the data is that fairly steady increases in locality can be obtained for P up to about 128. On the other hand, in a few cases the values of L are fairly low, below 4 for loops 7, 10, and 21. Although some of the curves suggest that larger P or larger δ might increase L still further, it is difficult to imagine the practicality of maintaining more than 128 contexts for more than 32 instruction cycles. For a good number of the curves, the data show that at a certain number of paths the locality strength shows no further increases, even decreases—not unexpectedly. This "knee" effect is fairly pronounced in all cases except loop 10. Also of interest is the fact that the best locality is not for the highest δ. In fact, the worst performance is for the lowest and highest values. This fact, together with the "knee" at which most locality is captured, suggests that a certain "working set," both temporally and spatially, may be optimal for capturing the locality we seek.

Loop 3 shows strangely unstable behavior. Further, the effect of different new path initiation policies has yet to be clarified. Additional simulations, currently under way, should help answer these questions.

6. Conclusion

In general, a low value of L translates into marginal cost effectiveness for multithreading. For example, if a short pipeline is assumed, and taking $R/I = 4$—a typical value, the data yield approximately one-to-one cost/performance, i.e., a k-fold speedup has a cost of k times the processor state size. Note that the result lifetime δ allows us to include cooperation between threads as we have defined them, and hence the model given here should subsume the locality attributable to the type of compiler partitioning which has been reported to date in the literature. This would appear to be a significant challenge to be overcome by the multithreaded approach for non-strict implementations. On the other hand, the sensitivity of cost effectiveness to locality strength means that even a small improvement, to about $l = 10$, would make the approach attractive. We are experimenting with different state change policies that may have a significant tuning effect on the locality behavior.

References

[1] D. Culler, A. Sah, K. Schauser, T. von Eicken, and J. Wawrzynek, "Fine Grain Parallelism with Minimal Hardware Support: A Compiler Controlled Threaded Abstract Machine," *Proceedings of the 4th Int'l Conference on Architectural Support for Programming Languages and Operating Systems*, Santa Clara, California, April 1991.

[2] R. Iannucci, "A Dataflow-von Neumann Hybrid," Technical report, MIT Lab. for Computer Science, Cambridge, MA, May 1988.

[3] K.R. Traub, "Sequential Implementation of Lenient Programming Languages," Technical Report TR-417, MIT Laboratory for Computer Science, September 1988.

[4] L. Bic, "A Process Oriented Model for Efficient Execution of Dataflow Programs," *Proceedings 7th International Conf. on Distributed Computing*, Berlin, W. Germany, September 1987.

[5] G.M. Papadopoulos and D.E. Culler, "Monsoon: An Explicit Token Store Architecture," *Proceedings of the 1990 Int'l Symposium on Computer Architecture*, Seattle, Washington, May 1990.

[6] T. von Eicken, R.H. Saavedra-Barrera, and D. Culler, "Analysis of Multithreaded Architectures for Parallel Computing," *Proceedings of the 2nd Annual ACM Symposium on Parallel Algorithms and Architectures*, Crete, Greece, July 1990.

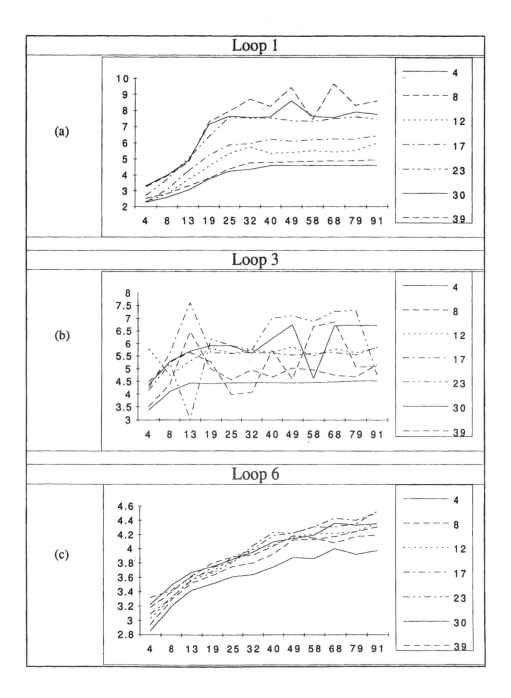

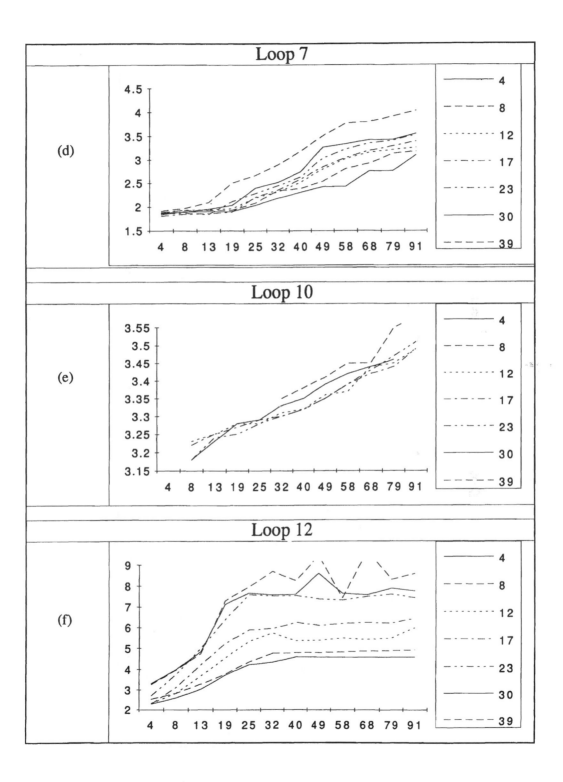

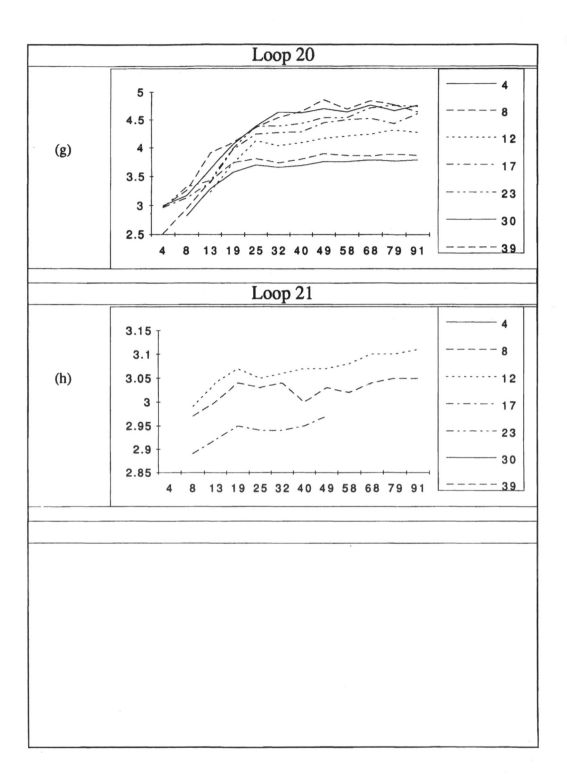

Locality and Latency in Hybrid Dataflow

Walid A. Najjar, William Marcus Miller, and A.P. Wim Böhm
Department of Computer Science
Colorado State University
Fort Collins, CO 80523

Recent evidence indicates that the exploitation of locality in dataflow programs could have a dramatic impact on performance. The current trend in the design of dataflow processors suggest a synthesis of traditional non-strict fine-grain instruction execution and a strict coarse-grain execution in order to exploit locality. While an increase in instruction granularity will favor the exploitation of locality within a single execution thread, the resulting grain size may increase latency among execution threads. We define fine-grain intra-thread locality as the inverse of the number of time steps one token has to wait for the other, in a dyadic instruction, in the matching store and quantify it using a set of numeric and non-numeric benchmarks. The results point to a very large degree of thread locality: for example, over 70% of the instructions have to wait less than 5 instruction execution steps for their input data. Furthermore, the remarkable uniformity and consistency of the distribution of thread locality across a wide variety of benchmarks suggests that thread locality is highly dependent on the instruction set, the compilation strategy and programming language. The resulting latency incurred through the partitioning of fine-grain instructions into coarser grain threads is evaluated. We define the concept of a cluster of fine-grain instructions to quantify coarse-grain input and output latencies. The results of our experiments offer compelling evidence that the inner loops of a significant number of numeric codes would benefit from coarse-grain execution. Based on cluster execution times, more than 60% of the measured benchmarks favor a coarse-grain execution. In 63% of the cases the input latency to the cluster is the same in coarse- or fine-grain execution modes. These results suggest that the effects of increased instruction granularity on latency is minimal for a high percentage of the measured codes, and in large part is offset by available intra-thread locality. Furthermore, simulation results indicate that strict or non-strict data structure access does not change the basic cluster characteristics.

1. Introduction

The fine-grain dataflow execution model has the ability to maximize the exploitation of parallelism as well as processor utilization while masking the latency of non-local accesses and inter-processor communication [1]. Despite these promises, an actual implementation of this model would suffer from significant amounts of unnecessary overhead: a substantial number of instructions executed by classical fine-grain architectures are non-compute actors [19]. Token matching is a major bottleneck in the dataflow circular pipeline: because matching is the only mechanism for instruction enabling, simple sequential threads of instructions would suffer unnecessary overhead [2], [25].

Second generation hybrid von Neumann-dataflow architectures have designs that aim at increasing task granularity and thereby reducing matching store overhead and

This work is supported in part by NSF Grants CCR-9010240 and MIP-9113268.

allowing locality to be exploited within a multi-instruction execution thread [13], [24], [10]. So far, however, very little is known about the qualitative and quantitative nature of locality in dataflow programs and of its impact on the performance of hybrid architectures. Section 2 of this paper addresses this issue. We define *intra-thread locality* as one form of instruction level locality in a dataflow graph execution and measure it across a suit of numeric and non-numeric benchmarks. The results show the existence of a large degree of intra-thread locality that can be exploited to reduce matching overhead.

In a multithreaded model a sequential thread of execution can block on a remote memory access (typically to a structure store); the execution is then switched to another ready thread. This model is implemented, with several variants, in the Monsoon, the *T, and the EM-4/EM-5 architectures. The other alternative, the non-blocking approach, requires that all input tokens to a grain be present before any instruction in that grain can start executing.

Blocking threads can block in the middle of their execution, e.g., because of a read-structure store. Execution switches to another thread. When the result of the remote read comes back, the blocked thread can be resumed. This model is used in HEP, TERA, and in the run time system of SISAL on conventional multi-processors.

Non-blocking threads have "variable delay" instructions only as their last instruction. Therefore, non-blocking threads do not need to be resumed. All the data values needed to execute the thread are available before the thread starts executing. Non-blocking threads are implemented with several variants, in dataflow machines (Monsoon, EM-4, *T, EM-5).

The non-blocking thread model has a higher potential for masking latency, while the blocking thread model can better exploit locality and therefore can further reduce matching overhead. The non-blocking model, however, could suffer from an increase in the latency of the input tokens to a grain. Section 3 of this paper provides a quantitative evaluation of the added latency in the non-blocking. The results show that in the majority of cases there is no added latency and that where any additional latency is incurred its effect compounded with the gain from reduced matching overhead is negligible.

2. Evaluation of Thread Locality

The asynchronous nature of dataflow execution tends to obscure the presence of program and data locality. There is, however, substantial empirical evidence that points to the existence of large amounts of locality that can be exploited to enhance performance. In this paper we focus on one form of locality: *intra-thread locality*, which is the locality among the instructions constituting a thread. In the rest of the paper we will refer to it simply as thread locality.

There are other forms of locality that can be identified in dataflow execution such as data structure, inter-thread, and producer-consumer forms of locality. These, however are more dependent on machine architecture and strategies for program partitioning, data allocation, and task scheduling.

In this paper we quantify thread locality in order to evaluate the potential benefit of using registers for temporary data storage and thereby reduce matching store overhead and token queue traffic. Dataflow programs exhibiting a high degree of locality would benefit from the conglomeration of tightly coupled fine-grain instructions into coarse-grain, von Neumann style execution threads.

2.1 Definitions

Measuring temporal data and instruction locality for a single thread of von Neumann code involves tracking the time between successive references to the same memory address (data and instruction references). This is normally done through data and instruction breakpoints. These values are sorted by increasing reference times to form a locality profile. The asynchronous, fine-grained, multithread nature of dataflow execution, complicates similar measurements on a dataflow processor (The scheduling of PEs is not based on instruction sequencing, multiple PEs are scheduled on single instructions when data become available). The execution of an instruction in the dataflow model generates a data token that is forwarded to one or more target instructions. This can in turn trigger the execution of some or all of these instructions. A dyadic instruction is enabled for execution when both its operands are available. The matching unit stores the first arriving operand and sends both operands off upon the arrival of the second operand.

Definition 1 *Given a dyadic instruction, thread locality is defined as the inverse of the time delay between the arrival of its first input data value and that of the second assuming the availability of infinite resources.*

Just as the delay between two successive memory references characterizes the temporal locality in a von Neumann thread, the delay between the arrival of an instruction's first and second operand is a measure of the locality that exist between the nodes of a dataflow graph. At the graph interpretation level this is a relatively simple measure to obtain; however, the assessment of thread locality on real dataflow processors is complicated by resource management, allocation policies, and variable instruction execution times.

In order to mask the effects of program partitioning and allocation, we will measure the waiting time of a token in the matching store as the number of *generations*. A generation is the execution time of a single instruction assuming:

- an infinite number of processors are available, and

- all instructions have the same execution time.

It follows that the number of generations necessary to execute a program graph is the size of the critical path through that graph in number of instructions. The proposed measure of locality is therefore an intrinsic characteristic of the program graph itself.

As an example of thread locality, a fine-grain representation for the expression $\sqrt{b^2 - 4ac}$ is shown in Figure 1. In this example, the waiting time between all tokens except those on arcs 5 and 7 is zero (1 matching cycle). Tokens on arcs 5 and 7 each wait one generation in the matching store (token generation numbers are listed in brackets).

The waiting time of a token is the number of generations the token spent in the matching store. Waiting times are a direct consequence of the partial ordering that exist between the nodes in the dataflow graph. As a result, the matching store occupancy relative to the number of execution threads is a measure of the degree of locality that exists between executing dataflow nodes. Periods of high matching store occupancy indicate limited locality, while periods of low occupancy indicate a high degree of locality. In general, this is not true on real machines because of resource limitations, and the disparity between the matching units cycle time and that of the processing elements causes the matching store to become saturated during times of

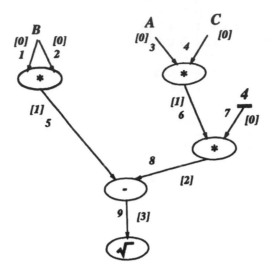

Figure 1: Token generations.

high program parallelism [7]. The underlying data dependencies determine the target machines dataflow graph, hence thread locality is an intrinsic property of the program graph. The simulator measures thread locality by tracking each token's matching store waiting time.

Similar locality measurements were reported in [6] where the waiting time in the matching store was measured for a single iteration of the Simple code on 10×10 mesh executing on a simulated Tagged-Token dataflow architecture. The results were used to evaluate token store capacities for various loop unrolling strategies. Related research is reported in [11] where a high-speed register-cache memory design is proposed for a multithreaded architecture. In this design registers are allocated at runtime and exploit the locality within *super-actors*.

2.2 Evaluation

The following benchmarks were used in our analysis of thread locality:

- Lawrence Livermore Loops (1 to 15) [15], [8]

- Purdue Benchmarks (1 to 12) [21], [22]

- Sieve of Eratosthenes

- Quicksort

The benchmarks were compiled into Manchester Dataflow machine code from SISAL [16] source code. The execution of each loop in the benchmarks was simulated for 50 and 100 iterations. Since the majority of time in numeric scientific programs is spent in inner loop execution (the 90/10 temporal locality rule [12]), only data on inner loop execution were collected. To isolate locality measurements to inner loops, the effects of loops initialization and control bias were removed.

The measurements for each test suite were averaged over all token generations and then weighted by the total number of matches per loop and the total number of instructions in each loop.

Livermore Loops	48.2%
Purdue Benchmarks	35.6%
Sieve	52.6%
Quicksort	46.9%

Table 1: Percentage of single input instructions.

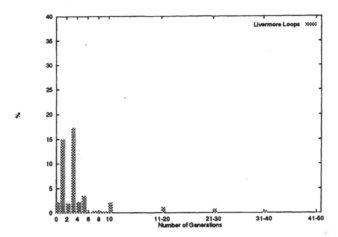

Figure 2: Locality distribution (% matches), Livermore loops.

Simulation results are reported through 50 token generations, beyond that no histogram value exceeds 0.5% of the total number of matches. The plots in Figures 2 to 5 show the distribution of the loop thread locality in all four benchmarks suites as a percentage of the total number of matches in each suite. Single input instructions are therefore not counted in these figures. They, however, represent a significant proportion of all instructions executed as can be seen from Table 1.

Figure 6 shows the cumulative locality distribution profile for all four benchmarks as the percentage of all matches. Figure 7 shows the cumulative locality distribution profiles as a percentage of the number of executed instructions.

2.3 Discussion of Results

These results indicate that considerable thread locality is present in dataflow programs. The following observations can be made based on the reported measurements:

- The measurements tend to cluster in the lower values of the delay. For the Livermore Loops 42% of all two-input instructions have waiting times less than 5 generations. If we include single input instructions, more than 70% of the instructions have waiting times less than 5 generations. Similar results were obtained for the Purdue Benchmarks, Quicksort, and the Sieve of Eratosthenes.

- The degree of locality shown in these figures in significantly large. Here a large degree of locality corresponds to a small value of the measured delay. In all four suites the percentage of matches that have a delay ≤ 2 is 20% or more.

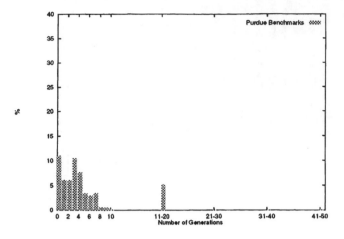

Figure 3: Locality distribution (% matches), Purdue benchmarks.

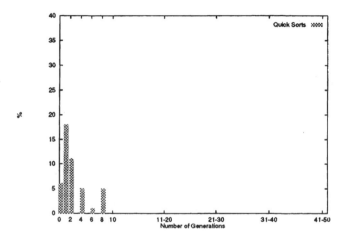

Figure 4: Locality distribution (% matches), Quicksort.

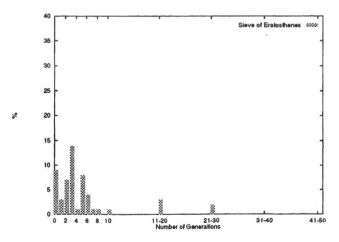

Figure 5: Locality distribution (% matches), Sieve.

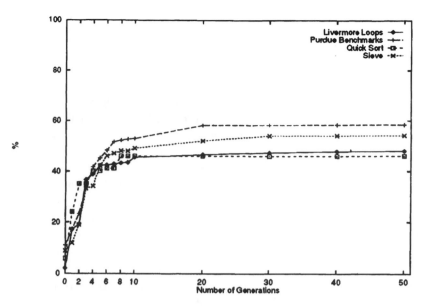

Figure 6: Cumulative locality distribution, (% matches).

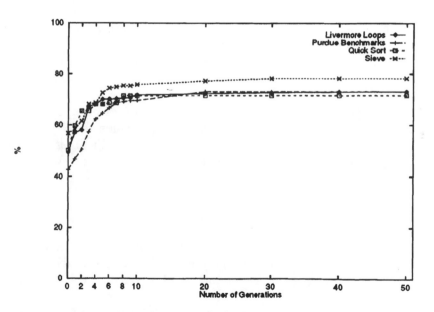

Figure 7: Cumulative locality distribution, (% instructions).

- The simulation results seem to be remarkably uniform across all four benchmarks as can be seen in Figures 6 and 7. This consistency in the measurements seems to suggest that the degree and distribution of thread locality is in part determined by the instruction set architecture and in part by the actual algorithm.

These results indicate that there is much to be gained by incorporating specific architectural and compiler features to exploit thread locality in a hybrid dataflow machine. One obvious approach is the grouping of fine-grain instructions into a single coarse-grain instruction with multiple inputs and outputs. Coarse-grain instructions would be beneficial in eliminating a large percentage of single input instructions and non-compute overhead instructions. On the average, single input instructions accounted for almost half of all executed benchmark instructions. In addition, increasing instruction granularity would reduce the load on the matching unit, the queue, and the communication network. It will also reduce the overall run time execution overhead by reducing the MIPS/MFLOPS ratio.

Coarse-grain instructions would allow thread locality to be exploited through the use of register banks; data structure locality could be exploited through pipelining. In [2] it was shown that the introduction of iterative instructions (instructions that produce a sequence of outputs when presented with a single set of inputs) was beneficial in reducing program execution times on the Manchester Dataflow Processor. The partitioning of fine-grain instructions into coarse-grain instructions would be based on several complex tradeoffs such as: matching cycles saved, instruction input latency, the ratio of the number of operands to the instruction operation and the coarse-grain instruction execution time. The percentage of fine-grain instructions that can be partitioned in this manner and their effect on fine-grain instructions is a subject of future research. The matching unit itself should be altered to exploit locality through the use of a token cache. The cache should employ a direct matching scheme using a different segment for each token color and a directly computable offset within the segment based on the instruction address.

The uniformity of results across such a varied collection of benchmarks suggests that locality is to a large extent determined by the instruction set architecture. This implies that an instruction set specifically designed for coarse-grain dataflow execution might have a significant impact on performance.

3. Measurements of Loop Latency

3.1 Definitions and Models

Our objective is to quantitatively evaluate the added latency cost that is incurred in a coarse-grain dataflow execution model. In this section we define the execution models as well as the graph and timing parameters that will be used in the evaluation.

Definition 2 *A **cluster** of instructions is a connected directed acyclic graph with only one output arc. In a cluster each node is a fine-grain instruction and the output is always generated by the last executing node.*

An example of a cluster is depicted in Figure 8. While a cluster could be any collection of fine-grain instructions, in this paper we will focus on the body of loops as a specific type of cluster. Figure 10 shows the body of loop number 7 in the Livermore loops benchmark suite. Two parameters are associated with the graph of a cluster:

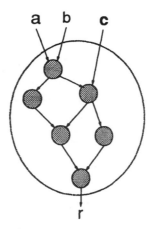

Figure 8: Typical cluster of fine-grain instructions.

- S_1 is the total number of instructions in the cluster; it is also a measure of its execution time on a sequential machine.

- S_∞ is the cluster critical path length; it is also a measure of its execution time on a machine with infinite hardware parallelism.

$\Pi = S_1/S_\infty$ is the average fine-grain parallelism in the cluster. In the example of Figure 8 $S_1 = 6$, $S_\infty = 4$ and $\Pi = 1.5$.

Two execution models of a cluster are defined:

- *Fine grain* cluster execution model: any instruction in the cluster will execute as soon as its inputs are available; instructions execute in parallel assuming infinite hardware parallelism.

- *Coarse grain* cluster execution model: no instruction will execute until all the input tokens to the cluster have arrived. Instructions in the cluster are executed in a sequential non-pipelined mode.

For the sake of simplicity, we will assume, in both models, that all instructions execute in one time step and that communication overhead is negligible. The *ideal execution* model of a cluster is therefore a fine-grain execution with infinite matching bandwidth. A *token generation* is the execution time of a single instruction under ideal execution; it will be used as the basic time unit in the remainder of this paper.

Next we define a number of timing parameters that characterize the execution of a cluster under either fine- or coarse-grain models.

- t_0: the arrival time of the first input to the cluster,

- t_n: the arrival time of the last token in the cluster,

- t_r: the time at which the result is generated.

The relationships between these values, shown in Figure 9, are defined by:

- l: the delay between t_0 and t_n, $(l = t_n - t_0)$,

Figure 9: Relationship between input latency and output delay.

- d: the delay between the arrival of the last input token (t_n) and the first result token (t_r), ($d = t_r - t_n$),

- l': the delay until the first fine-grain instruction in the cluster can fire.

Notice that l and l' are not parameters of the cluster itself but rather depend on the execution of the program graph containing it.

For a cluster executed on a machine with infinite resources, $l \geq 0$, $l' \leq l$, and $1 \leq d \leq S_\infty$. For fine-grain execution, $d < S_\infty$ implies some instructions may fire before all of the cluster's inputs have arrived, hence there will be some degree of pipelining and latency masking occurring within the cluster. The net effect is one of pipelining, in which one or more instructions begin execution before all cluster inputs have arrived thereby keeping the pipeline busy. Pipeline starvation could occur due to insufficient program parallelism in a dataflow machine [2]. Dataflow architectures such as the Monsoon circumvent the pipeline starvation problem by allowing the concurrent execution of multiple clusters (threads) per processor [26].

In general, for a cluster to be efficiently executed under a fine-grain model, $\Pi \gg 1$, $S_\infty \gg d$, and $l \gg l'$. These conditions guarantee that the dataflow circular pipeline stays full, hence the cost of token matching and structure store latency can be hidden by fast context switching. A cluster may favor a coarse-grain execution strategy for $l \approx l'$ or $d \approx S_\infty$, provided the average cluster parallelism Π is reasonably small and the available intra-thread locality is high.

Based on these parameters, we can derive the following properties for an ideal execution model (i.e., with zero matching costs):

[1] $l = 0 \Rightarrow d = S_\infty$. By the definition of d, if no instruction in the cluster incurs any input latency, the cluster output delay will be equal to its critical path length.

[2] $l' = l \Rightarrow d = S_\infty$. If $l = l'$, no instruction in the cluster can fire until all inputs have arrived, hence the number of generations between the nodes with input time t_n and the output time t_r is S_∞, and therefore $d = S_\infty$.

[3] $l' + S_\infty \leq l + S_1$. This follows directly from the definitions of l' and l. $l' \leq l$ and $S_\infty \leq S_1$, hence for a dataflow machine with infinite resources, $l' + S_\infty \leq l + S_1$. Evidently, $l' + S_\infty$ is the lower bound on the execution time in the fine-grain model and $l + S_1$ the upper bound on the execution time in the coarse-grain model. This relationship will be investigated further in Section 5.

3.2 Latency Measurements

To quantify the cluster parameters, l, l', and d, a dataflow machine simulator based on the Manchester Dataflow Machine (MDFM) instruction set [3] was used to trace the execution of clusters in a suite of benchmarks consisting of:

- Lawrence Livermore Loops (1–10, 13–15) [15], [8]

- Purdue Benchmarks (1–4, 7–14) [21], [22]

The clusters were simply chosen as the inner loop in each benchmark. The cluster boundary was chosen such that the top level instruction in each cluster is an arithmetic instructions. In other words all the inputs to the cluster are inputs to an arithmetic instruction within that cluster.

Benchmarks were compiled from the single assignment language SISAL [16] into MDFM machine code. To study the effects of both strict and non-strict structure store access on cluster latency, all benchmarks were compiled using both strict and non-strict/no garbage collection options (see Section 4).

As an example, the SISAL code for Livermore Loop 7 as well as the cluster of instructions of its inner loop are shown in Figure 10. The opcodes MLR and ADR are multiply reals and add reals, respectively. With each input is also specified its arrival time, in generation numbers, obtained from the simulator after compiling the source code using strict structure store access and garbage collection enabled. For this loop $l' = 13, l = 14, d = 8, S_\infty = 8$, and $S_1 = 16$, yielding an average cluster parallelism of $\Pi = 1.8$.

Simulation results obtained for code generated using strict structures with garbage collection active are summarized in Table 2. The values in column SP will be discussed in Section 5. The following observation can be made:

- l and l' are the same for 63% of the simulation runs, implying the token arrival to token result delay, d, is very nearly equal to S_∞ for these clusters. In these cases a coarse-grain execution would not incur any additional latency over a fine-grain one. Under these conditions there can be little pipelining of instruction execution, and therefore the overall execution time of the cluster is not affected by its execution mode.

- The average value of Π is small ≈ 1.3 for the Livermore loops, and ≈ 1.1 for the Purdue benchmarks. This indicates that there is very little parallelism to exploit within these clusters (this result has been reported in [14]). Because Π is small, token matching and structure store latency cannot be masked in the fine-grain execution of a single cluster per processor. One alternative is to exploit inter-thread concurrency by executing multiple threads per processor as in the Monsoon architecture [26]. Another alternative is a sequential non-blocking execution strategy which offers great potentials for exploiting intra-thread locality and also reducing matching store costs.

3.3 Strict and Non-Strict Structures

The MDFM code generation system can be configured to generate code for both strict and non-strict access to the structure store. The structure store accesses data without the use of tags, implementing the I-structure paradigm through a deferred read mechanism [9]. The structure store consists of an allocation unit, structure

```
type double = double_real;
type OneD  = array[double];
function Loop7(n:integer;R,T:double; U,Y,Z:OneD; returns OneD)
    for k in 1,n returns
        array of U[k]+R * (Z[k]+R * Y[k])
                +T * (U[k+3]+R * (U[k+2]+R * U[k+1])
                +T* (U[k+6] +R * (U[k+5]+R * U[k+4])))
    end for
end function
```

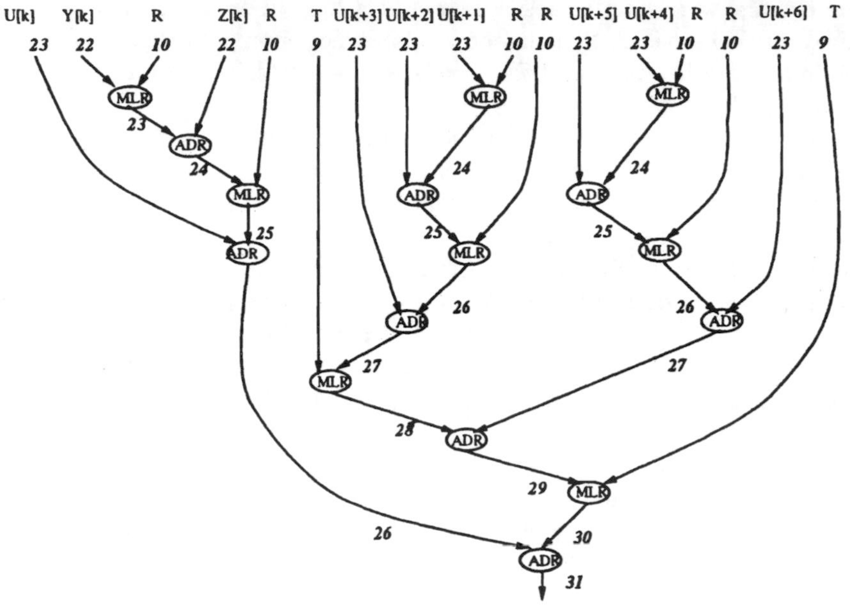

Figure 10: Cluster of instructions for Livermore Loop 7.

memory, a deferred access queue and a clearance unit. The allocation unit manages storage allotment, while the clearance unit performs garbage collection. Structure store access can be made asynchronously via a deferred access queue. When a read request is made for data not yet written, the request is held in the deferred access queue until the required data arrive. To compare the effects of strict and non-strict structure store access on cluster parameters, each benchmark was compiled to generate code for both paradigms.

For strict structure store access, the compiler generates code to ensure strictness, i.e., no instruction can access an array element until the entire data structure is built. The effect of strictness on cluster inputs is to delay the arrival of tokens transporting data structure elements. Simulation results indicate that the basic cluster characteristics do not change. Table 3 shows the timing parameters for a non-strict execution of some Livermore loops. Comparing these with the values in Table 2, the main conclusions that can be drawn are:

- The token arrival latencies l' and l, are in general longer for code compiled with strict structure store accesses than non-strict. This result is to be expected since no array element is available prior to completion of the whole array.

Benchmark	l'	l	d	S_∞	S_1	Π	SP
LL Loop #							
1	13	13	4	4	5	1.25	0.90
2	9	9	3	3	4	1.33	0.93
3	13	13	2	2	2	1	0.94
4	5	5	8	8	8	1	0.67
5	6	6	2	2	2	1	0.90
6	19	19	2	2	2	1	0.96
7	13	14	8	8	16	1.78	1.03
8	43	43	6	6	14	2.33	1.05
9	29	29	10	10	17	1.70	0.96
10	1	1	9	9	9	1	0.58
15	0	12	6	11	13	1.18	1.08
Purdue #							
1	0	0	4	4	4	1	0.62
2	0	12	2	6	6	1	1.19
3	1	1	41	41	41	1	0.52
4	0	1	2	3	3	1	1.00
7	0	7	4	5	6	1.2	0.93
8*	0	9	1	2	2	1	1.09
9	0	0	6	6	6	1	0.58
10*	0	0	2	2	2	1	0.75
11*	2	2	6	6	6	1	0.64
13	0	1	4	5	6	1.2	0.89
14*	1	17	8	15	17	1.13	1.06

*Significant loop only.

Table 2: Timing and cluster parameters per benchmark—Strict structures.

LL Loop #	l'	l	d
1	7	7	4
2	0	1	3
3	7	7	2
4	6	8	8
5	2	2	2
6	6	6	2
7	7	8	8
8	13	13	6
9	10	12	10
10	1	1	9
15	0	17	6

Table 3: Timing and cluster parameters, Livermore loops—Non-Strict structures.

- In most of the cases in the strict execution we have $l = l'$ whereas this is not the case in the non-strict execution. Again this is to be expected since strict array creation makes all array elements available at the same time.

From these initial results we can conclude that a coarse-grain execution is not hampered by strict array implementation whereas a non-strict array implementation would enhance fine-grain execution. These initial results, however, must be confirmed by larger benchmark programs.

3.4 Analysis of Results

The results in the previous section describe the latency of input token arrival at cluster boundaries. In this section we analyze the effects of the input latency on the execution time of a cluster under the fine- and coarse-grain models of execution. Let T, $T_{\min}$, $T_{\max}$ and Δ be defined as

$$
\begin{aligned}
T &= t_r - t_0 \\
T_{\min} &= l' + S_\infty \\
T_{\max} &= l + S_1 \\
\Delta &= l - l' + S_1 - S_\infty.
\end{aligned}
$$

T is the total delay in the cluster execution from the arrival of the first input to the availability of its output. $T_{\min}$ is the lower bound on T under the fine-grain execution model and $T_{\max}$ is the upper bound on T under sequential coarse-grain execution. The difference Δ can be viewed as a measure of the potential loss in performance between the coarse- and fine-grain models. Surprisingly, for the combined benchmarks, $T_{\min} = T_{\max}$ in 45% of the cases. Figure 11 plots the distribution of Δ for the Livermore loops and the Purdue benchmarks. Both sets of data exhibit similar behavior: a high percentage of benchmarks have values of $T_{\min}$ and $T_{\max}$ that are nearly equal. For the Livermore loops, $\Delta \leq 10$ for 85% of the measured code. For the Purdue benchmarks, $\Delta \leq 10$ in 75% of the cases. None of the measured values exceeded 20 token generations for either test suite.

The analysis following is based on a number of simplifications such as negligible matching costs and the pipelined nature of dataflow execution. The following analysis is based on a hypothetical dataflow machine depicted in Figure 12 where the matching stage and the execution stage both have a unit time delay. The machine can operate in both coarse- and fine-grain modes as defined in Section 2. In both modes an instruction will execute in one time step.

Let T_f and T_c represent the execution time in the fine- and coarse-grain modes, respectively. They can be derived as

$$
\begin{aligned}
T_f &= l + 2d \\
T_c &= l + 1 + S_1.
\end{aligned}
$$

For a cluster of instructions executed in fine-grain mode, a latency l' is incurred until the first instruction packet can fire. At time $t_0 + l$ there will be d instructions that will have to go through the two stages of the machine. In coarse-grain mode the execution unit incurs a startup latency of l, until the matching unit collects all cluster inputs. The first instruction is ready to execute at time $l + 1$, all others instructions requiring an additional S_1 cycles to produce the final result.

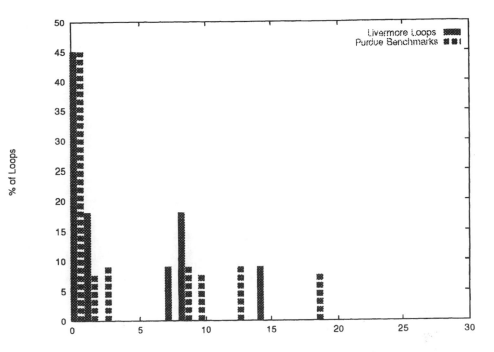

Figure 11: The distribution of Δ across benchmarks.

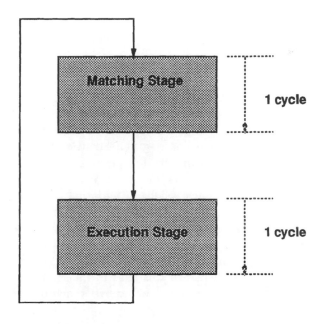

Figure 12: A two-stage hybrid machine.

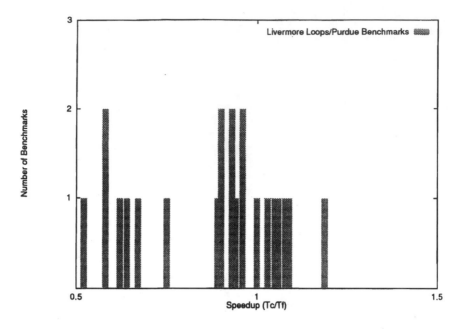

Figure 13: Distribution of speedup.

Let the speedup achievable in the fine-grain mode over the coarse-grain one be defined by

$$SP = \frac{T_c}{T_f} = \frac{l + 1 + S_1}{l + 2d}.$$

The fine-grain mode outperforms the coarse-grain mode when

$$T_c > T_f \iff l + S_1 + 1 > l + 2d \iff S_1 > 2d - 1.$$

The values of SP are shown in Table 2, indicating that 60% of the benchmarks would benefit from a coarse-grain execution. The distribution of the speedup SP across the benchmarks is shown in Figure 13. It can be noted that all values of SP lie between 0.5 and 1.2 implying that a coarse-grain execution would outperform a fine-grain one by at most a factor of 2, while the fine-grain execution will perform at most 20% better and that in only one case. While a factor of 2 is very significant in real architectures, it does not carry much weight in hypothetical architectures based on highly simplified approximations. These results are even more compelling considering that communication costs or resource conflicts have not been accounted for in the fine-grain execution model.

A fine-grain model of execution will perform well for small input latency l, and sufficiently large cluster parallelism. In this case a fine-grain execution model can mask memory latency through fast and inexpensive synchronization. However, if cluster parallelism is small and input latency high, the fine-grain model performs poorly because there is insufficient useful work to mask input latency. The full cost of token matching is incurred because there are no instructions in the execution unit's ready queue. By exploiting intra-thread locality, a coarse-grain model can efficiently execute clusters consisting of sequential code with few synchronization points.

4. Conclusion

The ability of the dataflow paradigm to exploit program parallelism at all levels while implementing implicit synchronization and resolving data dependencies at run time has been demonstrated by several research projects. The fine-grain execution model, however, fails to exploit the inherent locality in programs and thereby introduces excessive run time overhead in the matching stage. Hybrid von Neumann-dataflow architectures that alleviate the run time overhead have been proposed as alternatives to the fine-grain model. This paper addresses the issue of quantitatively evaluating the dynamic instruction level locality present in dataflow graphs and the added latency introduced by a non-blocking execution of coarse-grain dataflow graphs. The experimental measurements evaluate thread locality on a dataflow machine simulator based on a set of numeric and non-numeric benchmarks.

We have defined and quantified *intra-thread locality* in dataflow execution. The results present compelling quantitative evidence that high degree intra-thread locality exists in dataflow programs. It is also shown that a substantial percentage of tokens have very large waiting times, indicating the need for long-term secondary storage. Furthermore, the distribution of the locality appears to be quite consistent across a wide variety of benchmarks.

We have used the concept of a *cluster* of fine-grain instructions to quantify input and output latencies under both coarse- and fine-grain execution models. The results show that in a large percentage of the cases (63%) there was no increase in latency between fine- and a coarse-grain execution models. An analysis of the execution of these clusters on an idealized hypothetical dataflow machine shows that a coarse-grain execution will outperform a fine-grain one in over 60% of the cases. In those cases where the fine-grain model has a smaller execution time, the speedup is less than 1.2 for the large majority of cases.

Further research results by our group, on this and related topics, since the ISCA 1992 Workshop, have been published in [4], [5], [17], [18], [20], [23].

References

[1] Arvind and R.A. Iannucci, "Two Fundamentals Issues in Multiprocessors: The Data-Flow Solutions," Technical Report LCS CSG 226-6, Laboratory for Computer Science, MIT, Cambridge, Massachusetts, May 1987.

[2] A.P.W. Böhm and J.R. Gurd, "Iterative Instructions in the Manchester Dataflow Computer," *IEEE Trans. on Parallel and Distributed Systems*, Vol. 1, No. 2, 1990, pp. 129–139.

[3] A.P.W. Böhm, J.R. Gurd, and C. C. Kirkham, "The Manchester Dataflow Computing System," in *Experimental Parallel Computing Architectures*, J. Dongarra, Ed., North Holland, 1987, pp. 177–219.

[4] A.P.W. Böhm, W.A. Najjar, B. Shankar, and L. Roh, "An Evaluation of Bottom-Up and Top-Down Thread Generation Techniques," *26th ACM/IEEE International Symposium on Microarchitecture* (MICRO-26), 1993.

[5] A.P.W. Böhm, W.A. Najjar, B. Shankar, and L. Roh, "An Evaluation of Coarse-Grain Dataflow Code Generation Strategies," in *Working Conference on Massively Parallel Programming Models*, Berlin, Germany, September 1993.

[6] S. Brobst, "Organization of an Instruction Scheduling and Token Storage Unit in a Tagged Token Dataflow Machine," *Int. Conf. on Parallel Processing*, S.K. Sahni, Ed., 1987, pp. 40–45.

[7] D.E. Culler, "Resource Management for the Tagged Token Data Flow Architecture," Technical Report TR-332, Laboratory for Computer Science, MIT, January 1985.

[8] J.T. Feo, "The Livermore Loops in SISAL," Technical Report UCID-21159, Computing Research Group, Lawrence Livermore National Laboratory, Livermore, CA 94550, August 1987.

[9] J.R. Gurd and A.P.W. Böhm, "Implicit Parallel Processing: SISAL on the Manchester Dataflow Computer," in *Parallel Systems and Computation*, G. Paul and G.S. Almasi, Eds., North Holland Publishing Company, 1988, pp. 179–204.

[10] V.G. Graffe and J.E. Hoch, "Implementation of the Epsilon Dataflow Processor," *Proc. of the Twenty-third Ann. Hawaii Int. Conf. on System Sciences*, Vol. 1, 1990, pp. 19–29.

[11] H.J. Hum and G.R. Gao, "A Novel High-Speed Memory Organization for Fine-Grain Multi-thread Computing," *Conf. on Parallel Architectures and Languages*, Europe, 1991.

[12] J.L. Hennessy and D.A. Patterson, *Computer Architecture: A Quantitative Approach*, Morgan Kaufmann Publishers Inc. 1990.

[13] R.A. Iannucci, "Toward a Dataflow/Von Neumann Hybrid Architecture," *Int. Ann. Symp. on Computer Architecture*, 1988, pp. 131–140.

[14] N.P. Jouppi and D.W. Wall, "Available Instruction-Level Parallelism for Super-Scalar and Superpipelined Machines," Technical Report WRL Research Report 89/7, Western Research Laboratory, Palo Alto, CA, July 1989.

[15] F.H. McMahon, "Livermore FORTRAN Kernels: A Computer Test of Numerical Performance Range," Technical Report UCRL-53745, Lawrence Livermore National Laboratory, Livermore, CA, December 1986.

[16] J. McGraw et al., *SISAL: Streams and Iterations in a Single Assignment Language, Reference Manual Version 1.2*, Manual M-146, Rev. 1, Lawrence Livermore National Laboratory, Livermore, CA, March 1985.

[17] W.A. Najjar, A.P.W. Böhm, and W.M. Miller, *Exploiting Locality in Hybrid Dataflow Programs*, Kluwer, 1993.

[18] W.A. Najjar, A.P.W. Böhm, and W.M. Miller, "A Quantitative Analysis of Dataflow Program Execution—Preliminaries to a Hybrid Design," *Journal of Parallel and Distributed Computing*, Vol. 18, No. 3, July 1993.

[19] W. Najjar and J.-L. Gaudiot, "Multi-Level Execution in Data-Flow Architectures," *Int'l. Conf. on Parallel Processing*, S.K. Sahni, Ed., St. Charles, Illinois, 1987, pp. 32–39.

[20] W.A. Najjar, L. Roh, and A.P.W. Böhm, "The Initial Performance of a Bottom-Up Clustering Algorithm for Dataflow Graphs," *Proc. of the IFIP WG 10.3 Conf. on Architecture and Compilation Techniques for Medium and Fine Grain Parallelism*, Orlando, FL, January 1993.

[21] J.R. Rice, "Problems to Test Parallel and Vector Languages," Technical Report CSD-TR 516, Purdue University, 1985.

[22] J.R. Rice, "Problems to Test Parallel and Vector Languages—2," Technical Report CSD-TR 1016, Purdue University, 1990.

[23] L. Roh, W.A. Najjar, and A.P.W. Böhm, "Generation and Quantitative Evaluation of Dataflow Clusters," *Conf. on Functional Programming Languages and Computer Architecture*, Copenhagen, Denmark, June 1993.

[24] S. Sakai, Y. Yamaguchi, K. Hiraki, Y. Kodama, and T. Yuba, "An Architecture of a Data-Flow Single Chip Processor," *Int'l. Ann. Symp. on Computer Architecture*, May 1989, pp. 46–53.

[25] S. Sakai, Y. Yamaguchi, K. Hiraki, Y. Kodama, and T. Yuba, "Pipeline Optimization of a Dataflow Machine," in *Advanced Topics in Data-Flow Computing*, J-L. Gaudiot and L. Bic, Eds., Prentice-Hall, 1991, pp. 225–246.

[26] K.R. Traub, G.M. Papadopoulos, M.J. Beckerle, J.E. Hicks, and J. Young, "Overview of the Monsoon Project," *Int'l. Conf. on Computer Design*, IEEE, October 1991, pp. 150–155.

Implementation of Manipulator Control Computation on Conventional and Dataflow Multiprocessors

S. Zeng[1] and G.K. Egan[2]
Laboratory for Concurrent Computing Systems
Swinburne University of Technology
John Street, Hawthorn 3122, Australia

There is an increasing demand for developing the manipulator dynamic control scheme. This control scheme involves the real-time computation of the desired generalized forces or motor torques required to drive all joints appropriately so that the manipulator follows the intended trajectory. To achieve the convergence of the control algorithm, this real-time computation must be repeated at the sample rate of greater than 60 Hz that is determined by the mechanical resonance. Given this and the non-linearity of a manipulator, the computation load on a controller is substantial and has in the past required an expensive minicomputer or even a super-minicomputer. One alternative approach is to decompose the computation load into a number of tasks which can be performed by inexpensive multiprocessors synchronously. This paper presents a number of implementations of the control computation of manipulators on multiprocessors. The results show that a moderate speedup has been achieved on a shared memory system and a good speedup on a dataflow system.

1. Introduction

The manipulator dynamic control involves real-time calculation of the desired forces or motor torques to allow the manipulator to follow the required trajectory [1]. These calculations are normally based on the manipulator dynamic equations and the feedback information about the actual motion of the manipulator. To achieve convergence of the control algorithm may require sampling rates greater than 60 Hz, with the upper limit being determined by the mechanical resonance. Given this and the high degree of non-linear characteristics of the manipulator, the computation load on the controller is substantial and has in the past required an expensive minicomputer or even a super-minicomputer.

An alternative approach is to decompose the computation load of the manipulator dynamic control into a number of tasks which will be performed by inexpensive multiprocessors concurrently [2], [3].

Success of such an approach requires an optimal algorithm to assign tasks to respective processors and an efficient configuration of multiprocessor systems to support concurrent computation.

This paper presents a number of implementations of the control computation of a manipulator on multiprocessor computer systems. Our research lies in exploring

---

[1]S. Zeng is a graduate student in the Laboratory for Concurrent Computing Systems at the Swinburne University of Technology, John Street, Hawthorn 3122, Australia.
[2]G.K. Egan is Professor of Computer Systems Engineering and Director of the Laboratory for Concurrent Computing Systems at the Swinburne University of Technology, John Street, Hawthorn 3122, Australia.

implicit parallel programming schemes for real-time control and as such is a departure from the more usual explicit solution techniques in the literature.

2. The Recursive Newton–Euler Equations

There are a number of ways to formulate the dynamic equations of manipulator motion; two main approaches that are widely used to systematically derive the dynamic model of a manipulator are the Lagrange–Euler (LE) formulation and the Newton–Euler (NE) formulation [4].

The LE formulation generates a set of closed form differential equations to describe motion. The computation method of the LE equations involves many matrix multiplications and is computationally inefficient.

The NE formulation yields a computationally efficient set of forward and backward recursive equations of motion. This algorithm is the fastest and the most efficient of existing algorithms for dynamic control computation [4].

The Newton–Euler equations are based on Newton's second law:

$$F_i = m_i a_i$$

and Euler's equation:

$$N_i = I_i \dot{w}_i + w_i \times (I_i w_i)$$

Furthermore, recursive Newton–Euler equations are derived with nine equations for each link [1].

$$A_i^0 w_i = A_i^{i-1}(A_i^0 w_{i-1} + z_0 \dot{q}_i) \qquad \text{if link i is rotational}$$
$$\text{or } A_i^{i-1}(A_i^0 w_{i-1}) \qquad \text{if link i is translational}$$

$$A_i^0 \dot{w}_i = A_i^{i-1}[A_i^0 \dot{w}_{i-1} + z_0 \ddot{q}_i + (A_i^0 w_{i-1}) \times (z_0 \dot{q}_i)] \qquad \text{if link i is rotational}$$
$$\text{or } A_i^{i-1}(A_i^0 \dot{w}_{i-1}) \qquad \text{if link i is translational}$$

$$A_i^0 \dot{v}_i = (A_i^0 \dot{w}_i) \times (A_i^0 p_i^*) + (A_i^0 w_i) \times [(A_i^0 w_i) \times (A_i^0 p_i^*)] + A_i^{i-1}(A_{i-1}^0 \dot{v}_{i-1}) \qquad \text{if link i is rotational}$$
$$\text{or } A_i^{i-1}(z_0 \ddot{q}_i + A_{i-1}^0 \dot{v}_{i-1} + (A_i^0 \dot{w}_i) \times (A_i^0 p_i^*) + 2(A_i^0 w_i) \times (A_i^{i-1} z_0 \dot{q}_i) + (A_i^0 w_i) \times [(A_i^0 w_i) \times (A_i^0 p_i^*)]$$
$$\text{if link i is translational}$$

$$A_i^0 \ddot{v}_i = (A_i^0 \dot{w}_i) \times (A_i^0 s_i) + (A_i^0 w_i) \times [(A_i^0 w_i) \times (A_i^0 s_i)] + A_i^0 \dot{v}_i$$

$$A_i^0 F_i = m_i A_i^0 \ddot{v}_i$$

$$A_i^0 N_i = (A_i^0 I_i A_0^i)(A_i^0 \dot{w}_i) + (A_i^0 w_i) \times [(A_i^0 I_i A_0^i)(A_i^0 w_i)]$$

$$A_i^0 f_i = A_i^{i+1}(A_{i+1}^0 f_{i+1}) + A_i^0 F_i$$

$$A_i^0 n_i = A_i^{i+1}[(A_{i+1}^0 n_{i+1} + (A_{i+1}^0 p_i^*) \times (A_{i+1}^0 f_{i+1})] + (A_i^0 p_i^* + A_i^0 s_i) \times (A_i^0 F_i) + A_i^0 N_i$$

$$\tau_i = (A_i^0 n_i)'(A_i^{i-1} z_0) + b_i \dot{q}_i \qquad \text{if link i is rotational}$$
$$\text{or } (A_i^0 f_i)'(A_i^{i-1} z_0) + b_i \dot{q}_i \qquad \text{if link i is translational}$$

where: A_i^{i-1} and I_i are 3×3 matrices, $\dot{q}_i$, $\ddot{q}_i$, τ_i, m_i and b_i are scalars, and the rest are 3×1 vectors.

The manipulator configuration chosen is a popular ASEA IRb-6 robot arm which has five degrees of freedom, so there are in total 45 equations.

3. Explicit Parallel Implementations on a Shared Memory Multiprocessor

In these implementations, the Pascal programs augmented explicitly with the synchronization primitives from the parallel programming library of Encore Multimax, a shared-memory multiprocessor system with six processors is used to implement the computation of manipulator dynamic control equations.

The primitives used were *fork, spinlock, spinunlock, fbarrier_init, fbarrier,* and the memory allocation directive *share* [5], where *fork* is used to create a new process. The new process (the child) is an exact copy of the calling process (the parent) except the child process has a unique process ID. In the program, one process runs on one physical processor. *Spinlock* and *spinunlock* are used where necessary to provide exclusive access to the data structures located in a shared memory. *Fbarrier_init* and *fbarrier* are used to synchronize the parallel processes on each iteration of the control loop.

3.1 Decomposition of the Computing Load into Tasks
The decomposing of the computing load is the first important step in the application of parallel processing. If we split the computing load into coarse grains, only a few tasks can be performed concurrently. On the other hand, if the grains are too small, the data transfer activities between the processors (hence the operating system overhead) will increase. This effect will lead to the performance degradation.

After a substantial number of experiments [15], we finally partitioned the recursive Newton–Euler equations into 51 tasks. A task graph was sketched to represent the ordering constraint arising from the data dependencies between the tasks (shown in Figure 1), where task 0 and 52 are dummy tasks, representing enter node and exit node respectively.

In a task graph, there is a longest path called critical path whose path length is defined as follow:

$$t_{cr} = \max_k \sum_{i \in \phi_k} t_i$$

The critical path length plays a principal role since once the critical path length is determined, no matter what scheduling is used and how many processors will be employed, the execution time will be not shorter than this critical path length.

Using UNIX-gprof, we can estimate the execution time of each task; furthermore, the critical path length can be inferred:

the critical path: 0->2->12->22->32->42->44->45->47
->37->39->29->19->9->10->52

the critical path length = 48.354 (sec) (40,000 iterations)

A task cannot start until all of its predecessors are completed. Threshold variables are used to determine when a task is ready to be executed and that task is then

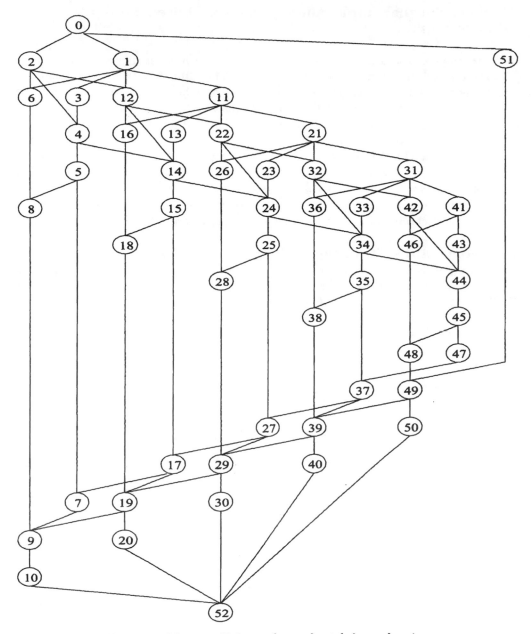

Figure 1: Newton–Euler task graph and dependencies.

scheduled. Two methods have been employed to schedule tasks. One is dynamic scheduling and the other is static scheduling.

3.2 Dynamic Scheduling

For dynamic scheduling, all of the processors share a common task queue which is located in a shared memory and the tasks are scheduled at run-time. If we denote:

T be a set of tasks, i.e., $T = (T_0, T_1, \cdots, T_i, \cdots, T_n, T_{n+1})$, where T_0 and T_{n+1} are dummy tasks, representing the enter node and the exit node in a task graph, respectively.

P be a set of processors, i.e., $P = (P_1, \cdots, P_j, \cdots, P_m)$; then the dynamic scheduling can be described as the following steps:

1. Initially, T_0 is put into the queue, and a shared variable *remaining_tasks* is set to equal to NoOfTasks;

2. P_j checks the variable *remaining_tasks*: **IF** *remaining_tasks*=0, then go to step 4, **ELSE** go to step 3;

3. P_j reads a task T_i from the queue, **IF** $T_i <> T_{n+1}$, i.e., T_i is not the exit node, then P_j performs T_i. After completing T_i, P_j checks the thresholds of successors of T_i and puts any task with threshold equal to its NoOPred (No Of Predecessors) into the queue, and go to step 2; **ELSE** P_j sets the variable *remaining_tasks*=0, and go to step 2;

4. stop.

Spinlocks were used to guarantee that only one processor can access the queue at each time.

The advantage of dynamic scheduling is that it is simple to program, and avoids manual work such as mapping tasks to specific processors. The drawback is that a processor spends quite a long time on scheduling and spinlock/spinunlock.

3.3 Static Scheduling

For static scheduling, tasks are allocated to specific processors. The order in which the tasks are executed on a given processor is predetermined. Tasks wait until the predecessors have finished before executing. In this case, the task itself monitors the threshold rather than being explicitly scheduled by a predecessor. In the program, we use the DHLF/MISF (Dynamic High Level First/Most Immediate Successive First) [16] method to generate a task order for each processor and then directly map the tasks to specific processors. If a task and its predecessor are allocated to the same processor, then the No Of Predecessors of this task can be reduced by 1.

The scheduling time for static scheduling has been greatly reduced, however, this method involves substantial manual work to map tasks to specific processors.

The results in Table 1 are for the dynamic control routine. It can be seen that for dynamic scheduling, using one processor, the execution time is worse than that of the sequential scheme, using more than two processors; only a slight speedup can be achieved. This is because processors spend quite a long time on scheduling and spinlock/spinunlock. It also can be seen that for static scheduling, moderate speedup has been achieved by using several processors.

	scheduling	processor number	execution time (sec)	speedup
sequential			142.3	
parallel	dynamic	1	186.9	
		2	130.7	1.09
		3	104.2	1.37
		4	87.2	1.63
		5	80.8	1.76
	static	1	142.3	1.00
		2	84.7	1.68
		3	66.3	2.15
		4	61.3	2.32
		5	60.0	2.37

Table 1: Times for dynamic and static implementations (40,000 iterations).

4. Implicit Parallel Implementations in SISAL

SISAL is a functional language which has been targeted at a wide variety of systems including current generation multiprocessors such as the Encore Multimax and research dataflow machines [6], [7]. The multi-targeting feature is accomplished by compiling SISAL to an intermediate language IF1. The IF1 representation is then compiled to the appropriate target instruction set. The textual form of SISAL, in terms of control structures and array representations, provides a relatively easy transition for those familiar with imperative languages. The optimizing SISAL compiler (OSC) from Colorado yields performance competitive with Fortran.

In SISAL programs, there two forms of Loop expression, one is of the form:

```
for initial
    index:=lowest_index;
    variable:=initial_value;
while index <= highest_index repeat
    index:=old index + 1;
    variable:=function1(old index, old variable);
return array of variable
end For
```

Another form of Loop expression is:

```
for index in lowest_index, highest_index
    variable:=function2(index);
return array of variable
end For
```

The first one performs sequential loops in which one iteration depends on the results of the previous iteration. The second form may be used when there are no data dependencies between iterations; this makes it is possible to execute several loops in parallel.

4.1 SISAL on a Conventional Shared Memory Multiprocessor

As we know, the dynamic control of the manipulator involves calculating nine equations for each link. The data dependencies between two equations among nine equations and between two links are so strong that it is difficult to write the calculation program in a second form of parallel SISAL loop. The manipulator program expressed in SISAL is presented below. It can be seen that there are no directives as to how the tasks should be scheduled.

```
type vector = record[x,y,z:real];
type matrix = record[n,o,p:vector];
        :
function VAV(a,b:vector returns vector)        %vector + vector
    let
        c:=record vector[x:a.x+b.x;y:a.y+b.y;z:a.z+b.z]
    in c
    end let
end function
        :
function dynamic_control(z0:vector;dq,ddq,m,bo:array[real];
                    po,s:array[vector];Tm,Tm_1,Im:array[Matrix]
                    returns w,dw,v,dv,dcv,Fe,Ne,fc,nc,t)
    let
        wj,dwj,dvj,dcvj,Fej,Nej:=
            for initial
                link:=0;
                wi:=record vector[x:0.0;y:0.0;z:0.0];
                    :
            while link <= repeat
                link :=old link+1;
                wi,dwi,dvi,dcvi,Fei,Nei:=
                if motion[link]=1 then                        %rotation
                    let
                        %compute angular velocity
                        zdq:=SMV(dq[link],z0);
                        value01:=VAV(old wi,zdq);
                        w1:=MMV(Tm_1[link],value01);
                            :
                        %compute external moment - Ne1
                    in w1,dw1,dv1,dcv1,Fe1,Ne1
                    end let
                else                                          %translation
                    let
                        %compute angular velocity
                        w1:=MMV(Tm_1[link],old wi);
                            :
```

processor number	execution time (sec)	speedup
1	116.5	
2	119.2	0.977
3	121.6	0.958
4	119.7	0.973

Table 2: Times for SISAL on a conventional multiprocessor (40,000 iterations).

```
                    %compute external moment - Ne1
                 in w1,dw1,dv1,dcv1,Fe1,Ne1
                 end let
              end if
              returns array of wi
                       :
                    array of Nei
           end for;
        w,dw,dv,dcv,Fe,Ne:=array_setl(wj,0),
                   :
                       array_setl(Nej,0)
        in let fcj,ncj,tj:=
                   :
              fc,nc,t:=array_setl(fcj,0),
                   :
                    array_setl(tj,0)
          in w,dw,dv,dcv,Fe,Ne,fc,nc,t
       end let
     end function
```

The current version of the SISAL compiler OSC (Optimizing SISAL Compiler) can only exploit the parallelism in *for* $\cdots$ *in* loops. Procedural level concurrency of the type found in the manipulator control program is not currently exploited as can be seen from the results in Table 2. It can be observed, however, that the run times for SISAL on a conventional multiprocessor compare favorably with the Pascal implementations. The slight increase in execution with additional processors is caused by operating system overheads.

4.2 SISAL on a Dataflow Multiprocessor

The dataflow model has been introduced to exploit the maximum parallelism inherent in algorithms since the early 1970s. Dataflow microprocessors are commercially available and other microprocessers such as the Inmos transputers may be used as dataflow processors [14]. Unlike the conventional control-flow model the course of a computation is determined solely by the availability of data; therefore, the dataflow model can avoid most problems existing in the conventional multiprocessor system, such as memory conflict, side effects, etc.

Dataflow programs are represented by a directed graph where the arcs denote paths over which data travel and the nodes of the computational function (instruction operations). A node "fires" as soon as all its operands arrive on all its input arcs. When the node fires, results are transmitted to successor nodes in data packets called token and these nodes will cause further firings. Potentially many nodes may be eligible to fire in parallel.

The hardware of the dataflow machine studied (CSIRAC II) consists of a homogeneous array of processing elements or processors interconnected by a modulo 4 multi-stage interconnection network (MIN). The graph describing the computation to be performed is partitioned and the partitions distributed to the processing elements [8], [9], [10]. In CSIRAC II, a processing element consists of two main functional units (Figure 2). If the destination node is monadic, the token can be directly passed to the evaluation unit. If the destination node is dyadic, then the matching unit retains the token and processes the next token; the retained token is retrieved when its partner arrives. In the evaluation unit the node function is evaluated and the results are dispatched through the communication network to their destinations [11]. CSIRAC II supports data structures stored in a distributed Object Store. The Object Store is partitioned and the partitions associated with processing elements. Objects are accessed by a pointer/descriptor usually requiring an indirect access and two network transits for each data item fetched, i.e., the request and response. This form of storage is variously called Structure Stores or I-Structures by other dataflow researchers. For stimulus response or flow through computations where the input data is continuously consumed by a computation producing a control or graphical output, CSIRAC II transmits data structures directly from producer to consumer.

The simulator for CSIRAC II has an internal time resolution of 10 nSec, with all other times being a multiple of this. Token packets traverse the network stage by stage with 100 nSec each stage. The network and processing elements combined is five stages or 500 nSec deep. The path taken by any given token is conservatively modeled as busy for the entire token transmission while in practice the path would be established and released stage by stage. Pipelining within processing elements is not modeled directly but approximated by commencing the processing of tokens at a time equal to half the transmission time after the token has been dispatched. The rate for reading tokens from the network queues is assumed as 50 nSec per word, and the time for tokens requiring a matching operation is 100 nSec if they are in the cache and a very conservative 500 nSec plus another 500 nSec for each further search of token storage if it is not in the cache. The node evaluation time for simple operations such as arithmetic is 100 nSec, or a peak of 10 MIPs. The more complex node operations, such as for loop range generators, are set to an appropriately longer time [18], [19]. The simulator also generates a number of graphics for performance analysis [8], some of which are used here.

For CSIRAC II, SISAL programs are compiled by the front end of OSC into IF1(an intermediate form). The IF1 is then translated into i2, an intermediate target language which directly represents a dataflow graph [9], [13].

The set of graphs in Figure 3 shows the machine activity during the simulation of 10 iterations. Only 16 processing elements are used for the study of a simulator maximum of 128. Graph 4(a) shows the number of tokens waiting in a processing elements Matching Stores and the number of tokens in transit through the network; Graph 4(b) shows the maximum, minimum, and average number of active processing elements during each simulation time sample; Graph 4(c) shows the activity of processing elements accessing the object store; Graph 4(d) shows the work-load distribution, a dark spot indicates that processing element is active [8].

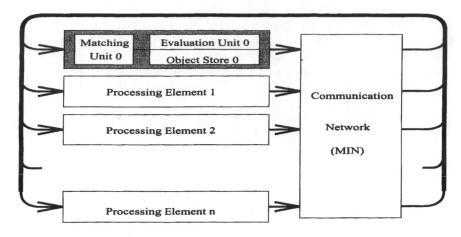

Figure 2: CSIRAC II organization.

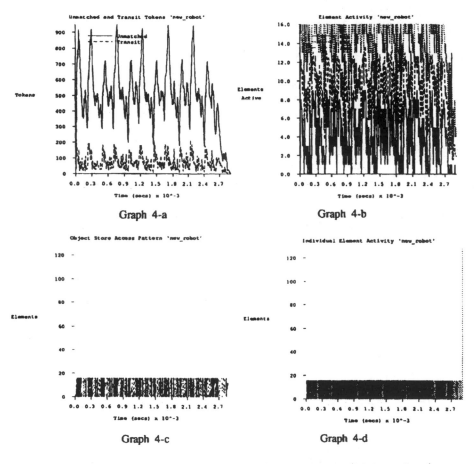

Figure 3: Machine activity during the simulation (10 iterations).

processing element number	execution time (sec)	speedup
1	110.0	
2	57.9	1.91
8	17.7	6.27
16	11.7	9.41
32	9.3	11.81
64	8.6	12.80
128	8.3	13.19

Table 3: Runtime for SISAL on dataflow (40,000 iterations).

Because there is no conditional execution in the control program each iteration takes the same time. Table 3 shows the times that CSIRAC II would take for 40,000 iterations for a varying number of processing elements.

5. Conclusion

We have investigated several computation models for the dynamic control of a manipulator. As we know, program parallelism involves the partition of a computing load. In theory, if we wish to speedup our program, we should cut down the critical path length; to do so, we should produce a fine-grained program to exploit low-level parallelism in tasks, further reducing the critical path. However, if the grains are too small, there will be substantial overhead associated with coordinate processes; the actual critical path length will increase. Therefore, the potential gain from parallelism will be overwhelmed by this lengthening of the critical path. This can be seen from our shared-memory schemes, where each processor can directly access a data structure located in shared memory, which also can be accessed by all other processors. Mutual exclusions using atomic test and set instructions or locks were used to protect these accesses. The locks were implemented as hard locks, meaning that processes were not suspended but they repeatedly retried locks until successful. This imposes a significant overhead leading to our only exploiting medium granularity for our shared-memory schemes. With the amount of concurrency available at this level of granularity, only a slight speedup was achieved by using dynamic scheduling and a moderate speedup by using static scheduling. Although part of the software scheduling can be replaced by task queues implemented in hardware, only a limited speedup can be achieved because of the number of tasks which can be executed concurrently.

The dataflow model of computation deviates from the conventional control flow in that the execution of an instruction is solely based upon the availability of its operands. The instructions in the dataflow model of computation do not impose any constraints on sequencing, except the data dependencies in the program. The advantage of the dataflow approach over the conventional control flow method stems from the inherent parallelism at the instruction level. This allows efficient exploitation of the fine-grain parallelism in an application program minimizing the critical path length of the manipulator dynamic control program. SISAL automatically partitions the program into very fine-grained tasks (instruction level) and their data dependencies. The CSIRAC II dataflow machine uses a dynamic scheduling policy very similar to the one used in the Pascal-based scheme. The simulation results demonstrate the potential and advantage of a dataflow machine to resolve a complicated and high performance real-time control problem such as manipulator dynamic control.

References

[1] J.Y.S. Luh, M.W. Walker, and R.P.C. Paul, "On-Line Computational Scheme for Mechanical Manipulators," *ASME Journal on Dynamic Systems, Measurement, Control*, Vol. 102, June 1980, pp. 69–76.

[2] J.Y.S. Luh and C.S. Lin, "Scheduling of Parallel Computer for a Computer-Controlled Mechanical Manipulator," *IEEE Transactions on Systems, Man, and Cybernetics*, Vol. 12, 1982, pp. 214–234.

[3] H. Kasahara and S. Narita, "Parallel Processing of Robot-arm Control Computation on a Multi-Microprocessor System," *IEEE Journal on Robotics and Automation*, Vol. RA-1, No. 2, June 1985, pp. 104–113.

[4] E.E. Binder and J.H. Herzog, "Distributed Computer Architecture and Fast Parallel Algorithms in Real-time Robot Control," *IEEE Transactions on Systems, Man, and Cybernetics*, Vol. SMC-16, No. 6, July/August 1986, pp. 543–549.

[5] *UMAX 4.3 Programmer's Reference Manual 1*.

[6] *SISAL Language Reference Manual Version 1.2*, March 1, 1985.

[7] J.T. Feo and D.C. Cann, "A Report on the SISAL Language Project," *Journal of Parallel and Distributed Computing*, Vol. 10, 1990, pp. 349–366.

[8] M.W. Rawling, *Implementation and Analysis of a Hybrid Dataflow System*, M. Eng thesis, Royal Melbourne Institute of Technology, Australia.

[9] G.K. Egan, N.J. Webb and A.P.W. Böhm, "Some Features of the CSIRAC II Dataflow Machine Architecture," in *Advanced Topics in Data-Flow Computing*, Prentice-Hall, 1991, pp. 143–173.

[10] D.A. Abramson and G.K. Egan "The RMIT Data Flow Computer: A Hybrid Architecture," *Computer Journal*, Vol. 33, No. 3, 1990.

[11] D.A. Abramson and G.K. Egan, "Design of a High Performance Dataflow Multiprocessor," in *Advanced Topics in Data-Flow Computing*, Prentice-Hall, 1991, pp. 121–141.

[12] M.L. Welcome et al., *IF2: An Applicative Language Intermediate Form with Explicit Memory Management, Lawrence Livermore National Laboratory Manual M-195*, Lawrence Livermore National Laboratory, Livermore, CA, November 1986.

[13] G.K. Egan, M. Rawling, and N.J. Webb "i2: An Intermediate Language for RMIT Dataflow Machine," Technical Report 31-004, Laboratory for Concurrent Computing Systems, School of Electrical Engineering, Swinburne Institute of Technology.

[14] A. Katbab, "A Multiprocessor Architecture for Robot-Arm Control," *Microprocessing and Microprogramming*, Vol. 24, 1988, pp. 673–680.

[15] S. Zeng and G.K. Egan, "Parallel Processor Implementations of the Recursive Newton–Euler Equations Used in the Dynamic Control of Robots," Technical Report 31-028, Laboratory for Concurrent Computing Systems, School of Electrical Engineering, Swinburne Institute of Technology.

[16] C.L. Chen, C.S.G. Lee and E.S.H. Hou, "Efficient Scheduling Algorithm for Robot Inverse Dynamics Computation on a Multiprocessor System," *IEEE Trans. Syst. Man., Cybern.*, Vol. 18, No. 5, September/October 1988.

[17] S. Zeng, *The Control of High-Performance Manipulators using Multiprocessor Computer System*, M. Eng. thesis, Laboratory for Concurrent Computing Systems, School of Electrical Engineering, Swinburne Institute of Technology, 1992 (to be published).

[18] C. Baharis, *Topographic Reconstruction on the CSIRAC II Dataflow Computer*, Master thesis, Department of Communication and Electrical Engineering, Royal Melbourne Institute of Technology, April 1991.

[19] G.K. Egan, "The CSIRAC II Dataflow Computer Simulation Suite," Technical Report 31-010, Laboratory for Concurrent Computing Systems, School of Electrical Engineering , Swinburne Institute of Technology, May 1990.

Biography

Guang R. Gao received his M.S. and Ph.D. degrees in Electrical Engineering and Computer Science from the Massachusetts Institute of Technology, in 1982 and 1986, respectively. Currently he is an associate professor of the School of Computer Science, McGill University, Montreal, Canada. He has published many technical and research papers in the field of computer architecture, compilers, parallel processing, and dataflow computations, and has served as a guest editor of a special issue on dataflow and multithreaded computers of the *Journal of Parallel and Distributed Computing,* 1993.

He has been a co-chairman of the *Second International Workshop on Dataflow Computation* held in conjunction with the *ACM ISCA-92,* and is a co-chairman of the *International Workshop on Multithreaded Computers* held in conjunction with *Supercomputing 1991.* Currently he serves as the program chairman of the *International Conference on Parallel Architectures and Compilation Techniques (PACT '94).* He has also served as a program committee member in a number of international conferences, most recently *Parallel Language and Architecture Europe (PARLE'94), IEEE International Conference on Application Specific Array Processors (ASAP'92), International Working Conference on Programming Models for Massively Parallel Computers (1993), International Parallel Processing Symposium (IPPS'95),* and the *International Conference on Parallel Architectures and Compilers (PACT'95).*

Gao is a member of ACM, SIGARCH, and the IEEE Computer Society.

Lubomir Bic received an M.S. degree in computer science from the Technical University Darmstadt, W. Germany, in 1976 and a Ph.D. in computer science from the University of California, Irvine, in 1979. He is currently Professor of Information and Computer Science at the University of California, Irvine.

Lubomir Bic's primary research interests lie in the areas of parallel processing and data engineering. He leads several projects aimed at developing new models of computation and tools for the programming of parallel and distributed systems for both scientific and symbolic applications, such as parallel and distributed databases and knowledge-based systems. He has published his work in a wide spectrum of books, journals, and conference papers, and has given many invited presentations and tutorials. He has also actively served the research community in a number of roles, including the editing of special journal issues and tutorial books, organizing workshops and conferences, and serving as a reviewer of numerous proposals and publications.

He is a member of ACM and IEEE. He was a Guest Editor of two special issues of *JPDC on Dataflow Computing.* He served as the co-chair of the *3rd International Parallel Processing Symposium (IPPS'89),* two *Dataflow Workshops,* and the *Architecture Workshops* at the *19th International Symposium on Computer Architecture (ISCA '92).* He will serve as co-chair at the *IFIP Working Conference on Parallel Architectures and Compilation Techniques (PACT'95),* and the *IEEE 1st International Conference on Algorithms and Architecture (ICA3PP-95).* He has also been a member of program/organizing committees of the *Sixth Annual Parallel Processing Symposium (IPPS'92),* the *Federated Computer Research Conference (FCRC),* the *IFIP Conference on Architectures and Compilation Techniques (PACT'93, PACT'94, PACT'95),* the *Fifth IEEE Symposium on Parallel and Distributed Processing (SPDC'93),* and the *21st International Symposium on Computer Architecture (ISCA '94).* He has been the general chair of the *20th International Symposium on Computer Architecture (ISCA '93)* and currently serves as one of the editors of the *IEEE Transaction on Knowledge and Data Engineering.*

Jean-Luc Gaudiot was born in Nancy, France, in 1954. He received the Diplome d'Ingenieur from the Ecole Superieure d'Ingenieurs en Electrotechnique et Electronique, Paris, France in 1976, the M.Sc. and Ph.D. in Computer Science from the University of California, Los Angeles in 1977 and 1982, respectively.

His experiences includes microprocessor systems design at Teledyne Controls, Santa Monica, California (1979–1980) and research in innovative architectures for the TRW Technology Research Center, El Segundo, California (1980–1982). Since graduating in 1982, he has been on the faculty of the Department of Electrical Engineering-Systems, University of Southern California, where he is currently an associate professor. His research interests include data-flow architectures, fault-tolerant multiprocessors, and implementation of artificial neural networks. In addition to his academic duties, he has consulted for several aerospace companies in the Southern California area.

Gaudiot is a member of the ACM, the ACM SIGARCH, the IFIP Working Group 10.3 (Parallel Processing), and a senior member of the IEEE. He was the general chairman of the *1992 International Symposium on Computer Architecture,* the Program Chairman for the *1993 IFIP Working Conference on Architectures and Compilation Techniques for Fine and Medium Grain Parallelism,* and the Systems Track Program Chairman for the *1993 IEEE Symposium on Parallel and Distributed Processing.* He is currently serving as Associate Editor of the *IEEE Transactions on Computers* and as Advisory Board member of the *IEEE Technical Committee on Computer Architecture.* He has also been appointed a Distinguished Visitor of the IEEE Computer Society (1994–1998).

IEEE Computer Society Press Publications

The world-renowned Computer Society Press publishes, promotes, and distributes a wide variety of authoritative computer science and engineering texts. These books are available in two formats: 100 percent original material by authors preeminent in their field who focus on relevant topics and cutting-edge research, and reprint collections consisting of carefully selected groups of previously published papers with accompanying original introductory and explanatory text.

Submission of proposals: For guidelines and information on CS Press books, send e-mail to csbooks@computer.org or write to the Acquisitions Editor, IEEE Computer Society Press, P.O. Box 3014, 10662 Los Vaqueros Circle, Los Alamitos, CA 90720-1314. Telephone +1 714-821-8380. FAX +1 714-761-1784.

IEEE Computer Society Press Proceedings

The Computer Society Press also produces and actively promotes the proceedings of more than 130 acclaimed international conferences each year in multimedia formats that include hard and softcover books, CD-ROMs, videos, and on-line publications.

For information on CS Press proceedings, send e-mail to csbooks@computer.org or write to Proceedings, IEEE Computer Society Press, P.O. Box 3014, 10662 Los Vaqueros Circle, Los Alamitos, CA 90720-1314. Telephone +1 714-821-8380. FAX +1 714-761-1784.

Additional information regarding the Computer Society, conferences and proceedings, CD-ROMs, videos, and books can also be accessed from our web site at www.computer.org.

Printed and bound by CPI Group (UK) Ltd, Croydon, CR0 4YY